American Political Culture

American Political Culture

AN ENCYCLOPEDIA

VOLUME 1: A–E

MICHAEL SHALLY-JENSEN, GENERAL EDITOR

MARK J. ROZELL AND TED G. JELEN,
ADVISORY EDITORS

 ABC-CLIO ™

An Imprint of ABC-CLIO, LLC
Santa Barbara, California • Denver, Colorado

Copyright © 2015 by ABC-CLIO, LLC

Library of Congress Cataloging-in-Publication Data

American political culture : an encyclopedia / Michael Shally-Jensen, general editor ;
Ted G. Jelen and Mark J. Rozell, advisory editors.
     volumes cm
 Includes bibliographical references and index.
 Contents: Volume 1. A-E — Volume 2. F-O — Volume 3. P-Y.
 ISBN 978-1-61069-377-6 (hardback) — ISBN 978-1-61069-378-3 (ebook)
1. United States—Politics and government—20th century.   2. United States—Politics and
government—21st century.   3. Political culture—United States—History—20th century.
4. Political culture—United States—History—21st century.   I. Shally-Jensen,
Michael, editor.
 E169.12.A428 2015
 320.97309'04—dc23   2014032452

ISBN: 978-1-61069-377-6
EISBN: 978-1-61069-378-3

19 18 17 16 15   1 2 3 4 5

This book is also available on the World Wide Web as an eBook.
Visit www.abc-clio.com for details.

ABC-CLIO, LLC
130 Cremona Drive, P.O. Box 1911
Santa Barbara, California 93116-1911

This book is printed on acid-free paper ∞
Manufactured in the United States of America

Contents

Organization of the Encyclopedia   xiii

Introduction   xv

Guide to Related Topics   xxi

Volume One

Abortion and Politics   1

Advertising, Political   8

Affirmative Action   14

African Americans and Politics   20

Air Quality and Politics   28

American Dream   33

American "Exceptionalism"   39

American Flag   45

American Indian Politics   49

Anti-intellectualism in American Life   54

Arts, Humanities, and Politics   60

Asian Americans and Politics   67

Baby Boom Generation and Politics   75

Banking Policy and Politics   81

Biotechnology and Politics   86

Border Protection and Politics   92

Budget Politics   98

Bureaucracy and American Political Culture   103

Campaign Finance   111

Campaigns and Campaigning   117

Catholics and Politics   125

Church–State Relations   131

Cities and Politics   139

Citizenship and Politics   145

Civil Liberties   152

Civil Religion   159

Civil Rights   165

Civil War (1861–1865) and Modern Memory   171

Class and Politics   176

Climate Change and Politics   180

Coastal Zones, Economics, and Politics   188

Cold War Political Culture   193

Congress and Congressional Politics   198

Conservatives and Conservatism   205

Conspiracy Theory and the "Paranoid Style"   213

Constitution and Constitutionalism   220

Consumer Culture and Politics   226

Corporate Behavior and Politics   232

Corruption in Politics   240

Courts and Court Politics   249

Crime, Punishment, and Politics   254

Crises, Emergencies, and Politics   262

Cultural Pluralism   268

Culture Wars   274

Cybersecurity and Politics   280

Death Penalty and Politics   287

Debates, Presidential   293

Debt, Deficit, and Politics   298

Democracy   304

Democratic Party   310

Desegregation and Politics   316

Disability and Politics   321

Disasters and Politics   328

Disinformation, Deception, and Politics   334

Drug Policy and Politics   340

Economic Policy and Politics   349

Education Policy and Politics   355

Electoral College   361

Endangered Species Act, Habitat Loss, and Politics   367

Energy Policy and Politics   373

Environmental Policy and Politics   379

Ethics in Government   385

Evolution, Creationism, and Politics   392

Executive Privilege   396

Volume Two

Guide to Related Topics   xiii

Factions and Intraparty Conflict   403

Family, State, and Politics   408

Farming, Food, and Politics   417

Far-Right Parties and Organizations   422

Fear Tactics in Politics   427

Federalism   433

Filibuster   439

Film and American Political Culture   445

First Lady   451

Foreign Policy and Politics   457

Free Speech   463

Gay and Lesbian Culture and Politics   469

Globalization   475

Governors and Gubernatorial Politics   481

Grassroots Activism   489

Green Movement and Politics   494

Gridlock, Legislative   500

Guns and Politics   505

Health Care and Politics   513

House of Representatives, United States   519

Housing Policy and Politics   525

Humor, Satire, and Politics   530

Immigration and Politics   537

Impeachment   546

Independent Voters   553

Individualism   558

Inequality and Politics   565

Information Leaks and Politics   572

Infrastructure and Politics   586

Initiatives and Referendums   590

Intelligence Community and Politics   597

Interest Groups and Lobbying   606

Internet, Society, and Politics   614

Islamophobia   619

Jews and Politics   625

Labor and Politics   631

Latinos and Politics   637

Leaders and Leadership   646

Left and Politics   650

Legislative Veto   660

Liberals and Liberalism   665

Libertarians and Libertarianism   670

Liberty   676

Literature and Politics   681

Midterm Elections   689

Military and Politics   693

Mining and Politics   700

Monuments, Memorials, and Public History   705

Mormons and Politics   710

Muslims, Arab Americans, and Politics   717

National Identity   725

National Parks, Wilderness Areas, and Politics   730

National Security Policy and Politics   736

Nationalism   743

Nominating Conventions   750

Nuclear Power and Politics   755

Nuclear Weapons and Politics   762

Oil, Natural Gas, and Politics   769

Volume Three

Guide to Related Topics   xiii

Pardons and Politics   775

Partisanship and Polarization   780

Personality and Politics   786

Political Communications   791

Political Consultants and Campaign Managers   796

Political Parties   801

Popular Culture and Politics   807

Poverty and Politics   812

Power and Politics   817

Pragmatism   821

Prayer and Religious Symbols in Public Places   827

Presidency and Presidential Politics   832

Presidential Appointments   839

Presidential Memoirs, Autobiographies, and Biographies   846

Primaries and Caucuses   858

Print Media and Politics   864

Privacy Rights and Politics   870

Privatization and Deregulation   875

Progressives, Progressivism, and President Barack Obama   882

Protest Movements   891

Protestants, Evangelicals, and Politics   899

Public Health and Politics   905

Public Opinion   912

Public–Private Partnerships   917

Race, Ethnicity, and Politics   923

Recall Elections   928

Recession and Politics   935

Redistricting   940

Regions and Regionalism: The Midwest   946

Regions and Regionalism: The Northeast   955

Regions and Regionalism: The South   960

Regions and Regionalism: The West   967

Religion and Politics   972

Republican Party   979

Right to Die and Politics   985

Scandals in Politics   993

Science, Technology, and Society   997

Senate, United States   1002

Separation of Powers   1008

Social Media and Politics   1013

Social Security and Politics   1020

Social Welfare and Politics   1025

Space Policy and Politics   1030

State and Local Politics   1037

State Secrets and Politics   1041

States' Rights   1047

Supreme Court, United States   1052

Surveillance, Society, and Politics   1057

Talk Radio and Politics   1063

Tax Policy and Politics   1069

Tea Party   1075

Television News, Opinion, and Politics   1081

Term Limits   1087

Terrorism, Torture, and Politics   1091

Theater and Ritual in American Politics   1097

Think Tanks and Politics   1103

Third Parties   1108

Trade Policy and Politics   1114

Veterans and Politics   1121

Veto Power   1125

Vice Presidency   1130

Violence and Politics   1135

Voter Turnout   1140

Voting and Politics   1147

War and Politics   1153

Water Policy and Politics   1158

White House and Capitol Hill   1163

Women and Politics   1168

Youth and Politics   1175

Bibliography   1183

Editor and Contributors   1243

Index   1265

Organization of the Encyclopedia

American Political Culture: An Encyclopedia is arranged alphabetically by entry to facilitate the easy lookup of topics of interest. We have taken care to begin each entry title with the most substantive word so as to reflect that topical interest; thus, there are entries covering "Foreign Policy and Politics," "Information Leaks and Politics," "Partisanship and Polarization," "Campaign Finance," and so on. Where necessary, we have provided stand-alone cross-references to help steer users to the appropriate entries. Thus, there is a cross-reference at "Conventions" to direct users to the entry "Nominating Conventions."

The three volumes of the encyclopedia contain nearly 200 entries, averaging about 3,500 words in length (though a few run less than that and several run considerably longer). Each entry begins with a description or definition of the topic at hand and proceeds to examine the subject's cultural, historical, and political context. The encyclopedia focuses particularly on the last 30 to 40 years of U.S. history, a period when cultural politics and the question of national identity have become especially important. Earlier periods are, of course, noted to the extent that they inform contemporary discussions of a topic.

While all of the entries draw on scholarly research, they have been written so that a reasonably diligent upper-level high school student, college undergraduate, or generally informed layperson can follow the discussion and findings. As much as possible, specialized terms are used only selectively and are defined in text as necessary. Subheadings help break down the topics into more easily understandable parts. An additional feature, employed in many entries, is the use of sidebars, or text boxes, to cover topics of interest related to the main topic of an entry but not necessarily integral to it. Most entries end with a concluding statement, and all provide a listing of related entries and a bibliography of useful print and electronic information resources. Also provided, at the front of the encyclopedia, is a Guide to Related Topics that groups entries under related themes and topics, and a basic Introduction that places the concept of "political culture" into historical context. At the end of the encyclopedia is a General Bibliography along with a detailed subject index.

The contributors, identified in each entry and listed at the back of the book, come from a wide range of disciplines and include political scientists, public policy specialists, communications and media professionals, sociologists, legal and constitutional scholars, historians, American studies specialists, and political economists. It is hoped that the work published here will inspire conversations among students and teachers as well as researchers and members of the general public. Readers will find thoughtful introductions to some of the most pressing and enduring issues confronting American society.

Introduction

The reason we employ the term "political culture" in the title of this work is to recognize that a subject as rich and exasperating as American politics is to be found not just in politics or political institutions per se but also in the culture. Thus, we examine here, along with traditional "political" topics such as political parties, public opinion, interest groups, constitutional questions, and campaigns and elections, various "cultural" elements and constituencies, including the media, religious groups, cultural symbols, ideologies, and historical influences. The materials we look at consist of political speeches, news accounts, opinion forums, memoirs, political rituals, films, and televised debates, among others. "Culture," as used here, refers not simply to the arts (though these are discussed) but to the ways in which society makes meaning of and interprets its own actions (Geertz 1973). The ways, say, that one responds to political figures—the feelings they evoke, the reactions they invite, the meanings they embody—are not the result of categorical imperatives or "natural" impulses but rather the stuff of political upbringing (political socialization) and experience. All of us import our values and experiences into our perceptions of the world. The images we form, the understandings we hold, regarding leaders, current events, economic conditions, and so on, shape and spur our political actions. From an external viewpoint, making sense of those actions entails capturing the ideas and understandings people have about their political world. In the present work, we accomplish that goal largely by throwing a wide net over American society and politics, seeing both as always already enmeshed in a cultural reality.

Development of the Concept of Political Culture

In Alexis de Tocqueville's *Democracy in America*, which some call the first study of political culture (although Tocqueville did not use that term), the author describes voluntary associations and how they shape (and are shaped by) the attitudes of their members. Tocqueville saw government itself as a kind of human association, an effort to come together—democratically, in the case of the United States—to order societal affairs. Tocqueville stressed the place of religion, individualism, and egalitarianism in the making of American political culture. He did not see these as "clear and distinct ideas," in the manner of many thinkers of his era. Rather, he understood each component or element as being in tension with others: religious faith was in tension with a sense of social and political autonomy; American individualism was in tension with a sense of community and democracy; and egalitarianism was in tension with the idea of freedom and individual "excellence," or achievement. Americans, in Tocqueville's view, were engaged in a constant balancing act. And the commitment to getting the balance right is what Tocqueville pointed to as the "dynamism" of American democracy—that, and the struggle to deal with an ever-changing set of social circumstances. As the author put it:

> [The] perpetual change which goes on in the United States, [the] frequent vicissitudes of fortune, [the] unforeseen fluctuations in private and public wealth, serve to keep the minds of the people in a perpetual feverish agitation, which admirably invigorates their exertions and keeps them, so to speak, above the ordinary level of humanity. The whole life of an American is passed like a game of chance, a revolutionary crisis, or a battle. As the same causes are continually in operation throughout the country, they ultimately impart an irresistible impulse to the national character. (1863, 548)

The modern concept of political culture emerged after World War II and was initially linked to theories of modernization. The idea among social scientists then was to identify the values, attitudes, and beliefs that supported the development of democracy in different regions and countries of the world—and, concomitantly, to find the factors that *hindered* democracy and fostered dictatorship instead (Pye and Verba 1965). There was relatively little interest in applying the new perspective to the United States, for it was generally assumed that America represented democracy in its ideal form. When the concept was applied here, the approach used was somewhat different. Instead of looking for markers of democracy, researchers sought to break down American society into various political *sub*cultures. The effort, according to its principal practitioner, Daniel Elazar (1966), served to shed light on regional differences and political differences among the states.

Elazar defined political culture as a "particular pattern of orientation to political action" (Elazar 1966, 78). He saw that pattern as composed of a set of underlying characteristics that could explain the activities of citizen-voters. Such characteristics were the result of ethnic and religious values held by various founding groups in the United States and maintained within specific regions of the country. These values were passed down from one generation to the next and produced a more or less stable set of social and political mores (manners, customs, and usages).

In general, argued Elazar, one could identify three principal political cultures (or subcultures) in the United States. In a *moralistic* culture, such as we find in the early New England states, emphasis was placed on creating a "good society" based on religious and moral principles. Citizens held that consensus and collective action were the way to get things done. The goal of politics was the betterment of all. Political activities centered on the community rather than the individual, and on issues rather than patrons and clients. There was a willingness to entertain novel policy solutions to problems—with little or no expectation of personal reward or payback. Political parties were viewed as less important than nonpartisan coalitions. Political participation was not only encouraged but generally expected of citizens.

In an *individualistic* culture, such as one finds in the early mid-Atlantic states, value was placed on individual achievement—particularly in the commercial arena—and on the building up of wealth and status. The focus was not the common good so much as the flowering of "virtue," evidenced by individual success. Politics was seen as a marketplace of competing interests whose actors used the system to better their own cause. An individualistic political culture was driven not by issues and societal needs but by political parties and systems of patronage. Politics, in this system, consisted in the collection of debts and the disbursement of rewards among those who played the game. Ordinary citizens were not necessarily welcome, except to offer their support to key players through voting.

Finally, in a *traditionalistic* culture, such as that found in the early South, stress was placed on preserving the status quo, largely to the benefit of elites. In the South, a plantation economy based on slavery developed and gave rise to a feudal aristocracy. Power within a traditionalistic culture was vested in an elite group of wealthy and influential families, all of whom strove to maintain their position and authority. Participation by persons outside this group was discouraged, and voter turnout was low. There was limited party competition, if any, because a single party could effectively represent the interests of the ruling elite.

Although Elazar tied each of these political cultures to geographic regions from the colonial era, he saw them as eventually being disbursed over wider areas. He described how migration during the expansion of the American frontier transported elements of those political cultures directly westward. By the time of his study, then, the northern tier of states was said to be predominantly moralistic, the southern tier was said to be traditionalistic, and the states in between were said to be individualistic.

Over the years, a number of researchers have sought to rework Elazar's early model by downplaying historic cultural differences and highlighting other elements. These researchers have found, for instance, that religious affiliation tends to override other cultural factors (Morgan and Watson 1991). Others have argued that present-day patterns of racial and ethnic geography are more critical to our understanding of political realities than any early settlement patterns (Hero 1998, 2007).

It should be recognized, as well, that although political cultures tend to change rather slowly, they can be "sped up" in that regard or take a new direction by means of an influx of immigrants. Joel Lieske (2010), extending Elazar's work, has sought to highlight these changing political subcultures in the United States. Lieske looks at racial-ethnic identity, religious affiliation, and social organization in order to classify American political subcultures at the county level. He finds five main subcultures, or types of political cultures, that he terms moralistic, individualistic, pluralistic, bifurcated, and separatist. These, in turn, encompass a number of subcategories that are based on a mix of ancestry (e.g., Nordic, Anglo-French), geography, and other factors. Lieske relates these different subcategories to varieties of political behavior and shows that they have predictive value: they can help one to identify likely political outcomes—policy choices and party preferences—at both the county and state levels.

The concept of political culture has been subject to criticism by those who argue that culture is too difficult to define. Rejecting that criticism, Anne Norton (2004) insists on the concreteness of culture, on its clear expression in institutions, artifacts, documents, language, behavior, and laws. Culture, says Norton, is not a "variable" like religious affiliation or annual income. You cannot, as a researcher, rub it up against other such categories and expect a return. Proposing that "politics is in culture" (i.e., that all politics takes place within a cultural "matrix") and that "culture is political" (i.e., that by its very nature culture is a political project), Norton concludes that the concept of political culture, as valuable as it might be, is nevertheless somewhat misleading. She worries that it suggests an underlying separation or distance between politics and culture. Norton would prefer that we avoid using the term "political culture" while continuing to focus on politics and culture as opposite sides of the same coin. Although I appreciate Norton's point (and admire her book), I find that thinking and writing about political culture can in fact be a useful enterprise.

One might usefully compare political culture to a similar concept—that of political economy. Back in the 18th and 19th centuries, what we today refer to as economics (or economic science) was known as political economy. Students of political economy looked at a wide array of things: production, trade, law, custom, and government in their analyses of national economies. The term "political economy" passed out of use with the rise of modern economics, and much of what it had encompassed came to be regarded as extraneous ("externalities"). Recently, however, political economy has enjoyed a resurgence, as researchers have found that its broad, interdisciplinary perspective has value in trying to understand a complex world (Cohen 2008).

Jeffrey Goldfarb (2012) describes political culture as the intersection of the "culture of power" and the "power of culture," or, in short, "power and culture related" (p. 72). Goldfarb has in mind a somewhat practical application of the concept, using it as a means to both understand and *change* an established political culture for the better. He provides an example along these lines for the United States—the transition from a culture of pervasive, overt racism to one of honoring (or at least recognizing) civil rights. Whereas racism was once a "primary marker" of American political culture (on par with that of South Africa), antiracism and the valuing of civil rights have since come to form the dominant paradigm (pp. 37–38). In each case it was the political culture that set the stage.

Indeed, historians have made productive use of the concept in looking at past eras and how they differ from our own, and in making historical comparisons between nations (Calhoun 2007; Fischer 2012; Kennon 1999; Neely 2005). In the end, I agree with William Lyons and John Scheb (2006), who argue that a political culture "gives people a sense of what government ought to deal with, what is appropriate, and what is not appropriate for public consideration" (p. 3). Political culture sets up the boundaries for debate regarding governance and how governance is to be achieved or realized. It also, one could add, supplies most or all of the terms of that debate. Lyons and Scheb go on to raise some fundamental questions which, they say, an appreciation of political culture can help us to address:

> What type of government will a society have? What role will government play? What functions will it perform? What values will it promote? Which groups will it favor? How much power will leaders have, and how will they use their power? The answers to these questions cannot be ascertained in a cultural vacuum. The role and scope of government reflect a people's view of human nature and of individual capability and responsibility. Few societies

are in complete agreement on these questions. Over time, however, societies develop answers to these questions. As a consensus emerges, these answers form a nation's political culture. (p. 3)

The phrase "over time," of course, refers to history and the evolution of government and society. We may possess some answers to key questions about governance, but at the same time we are engaged in a dialogue with our past regarding the viability of those answers. As the picture becomes more complex (through generational change, immigration, technological advancement, etc.), our questions become more persistent. Culture provides not only rules and norms—the "answers"—but also the ways of escaping or getting around them. In this way, policies and political actions inevitably become instances of affirmation or rejection. Moreover, the consequences of our actions extend into the future, producing something that we may neither have intended nor foreseen (Norton 2004, 79). It is in the arena of political culture, then, that we spell out where we are going as a society based on where we have been.

—*Michael Shally-Jensen*

Bibliography

Calhoun, Charles W. 2007. "The Political Culture: Public Life and the Conduct of Politics." In Charles W. Calhoun, ed. *The Gilded Age: Perspectives on the Origins of Modern America.* 2nd ed. Lanham, MD: Rowman & Littlefield, pp. 239–64.

Cohen, Benjamin J. 2008. *International Political Economy: An Intellectual History.* New York: Oxford University Press.

Elazar, Daniel J. 1966. *American Federalism: A View from the States.* New York: Thomas Y. Crowell Company.

Fischer, David Hackett. 2012. *Fairness and Freedom: A History of Two Open Societies: New Zealand and the United States.* New York: Oxford University Press.

Geertz, Clifford. 1973. *The Interpretation of Cultures.* New York: Basic Books.

Goldfarb, Jeffrey C. 2012. *Reinventing Political Culture.* Cambridge: Polity Press.

Hero, Rodney E. 1998. *Faces of Inequality: Social Diversity in American Politics.* New York: Oxford University Press.

Hero, Rodney E. 2007. *Racial Diversity and Social Capital: Equality and Community in America.* New York: Cambridge University Press.

Kennon, Donald R., ed. 1999. *A Republic for the Ages: The United States Capitol and the Political Culture of the Early Republic.* Charlottesville: University Press of Virginia.

Lieske, Joel. 2010. "The Changing Regional Subcultures of the American States and the Utility of a New Cultural Measure." *Political Research Quarterly* 63: 538–52.

Lyons, William, and John M. Scheb II. 2006. *American Government: Politics and Political Culture.* 4th ed. Mason, OH: Atomic Dog/Thomson Custom.

Morgan, David R., and Sheilah S. Watson. 1991. "Political Culture, Political System Characteristics, and Public Policies among the American States." *Publius: The Journal of Federalism* 21: 31–48.

Morone, James A. 2009. "Political Culture." In Michael Kazin and Rebecca Edwards, eds., *Princeton Encyclopedia of American Political History.* Princeton, NJ: Princeton University Press.

Moser, John E. 2001. "Political Culture." In George Kurian, ed., *Encyclopedia of American Studies*. Danbury, CT: Grolier.

Neely, Mark E., Jr. 2005. *The Boundaries of American Political Culture in the Civil War Era*. Chapel Hill: University of North Carolina Press.

Norton, Anne. 2004. *95 Theses on Politics, Culture, and Method*. New Haven, CT: Yale University Press.

Pye, Lucien, and Sidney Verba, eds. 1965. *Political Culture and Political Development*. Princeton, NJ: Princeton University Press.

Tocqueville, Alexis. 1863 (1835). *Democracy in America*. 2nd ed. Translated by H. Reeve. Cambridge: Sever & Francis.

Guide to Related Topics

CULTURE WARS

Abortion and Politics

Affirmative Action

American Flag

Arts, Humanities, and Politics

Biotechnology and Politics

Church–State Relations

Cultural Pluralism

Culture Wars

Desegregation and Politics

Disability and Politics

Education Policy and Politics

Evolution, Creationism, and Politics

Family, State, and Politics

Gay and Lesbian Culture and Politics

Guns and Politics

Immigration and Politics

Popular Culture and Politics

Prayer and Religious Symbols in Public Places

Right to Die and Politics

Social Welfare and Politics

DEMOGRAPHICS

African Americans and Politics

American Indian Politics

Asian Americans and Politics

Baby Boom Generation and Politics

Catholics and Politics

Cities and Politics

Class and Politics

Gay and Lesbian Culture and Politics

Immigration and Politics

Jews and Politics

Labor and Politics

Latinos and Politics

Mormons and Politics

Muslims, Arab Americans, and Politics

Protestants, Evangelicals, and Politics

Race, Ethnicity, and Politics

Regions and Regionalism: The Midwest

Regions and Regionalism: The Northeast

Regions and Regionalism: The South

Regions and Regionalism: The West

State and Local Politics

Veterans and Politics

Women and Politics

Youth and Politics

GOVERNMENT OFFICES AND INSTITUTIONS

Bureaucracy and American Political Culture

Congress and Congressional Politics

First Lady

Governors and Gubernatorial Politics

House of Representatives, United States

Intelligence Community and Politics

Military and Politics

Presidency and Presidential Politics

Presidential Appointments

Senate, United States

Supreme Court, United States

Vice Presidency

White House and Capitol Hill

IDEAS AND CULTURAL PRACTICES

American "Exceptionalism"

American Dream

Anti-intellectualism in American Life

Church–State Relations

Citizenship and Politics

Civil Liberties

Civil Religion

Civil War (1861–1865) and Modern Memory

Cold War Political Culture

Conspiracy Theory and the "Paranoid Style"

Consumer Culture and Politics

Cultural Pluralism

Democracy

Ethics in Government

Federalism

Free Speech

Humor, Satire, and Politics

Individualism

Islamophobia

Liberty

Monuments, Memorials, and Public History

National Identity

Personality and Politics

Power and Politics

Pragmatism

Privatization and Deregulation

Public Opinion

Religion and Politics

Right to Die and Politics

Scandals in Politics

Separation of Powers

Social Welfare and Politics

IDEOLOGIES

Conservatives and Conservatism

Democratic Party

Far-Right Parties and Organizations

Green Movement and Politics

Independent Voters

Left and Politics

Liberals and Liberalism

Libertarians and Libertarianism

Nationalism

Progressives, Progressivism, and President Barack Obama

Protest Movements

Republican Party

Tea Party

Think Tanks and Politics

LAW AND SOCIETY

Affirmative Action

Campaign Finance

Civil Rights

Constitution and Constitutionalism

Corporate Behavior and Politics

Corruption in Politics

Courts and Court Politics

Crime, Punishment, and Politics

Death Penalty and Politics

Drug Policy and Politics

Free Speech

Guns and Politics

Pardons and Politics

Prayer and Religious Symbols in Public Places

Privacy Rights and Politics

State Secrets and Politics

States' Rights

Supreme Court, United States

Surveillance, Society, and Politics

Violence and Politics

MEDIA AND COMMUNICATIONS

Advertising, Political

Campaigns and Campaigning

Debates, Presidential

Disinformation, Deception, and Politics

Fear Tactics in Politics

Film and American Political Culture

Information Leaks and Politics

Literature and Politics

Political Communications

Popular Culture and Politics

Presidential Memoirs, Autobiographies, and Biographies

Print Media and Politics

Public Opinion

Social Media and Politics

Talk Radio and Politics

Television News, Opinion, and Politics

Theater and Ritual in American Politics

POLITICAL ECONOMY

Banking Policy and Politics

Budget Politics

Coastal Zones, Economics, and Politics

Corporate Behavior and Politics

Debt, Deficit, and Politics

Economic Policy and Politics

Globalization

Health Care and Politics

Housing Policy and Politics

Inequality and Politics

Poverty and Politics

Privatization and Deregulation

Public–Private Partnerships

Recession and Politics

Social Security and Politics

Tax Policy and Politics

Trade Policy and Politics

POLITICS AS SUCH

Campaign Finance

Campaigns and Campaigning

Crises, Emergencies, and Politics

Electoral College

Executive Privilege

Factions and Intraparty Conflict

Filibuster

Grassroots Activism

Gridlock, Legislative

Impeachment

Initiatives and Referendums

Interest Groups and Lobbying

Leaders and Leadership

Legislative Veto

Midterm Elections

Nominating Conventions

Partisanship and Polarization

Political Consultants and Campaign Managers

Political Parties

Primaries and Caucuses

Protest Movements

Recall Elections

Redistricting

Term Limits

Third Parties

Veto Power

Voter Turnout

Voting and Politics

SCIENCE, ENVIRONMENT, AND TECHNOLOGY

Air Quality and Politics

Biotechnology and Politics

Climate Change and Politics

Coastal Zones, Economics, and Politics

Cybersecurity and Politics

Disasters and Politics

Endangered Species Act, Habitat Loss, and Politics

Energy Policy and Politics

Environmental Policy and Politics

Evolution, Creationism, and Politics

Farming, Food, and Politics

Infrastructure and Politics

Internet, Society, and Politics

Mining and Politics

National Parks, Wilderness Areas, and Politics

Nuclear Power and Politics

Oil, Natural Gas, and Politics

Public Health and Politics

Science, Technology, and Society

Space Policy and Politics

Water Policy and Politics

SECURITY ISSUES

Border Protection and Politics

Cybersecurity and Politics

Foreign Policy and Politics

Information Leaks and Politics

Intelligence Community and Politics

Military and Politics

National Security Policy and Politics

Nuclear Weapons and Politics

State Secrets and Politics

Surveillance, Society, and Politics

Terrorism, Torture, and Politics

War and Politics

A

ABORTION AND POLITICS

"Abortion" refers to the premature end or termination of a pregnancy after implantation of the fertilized ovum in the uterus and before fetal viability or the point in fetal development at which a fetus can survive outside a woman's womb without life support. The term refers to the expulsion of the fetus, fetal membranes, and the placenta from the uterus and includes spontaneous miscarriages and medical procedures performed by a licensed physician intended to end pregnancy at any gestational age.

Abortion as a Social Issue

As a contemporary social issue, elective abortion raises important questions about the rights of pregnant women, the meaning of motherhood, and the rights of fetuses. Since the late 1960s, abortion has been a key issue in the contemporary U.S. culture wars. The term "culture wars" refers to ongoing political debates over contemporary social issues, including not only abortion but also homosexuality, the death penalty, and euthanasia. Culture wars arise from conflicting sets of values between conservatives and progressives. The culture war debates, particularly those surrounding the issue of abortion, remain contentious among the American public. The debates have resulted in disparate and strongly held opinions and have resulted in the emergence of activist groups taking a variety of positions on abortion. Activists include those who support a woman's right to abortion (epitomized in groups such as the National Abortion Rights Action League—NARAL Pro-Choice America) and those who oppose abortion on religious or moral grounds (such as right-to-life organizations).

Researchers suggest that the continuing debates over abortion have called into question traditional beliefs about the relations between men and women, raised vexing issues about the control of women's bodies and women's roles, and brought about changes in the division of labor in the family and in the broader occupational arena. Elective abortion has called into question long-standing beliefs about the moral nature of sexuality. Further, elective abortion has challenged the notion of sexual relations as privileged activities that are symbolic of commitments, responsibilities, and obligations between men and women. Elective abortion also brings to the fore the more personal issue of the meaning of pregnancy.

Historically, the debate over abortion has been one of competing definitions of motherhood. Pro-life activists argue that family, and particularly motherhood, is the cornerstone of society. Pro-choice activists argue

American Opinions on Abortion
"Should abortion be . . .?"

	CNN/ORC	Gallup
Always Legal	27%	26%
Sometimes Legal	51%	52%
Always Illegal	20%	20%

Source: PollingReport.com (data aggregator), October 2014.

Pro-life and pro-choice demonstrators hold signs side by side during the annual "March for Life" on January 24, 2005, in Washington, D.C. Pro-life activists marched from the Ellipse to the Supreme Court building to protest the 32nd anniversary of the *Roe v. Wade* decision that legalized abortion. On February 22, 2005, the Supreme Court refused Norma McCorvey's—the "Roe" in the landmark case—request to overturn the 1973 ruling. (Brendan Smialowski/AFP/Getty Images)

that reproductive choice is central to women controlling their own lives. More contemporary debates focus on the ethical and moral nature of personhood and the rights of the fetus. In the past 30 years, these debates have become politicized, resulting in the passage of increasingly restrictive laws governing abortion, abortion doctors, and abortion clinics.

Abortion Procedures

An early abortion procedure, performed during the first trimester, or the first 12 weeks of pregnancy, is one of the safest types of medical procedures when performed by a trained health care professional in a hygienic environment. The risk of abortion complications is minimal, with less than 1 percent of all patients experiencing a serious complication. In the United States, the risk of death resulting from abortion is less than 0.6 per 100,000 procedures. The risks associated with abortion are less than those associated with childbirth.

There are two major types of procedures used to terminate a pregnancy. These procedures include both medical abortions and surgical abortions. The type of procedure that will be used is selected by the physician and the patient after determining the stage of pregnancy. Early-term abortions, or those occurring in the first trimester of pregnancy, may be either medical or surgical. Surgical abortions are used in later-stage abortions, or those occurring in the second or third trimester.

Early First-Trimester Abortions

Early first-trimester abortions are defined as those performed within the first eight weeks of pregnancy. Two procedures may be used: medical (nonsurgical) or surgical abortions. Medical abortions involve the administration of oral medications that cause expulsion of the fetus from the uterus (miscarriage). Medical abortions include the use of RU-486, commonly referred to as the abortion pill, as well as other combinations of drugs, depending on the stage of pregnancy. Typically, a combination of methotrexate and misoprostol is used to end pregnancies of up to seven weeks in duration. RU-486, a combination of mifepristone and misoprostol, is used to terminate pregnancies between seven and nine weeks in duration. Women opting for a medical abortion are typically administered methotrexate orally or by injection in a physician's office. Misoprostol tablets are administered orally or vaginally during a second office visit that occurs five to seven days later. The procedure is then followed up with a visit to the physician to confirm complete expulsion of the fetus and the absence of any complications. Many women find that medical abortions are more private and more natural than surgical abortions.

A surgical abortion involves the use of suction aspiration to remove the fetus from the uterus. Surgical abortion is generally used to end pregnancies between 6 and 14 weeks' duration. Vacuum aspiration uses suction to expel the contents of the uterus through the cervix. Vacuum aspiration is performed in a doctor's office or clinic setting and typically takes less than 15 minutes. Patients receive an injection into the cervix to numb the cervical area. The physician inserts dilators to open the cervix, where a sterile cannula is inserted. The cannula, attached to tubing that is attached to a vacuum or manual pump, gently empties the contents of the uterus. The procedure is highly effective and is used most often in first-trimester abortions.

Second-Trimester Abortions

Second-trimester abortions refer to abortions performed between the 13th and 20th weeks of pregnancy. In some cases, second-trimester abortions may be performed as late as the 24th week of pregnancy. Second-trimester abortions carry a greater risk of complications due to the later stage of fetal development and are performed under local or general anesthesia. The cervix is dilated and a curette or forceps are inserted through the vagina, and the fetus is separated into pieces and extracted. Second-trimester abortions are typically performed in cases where a woman has not had access to early medical care and has only recently had a pregnancy confirmed, or in cases where a recent diagnosis of genetic or fetal developmental problems has been made.

The available abortion procedures provide many options to women. Pregnancy terminations performed between the 6th and 12th weeks of pregnancy are safe and include both medical and surgical procedures. Medical abortions, accomplished with a combination of drugs that induce a miscarriage, provide women with the option of ending a pregnancy in the privacy of her home in a relatively natural way. Surgical abortion, by using vacuum aspiration, gently removes the fetus from the uterus and includes minimal risks. These risks are usually limited to cramping and bleeding that last from a few hours to several days after the procedure. Most women who abort during the first trimester are able to return to their normal routines the following day. Antibiotics are generally prescribed following a first-trimester abortion to decrease any risk of infection, and a follow-up visit several weeks later makes first-trimester abortions safer than childbirth.

Early Abortion Laws

Laws governing abortion up until the early 19th century were modeled after English Common Law, which criminalized abortion after "quickening," or the point in fetal gestational development where a woman could feel fetal movement. Prior to quickening, the fetus was believed to be little more than a mass of undifferentiated cells. Concurrent with the formal organization of the American Medical Association in the mid-1800s, increasingly restrictive abortion laws were enacted. In general, these laws were designed to decrease competition between physicians and midwives, as well as other lay practitioners of medicine, including pharmacists. A few years later, the New York Society for the Suppression of Vice successfully lobbied for passage of the Comstock Laws, a series of laws prohibiting pornography and banning contraceptives and information about abortion. With the formal organization of physicians and the enactment of the Comstock Laws, pregnancy and childbirth shifted from the realm of privacy and control by women to one that was increasingly public and under the supervision of the male medical establishment. Specifically, all abortions were prohibited except therapeutic abortions that were necessary to save the life of the pregnant woman. These laws remained unchallenged until the early 1920s, when Margaret Sanger and her husband were charged with illegally distributing information about birth control. An appeal of Sanger's conviction followed, and contraception was legalized, but only for the prevention or cure of disease. It was not until the early 1930s that federal laws were enacted which prohibited government interference in the physician–patient relationship as it related to doctors prescribing contraception for their women patients. Unplanned pregnancies continued to occur, and women who had access to medical care and a sympathetic physician were often able to obtain a therapeutic abortion. These therapeutic abortions were often performed under less-than-sanitary conditions because of the stigma attached to both the physicians performing them and the women who sought to abort.

By the 1950s, a growing abortion reform movement had gained ground. The movement sought to expand the circumstances under which therapeutic abortions were available; it sought to include circumstances in which childbirth endangered a woman's mental or physical health, where there was a high likelihood of fetal abnormality, or when pregnancy was the result of rape or incest. The abortion reform movement also sought to end the threat of back-alley abortions performed by questionable practitioners or performed under unsanitary conditions that posed significant health risks to women and often resulted in death.

By the 1960s, although the abortion reform movement was gaining strength, nontherapeutic abortion remained illegal, and therapeutic abortion was largely a privilege of the white middle to upper classes. A growing covert abortion rights collective emerged in the Midwest. Known as the Jane Project, the movement included members of the National Organization for Women, student activists, housewives, and mothers who believed access to safe, affordable abortion was every woman's right. The Jane Project was an anonymous abortion service operated by volunteers who provided counseling services and acted in an intermediary capacity to link women seeking abortions with physicians who were willing to perform the procedure. Members of the collective, outraged over the exorbitant prices charged by many physicians, learned to perform the abortion procedure themselves. Former members of the Jane Project report providing more than 12,000 safe and affordable abortions for women in the years before abortion was legalized.

Activists involved in the early movement to reform abortion laws experienced their first victory in 1967, when the Colorado legislature enacted less restrictive regulations governing abortion. By 1970, four additional states had revised their criminal penalties for abortions performed in the early stages of pregnancy by licensed physicians, as long as the procedures followed legal procedures and conformed to health regulations. These early challenges to restrictive abortion laws set into motion changes that would pave the way to the legal right to abortion.

The Legal Right to Abortion

Two important legal cases reviewed by the U.S. Supreme Court in the 1970s established the legal right to abortion. In the first and more important case, *Roe v. Wade* (1973), the court overturned a Texas law that prohibited abortions in all circumstances except when the pregnant woman's life was endangered. In a second companion case, *Doe v. Bolton* (1973), the high court ruled that denying a woman the right to decide whether to carry a pregnancy to term violated privacy rights guaranteed under the U.S. Constitution's Bill of Rights. These decisions, rendered by a 7–2 vote by the Supreme Court justices in 1973, struck down state statutes outlawing abortion and laid the groundwork for one of the most controversial public issues in modern history.

The Supreme Court decisions sparked a dramatic reaction by the American public. Supporters viewed the Court's decision as a victory for women's rights, equality, and empowerment, while opponents viewed the decision as a frontal attack on religious and moral values. Both supporters and opponents mobilized, forming local and national coalitions that politicized the issue and propelled abortion to the forefront of the political arena. Opponents of abortion identified themselves as "antiabortion" activists, while those who supported a woman's right to choose whether to carry a pregnancy to term adopted the term "pro-choice" activists. These two groups rallied to sway the opinions of a public that was initially disinterested in the issue.

The Early Years Post Roe

Following the *Roe* decision, antiabortion activists worked to limit the effects of the Supreme Court decision. Specifically, they sought to prevent federal and state monies from being used for abortion. In 1977, the Hyde Amendment was passed by Congress, and limits were enacted that restricted the use of federal funds for abortion. In the ensuing years, the amendment underwent several revisions that limited Medicaid coverage for abortion to cases of rape, incest, and life endangerment. The Hyde Amendment significantly impacted low-income women and women of color. It stigmatized abortion care by limiting federal and state health care program provisions for basic reproductive health care.

As antiabortion and pro-choice advocates mobilized, their battles increasingly played out in front of abortion clinics throughout the country, with both groups eager to promote their platforms about the legal right to abortion. Abortion clinics around the country became the sites of impassioned protests and angry confrontations between activists on both sides of the issue. Confrontations included both antiabortionists who pled with women to reconsider their decision to abort and pro-choice activists working as escorts for those who sought abortions, shielding the women from the other activists who were attempting to intervene in their decision. Many clinics became a battleground for media coverage and 30-second sound bites that further polarized activists on both sides of the issue. Moreover, media coverage victimized women who had privately made a decision to abort by publicly thrusting them into the middle of an increasingly public battle.

By the mid-1980s, following courtroom and congressional defeats to overturn the *Roe v. Wade* decision and a growing public that was supportive of the legal right to abortion, antiabortion activists broadened their strategies and tactics to focus on shutting down abortion clinics. Moreover, antiabortionist groups began identifying themselves as "pro-life" activists to publicly demonstrate their emphasis on the sanctity of all human life and to reflect their concern for both the pregnant woman and the fetus. The change in labels was also an attempt to neutralize the negative media attention resulting from a number of radical and militant antiabortion groups that emerged in the 1980s, many of which advocated the use of intimidation and violence to end the availability of abortion and to close down clinics. For these more radical groups, the use of violence against a fetus was seen as justification for violence that included the bombing and destruction of abortion clinics and included, in some cases, the injury or murder of physicians and staff working at the clinics.

The polarization of activists on both sides of the issue and the increased incidence of violence at abortion clinics resulted in the passage of the Freedom of Access to Clinic Entrance Act (FACEA). FACEA prohibited any person from threatening, assaulting, or vandalizing abortion clinic property, clinic staff, or clinic patients, as well as prohibited blockading abortion clinic entrances to prevent entry by any person providing or receiving reproductive health services. The law also provided both criminal and civil penalties for those breaking the law. Increasingly, activists on both sides of the issue shifted their focus from women seeking to abort and abortion clinics to the interior of courtrooms, where challenges to the legal right to abortion continue to be heard. Meanwhile, increasingly restrictive laws governing abortion and abortion clinics were passed.

The Later Years Post Roe

With the legal right to abortion established and the battle lines between pro-life and pro-choice activists firmly drawn, key legislative actions impacting the legal right to abortion characterized the changing landscape of the abortion debate. In the 1989 *Webster v. Reproductive Health Services* case, the Supreme Court affirmed a Missouri law that imposed restrictions on the use of state funds, facilities, and employees in performing, assisting with, or counseling about abortion. The decision for the first time granted specific powers to states to regulate abortion and has been interpreted by many as the beginning of a series of decisions that might potentially undermine the rights granted in the *Roe* decision.

Following the *Webster* case, the U.S. Supreme Court reviewed and ruled in *Planned Parenthood of Southeastern Pennsylvania v. Casey* (1992), a case that challenged five separate regulations of the Pennsylvania Abortion Control Act as being unconstitutional under *Roe v. Wade*. Specifically, the Pennsylvania act required doctors to provide women seeking abortion with a list of possible health complications and risks of abortion prior to the procedure, required married women to inform their husbands of an abortion beforehand, required parental or guardian consent for minors having an abortion, imposed a 24-hour waiting period before a woman could have an elective abortion, and mandated specific reporting requirements for clinics where abortions were performed. The court upheld four of the five provisions, striking down the spousal consent rule, which was found to give excessive power to husbands over their wives and possibly exacerbate spousal abuse. Moreover, the Court allowed for waivers for extenuating circumstances in the parental notification requirement. *Casey* was the first direct challenge to *Roe*, and the court modified the trimester framework that *Roe* had created. It also restructured the legal standard by which restrictive abortion laws were evaluated. *Casey* gave states the right to regulate abortion during the entire period before fetal viability, and they could do so for reasons other than to protect the health of the mother. The increased legal rights provided to states to impose restrictions on laws governing abortion resulted in a tightening of the requirements for clinics providing abortions and adversely affected many women who sought abortions, particularly low-income women and women who lived in rural areas. As a result of the increased power granted to states to regulate abortion, women were required to attend a pre-abortion counseling session before the procedure, in which they received information on the possible risks and complications from abortion, and they were required to wait at least 24 hours after the counseling session to undergo the procedure. For poor women or for women who lived in states where there were no abortion clinics, the costs associated with the procedure rose dramatically because of the associated travel and time off from work.

Since *Casey*, the Supreme Court has heard only one case related to abortion. In *Stenberg v. Carhart* (2000), the constitutionality of a Nebraska law prohibiting so-called partial birth abortions was heard by the high court. The Nebraska law prohibited this form of abortion—known as intact dilation and extraction (IDX) within the medical community—under any circumstances. Physicians who violated the law were charged with a felony, fined, sentenced to jail time, and automatically had their license to practice medicine revoked. The IDX procedure is generally performed in cases where significant fetal abnormalities have been diagnosed and represents less than one-half of 1 percent of all abortions performed. The pregnancy is terminated by partially extracting the fetus from the uterus, collapsing its skull, and removing its brain. In the *Stenberg* case, the court ruled that the law was unconstitutional because it did not include a provision for an exception in cases where the pregnant woman's health was at risk. However, in 2007, the decision was reversed in *Gonzales v. Carhart*, the ban reinstated. The court held that the IDX prohibition did not unduly affect a woman's ability to obtain an abortion.

The Shift in Recent Debates

The differences between activist groups involved in the abortion debates have traditionally crystallized publicly as differences in the meaning of abortion. Pro-life activists define abortion as murder and a violation against the sanctity of human life. Pro-choice activists argue that control of reproduction is paramount to women's empowerment and autonomy. More recently, the issues have focused on questions about the beginning of life and the rights associated with personhood. Technological advancements in the field of gynecology and obstetrics are occurring rapidly and influencing how we understand reproduction and pregnancy. Advances in the use of ultrasound technology, the rise in fetal diagnostic testing to identify genetic abnormalities, and the development of intrauterine fetal surgical techniques to correct abnormalities in the fetus prior to birth all contribute to defining the fetus as a wholly separate being or person from the woman who is pregnant.

These new constructions of the fetus as a separate person, coupled with visual technologies that allow for very early detection of pregnancy and images of the developing fetus, give rise to debates about what constitutes personhood and the rights, if any, the state of personhood confers upon the entity defined as a person. The issue of viability, defined as the developmental stage at which a fetus can survive without medical intervention, is complicated in many respects by these technological advances. Those who identify themselves as pro-life argue that all life begins at the moment of conception and point to technology to affirm their position. Many pro-life activists argue that the fetus is a preborn person with full rights of personhood—full rights that justify all actions to preserve, protect, and defend the person and his or her rights before and after the birth process. Such advocates have also argued for the recognition of fetal pain (or the capability to feel pain) as a litmus test with respect to abortion decisions.

Those who identify themselves as pro-choice argue that personhood can only be conferred on born persons and that a developing fetus is neither a born person nor a fully developed being. These contemporary debates concerning personhood and rights continue to divide the public and are particularly germane to the issue of fetal surgery. Fetal surgery is cost-prohibitive, success rates are very low, and some argue that the scarcity of medical resources should be directed toward a greater number of patients or toward the provision of services that have greater success rates.

At the state level, the battle has recently been fought in terms of pre-abortion counseling, including the issue of whether to require ultrasounds and whether pregnant women should be shown the ultrasound images. Twenty-three states now require that an ultrasound be done prior to an abortion and that the pregnant woman be given an opportunity to view the image. A few states require both that an ultrasound be done and that the woman view the image, although such laws are currently in litigation (National Right to Life Committee 2013).

Another battle has opened up in the area of the licensing of clinics that perform abortions. Some states, such as Texas, have passed restrictive laws requiring clinics to meet heightened quality and service standards. The effect is to cause many clinics to shut down because they do not have the resources to upgrade their facilities. Opponents argue that the new laws are medically unnecessary and will force women to resort to older, unregulated methods. The U.S. Supreme Court, in October 2014, agreed with the abortion rights activists and ordered that the clinics remain open.

The Impact of Restrictive Abortion Legislation

Abortion is one of the most common and safest medical procedures that women aged 15 to 44 can undergo in the United States. According to the U.S. Census Bureau's *2010 Statistical Abstract*, which combines figures reported by the Centers for Disease Control and the individual states, approximately 1.2 million abortions were performed in the United States in 2005. Among women aged 15 to 44, the abortion rate declined from 27 out of 1,000 in 1990 to 19.4 out of 1,000 in 2005. The number of abortions and the rate of abortions have declined over the years, partly as a result of improved methods of birth control and partly as a result of decreased access to abortion services.

The number of physicians who provide abortion services has declined by approximately 39 percent, from 2,900 in 1982 to less than 1,800 in 2000. Although some of the decline is the result of a shift from hospital-based providers to specialized clinics offering abortion procedures, this shift is further exacerbated by the number of clinics that have closed in recent years due to increased regulatory requirements that make remaining open more difficult. Moreover, the decline in providers of abortion services means that some women will experience a more difficult time in locating and affording services. Today, only 13 percent of the counties in the United States provide abortion services to women; that is, abortion services are unavailable in 87 percent of U.S. counties. Moreover, the Hyde Amendment preventing federal funds from being used to pay for abortion services was reaffirmed in March 2010 by President Barack Obama as part of an overall health care reform legislative package.

The Food and Drug Administration's (FDA) approval of Plan B, an emergency contraceptive best known as "the morning after pill," and mifepristone (RU-486) for early medication-induced abortions may be shifting the location of abortion procedures away from abortion clinics to other locations such as family planning clinics and physicians' offices. However, neither of these recent FDA approvals eliminates the need for reproductive health care that includes abortion care. While the issue of abortion may spawn disparate opinions about the meaning of motherhood, family values, the changing dynamics of male–female relations, and sexual morality, as well as raise issues about personhood and rights, unintended pregnancies disproportionately impact women and their children. This is especially true of poor women and women of color whose access to reproductive health care may be limited or nonexistent. Historically, women from the middle and upper classes have had access to abortion—be it legal, illegal, therapeutic, or nontherapeutic—while women from less privileged backgrounds have often been forced to rely on back-alley abortionists whose lack of training and provision of services cost women their health and, often, their lives.

See also Culture Wars; Evolution, Creationism, and Politics; Family, State, and Politics; Privacy Rights and Politics; Supreme Court, United States; Women and Politics.

Jonelle Husain

Bibliography

Ainsworth, Scott H., and Thad E. Hall. 2010. *Abortion Politics in Congress: Strategic Incrementalism and Policy Change*. New York: Cambridge University Press.

Ehrenreich, Nancy, ed. 2008. *The Reproductive Rights Reader: Law, Medicine, and the Construction of Motherhood*. New York: Routledge.

Ginsberg, Faye, D. 1998. *Contested Lives: The Abortion Debate in an American Community*. Rev. ed. Berkeley: University of California Press.

Herring, Mark Youngblood. 2003. *The Pro-Life/ Choice Debate*. Westport, CT: Greenwood Press.

Maxwell, Carol J. C. 2002. *Pro-Life Activists in America: Meaning, Motivation, and Direct Action*. Cambridge: Cambridge University Press.

McBride, Dorothy E. 2008. *Abortion in the United States: A Reference Handbook*. Santa Barbara, CA: ABC-CLIO.

National Right to Life Committee. 2014. "A Window to the Womb: A Guide to State Laws on Ultrasound." June 12. http://www.nrlc.org/uploads/stateleg/Ul trasoundFactsheet.pdf. Accessed May 16, 2014.

Page, Cristina. 2006. *How the Pro-Choice Movement Saved America: Freedom, Politics, and the War on Sex*. New York: Basic Books.

Pew Research. 2013. "A History of Key Abortion Rulings." January 16. http://www.pewforum.org /2013/01/16/a-history-of-key-abortion-rulings-of- the-us-supreme-court/. Accessed May 16, 2014.

Rose, Melody. 2007. *Safe, Legal, and Available? Abortion Politics in the United States*. Washington, DC: CQ Press.

Shrage, Laurie. 2003. *Abortion and Social Responsibility: Depolarizing the Debate*. New York: Oxford University Press.

Solinger, Rickie. 2013. *Reproductive Politics: What Everyone Needs to Know*. New York: New York University Press.

Wilson, Joshua. 2013. *The Street Politics of Abortion: Speech, Violence, and America's Culture Wars*. Stanford, CA: Stanford University Press.

ADVERTISING, POLITICAL

Broadly construed, political advertising in America is older than the Republic itself. Ben Franklin's "Join or Die" poster, widely thought to be America's first political cartoon, was published in 1754, during the French and Indian War (and later recycled when tensions grew between the colonies and Great Britain prior to the Revolutionary War). Today, political advertising, largely in the form of audiovisual 30-second spots, remains the principal vehicle by which political communicators tell the stories of American politics. These spots draw upon a deep array of research-tested content, spanning both policy and emotion. Ads attacking one's opponents are particularly common. Such "negative" spots can effectively demobilize those inclined to support the sponsor's opponent, though they may also contribute to a broader popular disdain for the craft of politics. The propensity for ads to distort the truth or perpetrate falsehoods engenders further antipathy and has given rise to the practice of ad-watch journalism, an attempt to police the most egregious transgressions of veracity. In an age of social media, activists and ordinary citizens are full participants in the generation of ads (content), in their dissemination, and in criticism and analysis of the ads. Emerging models reporting and communicating promise a more diverse and democratic discourse, albeit a noisier one as well.

Politics on Air

America's earliest purchases of airtime for political broadcasts featured candidate speeches. Both major party presidential nominees paid to air speeches on radio in the 1924 election. The Republicans aired the first nonspeech radio ad in 1928. Since the middle of the 20th century, advertising has turned to television and become an important audiovisual medium.

The first TV polispot was aired in 1950 by Connecticut senator William Benton, founder of a New York City ad agency who had been appointed to the state's vacant U.S. Senate seat and who was running in a special election against Prescott Bush (father of former U.S. president George H.W. Bush). In the 1952 presidential campaign, Republican nominee Dwight D. Eisenhower turned to seasoned Madison Avenue ad makers to craft a series of paid spots. Thomas Rosser Reeves Jr., a pioneer of TV advertising and the hard sell approach (including memorable but irritating ads), was a key architect of Ike's spots. The "Eisenhower Answers America" ad campaign featured the general's

Democratic presidential candidate Bill Clinton's counterstrike TV ad attacking President George H.W. Bush's attack ad, with a quote from *The Washington Post* calling the Bush ad "misleading." (Ted Thai/The Life Picture Collection/Getty Images)

taped "answers" to questions from ordinary Americans filmed after the answers had been recorded. Eisenhower's opponent, Illinois governor Adlai Stevenson, denounced the use of the techniques of soap-selling in promoting political candidates. The most famous paid advertisement of the 1952 campaign, however, was not a 30- or 60-second spot, but the 30-minute-long "Checkers" speech delivered by Republican vice presidential nominee Richard M. Nixon, viewed by nearly half of the nation's households with televisions. Nixon's defense against charges he personally profited from a secret fund was credited with saving his spot on the GOP ticket in the face of calls that he step down. (The fund was similar to those enjoyed by many politicians at that time, including, it was later learned, a larger one aiding Governor Stevenson).

In 1956, Madison Avenue advertising agencies avoided taking on the Democratic account for fear of alienating the Republican businessmen who comprised their corporate clients. While both parties would play down the significance of their advertising campaigns that year, the practice was beginning to evolve. Higher production values started to appear in political commercials (more action and imagery), and the Democrats pioneered the first true "attack" ads at the presidential level, featuring clips from candidate Eisenhower's 1952 ads and the tagline "How's that again, General?"

By 1960, 90 percent of homes had television sets. Thirty-minute ads were still common, perhaps most notably a recording of John F. Kennedy's speech before the Greater Houston Ministerial Association on September 12, 1960. In it, Kennedy responded to concerns that as a Catholic, he would be taking direction from the Pope on important questions of public policy. The speech has been described as one of Kennedy's greatest, and a 30-minute version was aired widely in states with large numbers of Catholic voters. One-minute and five-minute versions were aired in states with conspicuous Protestant resistance to Kennedy.

The 1964 campaign spawned what is to this day perhaps the most famous of all campaign commercials—even though it aired only once. Seizing on comments by GOP nominee Barry Goldwater suggesting his willingness to consider the tactical use of nuclear weapons, the ad juxtaposed a young girl counting the petals on a daisy with the voice of NASA's mission control in Houston in the countdown to a rocket launch. As the countdown reaches zero, the young girl looks up and the camera zooms in on her eye to reveal the reflection of the mushroom cloud of a nuclear explosion. It was an example of what the ad's creator, Tony Schwartz, saw as the primary characteristic of powerful advertising. For Schwartz, effective ads did not inject a message into the viewer (as posited by the hypodermic needle model of political communication that still informs a great deal of research on ads), but rather by drawing out what was already in the viewers' mind. Goldwater is never mentioned in the ad—but viewers familiar with his belligerent views on foreign policy readily drew the intended inference.

Initially, the Johnson campaign planned to air the spot on all three national television networks, but following its single airing on "Monday Night at the Movies" and the groundswell of reaction it created, those plans were shelved. Indeed, Republican attacks on the ad led to its repeated airing on all three network newscasts and various political commentary programs. Kathleen Hall Jamieson, perhaps the most distinguished student of political advertising, has called such an appearance of campaign spots in news "news ads." Their rebroadcast as news can magnify their reach even where sponsors themselves could not afford to.

The 1964 campaign included at least one other notable ad: a 30-minute speech by General Electric Company spokesman Ronald Reagan on behalf of candidate Goldwater. Reagan's speech drew upon the storytelling techniques the former actor honed while making thousands of speeches across the country for GE from 1954 to 1962. Many Republicans found Reagan more effective and appealing than Goldwater, and the speech would help propel the former union leader's political career to the highest levels.

Standard Fare

By 1968, the power of political advertising on television was widely recognized. Ads increasingly turned away from the "hard sell" approach and embraced the production values of more popular genres of programming. Journalist Joe McGinnis described the role of consultants including Roger Ailes in promoting the "New Nixon," while candidate Robert F. Kennedy hired an ad agency that enlisted filmmaker Charles Guggenheim to produce spots in his quest for the Democratic presidential nomination. Guggenheim's memorial film (Robert Kennedy Remembered) was shown at the Democratic National Convention and later won an Oscar.

Guggenheim would also be the principal ad maker for Democratic presidential nominee George McGovern in 1972. McGovern's ads employed the cinema verité or real-life school of ad making, which allowed the candidate to appeal to Democratic voters turning against the machine-politics establishment in their party. The trend away from carefully scripted spots would accelerate in the 1976 campaign when the legacy of Watergate enshrouded the politics of the nation. That year, both incumbent President Gerald Ford and challenger Jimmy Carter frequently turned to more personal appeals, often relying on ordinary citizens on the streets of the United States.

The late 1970s and 1980s would be marked by a proliferation in the number of groups sponsoring campaign ads. Changes in campaign finance law spawned the rise of independent groups that became major players in electoral politics. In 1978, the National Conservative Political Action Committee (NCPAC) used a state-of-the-art direct mail campaign to fund independent attack ads in a successful effort to unseat incumbent Democratic senators in Iowa and New Hampshire. NCPAC attacks in 1980 contributed to the defeat of four more Democrats, including Sen. George McGovern of South Dakota.

The potential power of political advertising was vividly on display in the 1984 Kentucky U.S. Senate race. There, challenger Mitch McConnell aired advertising (produced by Roger Ailes) asking "Where's Dee?" (a reference to incumbent Dee Huddleston), featuring bloodhounds tracking down the wayward senator for missing votes (though Huddleston's attendance was actually one of the strongest in Congress). The ads were credited with reversing what had been a large lead in the polls in favor of Huddleston.

The techniques behind ad making were also advancing, notably with the rising use of focus groups. As with the direct mail techniques, it was Republicans

and conservatives who were first off the mark in innovative campaigning. In the 1980 presidential campaign, the GOP used both focus group and selected market testing for pro-Reagan spots. Their data indicated that the old school "talking head" format worked for Reagan, conveying a sense of his character despite the broader trend in political advertising toward Madison Avenue production values. GOP operatives were astonished that their Democratic rivals were not doing testing of their own.

Democratic presidential advertising in the 1980s was demonstrably inferior to the Republicans'. Reagan's 1984 reelection campaigns featured emotionally resonant ads (only vaguely connected to specific policy claims) in support of a powerful narrative frame. It was "morning in America," again, and America was better off than it was four years before. The narrative is optimistic toward Reagan while implicitly critical of Democrats, the party of four years before. The ads' audiovisual texture—uplifting musical scores (including Lee Greenwood's "God Bless the USA") and warmly lit vignettes of traditional American life—was woven with the campaign's central emotional appeal.

New Tools

The effectiveness of focus groups was vividly demonstrated in 1988. The Bush–Quayle campaign hammered Democratic opponent Michael Dukakis with charges of being soft on crime and defense. Research had shown the attacks to be particularly damaging to Dukakis among the coveted swing voters known as "Reagan Democrats." Other ads targeted the Massachusetts governor on the environment, an issue where the Democratic advantage was substantial. A Dukakis photo op atop a tank in support of his vision of strategic defense policy was turned into a biting satire in another Bush ad.

Critics argued that Bush's advertising was false and misleading. Indeed, journalists attempted to point out the ads' distortions, yet they did so in ways that only further reinforced the very ads they sought to discredit. A team of researchers centered at the Annenberg School of Communication at the University of Pennsylvania directed by Kathleen Hall Jamieson would eventually devise a "visual grammar" to allow

TV journalists to critique an ad's false claims without simultaneously reinforcing them. Avoiding the use of full screen shots from the ads and using graphics to clearly convey claims deemed false were among the techniques that came to be adopted by practitioners of "ad watch" journalism. The approach has been sustained over the years, albeit against the challenges that frequent personnel turnover and dwindling resources have brought. As a result, campaigns are ever on notice that their claims may be questioned by the ad police. As one might imagine, the ad cops themselves engender frequent criticism, and their project is ever more complicated given the smoldering partisan flames of contemporary American politics. In the age of social media, the audience itself has emerged as a contributor to the discourse on truth in advertising and in politics in general. A second legacy of the 1988 Bush campaign was the lesson learned by Democrats, at least Bill Clinton, whose rapid response "war room" sought to counter attacks as soon as they appeared, ideally during the same news cycle, rather than to let them fester, grow, and ultimately define the candidate the way Bush had been able to do to Dukakis.

It is not just falsehoods that have stoked voter ire over campaign spots. Attack advertising in particular draws low marks, though it constitutes an ever-larger share of all political advertising. Attack campaigning is as old as the Republic (the Jefferson–Adams being an early variant of the form). Yet, while citizens denounce them, campaigns continue to air them, inviting the obvious inference that campaigns believe they work. While academic research has returned mixed evidence on the electoral and social impact of attack ads, the psychology of negativity is clear. Negative information is easier to recall, more able to alter existing impressions, and tends to carry greater weight than positive information. While criticizing one's opponents remains one of democracy's most cherished expressive freedoms, negative advertising typically blends other ingredients as well, notably emotionality, one-sidedness, and an approach to politics often seen as "dirty" or "by any means necessary," in addition to questionable fidelity to the truth.

One of the most powerful ways advertising can communicate with viewers is by drawing upon the readily recognizable audiovisual conventions of popular culture. The earliest audiovisual campaign communication mimicked the form of the popular newsreels of the day, such as those used in a Republican attack on Upton Sinclair, the 1934 Democratic candidate for governor of California. Early advertising also drew upon cartoons, relying upon broadly recognizable cultural archetypes. In 1952, Republicans used the familiar format of a trial to frame attacks on Democratic malfeasance. The audiovisual conventions of horror stories have been a particularly common trope in political advertising. Ominous music, stark (often black-and-white) imagery, and fear-provoking sound effects powerfully support the narrative. The stark "Daisy" ad with its nuclear cloud ending was clearly frightening to viewers familiar with the geopolitical tensions present at the height of the Cold War. The 1988 Bush ad titled "Revolving Door" invited viewers to contemplate the "Nightmare on Elm Street" that would await America if Massachusetts governor Michael Dukakis's soft-on-crime policies were to go nationwide.

A 1996 ad on immigration for GOP presidential hopeful Patrick Buchanan utilized the low-light hand-held video associated with surveillance video or the TV program *COPS* to highlight the threat posed by illegal immigration. Heroic biography and satire have been models for political spots over the years. In 2004, ads supporting President Bush adopted some of the audiovisual and narrative techniques of action thrillers like the series *24* to convey his steadfast opposition to terrorism. In the early phase of the 2008 campaign for the Democratic presidential nomination, a web mash-up of the "1984" Apple Computer ad (drawing on George Orwell's dystopian vision) went viral. Produced by an independent pro-Obama political operative, the ad placed Hillary Clinton in the big brother role. Her image appeared on the screen that is ultimately burst apart when hit by a hammer thrown from below, representing liberation. The ad's very nature, a viral web ad, embodied its narrative frame, turning the sense of machine-like inevitability of the Clinton campaign into a liability against an Internet-savvy upstart.

Attacks and Reality Checks

Recently, as voters have placed an increasing premium on "authenticity," campaigns have adopted the look and feel of reality TV in their spots, sometimes even staged around the proverbial kitchen table or on the factory floor. In 2012, a group supporting Barack Obama sponsored ads featuring personal testimonies of workers who ended up building the stage from which it was announced that they would lose their jobs.

The communications environment has expanded over the years, with increasing roles for varied media outlets and individual actors. In 2004, a series of ads produced by a group called the "Swift Boat Veterans for Truth" made false claims about Democratic presidential nominee John Kerry's heroic war record. The ads featured military veterans stating Kerry lied to get his medals. Perhaps more revealing than the ads themselves was the path by which they entered the public discourse. In the weeks after the ads were launched in late July and early August, the ads and their charges received little attention in the mainstream media, or from the Kerry campaign (which failed to adopt the rapid response approach that had proven so effective for Clinton's campaigns). The attacks, however, were prominently featured in conservative-oriented media outlets such as the Drudge Report and Rush Limbaugh's radio show and on FOX News. By mid-August, major news organizations began to document falsehoods and distortions in the ads, but by that time key voter blocs (including veterans) were moving away from Kerry. News reports about Kerry began to refer more frequently to Vietnam than to his home state of Massachusetts, and eventually the term "swift boating" would come to denote unscrupulous (yet effective) attack advertising.

From the very beginning, attacks using an opponent's (or their supporters') own words have proven particularly forceful. George H.W. Bush's 1988 declaration "read my lips, no new taxes!" was featured in a range of Clinton–Gore ads in 1992. In 2000, Bush mocked Al Gore's campaign refrain "I want to fight for you!" by splicing video of Gore in his convention speech mouthing the words "for you" right after a Bush ad's claim that Gore's health plan was "a prescription for disaster." John Kerry's explanation of his votes on the Iraq War (Kerry voted for a bill that included taxes to fund the war, but against one that did not) was reduced to the candidate's own poorly chosen phrase, "I voted for (the $87 billion in war

funding) before I voted against it" in highly evocative Bush ads reinforcing the Republican charge that Kerry was a flip-flopper. One vividly used footage of Kerry windsurfing ocean waters to signify his unmoored approach—or even his unmoored character.

Just four years later, however, Republican nominee John McCain refused to allow his campaign to air ads featuring the incendiary words of Rev. Jeremiah Wright, the minister at the church on the South Side Chicago that Barack Obama attended. Other groups, however, did air such spots. The use of a candidate's own words and image can lend credibility to an ad's charges, though clever juxtaposition can spin one's words out of context and twist their meaning. In 2012, Republicans seized upon President Obama's celebration of an American system that provided the opportunity allowing businesses to succeed, and that those who owned businesses "didn't build that" to imply Obama was claiming it was their own businesses they didn't build. Perhaps more decisively, the Obama campaign's use of 2012 Republican rival Mitt Romney's comments at a private fundraiser regarding the "47 percent" of Americans whose dependence on government left them impervious to the GOP message of lower taxes and less government clearly reinforced what had already been a main line of attack from the Democrats.

Electoral Effects and New Media

Scholars who have sought to explore the electoral effects of campaign ads, though, have found mixed evidence at best. Where effects have been found, they tend to be small. This is unsurprising given the wide range of influences on election outcomes and the way scholars frame their analyses. Long before the vote, deep underlying forces including the state of the nation's economy, the president's job approval and shifting partisan trends are evident, and typically election outcomes fall in line with these factors. Some have concluded campaigns do not matter much at all. In part, however, the role of campaigns and campaign advertising is to help make known to voters these very underlying dynamics. Further, it is likely that at least some of the diminished effect of political advertising owes to the fact that one side's ads cancel out the other side's ads.

Electoral effects, moreover, are not the only, or perhaps even the most important, effects of political advertising. Ads shape, reflect, and to some degree constitute the political discourse. The "Occupy Wall Street" movement emerged in the year after "Wall Street" was one of the most common themes found in campaign ads. Further, elected officials behave in anticipation of the ads their opponents may run against them, which can be a powerful constraint on public policy.

The grip of broadcast television on American politics is loosening with the advent of social media and the continued fragmentation of the old media environment. Audiovisual political advertising, however, is unlikely to disappear. In the future, some ads may be ever more narrow-casted (while others will go viral), and they may reach voters through their smartphones, tablet computers, or other devices, but they still promise to be the principal means by which political communicators tell the stories of American politics. With social media, audiences become participants. Such was the case with "Hillary 1984" and wil.i.am's "Yes We Can" music video in 2008. In this radically democratized communications world, audiovisual political communication, from paid advertising to crowd-sourced and user-generated viral content, is a vital element of fulfilling that democratic promise.

See also Campaign Finance; Campaigns and Campaigning; Debates, Presidential; Nominating Conventions; Political Communications; Political Consultants and Campaign Managers; Primaries and Caucuses; Public Opinion; Redistricting; Social Media and Politics.

Glenn Richardson

Bibliography

Brader, Ted. 2005. *Campaigning for Hearts and Minds: How Emotional Appeals in Political Ads Work*. Chicago: University of Chicago Press.

Diamond, Edwin, and Stephen Bates. 1984. *The Spot: The Rise of Political Advertising on Television*. Cambridge, MA: MIT Press.

Jamieson, Kathleen Hall. 1992. *Dirty Politics: Deception, Distraction, and Democracy*. New York. Oxford University Press.

Jamieson, Kathleen Hall. 1996. *Packaging the Presidency: A History and Criticism of Presidential Campaign Advertising*. 3rd ed. New York: Oxford University Press.

Nelson, John S., and G. R. Boynton. 1997. *Video Rhetorics: Televised Advertising in American Politics*. Urbana: University of Illinois Press.

Richardson, Glenn W., Jr. 2008. *Pulp Politics: How Political Advertising Tells the Stories of American Politics*. Lanham, MD: Rowman and Littlefield.

West, Darrell M. 2013. *Air Wars 1952–2012: Television Advertising in Election Campaigns*. Washington, DC: CQ Press.

AFFIRMATIVE ACTION

In the United States, the political turmoil over affirmative action policies has been inseparable from questions about the meaning of the nation's commitment to the principle of equality—or, as one historian of these policies has put the question: "What is fair in America?" (Anderson 2004, xi). The story of affirmative action grows out of the larger story of civil rights and race relations in America and centers on concerns over what should be done for a segment of the population who, after generations of slavery followed by a century of systematic discrimination, found themselves lagging far behind in the quest for the American dream of stable prosperity, relative to most of the nation's other recognized racial or ethnic groupings. Given this state of affairs, members of these groups often felt shut out of the American promise of equality.

Affirmative action as it is understood today refers to any race-conscious policy designed to give special consideration—in hiring, promotions, admissions, and so forth—to these historically disadvantaged groups. Under the rubric of "diversity," however, affirmative action has subtly shifted its focus away from the disadvantaged and toward those groups who are merely underrepresented in certain positions, career fields, or institutions. As a result of this shift, the basic image of affirmation action has changed. Once seen as a temporary exception to the principle of nondiscrimination on the basis of race—an exception allowed for strictly remedial purposes, it now carries the implication of a permanent state of affairs that makes racial or ethnic identity an official and integral part of an individual's place in the public sphere.

Objections to these policies have usually been strongest among those who believe themselves to be directly harmed by them. Far from being privileged, these objectors believe they are being individually punished for the national sins of generations past—sins to which they may have no other connection than having a similar shade of skin pigmentation to the historical perpetrators. Thus, more than being a mere amplification of one's disappointment about not getting a particular benefit, these objections tap into a powerful strain of American moral and political thought: the belief that every human being and citizen in this nation is to be judged as an individual, not as a member of a group—and that one's character and abilities (in other words, "merit") should be the measure of that judgment. This and only this they believe to be the genuine American promise of equality.

Civil Rights and the Origins of Affirmative Action

From its beginnings in the midst of the Civil War until the passage of the 1964 Civil Rights Act, the civil rights movement held fast to the view just described. In 1865, just days after the assassination of President Lincoln and less than six months prior to the final adoption of the Thirteenth Amendment, Frederick Douglass famously responded as follows to the question, "What shall we do with the Negro?"

> Do nothing with us! . . . All I ask is, give him a chance to stand on his own legs! Let him alone! If you see him on his way to school, let him alone, don't disturb him! If you see him going to the dinner table at a hotel, let him go! If you see him going to the ballot-box, let him alone, don't disturb him! If you see him going into a work-shop, just let him alone,–*your interference is doing him a positive injury.* (emphasis added)

Henceforward, strict legal equality and nondiscrimination—the ideas eventually encapsulated in Justice John Marshall Harlan's term "color-blind Constitution"—were the central pillars of the civil rights movement.

Thus it remained, up to that moment that President Johnson's signature on the 1964 Civil Rights Act accomplished these goals. "Almost at once," says legal historian Andrew Kull, "the ground of the debate shifted" (Kull 1992, 2). Once achieved, the movement's original goals seemed insufficient. Now that nondiscrimination and legal equality had displaced Jim Crow and segregation as the legal status quo, civil rights leaders felt the need to push for a "fuller measure of equality," one which would require active government support to help lift the black community out of its endemic economic poverty. But this required a "polar reversal" of the movement's century-old commitment to the ideal of the color-blind Constitution. This new goal required that government explicitly *see* and consider the race of its citizens to combat the inequality that, while no longer embedded in the law, was still deeply felt in the lives of most of the nation's black citizens.

Standing ready to be applied to these new goals, the term "affirmative action" had been around a number of years already. It had been originally fashioned for a different purpose, one perfectly in line with the old ideal of the color-blind Constitution. The first official use of the term was in March 1961 in President Kennedy's executive order 10925, which announced that his administration would not simply mouth the maxims of civil rights but would take "affirmative steps" and "affirmative action" to ensure compliance with "the national policy of nondiscrimination" (Anderson 2004, 61). Established by this order, the President's Committee on Equal Employment Opportunity would monitor employment practices and press for *neutral* hiring and promotion, in federal agencies and in private companies with federal government contracts.

Chosen for its alliterative qualities, affirmative action proved a catchy and attractive label for the Kennedy administration's efforts at combating discrimination against blacks in the workplace. For the same reasons, the term seemed the perfect label for the sure-to-be-controversial change from *non*discrimination to the "benign discrimination" that was to follow. The alliterative resonance of the term seems to have ensured its survival, even as the policies it refers to have changed. While none of the subsequent changes have been as drastic as this first one, affirmative action has continued to evolve over time.

Quotas and the "Irony" of Affirmative Action

While the groundwork may have been laid during the Johnson administration, it was during Richard Nixon's presidency that affirmative action became synonymous with quotas, and it was during this time also that it was most fully implemented. Historian Terry Anderson calls these years "The Zenith of Affirmative Action." Capping the already tumultuous sixties, the "widespread rioting in urban black ghettos of America" pushed many in the political class to think less in terms of principle on this issue and more in terms of practical results (Nieli 2012, 9). At one point, President Johnson had pleaded with a group of CEOs: "If they're working, they won't be throwing bombs in your homes and plants. Keep them busy and they won't have time to burn your cars" (Anderson 2004, 105). Thoughts like these led many business leaders and northern politicians to consider tactics they might not have otherwise.

Two such pragmatic, results-oriented men were Nixon's secretary of labor George Shultz and his assistant secretary, Arthur Fletcher, an African American businessman. Unsatisfied with nondiscrimination's ability to alleviate chronic economic inequality in the black community, they declared that "goals or standards for percentages of minority employees" were now considered necessary to prove that organizations were not shutting blacks out. These goals and standards would have to be enforced according to "targets and timetables," and those not meeting the table were to be considered noncompliant. The central and explicit goal of affirmative action had become to hire and promote more minorities, which meant preferential employment practices for certain racial categories.

Affirmative action had arisen from a civil rights movement dedicated to the color-blind Constitution ideal and its rule of strict nondiscrimination, and it was given a considerable boost by the 1964 Civil Rights Act—which focused attention, dedicated resources, and created whole new agencies dedicated to the goals of equality, justice, and opportunity for blacks (and eventually for women and other minorities). But now affirmative action had become a byword for employment practices that flatly contradicted the principles that gave it birth and appeared to violate the terms of the Civil Rights Act, to say nothing of the Fourteenth Amendment's equal protection clause.

This "irony of affirmative action," as it has often been called, was something politicians and bureaucrats often understood and were willing to accept (Anderson 2004, 117). But the majority of the American people was another matter. With a keen sense of the political winds, Nixon backed off his support for affirmative action toward the end of his first term, and during the 1972 election, "in a curious twist he now began calling Democrats the 'quota party'" (138). "Every man, woman, and child should be free to rise as far as his talents, energy, and ambition will take him" was the position he now embraced (139). An astounding poll by Gallup in 1977 proved Nixon's prescience. By a margin of 8 to 1 Americans opposed preferential hiring and admission. This included 82 percent of women and 64 percent of minorities. Gallup concluded: "Not a single population group supports affirmative action" (148).

The Supreme Court and the Development of Affirmative Action

The Supreme Court finally began to hear cases directly addressing the legality and constitutionality of affirmative action programs in the late 1970s, and the jurisprudence that resulted split into two basically different streams—one concerning admission procedures in state-funded higher education and the other concerning government contracting and employment practices. In 1977, when the Court handed down its opinion in *Bakke v. California*, it proved to be less definitive than many had hoped (or feared). On the one hand, Justice Powell's majority opinion states that the Constitution prohibits categorizing citizens by racial group. Every citizen must be treated as an individual. On the other hand, Powell saw nothing wrong with state schools considering various characteristics of its applicants (including racial background), as long as it served a purpose central to the school's educational mission. Schools must be allowed to seek student "diversity" because it contributed to the differing perspectives needed to create a dynamic learning environment. As long as it was only one among many of the characteristics considered, race could be considered as part of a "holistic" assessment of each individual applicant.

Affirmative action at many universities would need to be reformed to save it from the *strict scrutiny* that Powell's opinion said was constitutionally required, but it need not be discarded. The result was another subtle change in affirmative action's meaning. Quotas were out, but diversity was in. The saving mechanism of diversity had no apparent application in the area of employment, however. Affirmative action here would likely have to justify itself according to the original rationale of preventing present and overcoming past discrimination against minorities. Here the Court proved initially accommodating to affirmative action programs. But that accommodating spirit proved temporary, and the Court has since moved in the opposite direction.

In 1979, the Court upheld an affirmative action plan that sought to eliminate racial imbalances in Kaiser Aluminum and Chemical Corporation's workforce by reserving 50 percent of craftsman training slots for black employees (who had previously been relegated to manual labor)—despite the general rule that these slots were awarded on the basis of seniority. When white employees with more seniority were passed over, they sued. Their complaint pointed to the plain wording of Title VII of the 1964 Civil Rights Act, which prohibited any workplace discrimination on the basis of race. But Justice Brennan's majority opinion argued that voluntary, private affirmative action programs did not violate the *intent* of Title VII, particularly when the plan was a "temporary measure" that was "designed to eliminate conspicuous racial imbalance in traditionally segregated job categories" (443 U.S. 193, 209).

One year later the Court said that Congress need not always act in color-blind manner, and it gave the okay to government set-asides for minority contractors, but the badly splintered opinion (no more than three justices were able to agree with one another) was soon repudiated for being out of sync with the Fourteenth Amendment's equal protection clause. Over the course of the next decade the Court established that any racial classification by any level of government must be subject to strict scrutiny. With strict scrutiny being the most difficult level of review to overcome, this case effectively ended racial set-asides for government contracts and official racial preference programs in public employment.

Yet racial consciousness still exists in certain public jobs because of a statutory rule against employment practices discovered to have a "disparate impact" on minority hiring and promotion. Originally part of the Supreme Court's interpretation of the Civil Rights Act, Congress amended the statute in 1991 to include the rule, after the Court had recently discarded it. The point of the disparate impact rule was to prevent employers from covertly discriminating by instituting requirements (like tests) that would disproportionately exclude blacks but were not a relevant measure of an individual's ability to perform the job.

When the fire department of New Haven, Connecticut, dismissed all the results for its promotion exam because none of those who passed it were black, a group of white and Hispanic firefighters brought suit, arguing that they had been discriminated against in violation of the equal protection clause. For its part, New Haven claimed that it was merely trying to avoid a lawsuit under the disparate impact rule. In 2009 the Court found in favor of the suing firefighters but avoided pronouncing on the constitutionality of the disparate impact rule. Instead, it held that the fire department had no reason to fear disparate impact liability in the first place and thus had no legal basis for its action. As of yet, the Supreme Court has not definitively pronounced on the constitutionality of disparate impact lawsuits, and many view them as the last refuge of affirmative action in public employment.

Higher Education and the Face of Affirmative Action in the 21st Century

Thanks in part to Justice Powell's opinion in *Bakke*, affirmative action in the guise of diversity has thrived in the world of higher education, even while it has beat a steady retreat in other areas. For much of the time since, the Court seems to have been caught between two horns of Powell's opinion. It was Powell who first prescribed strict scrutiny for affirmative action policies, and the rollback of affirmative action generally was understood as an elaboration of the principles he laid down. Yet because Powell believed that a race-conscious pursuit of diversity in the student populations could potentially survive strict scrutiny, courts seemed hesitant to be quite as strict when scrutinizing admissions.

As case after case shot down affirmative action in employment and contracting, most observers at the turn of the century thought this trend would quickly overtake race-conscious admissions as well. But in a pair of cases decided together in 2003, the Court attempted to pursue a middle course. The University of Michigan had been sued for its preferential admissions process, both in its undergraduate school and in its law school. Because the undergraduate school automatically added 20 points to the admissions score of minority students, the Court deemed it a quota and struck it down as a violation of the equal protection clause. But Justice Sandra Day O'Connor broke from the other justices in the majority and joined the four dissenters to uphold the law school's admission policy in the next case. Unlike the undergraduate school, she argued in *Grutter v. Bollinger*, the law school properly considered applicants as individuals. And to the extent that race was considered, racial status was only one among many "plus factors" used to promote student diversity. The dissenters accused O'Connor of drawing distinctions between the two cases that had no basis in any genuine difference. Strict scrutiny was the rule, but they (and Justice Kennedy especially) argued that O'Connor merely gave lip service to this test without truly applying it.

In the aftermath of these cases, Michigan voters approved the Michigan Civil Rights Initiative (2006),

Agnes Aleobua, a sophomore at the University of Michigan, speaks out against a ruling on race-based admission policies on campus in Ann Arbor, Michigan, on March 27, 2001. U.S. district judge Bernard Friedmans ruled that the law school's admissions standards are unconstitutional because they use race as a factor in judging applicants. (AP Photo/Paul Sancya)

also known as Proposal 2, which amended the Michigan Constitution to forbid state affirmative action practices, joining the states of California (1996) and Washington (1998). Since then the total number of statewide affirmative action bans has risen to eight. While this kind of voter backlash stalled affirmative action in some states, others saw an increase in the use of race-conscious admissions programs. The University of Texas in particular reintroduced race-consciousness which it had previously abolished to comply with a 1996 decision by the 5th Circuit Court of Appeals.

In response to that decision, the Texas legislature had passed Texas House Bill 588 (1997), which implemented a "Top Ten Percent Rule," giving automatic admission to the University of Texas for all students in the top 10th of their high school graduating class. The demographic realities that feed the makeup of the state's high schools guaranteed that this policy would produce a diverse student body at the University of Texas. This diversity, moreover, included race but included economic, geographic, and other forms of diversity as well, and it was achieved without even taking race (or any of these other factors) into specific account.

But while the university was able to tout diversity in its general student body, this diversity was not reflected equally in all majors or programs. Seeing the Supreme Court's *Grutter* decision as an abrogation of the appellate ruling that had forbid its original race-conscious policies, the university reintroduced race-consciousness in the effort to bring diversity to all of its programs. This new policy led to the most recent Supreme Court case, *Fisher v. Texas* (2013). With Justice O'Connor retired, the stricter view of strict scrutiny held by the *Grutter* dissenters was now ascendant. Writing for the Court, Justice Kennedy remanded the case back to the lower courts with instructions that it apply the genuine strict scrutiny he said was intended by Justice Powell in *Bakke*.

Personal Interests, Principled Positions, and Practical Outcomes

Whether *Fisher* will lead to the ultimate demise of race-conscious policies in public higher education remains to be seen. Meanwhile, the debate over affirmative action continues to rage in our politics and our public life. Which side a person takes has almost always depended on which of the two moral positions identified at the outset one finds more convincing—whether one thinks the idea of *equality* is more offended by social disparities that persist between racial/ethnic groups or by policies that treat citizens differently on the basis of skin color or language background. Often reinforcing these positions is the perception that the personal interests of one's self, one's friends, or one's family may depend on the outcome of the question. Little common ground is possible between these positions, and political consensus is probably impossible so long as they remain thus entrenched. Recent developments, however, may hold forth some hope that empirical data and pragmatic approaches can begin "to bridge the chasm" between the two sides (Sander and Taylor 2012, xi).

Andrew Kull predicted in 1992 that the social and political costs of individual grievances caused by affirmative action in the long run will be seen as slight compared to the "unintended consequences" to poor minority communities and to society at large (Kull 1992, 221). The so-called mismatch theory argues that such harmful and unforeseen consequences are no longer hypothetical but have been borne out by the evidence. In the most comprehensive case for this theory, Richard H. Sander and Stuart Taylor argue that these policies harm those they intend to help, while they deepen inequality and kill social mobility.

The large preferences commonly granted to black and Hispanic applicants, they argue, set these students up for failure. They do so by putting them in competition with peers whose preparation far exceeds their own and with whom they quickly perceive they cannot keep up, in courses pitched to "the middle" student. Alienation from fellow students and self-doubt ensue. And the result is that black and Hispanic students who would have succeeded if they had attended a school better matched to their academic preparation often give up, fail out, or steer clear of demanding (and remunerative) fields like the sciences and engineering (Sander and Taylor 2012, 4).

The solutions proposed by Sander and Taylor include an end to all large admissions preferences (including nonracial "legacy" preferences that have the same effect as affirmative action) to shift instead to better preparation at the lower levels of education and in general to replace the focus on race with a focus on economic status and mobility. If their findings remain uncontroverted by further study, if the political class finds its way to addressing their proposed solutions to the problem of inequality, and if these proposals bear fruit, then perhaps Americans will finally be able to close this cantankerous chapter of American politics. Short of that, it is always possible that the next Supreme Court ruling will be more definitive than the last.

See also Civil Rights; Desegregation and Politics; Education Policy and Politics; Inequality and Politics; Labor and Politics; Race, Ethnicity, and Politics.

Anthony D. Bartl

Bibliography

Anderson, Terry H. 2004. *The Pursuit of Fairness: A History of Affirmative Action*. New York: Oxford University Press.

Kull, Andrew. 1992. *The Color-Blind Constitution*. Cambridge, MA: Harvard University Press.

Nieli, Russell K. 2012. *Wounds That Will Not Heal: Affirmative Action and Our Continuing Racial Divide*. New York: Encounter Books.

Sander, Richard, and Stuart Taylor Jr. 2012. *Mismatch: How Affirmative Action Hurts Students It's Intended to Help, and Why Universities Won't Admit It*. New York: Basic Books.

Cases

Gratz v. Bollinger, 539 U.S. 244 (2003).

Grutter v. Bollinger, 539 U.S. 306 (2003).

Fisher v. Texas, 132 S.Ct. 1536 (2013).

Regents of the University of California v. Bakke, 438 U.S. 265 (1978).

Ricci v. Destephano, 129 S.Ct. 2658 (2009).

United Steelworkers of America v. Weber, 443 U.S. 193 (1979).

AFRICAN AMERICANS AND POLITICS

The successful 2008 election campaign of Barack Obama for the presidency of the United States permeated contemporary African American political culture, demonstrating the interconnection between politics, government, and everyday life. The definition of politics ranges from an art of compromise to the science of governing, revealing its broad reach and ubiquitous nature. Government, by extension, describes the system set up by people and imbued with the power to make, interpret, and enforce laws that control and protect those people. Authority in the United States' system of governance, of course, is divided among the executive, legislative, and judicial branches. African Americans have challenged each of these branches to create, mandate, and enforce laws that make everyday life safer and more equitable for all the country's inhabitants.

Executive Branch

Though Obama's successful candidacy was remarkable in many respects, he was not the first African American to make strides toward holding the highest office in the land. The former-slave-turned-abolitionist, Frederick Douglass, received one nomination during the roll call vote held at the Republican National Convention, where he was invited to speak on June 23, 1888. In 1972, Shirley Chisholm, the first African American woman elected to Congress, also became the first African American woman to run for president of the United States. Chisholm helped pave the way for candidates like Jesse Jackson (Sr.), the civil rights activist and Baptist minister who ran two presidential campaigns in the 1980s. Both his 1984 and his 1988 attempt to win the Democratic Party nomination ended in losses, but in 1988 Jackson was a close second to the Massachusetts governor, Michael Dukakis. In 2004, civil rights activist, Baptist minister, and radio talk show host Al Sharpton also made a bid for the Democratic Party nomination. Conservative statesman Alan Keyes, furthermore, has campaigned for the Republican Party's nomination several times, including unsuccessful bids during the 1992, 1996, 2000, and 2008 elections. In 2012 Herman Cain did likewise.

Running for president is not the only way in which African Americans have engaged the executive branch of government. Scores of activists and leaders of coalitions have wielded considerable political influence over U.S. presidents from the mid-19th century to the present. Douglass, who began recruiting black soldiers for the Union Army after President Abraham Lincoln issued the Emancipation Proclamation, later advocated on those soldiers' behalf, petitioning Lincoln for equal pay for African American troops. After the Civil War, Douglass supported the presidential campaign of Ulysses S. Grant, who later signed a series of acts into law that protected African Americans from the violence of the Ku Klux Klan.

With her antilynching crusade, journalist, lecturer, and champion of human rights, Ida B. Wells-Barnett went even further than Douglass to protect the lives of African Americans. This crusade spanned three decades, 1890–1920, and included petitions to presidents William McKinley and Woodrow Wilson. In 1898, for instance, Wells secured a meeting with McKinley, after which he delivered a speech disparaging the practice of lynching. Despite her best efforts, however, the federal legislation Wells deemed essential to curing the lynching contagion was never passed by the U.S. Senate—a woefully regrettable aspect of that institution's history, which the Senate formally apologized for in 2005.

Both A. Philip Randolph, founder of the Brotherhood of Sleeping Car Porters, and Mary McLeod Bethune, founder of Bethune-Cookman University, lobbied President Franklin Delano Roosevelt on behalf of African Americans. A close friend of First Lady Eleanor Roosevelt, Bethune became an intermediary between the Roosevelt administration and African American voters, who were mostly Republican at the outset of Roosevelt's presidential tenure. Bethune excelled in what became an advising role to the president; she was instrumental in forming the Federal Council of Negro Affairs, commonly known as the "Black Cabinet," which was a collective of African American public policy advisors to the executive branch. During Roosevelt's 12 years in office, 1933–1945, African Americans began flocking to the Democratic Party and African American employment in the executive branch also swelled to 45 members—more than during any previous administration. Given these achievements it may seem surprising that Roosevelt was initially reluctant to formally ban discrimination in industries awarded federal contracts. He did eventually capitulate, however, issuing Executive Order 8802,

only after A. Phillip Randolph threatened to orchestrate what would have been the first March on Washington for Jobs and Freedom.

In the 20 years following Roosevelt's presidency, African Americans continued to effect broad social and political change by bringing their concerns before the nation's subsequent leaders. In 1948, President Harry Truman signed an executive order banning segregation in the armed forces. Soon after taking office, President John F. Kennedy banned racial discrimination in federal housing, signing Executive Order 11063. Not long after the 1963 March on Washington for Jobs and Freedom, the long-awaited rally that attracted approximately a quarter million civil rights supporters and at which Martin Luther King Jr. delivered his famous "I Have a Dream" address, President Kennedy also sent Congress a bill proposing a ban on segregation in schools, public facilities, and employment. After Kennedy's assassination, his vice president, Lyndon B. Johnson, now the president, carried forth Kennedy's legacy and ensured the passage of the Civil Rights Act of 1964.

The Voting Rights Act, which President Johnson signed a year later, was a hard-fought victory for advocacy groups such as the Student Nonviolent Coordinating Committee (SNCC), the Southern Christian Leadership Conference (SCLC), and the Mississippi Freedom Democratic Party (MFDP). These civil rights organizations had been working on grassroots voter registration campaigns throughout the rural South, where African Americans outnumbered whites in some districts two-to-one. Having been disenfranchised since Reconstruction by literacy tests, poll taxes, and white supremacist strategies like the "grandfather clause," many African Americans in these regions were unaware of or fearful about executing their constitutionally secured right to vote. Groups like SNCC, the SCLC, and the MFDP brought volunteers in from the North to canvass rural towns and cities throughout the South, informing African Americans about their rights and encouraging them to vote. This voter registration work caught national attention during a campaign in Selma, Alabama, wherein white segregationists violently attacked peaceful marches led by SNCC and SCLC leaders. Concurrently, three African American members of the MFDP, Fannie Lou Hamer,

Annie Devine, and Victoria Gray, spearheaded a campaign against the five congressional representatives sent from the state of Mississippi. The MFDP argued that the representatives sent from their state did not legitimately represent their constituency because African Americans were illicitly barred from voting, as well as from running for political office. Coinciding mass demonstrations and organized challenges such as the Selma campaign and the MFDP's Congressional Challenge illustrate the multifaceted approach African American leaders and advocacy groups have taken to reform the U.S. government—often targeting more than one branch at a time.

The Legislative Branch

Once the Voting Rights Act passed, federal examiners were sent to areas suspected of withholding the ballot from African Americans. Though involving the examiners in the registration and voting processes was not a cure-all for generations of white supremacist suppression, it did help secure African Americans' constitutionally guaranteed right of suffrage. In Alabama, for instance, voter registration rates increased from a little over 2 percent of eligible African American voters prior to 1965 to 67 percent by 1972. Increased voter registration among eligible blacks ushered in an increase in black elected officials. Only a handful of African Americans held an elected office in Alabama in 1965, but 10 years later the state boasted 161 African American officials. The notable progress in Alabama echoed throughout the nation, as the number of African Americans holding an elected position more than tripled in the 10 years following the passage of the Voting Rights Act.

Although this piece of legislation was highly influential and sorely needed in its time, in many ways the Voting Rights Act of 1965 simply reinforced the Fifteenth Amendment to the Constitution, which was ratified almost 100 years earlier. In fact, the first African Americans to serve in the U.S. Congress began their tenure after the Civil War. Ratified in 1870, the Fifteenth Amendment granted African American men the right to vote, declaring "the right of citizens of the United States to vote shall not be denied or abridged by the United States or by any state on account of race,

color, or previous condition of servitude." The year it was ratified, two African American men, Hiram Rhodes Revels, a Republican from Mississippi, and Joseph H. Rainey, a Republican from South Carolina, were elected to the House and Senate, respectively. During the Reconstruction period in American history (1865–1877), African American men were sent to the U.S. Congress from states including Alabama, Florida, Georgia, Louisiana, Mississippi, North Carolina, and Virginia. After federal troops were removed from the South in 1877, however, measures to prohibit African American suffrage abounded, resulting in little to no congressional representation for African Americans from southern states by the turn of the century.

Strictly enforced codes of racial segregation made it difficult for African Americans not only to participate in the political process but also to find housing and gainful employment, to borrow money from banks, or to patronize restaurants, theaters, and hotels. During the period from 1910 to 1930, known as the Great Migration, over 1 million African Americans moved out of southern states in search of a better life in northern, midwestern, and western regions of the country. Once the migrants settled into their newfound communities, the U.S. Congress began to see a slight resurgence of African American participation, with a few representatives sent from places like Illinois, New York, and Michigan. Oscar DePriest from Chicago, for example, made history in 1928, becoming the first African American sent to Washington from a congressional district located north of the Mason-Dixon Line.

As more African American representatives began integrating the legislative branch, they developed a rich legacy not only of advocating issues that impacted members of their race, but of introducing, debating, and helping to enact legislation that benefited all American citizens. Augustus Hawkins, the first African American to serve in the U.S. Congress from the state of California, for instance, introduced a bill that became the Equal Employment section of the 1964 Civil Rights Act. This section introduced by Hawkins, Title VII of the act, developed into the Equal Employment Opportunity Commission. Over 40 years later, this federal agency remains committed to combating discrimination, harassment, and retaliation on the basis of not only race but also such factors as age, pregnancy, disability, and religion.

Sen. Edward Brooke from Massachusetts, the first African American elected to the Senate by popular vote, advocated the final civil rights bill of the 1960s. This bill was Congress's response to the report issued by the National Advisory commission on Civil Disorders, known as the Kerner Commission. The commission found that one of the major forces propelling Race Riots was white racism. In major cities throughout the nation, this racism manifest itself in forms of housing discrimination that left blacks segregated in urban ghettos. Title VIII of the Civil Rights Act of 1968, known as the Fair Housing Act, gave all Americans legal recourse to battle housing discrimination by explicitly prohibiting such discrimination based on race, religion, or national origin in the sale, rental, or financing of property. The act also instructed the Department of Housing and Urban Development as well as the U.S. attorney general to enforce these provisions and to assist victims of discrimination in securing redress. Although Senator Brooke had been promoting aspects of this bill for two years, it was ultimately the assassination of Martin Luther King Jr., and the racial unrest that ensued, which provided the final push to get the bill passed through Congress. President Johnson signed this act into law on April 11, 1968, one week after King's death.

By the election of 1970, the total number of African American congressional members grew to 13, and these representatives came together to form the Congressional Black Caucus. This nonpartisan coalition refers to itself as the "conscience of the Congress," a moniker reinforced by members of the organization who have bravely confronted controversial issues and fought to uphold sacred American values. In 1974, the first southern African American woman to serve in the U.S. Congress, Rep. Barbara Jordan, caught the nation's attention during the nationally televised impeachment hearings for President Richard Nixon. As a member of the House Judiciary Committee, Jordan delivered a speech that was a bold indictment, about the value of the Constitution and the need to preserve its authority in the face of violation. More recently, Rep. Barbara Lee delivered the lone speech opposing the use-of-force resolution brought before the House three days after the September 11, 2001, attacks on the World Trade Center. Though their remarks were controversial in nature, both of these African American congressional representatives rooted their positions in core American principles and expressed their desire to preserve what is best about the nation in moments of crisis.

In the 113th Congress, serving during the 2013–2015 session, there were 44 African Americans. This included 2 senators—Tim Scott, a Republican from South Carolina, and Cory Booker, a Democrat from New Jersey—and 42 representatives, 2 of whom are nonvoting delegates (from the District of Columbia and the U.S. Virgin Islands). Of the 42 House members, none were Republican, making Scott the only black Republican member of Congress.

Judicial Branch

In addition to drafting, debating, and passing legislation, the U.S. Senate is required by the Constitution to

Barbara Jordan, a noted figure in the U.S. political scene, in 1972 became the first African American woman ever elected to Congress from the Deep South. (Library of Congress)

advise the president regarding Supreme Court nominations. Since the Supreme Court was established in 1789, there have been two African American nominees confirmed by the Senate to join the judicial branch of government, which is charged with interpreting, adjudicating, and mandating the laws of the land. Thurgood Marshall, the first African American Supreme Court justice, was nominated by President Johnson and confirmed by the Senate on August 30, 1967. Justice Marshall served the high court for nearly a quarter century. After Marshall's retirement, President George H.W. Bush nominated Clarence Thomas, whom the Senate confirmed by a narrow margin after a contentious hearing, which included allegations of sexual harassment, as well as opposition from groups such as the National Association for the Advancement of Colored People (NAACP) and the National Organization for Women. Justice Thomas began his tenure on the Supreme Court as an associate justice in 1991 and continues to serve today.

Long before the Supreme Court had African Americans seated on its bench, this governmental body was making decisions that affected the daily lives of African Americans. In 1883, for instance, the Supreme Court declared the Civil Rights Act of 1875—a law that stipulated all persons, regardless of race, had a right to the "equal enjoyment" of public accommodations—unconstitutional. The court reasoned that although the Fourteenth Amendment granted equal protection under the law to all citizens of the United States, this particular statute exceeded constitutional reach by mandating that private persons, not states, refrain from discriminatory action. In 1896, moreover, the Supreme Court upheld the constitutionality of segregation, reinforcing the infamous "separate but equal" doctrine in its landmark *Plessy v. Ferguson* decision. This doctrine undergirded the widespread racial segregation of public facilities for the next 50 years, until the court's *Brown v. Board of Education* ruling. The "separate but equal" ruling in *Plessy* was unanimously overturned in 1954, when the court contended that separate schools for black children denied them the basic citizenship right of equal educational opportunity. This decision, which declared de jure segregation a violation of the equal protection clause of the Fourteenth Amendment, provided a firm foundation upon which the civil rights movement of the 1950s and 1960s was built.

In addition to *Brown*, the court has handed down several significant decisions influencing educational opportunities for all American citizens. In the 1978 *Regents of the University of California v. Bakke* decision, a divided (5–4) court ruled that the use of special admissions processes to increase acceptance rates of minority applicants was unconstitutional. The court did, however, uphold the practice of affirmative action, suggesting that race could be used as one factor among others in "narrowly tailored" admission decisions. Justice Marshall, who had argued *Brown* before the court as a lead NAACP lawyer decades earlier, penned an impassioned dissenting opinion to the *Bakke* ruling. In this opinion, Marshall combined historical and sociological data with legal precedent and constitutional principles to explain his disbelief that the very judicial body which refused to prohibit myriad forms of discrimination against African Americans was now standing in the way of a state's effort to remedy this past injustice.

The precedent set with the contentious *Bakke* decision was tested in two cases brought against the University of Michigan, both of which came before the court in 2003. Taken together, the rulings in *Grutter v. Bollinger* and *Gratz v. Bollinger* uphold the two-pronged reasoning in *Bakke*. Specifically, the court upheld its previous position that while affirmative action in college admissions is necessary to remedy the unjust exclusion of the past, racial quotas or set-asides that insulate minority applicants from competition violate the equal protection clause. Disagreeing with the court on much different bases than his predecessor had, Justice Thomas wrote a dissenting opinion to the *Grutter* decision. Though Thomas agreed with the court that racial quotas and set-asides are illegal, his opinion went a step further, arguing that all race-based admissions decisions—even narrowly tailored ones—violate the color-blind principle embedded in the U.S. Constitution. Subsequent court rulings (e.g., *Fisher v. Texas*, 2013) affirmed the latter view.

As the examples provided here demonstrate, the decisions, deliberation, and leadership of the executive, legislative, and judicial branches of the U.S. government affect the African American experience.

African American protest of and participation in these governmental branches, moreover, has simultaneously transformed politics in the United States.

History: The Black Power Movement

During the 1950s and 1960s Martin Luther King Jr. and others emerged as leaders of the civil rights movement. For more than a decade, an unprecedented number of marches, sit-ins, and other protest activities took place demanding an end to segregation. King's nonviolent protests were predicated on an integrationist ideology in which African Americans would "not be judged by the color of their skin but by the content of their character." During the mid-1960s, however, a different and competing philosophy emerged. The Black Power Movement advocated unity, community building, a recognition of blacks' African heritage, and the development of independent black organizations.

The integrationist goal of the civil rights movement was rejected. Black Power advocates believed that African Americans should focus on improving their own communities rather than integrating into white society. Where Martin Luther King Jr. and his followers found their inspiration in the nonviolent teachings of Mohandas Gandhi, Black Power advocates preferred Malcolm X, Marcus Garvey, and Franz Fanon.

The posthumously published *Autobiography of Malcolm X* was widely read and highly influential. During his life and after his death, Malcolm X influenced black activists. Malcolm X was a minster for the Nation of Islam. He was a separatist who believed that African Americans should control their own communities. He also rejected nonviolent protest. Malcolm X was, in many ways, the inspiration for the Black Power Movement.

Kwame Ture, then known as Stokely Carmichael, was the first to utter the phrase "black power," which became the movement's slogan. Carmichael was the SNCC's charismatic leader. Frustrated by the lack of progress toward desegregation in the late 1960s, some SNCC insiders rejected the commitment of Martin Luther King Jr. and other black leaders to nonviolent protest. They advocated a strategy of self-determination and self-defense. During a 1966 protest march in

Mississippi, SNCC field workers Stokely Carmichael and Willie Ricks used the chant of "Black Power" to distinguish their new direction from Martin Luther King's nonviolent approach. To them the phrase "Black Power" meant blacks taking political and economic control of their own communities in the Deep South and elsewhere.

The 1960s was a decade of turmoil and change. Images ranging from police dogs attacking peaceful civil rights protesters to cities burning during urban riots were staples of nightly newscasts. Malcolm X and Martin Luther King Jr. were assassinated. Thousands of students protested the Vietnam War on college campuses across the nation. The Black Panthers, another group associated with the Black Power Movement, were organized in Oakland, California, by Huey P. Newton and Bobby Seale. They advocated armed confrontations with the authorities but they also focused on issues that adversely affected the black community, including access to health care, housing, and the treatment of prisoners.

African American artists and writers were inspired by the Black Power Movement. They believed that the cultural heritage, history, and the African roots of black Americans were critical to redefinition of black identity. The negative connotations long associated with dark complexions were rejected. Black became beautiful. The Black Arts Movement was, as Larry Neal explained, "a cultural revolution in art and ideas." Writers and artists challenged traditional Western standards for art and literature and sought to develop a "black aesthetic." It was, as Neal stated, the "aesthetic and spiritual sister of the Black Power concept." The Black Power salute, consisting of an upraised arm and a clenched fist, became a symbol of solidarity.

Spiral, a collective of African American artists, was established in 1963 to discuss the commitment of African American artists to the civil rights movement and to debate the necessity of defining a black aesthetic in the visual arts. Artists used protest themes in their work. Black Liberation Theology was another outgrowth of the Black Power Movement. James Cone, the originator of Black Liberation Theology, promoted the use of Christianity to advance racial consciousness and empowerment. The Black Power Movement faded almost as quickly as it appeared.

By the end of the 1960s the civil rights movement had achieved its goal of eliminating the legal barriers to racial equality. The Civil Rights Act of 1964, the Voting Rights Act of 1965, and the Fair Housing Act of 1968 ended the era of state-sanctioned discrimination and segregation. Mass protests declined after the assassination of Martin Luther King, Jr. Ideological feuds among civil rights organizations hastened the movement's demise. The Federal Bureau of Investigation's Counterintelligence Program, which used covert methods to sabotage protest activities, contributed to the Black Power Movement's disintegration. By the early 1970s the Black Power Movement was eclipsed by antiwar protests.

The Black Power Movement was short lived, but it had a lasting influence on America's economic, political, and social institutions. The movement suffered from rhetorical excesses of some of its adherents. However, many who were seen as radicals in the 1960s used their organizational and leadership skills to become elected officials at the state, local, and national levels. Others moved into academia where they pioneered Black Studies programs. The continuing influence of the Black Power Movement can be seen in literature and the arts, on stage and on the screen. Echoes can be heard in musical genres ranging from jazz to hip-hop. One important legacy is the way in which African Americans view themselves: as individuals with pride and dignity comprising an integral part of the American mainstream.

Politics and the Black Church

If in its simplest form, politics is about influencing governmental policy or protesting against it, the black church has certainly played an important role in doing just that. Typically, the term "black church" has referred to predominantly black Christian congregations, collectively. Irrespective of religious denominational ties, these congregations tend to exhibit a black religious culture honed by the commonality of shared historical experiences. It is these experiences that have propelled the black church to be actively involved in the political process. Furthermore, such involvement is viewed as an integral part of the church's prophetic witness to the world.

To better understand how and why the black church participates in politics, one should consider three factors: the historical context of race relations vis-à-vis blacks and whites; its perception of what politics entails and the variety of ways in which it participates; and its understanding of the role of the black church in relationship to the secular world.

By far, the greatest factor propelling the black church to keep its membership aware of and actively involved in the political process has been the hegemonic crusade to oppress black Americans since the time of slavery. It is this experience of oppression and neglect that has motivated the black church to work for the achievement of justice for its constituency. Ironically, the collaboration and cooperation found among black churches surrounding civil rights and economic issues has given an impression that black churches have similar political stances when in fact they have always maintained varying political positions. Their memberships are politically diverse, both in their affiliations and in their political views. Yet, despite this distinctiveness, the common threat of political disenfranchisement makes political involvement not a choice but a survival tactic.

To the black church the customary discourse about secular or sacred or, similarly, about separation of church and state is theoretical, but not useful, constructs from which to carry out its mission within the world. Black communities, battered by the ferocity and vicissitude of acts of hatred stemming from society, were buttressed by the hope and affirmation emanating from pulpits. It was the church that provided relief, whether financial or spiritual. It was the church that addressed the concerns of the people, whether social or religious. The church became the lifeblood of the black community, involving itself in every aspect of the lives of its members, and thus not being a stranger to the political dimension as well.

Politics was more than exercising power on behalf of another; it was about building community and about finding ways to declare the humanity of black people in life-giving, soul-building ways. Whereas the United States through its laws sought to diminish the constitutional rights of African Americans, the black church sought to help them find independence and freedom through and beyond the Constitution. This was more than engagement in a political process; this was a moral imperative because denial of rights impeded the ability of individuals to be whole persons.

Paradoxically, black churches act in and upon the world although they claim not to be a part of the world. The influence that they seek to exert within the political arena is part of the dynamic spiritual redemptive process that they, too, undergo so that the process and the players, whoever they may be, can live up to the highest democratic standards. Holding government accountable for its actions is seen by the black church as part and parcel of the church's role to develop leadership and citizenship skills among its members.

The mission of the black church is multifaceted and presents challenges that require it to balance the worship of God and the spiritual care of its members with the redemptive restoration of the nation. With such challenging tasks, the black church engages in a variety of activities, some of which are typically viewed as political, such as seeking better voting rights or developing local community programs, and some of which seek to solidify community partnerships and ecumenical ties. All fall within the realm of a larger definition of politics that recognizes the importance of resource development.

As the institution upon which black communities have entrusted their hopes and aspirations, their spiritual development, and their legacies, the church seeks to ensure that fairness and access to opportunities for black communities is obtained. Thus, black preachers have run for political office, among them Adam Clayton Powell Jr., Walter Fauntroy, Floyd Flake, and Emmanuel Cleaver. Black church laypersons have run for office or become outspoken leaders on the national political arena, for example, Mary McLeod Bethune, Nannie Helen Burroughs, Shirley Chisholm, Parren Mitchell, Barbara Jordan, and Harold Washington. Black preachers have been instrumental in challenging unjust laws, as seen, for example, in the work of Martin Luther King Jr., and Oliver Leon Brown. Though some have posited that the black church is apolitical, it is far from being so. Even today, as the fear of complacency hauntingly threatens future attentiveness to political issues, the common soul of the black church and its legacy as the drum major for justice suggests that it will continue to follow spiritual directives that call the nation to perfect the American system of democracy, thereby shaping persons and policy for the betterment of all.

Conclusion

The election of Barack Obama was a turning point, but it does not mean that all problems for African Americans have been solved. During the campaign, Obama said that today's most difficult racial problems involve the present effects of past discrimination. The despair, grinding poverty, and the lack of educational and other opportunities in America's inner cities are the lingering vestiges of a segregated past. Addressing these conditions will continue to be a formidable challenge, even after Obama leaves office.

Over 40 years ago, on the night before his assassination in 1968, Martin Luther King Jr. spoke to a group of black sanitation workers who were in the midst of a tense strike. King comforted the workers with a sermon. Invoking an inspirational metaphor, King told the strikers he had been to the "mountaintop" where he had seen the "Promised Land." He said "I may not get there with you. But I want you to know tonight, that *we, as a people*, will get to the Promised Land." In many ways President Obama's election represents reaching that mountaintop and seeing the Promised Land, even while we realize that we still have miles to go before we rest.

See also Civil Rights; Cultural Pluralism; Inequality and Politics; Leaders and Leadership; Protest Movements; Religion and Politics; Voting and Politics.

Maegan Parker Brooks, Leland Ware, and Vivian C. Martin

Bibliography

Calhoun-Brown, Allison. 2000. "Upon This Rock: The Black Church, Nonviolence, and the Civil Rights Movement." *PS: Political Science & Politics* 33 (June): 168–74.

Carmichael, Stokely, and Charles V. Hamilton. 1967. *Black Power: The Politics of Liberation in America.* New York: Vintage.

Carson, Clayborne, general ed. 1991. *The Eyes on the Prize Civil Rights Reader.* New York: Penguin.

Congressional Black Caucus. http://www.thecongres sionalblackcaucus.com/. Accessed May 16, 2014

Fitzgerald, Scott T., and Ryan E. Spohn. 2005. "Pulpits and Platforms: The Role of the Church in Determining Protest among Black Americans." *Social Forces* 84 (December): 1015–48.

Fowler, Robert B., et al. 2010. *Religion and Politics in America: Faith, Culture, and Strategic Choices*. Boulder, CO: Westview Press.

Gilmore, Glenda Elizabeth. 1996. *Gender and Jim Crow*. Chapel Hill: University of North Carolina Press.

Harris-Lacewell, Melissa V. 2007. "Righteous Politics: The Role of the Black Church in Contemporary Politics." *Cross Currents* 57 (Summer): 180–96.

Jones, Angela. 2012. *The Modern African American Political Thought Reader: From David Walker to Barack Obama*. New York: Routledge.

Kelley, Robin D. G., and Earl Lewis, eds. 2001. *To Make Our World Anew*. Vol. 2. New York: Oxford University Press.

Lincoln, Eric C., and Lawrence H. Mamiya. 1990. *The Black Church in the African American Experience*. Durham, NC: Duke University Press.

Malcolm X, and Alex Haley. 1965. *The Autobiography of Malcolm X: As Told to Alex Haley*. New York: Ballantine Books.

Ogbar, Jeffrey O. G. 2004. *Black Power: Radical Politics and African American Identity*. Baltimore: Johns Hopkins University Press.

Payne, Charles M. 1995. *I've Got the Light of Freedom*. Berkeley: University of California Press.

Peniel, Joseph E. 2006. *Waiting 'Til the Midnight Hour: A Narrative History of Black Power in America*. New York: Henry Holt.

Seale, Bobby. 1996. *Seize the Time: The Story of the Black Panther Party and Huey P. Newton*. Baltimore: Black Classic Press.

Supreme Court of the United States. http://www.supreme courtus.gov/. Accessed May 16, 2014.

White House. (n.d.) "Our Government." http://www .whitehouse.gov/our_government/. Accessed May 16, 2014.

Wilmore, Gayraud S. 1998. *Black Religion and Black Radicalism: An Interpretation of the Religious History of African Americans*. Maryknoll, NY: Orbis Books.

AIR QUALITY AND POLITICS

Smog, acid rain, methane, and other forms of outdoor air pollution, as well as air pollution inside homes and other buildings, can all affect the environment. Cars, trucks, coal-burning energy plants, and incinerators all make controllable contributions to air pollution. New environmental air pollution regulations continue to decrease emissions but with industry resistance.

Air quality has been a driving force for U.S. and global air pollution control. It can be quite different from region to region and over time. Geological features such as deep mountain valleys may facilitate dangerous atmospheric conditions when on the downwind side of industrial emissions, heavy car and truck traffic, and wood and coal stoves. Points of contention in the air quality debate are scientific monitoring of air quality conditions, debate over what chemicals to regulate as pollution, and environmentalists' concerns over weak and incomplete enforcement. Each one of these is a controversy itself.

Public Health Issues

One of the primary criteria for an airborne chemical to be a pollutant is its effect on public health. One of the first areas of public concern about air pollution is breathing.

Asthma is becoming more common. This is true even though some air pollutant concentrations have decreased. The increase in asthma is concentrated in people of color and low-income people. The incidence of acute asthma attacks in children doubled in the past 13 years even as very effective medicines were developed. About 5 million child hospitalizations were children who had asthma attacks. It is the most frequent cause of childhood hospitalization. Deaths of children with asthma rose 78 percent from 1980 to 1993. It is concentrated in high-population urban areas. This one environmental effect of air pollution can spread to inner-ring suburbs, then to air regions over time. Asthma is described as like breathing through a straw.

The serious public health issues around air pollution highlight the gravity of the problem as a whole.

Air pollution can have short-and long-term health effects. Asthma from air pollution can have short-and long-term effects. Short-term effects of asthma are irritation to the eyes, nose, and throat. Long-term reactions to air pollution can include upper respiratory infections such as bronchitis and pneumonia. Other symptoms of exposure to air pollution are headaches, nausea, and allergic reactions. Short-term air pollution can aggravate underlying medical conditions of individuals with asthma and emphysema. Long-term health effects are more controversial. Depending on the type of air pollution, there is general consensus that exposure can cause chronic respiratory disease, lung cancer, heart disease, and damage to the brain, nerves, liver, or kidneys. Continual exposure to most kinds of air pollution affects the lungs of growing children by scarring them at early stages of development. Recent studies suggest that the closer one is raised to a freeway in Southern California, a notoriously low-quality air region overall, the greater the chance of having one of the listed long-term effects.

Cumulative exposure to polluted air does aggravate or complicate medical conditions in the elderly. Most air pollution risk is involuntarily assumed. The involuntary assumption of health risks is something most communities strongly object to. With the advent of the Toxics Release Inventory, many communities can track airborne industrial emissions. Citizen monitoring of environmental decisions has increased, especially around air quality issues.

State of Air Pollution

The air becomes polluted in different ways. How the air becomes polluted determines the types of problems it causes. Different sources of emissions contain different chemicals. These may interact with other airborne chemicals in both known and unknown ways. Moreover, air pollution can expose populations to more than just airborne pollution. As the chemicals

A view of downtown Los Angeles, California, on a smoggy afternoon, November 2, 2006. The city's geography, and its heavy reliance on pollution-causing automobiles for transportation, leads to an excess of smog. (Gabriel Bouys/AFP/Getty Images)

mix with moisture in the air, they can become rain. The rain can move the chemicals through the ecosystem, including crops and livestock. Mercury, lead, and aluminum all move in this way, with adverse ecological effects. There may be other chemicals with adverse ecological effects that do not last as long as metals do and may therefore be hard to detect while present.

The term "pollution" has important legal and environmental meanings. Legally, it means that a person or business is not complying with environmental laws. Many environmentalists do not think this is extensive enough and believe that large environmental impacts can be considered pollution even if they are legal. Many permits do not in fact decrease emissions but permit more emissions.

Many permits have numerous exceptions to emissions. The petrochemical industry is allowed *de minimus*, fugitive, and emergency emissions beyond the permit, and that industry is leaking a valuable commodity. Industry argues that if it complies with all the environmental laws, then its emissions are not pollution because they are part of the permit issued by the Environmental Protection Agency (EPA) via the respective state environmental regulatory agency. Although state and federal environmental agencies argue with the regulated industries, communities, and environmentalists, the actual environmental impact has worsened. Whereas many environmental decisions are made behind closed doors, more and more communities are monitoring the environment themselves.

One type of air pollution is particulate matter. The particles are pieces of matter (usually carbon) measuring about 2.5 microns or about 0.0001 inch. Sources of particulate matter are the exhaust from burning fuels in automobiles, trucks, airplanes, homes, and industries. This type of air pollution can clog and scar young, developing lungs. Some of these particles can contain harmful metals. Another type of air pollution is dangerous gases such as sulfur dioxide, carbon monoxide, nitrogen oxides, and other chemical vapors. Once in the atmosphere they follow the prevailing winds until they condense and fall to the ground as precipitation. This type of pollution can participate in more chemical reactions in the atmosphere, some of which form smog and acid rain. Other atmospheric chemical reactions are the subject of intense scientific controversy

and are part of the debates of global warming and climate change.

Most air pollution comes from burning fossil fuels for industrial processes, transportation, and energy use in homes and commercial buildings. Natural processes can emit regulated chemicals at times. How much of a given chemical is naturally emitted versus how much of the emission is from human actions is a subject of continuing scientific debate.

The Natural Resources Defense Council closely tracks the air emissions of the biggest polluters. The council calls this tracking its benchmarking project. It is a nonprofit environmental advocacy organization that believes in keeping track of environmental conditions to establish a baseline. Its research is based on publicly available environmental information, much of it available in the Toxics Release Inventory. Key findings of the benchmarking project's 2013 report include the following:

- Emissions of sulfur dioxide and nitrogen oxides have decreased by 72 percent and 70 percent, respectively, since the stricter pollution-control standards of the 1990 Clean Air Act went into effect.
- Carbon dioxide emissions increased 20 percent over the same period.
- In recent years (2008–2011), carbon dioxide emissions decreased by 7 percent as the building and use of coal plants have leveled off.
- Significant disparities in pollution rates persist throughout the electricity industry, with a small number of companies producing a relatively large amount of emissions.
- Not all power plants use currently available, state-of-the-art emission control technologies.
- The electric power industry remains a major source of mercury emissions in the United States, though such emissions have decreased by 40 percent since 2000.

The Natural Resources Defense Council's benchmarking project uses public data to compare the emissions performance of the 100 largest power producers in the United States. They account for 86 percent of reported electricity generation and 88 percent of the industry's reported emissions. Emissions performance is examined with respect to four primary power plant pollutants: sulfur dioxide, nitrogen oxides, mercury, and carbon dioxide. These pollutants cause or contribute to global warming and to environmental and health problems, including acid rain, smog, particulate pollution, and mercury deposition.

Recently, the U.S. Supreme Court ruled that the EPA may impose stricter emissions and air quality standards on several Midwestern Rust Belt and Appalachian states to protect "downwind" northeastern states from the effects of migrating air pollution.

Automobile Energy Efficiencies

Emissions from cars and trucks are central to debates about air quality and to what extent air pollution poses a risk. The first federal clean air laws were passed in the late 1960s and early 1970s. Pollution-control devices and lead-free gas have decreased some emissions. The onus is on the automobile industry to produce more efficient cars that use less gas and to decrease the environmental impact of vehicles. Emissions from cars and trucks continue to accumulate in land, air, and water. Continued retail sales of fuel-inefficient vehicles, combined with overall high numbers of vehicles, act to generate emissions that degrade air quality.

The battle between the government and industry over legislating the production of more efficient vehicles is a long-standing one. Most of this legislation requires minimal compliance by industry at some date years in the future. Manufacturers claim that it takes resources from research and development right now to try to change production technologies to meet those standards. Sometimes they get tax breaks and other public policy–based encouragement to do so. One area of contention is the free market. Market demand is for more cars, trucks, airports, and other petrochemical-based activities. Does legislation from democratically elected representatives constitute market demand? Many economists would say that it does not. Environmentalists claim that the minimal requirements are not fast or stringent enough.

In early April 2010, President Barack Obama changed fuel economy standards in the United States. The administration issued final regulations compromising fuel economy standards set in the Clean Air Act requiring fuel efficiency to increase to over 40 miles per gallon (mpg) by 2015 and 55 mpg by 2025. The compromise, which required an increase instead to 35.5 mpg by 2016, was celebrated by the auto industry for creating a unified national program from a patchwork of varying state and federal standards. It prompted the industry to voluntarily dismiss lawsuits challenging California's motor vehicle greenhouse gas emission standards, which were more stringent than federal standards when adopted a few years ago. With the compromise, California amended its regulations to match federal standards. Rising gas prices, the slowly deepening effects of rising gas prices on food and other consumer goods, and concern about air pollution all increased public involvement. In 2005, California and 16 other states sued the EPA for refusing to allow them to raise fuel economy standards beyond federal limits. Federal law can preempt state law.

Adopting fuel-efficient or alternative fuel technologies to meet the Clean Air Act standards would, in theory, save enormous amounts of gas and oil. A series of environmental disasters involving offshore oil drilling and ocean tankers in 2008 and 2009 may have pushed attention in the direction of acceptance. The sinking of the BP–Deepwater Horizon oil rig in the Gulf of Mexico near Louisiana in April 2010 caused the Obama administration to halt its plans to expand offshore drilling pending further investigation. A major controversy over alternative fuel solutions is whether they would prevent further environmental degradation. Global warming controversies are also pushing this issue into the public view. Some contend the United States needs to do more in terms of addressing mobile emissions sources and their environmental impacts. The exploration of alternative fuels for vehicles can be controversial in terms of environmental impacts. The removal of lead from U.S. gasoline was a major step forward, not yet replicated around the world. It greatly reduced airborne lead emissions. However, with current standards and the volume of driving, assuming complete environmental compliance, U.S. vehicles would still emit 500,000 tons of smog-forming pollution every year.

The United States is among the leading nations for both pollution and pollution-control technology. Diesel-powered vehicles are major polluters. They emit almost 50 percent of all nitrogen oxides and more than two-thirds of all particulate matter (soot) produced by U.S. transportation. Because the United States is more reliant on trucks (which tend to be diesel-fueled) for the shipment of goods and raw materials than other nations, diesel emissions can be large contributors to an air stream, along with many other pollutants. Some of these regulated pollutants are from industry and some from the environment.

The scale of diesel usage and its known emissions make it an environmental issue. Nitrogen oxides are powerful ingredients of acid rain. Acid rain can cause nitrogen saturation in crops and wilderness areas. Soot, regulated as particulate matter, irritates the eyes and nose and aggravates respiratory problems, including asthma. Urban areas are often heavily exposed to diesel fumes. While diesel is a polluting fuel, regular unleaded gasoline can also pollute. Overall, the environmental impacts of the combustion engine remain largely undisputed. What is disputed is whether the environmental regulations go far enough to mitigate environmental impacts from these sources. The controversy about automobile energy efficiencies opens this aspect of the debate.

Commercial hybrid electric vehicle (HEV) models use both batteries and fuel. In the past few years they have been produced and marketed to the public. More recently, HEV drive trains have been used successfully in heavy-duty trucks, buses, and military vehicles.

Researchers also want to move HEV technology into a more sustainable lifestyle. They would like to produce and market plug-in hybrids that can plug in to household outlets. They want such hybrids to be able to store electricity and operate as clean, low-cost, low-environmental-impact vehicles for most of their normal daily mileage. Right now electric cars are limited by their batteries. Combining engines with them and using braking power to recharge the batteries does extend their range and power but also increases their emissions. Transportation is conceptualized as part of an environmental, low-impact, and sustainable lifestyle. These communities unite plug-in hybrids, other low-impact transportation alternatives (bicycles, mass transit stops), zero-energy homes, a range of renewable energy technologies, and sustainable environmental

practices. One example of such a community is the Pringle Creek Community in Salem, Oregon.

Oil and Power: Impacts on Automobile Energy Efficiency

The primary resistance to increasing the efficiency of automobile and truck engines is the petrochemical industrial complex. Large oil companies are the backbone of U.S. industry and part of a thriving economy. They are multinational corporations that exert political power here and abroad. Some have revenues larger than those of most nations. Their only legal motivation is to make profit from dispensing a limited natural resource. Environmental and ecological integrity and consumer quality-of-life issues are not their concern. The oil industry has been a strong industrial stakeholder and exerted power at the local, state, and federal levels of government for almost a century. Many state legislatures have passed laws exempting oil companies from releasing their environmental audits or helping oil companies avoid compliance with environmental regulation or enforcement action. Oil companies are not responsive to community concerns and can litigate any issue with vast financial resources. The petrochemical industrial complex has also become part of social institutions such as foundations, churches, schools and universities, and athletic contests. Some employment opportunities, some infrastructure, and the hope of more economic development are offered to communities by oil companies.

No oil company seems to be turning its profits into consumer savings. Some are just starting to research more alternative energy sources, but this is controversial. Some environmental groups have recently challenged this assertion. To many U.S. consumers it seems there is a direct correlation between record prices paid by consumers and record profits enjoyed by oil companies.

Conclusion

The controversies around air pollution show no signs of abating. Points of concentrated air pollution are getting more attention and becoming political battlegrounds.

The environmental policies and laws do have the intended effect of reducing the emissions of some chemicals emitted by most industries. However, asthma rates increase and so too does community concern. It is likely that the costs of further decreasing emissions from industry, from municipalities, and from all of us will be more expensive. The current context of global warming and rapid climate change drives many air pollution controversies to center stage.

Continued dependence on fossil fuels guarantees increased controversy. As oil becomes depleted, multinational oil corporations exert their huge influence on the United States to protect their sources, even if it means harm to the environment and to citizens. The dissatisfaction of environmentalists and communities with the petrochemical industry, the dependence and demand of the United States for oil, the lack of governmental support for alternative energy development, and the inability to keep large environmental impacts secret all fuel this ongoing controversy.

See also Climate Change and Politics; Green Movement and Politics; Oil, Natural Gas, and Politics; Public Health and Politics.

Robert William Collin and Debra Ann Schwartz

Bibliography

Clifford, Mary, and Terry D. Edwards, eds. 2011. *Environmental Crime.* 2nd ed. Sudbury, MA: Jones and Bartlett.

Dobson, Andrew P. 2004. *Citizenship and the Environment.* New York: Oxford University Press.

Galambos, Louis, Takashi Hikino, and Vera Zamagni. 2006. *The Global Chemical Industry in the Age of the Petrochemical Revolution.* Cambridge: Cambridge University Press.

Miller, Norman, ed. 2009. *Cases in Environmental Politics: Stakeholders, Interests, and Policymakers.* New York: Routledge.

Natural Resources Defense Council. 2013. *Benchmarking Air Emission in the 100 Largest Electrical Power Producers in the United States.* New York: NRDC/M.J. Bradley & Associates.

Rom, William N. 2011. *Environmental Policy and Public Health: Air Pollution, Global Climate Change, and Wilderness.* San Francisco: Jossey-Bass.

Schwartz, Joel M., and Steven F. Howard. 2007. *Air Quality in America.* Washington, DC: AEI Press, 2007.

Simioni, Daniela. 2004. *Air Pollution and Citizen Awareness.* New York: United Nations Publications.

AMERICAN DREAM

The "American Dream" is one of the most strongly held and enduring ideals in American political culture. It encompasses a constellation of ideas such as religious liberty, political equality, social mobility, economic opportunity, and the pursuit of happiness. On the whole, the American Dream is essentially an optimistic and future-oriented ideal that holds out the promise that all Americans can build a better life for themselves and their children if they work hard and "play by the rules." A core thread woven throughout the tapestry of the American Dream is the belief that the future will always be better than the present, and each generation will have a better life than its predecessors. For immigrants to the United States, whether they are fleeing poverty and persecution or chasing their dreams of economic opportunity, the American Dream has historically been connected to the belief that the United States is a "land of opportunity." Thus, for native-born and immigrant alike, the American Dream is closely connected to the idea of "success." Living the American Dream, in short, means that individuals can "pursue their dreams" and "make something of themselves."

The "American Dream" in History

While the term "American Dream" was not coined until the 20th century, it has roots tracing back to the colonial era and the American Revolution. In the Declaration of Independence of 1776, Thomas Jefferson famously stated that all men are born with inalienable rights to "life, liberty, and the pursuit of happiness." And in 1782, Frenchman Hector St. John de Crèvecoeur wrote his "Letters from an American Farmer" in which he described the idea that immigrants fleeing the rigid feudal orders of Europe could start anew, shed their old identities and customs, and build a better life for themselves in America. To this day, the pursuit of happiness and the freedom to reinvent oneself and pursue one's dreams are linked to social and economic mobility and personal fulfillment, as well as material comforts such as home ownership. Indeed, home ownership became a hallmark of achieving the American Dream in post–World War II American life.

While elements of the American Dream have deep roots in American political culture, the term "American Dream" was first popularized by James Truslow Adams in his book *The Epic of America*. Written during the Great Depression, Adams set out to describe and defend that American dream of a better, richer, and happier life for all of our citizens of every rank, which is the greatest contribution we have made to the thought and welfare of the world. That dream or hope has been present from the start. Ever since we became an independent nation, each generation has seen an uprising of ordinary Americans to save that dream from the forces which appeared to be overwhelming it (1938, 415).

While the American Dream contains a theme of economic success and the consumer goods it can purchase, Adams warned that it should not be reduced to simple materialism. He stated:

> It is not a dream of motor cars and high wages merely, but a dream of a social order in which each man and each woman shall be able to attain to the fullest stature of which they are innately capable, and be recognized by others for what they are, regardless of the fortuitous circumstances of birth or position. . . . It has been a dream of being able to grow to the fullest development as man and woman, unhampered by the barriers which had slowly been erected in older civilizations, unrepressed by social orders which had developed for the benefit of classes rather than for the simple human being of any and every class. And that dream has been realized more fully in actual life here than anywhere else, though very imperfectly even among ourselves. (1938, 415–16)

In this passage Adams brings together the core elements of the American Dream: individualism, equality, merit, opportunity, and mobility are invoked as uniquely American and opposed to rigid social orders and status that is unearned by hard work or merit. And while the American Dream contains these core ideals, he also acknowledges that the United States has often fallen short of these ideals in practice. Much of American history can be understood as a struggle to close the gap between the principles of the American Dream and the imperfect practices of American democracy. For example, over time Americans have struggled to expand and clarify Jefferson's idea that "all *men* are created equal" to include men *and* women of all racial, religious, and ethnic backgrounds.

While Adams was critical of President Roosevelt's New Deal programs designed to ameliorate unemployment and spur the economy back to life, he believed that the characteristics of hard work, individualism, and self-reliance would enable Americans to work through challenging and difficult times and ultimately make themselves, their country, and the next generation better off in the long run. To this day, those who believe in the American Dream agree that there is something unique in the character of ordinary Americans that enables them to persevere and build a better, brighter, and richer future for themselves and their posterity.

Multiple American Dreams

The American Dream transcends political parties and ideologies by acting as a form of "social glue" that binds Americans together around a shared ideal. Yet Americans who align themselves with competing parties and ideologies often emphasize specific elements of the American Dream over others. For example, in 1983 Republican president Ronald Reagan highlighted what he saw as central to the American Dream: "What I want to see above all is that this country remains a country where someone can always get rich. That's the one thing we have and that must be preserved" (1983). And in 1993 Democratic President Bill Clinton stated his belief in the American Dream: "The American dream that we were all raised on is a simple but powerful one—if you work hard and play by the rules you should be given a chance to go as far as your God-given abilities will take you" (Hochschild 1996, 18). Many Americans likely agree with both statements since they each tap into the notion of upward mobility and economic success. However, it is clear that Reagan's version of the American Dream is strongly linked to the singular idea of the individual pursuit of wealth. By contrast, Clinton's version emphasizes themes of individual success within the framework of equal opportunity, merit, and fairness.

These alternative visions were on display during the 2012 presidential campaign. At the Republican national convention, Republicans emphasized the American Dream of economic success in which entrepreneurs and rugged individualists succeed without government interference or assistance. Describing his view of the American Dream, Republican presidential candidate Mitt Romney stated:

In America we celebrate success, we don't apologize for success. . . . Now is the moment when we can stand up and say, "I'm an American. I make my destiny. And we deserve better! My children deserve better. My family deserves better. My country deserves better." (Weinger 2012a)

At their national convention, Democrats invoked the American Dream of the equal opportunity to succeed which requires the government to enforce the rules and ensure that individuals have access to resources such as education that are necessary for success. First Lady Michelle Obama described the American Dream she shares with President Obama:

For Barack, success isn't about how much money you make, it's about the difference you make in people's lives. . . . Barack knows the American dream because he's lived it, and he wants everyone in this country, everyone to have that same opportunity, no matter who we are, or where we're from, or what we look like, or who we love. . . . And he believes that when you've worked hard, and done well, and walked through that doorway of opportunity, you do not slam it shut behind you. You reach back and you give other folks the same chances that helped you succeed. (Weinger 2012b)

These visions overlap as well as compete, and each vision taps into core themes of the "American Dream" as first described by James Adams.

Because the American Dream is an ideal that ties together many principles, it is no surprise that there are different versions of it. In his book *The American Dream: A Short History of an Idea That Shaped a Nation* (2003), James Cullen identifies at least seven distinct versions of the American Dream. First, there is the dream of religious liberty that traces back to the Puritans who founded the Massachusetts Bay Colony. Ever since, Americans like to think of the United States as a land of religious liberty, pluralism, and tolerance, especially for immigrants fleeing persecution. Second, there is the dream of political freedom articulated in the Declaration of Independence and the U.S. Constitution. This version of the dream stresses political equality and self-determination in which all citizens participate as equals. Third, there is the dream of social and economic mobility. This dream is exemplified in tales such as Abraham Lincoln's rise from his birth in a log cabin to his presidency as well as Horatio Algiers stories of "rags to riches" by luck and by pluck. Fourth, there is the dream of geographic mobility. This includes the dream of Westward expansion, the Great Migration, and what Cullen describes as the "Dream of the Coast" in which California symbolizes the dream of personal fulfillment, the pursuit of happiness, and the glamor of Hollywood. Fifth, there is the dream of equality under the law that is most vividly described by Martin Luther King Jr.'s "I Have a Dream" speech in 1963 in which he invokes racial equality and brotherhood to challenge the nation to live up to the Jeffersonian ideal that *all* men and women are created equal. Sixth, there is the dream of home ownership that flows from the Homestead Act through the growth of suburbia and individual homeownership in post–World War II American life. And seventh, there is the dream of the immigrant, a dream that is older than the nation itself, and one that is marked by acceptance and opportunity for some immigrants but ambivalence and discrimination toward others (Cullen 2003, 188).

All of these American Dreams are optimistic and forward looking. And while each of these dreams embody an ideal that has not always been practiced or applied equally to everyone, they are powerful ideals that reformers, abolitionists, suffragists, and champions of civil rights and equal opportunity can invoke to mobilize social, political, and legal changes that close the gap between the ideals of the American Dream and historical practices that often fall short of those ideals. For instance, while the dream of religious liberty remains powerful, over the course of U.S. history religious groups such as Catholics, Jews, and Muslims have faced discrimination but have also defended religious liberty in ways that renew America's commitment to religious liberty. And while the dream of equality was historically denied to women, African Americans, Asians, Native Americans, and Latinos, various social movements formed to ensure that all Americans could partake of the American Dream with equality under the law, equal rights, and equal opportunities. Although the United States has an imperfect record of living up to all of the ideals and principles embodied in the American Dream, these ideals and principles are often renewed as Americans work to close the gap between its principles and its practices.

Ironically, while Americans invoke history when asserting their inalienable right to pursue happiness, the actual pursuit of happiness often rests on reinvention and overcoming the limits of the past. As Cullen describes this paradox, "At the core of many American Dreams . . . is an insistence that history doesn't matter, that the future matters far more than the past. But history is in the end the most tangible thing we have, the source and solace for all our dreams" (2003, 184). While the American Dream is forward looking and optimistic, it is anchored in ideals and principles that were forged in the early years of an American history that we revere.

Is the American Dream at Risk of Fading?

There are, however, signs that the American Dream is either fading or is at risk of disappearing for some Americans. Many gaps remain between the ideals of the American Dream and social, economic, and political practices. For instance, there remains evidence of religious intolerance as well as gender and racial discrimination. In addition, there are signs that the core ideas of economic mobility and opportunity are slipping away from middle-class Americans (Isaacs, Sawhill, and Haskins 2008; Pew Charitable Trusts 2012). In addition, books such as *Who Stole the American Dream?* (Smith 2012) and *The Betrayal of the American Dream* (Barlett and Steele 2012) provide further evidence that the American Dream is slipping out of reach for most Americans owing to declining wages, the decline of labor unions, the hollowing out of the middle class, economic competition under globalization, and public policies that favor investors over wage earners and the wealthy over the middle class. Taken together, there is ample evidence that key elements of the American Dream are at risk of becoming more myth than reality.

First, American optimism rests on a core belief in individualism. However, extreme individualism often generates negative consequences. In his famous book *Democracy in America*, Alexis de Tocqueville observed that extreme individualism can lead Americans to believe that "they owe nothing to any man, they expect nothing from any man; they acquire the habit of always considering themselves as standing alone, and they are apt to imagine that their whole destiny is in their own hands" (1990 [1831], 98). So while Americans defend their individual rights and liberties they often fail to recognize their responsibilities and duties to their fellow citizens. This strong belief in individual responsibility also means that individuals are praised or blamed for their own success or failure (Hochschild 1996). This belief overlooks the social structures that enhance or limit the resources and opportunities to which each individual has access and it also negates the importance of collective action such as the modern civil rights movement. While Americans struggle to succeed and play by the rules, too often larger social, economic, or political forces such as poverty, recessions, discrimination, or glass ceilings restrict their opportunities and limit their life chances to succeed.

While Americans are firm believers in individualism and individual responsibility, there is a slight increase in the number of Americans who are skeptical that individual effort is all one needs to succeed. In 2009, 82 percent of Americans agreed that "everyone has it in their own power to succeed," but by 2011 this number had dipped to 75 percent (Pew Research Center 2012). And while only 12 percent of Americans agreed that "success in life is pretty much determined by forces outside of our control" in 2009, by 2011 this number had risen to 19 percent (Pew Research Center 2012). Alternatively, in 2000 about 74 percent of Americans agreed that "most people who want to get ahead can make it if they're willing to work hard," but by 2011 this had dropped to 58 percent (Pew Research Center 2012). And in 2000, 23 percent of Americans agreed that "hard work and success are no guarantee of success for most people," but by 2011 this had jumped to 40 percent (Pew Research Center 2012). While Americans are still strong believers in individualism and hard work determining one's success, there is a growing realization that individual effort does not necessarily guarantee success and upward mobility; instead, structural forces beyond their control block success even when individuals work hard and play by the rules.

Second, avenues of success and upward mobility are being threatened by growing economic inequality. Americans are typically quite tolerant of economic inequality provided that it is the result of hard work, fair play, and equal opportunity. Indeed, 90 percent of Americans "admire people who get rich by working hard" (Pew Research Center 2012). However, 77 percent of Americans agree that too much power is in the hands of a few rich people and large corporations, 71 percent agree that the rich keep getting richer while the poor get poorer, and 61 percent agree that the country's economic system unfairly favors the wealthy (Pew Research Center 2012). In fact, the top complaint—57 percent in 2011, up from 51 percent in 2003—against the U.S. tax system is that "wealthy people are not paying their fair share" (Pew Research Center 2011). In short, many Americans are increasingly aware of and concerned about growing inequality and how this allows concentrated economic power to wield undue political influence (Hacker and Pierson 2010).

Third, mobility and opportunity for many Americans have been blocked by a trend of declining wages for working- and middle-class Americans, which makes it harder to pursue the dream of homeownership or sending their children to college. Since the 1970s, the purchasing power of the average wage for an American worker has declined, while the gap between worker's wages and CEO salaries has skyrocketed.

While American workers remain highly productive, average family incomes have not kept up with inflation since the 1970s. In addition, public policies such as less funding for public and higher education have shifted the costs onto working- and middle-class families. As a result, the United States now has one of the lowest rates of upward mobility in the developed world. A recent study by the Organization for Economic Co-operation and Development found that the United States is now the only major country in the world in which the younger generation will *not* be better educated than the older generation. Indeed, about one in five young adults are now classified as "downwardly mobile" in educational terms, meaning that they will be less educated than their parents. This runs counter to the American Dream that education opens doors to economic success and upward mobility. As a result, within one generation, the United States went from number 1 in college graduation rates to 14.

Many Americans are beginning to lose faith in the power of individual effort in "pulling themselves up by their bootstraps," and this intuition is supported by recent reports documenting a decline in economic mobility. The Brookings Institution found that economic inequality is increasing at the same time that intergenerational mobility is decreasing:

> Contrary to American beliefs about equality of opportunity, a child's economic position is heavily influenced by that of his or her parents. Forty-two percent of children born to parents in the bottom fifth of the income distribution remain in the bottom, while 39 percent born to parents in the top fifth remain at the top. Children of middle-income parents have a near-equal likelihood of ending up in any other quintile, presenting equal promise and peril for those born to middle-class parents. Only 6 percent of children born to parents with family income at the very bottom move to the very top. (Isaacs, Sawhill, and Haskins 2008, 7)

In an ironic reversal, the Brookings report found that many European countries now have greater mobility than the United States For example, Sweden and

Denmark have a more equal distribution of wealth across their quintiles as well as higher rates of inter-generational economic mobility across those quintiles than the United States (Isaacs, Sawhill, and Haskins 2008, 39–40).

Further, by 2012, four years after the recession began in 2008, inequality and the lack of mobility in the United States became even more apparent. A Pew report found that "only 4 percent of those raised in the bottom quintile make it all the way to the top as adults, confirming that the 'rags-to-riches' story is more often found in Hollywood than in reality. Similarly, just 8 percent of those raised in the top quintile fall all the way to the bottom" (Pew Charitable Trusts 2012, 2). In short, children born into low-income families will very likely be low-income themselves, while children born into high-income families will in all likelihood be high-income themselves. This trend goes contrary to James Truslow Adams's original description of the American Dream in which all individuals can succeed "regardless of the fortuitous circumstances of birth or position" (1938, 415). The Pew report finds an on-going racial disparity in family income, wealth, and mobility and concludes that "the persistence of the black-white mobility gap undercuts the ideal of equality of opportunity, a concept central to the idea of the American Dream" (Pew Charitable Trusts 2012, 27).

Findings such as these support the growing realization among many Americans that individual effort alone no longer determines one's fate. Rather, the socioeconomic status into which an individual is born increasingly determines his or her future prospects of success and mobility. Indeed, 46 percent of Americans (32 percent of Republicans, 58 percent of Democrats) agree that the rich are wealthy mainly because "they know the right people or were born into wealthy families," while 43 percent of Americans (58 percent of Republicans, 32 percent of Democrats) agree that the rich are rich mainly because "of their own hard work, ambition or education" (Morin 2012, 8). These numbers indicate that a plurality of Americans "feel" what recent studies have documented: contrary to the ideal of upward mobility that is at the core of the American Dream, there is a growing recognition that one's future is shaped on the basis of the quintile one is born

into. If this is the case, the American Dream is at risk of fading for too many Americans.

Conclusion

The American Dream, even if elusive in reality, remains a guiding ideal for Americans. As James Cullen concludes, "What makes the *American* Dream American is not that our dreams are any better, worse, or more interesting than anyone else's, but that we live in a country constituted of dreams, whose very justification continues to rest on it being a place where one can, for better and for worse, pursue distant goals" (2003, 182, emphasis in original). Thus, despite recent evidence that the American Dream is slipping out of reach for many Americans, it remains a central ideal that Americans want to believe in. If the American Dream is to survive and be open to all, Americans will have to do exactly what James Adams described: persevere through difficult times and struggle to ensure that the principles embodied in the American Dream are open not to a lucky or wealthy few but to all individuals regardless of their race, gender, religion, or socioeconomic status.

See also American "Exceptionalism"; Class and Politics; Consumer Culture and Politics; Family, State, and Politics; Individualism; Liberty; National Identity.

Gregory W. Streich

Bibliography

Adams, J. T. 1938. *The Epic of America*. New York: Taylor & Francis.

Barlett, D., and J. Steele. 2012. *The Betrayal of the American Dream*. New York: Public Affairs.

Cullen, J. 2003. *The American Dream: A Short History of an Idea That Shaped a Nation*. New York: Oxford University Press.

Hacker, J., and P. Pierson. 2010. *Winner-Take-All Politics: How Washington Made the Rich Richer—And Turned Its Back on the Middle Class*. New York: Simon & Schuster.

Hanson, S., and J. White, eds. 2011. *The American Dream in the 21st Century*. Philadelphia: Temple University Press.

Hochschild, J. 1996. *Facing Up to the American Dream: Race, Class, and the Soul of a Nation*. Princeton, NJ: Princeton University Press.

Isaacs, J., I. Sawhill, and R. Haskins. 2008. "Getting Ahead or Losing Ground: Economic Mobility in America." http://www.brookings.edu/~/media/Files/rc/reports/2008/02_economic_mobility_sawhill/02_economic_mobility_sawhill.pdf. Accessed May 23, 2014.

Morin, R. 2012. "Rising Share of Americans See Conflict between Rich and Poor." January 11. http://www.pewsocialtrends.org/files/2012/01/Rich-vs-Poor.pdf. Accessed May 23, 2014.

Pew Research Center, 2011. "Tax System Seen as Unfair, in Need of Overall: Wealthy Not Paying Fair Share Top Complaint." December 20. http://www.people-press.org/files/legacy-pdf/12-20-11%20Taxes%20release.pdf. Accessed May 23, 2014.

Pew Research Center. 2012. "Poll Analysis: For the Public, It's Not about Class Warfare, but Fairness." March 2. http://www.people-press.org/2012/03/02/for-the-public-its-not-about-class-warfare-but-fairness/. Accessed May 23, 2014.

Pew Charitable Trusts, 2012. "Pursuing the American Dream: Economic Mobility across Generations." http://www.pewstates.org/research/reports/pursuing-the-american-dream-85899403228. Accessed May 23, 2014.

Reagan, R. 1983. "The President's News Conference." June 28. http://www.presidency.ucsb.edu/ws/index.php?pid=41535. Accessed May 23, 2014.

Samuel, L. R. 2012. *The American Dream: A Cultural History*. Syracuse, NY: Syracuse University Press.

Smith, H. 2012. *Who Stole the American Dream?* New York: Random House.

Tocqueville, A. 1990 [1831]. *Democracy in America*. Vol. II. New York: Vintage Classics.

Weinger, M. 2012a. "Mitt Romney's Speech: 12 Most Rousing Lines." August 30. http://www.politico.com/news/stories/0812/80507.html. Accessed May 23, 2014.

Weinger, M. 2012b. "Michelle Obama's 10 Most Memorable Lines." September 4. http://www.politico.com/news/stories/0912/80715.html. Accessed May 23, 2014.

AMERICAN "EXCEPTIONALISM"

American "exceptionalism" is an ideal that is central to America's self-image. In general, it views the United States as an exceptional and unique nation in the world because of its history, resources, ideals, people, and purpose. With roots tracing back to colonial times, American exceptionalism emerged as a full-blown ideal in the post–World War II era to describe how the United States is unique when compared to other nations and how it plays an indispensable role in global politics. While the United States remains a unique nation in many ways, there is a lively debate as to whether the United States will remain "exceptional" in the 21st century.

Moderate and Strong Forms of American Exceptionalism

American exceptionalism has a moderate and a strong version. The moderate version views the United States not as superior to other nations but one that is "qualitatively different" (Lipset 1997, 18). On this basis, Seymour Lipset argues that America is exceptional because its successful revolution established the United States as the first "new nation" in modern times and because it developed a unique set of unifying ideals embodied in the "American Creed" that includes the principles of liberty, individualism, egalitarianism, populism, and laissez-faire economics (Lipset 1997, 17–19). While Lipset believes the United States is unique and exceptional, he does not argue that it is an inherently superior country. Instead, he notes that American exceptionalism is a "double-edged sword" whereby key principles of the American Creed can conflict with—and undermine—each other: for instance, the principle of populism can lead to majority tyranny, which can undermine individualism and liberty; excessive individualism and laissez-faire economics can produce extreme inequality that undermines egalitarianism; and egalitarianism is undermined by a history of slavery and discrimination (Lipset 1997).

By contrast, the strong form of American exceptionalism views the United States as unique *and* superior to other nations. As Stephen Walt writes, "Most statements of 'American Exceptionalism' presume that America's values, political system, and history are unique and worthy of universal admiration. They also imply that the United States is both destined and entitled to play a distinct and positive role on the world stage" (Walt 2011). In the post-9/11 era, this form of American exceptionalism is expressed by pundits and politicians who argue that the United States must embrace its role as the global leader in promoting peace and prosperity and never apologize for its values or policies (Krauthammer 2009; Romney 2011). Any mistakes the United States makes are part of the price of global leadership: "For all our fumbling," journalist Michael Hirsh concludes, American global leadership is "the greatest gift the world has received in many, many centuries, possibly all of recorded history" (Hirsh 2003, 254). At the 2004 Republican national convention, President George W. Bush hinted at a divinely inspired justification of U.S. global leadership:

> I believe that America is called to lead the cause of freedom in a new century. . . . I believe all these things because freedom is not America's gift to the world; it is the Almighty God's gift to every man and woman in this world. . . . Like generations before us, we have a calling from beyond the stars to stand for freedom. . . . Now we go forward, grateful for our freedom, faithful to our cause, and confident in the future of the greatest nation on Earth. (Bush 2004)

Given this view of global leadership, advocates of strong American exceptionalism often worry that multilateral diplomacy unnecessarily limits the ability of the United States to act on the world stage.

What Do Americans Think about American Exceptionalism?

American citizens are strongly committed to the ideal of American exceptionalism, but recent surveys find they are split between its moderate and strong versions. A Gallup survey found that 80 percent of Americans agree with the statement that because of its history and its Constitution the United States has "a unique character that makes it the greatest country in the world" (Jones 2010). Moreover, 66 percent of Americans agree that the United States has "a special responsibility to be the leading nation in world affairs" (Jones 2010). By using phrases such as "the greatest country in the world" and "special responsibility" to lead, Gallup measured the degree to which Americans believe in the strong form of American exceptionalism.

However, surveys conducted by the Pew Research Center highlight the difference between the strong and moderate forms of American exceptionalism. Pew found that 53 percent of Americans agree that the United States "is one of the greatest countries in the world, along with some others" (Pew Research Center 2011), a phrasing that measures the moderate form of American exceptionalism in which the United States is unique but not superior; and 38 percent of Americans agree that the United States "stands above all other countries in the world" (Pew Research Center 2011), a measure of the strong form of American exceptionalism in which the United States is unique and superior. Pew also found that in 2011 about half of Americans (49 percent) agreed with the statement, "Our people are not perfect, but our culture is superior to others," but support for this view has declined from 60 percent in 2002 and 55 percent in 2007 (Pew Global Attitudes Project 2011, 5).

Partisan identity, ideology, and age shape how Americans view American exceptionalism. For example, 52 percent of Republicans but only 33 percent of Democrats agree that the United States "stands above all others," while 43 percent of Republicans and 59 percent of Democrats agree that the United States is "one of the greatest countries, along with some others" (Pew Research Center 2011). Among "Staunch Conservatives" 67 percent believe that the United States "stands alone above all other countries" and 32 percent believe it is "one of the greatest, along with some others." By contrast, 19 percent of "Solid Liberals" believe that the United States "stands alone above all other countries," while 62 percent believe it is "one of the greatest, along with some others" (Pew Research Center 2011). And among Americans aged 65 and older, 50 percent believe the United States "stands above all others," while 46 percent believe the United States is "among the greatest" nations. By contrast, 59 percent of Americans aged 18–29 agree that the United States is "among the greatest" nations, 27 percent agree that the United States "stands above all others," and 12 percent say that there are "other countries" that are better than the United States (Pew Research Center 2011). When asked whether they believed that American culture is superior to others, 60 percent of Americans aged 50 and over agree compared to 37 percent of Americans aged 30 and under (Pew Global Attitudes Project 2011, 6). By ideology, 63 percent of conservatives agree with the view that American culture is superior compared to 45 percent of moderates and 34 percent of liberals (Pew Global Attitudes Project 2011, 6).

In short, Americans believe in American exceptionalism. However, Republicans, conservatives, and older Americans are more likely to believe in its strong version, while Democrats, liberals, and younger Americans are more likely to support its moderate form.

The Domestic Roots of American Exceptionalism

American exceptionalism has deep roots in American political culture. It can be traced to Puritan leader John Winthrop, who in 1630 described the Massachusetts Bay Colony as a divinely ordained step toward building a "City upon a hill." American exceptionalism was also expressed by Thomas Jefferson in his first inaugural address in 1801, in which he observed that America represented the "world's best hope." In 1831, Frenchman Alexis de Tocqueville observed that Americans occupied an exceptional position because the nation was founded on principles of democracy and equality. And as America expanded westward in the mid-1800s to acquire land from Native Americans, the notion of Manifest Destiny was invoked as a divine mandate for westward expansion. And in his second annual address to Congress in 1862, Abraham Lincoln invoked the idea that America remained the "last best hope" for mankind. During his term President Ronald Reagan updated John Winthrop's claim that the United States remains a "shining city on a hill." George W. Bush repeatedly invoked the responsibility of the United States to spread liberty and freedom around the world. And during the 2012 presidential campaign, both President Obama and his challenger Republican Mitt Romney defended their belief that the United States remains an exceptional and "indispensable" nation on the world stage.

American Exceptionalism from a Comparative Perspective

Surveys consistently find that on a number of important political attitudes and policies the United States is exceptional and unique when compared to Great Britain and other Western European countries.

First, Americans are much more individualistic and less supportive of a strong social safety net provided by the government than their counterparts. When asked which is more important, 58 percent of Americans agree with the statement "freedom to pursue life's goals without state interference," while 35 percent of Americans support an active government that guarantees "nobody is in need" (Pew Global Attitudes Project 2011, 1). By contrast, 67 percent in Spain, 64 percent in France, 62 percent in Germany, and 55 percent in Britain say the state should ensure that nobody is in need (Pew Global Attitudes Project 2011, 1). In addition, 36 percent of Americans believe that "success in life is determined by forces outside our control," a number that illustrates a strong belief in individual responsibility for one's fate. However, this number is low compared to Britain (41 percent), Spain (50 percent), France (57 percent), and Germany (72 percent) (Pew Global Attitudes Project 2011, 1). Americans are unique in their strong belief in individualism, and this belief makes them less likely than their European counterparts to support government-sponsored safety nets and more likely to believe that individuals control their own destiny.

Second, Americans are comparatively more likely to support the use of unilateral military force. While 75 percent of Americans agree that it is "sometimes necessary to use military force to maintain order in the world," this view is shared by 70 percent in Britain but only 62 percent in France and Spain (Pew Global

Attitudes Project 2011, 2). Moreover, on the question of unilateralism, Americans are divided: 45 percent say that the United States should have United Nations' approval prior to military action, while 44 percent say this would make it too difficult to deal with threats (Pew Global Attitudes Project 2011, 3). In contrast, 74 percent in Spain and 76 percent in Germany say their country should have UN approval before taking military action (Pew Global Attitudes Project 2011, 3). And on the question of whether the United States should use drone strikes to attack and kill terrorist suspects in countries such as Pakistan and Yemen, 62 percent of Americans favor it, while 28 percent oppose this policy (Pew Global Attitudes Project 2012, 2). Even in Great Britain, the United States' closest ally, only 44 percent support drone strikes, while 47 percent oppose them. In other European publics there is even stronger opposition: in Germany 38 percent support but 49 percent oppose; in France 37 percent support but 63 percent oppose; and in Greece 5 percent support and 90 percent oppose them (Pew Global Attitudes Project 2012, 2). Drone strikes are a vivid example of the type of unilateral action that Americans typically support while majorities of their European counterparts oppose.

Third, Americans are more intensely religious than their European counterparts. While half of Americans say religion is "very important" in their lives, this number is high compared to Spain (22 percent), Germany (21 percent), Britain (17 percent), and France (13 percent) (Pew Global Attitudes Project 2011, 8). And 53 percent of Americans believe that one must believe in God to be moral and have good values compared with Germany (33 percent), Britain (20 percent), Spain (19 percent), and France (15 percent) (Pew Global Attitudes Project 2011, 9). Also, American Christians are more likely to prioritize their religious identity over their national identity: 46 percent identify themselves *primarily* as Christians, while 46 percent identify themselves *primarily* as Americans. By contrast, the majority of Christians in France (90 percent), Germany (70 percent), Britain (63 percent), and Spain (53 percent) identify themselves primarily by their nationality rather than their religion (Pew Global Attitudes Project 2011, 10).

Fourth, American public opinion is unique on important policy questions. While tolerance for homosexuality is widespread in the United States and Western Europe, Pew finds that "far more Western Europeans than Americans say homosexuality should be accepted by society; at least eight-in-ten in Spain (91%), Germany (87%), France (86%) and Britain (81%), compared with 60% in the U.S." (Pew Global Attitudes Project 2011, 11). And on the issue of global warming, while 67 percent of Americans agree that there is solid evidence the earth is warming and 42 percent agree that this is mostly due to human activity, only 44 percent of Americans think that global warming is a "serious problem" compared to 68 percent in France, 65 percent in Japan, 61 percent in Spain, and 60 percent in Germany (Pew Global Attitudes Project 2009, 87–88). And, finally, Americans are more likely to think of their culture as "superior" compared to others. While 49 percent of Americans and 47 percent of Germans agree with the statement "Our people are not perfect, but our culture is superior to others," this view is shared by 44 percent in Spain, 32 percent in Britain, and 27 percent in France (Pew Global Attitudes Project 2011, 5).

Findings such as these shed light on how America remains exceptional and unique from a comparative point of view. When compared to European publics, Americans take measurably different positions on important political attitudes and policies.

The International Dimension of American Exceptionalism

After World War II, it became popular to invoke the idea of the "American Century" because the United States became a central political, economic, and military actor on the world stage. American leaders helped craft international trade and economic institutions such as the International Monetary Fund and the World Bank, political entities such as the United Nations, and military alliances such as NATO that each played a part in creating a long era of peace, growth, and prosperity (Kagan 2012). And after emerging victorious from the Cold War, Americans once again reaffirmed their belief in American exceptionalism.

As the sole military superpower in a post–Cold War world, it became popular to describe the United States as "the indispensable nation" on the world stage. In 1998, President Bill Clinton's secretary of state, Madeleine Albright, was asked what she would say to parents of soldiers who may be sent into harm's way. She answered:

> Let me say that we are doing everything possible so that American men and women in uniform do not have to go out there again. It is the threat of the use of force and our line-up there that is going to put force behind the diplomacy. But if we have to use force, it is because we are America; we are the indispensable nation. We stand tall and we see further than other countries into the future, and we see the danger here to all of us. I know that the American men and women in uniform are always prepared to sacrifice for freedom, democracy and the American way of life. (1998)

As the indispensable nation, American exceptionalism views the United States as uniquely able to take a longer view of history and endowed with a duty to act globally to defend its way of life. President George W. Bush also promoted the notion that the United States is indispensable in fighting terror and spreading freedom; however, his supporters defended his use of unilateral power to pursue the War on Terror while critics worried that he was pursuing policies that went contrary to American ideals and international treaties.

President Obama has also defended the notion that the United States is exceptional and indispensable. Early in his first term, he was asked whether he believed in American exceptionalism. President Obama answered:

> I believe in American exceptionalism, just as I suspect that the Brits believe in British exceptionalism and the Greeks believe in Greek exceptionalism. I'm enormously proud of my country and its role and history in the world. . . . I don't think America should be embarrassed to see evidence of the sacrifices of our troops,

the enormous amount of resources that were put into Europe postwar, and our leadership in crafting an Alliance that ultimately led to the unification of Europe. We should take great pride in that.

> And if you think of our current situation, the United States remains the largest economy in the world. We have unmatched military capability. And I think that we have a core set of values that are enshrined in our Constitution, in our body of law, in our democratic practices, in our belief in free speech and equality that, though imperfect, are exceptional.

> Now, the fact that I am very proud of my country and I think that we've got a whole lot to offer the world does not lessen my interest in recognizing the value and wonderful qualities of other countries, or recognizing that we're not always going to be right, or that other people may have good ideas, or that for us to work collectively, all parties have to compromise and that includes us.

> And so I see no contradiction between believing that America has a continued extraordinary role in leading the world towards peace and prosperity and recognizing that leadership is incumbent, depends on, our ability to create partnerships we create partnerships because we can't solve these problems alone. (Obama 2009)

In this answer President Obama nicely summarizes what makes the United States exceptional. However, for his critics, this answer was too nuanced because even while defending American exceptionalism he implies that other countries also believe they are exceptional (an echo of the moderate version of American exceptionalism) and that U.S. leadership requires multilateral cooperation rather than unilateralism.

President Obama later responded to critics who accused him of opting for a path of decline. To Air Force Academy graduates he stated, "Let's start by putting aside the tired notion that says our influence has waned or that America is in decline" (Obama 2012). He then reminded his critics to "never bet against the United

States of America. And one of the reasons is that the United States has been, and will always be, the one indispensable nation in world affairs" (Obama 2012). Obama then claimed that the United States still has the economic resources, military strength, diplomatic standing, and political ideals that will make the 21st century another "American Century" (Obama 2012).

Conclusion

As we enter the 21st century there is a wide-ranging academic and political debate over the status of American exceptionalism.

First, some argue that American exceptionalism is mostly a self-congratulatory myth (Hodgson 2009; Walt 2011). While the United States has enormous powers and admirable ideals, by invoking notions of exceptionalism and indispensability the United States is doing what previous great powers have done: mistaking its temporary power as a sign of universal and exceptional character. For Steven Walt, when Americans are willfully blind to their limits, the belief in American exceptionalism leads the United States to pursue counterproductive policies such as propping up friendly dictators and failing to lead on issues such as global warming (Walt 2011).

Second, others argue that while the United States was an exceptional nation after World War II because of its political, economic, and military power, this status is slipping away due to internal domestic economic troubles and/or the emergence of countries such as China, India, and Brazil as economic powers (Friedman 2005; Zakaria 2008). As Fareed Zakaria famously observed, we are witnessing the "rise of the rest" rather than the decline of the United States In other words, countries such as Brazil, India, and China are "catching up" to the United States economically, and countries such as Finland, South Korea, and Canada are "passing" the United States educationally. Given that the strength of the U.S. economy rests on an educated and innovate workforce, this trend worries many observers. However, those who take this view argue that the United States still has the resources but simply needs the political leadership to meet these challenges and reclaim its exceptional standing (Friedman and Mandelbaum 2011).

Third, some argue that American exceptionalism is at risk if the United States opts for a path of "decline" and premature superpower suicide (Kagan 2012; Krauthammer 2009; Romney 2011). In particular, these critics argue that President Obama is steering the United States into an era of decline by shying away from global leadership, avoiding unilateral military force in favor of multilateral diplomacy, and failing to increase military spending. Instead, they argue that the United States must protect its unique global position by maintaining a dominant military role throughout the world and a willingness to project unilateral force when necessary. To be sure, President Obama has continually defended American exceptionalism but does so by emphasizing multilateral cooperation while reserving unilateral action as the option of last resort. Seen in this light, this debate is less about American exceptionalism and more about unilateralism versus multilateralism as the proper means to promote U.S. interests.

In conclusion, while there may be a rigorous debate over the future of American exceptionalism among academics, American citizens and presidents continue to defend it as an ideal. Even with a split between the moderate and strong versions of American exceptionalism, Americans remain committed to the ideal that the United States has been and remains unique and exceptional.

See also American Dream; Constitution and Constitutionalism; Democracy; National Identity; Nationalism; Religion and Politics.

Gregory W. Streich

Bibliography

Albright, M. 1998. "Transcript: Albright Interview on NBC-TV February 19." February 19. http://www .fas.org/news/iraq/1998/02/19/98021907_tpo .html. Accessed May 23, 2014.

Bacevich, A. 2008. *The Limits of Power: The End of American Exceptionalism*. New York: Metropolitan Books.

Bacevich, A., ed. 2012. *The Short American Century: A Postmortem*. Cambridge, MA: Harvard University Press.

Bush, G. 2004. "Remarks Accepting the Presidential Nomination at the Republican National Convention in New York City." September 2. http://www.presi dency.ucsb.edu/ws/index.php?pid=72727#axzz1 Xs4CwFYP. Accessed May 23, 2014.

Friedman, T. 2005. *The World Is Flat: A Brief History of the Twenty-First Century*. New York: Farrar, Strauss and Giroux.

Friedman, T., and M. Mandelbaum. 2011. *That Used to Be Us: How American Fell behind in the World It Invented and How We Can Come Back*. New York: Farrar, Strauss and Giroux.

Hirsh, M. 2003. *At War with Ourselves: Why America Is Squandering Its Chance to Build a Better World*. New York: Oxford University Press.

Hodgson, G. 2009. *The Myth of American Exceptionalism*. New Haven, CT: Yale University Press.

Ikenberry, G. John. 2011. *Liberal Leviathan: The Origins, Crisis, and Transformation of the American World Order*. Princeton, NJ: Princeton University Press.

Jones, J. 2010. "Americans See U.S. as Exceptional; 37% Doubt Obama Does." http://www.gallup.com /poll/145358/Americans-Exceptional-Doubt-Obama .aspx. Accessed May 23, 2014.

Kagan, R. 2012. *The World America Made*. New York: Knopf.

Krauthammer, C. 2009. "Decline Is a Choice: The New Liberalism and the End of American Ascendancy." *The Weekly Standard*, http://www .weeklystandard.com/Content/Public/Articles/000 /000/017/056lfnpr.asp. Accessed May 23, 2014.

Kupchan, Charles. 2012. *No One's World: The West, the Rising Rest, and the Coming Global Turn*. New York: Oxford University Press.

Lipset, S. 1997. *American Exceptionalism: A Double-Edged Sword*. New York: W.W. Norton.

Mead, W. 2001. *Special Providence: American Foreign Policy and How It Changed the World*. New York: Knopf.

Obama, B. 2009. "News Conference by President Obama." April 4. http://www.whitehouse.gov/the-press-office /news-conference-president-obama-4042009. Accessed May 23, 2014.

Obama, B. 2012. "Remarks Made by the President at the Air Force Academy Commencement." May 23. http://www.whitehouse.gov/the-press-office/2012/05/23/remarks-president-air-force-academy-commencement. May 23, 2014.

Pew Global Attitudes Project. 2009. "Confidence in Obama Lifts U.S. Image around the World: Most Muslim Publics Not So Easily Moved." July 23. http://www.pewglobal.org/2009/07/23/confidence-in-obama-lifts-us-image-around-the-world/. Accessed May 23, 2014.

Pew Global Attitudes Project. 2011. "The American-Western European Values Gap: American Exceptionalism Subsides." November 17. http://www.pewglobal.org/2011/11/17/the-american-western-european-values-gap/. Accessed May 23, 2014.

Pew Global Attitudes Project. 2012. "Global Opinion of Obama Slips, International Policies Faulted." Washington, DC: Pew Charitable Trust.

Pew Research Center. 2011. "U.S. Seen as Among the Greatest Nations, But Not Superior to All Others." June 30. http://www.people-press.org/2011/06/30 /u-s-seen-as-among-the-greatest-nations-but-not-superior-to-all-others/. Accessed May 23, 2014.

Romney, M. 2011. *No Apology: The Case for America's Greatness*. New York: St. Martin's.

Walt, S. 2011. "The Myth of American Exceptionalism." *Foreign Policy*. November 11. http://www.foreignpolicy.com/articles/2011/10/11/the_myth_of_american_exceptionalism?page=full. Accessed May 23, 2014.

Zakaria, Fareed. 2008. *The Post-American World*. New York: W.W. Norton and Company.

AMERICAN FLAG

The American flag is the national flag and ensign of the United States of America. It has 13 horizontal alternating red and white stripes and 50 white stars against a blue rectangle in the upper left corner. The American flag has varied in appearance since its original design, which dates back to before the United States' independence from Great Britain. Despite its variation over the decades, its place as a central figure in American culture has remained firm. The pledge of allegiance to the flag is taught across the nation and recited daily by children attending public school from kindergarten through graduation. The United States' National Anthem, "The Star Spangled Banner," venerates no leaders or attributes of the country, but rather its flag. Federal codes exist, which specifically outline how the flag is to be displayed and cared for. The shapes and colors of the flag are symbolic in a practical sense; however to many Americans, this symbol has deeper meaning than its superficial design. Not only is it flown atop flagpoles, but its likeness is often reproduced on apparel, stickers, and other merchandise. The American flag was originally referred to as the Continental Colors or the Grand Union Flag. It is sometimes called "Old Glory," "Stars and Stripes," or "The Star Spangled Banner."

Evolution

The Continental Colors, the first incarnation of the American flag, was flown during the Revolutionary War to distinguish vessels belonging to the U.S. Navy from those belonging to Great Britain. It closely resembled the flag of the British East India Company and was sometimes called the "Grand Union." The Continental Colors featured 13 alternating red and white horizontal stripes, resembling the modern American flag. In 1777, the Flag Resolution was passed by the Second Continental Congress, which determined that the U.S. flag would maintain the red and white stripes, but would contain 13 white stars in the upper left corner against a blue background. The stripes represented the original colonies, as they do on the modern flag. The stars were symbolic of the 13 states of the nation. As no particular arrangement for the stars was specified, flags from this era sometimes feature the stars arranged in staggered rows, while others feature them arranged in a circle. Betsy Ross is credited with sewing the first American flag to feature stars and stripes and changing the stars from six-pointed to five-pointed. There is no credible documentation proving the legend of Betsy Ross; however, nobody else has been alternately given credit. The blue and white rectangle is called the "union." In 1795, the design was altered to contain 15 stars, acknowledging the statehood of Vermont and Kentucky. As states were added to the union, the flag evolved to represent the number of states that comprised America.

The U.S. flag that is currently used was adopted in 1960. As a prized symbol of America, federal codes

dictate that it be treated with respect. According to United States Code, The Pledge of Allegiance to the flag is to be rendered by standing, facing the flag, and placing the right hand over one's heart. Nonreligious head coverings should be removed. Military personnel in uniform are to stand at attention and salute. United States Code dictates that the flag be flown only from sunrise to sunset, unless illuminated. The Code outlines regulations for display of the flag in various scenarios, including when it is among other flags, when flown from a staff projecting from a building, and when displayed against a wall. The flag is never to touch the ground or surface beneath it, to be worn or used for advertising, or to be displayed or stored in a way it could easily be damaged. The American flag is flown at half-staff as a sign of respect for and in memoriam of deceased public or government officials. The president may declare that all national flags are to be flown at half-staff as he or she deems fit upon the death of a leading citizen. Private institutions or organizations and individuals are not restricted from flying their flags at half-staff as a display of respect of mourning when this is not expected according to the Flag Code.

Controversies

Some acts with regard to the American flag are not clearly outlined in the Flag Code, which acknowledges it may have failed to address certain scenarios. Some controversial acts that have come to the attention of Americans in recent decades include flag burning. The Flag Code recommends the burning of American flags that are in poor condition, referring to this method of destruction as "dignified." The Code does not discuss flag burning for any purpose other than dignified disposal.

In 1984, Gregory Lee Johnson was arrested for burning a flag outside of the Republican National Convention in Texas in protest of President Reagan's policies. He was charged with "desecration of a venerated object, including the American flag, if such action were to incite anger in others" (U.S. Courts 2014). Johnson appealed, arguing that his First Amendment rights were being violated. The Supreme Court determined that Johnson's actions were indeed protected by the First Amendment. This amendment prompted the flag desecration laws that existed in 48 states at the time to be determined unconstitutional.

In 1989, Congress passed the Flag Protection Act, which was essentially the same as the state laws that were struck down by the *Texas v. Johnson* ruling, but on a federal level. In protest of this act, thousands of citizens burned American flags. Two men, Shawn Eichman and Mark Haggerty, were arrested and charged with violating the Flag Protection Act. As in the case of Johnson, Eichman and Haggerty appealed. Their cases were consolidated and heard by the Supreme Court, which found the Flag Protection Act unconstitutional, just like its state law predecessors, and struck it down. Since these two Supreme Court cases, numerous attempts have been made to pass an amendment to the U.S. Constitution which would ban flag desecration. None of them have been successful.

Other first amendment cases that have involved the American flag were the instances of two children who, for religious reasons, refused to salute the flag. The Supreme Court ruled in favor of the children. It was determined to be unconstitutional to force an individual to salute the flag in violation of his or her religious beliefs.

Another controversial act was the infamous raising of the American flag at Ground Zero on September 11, 2001, the day of the World Trade Center attacks in New York City. To many, this symbolized survival, hope, and triumph in the wake of tragedy. To some, however, it was a violation of the Flag Code, which states that flags that are no longer in acceptable condition are to be destroyed in a respectful manner. The flag that was raised upon Ground Zero was found in the wreckage and was itself damaged. Despite the controversy, the image of New York firefighters hoisting the symbol of our country was and remains a powerful one. This image has been compared with that of the Marines and Navy Corpsman raising a U.S. flag on Iwo Jima during World War II. Both images depict men demonstrating patriotism and respect for their flag in spite of unthinkable conditions. They have each been featured on postage stamps and have been reproduced as photographs, prints, posters, and other memorabilia.

Resurgence

Following the events of September 11, 2001, the American flag has enjoyed a renewed popularity. As a show of patriotism, Americans have been buying and displaying flags at an increased rate. The unprecedented attacks served as a reminder that America is vulnerable and must be defended. The slogan "freedom isn't free" often accompanies images of the American flag and other national symbols. The flag is displayed as a show of support to troops serving overseas and stateside to defend the values it represents to many Americans. Liberty, justice, freedom, and national pride are among the values American flag is believed to stand for. Studies have even suggested that the image of the American flag evokes a sense of nationalism, defined as a sense of national superiority to other nations.

George W. Bush, the president of the United States at the time of the September 11 attacks, could be seen wearing an American flag pin on his lapel shortly after the events. His aides, as well as some news anchors, also began wearing the flag pins. Although the Flag Code states that the American flag is not to be worn as clothing, a pin that represents the flag is permitted. The Flag Code states that the appropriate location for a flag pin is on the left lapel (above the heart), which is where it is typically seen on politicians and reporters. This trend began during the Nixon administration, waxing and waning in popularity over the following decades. The trend of wearing flag pins has risen during times of conflict, such as the Gulf War of the 1990s and the War on Terror (Overseas Contingency Operations). The American flag pin is now something of a wardrobe staple for politicians. The flag pin has become so synonymous with patriotism that when Barack Obama was observed without one in 2007, he was harshly criticized by the media, citizens, and other politicians. Obama explained that his decision was based on his belief that wearing the pin had become a substitute for actual patriotism, and he intended to express his loyalty and love for America through his words and actions. Following the controversy and criticism that ensued, Barack Obama would always be seen wearing the American flag pin upon his left lapel.

The famous statue of the Wall Street bull is decorated with American flags as members of the National Guard patrol the neighborhood following the September 11 terrorist attacks, September 17, 2001. (AP Photo/Beth A. Keiser)

Conclusion

The American flag has been a symbol of the United States since its inception during the Revolutionary War. Its design has been altered many times since then, but its symbolism remains the same. Its 13 stripes have represented the original 13 colonies since the flag was called the Continental Colors. The union, or the blue rectangle in the upper left corner, has maintained the same symbolism as well. Stars have been added to the flag, but have always stood for the number of states in the union. The American flag is a symbol of patriotism, and for some, one of nationalism. Ownership of an American flag in some form has been on the rise since the tragedies of September 11, 2001. Displays of the American flag and its image have increased by

individuals, businesses, and other institutions as well. As patriotism has become a more widely held American value, increasing emphasis has been placed on buying American-made products and making efforts to ensure others are certain of one's patriotic stance. Public figures, especially politicians and news anchors, have chosen the flag lapel pin as the primary means of nonverbally communicating their identification as a loyal, patriotic citizen. The American flag has been found to stir up a sense of nationalism in some. Extensive guidelines exist for the ways in which respect for the flag is to be demonstrated, including the pledge of allegiance to the flag. Much controversy has arisen regarding symbolic expressions involving the American flag, and efforts continue to be made to amend the Constitution of the United States to further limit how the flag may be treated. The American flag is, to many Americans, more than a national symbol. It represents the core values upon which the nation was founded: liberty, justice, and freedom.

See also Citizenship and Politics; Civil Religion; Liberty; Monuments, Memorials, and Public History; Nationalism; Presidency and Presidential Politics; Theater and Ritual in American Politics.

Jennifer Henry

Bibliography

Abrams, Floyd. 1997. "Look Who's Trashing the First Amendment." *Columbia Journalism Review* 36: 53.

Cruz, Gilbert. 2008. "A Brief History of the Flag Lapel Pin." *Time* (July 3). http://content.time.com/time/nation/article/0,8599,1820023,00.html. Accessed April 29, 2014.

Franklin, Tom. 2002. "The After-Life of a Photo That Touched a Nation." *Columbia Journalism Review* 40 (2002): 64.

Goldstein, Robert Justin. 2013. *Burning the Flag: The Great 1989–1990 American Flag Desecration Controversy*. Kent, OH: Kent State University Press.

Henderson, Jennifer Jacobs. 2005. "Conditional Liberty: The Flag Salute before Gobitis and Barnette." *Journal of Church and State* 47, no. 4: 747.

Holzer, Harold. 2002. "New Glory for Old Glory: A Lincoln Era Tradition Reborn." *White House Studies* 2: 203.

Kemmelmeier, Marcus, and David Winter. 2008. "Sowing Patriotism but Reaping Nationalism? Consequences of Exposure to the American Flag." *Political Psychology* 29: 859–79.

Luckey, John. 2008. "The United States Flag: Federal Law Relating to Display and Associated Questions." http://www.senate.gov/reference/resources/pdf/RL30243.pdf. Accessed April 29, 2014.

"Speech Exceptions." 2005. *Harvard Law Review* 118 (March): 1709–30.

U.S. Courts. 2014. "First Amendment: Free Speech and Flag Burning." http://www.uscourts.gov/educational-resources/get-involved/constitution-activities/first-amendment/free-speech-flag-burning.aspx. Accessed April 29, 2014.

Wilkins, Roger. 2002. "What Patriotism Means Today in the Wake of 9/11/2001." *Social Education* 66: 350.

AMERICAN INDIAN POLITICS

American Indian policy is linked to the tension between and among the several constituencies that form political relationships in the United States and their perspectives of self-determination, sovereignty, assimilation, and trust. Originally, the United States dealt with tribal nations as sovereign entities and the core policy relationship was one of reciprocal nationhood. Nations existed, with governing systems, prior to white contact, and these nations had 1,000-year histories of governance structures that had served them well. Today, American Indians represent a group subjugated consistently since European contact even while the politics that frame contemporary U.S. policies continue to encounter the resiliency of American Indian nations.

American Indians and the President

Early treaties gave the American president discretionary authority to establish trading posts and military outposts, to appoint agents, and to advise and to direct the Indians in land claim disputes. Early examples of authority, found in treaties, exercised by the president are comprehensive and reflect the federal policies of extermination and limiting tribes' access to their lands. The federal Constitution does not stipulate authority in this matter for the president of the United States; rather, his authority is derived from the delegated powers of Congress. Historically, the president in turn has delegated authority to Indian agents through the secretary of war (later, secretary of the Interior), effectively determining the day-to-day life of Indian peoples even as land was removed from their use. Today, the president and executive branch exercise authority, as delegated by Congress, primarily through the Interior Department's Office of the Assistant Secretary for Indian Affairs, which oversees the Bureau of Indian Affairs (BIA).

For the past two decades, the president has exercised most of his power over the day-to-day oversight of Indian affairs through the use of executive orders. Executive orders on tribal colleges, eagle feather use, education, and agency consultation are examples.

Presidential support for tribal sovereignty and Indian rights has ranged from negative to positive. President Andrew Jackson presided over Indian removal policies, but President Richard Nixon supported the Indian Self-Determination and Education Assistance Act. Other presidents' support has fallen somewhere in the middle of that continuum.

The powers inherent in the president's office to veto legislation, to appoint federal judges, and to appoint the Interior secretary (and others) provide a de facto set of authorities that affects federal Indian policy.

The appointment of the secretary of Interior and the assistant secretary for Indian Affairs is as critical today as it was during westward expansion. The Department of the Interior also houses other agencies, some of whom compete for resources found on tribal lands. The most critical policy within Interior Department impacting tribes today is Indian preference in hiring. The Supreme Court in *Morton v. Mancari* affirmed the government's obligation to tribes, linking the policy of Indian preference in hiring to self-determination.

The BIA, originally established in the War Department, has a consistent record of failure and abuse in its services to Indian people. Two of the most egregious examples are the failure to provide oversight for trust monies (now in settlement following a 2009 class-action suit, *Cobell v. Salazar*) and the education of Indian children through on-and-off reservation boarding facilities and peripheral dormitories.

Of note, Assistant Secretary Kevin Gover (Pawnee), in commemorating 175 years of the existence of the BIA in 2000, officially apologized for federal treatment of tribal peoples. While it did not represent an official apology from the federal government, it led to a 2009 joint resolution, S.J. Resolution 14, the "Native American Apology Resolution."

The scope of federal executive power over tribes and individual Indians remains very broad, and the ability of the BIA, as the primary representative of the federal government in Indian Affairs, to provide data to the judicial branch continues to affect the ability of tribes to actualize the Indian Self-Determination Act (1975) and the Tribal Self-Governance Act (1994).

American Indians and the Judiciary

The U.S. Supreme Court has a long history of reasserting congressional authority over the affairs of Indian people in case law. The Court has, for example, consistently upheld the power of Congress to abrogate Indian treaties; yet in recent years, the Court has asserted that Congress's intention to abrogate the provisions of a treat must be beyond doubt. "Absent explicit statutory language, we have been extremely reluctant to find congressional abrogation of treaty rights" (quoted in *United States v. Dion*).

The Supreme Court created several doctrines of law that impact American Indian politics; for example, the decision that Indian treaties are equal in stature to foreign treaties is an important construct for federal legal decisions. Equally as important is the Supreme Court's recognition of the doctrine of discovery, which gives the United States legal title to Indian-occupied land. There is also, of course, the legal designation of "ward" of the government, empowering Congress to act as "guardian." The Supreme Court's role in shaping American Indian policy has, like the other branches of the federal system, seen a wide range of decisions.

In 1903, the Court instituted "plenary authority" over Indian affairs by establishing that the consent of Indians was not necessary to obtain cessions of land and that Congress had the power to abrogate treaty provisions.

The decisions of the Supreme Court are only as effective as their enforcement, either through legislation and appropriations or through executive order. The role of the Court in affirming or restricting tribal rights continues to be debated by legal scholars, and the judicial appointments to the Court in the next decade will have lasting effect on the ability of tribal nations to reaffirm their status in court.

American Indians and Congress

Congress acts with constitutional authority to deal with tribes by Article 1, Section 8, Clause 3, where the legislative branch of the government is vested with the power "to regulate Commerce with foreign Nations, and among the several States, and with the Indian Tribes." The U.S. Constitution provides a framework for the relationship with U.S. tribes, yet this framework remains ambiguous in its definition of "commerce." Tribal treaties and the commerce clause of the U.S. Constitution provide the foundation for policies affecting Indian tribes and individuals. The sovereignty of Indian tribes is compromised by provision found in treaties that left many decisions to the discretion of Congress. The Senate monitored these early treaties and amended or modified the land payments or other provisions thought to be excessive. Beginning in the early 1800s, Congress began to pass laws to regulate the assimilation of Indians. This type of lawmaking escalated at the end of the treaty-making era in 1871, culminating in the passage of the Indian Reorganization Act (IRA) of 1934. By the end of World War II, and extending through the Civil Rights era in the United States, Congress enacted a litany of laws and policies aimed at the ultimate dismantling of tribal sovereignty.

The IRA of 1934 and the Indian Civil Rights Act of 1968 appear to begin a reversal of the dominant policies to destroy tribalism. Policies are the products of congressional committees, specifically those related to Indian Affairs. The first Standing Committee on Indian Affairs was created in 1920 in the Senate. A year later, the House of Representatives created a similar committee. Congress retains the sole authority to appropriate funds to fulfill the government's treaty obligations and to develop an appropriate plan to interact with tribal nations under the self-assumed "trust" obligation.

The congressional committee structure provided oversight for policies on land and land claims, health care, housing, education, economic development, water, trust accounts, gaming, tribal recognition, national resource and environmental impact, religious freedom, Indian child welfare, and tribal-state relationships. This committee structure remains in place currently.

Since 1975 and that year's Indian Self-Determination and Education Assistance Act, self-determination has been the official policy of the U.S. Congress. Although the federal government remains the final authority, the Self-Governance Act, passed in 1994, affirms a government-to-government relationship that continues to influence contemporary policy.

Very few American Indians have ever been elected to serve in the U.S. Congress. In 2014, the only senator, Tom Cole (Chickasaw) from Oklahoma, announced his retirement. Today's Congress works through the federal compacting process and appears open to supporting tribes. In recent years the Senate Indian Affairs Committee has reaffirmed tribal trust reform, but tribes remain watchful as the nation's economic strength remains tenuous and stands to affect the trusts.

Congress continues to set policy that establishes tribal–federal relationships and is historically bound to the perpetuation of tribal sovereignty and the unique rights provided in treaties to create the trust relationships defined by the federal government. This policy is declared through legislation that is subject to review by the Supreme Court.

American Indians and Political Parties

American Indians have made strides over the past few cycles in building voting participation and political representation. Candidates and elected leaders are, in turn, increasingly cognizant of the value of these voters as a constituency. More importantly, the growing influence of Indian Country is giving a voice to the too-long-neglected challenges facing today's Indians, from poverty to inadequate health care to substandard housing and access to education.

Although American Indians are active political participants who are asserting whatever political influence they might possess, relative to the larger political society American Indians can still be defined as somewhat politically powerless. American Indian history is one of genocide, exploitation, and subjugation. Present-day American Indian politics must be understood in light of this historical reality. As victims of conquest, American Indians have had to adapt to historical circumstances; Indians have always had to *react* to social, economic, and political pressures rather than being in the position of creating or initiating major policies. In addition, American Indians will always be a numeric minority (with a few congressional district

Dr. David Gipp, member of the Standing Rock Sioux Tribe, addresses the Democratic National Convention in Denver, Colorado, August 26, 2008. (MCT/Tribune News Service/Getty Images)

exceptions, as discussed earlier), and American democracy will continue to hold strong to the notion that "one person, one vote" is a sufficient calculation for representing the interests of the people.

The Native vote is key in several states; geographically decentralized areas have a propensity to swing elections in close races. Mainstream political parties are now providing opportunities for American Indian participation.

American Indian political activism has grown in the last two decades and so has engagement in political parties. From large political donations to major American political parties and grassroots Native voter rights advocacy, American Indians are engaged in—are becoming players in—mainstream politics. David Gipp, a member of the Standing Rock Sioux Nation, was the first American Indian to nominate a president in a major political party in 2008. The 2012 Democratic National Convention in Charlotte, North Carolina, saw

a record 161 Native delegates cast their votes in support of President Barack Obama's nomination. Denise Juneau, a citizen of the Mandan and Hidatsa tribes, delivered an impassioned speech on Indian education on the convention floor.

While a substantial number of American Indians do not participate in formal, mainstream political activities, tribes' experience of economic success in recent decades through tribal gaming enterprises has led some to become more politically active. Nationally, tribes are engaging more with political parties at the federal and state levels through campaign contributions.

American Indians and State Governments

Tribal governments work primarily with the federal government, and their relationships with the states where they are located are often contentious as tribes resent actions where states attempt to tax businesses and regulate their economies. In 1832, the Supreme Court in *Worcester v. Georgia* held that state laws had no force in Indian Country unless specifically authorized by Congress. This case affirmed federal exclusivity and barred state intrusion into internal tribal actions. Known as the Marshall Doctrine, this policy has been tested, and some states with historical circumstances that dictate openly intrusive policies have weakened the doctrine as they attempt to broaden their jurisdiction throughout Indian Country.

Recent disagreements were tested in courts using the federal preemption test, which voids state laws that are inconsistent with federal law or otherwise interfere with overriding federal and tribal interests. In addition, courts look to the infringement test to determine whether a state action infringes on tribal self-government. However, the current Supreme Court's presumptive favoring of states' rights stands to impact the doctrine of tribal sovereignty and to threaten the progress made by tribal self-determination policies.

Inter-tribal and Intra-tribal Politics

Most tribal governments receive few funds for administrative and governmental needs. While some tribal governments struggle to serve the needs of their populations, other tribes have been more fortunate in this regard—whether through making use of special BIA programs or through fostering successful economic development strategies. Yet most tribes have gone underserved and have faced a legacy of administrative neglect. This makes it all the more difficult to assert their tribal power or to develop politically and assert such power both locally and nationally. However, recent changes to the economic and political situation among tribal nations have presented new challenges to current tribal administrations.

Most contemporary tribal government constitutions or bylaws were created when Indian communities exercised little political self-sufficiency or legal autonomy. Such documents did not provide a structure for economic and community development, or for the protection of political and cultural rights. Current efforts by American Indian governments to engage in economic and political development as well as to assert more effective administrative and legal control over their tribal communities thus may require change or modification to their constitutional, legal, and administrative institutions. Change does not come easy or without conflict. Therefore, as tribal governments move forward to establish more governmental powers, disagreements will undoubtedly arise.

Knowledge and education of tribal government's past, present, and possible future is key in increasing the political power of tribal governments. This includes an understanding of the internal and external policies that have affected not only one's own tribe but American Indians and indigenous peoples as a whole. It is important for the general membership of tribal nations to understand these issues so as to avoid replicating any of the negative policies of the past. In a brief amount time, many tribal governments have been propelled into local, state, and national politics, leaving little time to learn the ropes. Yet, to the surprise of many, tribal governments are resilient and have effectively protected and preserved their tribes' sovereignty. Some tribes, again, have been less successful than others. More than ever, then, tribal leaders must educate themselves in a multiplicity of capacities, including environmental, political, economic, and governmental affairs. Just as tribal governments today are engaged in administering multimillion-dollar economic development projects and significant government finances, so they must devote themselves to increasing their own and their constituent's level of educational opportunity and achievement to move forward and lessen or avoid internal conflicts arising from change.

A lack of knowledge among tribal members who may not understand contemporary mainstream politics or mainstream economic development strategies can lead to division and time-consuming rivalry among the tribal nations' population. This situation can prohibit a tribal nation from advancing in its administrative, political, economic, and legal operations. Critical to this matter is an understanding of the dependency created through federal Indian policies of the past. In the 19th century and the first part of the 20th century, the "Indian Agent" exerted enormous power under the direction of the federal government and the BIA. Although many of the functions of the BIA were taken over by tribal governments under the IRA of 1934, the tribal councils and reservation business committees often exerted the same kind of unlimited power. Thus, today, some are still content with having federal bureaucrats determine their destiny rather than trusting in themselves and their elected leadership. Either that, or they remain suspicious of their own leadership if they wield too much political, legal, or economic power. Leaders with good intentions can face conflicts from their own people who do not understand how the political system and economic system work.

Some scholars and historians rest the blame on a federal government that approved the IRA's concept in principle but declined to fund its second, important component—which was to have professional ethnologists tailor new, boilerplate constitutions to fit the individual tribes. Lacking that component, tribes were left with restricted choices.

There are many internal dynamics that play a role in the maintenance, exercise, and limit on tribal sovereignty and tribal political and economic power. As American Indians have begun to take on more power over their own affairs, there has been a reemergence of the democratic principle that every member of the tribal citizenry should have the ability to participate in tribal government. However, with this reemergence must come a reeducation of tribal values, language, culture, and principles, including an education in the historical, political, and economic issues currently facing tribal nations and tribal citizenry.

An additional challenge to tribal political power is the ever-increasing tribal economic power gained, in large measure, through gaming enterprises. Much of the success in this area is owing to location, market monopoly, and effective political participation. However, some states and business entities oppose the monopolies that tribes have often realized and seek to tax and regulate them as a means of generating state revenue for cash-strapped states. This area of the law remains a work in progress for both sides and is brought into relief with each new casino that is proposed.

Conclusions

American Indian politics is perhaps best characterized by their continual flux. The complexity of 566 federally recognized tribes and their separate and combined interactions with states as well as with the courts

and the federal bureaucracy create an ever-changing landscape for American Indian politics. However, it is in moving through such a landscape that tribes have proven themselves to be resilient even as they remain both watchful and hopeful.

See also Federalism; Race, Ethnicity, and Politics; State and Local Politics.

Joely Proudfit

Bibliography
Indian Reorganization Act, June 18, 1934 (Wheeler-Howard Act—48 Stat. 984–25 U.S.C. § 461 et seq).
Indian Self-Determination and Education Assistance Act of 1975 (Public Law 93–638).
Morton v. Mancari 417 U.S. 535 (1974).
Tribal Self-Governance Amendments (Public Law 106–260).
United States v. Dion 476 U.S. 738–40.
Wilkins, David E., and Heidi Kiiwetinepinesiik Stark. 2011. *American Indian Politics and the American Political System.* Lanham, MD: Rowman & Littlefield.
Worcester v. Georgia 31 U.S. (6 Pet.) 515 (1832).

ANTI-INTELLECTUALISM IN AMERICAN LIFE

Anti-intellectualism, as both an ongoing sensibility and a phenomenon subject to occasional flare-ups, has existed from almost the start of the American project. But the consequences have not always seemed as dire, nor the manifestations as diverse and widespread, as they have in the last half of the 20th century.

Insofar as antielitism has intersected with anti-intellectualism, some events and movements have been interpreted as positives by a spectrum of historical actors. Calls for common sense, for instance, in late 18th-century philosophy and politics resulted in a leveling of participation in the pursuit of truth and the common good, respectively (Rosenfeld 2011). The "opinion of the multitude" (i.e., populism), at its best, gifted politics what Francis Galton would later call, in 1906, the "wisdom of the crowd." Of course some advised caution, with Immanuel Kant calling common sense "convenient" and a philistine form of anti-intellectualism. And Joseph Priestly warned that common sense would lead to new forms of dogmatism, intolerance, and demagoguery (Rosenfeld 2011, 88).

Later historians would say Priestly's devolution occurred as early as the Jacksonian era, during the election and presidency of Andrew Jackson. Richard Hofstadter, the earliest and foremost historian to write about anti-intellectualism, wrote: "As popular democracy gained strength and confidence, it reinforced the widespread belief in the superiority of the inborn, intuitive, folkish wisdom over the cultivated, oversophisticated, and self-interested knowledge of the literati and well-to-do." The collective "wisdom of the common man" was the new priority. At least one of Jackson's contemporaries, the historian George Bancroft, saw Jackson as a representative of the natural wisdom of the natural man, "unlettered" and "little versed in books" but "raised by the will of the people to the highest pinnacle of honour." Jackson embodied the democratic powers of intuition, vigor, action, genuineness. His judgment, and that of his followers, was unclouded by philosophical and academic speculations (Hofstadter 1963, 154–55, 158–59).

The emotional and occasional anti-intellectual fervor of the First and Second Great Awakenings, furthermore, created a new kind of Protestantism in the United States. Revivalist preachers loosened the hold of dominant learned clergy in Anglican, Presbyterian, and Congregationalist churches. Those preachers enabled citizens with a more direct access to God. Even Hofstadter, whose view of the Great Awakening was mostly negative about evangelical religion's effects on American intellectual life, conceded: "the Awakening quickened the democratic spirit in America . . . the revivalists broke the hold of the establishments and heightened that assertiveness and self-sufficiency which visitor[s] . . . from abroad . . . later [found]

Sacking Political Science

One example of anti-intellectualism operating in government circles involves the discipline of political science itself. In 2009 Senator Tom Coburn (R-OK) launched an effort to force the National Science Foundation (NSF) to cease offering research grants to scholars working in political science. The senator's concern was that political science was not science but politics dressed up as science. He observed that if Americans had an interest in politics, they could turn to a wide variety of print and electronic media outlets; they did not need political scientists (at least not government-funded ones) to explain things to them.

Coburn's initial effort failed, partly due to a large-scale e-mail campaign mounted by the American Political Science Association. In 2013, however, amid heightened concerns over government spending (particularly among Tea Party supporters), the senator renewed his effort and, without much debate, saw the measure passed and signed into law. Under the new regime at NSF there was to be only one exception regarding the funding of political science research. Whereas previously the agency's Political Science Program could consider funding for any study of "citizenship, government, and politics," now it could only fund research geared toward "promoting national security or the economic interests of the United States."

The funding cutback affects, among other things, important studies of American electoral behavior and legislative voting. For instance, the American National Election Studies project began in 1970 and is widely regarded as having successfully generated, through its surveys and interviews, some of the most important data on voting behavior to date. Another project, on roll-call votes in Congress (going back to 1789), has produced information used by scholars to study partisanship and polarization, among other things. Now, however, these projects and others like them must seek new sources of funding or cease operating.

characteristic of the American people. [And] the impulse given to humanitarian causes . . . must also be chalked up to . . . the Great Awakening" (Hofstadter 1963, 74). Those humanitarian causes included abolitionism and the antislavery movement.

But, in recent times, the varieties of anti-intellectualism have instigated more negative than positive cultural, educational, social, and political consequences. The prevalence of political ideology and the mistrust of expert judgment have contributed to a gridlocked Congress, human-made global climate change, the culture wars, renewed antiscience sentiments in schools, and a fractured system of higher education. Even if anti-intellectualism is something inherent to democracies and has some positive formulations, and even if ignorance is considered by some to be a part of the human condition (i.e., a consequence of "original sin"), it is clear that the presence and effects of anti-intellectualism need to be understood to be mitigated. The last is important to renewing some sense (however chastened) of the possibilities of cultural, social, and political progress.

What follows is a consideration of terminological, theoretical, and historiographical problems on the subject anti-intellectualism. After those problems are explored, instances and trends will be considered in relation to the recent history of presidential politics.

Definitions, Theory, and Historiography

In terms of beginnings it is useful to state the obvious: anti-intellectualism is, foremost, a negative proposition. The term itself posits an elite category which, from the point of view of the nonintellectual, is about margins, boundaries, and flaws of both intellectuals themselves and the intellectual life. The *Oxford English Dictionary* (*OED*) traces the origins of the term (a noun) to a 1909 article that appeared in the *Catholic Encyclopedia*. The *OED* provides no definition, but an excerpted example sentence links anti-intellectualism to both agnosticism and "fideism." The latter term, however, helps in thinking about anti-intellectualism. Fideism is defined by *OED* as "any doctrine according to which all (or some) knowledge depends upon faith or revelation, and reason or the intellect is to

be disregarded." Turning to other sources, *Webster's New World Dictionary* defines the "anti-intellect*ual*" as both an adjective, denoting "hostil[ity] to or oppos[ition] to intellectual personas or matters, activities, etc." and a noun as "an anti-intellectual person." Anti-intellectualism is simply listed as an additional related noun. The online *Merriam-Webster Dictionary* dates "anti-intellectual" to 1821 and provides this definition: "opposing or hostile to intellectuals or to an intellectual view or approach."

Several interesting considerations—keywords, themes, and topics—arise from these definitions. Notice the following terms (directly quoted or implied): faith, revelation, reason, hostility, opposition, personas, matters (e.g., ideas), activities, approaches to (or views of) issues, and so on. Both "hostility" and "opposition" imply action, which seem to downplay passive ignorance. But on ignorance, we could most certainly classify the willful variety as active—when that condition can really be discerned or reasonably suspected. Indeed, Robert Proctor's and Londa Schiebinger's study, *Agnotology* (2008), asserts that ignorance is an active, vigorous force in the world. It is socially produced and socially productive. Proctor discusses three kinds of ignorance: "native state," "lost realm," and "strategic ploy." The last is self-explanatory, but the first denotes an originary lack or deficit, and the second suggests a kind of selective neglect (Proctor and Schiebinger 2008, 3, 4, 6).

Returning to terms from the definitions, notice the implied ad hominem in relation to personas and activities. This goes to the oldest and traditional view of anti-intellectualism as against the person perceived to be, or desiring to be, an intellectual. Hofstadter's 1963 text, *Anti-intellectualism in American Life*, opens with the abuse of intellectuals perpetrated by Sen. Joseph McCarthy, the denigration of 1952 presidential candidate Adlai Stevenson, and the definition of an "egghead" and "disdain for pure science" forwarded by Secretary of Defense Charles E. Wilson (Hofstadter 1963, 3–5, 10–11). These "intellectuals" are, to the opposed, pretentious, effete, and inauthentic figures who forward themselves as "experts." Aaron Lecklider recently complicated this view by arguing that these slurs, however colorful, simply underscore the fact that intelligence is a contested domain. Anyone who assigns, defends, or takes on the mantle of "intellectual," then, simply perpetuates elitism by bracketing off and divorcing brainpower from ordinary men and women. Anti-intellectualism becomes a strategy to remind elites and managers of the brainpower of labor (Lecklider 2013, 4, 222). Anti-intellectualism also becomes less about individuals and people, and more about protecting masses, the power of common people, and, in the end, democracy.

Notice also, from the definitions, the topics of faith and revelation. These go to the old conflict between faith and reason, or between dogma and science. It is familiar history, but some Catholics and Protestants have been battling reason, science, and the perceived secularism of both since the Enlightenment. The recently published *United States Catholic Catechism for Adults* speaks of the "Age of Reason" and the Enlightenment, as well as Deism and the "scientific revolution," as prominent influences in the American project and as challenges to faith. This catechism asserts that these movements posit "reason and common sense" as "our only guides" to life. It also restates the old fear that "the principle of religious freedom" has "evolved into a 'wall of separation' that seems to say that faith should have no impact on the state or society" (*United States Catholic Catechism for Adults* 2006, 41–43).

These statements underscore the ongoing problem of how intellectuals, or thoughtful politicians, discuss and consider religion in the public square. If those discussions take place without care or with too much skepticism, hostility and charges of secularism (as well as elitism) will follow. And from the point of view of the religious, charges of anti-intellectualism are, at times, used as a cudgel or term of abuse. The label is attached to even thoughtful Christians who insert matters of faith in civil affairs. But, in this case, the work done for the secular thinker is often emotional. This is analogous to how "pseudoscience" is used, without rigor, by scientists to demarcate legitimate from illegitimate science. But, as Michael Gordin recently noted about problem of demarcation in the sciences, there is, analogously, "no bright line" that separates intellectualism from anti-intellectualism. As with science, all thought exists on a continuum (Gordin 2012, 11–12). This point correlates with Hofstadter's assertion that anti-intellectualism is not "commonly found in a pure or unmixed state" (Hofstadter 1963, 21). Returning to religion, and Christianity in particular, disagreements about religion, faith, and dogma lie behind many charges of anti-intellectualism.

Conflicts about approaches to problems, public and private, feed historical instances of anti-intellectualism. Because thoughtful people, whether or not they have been ordained with the title "intellectual," often see and emphasize complexity, those same may earn the scorn or hostility of those searching for immediate and applicable answers. This points to idea of "time" as being in conflict with the pursuit of truth. A certain impatience, then, feeds anti-intellectual moments and movements. Because the political sphere is about compromise, deliberation, and the search for practical solutions to problems, the thoughtful person is seen as an obstacle to efficiency and progress. Questions about means and ends slow down the process. Intuition and ideology become substitutes for complex thinking. Indeed, ideology provides a potent combination of focus, belief, and certainty. All of this puts reason and careful empiricism in permanent conflict with modern politics. Instances of anti-intellectualism, then, are signs of a paradox in modernity as applied to democratic politics, state building, and state maintenance. The "wisdom of the crowd" must prevail, sometimes as a force hostile to democratic deliberation.

What other considerations matter in terms of definitions? Given the authoritative nature of his *Anti-intellectualism in American Life*, it is productive to return to Hofstadter. How did he define anti-intellectualism in his 1963 classic? He began by noting that the term, despite its earlier empirical roots, only "became a familiar part of our national vocabulary" in the 1950s. Aside from being a kind of anti-rationalism, Hofstadter noted that anti-intellectualism was a "cyclical" phenomenon centered on intellectuals themselves—a specific kind of ad hominem. The later attitude had to do with "ambivalence" rather than pure dislike. Hofstadter continued: "The common strain that binds together the attitudes and ideas which I call anti-intellectual is a resentment and suspicion of the life of the mind and of those who are considered to represent it, and a disposition constantly to minimize the value of that life." With this distinction in mind, Hofstadter excludes the "philosophical anti-rationalism" of Whitman, Emerson, Nietzsche, and their followers from his work (Hofstadter 1963, 6–8). Based on the subsequent rise of anti-foundational language theory and poststructuralism, such as in the works of Jacques Derrida, Michel Foucault, and others published in the 1960s and afterward, this distinction remains relevant.

Hofstadter also lengthened the chronology to anti-intellectualism to a time before the American project. He asserted that anti-intellectualism is "a part of our English cultural inheritance" (Hofstadter 1963, 20). Precursors to Hofstadter did likewise. In a 1913 essay "The Moral Obligation to Be Intelligent," John Erskine asserted that "the disposition to consider intelligence a peril is an old Anglo-Saxon inheritance." In a sweeping statement that assumed the dominance of the English heritage in the United States, he added: "If we love Shakspere [sic] and Milton and Scott and Dickens and Thackeray, and yet do not know what qualities their books hold out for our admiration, then—let me say it as delicately as possible—our admiration is not discriminating; and if we neither have discrimination nor are disturbed by our lack of it, then perhaps that wise man could not list intelligence among our virtues" (Erskine 1913). After diagnosing the problem of anti-intellectualism at Columbia University and beyond, Erskine would go on, in his later works, to prescribe "great books" as a remedy. Erskine's prescription influenced a number of educators, most prominently Mortimer J. Adler and Robert Hutchins, to promote the great books idea to adults. From the 1940s and onward, Adler and Hutchins used that idea to fight anti-intellectualism both in and outside higher education (Lacy 2013).

In discerning iterations of anti-intellectualism through the early 1960s, Hofstadter noted 12 "exhibits" (A–L) that revealed variables and varieties. They were time bound in that they were definitions, of sorts, supplied by his contemporary anti-intellectualists. But each exhibit underscored themes that, if not universal, have nevertheless persisted to the present. Hofstadter said they "collectively display the ideal assumptions of anti-intellectualism." Here is a version of Hofstadter's list, cast as 12 things anti-intellectualists oppose. They are as follows: (1) against pretentious elites (i.e., "eggheads"); (2) against witty blowhards in politics; (3) against political expertise; (4) against pure research

(in favor of applied); (5) against the educated classes (meaning also any "cultivation"); (6) against academia (especially at colleges and universities); (7) against specialists and experts; (8) against cosmopolitanism (especially as represented by foreign art); (9) against secularism and moral complexity; (10) against knowledge for its own sake; (11) against education for academic rigor; and (12) against core knowledge in education (e.g., the three Rs). The last three arose from Hofstadter's opposition to Deweyan-inspired "life adjustment" education theory that had become prominent by the 1950s (Hofstadter 1963, 9–18).

To thin this herd and translate them into present terms, one can collapse the 12 into five or so deeper currents that run in and out of anti-intellectualism: against elitism (either as an affect or exclusionary principle), against expertise, against academia (wherein pure research is conducted), against cosmopolitanism, and against secularism (or atheism). The former animus to education rigor and basics has been transformed into an opposition to professional educators (especially unionized). In addition to that series of oppositions, one should add a host of relevant variables that distort and nuance the anti-intellectual sensibility: emotions (or passions), gender, race, sexuality, and ideology (aforementioned).

Among practitioners of anti-intellectualism, some theoretical considerations are in order. Hofstadter noted that if anti-intellectualism is "articulate enough to be traced historically or widespread enough to make itself felt . . . it has to have spokesmen who are at least to some degree competent." Thus, it is an irony: some intellect is requisite among practitioners of anti-intellectualism. He added that "few intellectuals are not without moments of anti-intellectualism," and few anti-intellectuals are "without single-minded intellectual passions." Hofstadter nuances the spectrum of anti-intellectuals by positing "ambivalence" about the intellect as a universal characteristic. Anti-intellectualists are not "categorically hostile to ideas." Rather, they are "often obsessively engaged with this or that outworn or rejected idea." They are devotees to "some ideas" and "long dead" thinkers such as Adam Smith, Thomas Aquinas, John Calvin, or Karl Marx. Hofstadter went on to call these practitioners "marginal intellectuals, would-be intellectuals, [and] unfrocked or embittered intellectuals."

He noted that they fall among the ranks of ministers, politicians, businessmen, marginal writers, and so on. Finally, Hofstadter charitably notes that, among practitioners, "anti-intellectualism is usually the incidental consequence of some other . . . justifiable intention" (Hofstadter 1963, 21–22).

A noteworthy development since Hofstadter's accounting is the appearance and increased usage of the category of "pseudo-intellectual." Todd Gitlin argued that "a central force boosting anti-intellectualism" since the 1960s was the creation of "faux cerebration," especially among political pundits. And this works in the United States because punditry pays tribute to "the democratic ideal of discourse" (Gitlin 2000). As discussed earlier, however (in relation to the pseudoscience), one suspects that the designation of "pseudo-intellectual" does more emotive than actual work. Demarcation requires consensus about legitimacy, and authoritative convocations of deep thinkers rarely convene to make those kinds of designations.

Instances, Trends, and Sites of Anti-intellectualism in Presidential Politics, 1968–2008

The political turmoil of the 1960s resulted in an intense localization of politics in the 1970s. The Nixon resignation and the continuing Vietnam War caused a loss of faith in progress by government, through normal state and national political processes. In 10 short years, the United States went from enthusiasm for Great Society programs to embracing the antigovernment rhetoric of suspicion in politics. Several ironies and paradoxes resulted.

The earliest evidence of political anti-intellectualism came with the Nixon administration's intense antielitism, particularly evident in the rhetoric Nixon's vice president Spiro T. Agnew. But even before Agnew, Nixon's political career had been associated with antielitism attached to anti-Communism. Republicans, through their neoconservative thinkers, evolved into a "New Right" and created an updated "New Class" theory. This sensibility involved seeing Democrats, journalists, civil servants, and academics as a unified liberal establishment out of touch with regular working-class people, otherwise called "the silent majority." With

that, Agnew castigated "pointy-headed liberals," "limousine liberals," the "radical chic," and an "effete corps of impudent snobs that characterize themselves as intellectuals" (Jacoby 2008, 150–52; Mattson 2008, 81–82, 86–87; Schulman 2001, 200–201). Agnew brought an updated McCarthyism to New Right politics, thereby continuing the relevance of Hofstadter's analysis.

The election of Ronald Reagan became a sign, and site, of anti-intellectualism put into political practice. The success of what Susan Jacoby called "the right-wing egghead establishment" depended on "conservative strategists . . . masking their own elite class status, at least in front of the general public, and defining 'the elites' as liberals." In addition the New Right fostered the "popular identification of intellectualism with the left" even while presenting themselves as "an aggrieved minority" (Jacoby 2008, 287, 290). The public, then, barely noticed Reagan's contradictory rhetoric promising results, decreasing the size of government, and expanding deficits and federal spending. Reagan's right-wing populism was enabled by a well-constructed and deliberate anti-intellectual approach to politics.

Recently, in the 2008 election cycle, anti-intellectualism via antielitism remained a popular, if less effective, tool in presidential politics. Candidate and Senator Barack Obama embodied, in Jacoby's words, "soaring oratory and soft-spoken reasonableness"—which made him a prime target for anti-intellectualism-style opposition. Obama's Harvard Law School education left him vulnerable to antielitist attacks, no matter the merit or "earned privilege" behind his attainments. And those same attacks had been used effectively against Al Gore and John Kerry, in the 2000 and 2004 presidential campaigns, respectively. When attacks based on Obama's friendship with the former Weatherman William "Bill" Ayers failed, the opposition—John McCain and especially his running mate Sarah Palin—turned to anti-intellectualism. Palin quipped that she and her family had not obtained their wealth "by writing books" (Jacoby 2008, 285–87). But that angle also proved unsuccessful. Yet even after Obama won the White House, an association with elitism recurred through the anti-intellectual tactics of the so-called Tea Party. And Obama's connections to elite-intellectual circles continued when a Harvard historian analyzed the president's intellectual influences, even before the completion of his first term, in the 2011 book, *Reading*

Obama. That book cemented an association with thinkers (e.g., Nietzsche, Rawls, William James, John Dewey) long derided by conservatives (Kloppenberg 2011).

There can be little doubt that anti-intellectualism and popular ignorance remain objects of study and concern in politics. Elvin T. Lim's *The Anti-intellectual Presidency* analyzed the historical decline of presidential rhetoric—from the earliest days to the present occupant of the White House. Lim's concern is the ever decreasing density *and* substance in presidential discourse. These traits have been replaced by appeals to emotion, "common sense," and references to children. On a related note, Susan Jacoby has also lamented the increased use of the term "folks" in presidential politics since the 1980s as a "debasement of public speech" (Jacoby 2008, 3–5; Lim 2008). History News Network editor and George Mason University professor Rick Shenkman recently tackled the paradox of empirical evidence of voter ignorance in light of the flattery attributed to voters by politicians. His book was provocatively titled *Just How Stupid Are We? Facing the Truth about the American Voter* (Shenkman 2008).

See also Conspiracy Theory and the "Paranoid Style"; Disinformation, Deception, and Politics; Humor, Satire, and Politics; Personality and Politics; Pragmatism; Public Opinion; Talk Radio and Politics.

Tim Lacy

Bibliography

Erskine, John. 1913. "The Moral Obligation to Be Intelligent." *The Hibbert Journal* 12 (October): 174–85. http://home.uchicago.edu/~ahkissel/education/erskine.html. Accessed May 16, 2014.

Gitlin, Todd. 2000. "The Renaissance of Anti-intellectualism." *The Chronicle of Higher Education* 47, no. 15 (December 8): B7.

Gordin, Michael D. 2012. *The Pseudoscience Wars: Immanuel Velikovsky and the Birth of the Modern Fringe*. Chicago: University of Chicago Press.

Hofstadter, Richard. 1963. *Anti-intellectualism in American Life*. New York: Alfred A. Knopf.

Jacoby, Susan. 2008. *The Age of American Unreason*. New York: Pantheon Books.

Kloppenberg, James T. 2011. *Reading Obama: Dreams, Hope, and the American Political Tradition*. Princeton, NJ: Princeton University Press.

Lacy, Tim. 2013. *The Dream of a Democratic Culture: Mortimer J. Adler and the Great Books Idea*. New York: Palgrave Macmillan.

Lecklider, Aaron S. 2013. *Inventing the Egghead: The Battle over Brainpower in American Culture*. Philadelphia: University of Pennsylvania Press.

Lim, Elvin T. 2008. *The Anti-intellectual Presidency: The Decline of Presidential Rhetoric from George Washington to George W. Bush*. New York: Oxford University Press.

Mattson, Kevin. 2008. *Rebels All! A Short History of the Conservative Mind in Postwar America*. New Brunswick, NJ: Rutgers University Press.

Proctor, Robert N., and Londa Schiebinger, eds. 2008. *Agnotology: The Making and Unmaking of Ignorance*. Stanford, CA: Stanford University Press.

Robin, Corey. 2011. *The Reactionary Mind: Conservatism from Edmund Burke to Sarah Palin*. New York: Oxford University Press.

Rosenfeld, Sophia. 2011. *Common Sense: A Political History*. Cambridge, MA: Harvard University Press.

Schulman, Bruce. 2001. *The Seventies: The Great Shift in American Culture, Society, and Politics*. Cambridge, MA: Da Capo Press.

Shenkman, Rick. 2008. *Just How Stupid Are We? Facing the Truth about the American Voter*. New York: Basic Books.

United States Catholic Catechism for Adults. 2006. Washington, DC: United States Conference of Catholic Bishops.

Appointments. *See Presidential Appointments*

ARTS, HUMANITIES, AND POLITICS

According to classical liberal theory, the state pursues a number of limited goals, such as safeguarding its citizens' lives, liberties, and properties and allowing religious worship, scientific study, and other cultural pursuits to be taken up in civil society. Among these pursuits are the fine arts and humanities, which range from theater and visual arts to the study of philosophy, literature, and other disciplines focusing on humanity. While respecting the fundamental distinction between state and society, many have argued that the liberal state cannot achieve its goals without moral and intellectual support from its citizens. Concerned that civil society, left to itself, cannot provide the state with all the support that it needs, some have argued that the state must give financial support and even substantive guidance to those who pursue the sciences, arts, and humanities. Since the middle of the past century, the public has generally endorsed governmental support for the natural sciences. But disputes have arisen over governmental funding to the arts and humanities at the federal level. The present entry will focus on controversies that have arisen with federal funding of the arts and humanities, especially at the nation's colleges and universities.

The Founders on the Arts and the Humanities in Political Life

The American founders reflected deeply about the role that education in the arts and in the humanities should play in the life of the new republic. Supported by modern political philosophers such as Locke and Montesquieu, the American founders argued that political societies should manage political conflict not by regulating the arts and humanities but by establishing a system of institutional checks and balances (Madison, *Federalist Papers*, 11). In adopting this new form of republicanism, the founders did not fully reject claims made by classical republicans that citizens need a range of moral and intellectual virtues to govern themselves freely. Many expected that life in the modern republic would promote the qualities of character needed to sustain a liberal democracy. Out of the rough and tumble of political and social interaction, free citizens would develop virtues such as enterprise, self-discipline, and prudence. John Adams wrote:

> The best republics will be virtuous, and have been so; but we may hazard a conjecture that the virtues have been the effect of the well-ordered constitution rather than the cause. And, perhaps, it would be impossible to prove that a republic cannot exist even among highwaymen, by setting one rogue to watch another; and the knaves themselves may in time be made honest men by the struggle. (Adams. "Defense of the Constitution." *Works* 6: 219)

Other, less sanguine founders thought that the modern republic would need positive support from those who pursue the sciences, arts, and humanities. Some endorsed Washington's call for a national university to cultivate the qualities necessary for leadership or statesmanship in public affairs, but Congress never appropriated money for the project (Pangle and Pangle 1995). While a majority of national leaders recognized the need to establish a national military college at West Point, New York, in 1785 and to promote agriculture, science, and engineering through land grant colleges in 1862 and 1890, they did not attempt to promote the arts and the humanities through the first half of the 20th century. Instead, they left it to state and local governments to help civil society cultivate the arts and humanities. And for well over 100 years, state and local governments sought to support the arts and humanities by funding public schools and institutions of higher learning as well as by guiding, through censorship, literature, the visual arts, and the theater.

Twentieth-Century Academics and National Politics

During the Great Depression, the federal government supported writers, painters, and other artists through programs such as the Works Progress Administration, the Federal Arts Project, and the Federal Writers Project, but these programs came into being more out of a need to stimulate employment than from a newfound need for public art. During the Cold War, political leaders sought to give vigorous state support to higher education. The Soviet Union's military and scientific successes spurred Congress to fund a range of scientific projects and fields. By 1950, the federal government funded scientific study through the National Institutes of Health, the National Science Foundation, and the U.S. Atomic Energy Commission. When the Soviets moved ahead of the United States in the space race, Congress funded the Defense Advanced Research Projects Agency and the National Aeronautics and Space Administration.

Alarmed at how the focus on the sciences was eclipsing the study of the arts and humanities, in 1963 the American Council of Learned Societies, the Council of Graduate Schools in America, and the United Chapters of Phi Beta Kappa established the National Commission on the Humanities and charged it with making a report on the state of the humanities in America. Their 1964 report emphasized primarily that the expansion and improvement of "activities in the humanities" are in the national interest. The report says that federal financial support is needed not only to meet the needs of the humanities but also to correct the view that America is a nation interested only in the "material aspects of life." It argued that the heavy emphasis placed on the study of science was tending to diminish the study of the humanities and called for establishing a National Humanities Foundation to give financial support to redress the imbalance. It recommended that the agency be directed and staffed by "men who enjoy the confidence of the scholarly community" because they offered "the best assurance against the dangers of government control." Thus, the initial justification for federal support for the humanities was that disinterested support for them would broaden and strengthen American cultural life, which could then temper Americans' enthusiasm for material goods and enjoyments to the benefit of social and political life (American Council of Learned Societies 1964).

In August 1964, Congressman William Moorhead of Pennsylvania introduced a bill to implement the commission's recommendations. In March 1965, the Johnson administration proposed that Congress establish a National Foundation on the Arts and Humanities and requested $20 million in support. It also proposed that Congress create two separate agencies, one devoted to "the arts" and another to the remainder of the humanities, with each reporting to a governing body. In September 1965, Congress passed the bill sponsored by Sen. Claiborne Pell and Congressman Frank Thompson Jr. (NEH website 2014).

The original National Foundation on the Arts and the Humanities Act began by acknowledging that the "encouragement and support of national progress and scholarship in the humanities and the arts is primarily a matter for private and local initiative." But the act goes on to recognize three reasons why the arts and humanities merit public support. The first reason given is the timeless truth that a "high civilization must value and support man's scholarly and cultural activity." The second reason comes to sight in response to an urgent and developing political need. According to the act, "democracy demands wisdom and vision in its citizens" and it must therefore "foster and support a form of education designed to make men masters of their technology and not its unthinking servant." As our society's technological prowess continues to grow, we need even more civic wisdom and vision to guide its use. The third reason why federal action is needed is that America's emergence as a superpower compels it to develop an intellectual and artistic culture that is worthy of its prominent status in world affairs. According to the act, the world leadership which has come to the United States cannot rest solely upon superior power, wealth, and technology, but must be solidly founded upon worldwide respect and admiration for the Nation's high qualities as a leader in the realm of ideas and of the spirit. How would the act promote the civic wisdom and insight that we need to rule ourselves and the intellectual and spiritual excellence that we need to lead the free world? According to the act, the government can do this by establishing a "climate for free thought" and by providing the "material conditions encouraging the release of creative talent." Thus, the thinking behind the law seems to be that if artists and scholars are given the time and the resources to pursue their work, they will, on their own, bring forth a wisdom that will help us to rule ourselves and our technology and that will be fully compatible with our leadership in international affairs. The act says that it is necessary for the federal government to complement, assist, and add to programs for the advancement of the humanities and the arts. In its original language, the act says that this assistance will go to local, state, regional, and private agencies and organizations. Moreover, the assistance will be administered by two separate agencies, the National Endowment for the Humanities (NEH) and the National Endowment of the Arts (NEA).

The Endowments, 1965–1980

In 1966, Congress appropriated $2.8 million to the NEA and $5.9 million to the NEH. Throughout the 1960s and 1970s, the endowments' funding grew to

$158 million in 1981 for the NEA and $151 million for the NEH. During this era, the most significant change in programing at the NEH came when President Jimmy Carter appointed Joseph Duffy as director of the NEH. Duffy led the endowment to give support not only to "high scholarship" in the humanities but also to a wide variety of groups across the country. The NEH's 1979 report described its new Expansion Arts Program as "a point of entry for developing groups that are established in and reflect the culture of minority, blue collar, rural and low-income communities." With this new "populist" focus, the endowment funded local history and cultural fairs and promoted the collection of oral histories.

The Reagan Era

Ronald Reagan's conservative advisors believed that both endowments were failing to support excellence in the arts and humanities. A Heritage Foundation report that was said to reflect these advisors' thinking claimed: "Because the current direction of the N.E.A. is in the hands of those with few esthetic commitments and less discernment, art is increasingly seen as mere entertainment, a diversion whose importance—and the amount of money it receives—is measured by the number of people who can be found to make up its audience." The report concluded that more funding should go to individuals who pursue "serious art" and less to those who use art to provide a "social service" or to those who merely seek to "fossilize the popular culture of the past." It says that the NEA's major problem is that it needs to "redefine its mission as support of art and artists, nothing less, and nothing else" (Kramer 1980).

Regarding the NEH, the report again argued that the endowment should use "the criterion of excellence" in funding grants and added that the endowment should abandon "guidelines for racial or ethnic quotas applied to the grant review and evaluation processes." Furthermore, the report cautioned that some of the NEH's programs had been used to "serve political or politicized ends." According to *The New York Times*, conservative critics were troubled by grants such as the $200,000.00 awarded to an organization that championed the struggle of women to improve conditions in the workplace (Kramer 1980).

The New York Times also reported that Reagan's cultural advisors were divided, some advocating cutting the endowments' funding, while others cited classical liberal doctrines and called for their elimination. In the end, the federal budget cut NEA funding from $158.8 million in 1981 to $143.5 million in 1982, and the NEH budget dropped from $151.3 million to nearly $130 million, a cut of 14 percent. While the NEA was able to reverse this trend and to recover what had been cut from its budget by 1984, the NEH continued to operate with less funding for the rest of the decade.

The Endowments in the 1980s and 1990s

Soon after Reagan appointed William J. Bennett as chairman of the NEH in 1981, Bennett announced his intention to reform the endowment. He argued that the endowment should support quality, nonpolitical work and that federal funds should never be used to support tendentious partisans. According to Bennett, beginning in the 1960s, America's intellectual elite had come to feel contempt for the values of the middle class. Rejecting America's traditional culture and morality, many academicians sought to discredit the truths that most Americans had been passing down from one generation to the next. But Bennett argued that neither those who framed the National Foundation on the Arts and Humanities Act nor the taxpayers who fund its programs ever intended it to promote "left-wing" or "anti-American" propaganda. Consequently, Bennett charged the endowment with funding projects that were both nonpartisan and consistent with the country's traditional political culture (Bennett 1992).

Bennett's successor at the NEH was Lynne Cheney, who seconded her predecessor's alarm at how many leading thinkers at the nation's institutions of higher learning had become stridently anti-American. She subsequently used the endowment to promote the study and appreciation of America's political and cultural tradition. Reports circulated that she personally rejected applications that seemed too partisan. Publicly, Cheney joined Bennett in decrying how the nation's colleges were no longer requiring their students to teach the great books of Western culture. Following Bennett's lead, she advocated the study of great books that help us think through permanent questions and enduring concerns. Among Cheney's more controversial moves concerned her efforts to elaborate national standards for the teaching of history in secondary schools. She approved a $500 million grant to scholars at UCLA to develop a set of National History Standards, but she later objected to its recommendations on the grounds that they emphasized the plights of the marginalized while significantly understating or ignoring the roles that figures such as Washington, Lee, Grant, Edison, and Einstein played in American history. After drawing attention to the issue, she campaigned successfully against their adoption by the U.S. Congress.

Critics on the left objected that Bennett, Cheney, and other conservatives were using the NEH to promote a political agenda of their own. Some blamed Bennett in particular for disrupting and abandoning the consensus about the proper use of the endowments

that had prevailed since the mid-1960s. But this objection overlooked how any consensus about culture and the fine arts that might have existed in the early and mid-1960s had given way to a serious intellectual dispute about the nation's political institutions and culture. Influenced by wide range of movements, including Marxism, critical theory, historicism, postmodernism, deconstructionism, multiculturalism, and environmentalism, many in the academy raised serious questions about the legitimacy of middle-class values and traditional institutions. Acknowledging how America's intellectual elites often challenged the country's moral and political culture, some argued that conservatives who assert that the endowments should fund only nonpartisan or nonpolitical projects fail to grasp that such an approach is impossible. They said that what Bennett and Cheney regard as the timeless truths contained in the great books are, in fact, beliefs that presuppose and support particular social structures, such as America's

A Robert Mapplethorpe exhibit. The artist's work was among those that spurred opposition to federal funding of the arts in the 1980s. (AP Photo/Julia Malakie)

traditional political, economic, and religious institutions. Because truth is historically situated, there is no canon of great works to be studied throughout time. Consequently, claims made by Bennett, Cheney, and other conservative critics that the endowments should support only nonpartisan or nonpolitical scholarship are both misleading and in themselves inherently partisan and political (Johnston 1992).

In May 1989, members of the U.S. Senate objected to the NEA making grants to the Southern Center for Contemporary Art, which sponsored the work of Andres Serrano. Twenty-one senators argued that Serrano's photograph of a crucifix submerged in a container of urine was "shocking, abhorrent and completely undeserving of any recognition whatsoever" (Vance 1998). Several weeks later, numerous Congressmen objected to NEA funding supporting an exhibit containing homoerotic photographs taken by Robert Mapplethorpe. In the subsequent federal budget, NEA appropriations were cut by the amount that had been granted for the Serrano and Mapplethorpe. With the Serrano and Mapplethorpe cases, the controversy over NEA funding spread from the nation's political elites to the public at large. When Republicans won control of the House of Representatives in 1994, Speaker Newt Gingrich successfully pushed to cut the budgets of both endowments by 40 percent (NEA: $162.3 to $99.4; NEH: $172 to $110.7). Along with conservatives' complaints about the teaching of the humanities in America, the obscenity controversies involving the NEA ushered in the contentious debates about the relationship between politics and culture that became known as the "culture wars" of the 1880s and 1990s.

Reforming the Act

The original supporters of the 1965 Act thought that if the arts and humanities were sufficiently funded and left to themselves, they would generate the civic wisdom needed to manage the nation's expanding powers both at home and abroad. The original act does not describe the character of that wisdom, except that it is to be democratic and that it is to be compatible with the nation's status as a superpower. What they failed to anticipate is that the post–World War II consensus on domestic policy and foreign affairs would break down as quickly and as radically as it did.

By 1990, Congress revised the original language of the act so that it would reflect competing concerns about how the endowments should support the arts and humanities (Public law 1990 [P.L. 101–512]). Legislators stipulated that funds should not support projects that concern any form of pending legislation. Acknowledging the importance of inclusiveness, legislators inserted a clause saying that the arts and humanities ought to reflect both "the nation's rich cultural heritage" and "the diverse beliefs and values of all persons and groups." An additional clause underscored the importance of the democracy's "multicultural artistic heritage" and of "new ideas." At the same time, legislators addressed two concerns that troubled conservative critics. In response to those who objected to using the taxpayers' money to fund avant garde or radical projects, the act observes that "the Government must be sensitive to the nature of public sponsorship." Recognizing the need for public support for the use of taxpayer funds, the act stipulates that public funds must "ultimately serve public purposes the Congress defines." Specifically, the act enjoins the chairperson of the NEA to ensure that "artistic excellence and artistic merit are the criteria by which applications are judged, taking into consideration general standards of decency and respect for the diverse beliefs and values of the American public."

In addition, legislators recognized that the endowments are responsible for helping artists and scholars to make the public aware of the great works of American culture and of civilization itself. The amendment acknowledged that the federal government cannot fulfill its educational mission, maintain a society that is orderly and free, and prove the American people with "models of excellence" unless it transmits "the achievement and values of civilization from the past via the present to the future." Presumably, the achievements and values of "civilization" would include those associated with either Western or non-Western civilizations.

With these amendments, Congress sought to address concerns from across the political spectrum. The law now openly endorsed using federal funds to promote work both on non-Western cultures and on the multiplicity of cultures that operate within America itself. Yet the law also cautioned that the endowments must exercise discretion in funding projects: public money must be used to serve public ends, which, it says, do not include the production and distribution of obscenity but do include promoting continuity and order in a free society.

Following the passage of this amendment, the NEA overturned its own peer review process and denied grants to performance artists Karen Finley, Holly Hughes, John Fleck, and Tim Miller because their work seemed likely to fall outside general standards of public decency. When these artists sued, in 1998 the Supreme Court upheld the amendment's "obscenity clause" as constitutional. As a result of the controversy, the NEA subsequently ceased making grants to individual artists and focused instead on supporting institutions.

Changes since 2000

In 2001, Bruce Cole became chair of the NEH and introduced a program called *We the People* that would foster greater understanding of America's founding principles, especially among the young. In the wake of 9/11, the program's goals met with widespread approval, evidenced by the extension of its initially proposed 3-year term to 10 years. While *We the People* was not the NEH's first agency-wide initiative, it marked a new era of centralized guidance and funding strategies. The NEH used supervisory review of peer review panels to ensure that funding decisions were consistent with public goals. Under Jim Leach, the NEH's director under Barack Obama, a program called *Building Bridges* aimed to promote understanding of diverse cultures both here and abroad, with a programmatic focus on the dual themes of civility in democratic society and the Muslim world.

Following these strategies, the endowments sparked relatively few controversies in the first decade of the 21st century. *From 2000 to 2010*, both endowments saw rising annual appropriations, but the Great Recession that began in 2009 led to cuts each year from 2011 to 2013. In both endowments, 2014 funding remains 13 percent lower than 2010 levels. And, while leaders in both parties tend to recognize that the endowments play an important role in supporting the arts and humanities

in the United States, in 2013 the Republican-led House Appropriations Committee proposed at 49 percent cut to the NEH.

Neither classical republicans nor classical liberals would be surprised that disputes have erupted over federal funding for the arts and the humanities. Both recognize that the arts and humanities often reflect and shape political beliefs and for this reason can become the focus of intense political scrutiny and debate. To temper disputes over the endowments, their leaders have worked to make the grant process even-handed and avoid awarding grants that seem needlessly provocative. Remarkably, what is most at issue today is not the content of the grants but the level at which the federal government can afford to make them.

See also Anti-intellectualism in American Life; Conservatives and Conservatism; Film and American Political Culture; Liberals and Liberalism; Literature and Politics; Monuments, Memorials, and Public History; Pragmatism; Science, Technology, and Society.

Mark J. Lutz and Kelly G. Lutz

Bibliography

American Council of Learned Societies. 1964. *Report of the Commission on the Humanities*. New York: American Council of Learned Societies.

Bauerlein, Mark, and Ellen Grantham. 2009. *National Endowment for the Arts: A History, 1965–2008*. Washington, DC: National Endowment for the Arts.

Bennett, William J. 1992. *The De-valuing of America*. New York: Touchstone Books.

Frohnmayer, John. 1993. *Leaving Town Alive: Confessions of an Art Warrior*. Boston, MA: Houghton Mifflin.

Glenn, David. 2009. "Humanities Endowment Should Get Back to Basics, Scholars Say." *Chronicle of Higher Education* 55, no. 23: A8–A10.

Jensen, Richard. 1995. "The Culture Wars, 1965–1995: A Historian's Map." *Journal of Social History* 17: 37.

Johnston, Kenneth R. 1992. "The NEH and the Battle of the Books." *Raritan* 12, no. 2: 118–32.

Koch, Cynthia. 1998. "The Contest for American Culture: A Leadership Case Study on the NEA and

NEH Funding Crisis." *Public Talk: Online Journal of Discourse Leadership*. Philadelphia: Penn National Commission. www.upenn.edu/pnc/ptkoch .html. Accessed April 4, 2014.

Kramer, Hilton. 1980. "Reagan Aides Discuss US Role in Helping Arts and Humanities." *New York Times*, November 26, p. 1.

National Endowment for the Arts. arts.gov

National Endowment for the Humanities. www.neh.gov

National Endowment for the Humanities. 2009. "Renaissance Scholar at Work." *Humanities* [Online], 30, no. 2.

Pangle, Thomas L., and S. Lorraine. 1995. *The Learning of Liberty*. Lawrence: University of Kansas Press.

Vance, Carole S. 1998. "The War on Culture." In Richard Bolton, ed. *Culture Wars: Documents from Recent Controversies in the Arts*. New York: New Press.

ASIAN AMERICANS AND POLITICS

The relationship between Asian Americans and politics is a complex and dynamic one. Depending on how politics is defined, as well as when and where it is practiced and by whom, Asian Americans may be considered as either politically hyperactive or apathetic. They may be characterized as politically conservative in one time period but progressive in another, while being condemned as radical in-between. Throughout history, some ethnic groups invested heavily in promoting workers' rights and equal rights in the United States, while others showed a greater interest in involvement in homeland independence and modernization projects occurring in Asia. This chameleon-like nature of the relationship has made the term "Asian American politics" difficult to define and comprehend in a simple and straightforward manner, while it simultaneously explains the community's vulnerability to suspicion, misunderstanding, and racial stereotyping by the American mainstream regarding Asian Americans' political identities and motivations. Paradoxically called, in different times and places, the "model minority," "perpetual foreigners," and the "yellow peril," Asian Americans have been relegated to a racial third space whose relationship to the U.S. political order cannot be captured by the two best known social scientific models, those applied to white immigrant assimilation and to black subordination. To help unpack the complicated, multifaceted, and shifting phenomenon, this entry provides a quick review of community formation and political activism over time, followed by a discussion of patterns of political attitudes and behavior in the post-1965 era, including results from recent surveys.

Defining the Asian American Population

The term "Asian Americans" refers to any individual of Asian descent who resides in the United States on a permanent or long-term basis, regardless of citizenship or other legal status. The definition of who is an Asian has undergone significant changes over the past 165 years of group history and reflects the convergence of influences that include U.S. immigration and naturalization policies, U.S. race relations, political turmoil and U.S. military engagements in Asia, and global labor market conditions and other forces in global economic restructuring. Factors within the community such as class, gender, culture, and generational cleavages, as well as grassroots activism and group consciousness, also play a part in structuring group identity.

The 2010 Census shows that over 17 million or close to 6 percent of Americans can claim to be of Asian descent, either alone or in combination with other races. There are 23 distinct ethnic groups identified by the U.S. Census, but the six largest Asian ethnic groups are Chinese, Filipinos, Japanese, Asian Indians, Vietnamese, and Koreans. Only the first three groups had a significant presence prior to 1965, owing to racist anti-Asian immigration quotas and other discriminatory policies. Today, compared to other major racial and ethnic groups, the Asian American population is distinguished by the rapid growth and predominance of the foreign-born. Primarily due to new and continuous migration from Asia, its 46 percent growth rate between 2000 and 2010 is the highest of all racial groups. The 68 percent foreign-born rate is more than five times the national average. One other notable trend is the continuous concentration of the population in the western region of the United States (particularly on the West Coast), with the South, however, being the region of highest growth.

Major Political Periods and Types of Political Activism

In 1882, Congress passed the Chinese Exclusion Act and inaugurated the ubiquitous era of Asian exclusion. Fear of the "Yellow Peril," perceived economic competition, and racial prejudice were main reasons behind the draconian legislation. During this era, groups of immigrant Asians who were banned from U.S. citizenship and the vote managed to flex their political muscles by forming umbrella community organizations and challenged almost every unjust law and policy through the American court system. They also lobbied elected officials, rallied against ethnic violence, staged strikes for workers' rights, and raised funds for homeland liberation and moderation projects. For Japanese Americans interned during World War II for their suspected "enemy within" status, most followed Nisei (first U.S.-born generation) leaders and practiced a politics of accommodation, even if there were heroic acts of resistance as well. In particular, the wartime convictions of three Japanese Americans for violating the internment order provided grounds for a key legal breakthrough in the early 1980s and helped propel the eventual triumph of the Japanese American redress movement, whereby the government acknowledged its flawed policies of the past.

Because of prolonged immigration exclusion, Asian Americans were less than 1 percent of the U.S. population in the 1960 Census and the majority were U.S.-born. These U.S.-born college students, social activists, and community youth formed the first stage of the Asian American Movement. Inspired by the black liberation movement, these Asian Americans protested against the Vietnam War, participated in the San Francisco State hunger strike that led to the nation's first ethnic studies program, and demanded fundamental social change to "serve the people." The awakened racial consciousness to the possibility of "yellow power" led to the coinage of the term "Asian American" in the late 1960s; as a pan-ethnic identity label, one of its primary purposes was to bond together the multiethnic community. Although the end of the Vietnam War, the onset of economic recession, and the advance of corporate interests seem to have beheaded the radical movement in recent years, some scholars insist that it has lived on and been reincarnated in numerous community-based organizations and campaigns for justice, equality, and empowerment, albeit under more subdued, sophisticated, and professional operations.

Meanwhile, with the advent of minority voting rights and the influx of well-educated and skilled immigrants from Asia made possible by the passage of

A Woman of Many Firsts

When Senator Mazie Keiko Hirono (D-Hawaii) was sworn in office in 2013, she established many firsts in U.S. history. She is the first Asian American woman in the U.S. Senate, the first female Senator from Hawaii, the first Buddhist in Congress, and the first Japan-born person in the Senate. Hirono also joined a record-high number of six other Asian American women to form the first female majority of any racial group in Congress. Armed with a law degree and experience in the state's attorney general's office, her first elective office was with the Hawaii House of Representatives in 1980, followed by two terms of service as Lieutenant Governor. Before becoming a U.S. Senator, Hirono served in the U.S. House of Representatives (representing Hawaii's second district). Hirono has had a solidly liberal voting record as a legislator, something that she attributed to her early-life hardships as a child immigrant who went to work at age 10 to support a mother who fled to the United States from an abusive husband.

landmark legislation in 1965, Asian Americans on the mainland began to emerge as voters, candidates, campaign donors and volunteers, and elected officials in the 1970s and onward. In Hawaii, the rise of Asian Americans in electoral politics began about two decades earlier, thanks in part to a large and stable ethnic population base and the World War II heroism of Japanese American servicemen. Today, Hawaii Asians continue to dominate state politics, and Asian American congressional delegates from the Aloha state have been a constant staple in Capitol Hill. Nationally, between 1978 and 2008, the number of key Asian American elected officials expanded from 120 to 410. The growth rate is particularly sharp at the local level, where nearly 7 in 10 Asian elective officials are found. The number of Asian American–elected officials in municipal governments and on local school boards surged from 52 to 298 during this same 30-year period.

Present-Day Participation in Voting and Other Political Activities

Research on American political behavior generally emphasizes the role of basic socioeconomic status such as education and income, other political resources such as time and civic skills, political interest and engagement, and political mobilization and contacts in determining the extent of voting and other acts of political participation. Although these factors have been found to influence Asian American voting behavior, for the majority of members of the community who were not U.S.-born, their voting and other participation are additionally impacted by international migration-related factors such as country of birth, age of migration, length of U.S. residency, English proficiency, and maintenance of contacts with the home country.

Because presently as many as three-fourths of voting-age Asian Americans were born outside of the

Election official Henry Tung helps a voter drop her vote into the ballot box at a polling station at St. Paul's Lutheran Church in Monterey Park, Los Angeles County, on November 6, 2012. (Frederic J. Brown/AFP/Getty Images)

United States, their ability to participate fully in the U.S. electoral process needs to be understood as a three-step process. To physically cast a ballot in an election, a foreign-born person who resides permanently in the United States must engage in the process of becoming naturalized first, followed by becoming registered to vote, and by casting a ballot either in person on or via postal service before Election Day. A set of barriers or costs is involved at each step of the process. For those immigrants who have survived the naturalization process, their franchise can be wasted by their failure to become registered to vote, which is a procedure foreign to many Asian immigrants. Registering to vote and casting a vote, either in person or by mail, may be particularly onerous in a referendum-heavy state such as California, where an estimated 40 percent of the Asian American population lives. When one adds to the equation such unique factors as language barriers, lack of familiarity with the American system, social discrimination, and economic hardship for working-class immigrants, it becomes hardly surprising that Asian Americans have one of the lowest citizenship, voting registration, and turnout rates among voting-age persons.

In the November 2012 elections, for example, 68 percent of Asians as compared to 93 percent of (non-Latino) whites and 94 percent of blacks among voting-age persons were U.S. citizens by birth or by naturalization. As high as 58 percent among Asians, but only 6 percent among whites and 7 percent among blacks, acquired U.S. citizenship through naturalization. Among voting-age persons, only 39 percent of Asians as compared to 67 percent of whites were registered to vote. This registration gap between the two racial groups narrows to 15 percentage points when counting only holders of citizenship. Whereas only one-third among voting-age Asians reported voting in the elections, as compared to 58 percent among voting-age whites and 62 percent among voting-age blacks, as high as 84 percent of Asians who were registered to vote turned out to vote—a rate only 3 percentage points below the national average. By taking into consideration layers of legal barriers to voting, Asian Americans are found to turn out at the polls at nearly as high a rate as most other American voters.

In addition to voting, Asian Americans are involved in a variety of political and civic activities that do not require U.S. citizenship but may require more time, skills, knowledge, and interest. As a result, in a post-2000 election survey, relatively few Asian Americans are found to participate in activities such as working with others in the community to solve a problem (21 percent); signing a petition for a political cause (16 percent); attending a public meeting, political rally, or fundraiser (14 percent); donating to a campaign (12 percent); or writing or phoning a government official (11 percent). Still fewer report taking part in a protest or demonstration (7 percent); contacting an editor of a newspaper, magazine, or television station (7 percent); serving on a governmental board or commission (2 percent); or working on a political campaign or other electoral activities (2 percent). Similar findings are reported in surveys conducted for the 2008 and 2012 election cycles, and ethnic communities differ in their most frequent mode of participation beyond voting. For example, about one-fourth of Asian Indian and Filipino Americans report having volunteered to work on community problems or made contacts with government officials or the media. A higher percentage of Japanese Americans than other Asian Americans report making donations to political campaigns, but that number is no higher than 20 percent. A higher percentage of Vietnamese Americans report having participated in protest rallies, even if that number is no higher than 10 percent.

Participation in Home Country Politics

Being majority foreign-born and nonwhite and originating from a world region that has a contentious history with the United States, Asian Americans have received the most amount of scrutiny in the popular media and mainstream politics regarding their loyalty and citizenship as well as their ability to become socially, culturally, and politically "assimilated." Recent surveys on Asian Americans consistently find that just over half report having paid very close or fairly close attention to news events happening in Asia. But respondents are just as likely to follow news events about Asian Americans as they are to keep up with news about events in Asia. Most respondents are also found to maintain strong social ties with people in their countries of origin and about one-third have sent money back to Asia.

Again, ethnic groups differ in levels of homeland contacts. In 2012, over 8 in 10 Asian Indian and Korean Americans report having maintained frequent contacts with friends or family in home country, but only 35 percent of Hmong Americans do. More than 3 in 5 Chinese Americans and 55 percent Vietnamese Americans, but fewer than 3 in 10 Asian Indian and Cambodian Americans, are found to closely follow news of home country politics and U.S. foreign policy regarding the home country. Just over half of Filipino, Vietnamese, and Cambodian Americans report having sent money to the home country, but only one-fifth of Japanese Americans indicate having done so. In 2008, that number among Japanese Americans is 12 percent. Finally, when immigrants were asked if they had ever participated in any activity dealing with the politics of their home countries after arriving in the United States, a lofty 94 percent answered "no" to the question in 2000 and 96 percent in 2008.

Does involvement in homeland society and politics take away interest in participating in U.S. elections? Past research has found that incidences of participation in homeland politics after an immigrant's arrival in the United States do not have a significant relationship to his or her acquisition of U.S. citizenship or voting. An immigrant's political activism prior to emigration also does not have a significant relationship to his or her rate of naturalization, voting, or participation beyond voting. Nonetheless, an immigrant's participation in homeland politics after arriving in the United States has a positive and significant relationship to his or her incidence of participation in politics beyond voting as well as to his or her participation in ethnic community organizations or related activities in the United States. This last set of relationships does not change after controlling for an assortment of possible confounding factors related to transnational political participation, such as transnational social, cultural, and political ties, degree of social and political incorporation, and personal skills and resources related to international migration. Thus, everything else being equal, an immigrant's engagement in homeland politics is associated with a greater, not lower, likelihood to participate in non-electoral activities in the United States, while it has no significant impact on voter registration and voting. These results clearly show not only that an immigrant's connections with his or her country of origin do not take place at the expense of his or her voting participation in the United States but that there may even be a complementary relationship to political activities beyond voting.

Political Preferences: Presidential Candidate Choice, Partisanship, and Political Ideology

Being stereotyped as the inscrutable and alien race, Asian Americans' political preferences have been the subject of much (wrongful) speculation until recent years, after the emergence of large-scale, scientifically designed, national opinion surveys centering on the Asian population. From these and other survey data that include a significant number of Asians in the pool of respondents, we now have a clearer picture of the candidate choice, political party affiliation, and political ideology of this rising community in American politics.

Presidential Vote

Most of the research on Asian Americans' candidate choices concerns this population's vote for U.S. president. In the National Asian American Survey (NAAS), a major preelection survey conducted between August and September, 2008, 41 percent of Asian Americans indicated their likelihood to favor Barack Obama, 24 percent for John McCain, while the rest were undecided. The same study finds that the majority of Asian Americans who voted in the 2008 primary elections supported candidate Hillary Clinton over candidate Barack Obama by a nearly 2 to 1 margin. In the 2008 general elections, national exit polls sponsored by the mainstream media found Asian American voters to have supported Obama over McCain by a roughly 2 to 1 margin. In the 2012 general elections, President Obama increased his vote share among Asian Americans by receiving 73 percent of their vote, which is 20 percentage points above the national average vote for Obama.

This pattern of a clear edge for Democratic Party candidates among Asian American voters nationwide is first reported in the Pilot National Asian American Political Survey, which is the nation's first multiethnic, multilingual, and multisite survey of the political attitudes and behaviors of Asian Americans. Among Asian American voters in the November 2000 election, for example, 55 percent report casting a vote for Democratic candidate Al Gore, and 26 percent for Republican candidate George Bush. Across Asian American groups, the percentage of voters favoring candidate Gore ranges from as high as 64 percent among Chinese Americans to as low as 44 percent among Korean Americans. In 2008, at least 8 in 10 Asian Indian, Cambodian, and Hmong American voters cast their vote for Democratic candidate Barack Obama, while close to half of Filipino and Vietnamese American voters cast their vote for Republican candidate John McCain. Nonetheless, the Democratic candidate received a higher proportion of the vote than the Republican opponent from each of the Asian groups in both 2000 and 2008. Similar ethnic patterns are found among likely voters in the 2012 elections.

Political Party Affiliation

Political party identification is traditionally the most reliable and important measure of political behavior. Extensive research done with American voters as a whole has found party identification to be a strong predictor of their candidate choice, political ideology, and issue position. Targeted research on Asian Americans affirms the utility of the party concept in studying their voting behavior—that is, Republican/Democratic identifiers would be more supportive of Republican/Democratic candidates and the respective party platform; voters with a stronger sense of partisanship are more likely to turn out and vote than those with a weaker sense of partisanship. However, these observations are made only among those Asians who identify with mainstream American parties. The challenge in understanding the political behavior of voting-age Asian Americans is that about half of them do not identify with either of the major American parties.

In the 2008 NAAS, 32 percent of all Asian Americans identified themselves as Democrat, 14 percent as Republican, 19 percent as Independent, and 35 percent as nonpartisan. Compared to other Asian ethnic groups, Vietnamese Americans have the highest share of Republican identifiers at 29 percent, while both Asian Indian Americans and Korean Americans report the highest share of Democratic identifiers at 39 percent and 39 percent, respectively. Results from the 2012 round of the NAAS show virtually the same partisan pattern for Asians as a whole. However, Filipino Americans report the highest share of Republican identifiers (27 percent) than the Vietnamese (20 percent). In contrast, close to or over half of Korean, Asian Indian, Hmong, and Samoan Americans report identification with the Democratic Party.

Political Ideology

Whereas about half of Asian American adults do not identify with the two major parties, they have little problem identifying themselves using mainstream ideological labels. In 2012, as in previous endeavors to gauge ethnic public opinion, Asian Americans were found to lean left and more liberal than conservative in political orientation. In a daily tracking poll conducted by Gallup for the entire year of 2009, Asian Americans were found to be the only major racial and ethnic group to have a higher proportion of liberals than conservatives (31 percent vs. 21 percent). However, a higher proportion of Asians than in any other racial group also call themselves politically moderate. These statistics seem to explain simultaneously their Democratic-leaning partisanship, their collective lack of identity with the major parties, and their support for a more activist government in providing social services to immigrants and language minorities and the general goal of affirmative action in helping eradicate social inequality.

Conclusion

Asian Americans have grown rapidly in visibility and influence in the post-1965 era, but their rise in U.S. mainland electoral politics has been a wobbly one vulnerable to the whims of racial politics. Two prominent cases in recent memory are the campaign finance investigations associated with President Bill Clinton's 1996 reelection effort (which purportedly involved Chinese funds going to the Democratic National Committee) and the unlawful detention in 1999 of a Taiwan-born American scientist, Dr. Wen Ho Lee, for allegedly spying for China. The political participation of Asian Americans has also been handicapped by structural disadvantages associated with the large presence of noncitizens and the continuous replenishment of new arrivals and to-be Americans as well as the collectively small and extremely diverse population. As a result, despite evidence to the contrary, both their political loyalty and their bloc-vote potential have been cast in constant doubt. And, like other U.S. minorities, they continue to endure severe underrepresentation at all levels of government. The good news from recent research is that Asian American candidates may win without a strong ethnic base, but they are more likely to win if they campaign in small- and medium-sized cities (such as Cupertino, California, and Sugar Land, Texas) that are majority or plurality Asian, have friendly election systems, and feature strong community organizations and ethnic media.

See also American Dream; Citizenship and Politics; Grassroots Activism; Immigration and Politics; Race, Ethnicity, and Politics; Regions and Regionalism: The West.

Pei-te Lien

Bibliography

Aoki, Andrew, and Don T. Nakanishi, eds. 2001. Symposium on "Asian Pacific Americans and the New Minority Politics." *PS: Political Science and Politics* 34, no. 3: 605–44.

Aoki, Andrew, and Okiyoshi Takeda. 2008. *Asian American Politics*. Malden, MA: Polity Press.

Chang, Gordon, ed. 2001. *Asian Americans and Politics: Experiences, Perspectives, and Prospects*. Stanford, CA: Stanford University Press.

Collet, Chris, and Pei-te Lien, eds. 2009. *The Transnational Politics of Asian American*. Philadelphia: Temple University Press.

Kim, Claire. 2000. *Bitter Fruit: The Politics of Black-Korean Conflict in New York City*. New Haven, CT: Yale University Press.

Kim, Thomas. 2007. *The Racial Logic of Politics: Asian Americans and Party Competition*. Philadelphia: Temple University Press.

Lai, James. 2011. *Asian American Political Actions: Suburban Transformations*. Boulder, CO: Lynn Rienner Publishers.

Lien, Pei-te. 2001. *The Making of Asian America through Political Participation*. Philadelphia: Temple University Press.

Lien, Pei-te, M. Margaret Conway, and Janelle Wong. 2004. *The Politics of Asian Americans*. New York: Routledge.

Liu, Michael, Kim Geron, and Tracy Lai. 2008. *The Snake Dance of Asian American Activism: Community, Vision, and Power*. Lanham, MD: Lexington Books.

Nakanishi, Don T., and James Lai, eds. 2002. *Asian American Politics: Law, Participation, and Policy*. Lanham, MD: Rowman and Littlefield.

Wong, Janelle. 2006. *Democracy's Promise: Immigrants and American Civic Institutions*. Ann Arbor: The University of Michigan Press.

Wong, Janelle, et al. 2011. *Asian American Political Participation: Emerging Constituents and Their Political Identities*. New York: Russell Sage Foundation.

Wu, Frank. 2002. *Yellow: Race in America beyond Black and White*. New York: Basic Books.

B

BABY BOOM GENERATION AND POLITICS

It is telling that the focus of research on children and their institutions turned from early childhood in the first decades of the 20th century to adolescents and young adults by the onset of World War II. The escalation of births after World War II, called the baby boom, witnessed the emergence of what was termed a "generation gap" between parents born after World War I and their offspring. And the years between the late 1950s and the late 1970s represented the heyday of the radical political youth movement and cultural revolution in the United States. The 1960s and 1970s were a critical evolutionary period, which was at once unique and of lasting consequence for the history of 20th-century youth and society at large. The long-term outcome of the youth rebellion was primarily social rather than political and can be viewed as constituting a new system of morals and values that diffused throughout American culture (to one degree or another) by the mid-1970s.

The Demographics of Youth after World War II

In 1960, the median age of population was between 35 and 40 years, which was older than ever before in the history of the United States. This reflected in part the post–World War II escalation of the birth rate as well as the contributions of medical research and preventive public health education in reducing child mortality and health-threatening diseases of the young and old. Births doubled between 1948 and 1953, swelling the number of individuals in the younger age groups and reducing the most common age to 17 by 1964. While the birth rate crested in 1953, it continued to grow until 1970. The cohort of teenagers between 13 and 19 years expanded along with a distinctive age-related culture. The impact of a growing youth population along with a distinctive culture separate from adults was heightened by the fact that school expansion had succeeded in increasing access to high schools in all regions in the nation. Of significant importance for the formation of a teen culture was the growth of the high school population during the Great Depression when jobs were scarce for adults, much less adolescents. Consequently, working-class youth who would have sought work instead stayed in school. The presence of unemployed working-class high school youth in cities created concerns over gangs and delinquency in the 1950s. In this same period, the prosperity of suburban areas, new shopping centers, and modern high schools also favored the new phenomena of affluent middle-class teenagers.

Postsecondary education also expanded significantly in this period first with GI's and then with increasing numbers of high school graduates who sought education beyond high school in universities and colleges. Supported by parents, they remained independent of adult responsibilities in their 20s or later by entering graduate school to avoid being drafted into the war in Southeast Asia. At the same time, the presence of working-class kids eligible for GI benefits (having completed high school and served in the military) raised alarms that followed from a long-term concern with the potential for maladjustment in the young and its potential for social disruption (Richardson 2006).

Never before had a cohort of young people in their teens and 20s differed so radically from their parents, who were born after World War I. They experienced the instability of the economy as the Roaring 20s ended in the Stock Market Crash and the Great Depression followed, which was resolved only by the onset of World War II with its unprecedented nuclear weaponry. Life uncertainty and tragedy was countered by unexpected opportunity and prosperity after the war, allowing upward mobility and the opportunity to become part of a growing middle and upper middle class. Their children were born into a world of relative affluence not experienced previously by them. In spite of, or maybe because of, the demographics of school expansion and prosperity, the 1950s were also known as an era of "conformity, flight from conflict, political quietism, the cult of the nuclear family, and embrace of class privilege," satirized in fiction by Sloan Wilson (1955) in his novel: *The Man in the Gray Flannel Suit*. New behaviors such as dating, teenage love, joy riding or drag racing in cars, street gangs, and competition emerged. Music, dance, movies, and television encouraged the view that teens were special producers as well as consumers of targeted products. The 1950s saw this group idealized as special vanguards of the future and condemned as delinquent sources of antiauthority criminality. Some argued that delinquency was, on one hand, proof of the inability of working- and lower-class parents to control their offspring while the heirs of affluence were condemned as spoiled brat products of Dr. Spock's parent education with its supposedly overindulgent practices, which Spock strongly denied (Cover Feature 1971; Spock 1971).

The complacency of the 1950s was undercut by the presence of real dangers that escalated the positive and negative aspects of modern technology and the desperate feeling of a crossroad in human existence. This included the Korean War, Cold War escalation with the USSR military and space race buildup, the "bomb" threat of nuclear annihilation, and Communist witch hunts on the part of Sen. Eugene McCarthy's Un-American Activities' probes and hearings designed to intimidate and destroy open debate and protest. It can be argued that the discrepancy between children of affluence and children sorted to poverty and lack of opportunity was the source of the idealism of the rebellious middle-class university cohort of the 1960s. Born of relative affluence they entered college to find that the American Dream they had experienced had vast and perhaps deadly shortcomings. The escalating war in Southeast Asia, lack of civil rights at home, urban decay, racism, sexism, and environmental destruction were a call to action for many. The "Port Huron Statement" released by the Students for a Democratic Society (SDS), formed in 1960, was written at their first national convention held in Port Huron, Michigan, June 11–15, 1962. It began with the words: "We are a people of this generation, bred in at least modest comfort, housed now in universities, looking uncomfortably to the world we inherit" (Miller 1987; SDS 1962).

Lieutenant Anthony Biddle Duke poses with his wife on a sidewalk in Palm Beach, Florida, during World War II. When the conflict ended, thousands of young couples like the Dukes moved to the suburbs and started families. (Bert Morgan/Premium Archive/Getty Images)

The Counterculture and Radical Politics

Under normal circumstances adults in their 20s and early 30s tended to be fairly conventional societal members given their everyday concerns with concrete and immediate problems of life, including getting married, having children and raising them, advancing careers, running a household, paying bills, attending to medical care, and insurance. Unmarried college-age and older students lacked these tethers to conventional concerns and often had acquired a disdain for the social, political, and economic materialism that in fact had buoyed their journey through the 1950s.

Raised with conventional American optimism, young-adult college students often found reality wanting in terms of the lives and treatment of those not so well birthed as themselves. The burgeoning civil rights movement exploded with the Supreme Court's *Brown v. Board of Education* decision of 1954. Southern resistance to desegregation brought student action in the form of the Freedom Riders of the early 1960s (Arsenault 2006; McAdam 1988). On May 21, 1961, 13 volunteers organized by the Student Non-violent Coordinating Committee got on a bus in Washington, D.C., headed for Mississippi to register black voters. These were the first "Freedom Riders." There were radicalizing events to follow. By June 1964, the so-called Freedom Summer, 1,000 young volunteers headed to Mississippi to continue their campaign to promote voter registration in poor black communities. Ten days after arriving, three volunteers, James Chaney, Andrew Goodman, and Michael Schwerner, were kidnapped, beaten, and killed by segregationists led by Mississippi law officers. By August 4 people were dead, 80 had been beaten, 1,000 people were arrested, and 67 businesses or homes had been bombed or burned (McAdam 1988).

Freedom Riders returned to their college campuses to join with other civil rights activists to inform others, engage in debates, and collect money to continue the work. Jack Weinberg of Congress of Racial Equality, originally established in 1942, set up tables at the University of California Berkeley in Sproul Plaza between the administration building and Student Union. The administration ruled that political activities were illegal, and the tables were moved to a site between Telegraph Avenue and Bancroft Avenue, an area considered a part of the city of Berkeley rather than university property. When the administration claimed jurisdiction over and a ban on political activity near the university, students rose in protest and in defense of the rights of students to free speech and political expression as well as academic freedom. The movement expanded into the Free Speech Movement, 1964–1965, which spearheaded student activism and official resistance that increasingly crossed into violence. The other most radicalizing series of events that paralleled the civil rights movement was the escalating Second Indonesia War, or Vietnam War, which began in 1959 and ended in April 1975. The issue of the draft, forced induction of able-bodied males of college age into military service, spread into nationwide as well as international student activism and protest.

Urban riots such as those in Watts, Los Angeles, and other cities in 1965 made the lack of opportunities and barriers to the advancement of minorities including poor urban blacks tangible to the general public. Vast discrepancies in income and power by social class and status were also made evident. The Black Power Movement of 1965 was not alone in an era when the Women's Liberation Movement, United Farm Workers, and the American Indian Movement raised consciousness of the oppression and lack of opportunities available to a variety of minorities in the intersecting levels of race, class, and gender. The lack of availability for the provision of basic human rights and needs in the wealthiest country in the world fed into a global awareness.

University students studied new English translations and reinterpretations of classic texts by social theorists such as Karl Marx, Max Weber, and Émile Durkheim. The popularization of the social sciences away from functionalism and behaviorism brought new analytical *and* political perspectives to the classrooms and streets. Popular forums addressed Eastern philosophies and theologies distinct from the Judeo-Christian tradition. The new forms of popular analysis made the hysteria of McCarthyism and the Cold War intolerances of the 1950s seem unacceptable and un-American in their own right. Optimism and a new utopian vision of a better, more humane world made change seem possible, even imminent.

Arguments for the Limited Future of the Youth Rebellion

As conservative and even liberal American leaders in business, government, and private-sector nonprofit institutions came under fire by student radicals, public and private concern at the upper levels of governmental and corporate leadership rose, enflamed also by media coverage of the increasing violence on the part of students and authorities. Some historians of the era point out, however, that the majority of the young involved in protests were not radicals but liberals—reformers rather than revolutionaries. The majority believed in an ethos of interracial nonviolence and a liberal/left coalition and had a progressive vision typical of the era of the 1960s (McAdam 1988). Even if the youth rebellion was not as extreme as might have been thought, it produced a significant cultural transformation that was not fleeting (Arsenault 2006; Carson et al. 1987; Hall 2005; Lewis 2006; McAdam 1988; Miller 1987).

Others disagreed and argued that youth activism would de-escalate by itself of natural internal forces. In July 1971, Peter F. Drucker wrote on "The Surprising Seventies" in *Harper's Magazine* (35–39) in an effort to provide a template for establishment responses to the rebellious youth of the 1960s. "Youth culture," he pointed out, "was not here to stay." Responding with violence—whether calling out the National Guard against demonstrators or engaging in heavy-handed police work with individuals and groups—was counterproductive and tended only to radicalize nonviolent individuals and movements and turn them violent. Most of the young rebels had attended college on their parent's discretionary income, Drucker reasoned. They had their necessities provided and were raised to expect health care, decent schools, housing, and a clean environment. Their outrage toward society stemmed partly from the realization that this condition was not universal and that equality and social justice were illusive. The hippies, dropouts, and radicals, Drucker pointed out, would grow up, get married, and want to provide for their children the way they had been provided for. They were, on this view, more likely to join Ralph Nader's "Raiders" over their concern with consumer product quality as they were to join the Weathermen, the violent offshoot of the

once-peaceful SDS. Their values would, said Drucker, return to the conventional wisdom as part of the oldest American tradition, namely, populism grounded in economic growth.

Drucker argued that the division in society was not generational and that there was more to worry about with respect to working-class, blue-collar youth than to affluent college students–turned counterculture protesters. He advised those in power to shift their efforts from punishing and alienating youth to providing incentives for a return to tradition. The real problem, Drucker argued, is that the group of well-educated college grads would need jobs if they were to settle down. Otherwise, faced with unemployment they were likely to join the displaced blue-collar workers and youth, who stood to revive the labor movement against capital and management. The college educated, he noted, would soon face a problem of their own, as teaching positions and other white-collar jobs could not necessarily absorb the overabundance of baby boomers looking for careers. Students considering the liberal arts were advised to shift to subject areas of increasing demand in the economy, such as technology, math, and science. Capital and government, Drucker argued, had to create new opportunities and new sources for investment to avoid massive unemployment and an economic crisis. They had to protect and expand capital reserves, he argued, by preserving their profits and investing wisely. Government needed to favor the interests of capital so that capital could do its job in protecting employment. The challenge to maintain productivity, he claimed, was a central issue, a conventional old-fashioned value, and a cornerstone of capitalism in a democracy. While the problems of race and civil rights, urban crisis, and the environment would remain, these issues could not be addressed without first easing the baby boom generation into being compliant with the realities of American capitalist enterprise.

Jack Rosenthal writing in *The New York Times* was less optimistic about there being an early solution to these issues, as the 1970 census indicated that 36.3 percent of the population was between 5 and 23 years. This situation meant that the last of the baby boomers would leave high school and enter college in 1985. There would be 17.8 million 15- to 19-year-olds still coming through the system—more than enough to be drawn to revolutionary activities (Rosenthal 1971).

Establishment Investigations into Youth Culture

Concern over the impact of this unprecedented generation attracted the attention of the political, economic, and social elites. Popular media were also interested in the story. Daniel Yankelovich, a leading figure in social science survey research, was hired by Time Inc. and Columbia Broadcasting Corporation (CBS) in 1968 and 1969, respectively, to follow the youth story. A 1969 survey became the basis of a television program called *Generations Apart* (Yankelovich 1969a,b). Yankelovich was subsequently asked by business leaders and their philanthropic counterparts to assess the depth of the youth rebellion and propose ways to bring young people back into the mainstream.

Yankelovich began by reanalyzing the surprising earlier research on youth, including a study conducted by Standard Oil, a Roper study published in *Psychology Today*, a Gallup Poll administered by Douglas Williams of Cornell, a study by the Bureau of Applied Research at Columbia, and studies by IBM, AT&T, and the Institute of Life Insurance, as well as his own studies for *Fortune* magazine and CBS (Yankelovich 1969a). The focus was on the generation gap between adults and youth, especially with respect to values and lifestyles. The earlier studies sponsored by businesses revealed the conflicting attitudes among established business and political leaders toward social problems, particularly the politics of youth and its potential (as they saw it) to threaten national security and prosperity (Yankelovich 1969a). Perhaps the most important question for investigation was, What happened to student radicals after they graduated? Did their radicalism wane once they were outside the college environment?

A third youth survey was conducted by Yankelovich in 1970, called "Youth and the Establishment." The findings were released in early 1971. The study found that slightly more than half of the student population, 56 percent, adhered to traditional values. The remaining 44 percent represented the new youth culture that included the politics of protest and reform. Additional information suggested that a large proportion of

adolescents and young adults were idealists and activists, but only a small percentage were "radical" in their views or actions.

The study attracted criticism from young people when it was reported in popular magazines such as *The Saturday Review*. Daniel J. Sobiesk of Chicago, for example, critiqued what he called a false assumption embedded in report having to do with the notion that youth needed to be fixed or corrected somehow. Another youthful reader admonished the magazine for publishing a report that looked to control young people who sought only to have a democratic voice. He called for more, not less, "power to the people," including youth. Martin E. Cornman, principal of Columbus High School in East Greenbush, New York, made the observation in another letter to *The Saturday Review* published February 27, 1971:

> Youth wants basic change in the Establishment not surveys, talk, and meetings. Cooperation will not solve alienation. Errors are not seen as errors but policies, at heart is that youth see poverty, racism, pollution, drug addiction, and warfare not as mistakes but deliberate actions that need basic changes in the philosophy of society dedicated to economic justice, brotherhood, appreciation of the environment, self respect and peace.

The "Youth and the Establishment" study was published in book form in 1972 as *The Changing Values on Campus: Political and Personal Attitudes of Today's College Students*. The book argued that there was a trend among young people toward more moderate political positions and that the level of activities on campus was declining. With the de-escalation of the Vietnam War, the force of the student movement began to decline along with the need for protestation.

The New Morality

A new study was undertaken on American youth in 1973 to address the seeming shift and "correction" among young people (Yankelovich 1974). The study was supported by the Edna McConnel Clark Foundation, the Carnegie Corporation of New York, the

Hazen Foundation, the Andrew W. Mellon Foundation, and John D. Rockefeller 3rd Fund. The findings were published in 1974 as *The New Morality: A Profile of American Youth in the 1970s*.

Social changes from 1967 to 1973 bore witness to the peak of the protests against the Vietnam War. It also encompassed the Women's Movement and sweeping changes in the sexual mores of the nation. In addition, there were major changes in the climate of trust in basic institutions and work-related values. The campus rebellion ended, but the significant lifestyle changes were not limited to youth. The Women's Movement in particular penetrated into social perspectives on gender roles. The largest difference in adherence to the views of the Women's Liberation Movement was between college women and noncollege women, or between professionals on the one hand and homemakers and blue-collar workers on the other. These groups, of course, also were widely separated in terms of their demographic profiles and potential voting behaviors.

The new crop of students no longer considered civil disobedience and violence an alternative to conventional politics. They valued a violence-free campus and rejected the idea that violence is sometimes justifiable given a worthwhile objective. The value of higher education was reinforced even though access was still limited for blue-collar workers. The gap between the values, morals, and outlook of youth and the general population was shrinking and leveling out with significant shifts apparent for all groups toward a new, more moderate political consensus. These new norms included (1) more liberal attitudes toward sex, authority, and religion; (2) more individualistic and less traditional social values concerning money, work, marriage, and the family; and (3) "self-fulfillment," or a loosening of role obligations and an opening up of life beyond the traditional nose-to-the-grindstone quest for economic security.

Radicals, who had constituted only an estimated 10 percent to 15 percent of the college population, took the lead in the years of ferment in their "harshly critical" views of the United States and its motives, institutions, and moral principles. The movement of the New Left had been largely associated with the Vietnam War protests but was also associated with broader critiques of corruption, immorality, and the misuse of power by those of high social status in political and economic circles. A more moderate majority of youth had participated in civil rights and other movements, attracted by antiwar and antidraft issues and repressive actions by authorities. The 89 percent of students who did not identify with the New Left nevertheless retained the countercultural values of new lifestyles and new social perspectives that had their genesis in the 1960s.

Private motivations now involved self-fulfillment, and public motivations involved views of a just and harmonious society and what that might entail. These twin motivations could be tapped and used productively to engage youth in participating in reform through traditional institutions. As youth created a synthesis between the old and the new and were willing to seek self-fulfillment and personal satisfaction in conventional careers, they also sought a rich and full life outside of work where they could express themselves and contribute meaningfully to social reform. There were significant lessons for the older generation and for corporate leaders: it was now imperative that the private sector recognize and take advantage of the newfound "appeal of non-financial rewards" for workers; that they find ways to increase "participation in decision making"; and that they open up the workplace in terms of an increased "tolerance of varied styles of dress, outlook, and life style, and make an effort to make work more interesting and meaningful."

Conclusion

What happened to the radical youth counterculture? As activist SDS leader, Tom Hayden, in an interview conducted in 1972 for *The Rolling Stone* magazine noted: "We ended a war, toppled two presidents, desegregated the South, broke other barriers of discrimination. How could we have accomplished so much and have so little in the end?" (Findley 1972). To the extent that the social and cultural dynamics of the 1960s survived, they have been diffused into the mainstream through changes in educational policies, lifestyle options, and popular culture. That does not necessarily mean, however, that the age cohorts or generational dynamics have lost their potential to once again alter the future in unforeseen ways.

See also American Dream; Civil Rights; Cold War Political Culture; Consumer Culture and Politics; Gay and Lesbian Culture and Politics; Labor and Politics; Left and Politics; Progressives, Progressivism, and President Barack Obama; Protest Movements; Youth and Politics.

Theresa Richardson

Bibliography

Arsenault, Raymond. 2006. *Freedom Riders, 1961 and the Struggle for Racial Justice.* New York: Oxford University Press.

Carson, Clayborne, et al., eds. 1987. *The Eyes on the Prize Civil Rights Reader.* New York: Penguin.

Cornman, Martin E. 1971. Letter to *Saturday Review*, February 27.

Cover Features. 1971. "Can the Old and Young Cooperate? What an In-Depth Study Shows" and "Youth in Protest." *Current Magazine*(March): 15.

Drucker, Peter. 1971. "The Surprising Seventies." *Harper's Magazine* (July): 35–39.

Findley, Tom. 1972. "Tom Hayden: Rolling Stone Interview, Part 2." *Rolling Stone* (November 9): 28.

Hall, Simon. 2005. *Peace and Freedom: The Civil Rights and Antiwar Movements in the 1960s.* Philadelphia: University of Pennsylvania.

Lewis, George. 2006. *Massive Resistance: The White Response to the Civil Rights Movement.* London: Hodder Arnold.

McAdam, Doug. 1988. *Freedom Summer.* New York: Oxford University Press.

Miller, James. 1987. *Democracy in the Streets: From Port Huron to the Siege of Chicago.* Cambridge, MA: Harvard University Press.

Richardson, Theresa. 2006. "Rethinking Progressive High School Reform in the 1930s: Youth, Mental Hygiene, and General Education." *American Educational History Journal* 33(1): 77–87.

Rosenthal, Jack. 1971. "New Census Trend Bulging Generation." *New York Times* (November 5).

Spock, Benjamin. 1971. "Spock Speaks Out: Don't Blame Me." *Look Magazine* (January 26): 15.

Students for a Democratic Society (SDS). 1962. "Port Huron Statement." National Convention Meeting at Port Huron, Michigan, June 11–15.

Wilson, Sloan. 1955. *The Man in the Gray Flannel Suit.* New York: Pocket Books.

Yankelovich, Daniel. 1969a. "A Special Kind of Rebellion," *Fortune Magazine* (January), copyright Time, Inc.

Yankelovich, Daniel. 1969b. "Generations Apart." 3 hour Television Special, Columbia Broadcasting System (CBS).

Yankelovich, Daniel. 1971. *Youth and the Establishment: A Report on Research for John D. Rockefeller 3rd and the Task Force on Youth.* New York: JDR 3rd Fund.

Yankelovich, Daniel. 1972. *The Changing Values on Campus: Political and Personal Attitudes of Today's College Students: A Survey for the JDR 3rd Fund by Daniel Yankelovich, Inc.* Introduction by John D. Rockefeller 3rd. New York: Washington Square Press.

Yankelovich, Daniel. 1974. *The New Morality: A Profile of American Youth in the 1970s.* New York: McGraw-Hill.

Yankelovich Studies. 1971–1972. "Youth and the Establishment," Promotion and Publicity, JDR 3rd Fund, Spec. Collection IV 3B 10, Series 3, Box 41, Folder 379 Rockefeller Archive Center, Sleepy Hollow, New York.

BANKING POLICY AND POLITICS

American political culture in the area of banking policy and politics is riddled with many of the same contradictions that exist in other aspects of American political economy. Chief among them is a lack of ease with the concentration of power in the government or the financial system, while needing a degree of concentration in both to survive in the postwar global marketplace. Given these contradictions, the essence of banking policy and politics is how the government walks the line between protecting the country's deposit base from speculative activity while allowing for it in clearly demarcated areas so that banks can still make a profit.

The problems with banks are specific to their nature. They are financial intermediaries. As such, when depositors put their money in a bank, the bank pays them interest and lends their deposit to borrowers, charging the latter a higher rate of interest. Therefore, the bank makes a profit on the difference between what it pays the depositor in interest and what it earns from borrowers. Since riskier loans tend to earn higher rates of interest, financial intermediaries have every incentive to lend to riskier borrowers and earn a higher profit for their own investors. Yet riskier borrowers also raise the possibility that the bank will lose the investment and thus the deposits. The dilemma of risks and rewards creates an inherent conflict of interest between taxpayers and depositors on one hand and bankers on the other. Because the general public insures bank deposits, and depositors expect to have access to their money, the government resolves the conflict by regulating the activities of banks.

Regulation is driven by the political system. While many analysts point to the importance of campaign contributions and lobbying in terms of banks (and other interested parties) getting what they want out of the American system, there is a layer of bureaucratic politics at the federal level that operates between these activities and the outcomes within the government agencies that govern finance. That is, these agencies have their *own* interests within the American political system. They must accomplish their mandates and obtain the necessary budgets and staff from Congress and the presidential administration. Hence, congressional committee jurisdictions (who oversees what) and the rulemaking activities of agencies (how laws and regulations are carried out) play a significant role in determining what happens (Lavelle 2013). The same political party does not necessarily control each part of the government, nor do all banking interests necessarily coalesce within one party. This complexity makes it difficult to fix any problem easily.

American complexity reflects the country's economic development and experience with war that has shaped its financial system over many years. In other industrial democracies, interest groups, parties, and government agencies are arranged differently and may be equally complex, but not in the same way. The unique American historical legacy has resulted in a tension between state and federal governments and the country's strong capitalist orientation, resulting in a deep distrust of government intervention into business decision making. Similarly, political ideologies at different moments in American history produced distinct

depository institutions—banks, savings and loans, and credit unions—which came to play unique roles in taking the deposits of individuals and channeling them to borrowers (Hoffman 2001). The fragmented regulatory framework within which these institutions operated was likewise tied to a particular political ideology of the day.

In the United States, this legacy has been termed the "dual banking system"—or the parallel set of state and federal banking regulators—that has endured since the Civil War. Under the dual banking system, the "doctrine of choice" operates to allow a diverse set of financial institutions the freedom to choose their own federal regulator. Advocates of the system view this freedom as protection from unreasonable regulatory behavior and a means to promote a healthy dynamic among regulators. Critics argue that it can create an unnecessary duplication of regulation and lack of consistency among them.

Banking Policy

Banking policy encompasses a wide range of government activities that have many effects on the macro-economy not limited to the day-to-day supervision of banks. Banking policy includes government taxing and spending related to financial institutions; the government's regulation of the banking, securities, and insurance industries; and its management of the money supply and interest rates charged in lending activities. Banking politics similarly operate across a wide range of activities. Since different agencies, independent regulatory commissions, single-headed regulatory agencies, and government-sponsored enterprises (GSEs) handle specific aspects of banking policy, the bureaucratic politics among them matters because they define the tasks and determine the way specialized knowledge is brought to bear on agencies, private associations, and organized constituencies (Eisner 1993, 10).

The splintered nature of the agencies that charter, regulate, and supervise banks reflects the various experiments with national banking in American history. The oldest, the Office of the Comptroller of the Currency (OCC), was established in 1863 as an independent bureau of the Department of the Treasury.

(In 2011, it absorbed the former regulator of savings and loan associations, the Office of Thrift Supervision, under the provisions of the Dodd-Frank Wall Street Reform and Consumer Protection Act.) A financial panic in 1907 prompted discussions for a central banking authority in the United States. In 1913, the Federal Reserve Act created a central banking system that would also issue Federal Reserve Notes that are legal tender. In addition to acting as the American central bank, the Federal Reserve is a regulator with primary responsibility for state-chartered member banks. Moreover, the Federal Reserve is responsible for regulating bank-holding companies. All large banks, and many small ones, are affiliated with a bank-holding company (which does not directly engage in banking itself).

Newer regulators emerged from the dislocation of the Great Depression of the 1930s. For example, the Federal Deposit Insurance Corporation (FDIC) is an independent agency of the federal government that was created in response to the bank failures of the 1920s and 1930s. A five-person board of directors who are appointed by the president and confirmed by the Senate manages the FDIC. In addition to providing deposit insurance for the system, it serves as the backup supervisor for the remaining banks and thrift institutions that are not regulated by the OCC and are not members of the Federal Reserve System. This group represents more than half of the institutions in the system. The Securities and Exchange Commission (SEC) was also created during the Depression to require public companies to disclose information to the public that might affect investment decisions. It oversees securities exchanges, brokers, dealers, investment advisors, and mutual funds. In these areas, the SEC has enforcement authority, where it can bring civil enforcement actions against individuals and companies for violation of the securities laws.

At different times in American history different advantages accrued to banks holding either state or federal charters. Therefore, the total number of state or national banks rises and falls according to a variety of factors. A bank with a federal charter has powers defined under federal law, operates under federal standards, and is supervised by a federal agency. Conversely, a bank with a state charter has powers defined by state law, operates under state standards, and is overseen by a state supervisor and/or the Federal Reserve if it is a member. The situation can become confusing when national banks operating in multiple state jurisdictions must comply with different state banking laws.

The newest regulator, the Consumer Financial Protection Bureau (CFPB), was created by the legislation that followed the financial crisis of 2008 under the umbrella of the Federal Reserve System. The CFPB's core mission is to provide consumers with the information they need to understand the terms of their agreements with financial companies. In addition, the new CFPB works to make regulations as clear as possible so that consumers can follow the rules on their own.

Banking Politics

Banking politics take place within and among the branches of government as well as the regulatory agencies. The separation of powers that is the hallmark of the U.S. government operates in the governance of finance at its most basic level: the U.S. Constitution gives the legislature the power to print money, whereas the executive branch and the courts retain their own spheres of influence.

In the American political system, the president serves as both head of state and head of government, and he or she is elected completely independent of the legislature. This arrangement between the executive and legislative branches of government fails to ensure that the same political party will control each branch, or even each chamber of Congress. In fact it is more often the case that different parties control one or another aspect of the legislative process, and with it oversight of monetary and regulatory policy as well as fiscal policy. At times those in office need to cooperate among themselves to get results and be reelected; however, at other times they can seem to be working at cross-purposes with each other. To add another layer of complexity to the system, just as the American political system spreads out power among the different branches of government, the legislature also divides power among various committees that do the work of the institution. Although the central bank of the United States, the Federal Reserve, is a creation of Congress and could be terminated by law and not by a constitutional amendment, the two branches—legislative and executive—share oversight of the central bank in a complex arrangement designed to keep it out of the politics of the day. The arrangement makes it possible for Congress to claim oversight of almost every aspect of monetary and regulatory policy, yet at the same time stand outside of the decisions that the Federal Reserve makes.

Theorists explain the relationship between the executive and legislative branches by arguing that if a policy results in an outcome that benefits everyone, the president will focus on that issue; if it offers an outcome that benefits only a select group of citizens, members of Congress will focus on it. According to this logic, monetary policy outcomes (money supply, interest rates, etc.) associated with the Federal Reserve are macroeconomic and will be the preserve of the presidency (Corder 1998, 155). In addition, the president does not have many other instruments that affect macroeconomic or credit market outcomes. The central bank's work naturally benefits or hurts the president, so the executive pays attention and Congress does not. Conversely, members of Congress focus their efforts on individual benefits through credit or tax policy (fiscal policy) because they can thus work more closely to aid the constituencies that keep them in office (Beck 1990, 143). Moreover, as with the president, Congress may choose to affect banking and credit policy with particularistic programs because they lack other, more effective, mechanisms to influence central bank activity.

Although there is no one part of the American government that actually decides who gets a loan—because private banks are left to make such decisions for themselves in the American capitalist system—Congress and the political system at large play a role in ensuring access to credit for specific political constituencies that might otherwise be denied access to it under purely market terms: chiefly homeowners, students, and farmers.

What types of intervention does Congress offer? Too numerous to elaborate here, each type operates through both loan guarantees and direct loan programs that are overseen by numerous congressional committees. These credit programs are not limited to the jurisdiction of the banking committees. For example, the Senate Committee on Health, Education, Labor and Pensions and the House Committee on Labor and Education oversee student loan programs that grant easier terms to individuals who might not otherwise be a good bet for the market. The House Committee on Agriculture and the Senate Committee on Agriculture, Nutrition and Forestry subsidize credit to the agricultural sector through the "Farm Bill." Agricultural policy is designed to allow farmers to borrow at below market rates or to value their security (i.e., crops) above market valuation (Beck 1990, 142). Other forms of intervention have been through agencies such as the Small Business Administration's loan guarantee program, which is the largest source of federal subsidies to small businesses. Arguably, the largest interventions have been through GSEs known as Fannie Mae (Federal National Mortgage Association) and Freddie Mac (Federal Home Loan Mortgage Corporation), which created and support a secondary market for mortgages. These enterprises operate by borrowing money at a lower rate and using it to buy mortgages and mortgage-backed securities so that lenders can move the assets (loans) off of their balance sheets and offer more loans.

The judicial branch of government can serve as a source of both politics and policy. Financial regulation involves restrictions on how financial assets may be used and the kinds of contracts that can be issued and enforced. Therefore, some views on the sanctity of property and contracts, such as those of fundamentalist free market conservatives, are incompatible with any serious regulation of the financial sector. Other ideological commitments to federalism have made it difficult to supervise some institutions at the federal level. Judicial conservatives do not always reach conclusions that support the financial sector, however, since state regulatory powers may work against predatory lending (McCarthy, Poole, and Rosenthal 2013, 108).

The political sources of financial instability can be found in the exchange between the network of bureaucratic agencies that govern finance and financial innovation in American capitalist financial markets. The exchange provides opportunities for regulatory arbitrage—essentially, the exploitation of gaps or loopholes—that can destabilize the system. Nonetheless, innovation is not necessarily bad. At times, it has meant that ordinary people have access to credit that allows them to make payments easily and to finance large purchases, such as homes and cars. Without it, they would have to rely on friends or family to provide a loan. In a capitalist democracy where banks, and not the government, make individual lending decisions, this innovation has contributed to economic growth and opportunities for people to move into the middle class.

Yet at a certain point, innovation in the financial services industry poses challenges to the regulatory framework within which it operates. From the end of World War II to the 1970s, the United States had financial sectors that were demarcated by regulations in such a way that bankers could make a profit on the business they were conducting, but that profit was limited by regulation. Over time, more and more providers could offer products they were previously not allowed to—home loans, car loans, credit cards, checking accounts, and so on—and yet the old regulations and agencies that administer them were left in place. The structure that was left to govern the new financial services marketplace—an ever-growing and evolving marketplace—meant that opportunities to evade regulations proliferated.

International Issues

The absence of an international regulator makes domestic institutions all the more important. A financial crisis is unlike other types of international crises, such as wars or hostage-taking, because the response must result from bargaining among political and economic players that are within the United States and that most likely played a role in causing it. Therefore, unlike an international crisis where two or more countries act in adversarial roles, in a financial crisis the U.S. government must respond to those it does not consider adversarial. And it must respond in the face of a large amount of citizen's anger at what they perceive to have led to the crisis.

Each government must first turn to the internal institutions that result from its historical legacy, such as its central bank, providers of credit, and regulatory agencies. Nonetheless, the American government must also consider international actors, such as other countries' central banks, transnational commercial banks, foreign governments, and the International Monetary

Fund (IMF), because its internal institutions may lack sufficient resources to address the crisis or because the actions may affect the stability of banks in other countries. Hence, the distinctive feature of a financial crisis where there is no inherent internal or external adversary means that at the international level, the most realistic policy goals will be to limit opportunities for transnational actors to play off national regulatory systems against each other prior to a crisis, and to determine appropriate bail-out strategies across state lines when a crisis does occur.

The world system's political institutions that govern finance are only emerging in their earliest forms, yet they reflect the contradictory tendencies with respect to multilateralism. The original international institutions that addressed the problem of global finance were among merchants and thus outside the state system. Since World War II, the United States has been a leader in establishing international organizations such as the IMF that promote coordination. At present, the IMF lacks the capacity to regulate banks. In other circumstances, the United States prefers to operate through more informal arrangements. The Financial Stability Forum, founded in 1999, shows promise in the area of coordination but lacks any real enforcement capability.

Regulatory arbitrage thus takes place in the international system just as it does within the United States. Opportunities have multiplied as the world's financial systems integrate. Europeans have commenced discussions of their own concerning how to distinguish banking from investment banking functions and thus address the problem of banks that are "too big to fail." As we have seen in the Eurozone crisis of 2010–2012, and more recently in the 2013 Cyprus bailout, the system ultimately puts everyone's deposits at risk.

See also Debt, Deficit, and Politics; Economic Policy and Politics; Federalism; Globalization; Privatization and Deregulation; Separation of Powers; Tax Policy and Politics; Trade Policy and Politics.

Kathryn C. Lavelle

Bibliography

Beck, Nathaniel. 1990. "Congress and the Fed: Why the Dog Does Not Bark in the Night." In Thomas

Mayer, ed. *The Political Economy of American Monetary Policy*. New York: Cambridge University Press, pp. 131–50.

Corder, J. Kevin. 1998. *Central Bank Autonomy: The Federal Reserve System in American Politics*. New York: Garland Publishing, Inc.

Eisner, Marc Allen. 1993. *Regulatory Politics in Transition*. Baltimore: Johns Hopkins University Press.

Hoffman, Susan. 2001. *Politics and Banking: Ideas, Public Policy, and the Creation of Financial Institutions*. Baltimore: Johns Hopkins University Press.

Lavelle, Kathryn C. 2013. *Money and Banks in the American Political System*. New York: Cambridge University Press.

McCarthy, Nolan, Keith T. Poole, and Howard Rosenthal. 2013. *Political Bubbles: Financial Crises and the Failure of American Democracy*. Princeton, NJ: Princeton University Press.

BIOTECHNOLOGY AND POLITICS

The United States remains at the forefront of biotechnology development in such fields as assisted reproduction, stem cell research, genomics, and genetically modified animals and agricultural products. This success, in part, is due to a political culture that values an open marketplace, the freedom of individuals and industry to research and market new developments, and a limited role for government oversight. Despite private industry efforts at self-regulation, challenges to this laissez-faire approach to biotechnology advancement and its marketization have emerged from a number of different quarters. Opponents of this system express concerns including the health and safety of individuals—patients, research participants, and consumers—as well as the long-term impact on society, the earth, and our understanding of human nature and the natural world.

The philosophical tradition that shapes this environment reflects the dominant cultural paradigm of the United States—the protection of individual liberty and autonomy with a limited role for government intervention in individual decision making, the marketplace, and scientific research. This approach facilitates incredible technological advances, yet creates a permissive environment where legal disputes are settled on a case-by-case basis with little move toward a framework or basic principles to govern current and future biotechnologies. This absence reflects and reinforces ambivalence toward government regulation, infusing businesses and individuals with the freedom to pursue the science largely on their own terms. The struggle to define and respond to these various biotechnological developments, both within government and among the general public, illustrates the collision of the dominant political culture with competing interests and values. The present entry examines a subset of emerging biotechnology developments directly affecting individuals and society that contribute to significant conflict between traditional cultural values with competing demands for oversight and regulation of the marketization of new technologies.

Biotechnology and Reproduction: Assisted Reproductive Technologies and Reprogenetics

Assisted reproductive technologies (ARTs) and genetic research are intricately intertwined practices, with advances by genetic researchers in cloning and embryo manipulation providing significant enhancements for clinical work. Genetic research involving gametes or embryos engenders a conflict similar to that of abortion and reproductive rights, inserting a religious or moral dimension into the public's understanding of this research. The ethical, legal, and moral issues at stake in both assisted reproduction and genetic research generate a deeply divisive conflict that continues unabated and intensifies as the science progresses.

Within this environment, research on embryos for reproductive and nonreproductive purposes has flourished, introducing an array of options for the creation, use, and alteration of gametes (sperm and egg) and embryos. These advances in reproductive medicine elicit concerns regarding the health and safety of the various clinical participants (egg donors and gestating mothers), the fetus and potential children in the absence of rigorous, systematic oversight. The political system is largely unable to keep pace with the rapid progress of the science, and coupled with the pressures of the marketplace for greater innovation and application, experimental procedures quickly move to accepted clinical practice often without the benefit of long-term study.

In vitro fertilization (IVF), or the fertilization of the egg outside the womb, provides the medically infertile, single individuals, same-sex couples, and alternative family arrangements the opportunity to bear children. Despite the repeated use and refinement of the procedures associated with IVF, a number of tangible and intangible safety concerns remain, particularly for women. IVF requires both eggs and sperm, retrieved from the individuals undergoing this procedure, or in cases of poor gamete quality, donor gametes will be used to create an embryo for implantation. Egg retrieval is a medically invasive procedure consisting of a series of daily hormone injections and outpatient retrieval surgery, both of which carry a number of associated medical risks, both immediate and long term. Potential drug-related side effects include ovarian hyperstimulation syndrome (the most severe) to discomfort, bloating, and nausea (the least severe); in addition, some evidence suggests a relationship between egg retrieval and an elevated risk for ovarian cancer (Giudice, Santa, and Pool 2007).

Given the potential risk to health and well-being for egg donors as well as the significant time and energy necessary for the donation process, the fertility industry's professional association recommends compensation of $7,000–$10,000 per donation cycle (Ethics Committee of the American Society for Reproductive Medicine 2007, 308). Although many egg donor agencies and clinics abide by this standard, advertisements abound in college newspapers that solicit donors with particular abilities and backgrounds, promising payments ranging anywhere from $5,000 to $100,000. In addition, those donors who command some of the highest offers include young women at prestigious universities with strong academic credentials and exceptional athletic or artistic abilities (Levine 2010, 29–31). Although there is some concern that excessive compensation may lead egg donors to ignore or discount the medical and psychological risks involved, egg donation remains a practice bound to the vicissitudes of the marketplace. While many feminists and feminist bioethicists advocate for prohibitions or greater restrictions on compensation for donors to ensure safety and prevent exploitation, many young women continue to donate their eggs to others.

As is the case with assisted reproduction, human embryonic stem cell research (hESCR) is practiced

Fertility Financing in the Private Market

Compared to most ART patients in the developed world, Americans encounter a unique set of circumstances when attempting to finance fertility treatment. Few states require insurance coverage, and in the absence of national health insurance, most patients bear the full cost of treatment. Until most recently, the expense of treatment effectively limited access to the wealthy; today, the emergence and proliferation of private lenders specializing in fertility loans ensures access to a multitude of new patients. Although this situation is seen as a positive development by infertility support advocates, a growing trend of business partnerships between fertility clinics and physicians with private lending companies introduces a potential conflict of interest. Some fertility clinics allow select private lenders onsite or online access to patients, with financing arrangements promoted by participating clinics and medical professionals. The intertwining of a physician's clinical role with the obligations to a private lending firm, in light of the vulnerability of many infertile patients, suggests the need for some measure of oversight regarding these business arrangements. Growing use of these lending schemes may lead the public to question the ability of physicians to provide objective, need-based care as well as the integrity of the fertility industry.

in an environment devoid of significant government oversight, allowing private industry to drive research and development. Although many of the projected therapeutic uses of hESCR are speculative, bioethicists and scholars continue to debate the ethics of current and potential developments in stem cell research. One of the central challenges to hESCR centers on the use and procurement of stem cells necessary for this research, a process that results in the destruction of the embryo. This procedure generates significant ethical conflict, akin to the battle over reproduction rights, creating a highly politicized research environment as well as legal uncertainty for scientists despite a cultural ethos that privileges freedom and autonomy for scientists and researchers (Robertson 2010).

In the United States, this research continues in fits and starts as scientists encounter a number of barriers, both legal and practical, to the procurement, use, and disposal of embryos for research purposes. Researchers gained the ability to create embryos in a laboratory setting in the 1990s, although an executive order issued by President George W. Bush in 2000 prohibited the creation of new embryonic stem cell lines. This prohibition had a significant impact given the limited number of stem cell lines in existence, some of dubious quality, thus in effect, restricting the development of this line of research (NIH 2009). Currently, this prohibition no longer stands, but the development of new lines remains problematic given the difficulty in procuring eggs. Compensation for eggs donated for research purposes is prohibited, despite the allowance of compensation for eggs for reproductive purposes. Support for this prohibition represents the coupling of strange bedfellows; concerned for the health of egg donors, feminist bioethicists support prohibitions on payment for egg donation for either reproductive or nonreproductive purposes. Conversely, politicized religious interest groups oppose compensation as a means to impair the creation of new embryos for this research. Moral objections to this research have ignited religious groups around the nation, and their efforts to limit this form of research have led to some policy changes, primarily along the edges of this issue area. Despite the moral and ethical controversies surrounding stem cell research, such research continues to progress within the United States, albeit most often in states that support and fund stem cell research institutions.

Somatic cell nuclear transfer (SCNT), or cloning, is a practice often used in hESCR, allowing genetic material to be inserted in the nucleus of a stem cell to produce a replicate or clone. Also referred to as therapeutic cloning, this technique is most often used to develop human tissues for transplant in cases of organ failure or degenerative diseases. Of greater political and moral consequence is the use of SCNT for reproductive cloning in animals and humans. Since the birth of Dolly, the first cloned mammal, scientists continue to refine this science as cloned animals still experience significant health problems and shortened lifespans (FDA 2009). While many nations have preemptively prohibited the reproductive cloning of humans, scholars have begun to discuss the relative merits of such a procedure for reproductive purposes. Although public opinion and political officials in the United States remain opposed to human cloning, theorists and health care professionals have begun to consider the implications of the future development and use of this practice on humans (Morales 2009).

The creation of embryos outside of the womb for reproduction leads to a number of ethical, moral, and legal concerns, but it is the manipulation of gametes and embryos for directed reproduction that leads to significant points of controversy regarding this new frontier in biomedicine. Currently, two methods for directed procreation are in use:(1) sperm sorting used to select for fetal sex and (2) genetic testing used for screening purposes. As to the latter, genetic tests such as preimplantation genetic diagnosis serve as valuable diagnostic tools that detect and prevent the passing of genetic disorders to offspring. Commonly used to prevent the transmission of Tay-Sachs or chromosomal abnormalities, commentators have begun to evaluate the ethical and social consequences of the genetic manipulation of embryos, with whole genome sequencing used to select for particular traits or abilities in future children (Davis 2009).

While these concerns are speculative, their potential emergence suggests the need for a comprehensive discussion regarding the permissibility of this technology for clinical use. The culture of egg donation indicates the expectations parents can bring to assisted reproduction, illustrated in the extraordinary efforts some take to find donors with particular traits and the consequent willingness to pay substantial sums for donated eggs. The concern that prospective parents may utilize genetic testing and the alteration of embryos to produce enhanced children introduces a number of immediate concerns for individual health and safety in addition to the broad implications of this potential science for society. While it is unclear the degree to which genetic manipulation can select for particular traits, the use of technology to perform such a task may lead to the objectification of children as well as further commoditization of reproduction (Hershberger et al. 2012). If some form of this science becomes a reality, it will be critical for the public to consider the consequences of genetic enhancement with regard to social inequality as well as the use of enhancement for specific purposes.

Currently, there is no government regulation to oversee or proscribe the use of current or potential techniques to manipulate genetic material in gametes or embryos. The absence of government intervention renders this a private choice—the choice of individuals to pay for this procedure, the choice of clinicians to perform such work, and the choice of researchers to develop advanced techniques in genetic manipulation. While many commentators maintain the need for procreative liberty to ensure the right of individuals to utilize reproductive technologies and as well maintain an environment conducive to scientific progress, the use of these and potential biomedical advances remains controversial, raising questions regarding the ethics of the manipulation of an embryo's genetic material to broader queries into the marketization of childbearing, equality, and the well-being of society (Steinbock 2008).

Genomics: Genetic Research for Nonreproductive Purposes

Genomics, or the study of DNA and the human genome, holds the promise of vast medical advances benefiting the general public as well as increased diagnostic capabilities for more advanced patient care.

Genetic research, ranging from the genetic testing of a single gene to whole genome sequencing, is expected to provide clinicians and researchers the tools to uncover the location of genetic predispositions for diseases such as cancer, diabetes, and psychiatric conditions as well as improve diagnosis and treatment of genetic disorders. This research introduces a number of logistical and broader ethical issues for individuals and the general public, concerns that are distinct from those associated with genetic research for assisted reproduction. While the range of potential problems or ethical issues that arise in the course of genomic research suggests the need for some degree of oversight of research and clinical treatment, the federal government has not moved toward policy development or systematic regulation of this field.

As is the case with many new developments in biotechnology, individuals and industries within the private market have been quick to capitalize on many different aspects of genetic research. One development incurring concern among researchers and consumer advocates is the sale of over-the-counter genetic testing kits that allow individuals to privately access their own genetic information. As of October 2012, the website for 23andMe, one of the industry leaders, attracts clientele through emphasizing the importance of information on one's current health, genetic predisposition to particular diseases, and information about one's ancestry. Over-the-counter genetic testing provides individuals access to this information; however, the use of such data for unintended purposes may lead to privacy violations and genetic discrimination. In addition, it is unclear how consumers interpret or understand the information gleaned from genotyping, and problems could develop from such an incomplete understanding of genetic information. The freedom to make use of such tests provides individuals with an exceptional amount of personal genetic information; currently, however, the full utility and value of this information remain unclear.

Whole genome sequencing, as opposed to genetic tests on one or two genes, provides the most comprehensive information of an individual genome. The sequencing process produces an incredibly refined analysis of genetic determinants of particular traits and predispositions, although, again, the full utility of this science may not emerge until a greater number and diversity of human genomes are sequenced. The Presidential Commission on Bioethics, a panel convened to evaluate newly emerging bioethical issues, has initiated a review of concerns that may arise with increased use of this technology. The commission recommends the promotion of data access and sharing between researchers and clinicians while working to ensure adequate protections for participating individuals. Whole genome sequencing amasses an unparalleled amount of information about an individual; for this information to have any utility for scientists, data sharing is necessary. The sharing of this information requires adequate security and protections for participating individuals, although it is unclear what the exact measures might be to ensure such protections while also affording researchers easy access to the data. A broader issue concerns the type of medical information obtained by this sequencing—some consider the unprecedented depth of knowledge exceptionally provocative and treat it as something that stands to challenge our subjective understanding of ourselves and the essence of human nature (Presidential Commission on the Study of Bioethical Issues 2012). Despite the move toward an identification and evaluation of the immediate and long-term risks and concerns of genomic research,

little action has been taken to outline policy proposals that respond to such potential risks.

Genetically Modified Organisms and Genetically Engineered Animals

Genetic modification has long been used to develop and enhance food products through genetic alteration, or recombinant DNA technology. This modification is used to develop new food products as well as enhance hardiness and shelf life, and increase crop yield and nutritional value. As is found with most new developments in biotechnology, the private market creates great incentives for innovation and advancement in this form of food technology. Such an environment, allowing for considerable profiteering by agricultural biotechnology companies, has also produced a movement against the use of genetically modified (GM) foods, primarily led by environmental, consumer, and farming organizations.

The U.S. Food and Drug Administration (FDA) reviews the safety of new food products prior to their introduction in the market. The standards established by the FDA regarding the testing of new GM food products are perceived by many opponents as insufficient, often due to the absence of extensive, long-term investigation of the effects of such products. The FDA

Biotech Profiteering and the Future of Farming in America

In 2011, a consortium of farmers filed a lawsuit against biotech giant, Monsanto. The lawsuit challenges Monsanto's primary business practice—the patenting and sale of genetically modified seeds. Farmers using these seeds must purchase new seeds every year from Monsanto; organic farmers are unable to prevent cross-contamination of their fields through unwanted pollination of genetically modified plant materials. Monsanto has issued statements that it does not pursue patent-infringement lawsuits against inadvertent contamination, although the Center for Food Safety reports that the company investigates approximately 500 farmers annually and has sued hundreds of farmers for GMO patent infringement over the past decade (Center for Food Safety 2012). The U.S. Court of Appeals reviewed the case in May 2013 and found on the side of Monsanto, because the lead plaintiff in the case had been replanting seeds intended as commodities, not seeds per se. The U.S. Supreme Court subsequently affirmed the Court of Appeals ruling. In any case, further rulings could have dramatic implications for the future of farming in America as well the acceptance of seed and other agricultural product patents.

also oversees research on genetically engineered (GE) animals, including both the development of new modifications and the introduction of GE animals into the food system. Although this research is still early in its development, scientists expect that the genetic modification of animals will lead to more healthy and environmentally friendly agricultural practices as well as to new areas of pharmaceutical and therapeutic research (FDA 2012). The freedom of the private market and the minimal role of the federal government overseeing the development and use of GM foods and GE animals have led activists to challenge both private industry and the federal government regarding the lack of appropriate oversight and research into the short- and long-term safety and environmental impacts of these products.

The development and use of biotechnology to engineer enhanced agricultural and animal products is an incredibly profitable yet controversial enterprise. The freedom of these companies has come under increased scrutiny as the array of forces opposed to this research and profiteering of private industry has mobilized. The long-term impact of these organizations is unclear, but their work represents one avenue to check the growth and power of this industry.

Conclusion

In the United States, the development and use of biotechnology moves at an exceptionally rapid rate, allowing for innovation and increased application of this new science. This rapid advance of science, however, means that technological innovations emerge and are used prior to a full public weighing of the relative costs and benefits for individuals and society. While many argue that such an environment is critical for scientific progress, it simultaneously sets the stage for ethical lapses, confusion regarding researcher and patient protections, and lengthy legal battles over rights and responsibilities of individuals and companies involved in these practices. Further, questions remain regarding the control and ownership of reproductive materials, technological developments, and the basic structures of cellular life. Such an environment, in part a product of American political culture and its emphasis on individual freedom and limited government,

is increasingly coming under scrutiny by a variety of competing interests and groups. Environmentalists, feminists, and religious activists represent some of the more ardent critics of many of these new biotechnology developments; it is these groups as well as other emergent voices opposed to the rapid deployment of these technologies that pose one of the more significant challenges to the continued development of biotechnology in the United States.

See also Drug Policy and Politics; Farming, Food, and Politics; Science, Technology, and Society.

Alisa Von Hagel

Bibliography

Center for Food Safety. "Monsanto vs. U.S. Farmers 2012 Update." 2012. http://www.centerfor foodsafety.org/wp-content/uploads/2012/11 /Monsanto-v-US-Farmer-2012-Update-final.pdf. Accessed December 12, 2012.

Davis, Dena. 2009. "The Parental Investment Factor and the Child's Right to an Open Future." *The Hastings Center Report* 39, no. 2 (March/April): 24–27.

Ethics Committee of the American Society for Reproductive Medicine. 2007. "Financial Compensation for Oocyte Donation." *Fertility and Sterility* 88, no. 30: 305–9.

FDA. U.S. Food and Drug Administration. 2012. "Animal and Veterinary Technology Overview: Somatic Cell Nuclear Transfer and Other Assisted Reproduction Technologies." http://www.fda.gov /animalveterinary/safetyhealth/animalcloning /ucm124765.htm. Accessed December 3, 2012.

FDA. 2009. U.S. Food and Drug Administration. *The Regulation of Genetically Engineered Animals Containing Heritable rDNA Constructs*. January 15. http://www.fda.gov/animalveterinary/de velopmentapprovalprocess/geneticengineering /geneticallyengineeredanimals/default.htm. Accessed December 12, 2012.

Giudice, Linda, Eileen Santa, and Robert Pool, eds. 2007. *Assessing the Medical Risks of Human Oocyte Donation for Stem Cell Research: Workshop Report*. Washington, DC: The National Academies Press.

Hershberger, Patricia, et al. 2012. "The Decision Making Process of Genetically-At-Risk Couples Considering Preimplantation Genetic Diagnosis: Initial Findings from a Grounded Theory Study." *Social Science and Medicine* 74, no. 10 (May): 1536–43.

Levine, Aaron. 2010. "Self-Regulation, Compensation, and the Ethical Recruitment of Oocyte Donors." *The Hastings Center Report* 40, no. 2 (March/April): 25–36.

Morales, Nestor Micheli. 2009. "Psychological Aspects of Human Cloning: The Identity and Uniqueness of Human Beings." *Ethics, Bioscience and Life* 4, no. 3 (November): 43–50.

NIH. National Institute of Health. 2009. *Human Embryonic Stem Cell Policy under Former President Bush (Aug. 9, 2001–Mar. 9, 2009)*. March 10. http://stemcells.nih.gov/policy/pages/2001policy.aspx. Accessed October 26, 2014.

Presidential Commission on the Study of Bioethical Issues. 2012. *Privacy and Progress in Whole Genome Sequencing*. October. http://www.bioethics.gov/cms/node/764. Accessed May 23, 2014.

Robertson, John. 2010. "Embryo Stem Cell Research: Ten Years of Controversy." *Law, Medicine and Ethics* 38: 191–203.

Steinbock, Bonnie. 2008. "Designer Babies: Choosing Our Children's Genes." *Lancet* 372, no. 9646 (October): 1294–95.

BORDER PROTECTION AND POLITICS

The contemporary period of heightened immigration enforcement began in the mid-1970s. Undocumented migration had been expanding for a decade by then, starting with the end of the Bracero legal temporary migrant labor program in 1964. The growth was accompanied by changes among U.S. employers (the global erosion of stable labor markets) that increased their demand for migrant workers. For reasons that are still not well researched, this became framed as a significant federal policy issue in 1975. Since the mid-1950s, the Immigration and Naturalization Service and its political counterparts in Congress and the Executive Branch had a policy of minimizing the size and cost of immigration enforcement, presenting low activity as a sign of success in immigration enforcement. That would change from 1975 on: failure of immigration enforcement to halt unauthorized migration would demonstrate the need for increases in size and funding. The more failure, the more growth—an ironic but profound driver of the escalation of unauthorized entry.

At the start of this escalatory period, certain key features of immigration enforcement were already in place and have continued to the present. Enforcement has been oriented toward those immigration violators who cross land borders without being inspected (entry without inspection [EWI]), rather than toward either the exclusion of selected persons entering at ports or the identification and deportation of people who entered with proper nonimmigrant visas but who violated their terms by overstaying, working without authorization, and so on (such enforcement activities do occur, with significant impact on the people involved, but we are characterizing broad trends here). Likewise, the enforcement emphasis has been on the southwestern land border, and thus on the Border Patrol, rather than other entry points or the national interior. As a result, the enforcement emphasis—in both practice and imagery—has been on Mexican and Central American EWIs rather than on a more diverse range of migrants that include visa violators from many countries.

Good demographic studies of this disproportionate emphasis are recent, finding that over 90 percent of arrests are for southwest border EWIs while unauthorized migrants are likely to be 40 percent (or more) visa violators from a diverse range of countries, but the pattern noted likely dates to the 1940s. (However, exclusion categories, such as against HIV-positive persons, in force until 2009, are forms of enforcement that are not as narrowly focused on the Mexican border, but impact visitors and immigrants at all ports of entry.) It is thus important to emphasize that this narrow emphasis on the southern border and Mexican enforcement is a specific policy choice and is only a small part of the overall unauthorized migration situation. However, it is portrayed as being the most significant factor in unauthorized entry.

The overall trajectory of the immigration enforcement apparatus from 1975 to the present is growth of size, intensity, and funding. At first, the growth pattern was wavy, with periods of increase in the mid-1970s and early to mid-1980s and periods of stasis in the late 1970s and 1988–1993. Since 1994, the growth has been continuous, with variations only in the rate of increase. By 2014, this trend resulted in a budget of $13 billion for Customs and Border Protection and $5.3 billion for Immigration and Customs Enforcement (ICE). The Border Patrol grew from 1,700 to 20,000 officers over this period and is now the largest uniformed Federal Police Agency. Even when events would seem to call for a redirection of policy approaches and enforcement emphases, such as the events of September 11, 2001, which involved the perpetration of mass terrorism by airport-entering, non-Latin American visa holders (some of whom violated those visas), border enforcement continues to focus mostly on Mexicans, Central Americans, and the southern border. Indeed, since 2005, there has been an unprecedented expansion in that region.

Legal and Policy Basis

Within this overall trajectory, a number of important laws, policies, and events merit discussion. Central Americans began to migrate to the United States in the 1970s, a flow that rapidly increased due to genocides, counterinsurgency campaigns, and revolutionary wars in the 1980s in that areas, as well as hurricanes, earthquakes, and widespread violence since that time. Haitians have fled similar conditions, whereas Cubans have fled an authoritarian government. U.S. asylum is not given for people fleeing violence, even with real fears of loss of life, but only for those with a specific fear of individual persecution. To put it differently, U.S. refugee policy has been characterized by a Cold War bias, granting asylum to those escaping communist governments, but ignoring the plight of other individuals and groups. Hence, the U.S. government in many cases has awarded asylum unequally, according to its foreign policy favorites and opponents. An example is the strikingly more generous arrangements for Cuban asylum than the comparable Haitian flow. Regional racism against Haitians in Florida has also

shaped federal enforcement policies. In this context, immigration enforcement has been deployed to limit access to asylum by catching, detaining, and removing masses of would-be refugees. In particular, south Texas has been used as an area to trap Central Americans who were caught coming through Mexico, at times forming a sort of open-air mass detention zone, whereas mass incarceration has been used against Haitians. Some legal and bureaucratic reforms were made in 1990, but the broad inequities and limitations in U.S. refugee policy have proven enduring.

Because of the effort to contain and expel would-be refugees, and because of the expansion of immigration enforcement more generally since the mid-1970s, the United States, from the 1980s to the present, has developed a large number of so-called detention centers (bureaucratic language for immigration prisons). These include both detention centers run directly by the government (Immigration and Customs Enforcement of the Department of Homeland Security) and private corporate prisons and rental spaces in local jails. They are often physically isolated and difficult for family, advocates, or lawyers to access, or even to find out basic information such as where a given person is being held. Health services have also been troubled, especially in private detention facilities. People are mostly held there mainly before they have been determined to be deportable, though some are held after final orders of deportation, while awaiting removal. This is because of the absence of and more recently limits on release while petitioning for asylum, as well as legal changes in 1996 described further on, that require many persons not yet brought to immigration hearings to be held without bond. This system has been termed an "American gulag" due to its vast size and hidden character.

In 1986, the Immigration Reform and Control Act (IRCA) was enacted into law. Among other provisions, this law for the first time made knowing employment of unauthorized workers itself an illegal act, so-called employer sanctions. Workplaces were available for government inspections and raids, and immigration officers could go into open fields and other open spaces that were private property. There was a long list of documents that employees could provide to employers to prove eligibility for employment. This approach quickly proved to be a major gap in the attempt to use employment as a control on unauthorized migration: workers soon learned how to acquire fraudulent documents, which employers were legally required to accept (to prevent arbitrary decisions and discrimination). To put it differently, employers were required to ask for documents but not to check their validity. At any rate, many employers "winked" at these sorts of arrangements—it gave them plausible deniability.

Furthermore, the government never devoted massive efforts at workplace enforcement the way it did for border interdiction, reflecting the enormous power and influence of the inequality between the business sector and would-be migrants at outer boundaries. While employment control has ebbed and flowed since 1986 (as described later), to the present it has not ever been a major part of U.S. immigration enforcement. For example, 2.7 million previously unauthorized migrants were legalized under IRCA, but there were no forward-looking provisions for increasing visas for low-skill workers and for Mexicans, Caribbeans, and Central Americans, the main sources of undocumented entrants. While IRCA was envisioned as a lasting solution to undocumented migration, this did not actually happen.

With respect to immigration enforcement, the period from 1986 to late 1993 was largely one of stasis, except for specific developments described previously. However, drug law enforcement, always a component of border enforcement, began to receive much greater levels of effort, technology, and funding, and the Immigration and Naturalization Service (INS), especially the Border Patrol and inspectors at ports of entry, was drawn more deeply into the so-called war on drugs. Drug interdiction opened the way for the U.S. military, both regular branches and the National Guard, to enter into border control activities and connect to civilian law enforcement activities and agencies. Military units supply intelligence, conduct surveillance, transfer technology, provide logistical and construction support, and periodically have operated in proximity to the Mexican border, but do not directly make arrests (this is forbidden to the military by the Posse Comitatus Act).

Militarization of the border goes beyond direct military involvement in border enforcement, to include counterinsurgency approaches to civilian policing, conceptualized as "low intensity warfare." Though the opening wedge has been drug interdiction, immigration has been the target of several National Guard call-ups and regular unit deployments in the 1990s and 2000s. Military involvement in civilian law enforcement, use of military arms and doctrines by civilian agencies, and the increased overlap between drug and immigration enforcement are troubling, because of the increased potential for violent force and diminished concern for human and civil rights.

The Immigration Act of 1990 reworked visa allocations and exclusion categories. It did not aspire, however, to resolve the basic enforcement dilemma of the United States, which is the mismatch between the work and family demands in this country and the numbers and kinds of legal immigrant visas. Instead, the United States returned to its long-standing "solution" of mass Mexican border enforcement, with the same frustrating lack of effectiveness. Historically, the Border Patrol operated a short distance back from the boundary. It used this spacing to circle around and arrest unauthorized entrants. The Border Patrol used high arrest rates to justify its budgets and mission. In late 1993, Silvestre Reyes, the chief patrol agent of the El Paso sector, relocated his officers directly up against the boundary, where their presence directly deterred many unauthorized crossers (Operation Blockade, later renamed Operation Hold the Line). With this tactic, reduced arrests came to be interpreted as a sign of success. The tactic, however, makes huge demands on the size of the workforce. It cannot be replicated outside of short segments in areas at or near main urban border crossings. The older, wide-ranging patrol tactics continued to be applied in rural small communities, farm and ranch areas, and open mountains and deserts.

This full frontal enforcement practice was replicated starting in 1994 in south San Diego County (Operation Gatekeeper), Douglas and Nogales, Arizona (Operation Safeguard), and areas of south Texas (Operation Rio Grande). Segments of border wall also were constructed. Relatively safe, relatively easy urban corridors were denied to migrants. But the main body of undocumented migrants (those who go long distances from interior Mexico/Central America to interior United States) were not deterred. They shifted to crossing points in remote areas of the border, especially Arizona. This situation involved considerably greater physical and climatic risks (overheating, freezing, thirst), and deaths in border crossing spiked, to around 400 per year (a conservative figure, since many deaths are unaccounted for). The crossing also required more skill, so the rate of use of smugglers greatly increased, from approximately 50 percent use to over 90 percent, and the price and likely profitability of smuggling also increased. Systematic surveys in Mexico found that with the help of smugglers, fewer migrants actually were contacted by U.S. authorities while crossing. Also, potential unauthorized migrants were not deterred from crossing by their awareness of ongoing U.S. enforcement, the cost of smugglers, or the risks of making the trip. The tactic likely has not been effective because the deterrence model of border control does not work for highly driven migrants.

The 1996 Illegal Immigration Reform and Immigrant Responsibility Act and the 1996 Antiterrorism and Effective Death Penalty Act increased and widened important penalties affecting migrants and drastically reduced discretion in their application. Among other components of these acts were considerable widening of the concept of deportable crimes, far beyond the standard meaning of aggravated felonies (e.g., crimes were categorized by maximum possible penalty rather than actual penalty, leading to deportation for some misdemeanors). Discretionary relief from deportation was largely eliminated, and appeals from the immigration courts (which are executive branch administrative tribunals, not judicial courts) to the federal courts were substantially reduced. Temporary and permanent bars to legal entry and migration were applied to persons previously removed from the United States, even if subsequently they had obtained the legal possibility of immigration (e.g., to reunite with family members). Release on bond before hearings was eliminated or greatly reduced. These acts rapidly amplified the detention and deportation activities of the U.S. government.

9/11 and After

The horrific attacks on 9/11 were done by a mix of holders of valid student and visitor visas and violators (overstays) of initially legal visas. No unauthorized border crossers were involved. After the attack, the immigration enforcement system was used against Islamic men in general. Men from Islamic majority countries were encouraged to register with the government, which many did to show their nonconnection with terrorism and their solidarity with the United States. Those people who had any immigration violation, some very narrow and technical, were held without bond and rapidly deported. (Ironically, would-be terrorists almost certainly did not register.) Other Muslim immigrants were also tracked and deported using the strong tools of federal law. A characteristic use of federal power was employing the unusual but important law enforcement provision for holding material witnesses likely to flee to seize individuals who are not witnesses to anything, hold them for substantial periods of time incommunicado, without arrest, bond, or proceedings, until they were moved into the deportation process or released without clear explanation.

The multiple failures leading up to September 11 also provided the political impetus for the creation of the Department of Homeland Security (DHS). Immigration and nonimmigrant entry functions affected by DHS include the breakup of the INS into three units in DHS. The border port functions (INS Inspections) were now combined with U.S. Customs; that and the Border Patrol were placed in Customs and Border Protection. Interior immigration policing (INS Investigations) and immigration Detention and Deportation were combined with interior customs enforcement into ICE. The legal immigration and naturalization processing segments were hived off into Citizenship and Immigration Services (however, nonimmigrant visas and some aspects of immigrant visas are still processed outside the United States by the Consular Service of the Department of State). More broadly, forming the DHS created a strong national security frame, in both practice and public meanings, over immigration, which in the past had not quite been so consistently cast as a matter of fundamental public survival.

As mentioned earlier, U.S. immigration enforcement has grown continuously and massively in terms of budget and labor force from 1994 to the present. During this period, however, there have been some interesting shifts in emphasis. The growth was largely devoted to the Mexican border from 1994 to 2001, due to the implementation of frontal enforcement operations described previously. From September 11, 2001, to 2005, the growth was slower, and it was dispersed more widely, including partial reallocations to the northern border and interior sites. In late 2005, however, a wave of emphatic anti-immigration politics swept over the Republican Party, which led to a renewed placement of rapidly expanding enforcement resources on the Mexican border. Systematic analysis of U.S. border security policy in the era of Al Qaeda and, more recently, the Islamic State (or ISIS), shows that the U.S. government has maintained its focus on labor and family migration from Latin America, via the Mexican border, and has largely not shifted its activities to focus on risks of terrorism.

One post-2005 initiative was a massive expansion of the southwestern border fence, which is also called a border wall (it is, in fact, a wall with some fence-like openings). Starting with about 70 miles of wall in 2005, it has grown to approximately 700 miles in the face of vigorous local opposition. The DHS overrode any other federal, state, and local laws and regulations in its construction. In addition, there has been a pilot system for electronic surveillance and targeting of enforcement units at the Mexican border. This has proven, so far, an expensive failure. The barrier and deterrence value of the physical wall is unknown, and the government does not claim that it will actually stop migrants, but rather will possibly slow them.

Another border initiative during this period, Operation Streamline, involves changes at some segments of the Mexican border. In the past, arrested migrants were usually offered voluntary departure, with no deportation record, or at most were put into the process for administrative deportation. In this new operation, such nonviolent arrestees were put into the federal criminal system and charged with EWI, filling federal prisons and courts with minor immigration offenders. It is not clear if the federal criminal justice and court system can sustain this program over time without large impacts on its other responsibilities.

From 2006 on, ICE increased its tempo of interior enforcement, especially arrests at homes. Other exemplary actions included a Danbury, Connecticut, case where an investigator pretended to be a contractor to entice unauthorized workers to their arrests. Although ostensibly aimed at deportable criminal aliens, many arrests were made opportunistically, such as noncriminals living in the same homes, apartment complexes, and neighborhoods. Safety against crime has provided important rhetorical cover for wider patterns of immigration expulsion. Systematic evidence shows that most arrested immigrants were not criminal aliens, and rules of entry, search, and seizure were commonly violated. More generally, formal deportation (with its effect of long-lasting or permanent bars to reentry) has increasingly been used, both in the interior and at the border, as opposed to earlier reliance on voluntary departure.

The introduction of employer sanctions, as well as the failure of these measures in the 1986 IRCA, is described earlier. In the face of flawed laws and emphatic business sector resistance, the level of effort at employer sanctions gradually dwindled in the 1990s. By the time of George W. Bush's administration from 2001 to 2005, employer sanctions enforcement efforts barely existed. With the anti-immigration political turn in late 2005, these enforcement efforts were revived. Workplace visits emphasized large visible raids over slow, systematic enforcement. Raids usually penalized immigrants, who were arrested and set up for deportation (and sometimes criminally charged also with using false identifications), but less often penalized employers, except for a small set of particularly abusive ones. These workplace raids are thus less employer sanctions than worker sanctions. In 2009 the Obama administration announced changes in which employment records (including identification documents) will be the focus of enforcement, rather than physical raids. This approach will reduce the controversial, visible enforcement actions, but may still lead to easily fired workers rather than penalizing businesses and managers. A centralized national identification database, accessed electronically, covering all persons (citizens as well as immigrants) may be the future of employment and movement control.

Since the late 19th century, immigration enforcement has been handled exclusively by the federal government. However, the 1996 Illegal Immigration Reform and Immigrant Responsibility Act deputized state and local law enforcement personnel to enforce immigration matters (the "287(g)" provision). State and local police also use various non-immigration stops and pretexts to identify suspected immigrants and detain them, often extra-legally, to turn them over to federal immigration officers. For many years, the INS (and then DHS) has checked state prisons and local jails for convicted criminals who are also immigrants (and, in some cases, persons who were not yet convicted of a crime). These individuals were then turned over for deportation (in the case of sentenced criminals, this was delayed until all or part of the sentence was finished). In 2009, the DHS began implementing Secure Communities, a standardized electronic check for the immigration status of everyone (convicted or not, low-or high-level charges) entering local jails. Prioritization of dangerous criminals has been poorly implemented. State and local enforcement of immigration laws has been criticized for inconsistent and inequitable application, racial-ethnic profiling, use against marginal and powerless communities, and disregard of constitutional processes and protections. Police chiefs have recommended against using state and local law enforcement agencies in immigration enforcement to maintain good relationships with immigrant communities (e.g., information gathering, crime reporting, and what is generally known as "community policing").

Conclusion

Enforcement of immigration laws as such cannot be directly equated to opposition to immigration in the wider social–political domain. Immigration laws vary according to wider social values, and any policy framework and set of laws and regulations would need to be enforced. Legal immigration, which allows many hundreds of thousands of people into the United States annually, also requires governmental implementation and enforcement. But the specific anti-immigrant politics of the period beginning in the late 1970s have found expression in a very massive policing apparatus, including hundreds of miles of border wall, 20,000 Border Patrol officers, huge interior workplace and home raids, and the so-called detention "gulag." It is a sign of a certain kind of value choice—subject to great struggles—in the contemporary United States. That massive enforcement apparatus also generates its own self-promoting and self-justifying set of bureaucratic

interests and an assiduous public relations apparatus that, in turn, affects American attitudes toward borders and immigrants. New controversies, such as fears about the Ebola virus entering the United States from abroad, continue to complicate the picture and make the issue of border protection ever subject to the ebb and flow of political tides.

See also Drug Policy and Politics; Immigration and Politics; Terrorism, Torture, and Politics.

Josiah McC. Heyman

Bibliography

Andreas, Andreas. 2001. *Border Games: Policing the U.S.-Mexico Divide*. Ithaca, NY: Cornell University Press.

Brotherton, David, and Philip Kretsedemas, eds. 2008. *Keeping Out the Other: A Critical Introduction to Immigration Enforcement Today*. New York: Columbia University Press.

Dow, Mark. 2004. *American Gulag: Inside U.S. Immigration Prisons*. Berkeley: University of California Press.

Dunn, Timothy J. 1996. *The Militarization of the U.S.-Mexico Border, 1978–1992: Low-Intensity Conflict Doctrine Comes Home*. Austin: CMAS Books, University of Texas at Austin.

Dunn, Timothy J. 2009. *Blockading the Border and Human Rights: The El Paso Operation That Remade Immigration Enforcement*. Austin: University of Texas Press.

Heyman, Josiah McC. 2008. "Constructing a Virtual Wall: Race and Citizenship in U.S.–Mexico Border Policing." *Journal of the Southwest* 50: 305–34.

Heyman, Josiah McC., and Jason Ackleson. 2009. "United States Border Security after September 11." In John Winterdyck and Kelly Sundberg, eds. *Border Security in the Al-Qaeda Era*. Boca Raton, FL: CRC Press, pp. 37–74.

Human Rights First. 2009. *U.S. Detention of Asylum Seekers: Seeking Protection, Finding Prison*. http://www.humanrightsfirst.org/wp-content/uploads/pdf/090429-RP-hrf-asylum-detention-report.pdf. Accessed May 16, 2014.

Human Rights Watch. 2009a. *Forced Apart (By the Numbers): Non-Citizens Deported Mostly for*

Nonviolent Offenses. www.hrw.org/sites/default /files/reports/us0409web_0.pdf. Accessed May 16, 2014.

Human Rights Watch. 2009b. *Locked Up Far Away: The Transfer of Immigrants to Remote Detention Centers in the United States*. www.hrw.org/sites /default/files/reports/us1209web.pdf. Accessed May 16, 2014.

Immigration Policy Center. http://www.immigration policy.org/. Accessed May 16, 2014.

Jimenez, Maria. 2009. *Humanitarian Crisis: Migrant Deaths at the U.S.-Mexico Border*. New York: American Civil Liberties Union. www.aclu.org /files/pdfs/immigrants/humanitariancrisisreport .pdf. Accessed May 16, 2014.

Kahn, Robert S. 1996. *Other People's Blood: U.S. Immigration Prisons in the Reagan Decade*. Boulder, CO: Westview Press.

Kenney, David Ngaruri, and Philip G. Schrag. 2008. *Asylum Denied: A Refugee's Struggle for Safety in America*. Berkeley: University of California Press.

Meissner, Dorris, and Donald Kerwin. 2009. *DHS and Immigration: Taking Stock and Correcting Course*. Washington, DC: Migration Policy Institute. www.migrationpolicy.org/pubs/DHS_Feb09 .pdf. Accessed May 16, 2014.

Migration Information Source Website. www.migra tioninformation.org. Accessed May 16, 2014.

Migration Policy Institute Website. http://www.migra tionpolicy.org/. Accessed May 16, 2014.

Payan, Tony. 2006. *The Three U.S.-Mexico Border Wars: Drugs, Immigration, and Homeland Security*. Westport, CT: Praeger Security International.

Pew Hispanic Center Website. pewhispanic.org. Accessed May 16, 2014.

U.S. Department of Homeland Security. 2013. "Immigration Statistics." www.dhs.gov/files/statistics /immigration.shtm. Accessed May 3, 2014.

BUDGET POLITICS

The U.S. budget process is enormous, arduously long, fraught with complexities, intentionally vague, and replete with politics every step of the way. When the budget battle begins anew, billions of dollars fly back and forth in a tug of war, settling wherever political clout is strongest. The budget process is determined by the constitutional principle of separation of powers, altered by laws, adjusted by various actors and intermittent crises, and implemented daily by millions of bureaucrats doling out money for the thousands of programs offered by the U.S. government.

Setting the Stage
The Players

The Constitution prescribes three branches of government: a bicameral legislature, a single elected executive, and an appointed national judiciary. Congress writes all of the laws and the budget is one of those laws. In the executive branch, the president signs the laws into action. Laws are then passed to the administrative arm of the executive branch: the cabinet departments and independent agencies. These offices carry out the policies and programs contained in the laws as indicated by legislative intent. There are two chambers in the Congress: the House of Representatives and the Senate. Within the executive branch there are 15 cabinet departments and at least 20 independent agencies, and of course each department or agency requires much money to operate the programs with which they are charged, programs such as Medicare, military systems, and Social Security.

Parties

Almost every member elected to Congress is a Democrat or a Republican. The party principle is all-important because it structures the leadership positions, the committees, the workflow, and, consequently, the size and structure of the budget.

Party is very influential in how the House and the Senate operate. Whichever party holds a majority of the seats in the chamber is the party that controls the committee assignments, the flow of legislation, and, thus, the outcome in that chamber. For example, if the Democrats have a majority of seats in the Senate, then at least 51 out of 100 seats are held by Democratic senators. In this example, the Senate's leadership will be headed by a Democrat and every committee in the Senate will have a majority of seats held by other Democratic senators. If a committee has 13 seats, for example, then at least 7 will be held by Democrats. If Republicans held a majority of seats in the Senate, then they would control the work flow, the committee assignments, and hold a majority of seats on every committee, and so on. The party in control in each chamber also elects, from among their members, the leader, called the majority leader. The party in the minority will also elect a minority leader. The two leaders assign members to committees in the spirit of cooperation, at least in theory. Usually, the upper hand belongs to the majority leader, who generally has enough political clout to schedule bills for discussion or a vote. The party principle works the same way in the House of Representatives. In many times throughout our history, one chamber of the Congress has held a majority of members of one party while the other chamber has a majority of the opposing party. When this division occurs, it is called "divided government."

Congress acts on an extremely wide variety of issues, and the budget reflects this breadth of responsibility. Each legislator hopes to be appointed to a committee that specializes in areas that will benefit the legislator's constituents. Reelection is never far from a legislator's mind. Given the breadth of legislators' responsibilities, there are approximately 276 committees, total, in the House and the Senate. To allow for specialization and to divide the workload, each representative and each senator serves on several committees.

The two parties' leaders will usually cooperate on committee assignments and workflow because the current majority leader realizes that if he or she does not cooperate at least in part with the minority leadership, then when or if the majority party becomes the minority they will likely not receive any cooperation either. Turnabout is fair play. Because every committee is controlled by the party that has a majority of seats in that chamber, legislation offered for consideration by minority legislators, including budget proposals, has a narrow chance of being acted upon by the majority party person in charge of the committee because politics usually rules. Each party seeks to get its proposals funded and enacted into the budget so that favors can be returned to the constituents who voted them in. In

so doing, each legislator "brings home the bacon" to his or her home district.

The Process

The Budget and Accounting Act of 1921 created the "executive centered" budget process, which means that the president coordinates his desired programs with the department and agency heads, forms a proposed budget, and then sends the proposed budget to Congress early in February. Within the Executive Office of the President is the Office of Management and Budget (OMB), which coordinates the departments' and agencies' budget requests over an 18-month time period. OMB's job is to assist the departments and agencies in building their requests for the upcoming fiscal year. OMB reviews their requests for efficiency, effectiveness, and congruence with the president's policies, the current political climate, and, sometimes, revenue availability. During this reconciling of executive branch interests, liaisons between the executive and legislative branches occur so that no one in Congress is truly surprised when the president's budget proposal arrives there in February.

When the leaders of each party in each house of Congress receive the president's budget, they begin their formal work on the budget by voting on a budget ceiling, that is, an expenditure limit for the coming fiscal year. This preliminary work is called a "budget resolution" that usually occurs a couple of months after Congress receives the president's proposal. Several laws structure the budget cycle inside of Congress and, according to those laws, Congress should pass a budget resolution by April 15. In both the House and the Senate there are substantive committees whose purpose is to deliberate legislation and appropriate money for the various programs. Each chamber's leadership divides the budget into subject areas such as education, health, and transportation and sends a proposal for that subject area of the budget to the committee that has jurisdiction for that subject. For example, a budget proposal about a highway program goes to the transportation committee and a school program proposal goes to the education committee. Each committee is tasked with deciding what programs are needed and how much should be spent on them, weighing and sifting the various needs and wants of the country, and, usually, considering the president's requests. By June 30, each committee in Congress is supposed to pass an appropriation bill that outlines these preferences for the many programs under its jurisdictions. It is rare that either chamber of Congress or either party completes all appropriation bills by June 30, before its July 4 recess. Generally, each chamber of Congress *eventually* passes its spending bills, and the two chambers try to negotiate their differences. It is also rare that the appropriations bills from the House of Representatives' committees will be identical to those of the Senate's committees and, when this happens, a conference committee must be convened. While the congressional committees are deliberating the fate of a huge variety of expenditure bills, the Congressional Budget Office (CBO) assists legislators by researching facts and data about those very same programs in those bills. Also, it is typically budget time when the thousands of lobbyists descend on Capitol Hill carrying information considered vital to their cause. Vocal public groups also take part by speaking out and calling attention to a wide variety of budget issues.

A conference committee is drawn from influential and expert members of each chamber, but politics also plays a big role in this committee both in its creation

Glossary of Budget Politics

appropriations bill: a substantive piece of legislation that spells out exactly what is to be spent on program X, Y, or Z.

"bringing home the bacon": a term for pork-barrel politics; both parties seek to enact programs to help their constituents' interests.

budget deficit: a "gap" between government expenditures and revenues; also, any underfunded obligation, or spending that exceeds budgeted amounts (and is not covered by revenues).

budget resolution: a spending ceiling for a subject area of the budget that is set by one or more committees in the House of Representatives.

conference committee: a joint committee comprising members of both the Senate and the House, organized to resolve differences between the two chambers' versions of a particular bill—in this case, a budget bill.

Congressional Budget Office (CBO): the legislative counterpart to the Office of Management and Budget (OMB); it is a powerhouse of intellectual talent.

debt ceiling: an agreed-to limit on the amount of debt that the U.S. Treasury can issue.

divided government: split party control of the two houses of Congress; it is both a result and a symptom of the political use of the natural differences of opinion found among people in every society.

fiscal year: a 365-day budget time period; the U.S. fiscal year begins October 1 and ends on September 30 of the following year.

Gramm-Rudman-Hollings (GRH) Act: a law passed in 1985 to sequester, or automatically cut, certain expenditures if a spending limit is exceeded; in practice, so many items were excepted from the law that GRH was rendered ineffective.

national debt: the total amount owed by the U.S. government.

Office of Management and Budget (OMB): an office within the Executive Office of the President that coordinates budget requests by the various cabinet departments and agencies and examines them in terms of the president's policies and priorities.

sequester: an automatic reduction in spending that takes effect at some predetermined time or under a specific condition.

and in its operation. For an appropriations bill to pass, a majority of the conference committee must vote for the bill. Majority rule is a major operating principle in the U.S. Congress and all of its committees. Assuming that the conference committee can agree on the wording of the bill and the funding level, the conference committee will pass the compromise appropriation bill by a majority and then the bill must go back through each chamber and be passed by a majority of the legislators in that chamber, again, or it is dead. Considering all the different subject-matter appropriations bills, one can see how terribly complex this weighing and sifting process can become. If both chambers of Congress can complete their work, pass all of their appropriations bills by the early deadline of August 30, the "budget package" then proceeds to the president's desk for him to sign. This is the ideal case, but it rarely happens so neatly.

Politics Rules

If the budget players and the budget process form the framework of budgeting, then politics in the ordinary sense hangs on that framework like little grenades waiting to explode. Divided government, presidential scandals, debt ceiling arguments, the cost of borrowing, lobbyists, media hype, domestic crises, and public apathy all have played their hand in contorting and politicizing our budget process.

The Decline of Compromise

Steadily, from the 1960s onward, conflict over the budget process grew. Partisan battles over entitlements and spending made new enemies. In earlier days those battles were resolved through compromise, perhaps in backrooms, but resolved nonetheless. Yet as Lyndon Johnson's Great Society Programs were passed, party members became entrenched, less willing to compromise. Between 1970 and 2014, the United States operated under divided government more than half the time. When this situation occurs, one house, dominated by one party, can stop the legislation of the other party dead in its tracks simply by refusing to send bills to committee or bring them to the floor for a vote. This intransigence retards the entire budget process.

While it is still possible to come to the table and strike deals over controversial legislation in the budget, as the 20th century wore on, fewer and fewer budget bills were passed on time in a proper fashion. Partisanship raged in the 1970s amid the Nixon presidency, the Watergate scandal, and subsequent inflation and gas rationing. By the time Jimmy Carter became president in 1977, inflation was 20 percent. During his reelection campaign in 1980, Carter was besieged by the Iranian hostage crisis. Although Carter presented budget problems in a logical and ordered way, the unresolved hostage crisis politicized the budget process and Carter was unable to tame the debt; instead of cutting the budget as the president had proposed, the government was forced to borrow even more funds at a higher rate.

Ronald Reagan's success at resolving the hostage crisis gained him popularity in Congress, which was now firmly held by the Republican Party. After the attempt on Reagan's life in March 1981, Congress rode the president's popular coattails and passed an even larger budget than Carter's; it included the largest military buildup since World War II. However, the dark side of the buildup was $4 trillion in new debt incurred by the government in the 1980s. Budget deficits grew again, but the public approved of the enhanced protection it perceived by means of the defense budget. When the budget deficits grew too large, numerous reforms were passed, such as the Gramm-Rudman-Hollings Act of 1985. Intended as a budget-balancing measure, this law, unfortunately, had little or no effect. Thus, although George H.W. Bush came into office on a pledge of "no new taxes," the deficit grew to several hundred billion dollars under him and Bush ended up breaking his promise, raising both the income tax and capital gains rates. Bill Clinton was the benefactor of the technology boom that brought in more income tax dollars and brought the deficit down substantially. However, by the fall of 1995, when the next fiscal year budget was due, Democrat Clinton and Republican House Speaker Newt Gingrich found themselves at odds. For the first time in history the U.S. federal government shut down for several days, doing so amid a political spectacle not outdone by any soap opera. Bowing to public pressure to compromise, Clinton and Gingrich finally agreed to disagree but moved forward over domestic versus military spending in the

1996 budget, and the government reopened. When the scandal over Monica Lewinsky broke in 1998, Clinton found himself once again at odds with a Republican Congress—this time, involving impeachment. The budget process suffered under the weight of the decline in congressional collegiality.

Shortly after George W. Bush became president in 2001, September 11 forced some major changes to the budget, and, temporarily, partisan politics subsided as the nation came together to face the disaster. By 2003, when it became apparent that the United States would invade Iraq and had already sent troops into Afghanistan, budget politics again became conflictual, and both budget deficits and the national debt rose precipitously. By the time Barack Obama assumed office in 2008, the United States was fullbore into a major financial crisis, to which the answer was a government bailout of the auto industry, banks, and financial firms, all to the detriment of the American taxpayer. About $3.8 trillion was expended in this bailout amid intense partisan political battles. Deficits grew and the debt rose. Between 2008 and 2014, several debt crises permeated any talk of restoring the budget to balance or rationality as civil service workers' pensions were raided and replaced with IOUs to close a temporary cash-flow gap. Severe partisan wrangling was a constant media theme, leaving the public to believe that argumentation was the way the Congress and the administration normally worked.

Outside Influences

Media Hype

The media plays a tremendous role in the budget debates and its history. C-SPAN shows the houses of Congress in action but few people watch, instead relying on incomplete and sensationalized sound bites from the network and cable channels. Hearing of stalemates and incessant nastiness, the public tunes out of the reality of the debate over spending and deficit control. An apathetic public is not an informed public. Thomas Jefferson said, "The price of democracy is vigilance." The public must be informed to be vigilant, but the average American knows little or nothing about the U.S. financial status except that the deficit and debt are large, the parties are fighting each other, and nothing is getting done. Polls from major survey organizations repeatedly indicate a very low level of public knowledge about the budget situation. Part of the fault lies with a media that seeks ever higher ratings. As private corporations, their shareholders demand profitability, and high ratings drive more advertising revenue, which in turn drives profits.

True news is available for the individual who seeks it. The website of the Treasury and the website of the Federal Reserve (which is a private corporation, not part of the U.S. government) each have abundant educational materials, including the budget, historical tables, explanatory notes, and other pertinent information. Though many are increasingly dependent on this technology, many prefer not to take time to read lengthy, complicated documents, as the polls reflect. The public is not maintaining its vigilance.

Lobbying

Another factor in the budget mess is the inordinate level of lobbying that takes places in the halls of each chamber and in congressional offices. There are over 40,000 registered lobbyists in Congress. Lobbying consists of gaining access to lawmakers, with the specific intent to persuade a legislator to push for a desired bill in his or her chamber of Congress. Lobbyists are inherently one-sided and frequently come carrying a partisan or ideological bent. Many are hired by large corporations, entire industries, or foreign governments or companies wishing to do business with the United States. Their tactics range from direct appeals, masses of data, gifts (which are regulated by law), criticism, threats, or the promise that the "other side" (usually the other party in the chamber) will take up its fight and work against them if they do not cooperate now. Sometimes, money trades hands. With the advent of the 2010 U.S. Supreme Court decision *Citizens United v. the Federal Election Commission*, the limit on the amount that unions and corporations could spend in helping their candidates get elected was removed, thus throwing open the floodgates to unfettered financial influence of lobbyists and political action committees.

Conclusion

Unfortunately divided government seems to be a new normal for the U.S. budget process; moreover, Congress can be full of relatively pig-headed personalities. Generally, both Democrats and Republicans try to outdo each other in their attempts to demonize the other party and exalt their own party's efforts. This antagonism slows down the budget process because time is spent pointing out the other party's budget faults instead of working together on a compromise position. In addition, the complexity of the process stymies even the most astute observer from getting a clear understanding of what is happening, but when one adds politics and games to the mix, it is impossible to know the players without a score card.

Congress knows the general public is unaware and uninformed and that only a small minority is intensely interested. While many in Congress and in presidential administrations are well-intentioned, diligent hard-working public servants, those who are not have derailed the budget process and made an already difficult process needlessly worse. The framers of the U.S. government warned people about the dangers of what they termed "factions" as instruments to divide rather than to unite. Unfortunately, their fears have been proved in nearly every Congress over the past 100 plus years. If the process is to be righted and our course made truer, legislators, the media, and the public must reawaken, take up their essential role in a democratic republic, and get their respective jobs done.

See also Banking Policy and Politics; Bureaucracy and American Political Culture; Congress and Congressional Politics; Debt, Deficit, and Politics; Economic Policy and Politics; Interest Groups and Lobbying; Partisanship and Polarization; Tax Policy and Politics.

Barbara L. Neuby

Bibliography

Budget of the United States. 2014. http://www.white house.gov/omb/budget. Accessed February 5, 2014.

Gallup Organization. 2014. "Gallup Politics." http://www.gallup.com/poll/167816/congress-low-job-approval-persists.aspx. Accessed March 10, 2014.

Ippolito, Dennis. 2013. *Deficits, Debt and the Politics of Tax Policy*. New York: Cambridge University Press.

Kettl, Donald F., and James W. Fesler. 2005. *The Politics of the Administrative Process*. Washington, DC: Congressional Quarterly Press.

Lee, Johnson, and Joyce Lee. 2013. *Public Budgeting Systems*. Sudbury, MA: Jones and Bartlett.

Rubin, Irene S. 2000. *The Politics of Public Budgeting*. New York: Chatham House Publishers.

Rubin, Irene S. 2003. *Balancing the Federal Budget*. New York: Chatham House Publishers.

Wildavsky, Aaron. 1992. *The New Politics of the Budgetary Process*. New York: HarperCollins.

Williams, John. 2014. Shadowstats.com. Accessed January 24, 2014.

BUREAUCRACY AND AMERICAN POLITICAL CULTURE

A bureaucracy is a type of organizational system that strives to coordinate the activities of large numbers of people to achieve a common objective. To qualify as a bureaucracy, an organization must possess several basic characteristics. Five of the most commonly identified bureaucratic traits are (1) clearly defined objectives; (2) a division of labor; (3) a formal structure tying together the various component parts of the organizations; (4) a set of procedures guiding organizational activity; and (5) specialized training, expertise, and experience.

First, bureaucratic organizations represent highly rationalized organizational forms (Weber 1958). They are established to address specific problems and achieve clearly articulated goals (Wilson 1989). As a result, the roles and responsibilities of bureaucratic agencies should be widely known, and the operations that guide bureaucratic actions should be explicitly stated.

Second, there is a straightforward division of labor within bureaucratic organizations. Each person who works in a bureaucracy cannot possibly perform all of the organization's tasks. Instead, each bureaucratic employee is assigned to a particular operation or function, enabling him or her to concentrate his or her efforts and develop high levels of expertise in his or her respective areas of activity. This division of labor also allows the entire bureaucratic organization to carry out relatively complex tasks in a rational, efficient manner.

Third, there must be an identifiable structural framework that links together all of the specialized units and operations within the organization. Several different types of bureaucratic structures have been identified. At the one extreme, there is the centralized, hierarchical pattern that is often identified as the hallmark of the classical bureaucracy (Gulick and Urwick 1937; Taylor 1911; Weber 1958). Here, a definite chain of command exists throughout the entire organization that produces a fairly rigid, vertical bureaucratic structure where decisions are made at the top and implemented by lower-level officials. At the other extreme, there are bureaucracies that have a more flexible, decentralized, horizontal form where power, control, and responsibility are dispersed throughout the organization. Top-level officials are still leaders, but they coordinate rather than direct organizational activity. Lower-level bureaucrats do not simply follow orders; instead, they are directly involved in organizational decision making (Barzelay 1992; Wilson 1989).

Fourth, a bureaucracy operates on the basis of established policies and the formalization of rules (Rourke 1984). These policies and guidelines are codified into a set of standard operating procedures(SOPs). SOPs facilitate the coordination of tasks within a bureaucracy. By clearly assigning responsibilities to administrative units and personnel, SOPs reduce redundancy and minimize the duplication of organizational efforts. SOPs also allow organizations to treat similar cases in a uniform, expedient manner, thereby reducing favoritism and inequitable treatment across different situations.

Finally, specialization, expertise, and experience are key components of modern bureaucratic organizations (Rourke 1984). Bureaucratic expertise stems from the concentrated attention that organizations give to particular problems and circumstances. Bureaucratic expertise also flows from the training, experiences, and skills of those who work in the organization. Each bureaucratic unit should be staffed by personnel with the requisite backgrounds, experiences, and capabilities to perform their preassigned tasks.

The preceding five characteristics define an "ideal" bureaucracy. In reality, no organization fully conforms to this description (Goodsell 2004). But many organizational structures possess most or all of these characteristics, and they clearly adhere to a common set of norms (Downs 1967). These norms provide guidance for individual and organizational activity. Moreover, they produce a form of administrative behavior that is quite unique and distinctive. It is this organizational behavior that sets bureaucratic institutions apart from all others.

Bureaucracies are involved in a wide array of activities in contemporary societies. This involvement is due to their ability to provide services, distribute benefits, and administer programs in an expeditious and effective manner. Therefore, they exist in almost all areas of the private sector (e.g., the production of automobiles, the distribution of telecommunication services, the development of food supplies, the marketing of clothing and other goods). They are prevalent in the nonprofit arena as well. Many humanitarian organizations, religious groups, and social services agencies qualify as bureaucracies administering programs within and across societies.

But the term "bureaucracy" is often used to describe *governmental* organizations. And many governmental organizations do fit the description of a bureaucracy: they are structured in such a way as to coordinate the activities of large numbers of people, who are all working to address a common problem or condition. And when most Americans think of a bureaucracy, they are often referring to the governmental organizations that exist in the public sector. Consequently, it is important to look at the governmental bureaucracies that exist in the United States.

The American Governmental Bureaucracy

The U.S. governmental bureaucracy is not one single organization. Instead, it is composed of numerous departments, divisions, agencies, bureaus, and offices that are spread across different levels of government. At the national level, there are over 2,000 units that comprise the federal bureaucracy with almost 3 million civilian, full-time employees. To comprehend the scope and operations of this bureaucratic activity, the federal bureaucracy is usually broken down into three groups: cabinet departments, government corporations, and regulatory agencies.

Cabinet departments are officially created by the U.S. Congress based on recommendations of the president. Currently, there are 15 cabinet departments that are responsible for guiding governmental activity in their respective policy areas. For example, the Department of Commerce is charged with promoting the economic growth of the country, while the Department of Energy helps develop and regulate the nation's energy resources. Some of these departments have existed since the beginning of the American republic (i.e., the Departments of State, Treasury, and Justice were created in 1789), while others were created fairly recently (e.g., the Department of Homeland Security, the newest federal cabinet department, was established in 2002). The size of these departments is also quite variable; the Department of Defense is the largest, with about 730,000 employees, while the Department of Education ranks as one of the smallest, with around 4,000 employees.

The federal bureaucracy is also made up of independent agencies, government corporations, and regulatory bureaus. These agencies have been created because their functions do not fit within the jurisdiction of existing executive departments (e.g., the National Aeronautics and Space Administration) or when there is a desire to remove an agency's activities from political pressure (e.g., the Environmental Protection Agency [EPA] and the Federal Reserve Board). These agencies, like cabinet departments, are created through the official actions of the U.S. Congress. However, as their name implies, independent agencies are able to operate with more independence than other bureaucratic departments, and many of them possess a broad set of powers with the ability to make policy decisions in their respective policy areas, implement those decisions, and then adjudicate any disputes that arrive over their actions. Currently, there are approximately 60 independent agencies and bureaus in the federal government.

Government corporations are created to perform specific operations, similar to private-sector business organizations. For example, AMTRAK (the National Railroad Passenger Corporation) provides passenger rail service and the Federal Deposit Insurance Corporation guarantees the financial deposits of American citizens. Like cabinet departments and independent agencies, government corporations are created by the U.S. Congress. However, government corporations function more as private companies with less legislative oversight.

Regulatory agencies establish administrative standards and procedures to ensure that the safety and well-being of the public is protected. These agencies cover a fairly broad set of activities, from regulating the quality of food that is produced to the disposal of nuclear waste materials. Some of the most well-known units of the federal bureaucracy are regulatory agencies, including the EPA, the Food and Drug Administration, the Interstate Commerce Commission, the Army Corps of Engineers, the Equal Employment Opportunity Commission, and the Federal Aviation Administration.

In addition to cabinet departments, government corporations, and regulatory agencies, the federal bureaucracy is made up of a set of offices that report directly to the president. These units were established in 1939 as part of the Executive Office of the President (EOP). The offices within the EOP assist the president in performing executive responsibilities. They have been created to strengthen the president's ability to coordinate and exert influence over the activities of other executive agencies. One of the main units within the EOP is the White House Office, which provides managerial assistance as well as policy advice to the president. The Office of Management and Budget (OMB) is another important unit within the EOP. The OMB prepares the federal budget for the president, oversees the financial activities of the executive branch, and evaluates the performance of executive agencies. Other units within the EOP provide advice to the president on specific policy issues, such as matters of national security (the National Security Council), the economy (the Council of Economic Advisers), and the environment (the Council on Environmental Quality).

At the state and local governmental levels, the bureaucracy is also composed of a myriad of departments, divisions, agencies, and offices. Many subnational bureaucracies are designed in a similar fashion to the federal bureaucracy: they are organized around a set of cabinet departments that have the responsibility for administering programs within respective policy areas. Yet, there is also quite a bit of variability in the number and type of bureaucracies that exist in state and local governmental jurisdictions. In addition, the power that chief executives and legislative bodies have over these bureaucracies also varies across the nation. In some states and cities, governors and mayors exert a great deal of influence over bureaucratic operations; however, in other state and local governments, chief executives have very little influence over what bureaucratic agencies do.

Bureaucrats

The individuals who work in governmental organizations are often referred to as "bureaucrats." These individuals are recruited, hired, and promoted because of their qualifications, experiences, and expertise. This enables them to perform their organizational responsibilities in a straightforward, more competent manner. Because bureaucracies are responsible for a variety of tasks, the individuals who work in bureaucratic organizations come from a wide cross section of society. There are highly educated professionals (i.e., lawyers, doctors, engineers, and scientists) as well as individuals who provide more basic, but still extremely important organizational functions (e.g., maintenance workers, custodial staff, and security supervisors).

About one in six Americans work in the government bureaucracy, which represents about 14 percent of the total labor force. The number of bureaucrats has increased over time. About 8.8 million people were employed in government bureaucratic agencies at the national, state, and local levels in 1960. That number increased to 16 million in 1980 and then to 20 million in 2000. By 2012, about 22 million Americans worked in the government bureaucracy (excluding military personnel). The growing number of state and local bureaucrats has been primarily responsible for this increase. For example, 6.4 million people worked in state and local government agencies in 1960, and

the number doubled to 13 million in 1980 and then increased to 19.2 million by 2012. Across this same time period, the size of the federal government's workforce increased much more modestly, growing from 2.4 million employees in 1960 to 3.1 million in 1990. The number of federal government employees even declined to 2.8 million in 2012.

In the United States, most public-sector bureaucrats are recruited through a competitive, merit-based selection process. This system was established with the passage of the Pendleton Civil Service Reform Act in 1983. The Pendleton Act changed the employment practices and procedures of the federal government. It eliminated the previous "spoils" system that focused on personal attributes and political connections, and it established a process where individuals were to be hired and promoted based on their expertise and qualifications. This system aims to promote political neutrality and enhances bureaucratic competency within government agencies. The merit system process is now a common feature of public employment across the U.S. bureaucratic system, spreading from the national level to state and local government agencies.

However, not all bureaucrats working in public agencies in the United States fall under these merit system principles and guidelines. A small percentage of public employees are political appointees. For example, cabinet secretaries and some assistant secretaries of executive departments in the federal bureaucracy are nominated by the president, subject to Senate confirmation. Individuals are recruited to fill these positions because of their special expertise and unique qualifications or because of long-standing relationships with political leaders. At the national level, the number of political appointees has grown as presidents try to exert influence over an ever-expanding bureaucratic system that has become difficult to manage and control.

In terms of the socio-demographic characteristics, the U.S. bureaucracy is now quite representative of the nation's population as a whole. The average age of employees in the federal government is 47 years, where the median age of the U.S. population is 37 years. About 44 percent of federal employees have attained bachelor's or advanced degrees (or equivalent types of higher education), compared to 27 percent in the total U.S. population. Women represent about 44 percent of all federal employees, with African Americans and Hispanics/Latinos comprising 17.5 percent and 7.7 percent, respectively. At the state and local levels, 45.8 percent of all public employees are women, 19 percent are African Americans, and 10 percent are Hispanics. Again, this matches quite closely the socio-demographic composition of the U.S. population: about 51 percent of the Americans are females, 13 percent are African Americans, and 16 percent are Hispanics (U.S. Census Bureau 2011, 2013).

The Role of the Bureaucracy in American Politics

In the American political system, governmental bureaucracies are the main administrators of public policies. They have the primary responsibility for making sure that governmental programs are actually put into place. Even though legislative bodies are the official law-making bodies, they do not have the ability to implement their own decisions. And public policies are not self-executing. Therefore, this task falls to bureaucratic organizations. Moreover, in the process of implementing policies, bureaucratic agencies are often in a position of deciding who or what the policy affects, as well as the rewards or penalties that should be dispensed. Thus, they are also able to make policy decisions, particularly in areas where they have more discretionary authority and greater expertise (Lowi 1969).

However, not all bureaucratic agencies have the same impact on the policy-making process. The level of political and public support that agencies have is an important factor in this respect, as is the degree of organizational cohesion and administrative leadership that they possess. In addition, bureaucratic influence varies by the agency's area of policy responsibility (Meier and Bothe 2007). For example, agencies in charge of implementing policies that provide benefits broadly across society (e.g., determining the support for farmers) generally have more discretion, because legislation dealing with these policies tends to be stated less precisely. This gives bureaucratic organizations that operate in these policy areas more leeway

and discretion to shape the development of public programs.

In addition, the influence of any particular agency on policy making is also dependent on the activities of *other* bureaucratic organizations that operate in the same policy area. Program implementation often involves coordination and cooperation of multiple bureaucratic agencies, across and within levels of governments. A specific bureaucratic organization may be designated as the lead agency for administering a public program. But the successful implementation of the program rests on an agency's ability to work closely with other bureaucratic units that are involved in the development of similar programs. In addition, bureaucratic units must also be able to maintain the support of legislative bodies (through budgetary allocations and statutory authorizations), as well as the scrutiny of their actions in the judicial system. Bureaucratic agencies are not autonomous, all-powerful actors in the political system that are able to operate in isolation from other organizations and actors.

Checks on Bureaucratic Influence

The bureaucracy is expected to respond to other political institutions, including chief executives, legislatures, and the courts. Therefore, these political institutions and elected politicians have several tools to influence and constrain bureaucratic behavior and to prevent the bureaucracy's abuse of power.

The president, as the nation's chief executive, has several ways to control bureaucratic power. Presidents can appoint bureau chiefs who are in line with their own political ideologies, they can recommend the reorganization of the federal bureaucracy to give greater or less power to agencies in charge of particular programs, and they can influence the budgetary allocations that agencies receive to implement programs. Governors, mayors, and city/county mangers use similar measures—appointment, reorganization, and budgetary mechanisms—to control bureaucratic actions at the state and local levels of government.

Legislative officials can constrain bureaucratic power through statutes, expenditure appropriations, and legislative oversight activities. For example, clearly stated laws and strictly worded program requirements give bureaucrats less leeway to shape policies. Legislatures also can reward or sanction agency behavior by increasing, decreasing, or even eliminating the financial resources needed to administer programs. Investigations and oversight activities provide another way to exert constraints or checks on bureaucratic behavior. Legislative committees and subcommittees oversee agency activities and gather information about the operation of programs under their jurisdiction by holding hearings, requesting reports, and informally communicating with agency officials. And legislative bodies are responsible for creating bureaucratic agencies, and they can terminate bureaucratic agencies if they feel the agencies are not doing what they should be doing. These are powerful weapons that could be used to limit bureaucratic authority.

The courts can also affect administrative activity by interpreting or reinterpreting the meaning of laws. They can also overrule bureaucratic decisions and actions. Thus, the courts have the ability to define the scope and impact of bureaucratic operations.

However, these external checks on bureaucratic power are, in reality, often quite limited. Elected officials are incapable of monitoring bureaucratic activity in all circumstances, for prolonged periods. They are restrained by the amount of time they can devote to bureaucratic oversight, their level of expertise relative to that of bureaucrats, and the difficulty of obtaining relevant and timely information about agency performance. Similarly, the ability of the courts to check bureaucratic activity is also constrained. The courts do not identify or solicit cases of bureaucratic abuse or noncompliance on their own. Instead, their check on bureaucratic power occurs when political institutions, organized groups, and individual citizens bring the issues to them.

There are, however, internal checks on the behavior and actions of bureaucracies that come from within the bureaucracy itself. Professional norms develop within bureaucratic organizations about how they should operate and the mechanisms that they should use to handle policy problems. In addition, bureaucrats are influenced by their personal values and orientations about ethical and appropriate ways of performing their responsibilities. These internal checks can provide important restraints on the actions of bureaucratic agencies.

Perceptions of Government Bureaucracy

The bureaucracy is often depicted quite negatively in American politics. The media describe bureaucracies as wasteful, unproductive, inefficient, and unresponsive. Presidents and other chief executives lament that they are unable to get bureaucratic agencies to act swiftly or smoothly. Legislators blame the public bureaucracy for program failures and policy breakdowns. Business leaders complain about the restrictions and inefficiencies of government regulations.

The American public also has a fairly negative image of the bureaucracy and of the government employees who work in bureaucratic agencies. Most Americans say they have little confidence in the ability of the bureaucracy to perform its responsibilities. They criticize bureaucratic agencies for their excessive paperwork and "red tape," and they dislike the "uncaring," inattentive attitudes that bureaucrats may exhibit when they administer programs (Hill 1992). A clear majority of the American public thinks that government bureaucrats cannot be trusted to do what is best for the country (NORC 2014).

However, public beliefs about the bureaucracy are much more complex than this when they are examined more closely (Goodsell 2004). The American public has more favorable attitudes about specific public agencies compared to its impressions of government bureaucracies in general. For example, a 2013 Pew Research Center survey reported that a majority of the American public say that they are frustrated with the federal government as a whole, but they have much more favorable attitudes toward specific federal departments and agencies (Pew Research Center 2013).

In addition, the American public wants the bureaucracy to be responsive to its needs and administer programs efficiently (Meier and Bothe 2007). Bureaucrats should not be biased or unduly influenced by special interests when they implement public policies. To achieve this goal, bureaucrats try to follow legislative guidelines, existing administrative policies, and SOPs. When they do exercise discretion, bureaucrats should use their professional judgment based on the norms of procedural fairness and equal treatment. However, some bureaucratic agencies are expected to be particularly attentive to certain groups and interests. For example, the Department of Agriculture should be responsive to the needs of farmers, and the Veterans Administration should address problems and concerns of those who have served in the military. Although it is important for public agents to listen to their clientele groups and respond to their needs, this situation can be a problem for bureaucratic organizations if they are overly attuned to these interests, ignoring the concerns of the general population.

The public also expects bureaucrats to possess the skills, knowledge, expertise, and ability to carry out their designated responsibilities in an effective and efficient manner (Meierand Bothe 2007). They should be able to implement programs to achieve policy objectives. But it is difficult to determine whether the bureaucracy is effective or efficient. Policy goals are often vague and indeterminate, and there are no other organizations that provide the same type of goods and services. So, it is extremely difficult to evaluate their performance and compare their actions to those of organizations in the private or nonprofit sectors.

The Importance of the Bureaucracy

The American public has more contact with the bureaucracy than with any other component of government. Public bureaucracies regulate the water that we drink and the food that we eat. Social service agencies distribute cash and noncash services to help stabilize our economic situations or offset periods of fiscal distress. Police units protect us from the harmful actions and behaviors of others; fire departments provide critical assistance so that we can get through extremely stressful, emergency situations. Indeed, a myriad of federal, state, and local bureaucratic organizations help guide us through our daily routines, shaping our actions and delivering needed services and benefits. In fact, it is difficult (perhaps even impossible) for the general public to avoid bureaucrats and bureaucratic organizations. Bureaucracies are integral components of modern-day societies and key actors in the contemporary public policy-making process.

See also Budget Politics; Federalism; Privatization and Deregulation; Public–Private Partnerships.

Saundra K. Schneider and Seoyoun Choi

Bibliography

Barzelay, Michael. 1992. *Breaking through Bureaucracy: A New Vision for Managing in Government*. Berkeley: University of California Press.

Downs, Anthony. 1967. *Inside Bureaucracy*. Boston: Little Brown, and Company. (Reissued by Waveland Press, Prospects Heights, IL, 1994).

Goodsell, Charles T. 2004. *The Case for Bureaucracy: A Public Administration Polemic*. 4th ed. Washington, DC: CQ Press.

Gulick, Luther, and L. Urwick. 1937. *Papers on the Science of Administration*. New York: Institute of Public Administration.

Hill, Larry B. 1992. "Taking Bureaucracy Seriously." In Larry B. Hill, ed. *The State of Public Bureaucracy*. Armonk, NY: M.E. Sharpe, pp. 15–58.

Lowi, Theodore. 1969. *The End of Liberalism*. New York: Norton.

Meier, Kenneth J., and John Bothe. 2007. *Politics and the Bureaucracy: Policymaking in the Fourth Branch of Government*. 5th ed. Belmont, CA: Thomson/Wadsworth.

NORC. General Social Survey. 2014. http://www.norc.org/Research/Projects/Pages/general-social-survey.aspx. Accessed October 26, 2014.

Pew Research Center. 2013. "Trust in Government Nears Record Low, but Most Federal Agencies Are Viewed Favorably." October 18. http://www.people-press.org/2013/10/18/trust-in-government-nears-record-low-but-most-federal-agencies-are-viewed-favorably/. Accessed April 15, 2014.

Rosenbloom, David H., Robert S. Kravchuk, and Richard M. Clerkin. 2008. *Public Administration: Understanding Management, Politics, and Law in the Public Sector*. 7th ed. Boston: McGraw-Hill.

Rourke, Francis E. 1984. *Bureaucracy, Politics, and Public Policy*. 3rd ed. Boston, MA: Little, Brown, and Company.

Rourke, Francis E. 1992. "Responsiveness and Neutral Competence in American Bureaucracy." *Public Administration Review* 52, no. 6: 539–46.

Stillman, Richard J., II. 2004. *The American Bureaucracy: The Core of Modern Government*. 3rd ed. Belmont, CA: Thomson/Wadsworth.

Taylor, Frederick W. 1911. *Principles of Scientific Management*. New York: Harper and Row.

U.S. Census Bureau. 2011. *Statistical Abstract of the United States: 2012*. 131st ed. Washington, DC. http://www.census.gov/compendia/statab/. Accessed April 15, 2014.

U.S. Census Bureau. 2013. "People and Households." http://www.census.gov/people/. Accessed April 15, 2014.

Weber, Max. 1958. *From Max Weber: Essays in Sociology*. Translated by H.H. Gerth and C. Wright Mills. New York: Oxford University Press.

Wilson, James Q. 1989. *Bureaucracy: What Government Agencies Do and Why They Do It*. New York: Basic Books.

Business. *See Corporate Behavior and Politics; Interest Groups and Lobbying*

C

CAMPAIGN FINANCE

The Election of 1896 and the Birth of Political Money

Although political money is a core focus in the United States in the 21st century, its potency as a force in American elections dates back to the 19th century. In 1896, for the first time since the end of the Civil War, the two major candidates for president offered a clear and stark choice for the voters. The Democrats' standard-bearer was 36-year-old former Nebraska Congressman William Jennings Bryan, who swept to the nomination on the heels of his spellbinding "Cross of Gold" speech at the party convention, in which he inveighed against a changing political and economic order that prioritized the corporations and the bankers over the farmer and the wage earner.

The Bryan nomination signaled that the Democrats would center the election explicitly on economic and class-based issues. A month earlier, the Republicans had nominated former Ohio governor William McKinley, a nondescript and safe choice at the time. Now, with Bryan's populist fervor galvanizing voters, especially in the South and Midwest, the Republicans realized that they had a seminal fight on their hands.

At this point, McKinley's campaign manager, Mark Hanna, embarked on a path that had never been traveled in American political history. Before the 1896 election, any money that flowed into American elections did so passively: candidates simply waited for whatever money might come in from outside parties and relied mostly on "assessments" on their party's officeholders to kick over a percentage of their salary. Nobody had ever gone out and tried to affirmatively raise money from outside donors. But now Hanna did exactly that, soliciting massive donations from financial tycoons and corporate leaders by forebodingly underlining the consequences for their business interests should Bryan win the election (Horner 2010).

Through this systematic fundraising effort, Hanna personally raised $7 million, a staggering sum equal to approximately $190 million in 2013, and a number which would not be equaled in real-dollar terms until 1936. Hanna then spent it on campaign posters, Republican speakers, newspaper ads, rallies, and parades, all to great effect: McKinley defeated Bryan, ushering in a generation of Republican dominance in presidential elections. Hanna had proved that political money could be harvested. In victory, McKinley proved that political money worked: outspending one's opponent could be the key to electoral success.

The Counterreaction, and the Cycle of Crisis and Reform

McKinley's cash-fueled victory also set off alarm bells. The idea that money could rule in politics and elections was anathema to many people who were schooled in the founding ideals. Candidates looking to buy their way to victory compromised the integrity of the political system; it was simply an unethical way to "do" politics. It took over a decade, but in 1907 Congress passed the Tillman Act—the first campaign finance law in American political history. The main provisions of the Tillman Act forbade corporations from making financial donations to political candidates.

However, it soon became clear that the Tillman Act would be of limited practical utility, mainly because it lacked an enforcement mechanism—there was no federal agency tasked with overseeing the electoral process. Its replacement, the Federal Corrupt Practices Act (FCPA), was hamstrung by the same problem, but was nevertheless something of an advance in campaign finance law. It was the basis of the prosecution of Truman Newberry, who had defeated Henry Ford for a U.S. Senate seat in Michigan in 1918, but Newberry's conviction was later thrown out by the Supreme Court.

That decision might have been the deathblow for campaign finance regulation were it not for the 1922 revelations that Warren Harding's secretary of the Interior, Albert Fall, had been secretly selling off federal land reserved for conservation purposes and taking bribes from oil executives in exchange for drilling leases. Although the "Teapot Dome" scandal was not directly connected to the electoral process, the corruption it represented led to a set of amendments to the FCPA in 1925.

A pattern had thus been established in American politics: the emergence of a crisis which prompts a public outcry about the toxic role of money in politics . . . which leads to the enactment of a campaign finance law . . . which is then parsed for loopholes . . . which are then exploited relentlessly by the political professionals until . . . the emergence of a crisis which prompts a public outcry about the toxic role of money in politics.

Just as Mark Hanna's innovations had led to the Tillman Act, and just as the Teapot Dome had led to the 1925 FCPA Amendments, another political scandal would produce the largest campaign finance law in American history.

Watergate, the Federal Election Campaign Act, and *Buckley v. Valeo*

The flawed FCPA was euthanized in 1971, replaced by the Federal Election Campaign Act (FECA). In its original form, FECA was only a marginal improvement on its predecessor, but that would change quickly. The catalyst for reform was the Watergate scandal, which began in 1972 when five men were caught breaking into the Democratic National Committee's (DNC) headquarters in the Watergate office complex, intending to bug the DNC's telephones.

It soon emerged that the break-in was part of a vast campaign of political espionage that was overseen by officials in Richard Nixon's administration. Nixon himself subsequently ordered a systematic cover-up that included hush-money payments and the manipulation of the American intelligence community. Nixon's perfidy eventually forced him to resign the presidency in the summer of 1974, and the Republican Party's image was so tainted that a wave of new Democratic senators and representatives was sent to Congress in that fall's midterm election.

The unfolding scandal also focused public attention on the broader implications of political corruption and the seamy side of campaign fundraising—the hush-money paid to the five Watergate burglars came from Nixon's campaign war chest. As Nixon's presidency was immolating, Congress moved to strengthen FECA with a series of powerful amendments. The new provisions placed hard caps on the amount of money candidates could spend when running for public office, on the amount of money individuals or political groups could donate to their preferred candidates, and on the amount of money individuals or political groups could independently spend to advance or hinder a candidate's campaign. And for the first time, an independent agency was established to oversee the system and enforce the rules: the Federal Election Commission (FEC).

As soon as Nixon's successor, Gerald Ford, signed the FECA amendments into law, New York senator James Buckley challenged them in court with a novel argument (see sidebar). In the more than 70 years of campaign finance regulation, nobody had ever seriously contemplated that limits on political money implicated the First Amendment, but now Senator Buckley insisted that by placing limits on how and how much money could be spent in elections, Congress had effectively placed direct limits on political speech.

The Supreme Court agreed and struck down key provisions of the amendments in its 1976 decision, *Buckley v. Valeo*. Rejecting the suggestion proffered by the law's sponsors that campaign spending and political donations were merely "symbolic speech" that could be liberally regulated, the Court instead declared that political money was in fact pure speech which merited maximum First Amendment shelter. Their analysis was centered on an observation that money

James Buckley

That James Buckley was even available to challenge the constitutionality of the Federal Election Campaign Act's 1974 amendments was a quirk of history. The Senate seat that Buckley held had been won by Robert Kennedy in 1966, only to become vacant upon Kennedy's assassination as he ran for president in 1968. Had Kennedy lived but not won the presidency, he would have been very difficult to defeat in a Senate reelection bid. But with Kennedy gone, New York governor Nelson Rockefeller selected a liberal Republican, Charles Goodell, to fill out the remainder of his term; as an appointed interim senator, Goodell was a much more inviting target. Buckley, who had launched an unsuccessful primary challenge in 1968 against New York's other Republican senator, Jacob Javits, now set his sights on capturing Goodell's seat in 1970. This time, Buckley ran as the nominee of the Conservative Party, and when Goodell split the state's liberal vote with Democrat Richard Ottinger, Buckley emerged as the victor. He held the seat for one term, before being defeated by Daniel Patrick Moynihan in 1976.

Oddly, two of the three candidates in the 1970 New York Senate race had relatives who proved to be much more famous. James Buckley's younger brother, William F. Buckley, was a writer and talk-show host, and the intellectual godfather of the American conservative movement; Charles Goodell's son, Roger Goodell, went on to become commissioner of the National Football League.

was absolutely necessary for electioneering communications. Commenting that "being free to engage in unlimited political expression subject to a ceiling on expenditures is like being free to drive an automobile as far and as often as one desires on a single tank of gasoline," the Court threw out the cap on a candidate's election spending.

The cap on donations, by contrast, survived, and it was here that the legacy of Watergate played its most dispositive role. In the scandal's aftermath, the Court was compelled to concede that preventing the appearance of corruption was a compelling governmental interest, and thus, the limits on the amount of money individuals or groups could directly give to specific candidates were upheld.

In addition, the court acknowledged that purportedly "independent" expenditures could function as virtual donations which brought the anticorruption rationale to the fore. If an interest group ran an ad urging viewers to vote for a specific candidate, then the candidate would naturally feel a sense of gratitude that could later be repaid with favorable legislation; the exact kind of quid pro quo corruption that could legitimately be combated. Consequently, the Court held that independent expenditures which advocated the election or defeat of a clearly identified candidate were subject to regulation.

Importantly, the anticorruption argument was the only rationale for campaign finance laws that was deemed to be constitutionally acceptable. The law's defenders had offered two other justifications for the regulation of political money: a need to level the playing field among rich and poor political actors and a desire to rein in the skyrocketing costs of political campaigns. Although both of these arguments were sensible and politically popular, the Supreme Court rejected them outright. The level-playing-field argument met with particular hostility: "the concept that government may restrict the speech of some elements of our society to enhance the relative voice of others is wholly foreign to the First Amendment." FECA had been narrowed and somewhat weakened, but it did put in place a regulatory scheme that governed American elections for over a quarter century.

From McCain-Feingold to *Citizens United*

The established pattern of crisis-regulation-loopholes-exploitation was next manifested by the discovery of the "soft money" loophole. In comparison to "hard money" gifts to candidates which were subject to FECA regulations, money that was given to political parties was not subject to limits. In the 1996 presidential election, presumptive Republican nominee Bob Dole was buffeted by so-called party-building television ads which clearly benefitted the reelection bid of President Bill Clinton, but which were not technically covered by campaign finance rules since they were paid for with money that had been donated to the Democratic Party, and not to the Clinton campaign.

Four years later, Arizona senator John McCain's insurgent bid for the Republican nomination hit the rocks with a defeat in the New York primary, a loss that many observers ascribed to a late buy of ads worth $2.5 million excoriating McCain, which were run by a heretofore-unknown environmental interest group called "Republicans For Clean Air." Upon further investigation, it turned out that the entire membership list of "Republicans For Clean Air" consisted of two names: Charles and Sam Wyly, Texas businessmen and associates of McCain's primary opponent, Texas governor George W. Bush.

FECA had been more successful than either the FCPA or the Tillman Act, but by now it had been obsolesced. Its limits on campaign contributions could be circumvented by donations to political parties; its rules for independent expenditures could not legally extend to shadowy groups that simply avoided the "magic words" of advocating election or defeat. The time had come for a new campaign finance regime, and John McCain himself brought that regime

A woman signs a giant banner printed with the preamble to the U.S. Constitution during a demonstration against the Supreme Court's *Citizens United* ruling at the Lincoln Memorial on October 20, 2010, in Washington, D.C. The protest was against the Court's decision to overturn a law barring corporations and unions from paying for political ads made independently of candidate campaigns. (Chip Somodevilla/Getty Images News/Getty Images)

to fruition. Teaming up with Wisconsin Democratic senator Russell Feingold, McCain helped to craft a replacement for FECA, and after a series of legislative false starts, the McCain-Feingold bill finally passed and was signed into law as the Bipartisan Campaign Reform Act of 2002 (BCRA).

The scope of BCRA's regulatory authority was sweeping. The soft money loophole was closed, and tight restrictions on interest group electioneering were crafted: now, "issue ads," which merely referred to a clearly identifiable candidate (whether or not they advocated the candidate's election or defeat), were covered by strict funding rules.

But BCRA was not confined to the imposition of fresh limits on campaign spending. Somewhat paradoxically, BCRA contained a provision that actually increased the amount of money in American elections: the "Millionaire's Amendment." Should a candidate for federal office find himself or herself matched up against a rich opponent who was liberally tapping his or her personal wealth to bankroll his or her campaign, the underfunded candidate could now take advantage of a sliding scale of adjusted rules. For example, if the underfunded candidate had been outspent by a certain threshold, his or her contribution limits trebled, meaning that he or she was now able to solicit exponentially larger gifts from donors.

Initially, BCRA was upheld by the Supreme Court, in *McConnell v. Federal Election Commission* (2003), an opinion jointly authored by John Paul Stevens and Sandra Day O'Connor. At the time of *McConnell*, Justice O'Connor held a particular distinction on the Court: of the nine justices, she was the only one who had ever run for public office (she was Arizona state senator in the 1970s) and thus was the only one with a direct experiential understanding of how electoral politics works.

Within two years, however, Justice O'Connor announced her retirement, and President Bush selected John Roberts as her replacement (upon the death of Chief Justice William Rehnquist, Roberts's nomination to O'Connor's seat was withdrawn, and he was resubmitted for the Chief Justiceship instead). This one change on the Court—Roberts in for O'Connor—would have dramatic and stunning consequences for campaign finance law.

The first sign that the Roberts Court would be hostile to campaign finance regulation was the 2008 decision in *Davis v. Federal Election Commission*, which threw out the Millionaire's Amendment by a 5–4 vote. While *Buckley v. Valeo* had rejected leveling the playing field as a justification for campaign finance law, that rejection was premised on the dangers of restricting the speech of one candidate as a means of enhancing the speech of another candidate. The "Millionaire's Amendment" did not restrict any candidates' speech; if anything, by hiking up the contribution limits, it facilitated the creation of more political speech. But the Roberts Court, which had already evinced a tendency to favor corporate interests (Rosen 2008), seemed keen on protecting the power of wealth, and that power was threatened by the "Millionaire's Amendment."

If *Davis* was a warning shot, then 2010's *Citizens United v. Federal Election Commission* was a nuclear detonation. Citizens United was a conservative advocacy group that produced a 2008 "documentary" about former First Lady—and imminent presidential candidate—Hillary Clinton. When Citizens United attempted to buy television airtime to advertise the film, the FEC held that the film was little more than an extended political commercial which referred to a clearly identified candidate for federal office, and ruled that ads for the film were covered by BCRA's rules.

By the same 5–4 split in *Davis*, the Court reversed the FEC, invalidated core provisions of BCRA, functionally overturned *McConnell*, and undid central principles of campaign finance reform that had stood for over a century.

The most controversial part of the *Citizens United* decision was the declaration that the longstanding limits on corporations' ability to spend money to influence elections violated the First Amendment. Corporations were still subject to rules restricting donations that could be made to specific candidates, but the restraints on corporate "independent expenditures" which had been in place since the Tillman Act of 1907 were now gutted.

Criticism of the decision was swift, loud, and very public. Less than a week after the decision was announced, President Barack Obama used a portion of his State of the Union address to express his disagreement with it; television cameras showed Justice Samuel Alito (who had been in the majority), seated down front in the chamber, shaking his head and mouthing the words "not true."

Analysis

A century of campaign finance law has been anything but a model of consistency. Commentators have labeled it "a patternless mosaic" (Lowenstein 1991) and an "illusion of coherence" (Hasen 2011), among other critiques. Judicial antagonism toward campaign finance legislation does have its cheerleaders; skeptics of restricting money in politics abound. But for every analyst who questions either the effectiveness or the very desirability of campaign finance laws (Smith 2001), there is an analyst who defends such laws and decries the political forces that make them seem necessary.

The post-*Buckley* era has been a transformational period in popular perceptions of campaign finance. What began in the early 20th century as a purely political cause championed by advocates of reform, by the late 1970s, had evolved into a constitutional question which pivoted on the most famous provision of the Bill of Rights: the free speech clause. This evolution, however, may not be healthy. As one constitutional scholar pointed out, "under existing constitutional ground rules, American judges, confronted by a hard constitutional case with implications for democracy, are not required—indeed, they may not even be permitted—to ask whether the outcome is good or bad for democracy. Rather . . . they are expected to resolve the case by shoehorning it into one or another doctrinal category, such as equal protection, freedom of association, or free speech, without ever asking what kind of democracy they are building" (Neuborne 2011). Indeed, were the justices inclined to even ask that question, it is doubtful that they could come up with a coherent and reliable answer. Upon Sandra Day O'Connor's retirement, the Supreme Court for the first time in history did not have a single justice who had ever run for public office. In contemporary politics, two things seem very clear: a majority of Americans want money's role in the political process circumscribed, and a majority of Justices on the Supreme Court do not.

Conclusion

The phenomenon of money and politics in the United States must be understood in historical context. America's founding generation saw the United States as a bold new experiment in human affairs, one which would leave behind the pathologies of the Old World and show how a virtuous polity ruled by leaders of their own choosing could govern itself via deliberative democratic processes. The founders were not naïve about human nature, but they were optimistic about how human nature could be induced to follow its better angels. They structured the American political order based on an awareness that impulses which mitigated toward corruption and self-interest were unavoidable, but also based on a belief that these impulses could be limited and controlled.

The founders felt that they had successfully engineered a system that would restrain the dark forces of partisanship and self-interest and allow for the emergence of practices and traditions in which personal talent and integrity could flourish. In turn, this approach meant that the founders abhorred any influences which would shift the political order away from these statesmanlike qualities. Their disdain for political parties, for example, was acute, as famously seen in Madison's admonitions about the dangers of faction in *Federalist #10*.

Just as factions and political parties could wrench the political system off of its meritocratic moorings, so too can political money upset the founders' expectations. Factions and parties were problematic precisely because they represented a means through which enlightened statesmen could be blocked from taking the helm. Were the founders to see how wealth can trump talent and qualifications, how the strategic raising and spending of money can alter the direction of the political system, they would likely see untrammeled political money as a threat to political integrity in similar terms.

Yet there is another historical context that is relevant. The United States, after all, is a capitalist nation. America embraces the capitalist spirit as more than merely an economic model; the primacy of competition as a motivating factor transcends its role in the financial system. Explaining the role of free speech in democracy, Oliver Wendell Holmes insisted in 1919 that "the best test of truth is the power of the thought to get itself accepted in the competition of the market" (*Abrams v. United States*).

America's preference for capitalism also reflects an acknowledgment, perhaps best expressed by the lawyers in one of the leading campaign finance court cases, that "our social system is based on the premise that inequalities of wealth serve valid and useful purposes" (Claggett and Bolton 1976). Given that this is an accurate insight, it can be argued that it is inconsistent for that social system to be managed by a political process which zeroes out inequalities of wealth as an operational dynamic. Thus, it is a fair question to ask: does the present-day dominance of money in American politics represent a betrayal of American political traditions, or a furtherance of them?

See also Advertising, Political; Campaigns and Campaigning; Interest Groups and Lobbying; Power and Politics; Supreme Court, United States.

Steven B. Lichtman

Bibliography

Baker, Paula. 2012. *Curbing Campaign Cash: Henry Ford, Truman Newberry, and the Politics of Progressive Reform*. Lawrence: University Press of Kansas.

Claggett, Brice, and John Bolton. 1976. "*Buckley v. Valeo*: Its Aftermath, and Its Prospects: The Constitutionality of Government Restraints on Political Campaign Financing." *Vanderbilt Law Review* 29: 1327.

Corrado, Anthony, et al. 2005. *The New Campaign Finance Sourcebook*. Washington, DC: Brookings Institution Press.

Hasen, Richard L. 2011. "*Citizens United* and the Illusion of Coherence." *Michigan Law Review* 109: 581.

Horner, William T. 2010. *Ohio's Kingmaker: Mark Hanna, Man and Myth*. Athens: Ohio University Press.

Lowenstein, Daniel Hays. 1991. "A Patternless Mosaic: Campaign Finance and the First Amendment after Austin." *Capital University Law Review* 21: 381.

Madison, James. 1787. *Federalist No. 10*.

Neuborne, Burt. 2011. "Felix Frankfurter's Revenge: An Accidental Democracy Built by Judges." In Monica Youn, ed. *Money, Politics, and the Constitution: Beyond Citizens United*. New York: The Century Fund.

Overacker, Louise. 1932. *Money in Elections*. New York: Macmillan.

Rosen, Jeffrey. 2008. "Supreme Court Inc." *New York Times Sunday Magazine*.

Smith, Bradley A. 2001. *Unfree Speech: The Folly of Campaign Finance Reform*. Princeton, NJ: Princeton University Press.

Williams, Hal R. 2010. *Realigning America: McKinley, Bryan, and the Remarkable Election of 1896*. Lawrence: University Press of Kansas.

Cases

Abrams v. United States, 250 U.S. 616 (1919).

Buckley v. Valeo, 424 U.S. 1 (1976).

Citizens United v. Federal Election Commission, 558 U.S. 50 (2010).

Davis v. Federal Election Commission, 554 U.S. 724 (2008).

McConnell v. Federal Election Commission, 540 U.S. 93 (2003).

CAMPAIGNS AND CAMPAIGNING

Political campaigns are the lifeblood of American democracy, pulsing outward through the elected organs of government from the beating heart of public opinion. Today, political campaigns in the United States constitute a multibillion-dollar industry, drawing upon experts in communication (including social media), brain science, opinion polling, data analytics, and fundraising. Campaigns have also become increasingly negative and vitriolic. The combination of attack politics and high-tech, and capital-intensive tactics has spread from the United States to other electoral democracies, spawning what has been termed the "Americanization" of political campaigns worldwide. Recent evolution in campaign practice also bears directly upon the enduring questions of wealth and power in a democracy. Nonetheless, person-to-person human contact still lies at the core of effective campaigning, and American political campaigns remain an integral part of the fabric of America's democracy and political culture.

When John F. Kennedy accepted his party's nomination for president at the Democratic National Convention in Los Angeles in 1960, he spoke of the policy challenges confronting the nation as it faced a "new frontier." The road Kennedy had taken to secure that nomination and eventually the presidency also represented a new frontier—in political campaigns. The 1960 race had one foot firmly planted in the past— the organizational strength of party machinery would loom large in places like Chicago and Texas—and one foot in the future: candidate-centered campaigns that would come to increasingly rely on television rather than party workers as the principal means of political communication, and on direct primaries rather than party leaders to secure nominations. The Kennedy campaign would also break new ground in the emerging science of voter contact and mobilization. All of these forces would escalate the costs of campaigning, a development of significant consequence.

The Party Machine Model: People Power

Since the emergence of mass democracy in the United States in the 1820s, political parties have provided the motive power of political campaigns. Before the progressive reforms began to take their toll, parties fielded vast armies of working-class volunteers at election time, many whom enjoyed such spoils of victory as patronage jobs and access to social services in their hours of need. Machine politics thrived in many of the nation's biggest cities. Small-town and rural machines also existed (particularly in the South), though they lacked the power and sweep of their urban contemporaries. The progressives, from their origins in the late 1800s to the present day, have seen parties as narrowly focused threats to the public interest. They pushed reforms including voter registration, the secret ballot, nonpartisan municipal elections, direct primary election of party nominees, and merit-based civil service, all explicitly designed to weaken parties' organizational strength. For many progressives, parties were seen as captive to the "unwashed masses," urban ethnics unfit to guide the ship of state. Other

progressives were less openly hostile to the working class and immigrants, but the cumulative impact of the progressive reforms has been to weaken working-class political clout as no new institutional framework for working-class politics has emerged to replace the machine party. This situation has skewed political participation and power in the United States toward the middle class and especially the upper class.

The Rise of Money Power in Politics

Party machines would remain critical mobilizers of the vote in the decades after the first wave of progressive reforms, but the axis of power was shifting toward money and mass communication. "Dollar Mark" Hanna, an Ohio industrialist and financier, became the first prominent big-money kingmaker in American politics during the late 1800s. He is particularly credited with contributing to the election of William McKinley to president in 1896.

At the same time, first with the "penny press," then with radio and eventually television, political campaigns would increasingly become exercises in mass communication. This would further leverage money power in politics.

The Rise of the Primary

Historically, the selection of party nominees for president has shaped the party nomination process more broadly. The nation's earliest nominations for president were decided by the parties' congressional delegations, a process that would ultimately be derided as "King Caucus." As part of the democratizing reform spirit that began to spread across the nation in the early 1800s, control of nominations was shifted to party conventions by 1832. The next major wave of reform would be driven by the progressive movement, and would lead to the emergence of direct primary selection of nominees by voters, an American innovation that to this day distinguishes party nominations in the United States from those in most democracies. The state of Florida held the first presidential primary in 1904, and within the decade, a majority of states had moved to primaries. The rising tide of primaries would ebb, however, and by 1936 only 14 states held primaries to select national convention delegates. Primaries, therefore, would play little role in the presidential nomination battles of the first half of the 20th century.

JFK's 1960 campaign marked a revival of the primary. While the number of delegates at stake was substantially limited, Kennedy was able to capitalize on the media coverage they generated and used his victories to demonstrate his electoral viability to the party leaders who still held decisive weight in the nomination process. In particular, Kennedy, who would become the nation's first Catholic president, pointed to his victory in the overwhelmingly Protestant state of West Virginia as proof of his electability.

The role of primaries would be considerably enhanced as a result of reforms instituted by the Democratic Party following the 1968 campaign. The party's presidential nominee, Vice President Hubert H. Humphrey, did not run in a single primary. The Democrats, like America as a whole, had been torn asunder by infighting over the Vietnam War and civil rights. The specter of Chicago mayor Richard J. Daley, arguably the nation's last old school party machine "boss," presiding over the party's national convention in his city with an iron fist, further helped to create the opening for a profound shift in the balance of power in the nomination process, specifically paving the way for the renewed growth of direct primaries. Following the Chicago Convention, the Democrats established a Committee on Party Structure and Delegate Selection to explore democratizing reforms, which became known as the McGovern-Fraser Commission (reflecting the names of its cochairs). The commission's reforms would propel many state parties to turn to direct primaries to select convention delegates, a move which would have deep consequences for the Democratic Party and American politics, some unforeseen.

The Political Consequences of Campaign Reform

While aggressive support for business has been a part of Republican Party DNA from the time it inherited the opposition party mantle from the Whigs, it is of more recent vintage in the Democratic case. Ironically, it was the party's push to "democratize" its nomination

process that set in motion the tilt toward capital. Candidates compete in direct primaries by appealing to voters largely through political advertising, the costs of which are met by prodigious fundraising from a donor pool skewed in favor of the wealthy. The policy preferences of Democratic donors pushed the party leftward on social issues but to the right on economics, both forces that would distance the party from its historical working-class base. At the same time, Republicans would become even more enthusiastic proponents of the corporate agenda as the business community itself became considerably more politicized beginning in the 1970s. The influence of organized labor on the Democratic Party, which rose to prominence during the New Deal, would begin to wane as campaign cash and mass communication began to supplant the role of organizational strength.

Media and Advertising

Political pundits and campaign pros often distinguish "free media" (news coverage and debates) from paid media (political advertising). In 1948, President Harry Truman's campaign purchased television time to air a recording of one his speeches, a first in American politics. It was the 1952 campaign, however, that witnessed the first major deployment of televised advertising, when Dwight Eisenhower's campaign turned to Madison Avenue advertising pro Rosser Reeves to craft his campaign spots. Yet throughout the 1950s, most Americans still relied on newspapers and radio for political news.

By the 1960 campaign a majority of American homes had television. While both candidates aired extensive ad campaigns, it was a series of televised debates (the first ever at the presidential level) that most acutely brought the power of the mass media to bear on the vote choice. That influence, while no doubt consequential, may have been exaggerated over the years by the potent myth that radio listeners thought Nixon won the first debate while television viewers thought Kennedy prevailed. That oft-repeated claim may have its origins in a single opinion poll that consisted of a small sample in which Republicans were overrepresented among radio listeners. Nor would such a poll clarify whether it was Nixon's stronger vocal presence on radio or Kennedy's visual appeal on television that was responsible for the disparity. In any event, with the dawn of the age of television, political campaigns would never be the same. Presidential debates, moreover, would come to occupy a key place in campaign discourse. Typically, it seems, challengers benefit more, as they are given an opportunity to stand on equal footing with an incumbent president. Yet some of those same challengers also seemed to succumb to the poor debate performances as incumbents. Presidents Carter, Ford, Reagan, Bush I, and Obama all suffered through subpar debates, perhaps owing to the distractions of office or false confidence in their lackluster preparations.

The role of advertising was particularly pronounced in the presidential campaign of 1988. Vice President Bush's team created a series of focus-group–tested spots that proved effective electorally, although not without controversy. Ads focusing on the case of a furloughed convict, William (a.k.a. "Willie") P. Horton Jr., were criticized for falsehoods, distortions, and race-baiting. An ad featuring video of opponent Michael Dukakis riding in a tank during a photo op also took liberties with the facts. As a consequence, journalists in subsequent campaigns would pay increased attention not only to the factual inaccuracies of political ads but to the way they communicated their critiques. The result was "ad watch" journalism, which has persisted in one form or another to the present day.

Capital-Intensive Campaigns I: The Rise of the Consultant

As early as the late 1960s, the emergence of a new class of campaign operatives who would become known as "political consultants" was coming into view. These campaign professionals drew upon expertise in opinion polling, ad-making, data analysis, and voter contact, especially in the emerging field of direct mail. What consultants offered candidates was in essence a shadow party, an off-the shelf, fully functional campaign apparatus that could be purchased on the fly, or "organization in a box." This would reduce the influence of the parties, which would soon face another body blow to their political prominence.

The Rise of PACs

In response to reports of corruption in the Nixon campaign, Congress passed the FECA in 1971, amended in 1974, in an attempt to reduce the influence of big money donors on the political process. Contributions to candidates and parties were capped, and corporations, unions, and other political interest groups would have to operate political action committees (PACs) if they wished to donate directly to candidates for federal office. (Direct contributions from corporate treasuries to candidates had been banned by the Tillman Act in 1907.) In short order, PACs would proliferate and become highly influential players in electoral politics—so influential, in fact, that they came to be seen as serious threats to the viability of the two major political parties.

Candidates were no longer tethered to the party apparatus, in terms of either funding or voter mobilization. PACs began to be seen as new kingmakers, calling into question the continued viability of political parties. In response, Congress would again amend FECA in 1979 to allow parties to raise essentially unlimited funds for "party-building" activities such as voter registration and mobilization and televised issue advocacy (so long as it did not specifically endorse or oppose candidates for federal office). Such contributions became known as "soft money," and their use exploded until they were banned by the BCRA (a.k.a. "McCain-Feingold").

BCRA also banned what it categorized as "electioneering communications" (ads that mentioned a specific candidate for federal office), aired up to 60 days before a general election (30 days before a primary) when funded by corporate or union treasuries. Instead, such communications would have to be funded through PACs and subject to federal disclosure and contribution limits. In 2010, in *Citizens United v. Federal Election Commission*, the Supreme Court struck down the ban on electioneering communications within 60 days of a general election as a violation of the free speech rights of associations of individuals (including corporations), allowing corporate and union funds to go directly into electioneering, bypassing PACs and their contribution limits and disclosure requirements. Also in 2010, the Court of Appeals for the District of Columbia Circuit struck down limits on the amount of money individuals could contribute to independent expenditure committees. The decisions have opened the floodgates on independent political spending and given rise to so-called Super PACs. In 2012, according to the Center for Responsive Politics, outside groups spent $1.1 billion, nearly as much as they had in the two previous decades combined. While at the presidential level, outside money was countered by prolific fundraising by both parties' nominees, at the state and local levels, the influence of outside money can be decisive. Critics, moreover, point to 501(c)4 organizations (designed originally for nonprofit social welfare organizations) that have emerged as major players in campaigns, describing their funding as "dark money" owing to the anonymity of its donors, and note the outsized role played by ultrarich contributors including the right-wing Koch brothers and left-leaning capitalist George Soros.

Campaign reform has altered the shape of American campaigns time and again, with each wave of reform spurring countermoves and adaptations. For example, by the late 1990s, in the face of repeated drubbings in the "air wars" of big money ad buys, organized labor returned in force to the "ground game," emphasizing armies of volunteers reaching out to contact voters directly. Their success was not lost upon the Republicans, who by the 2000s would meld person-to-person voter outreach with big data micro-targeting. The Obama presidential campaigns of 2008 and 2012 were seen as exemplars in the use of "big data" and personal contact in electioneering.

The Revival of Partisan Media

Not only has the environment for "paid media" (advertising) changed dramatically, but so too has the free media (news) landscape. In the early days of the American republic, the nation's newspapers emerged as partisan organs trumpeting the views of one side or another in the political debate. In the mid-1800s, spurred on by news organizations such as *The New York Times*, independent journalism would appear, promising reporting based on facts rather than opinions and presenting both sides to the debate rather than just one. It was a model that would hold sway for nearly a century. In the aftermath of World War II,

however, conservative intellectuals would come to see the nation's media, education, and governing institutions as ruled by a liberal elite, and they would eventually develop their own elite media organizations, think tanks, and electioneering infrastructure.

The conservative media wave began first with publications such as *National Review* and *Commentary* magazines. It would explode however, in the 1990s, first on talk radio (where Rush Limbaugh's outsized influence earned him status as an honorary Republican member of Congress) and then in cable news, where former political consultant Roger Ailes would fashion a media empire that would come to dramatically alter the nation's political discourse. Ailes' project (FOX News) received a substantial boost in 1998 when President Bill Clinton's affair with White House intern Monica Lewinsky poured fuel on smoldering partisan fires and boosted the viewing audience. What Ms. Lewinsky did for FOX, the Iraq War would do for MSNBC, which began to lean center-left politically. By 2008, cable viewers were sorting themselves into partisan tribes who viewed the same world in fundamentally different ways. Not only would partisan cable serve as an important driver in the campaign discourse (perhaps most notably and controversially with the coverage afforded to the incendiary accusations of the Swift Boat Veterans for Truth against presidential candidate John Kerry in 2004), but FOX itself would become the "go to" destination in Republican presidential nomination contests. The network was also influential in propagating the Tea Party insurgency during the early years of the Obama presidency.

Capital-Intensive Campaigns II: "Big Data"

By the second decade of the 21st century, political campaigns were increasingly defined by technological developments, including the computer-assisted drawing of district boundaries to enhance partisan advantage, the micro-targeting of voters (based on troves of personal data collected on citizens by corporations and sold to marketers in including political campaigns), and the use of experiments in electioneering allowing campaigns to test the effectiveness of their appeals in "real-time."

The combination of computers and data allows those charged with drawing election districts to carve out, block by block and even household by household, boundaries designed to ensure their electoral success. In most states, that process is partisan, and largely the province of the party in power. The Constitution requires congressional districts to be reapportioned every 10 years following the decennial census, and with their massive electoral gains in 2010, Republicans were situated to craft district boundaries that would maximize the number of seats they could garner. Indeed, in 2012, 1.4 million more Americans nationwide voted from Democratic House candidates than did so for Republicans, yet the Republican Party sustained a 234–201 House majority. In Pennsylvania, the impact was particularly notable, as tens of thousands more voters in the Commonwealth supported Democratic House candidates, but the state's congressional delegation tilted Republican by a margin of 13–5. The tactic is not limited to Republicans, as democratically controlled Illinois also obtained a slightly skewed congressional delegation when compared to the statewide congressional vote. Nonetheless, in 2012, the net advantage owing to partisan gerrymandering was considerably higher in Republican-controlled states than in Democratic ones. Further, while some of the disparity owes to patterns of residential segregation (Democratic voters are frequently clustered into densely packed urban areas), an analysis of Pennsylvania's extreme partisan gerrymander indicated its impact was five times greater than such structural influences as residential segregation. Notably, in California, where congressional district boundaries are drawn by the California Citizens Redistricting Commission and not by the legislature, the percentage of seats won by each party closely tracks their statewide popular vote.

One perhaps unintended consequence of "gerrymandering on steroids" has been the rising importance of the intraparty nomination contest. With defeat in the general election unlikely, many legislators have more to fear today from a challenge in their own party primary than they do from an opposition party challenger in November. In the primaries, caucuses, and conventions used to select party nominees, the voters are typically more ideologically extreme than in general elections. Many have linked this development to the high levels of polarization in the House of Representatives. While the boundaries of the state's senators represent are not subject to gerrymander, the polarization of political debate emerging from the House has infiltrated the upper chamber as well. Some GOP leaders fret over extremist Tea Party nominees in recent election cycles that could not prevail in otherwise winnable races, costing the party control of the U.S. Senate.

Micro-targeting

A second aspect of the big data revolution in political campaigning has been the emergence of a form of narrowly focused voter contact known as "micro-targeting" in the 21st century. Historically, campaigns analyzed voters in geographic or demographic blocs. They were limited to readily accessible metrics like census data, precinct voting returns, and opinion polling that did not allow for nuanced distinctions among voters. Once campaigns were able to draw upon the vast caches of consumer data collected by corporate vendors, however, they were able to move beyond primitive clusters toward ones better informed by behavioral and attitudinal data. The key step in the process was the development of computer algorithms that would identify the factors that drew segments of voters together. While some media accounts emphasized catchy titles such as "soccer moms" and links between consumer purchases and political predispositions, the reality was considerably more nuanced, based on the confluence of numerous variables that might otherwise seem unrelated.

Experiments in Electioneering

The power of micro-targeting is amplified when combined with carefully designed experiments testing which political appeals actually move and motivate voters. Republicans, smarting from the effectiveness of the voter mobilization success of the Democrats and labor in 2000, embarked upon their own effort to create a state-of-the-art turnout machine, a project that would become known as the 72-Hour Task Force (a reference to the crucial final three days of a campaign). They would test experimentally different combinations of message and methods in contacting voters. Their work achieved fruition in 2004 with the reelection of

George W. Bush. For political campaigns, moving as little as 2 percent of the vote can prove decisive. While earlier generations of consultants might have been nonplussed by such small margins, the narrow presidential vote in 2000 and the increasingly narrow divide among voters made such increments critical. In 2008 and 2012, the Obama campaign would take such tactics to the next level, integrating newly emerging social media platforms into the campaign arsenal and training that arsenal on house-to-house voter contact, fully returning the ground game to primacy in electoral politics. Now more than ever, it turns out, person-to-person contact is the most effective mobilizing tool in political campaigns.

Campaigns in the Age of Social Media

Twenty-first-century social media have placed a premium on candidate engagement with individual voters. Today campaigns stake a presence on dozens of social platforms such as Twitter, Facebook, YouTube, and Flickr. In 2008, Barack Obama became the first presidential candidate to have profiles on BlackPlanet and MiGente, social media sites popular in the black and Latino communities. Today, candidates and campaigns are well schooled in the art of effectively "tweeting" and in ways to avoid social media mishaps. Indeed, campaigns and interest groups have even begun to shift their approach to public policy questions to generate more social media–friendly content.

The Changing American Voter

The role of the voter is central to political campaigns. Perhaps the most fundamental finding of political scientists who have studied the American voter is that voters lack both detailed information about government and politics and philosophically consistent positions across issues. To the extent that voters engage in reasoning, it is through cognitive shortcuts or cues (like party or the perceived character of candidates for office). Moreover, the political brain is an emotional brain, in the words of political psychologist Drew Westen. It has long been recognized that negative information carries more weight than positive information in evaluation, and negative information is more

likely to alter existing impressions than positive information. Not surprisingly, many campaign appeals consist of emotional, negative appeals.

Perhaps the most pervasive emotional appeals in American politics turn on questions of race. Race has been a core conflict in the nation's politics from the time of the founding through the present day. Today, the politics of race is largely subterranean, operating through "dog whistle" campaign communication working below the level of consciousness. Perhaps the most significant manifestation of the politics of race in the postwar environment has been in the racial identity of the major parties. Since before the Civil War, the Democratic Party had been the party of the segregationist South. The Republican Party, the party of Lincoln, had freed the slaves and sustained the allegiance of majorities of African American voters until the mid-20th century. President Truman's executive order desegregating the armed forces split the Democrats, and in the decades following the passage of the Civil Rights Act of 1964, Republicans would become the dominant party in the South, and among white voters generally. No Democratic candidate for president has carried a majority of the white vote since Lyndon Johnson's landslide victory in 1964. Republicans enjoy majority white support among women and men and among rich and poor. The only demographic subgroup of whites to give majority support to Barack Obama was the young. The principal consequence of the latest turn in America's racial politics may be the linkage of support for government programs with racial and ethnic minorities and the chasm between the nation's racially mixed urban areas and largely white rural communities. A consequence of racialized campaigning has been a tilt toward policies favoring wealthy citizens.

As campaigns have embraced micro-targeting, experiments in electioneering and the analysis of "big data," they have increasingly come to realize that it is far more effective to identify a candidate's or party's nonvoting supporters and try to get them to the polls than it is to try to convert undecided voters or supporters of the opposition. This is especially true in midterm elections, contests for Congress in years when there is no presidential contest on the ballot. Mobilization of the party's base of supporters has long been a tenet of

Republican campaign operatives, in part because opinion polls have shown a greater percentage of voters on the far right than on the far left. Democratic campaigns have more typically attempted to position themselves in the political center, though more recently, they, too, have turned increasingly toward mobilization of their core supporters. Base mobilization may be contributing to the increased polarization observed in Congress and state legislatures.

The Political Consequences of Political Campaigns: Campaign Effects

In their attempt to isolate the effects of campaigns on election outcomes, political scientists have produced mixed findings. Many suggest campaigns do little to shape election results, which instead are determined by forces such as the state of the economy and public's assessment of the president's job performance. Nonetheless, it is hard to imagine that in the closest contests the quality and quantity of campaigning would not matter.

Perhaps even more consequential than the impact of campaigns on election outcomes is the impact of campaigns on governing and the political climate following the campaign. Anticipation of the next campaign (and its likely attack ads) also bears substantial weight in the minds of elected officials. Add to that the need for elected officials to raise significant amounts of money to fund their campaigns and the net impact of political campaigns on governing and our national discourse is substantial.

Recent campaigns have shaped national dialogue on issues such as the Affordable Care Act and U.S. wars. Shifting demographics, moreover, have become most visible in the context of campaigns, leading some Republicans in particular to challenge their party to move beyond its base of support among older, white voters in the face of an electorate roughly 2 percent less white with each passing presidential election.

The Political Consequences of Political Campaigns: Money, Power, and Democracy

For nearly 200 years, the long arc of American democracy tilted largely toward expanding the electorate. Voting rights were extended to all white males in the early

1800s, to all men after the Civil War, to women in 1920, and to 19-year-olds in 1971. The tools of disenfranchisement (including poll taxes and literacy tests) were gradually eradicated. Beginning in the early 2000s (and especially after Republican gains in the 2010 election cycle), however, numerous states (virtually all under Republican control) have adopted measures that make voting harder, at least for certain citizens. These efforts have been framed as protection against voter fraud, though court cases have repeatedly failed to document widespread or significant misconduct. Like the waves of progressive reforms before them, the new wave of voter laws disproportionally impact disadvantaged elements of society, particularly the young, the elderly, and the poor. The combination of voter suppression at the bottom of the social structure and the increased importance of money in politics comes at a time when economic inequality has reached record levels. The new restrictions on voter registration, early voting, and so on have been advocated by pressure groups allied with the nation's business elite, whose hostility to organized labor is self-evident. Some observers have begun to argue that a significant cause of the exploding gap between the super-wealthy and ordinary Americans is in fact growing political inequality.

The increased role of money in politics and the growing inequity in American life have spawned intense and passionate calls to reform the political system, especially the way campaigns are financed. Advocates argue that public financing of election campaigns produces "clean money," in contrast to private financing they see as creating the appearance if not the reality of corruption. Their opponents see the spending limits that accompany public campaign finance as unconstitutional restrictions on free speech. These conflicts are deep and intractable. Yet even if reformers were to succeed in securing public financing of political campaigns, serious issues would remain. It is likely, especially given the current state of government finances, that campaign subsidies would not reach the highest levels of campaign spending. This very reality has worked to undermine the existing federal funding regime for presidential elections as candidates of both parties have concluded it is easier and more advantageous to raise unlimited amounts of private contributions rather than accept public financing and the spending limits it entails.

Proposals to limit or reduce the amount one can contribute to a campaign can never be low enough to generate widespread contributions from poor citizens who simply lack the money to spend. Indeed, historically, "progressive" causes have been bankrolled by a small number of large donors rather than a large number of small ones. In sum, it is hard to see what set of reforms to campaign finance, given the constitutional protection of free speech and the Supreme Court's equation of money with speech (*Buckley v. Valeo*, 1976), can both address concerns of the corrupting influence of campaign cash while simultaneously providing enough funds to launch vigorous rounds of campaign communication. More plausibly, the legal environment that has increasingly been tilted against organized labor might once again seek to empower the unions that played such a significant role in building the American middle class and resisting the excesses of concentrated corporate power. The existing campaign finance system itself, however, serves to tilt the political playing field toward those with extreme wealth. In any event, as these battles are waged, political campaigns will continue to lie at the heart of the struggle for democracy.

See also Advertising, Political; Campaign Finance; Debates, Presidential; Nominating Conventions; Political Communications; Political Consultants and Campaign Managers; Primaries and Caucuses; Public Opinion; Redistricting; Social Media and Politics.

Glenn Richardson

Bibliography

Issenberg, Sasha. 2012. *Victory Lab*. New York: Crown Publishing.

Jamieson, Kathleen Hall. 1992. *Dirty Politics: Deception, Distraction, and Democracy*. New York: Oxford University Press.

Jamieson, Kathleen Hall. 1996. *Packaging the Presidency: A History and Criticism of Presidential Campaign Advertising*. 3rd ed. New York: Oxford University Press.

Nichols, John, and Robert W. McChesney. 2013. *Dollarocracy: How the Money and Media Elections Complex Is Destroying America*. New York: Nation Books.

Popkin, Samuel L. 1994. *The Reasoning Voter*. Chicago: University of Chicago Press.

Sides, John, and Lynn Vavreck. 2013. *The Gamble: Choice and Chance in the 2012 Presidential Election*. Princeton, NJ: Princeton University Press.

Westen, Drew. 2007. *The Political Brain: The Role of Emotion in Deciding the Fate of the Nation*. New York: Public Affairs.

CATHOLICS AND POLITICS

American Catholics began to exercise an important role in U.S. politics with the arrival of 750,000 Irish immigrants fleeing a potato famine during the 1840s. These politically active Catholics were augmented by millions of other Catholic émigrés from Eastern, Central, and Southern Europe, which began in 1890 and lasted until the early 1920s. During that period, more than 15 million people emigrated to U.S. shores—up to that time the largest number in U.S. history. Many became involved in local politics–including John F. Kennedy's grandfather, "Honey Fitz" (John F. Fitzgerald), who was elected mayor of Boston and had previously held many other elective offices including that of U.S. Congressman.

The vast majority of Catholic immigrants gravitated to the Democratic Party, thanks to Republican hostility to their presence. As the late Edward M. Kennedy once recalled, "As far back as the 1890s, when my grandfather John F. Fitzgerald ran for Congress, it would have been unthinkable for him to run as a Republican" (White 1983, 10). Two major reasons why Catholic immigrants gravitated toward the Democratic Party were (1) Republican support for Prohibition, which was much more than antialcohol and became an issue laden with anti-Catholic prejudice; and (2) GOP support for a restrictive immigration policy, which was approved by a Republican-controlled Congress and signed by President Coolidge in 1924.

As Catholic involvement in politics escalated, it was no surprise that one of them, Alfred E. Smith, would set his sights on the White House. In 1928, the Democrats nominated Smith, who personified the eastern, "wet" (anti-Prohibition), urban, and Catholic elements of the Democratic coalition. He was born on New York City's East Side, the son of an Irish immigrant. Smith ran for governor five times, losing only in the Republican landslide of 1920. Writing of his presidential nomination in 1928, *The New Republic* observed, "For the first time a representative of the unpedigreed, foreign-born, city-bred, many-tongued recent arrivals on the American scene has knocked on the door and aspired seriously to the presidency seat in the national council chamber" (quoted in White 1983, 10).

Smith lost the presidency in one of the greatest landslides in U.S. history. But Catholics gravitated to his candidacy in record numbers. In some Irish-dominated areas in Boston, Providence, and Hartford, for example, Smith received 91 percent, 71 percent, and 60 percent of the votes cast (White 1983, 10). Undoubtedly, ethnic and religious identities accounted for Smith's large majorities. The *Springfield Republican* reported that when voters discussed politics in 1928, they talked in "terms of French, Irish, Pole, and Yankee or Catholic and non-Catholic." The paper concluded, "Votes will undoubtedly be cast on other issues, particularly prohibition and prosperity, but when you get down to the ground there's 'dirt!'" (quoted in White 1983, 11).

Questions about Smith's patriotism, and the role the Pope might play in any Smith administration, were lingering concerns. While Smith won overwhelming Catholic support, he lost other bastions of the Democratic party—particularly in the "Solid South"—where white Protestant resistance to a Catholic president remained strong. Several states defected from Smith and voted Republican for the first time since the Civil War. Altogether, Smith won 8 states, and 41 percent of the national vote. His electoral drubbing—despite the enormous Catholic affection for him—guaranteed that the Democrats would not nominate another Catholic for decades to come.

A Catholic Resurgence: John F. Kennedy and the Election of 1960

That time came in 1960. That year, an ambitious John F. Kennedy had the presidency in his sights. Catholic immigrants, which now included their sons and daughters, had begun to drift away from the Democratic Party, as the Cold War escalated and the Iron Curtain left much of Eastern Europe impenetrable. Many Catholic immigrants had left relatives stranded behind in the Iron Curtain, and slowly their anticommunism

rose to new heights. Republicans had always taken a strong anticommunist stance. In 1956, the Republican National Committee established a Nationalities Division that distributed pro-Eisenhower "I Like Ike" campaign buttons in 10 languages, along with 500,000 pamphlets titled *The Republican Policy of Liberation*. Not surprisingly, Eisenhower captured 54 percent of the Catholic vote that year (White 1997, 142).

For Democrats, winning back wayward Catholics became a top priority. Connecticut Democratic party boss John Bailey circulated a memorandum arguing that John F. Kennedy's Catholicism was an asset that the next nominee needed to wrest the White House from the Republicans. JFK's father, former ambassador Joseph P. Kennedy, agreed, telling his son: "There's a whole new generation out there and it's filled with the sons and daughters of immigrants from all over the world, and those people are going to be mighty proud that one of their own is running for president. And that pride will be your spur, it will give your campaign an intensity we've never seen in public life" (Barone 1990, 310). Joseph Kennedy's advice was prescient. In 1960, John F. Kennedy won 78 percent of the Catholic ballots, while his Republican opponent, Richard M. Nixon, won 63 percent of the votes cast by white Protestants (Barone 1990, xii). A religious gap that had existed in earlier contests now became a religious canyon.

U.S. Catholics were attracted to John F. Kennedy for several reasons. As late as 1960, most Catholics were economic "have nots." Franklin D. Roosevelt's New Deal, which saved many from economic ruin, was still fresh in their minds. Thanks to FDR, Catholics were the beneficiaries of many government programs—especially Social Security—that provided an economic safety net. Moreover, the discrimination that immigrants were subjected to at the turn of the 20th century remained poignant. "No Irish Need Apply" wasn't just a page in a dusty history book, but a sign whose memories still rendered a stigmata of hurt and pain. Richard M. Nixon wrote in *Six Crises* that in 1960 he "could not dismiss from my mind the persistent thought that, in fact, Kennedy was a member of a minority religion to which the presidency had been denied throughout the history of our nation and that perhaps I, as a Protestant who had never felt the slings of discrimination, could not understand his feelings—that, in short, he had every right to speak out against even possible and potential bigotry" (Nixon 1979, 436). Kennedy tacitly agreed, telling delegates to the 1960 Democratic National Convention that his party had taken a "hazardous risk," and he reiterated his pledge to uphold the Constitution regardless of any religious pressure "that might directly or indirectly interfere with my conduct of the presidency in the national interest" (Kennedy 1960a).

Also helping Kennedy was the Cold War, which provided a source of issue-agreement between Catholics and the Democratic presidential candidate. For decades, Catholics had been ardent anticommunists. In 1930, Pope Pius XI asked Catholics to pray for the conversion of Russia—and they did (White 1997, 141). By 1949, 81 percent of Catholics saw Christianity and communism as incompatible (White 1997, 64). Republicans took notice. But Kennedy was not to be outdone in his anticommunist appeals—especially to those ethnic Catholics who had relatives behind the Iron Curtain. On the stump, Kennedy combined his anticommunism with an appeal to old-fashioned American nationalism: "I want a world which looks to the United States for leadership, and which does not always read what Mr. Khrushchev is doing or what Mr. Castro is doing. I want to read what the president of the United States is doing" (Sorensen 1966, 207).

Despite Kennedy's vehement anticommunism, religion remained the crucible around which the 1960 contest was fought. As one elderly woman told presidential chronicler Theodore H. White: "We've never had a Catholic president and I hope we never do. Our people built this country. If they had wanted a Catholic to be president, they would have said so in the Constitution" (White 1961, 125). The arguments both pro and con surrounding the question of whether a Catholic could serve as president galvanized U.S. Catholics. As the editors of *U.S. News and World Report* stated in their August 1, 1960, issue, "There is, or can be, such a thing as a 'Catholic vote,' whereby a high proportion of Catholics of all ages, residences, occupations, and economic status vote for a well-known Catholic or a ticket with special Catholic appeal" (Nixon 1979, 364). Looking back, *The New York Times* religion editor Peter Steinfels writes that the Roman Catholic

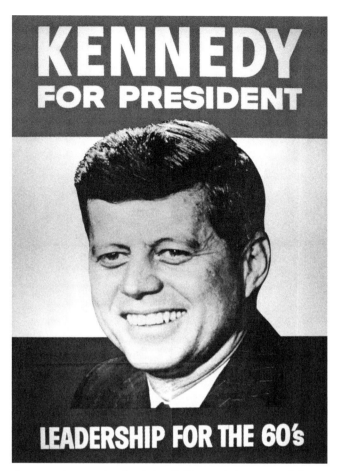

A campaign poster for John F. Kennedy's successful presidential bid in 1960. (John F. Kennedy Library)

Church provided a sense of security to newly arrived immigrants and, in so doing, reinforced their strongly held Catholic identities: "Catholic fraternal societies provided insurance while preserving ethnic cultures. Catholic reading circles and Catholic summer school programs of lectures, concerts, and dramas mirrored the nineteenth century Chautauqua Movement for cultural improvement. Catholic newspapers by the hundreds were printed in a babel of languages, often for small ethnic readerships but sometimes with national impact. Catholic publishers sprung up to serve a growing market for Bibles, prayer books, catechism, religious novels, and pious nonfiction" (Steinfels 2003, 104).

This strong sense of religious identity made Catholicism a unifying force. As Catholicism emerged as the primary issue in 1960, newspaper headlines reflected what was up front in voters' minds: "Democrats Hit

Back on Religion" (*The New York Times*); "Johnson Blasts 'Haters' Attacks on Catholics" (*The Washington Post*); "Creed Issue Must Be Met, Bob Kennedy Says Here" (*Cincinnati Enquirer*); "Mrs. FDR Hits Religious Bias in Talk to Negroes" (*Baltimore Sun*) (Nixon 1979, 465). Meanwhile, the National Association of Evangelicals sent a distressed letter to pastors, warning, "Public opinion is changing in favor of the church of Rome. We dare not sit idly by–voiceless and voteless" (Goodstein 2004). These headlines reflected and shaped the public's views of the candidates. The morning after the long election night, Nixon's daughter, Julie, awakened the exhausted candidate to ask, "Daddy, why did people vote against you because of religion?" (Nixon 1979, 465).

Ethnic Catholics Desert the Democrats, 1980–2012

Yet only three years after John F. Kennedy's narrow 1960 victory, there were signs that the old Catholic–Protestant divide was losing its salience. The final political meeting President Kennedy held in the White House occurred on November 13, 1963. It focused on the movement of urban-dwelling Catholics to the suburbs. Richard M. Scammon, then director of the Census Bureau, told Kennedy he would be well advised to focus on the new suburbanites (many of them Catholic) during the upcoming campaign. Kennedy was fascinated by Scammon's analysis and wanted to know at what point in their upward economic and social climb these former urban residents would become antitax Republicans. Scammon promised to find out, but that assignment was shelved when Kennedy was assassinated just nine days later (Dallek 2003, 691).

What Kennedy began to realize was the distinct possibility that the Catholic vote would break for the Republicans in the not-too-distant future if Democrats did not act. That proved prescient. Between 1976 and 2012, only twice did Democratic presidential candidates secure a Catholic majority: Jimmy Carter with 54 percent in 1976 and Bill Clinton with 53 percent 20 years later (Connelly 2004). In fact, the lack of Catholic support for the Democratic tickets was due in part to the suburban movement. When urban Catholics packed their belongings into station wagons and headed for the suburbs, new worries associated with being "haves" in American society (especially concerns about high property tax rates) dominated their thoughts. Beginning with Ronald Reagan in 1980, Republican presidential candidates consistently won Catholic majorities: 50 percent and 54 percent, respectively, for Reagan in 1980 and 1984; 52 percent for George H.W. Bush in 1988 (Connelly 2004).

The demise of a solid Democratic Catholic voting bloc became clear when another Catholic Democrat who, like John F. Kennedy, also happened to be a U.S. senator from Massachusetts (and even had the same initials) sought the presidency in 2004. That year, the Democratic Party nominated only the third Roman Catholic in its history for the presidency, John F. Kerry. But unlike 1928 and 1960, Kerry *lost* the Catholic vote, receiving just 47 percent to 52 percent for Methodist George W. Bush (Edison Media Research and Mitofsky International 2004). Just as Richard Scammon had predicted, Catholics were now "haves" in American society, with many residing in the prosperous suburbs. Today, just as many Catholics are as likely as Protestants to have graduated from college, and as a group Catholics earn slightly more on the whole than do Protestants (Greeley 1997, 73).

In addition to becoming haves, Catholics were also responding to the increased salience of social and cultural issues. In 1973, the Supreme Court in *Roe v. Wade* voted to legalize abortion during the first three months of a woman's pregnancy. Immediately, abortion became a hot-button issue, and Catholics (especially those who attended church regularly) began voting Republican—especially when the party embraced antiabortion planks in its platforms starting in 1980 that pledged to overturn *Roe*. In 2004, 56 percent of weekly church-attending Catholics voted for George W. Bush (Edison Media Research and Mitofsky International 2004). Four years later, John McCain captured 50 percent of weekly church-attending Catholics (Edison Research 2008). And in 2012, Mormon Mitt Romney won 57 percent support from weekly Catholic mass attendees (Edison Research 2012). The Catholic hierarchy also became more outspoken in its opposition to Democratic candidates. In 2004, Catholic prelates in Camden, New Jersey; St. Louis, Missouri; Lincoln, Nebraska; Denver, Colorado; and Colorado

Springs, Colorado, issued statements forbidding John F. Kerry from receiving Holy Communion should he attend mass in their dioceses because of his pro-choice abortion stance. The Colorado Springs bishop warned that Catholics who supported Kerry were jeopardizing their salvation by supporting any candidate who backed abortion rights. The Denver bishop went even further, chastising Kerry's Catholic supporters as "cooperating in evil" (Dowd 2004).

Hispanics and a New Catholic Demography

Speaking at the 1998 commencement exercises at Portland State University, President Bill Clinton cast his eye toward the 21st century and saw a nation transformed. Saying that the United States was experiencing a "great revolution" thanks to the influx of new immigrants, Clinton foretold a future when whites would no longer be a majority: "Today, largely because of immigration, there is no majority race in Hawaii or Houston or New York City. Within five years, there will be no majority race in our largest state, California. In a little more than fifty years, there will be no majority race in the United States" (Clinton 1998).

The facts bear out Clinton's argument. When Richard M. Nixon took the presidential oath in 1969, there were approximately 9.6 million foreign-born persons residing in the United States (White 2009, 59). By 2013, when Barack Obama raised his hand to take the presidential oath, that number had increased to 40 million (U.S. Census Bureau 2012). Today, the Latino proportion of the foreign-born population is 53 percent, the vast majority of whom are Catholic (U.S. Census Bureau 2012). In 2010, the Census Bureau counted 50.5 million Latinos, which constituted 16 percent of the total population (U.S. Census Bureau 2011). Today, for the first time in history, Latinos outnumber blacks, making them the nation's number one minority group. Latinos are projected to account for 60 percent of the U.S. population growth between 2005 and 2050. And in 2008, the Census Bureau issued a bulletin stating that by 2042 (eight years earlier than expected), whites will be the nation's new minority (White 2009, 63).

As always, children are harbingers of the future. According to the Census Bureau, 70 percent of the population increase among children aged 5 and younger is Hispanic. Should present trends continue, Hispanics will approach 29 percent of the total population in 2050 and could even reach 33 percent by 2100 (White 2009, 63). These trends have transformed the matter of who sits in the Catholic pews. According to the landmark survey of religious affiliation conducted by the Pew Research Center, 29 percent of U.S. Catholics are Hispanic (Pew Forum on Religion and Public Life 2008). There is hardly a Catholic church today in the United States that does not have a mass spoken in Spanish. Priests are under enormous pressure to learn the language, as they need to find ways to communicate with their new communicants.

The increased Hispanic presence across the land has transformed the nature of the Catholic vote. For much of U.S. history, the Catholic vote was defined by ethnic groups that included the Irish, Italians, Poles, French, Lithuanians, Portuguese, and others. Now Hispanic migrants from Mexico and Central and South America comprise an ever larger share of the Catholic vote. Back in 1980, Hispanics constituted less than 1 percent of the total presidential votes cast. In 2012, Hispanics constituted 10 percent of all votes cast, and they cast a remarkable 71 percent of their votes for Barack Obama (Edison Research 2012).

Hispanics have gravitated to the Democratic Party for the same reasons many of their Catholic forebears did: immigration. Beginning in 2007, Republicans have been obdurate opponents to any immigration reforms that would grant citizenship to the nearly 11 million illegal immigrants residing in the United States. During the 2012 campaign, Republican presidential nominee Mitt Romney advocated a policy that would have illegals "self-deport" (Alter 2013, 189). In June 2012, President Obama signed an executive order decreeing that 800,000 young people who had arrived illegally in the United States before age 16, had finished or would finish high school, and met other requirements be given temporary status and avoid deportation (Alter 2013, 276).

The result was to drive an already pro-Democratic Hispanic Catholic vote even higher with respect to Obama and other Democratic candidates and much lower with respect to Republican candidates. This was a change from the George W. Bush years, when the Republican president opposed English-only laws and advocated a humane immigration policy that won the support of senators John McCain and Edward M. Kennedy. Bush won an all-time GOP high of 44 percent of the Hispanic vote in 2004, but no Republican has achieved that number since. The result has been to place California in a safe-Democratic column. Other states, including New Mexico, have joined that category. And a large Hispanic presence in such diverse states as Colorado, Nevada, Arizona, Virginia, Florida, North Carolina, and Georgia (among others) is making these states even more competitive. Eventually, Texas is expected to join this group of competitive states (perhaps in the next decade). While older ethnic Catholics have gravitated toward the GOP, this dynamic group of younger, Hispanic Catholics sees the GOP as hostile to their very presence, and they have rallied behind Obama in two consecutive elections. Their overwhelming support helped make Obama the first president since Dwight Eisenhower to win more than 50 percent of the popular vote in two straight contests.

After the drubbing Republicans took in 2012, Republican members of Congress have pushed for immigration reform, believing that if they do not do something about the issue their party will be doomed to lose the presidency for years to come. Republican senator Lindsey Graham, a pro-immigration reform sponsor in the U.S. Senate, explained his reasoning: "I want to get reattached to the Hispanic community, to sell conservatism, pass comprehensive immigration reform and grow this party. The party has got to be bigger than Utah and South Carolina. The Hispanic community is close to our values, but we have driven them away over this issue" (Graham 2013).

Conclusion

Back in 1960, John F. Kennedy told the Southern Baptists that he dreamed of a country "where there is no Catholic vote" (Kennedy 1960b). Today, Kennedy's wish has come true in part. Ethnicity, not religious affiliation per se, is reshaping the Catholic vote. But the lack of a unified Catholic vote across its many constituencies does not signify an absence of religious conflict. As political scientist E.E. Schattschneider once wrote, "The substitution of conflicts is the most devastating kind of political strategy" (Schattschneider 1975, 71). Today, the ancient Catholic–Protestant divide has given way to a new conflict over the internalization and exposition of religious values. Thus, those who attend church regularly—be they Catholics or white Protestants—have consistently backed Republicans, while those who don't—be they Catholics or white Protestants—have usually supported Democrats. And Hispanics are supporting Democrats (regardless of church attendance) because they see them as the more welcoming party. As Schattschneider once foretold, the tearing apart of the old Catholic–Protestant conflict and its replacement by a new conflict is dangerously explosive because wounds have been ripped open that are exacerbating a new religious, ethnic, and racial divide that is likely to define our politics for some time to come.

See also Abortion and Politics; Church–State Relations; Civil Religion; Cultural Pluralism; Jews and Politics; Latinos and Politics; Religion and Politics.

John Kenneth White

Bibliography

Alter, Jonathan. 2013. *The Center Holds: Obama and His Enemies*. New York: Simon and Schuster.

Barone, Michael. 1990. *Our Country: The Shaping of America from Roosevelt to Reagan*. New York: Free Press.

Clinton, Bill. 1998. "Remarks by the President at Portland State University Commencement." Portland, Oregon, June 13.

Connelly, Marjorie. 2004. "How Americans Voted: A Political Portrait." *New York Times* (November 7).

Dallek, Robert. 2003. *An Unfinished Life: John F. Kennedy, 1917–1963*. Boston: Little Brown and Company.

Dowd, Maureen. 2004. "Vote and Be Damned." *New York Times* (October 17).

Edison Media Research and Mitofsky International. 2004. Exit poll, November 2.

Edison Research. 2008. Exit poll, November 4.

Edison Research. 2012. Exit poll, November 6.

Goodstein, Laurie. 2004. "How the Evangelicals and Catholics Joined Forces." *New York Times* (May 30).

Graham, Lindsey. 2013. *Real Clear Politics.* "Lindsey Graham: Pass Immigration Reform for the Good of the Republican Party." June 23.

Greeley, Andrew. 1997. *The Catholic Myth: The Behavior and Beliefs of Catholics.* New York: Touchstone Books.

Kennedy, John F. 1960a. Acceptance Speech. Democratic National Convention, Los Angeles. July 15.

Kennedy, John F. 1960b. "Address to Southern Baptist Leaders." *New York Times* (September 13).

Nixon, Richard M. 1979 edition. *Six Crises.* New York: Warner Brothers.

Pew Forum on Religion and Public Life. 2008. "U.S. Religious Landscape Survey: 2008." February 25.

Schattschneider, E. E. 1975. *The Semi-sovereign People: A Realist's View of Democracy in America.* Hinsdale, IL: Dryden Press.

Sorensen, Theodore C. 1966. *Kennedy.* New York: Bantam Books.

Steinfels, Peter. 2003. *A People Adrift: The Crisis of the Roman Catholic Church in America.* New York: Simon and Schuster.

U.S. Census Bureau. 2011. "The Hispanic Population: 2010." Washington, DC: U.S. Department of Commerce.

U.S. Census Bureau. 2012. "The Foreign-Born Population in the United States: 2010." Washington, DC: U.S. Department of Commerce.

White, John Kenneth. 1983. *The Fractured Electorate: Political Parties and Social Change in Southern New England.* Hanover, NH: University Press of New England.

White, John Kenneth. 1997. *Still Seeing Red: How the Cold War Shapes the New American Politics.* Boulder, CO: Westview Press.

White, John Kenneth. 2009. *Barack Obama's America: How New Conceptions of Race, Family and Religion Ended the Reagan Era.* Ann Arbor: University of Michigan Press.

White, Theodore H. 1961. *The Making of the President 1960.* New York: New American Library.

CHURCH–STATE RELATIONS

In many ways, concern about the relationship between church and state is a distinct American development. Influenced by the Enlightenment thinkers, the First Congress included two relevant provisions in the text of the First Amendment to the Constitution. The so-called Establishment Clause says that "Congress shall make no law respecting an establishment of religion," and the second clause prohibits Congress from making any law "prohibiting the free exercise" of religion. Taken together, these two clauses force the government to leave a significant amount of space for individuals to make their own choices regarding religion and other spiritual enterprises.

The brevity of these two passages, of course, has led to an important and protracted debate about the government's relationship with religion. Separationists argue that the religion clauses in the First Amendment require a strict separation between church and state. Accommodationists, on the other hand, view these clauses leave significant room for cooperation between government and religious groups—or at least government tolerance of religion expressed in the realm of public policy. The U.S. Supreme Court has long played an important role in defining the balance between these two positions.

In the founders' time, America was relatively homogeneous in terms of religion; the major debates were among various Protestant sects. Demographic and cultural changes in America have changed the discourse considerably. As a result, the modern debate often involves vastly different sets of religious and spiritual beliefs, including the interests of a growing number of distinctly nonreligious citizens (Lopez and Gonzalez-Barrera 2012). Even so, a strong majority of American citizens has always identified as Christian. Americans still report high levels of church attendance, and a large percentage of Americans report that religion is very important to them (Jelen 2010).

Thomas Jefferson suggested in 1802 that the First Amendment's religion clauses acted as a "wall of separation between church and state" (Jefferson 1998). However, throughout the country's history, the majoritarian branches of federal, state, and local governments have generally sought to accommodate the widely shared religious beliefs of American Christians. As early as 1897, the U.S. Supreme Court has acknowledged the importance of Jefferson's conception of the First Amendment's religion clauses (*Reynolds v. U.S.*). However, it was not until the middle of the 20th century that the Supreme Court actually struck down a law because it violated the principles of the First Amendment's religion clauses (*Engel v. Vitale*). Since that time, the Court's role in patrolling church–state relations has been the subject of controversy. But the debate is wider than just the First Amendment, and it extends beyond the Supreme Court. The 1973 landmark decision in *Roe v. Wade*, which greatly intensified the debate about the role of religious values in American law and society, did not implicate the First Amendment's religion clauses directly. In response to this and other Supreme Court decisions deemed hostile to America's Christian traditions, religious groups often turned to the political branches of government for relief.

Religious Groups and Public Policy—the 1970s and 1980s

To be sure, religious movements ebbed and flowed cyclically in 20th-century America (Jelen 2010), with the 1920s, the 1950s, and the 1980s being high points for such activism (Wilcox 2010). The most recent cycle started in the wake of the Court's decision in *Roe*, which served to invigorate religious opposition to the cultural liberalization of the 1960s and early 1970s. At about the same time, various government agencies were beginning to threaten the tax exempt status of religious institutions that engaged in racial discrimination, and the Supreme Court seemed unwilling to come to the aid of these religious groups (*Bob Jones University v. Simon*). This existential threat unified evangelical leaders, who were able to rally religious adherents around the cause by linking it to the abortion debate post-*Roe* (Balmer 2006).

The 1976 election was affected by this religious movement, even though the bulk of the formal organizing happened later in the decade. Newly mobilized Christians were driven to the ballot box to support the unabashed born-again Christian candidate, Jimmy

Carter (Hood, Kidd, and Morris 2011; Wilcox 1989). Evangelical religious leaders began to see the results of their organizational efforts in the late 1970s, and the result was a number of powerful groups such as the American Family Association, the Moral Majority, Focus on the Family, and Concerned Women for America. These newly organized religious groups became powerful forces in American electoral politics. They advocated for Christian morals to be reflected in American politics. They supported an accommodationist view of the First Amendment's religion clauses, which would allow for the government to allow significant religious presence in the public square. To achieve this vision, of course, they would also need to push for the election of likeminded policy makers.

Some of the first major successes for these religious affinity groups happened in the realm of local politics. Although the Supreme Court's religious establishment cases since the 1960s had declared many of their preferred policies to be unconstitutional, local governments were often able to avoid the implementation of these Supreme Court rulings (Canon and Johnson 1999). Throughout the 1970s, there was an orchestrated effort on the part of fledgling religious groups to fill local commissions and boards with people who would resist the push to remove religion from the public square. These efforts were very successful, particularly in shaping school district policies and curricula (Wills 1990). These wins at the local government level accommodated religious interests, allowing for traditional Christian morals to be reflected in local policy.

In the early 1970s, religious affinity groups were mostly politically unaffiliated; this was despite the fact that the Christian right had informally allied with the Republicans in the past (Martin 1996). Heading into the 1980s, both Republicans and Democrats courted the religious vote (Wilcox 1989). However, these organizations, and the voters they represented, were soon drawn toward the Republican Party as the Democratic Party deepened its alliances with liberal social activist movements and separationist tendencies. The Christian–Republican coalition was strengthened by then presidential candidate Ronald Reagan in the run-up to the 1980 election. Reagan emphasized his opposition to the *Roe* decision, and this helped him to garner support from the strong pro-life sentiments that dominated in many of these religious affinity groups. His campaign speeches also made frequent use of religious ideas (Wilcox 2010), as did his speeches once in office (Wills 1990).

While they have had success in organizing to influence elections, the ability of religious affinity groups to affect national policy has been limited (Bivins 2003). Even during the Reagan years, the progress made nationally was generally more rhetorical than substantive. Although the language of "traditional American Christian values" gained significant traction during the 1980s, no great strides in limiting abortion, returning prayer to schools, or curtailing the advancement of other liberal social policies happened during the Reagan administration. The rhetoric of religion was present, but there was little movement toward accommodation of religion in terms of national policy. One exception to this was Reagan's announcement of the "Mexico City Policy," in which he instructed the United States Agency for International Development to withhold development funds from groups that engage in promoting or providing abortions elsewhere in the world.

Some of the few victories for the Christian Right at this time came from the Supreme Court, to which Reagan had appointed two moderates and one strong conservative. In *Bowen v. Kendrick*, the Court upheld federal funding for abstinence-only education. In *Webster v. Reproductive Health Services*, the Court upheld restrictions on access to abortion; this decision set the stage for further weakening of the privacy right outlined in *Roe* (Baer 2005). *Widmar v. Vincent* held that religious groups must be given equal access to public school facilities after hours, and Congress extended this idea with the Equal Access Act of 1984. But many of the Court's important holdings regarding religion were separationist in nature during this time. The Court allowed tax deductions for private school expenses (*Muller v. Allen*), but it struck down a moment of silence (*Wallace v. Jaffree*) and the teaching of creationism (*Edwards v. Aguillard*) in public schools.

Although the national policy victories of the religious affinity groups were rather modest, the perceived strength of the Christian fundamentalist and evangelical groups became a national story. These groups were able to mobilize large swaths of likeminded voters at election time. In this way, the Religious Right became an important player in electoral politics. Reagan was able to unify the Religious Right's "family values" message with the "smaller government" message of the Republican Party at that time.

The 1990s and 2000s

During the tenure of Reagan's Republican successor, President George H.W. Bush, the Supreme Court's decision in *Employment Division v. Smith* inspired a rare coalition between groups on the Religious Right and liberal rights-based groups like the American Civil Liberties Union. In *Smith*, the Court held that the government could burden the free exercise of religion as long as it did so incidentally through the enforcement of a facially neutral law. Together, these groups fought for the passage of the Religious Freedom Restoration Act of 1993. This law would raise the standard of review for Free Exercise cases, making it more difficult for the federal government to burden religious exercise. But the Court also affirmed the constitutionality of the Equal Access Act of 1984, which mandated an accommodationist relationship between public facilities and religious groups (*Board of Education v. Mergens*).

The perceived electoral power of the partnership between religious groups and the Republican Party began to wane after the defeat of Bush in 1992. At the time of William Jefferson Clinton's election, he was a member of the Southern Baptist Convention— the same evangelical denomination to which Jimmy Carter had belonged. During his presidency, Clinton attended church services and consistently sought the council of religious leaders. Although his religious faith was more in line with Christian traditionalists than either of the previous two presidents, the Religious Right groups did not align themselves with Clinton or the Democratic Party. Clinton was comfortable putting his religious faith on display, but his policy positions tended to conflict with the goals of the Christian Right (Balmer 2008). But religious groups were able to win a partial victory during Clinton's first term. Although he campaigned on promises to allow homosexual people to serve in the military, but pressure from the Religious Right forced Clinton into the compromise policy that became known as "Don't Ask, Don't Tell." This policy was less desirable to the religious groups than an all-out ban, but in practice it became nearly the same thing. He also reversed the Reagan-era Mexico City Policy, which allowed federal international development funding to groups engaging in promoting or providing abortions overseas.

In 1994, the Republicans mounted a successful comeback campaign in which they took control of Congress for the first time in four decades. The Christian Right received much of the credit for the Republican Revolution of 1994. At this point, the coalition between the Republican Party and conservative religious affinity groups had consolidated to the point that the two were virtually indistinguishable (Rozell and Wilcox 1995). The details of the impeachment proceedings against President Clinton, which involved accusations of marital infidelity, served to help cement religious opposition to the president.

After the midterm elections, President Clinton was much more amenable to compromise, and the Religious Right groups were often the beneficiaries of this. Although Clinton was seen as "the most pro-gay president in the history of the United States" at the time, he maintained his steadfast opposition to same-sex marriage (Moss 1996). It was President Clinton who signed the Defense of Marriage Act 1996 into law. It was also in 1996 that the president signed the Personal Responsibility and Work Opportunity Act. This reform of the welfare system replaced the New Deal-Era Aid to Families with Dependent Children program with the Temporary Assistance for Needy Families. This reform was strongly supported by the Religious Right, as it embodied the Protestant work ethic that conservative Christian organizations lobbied for (Martin 2012). It also included a "Charitable Choice" provision, which required that states include secular charitable organizations when contracting for the provision of services.

Although Clinton made two socially liberal appointments to the Supreme Court during his presidency, the Court delivered some limited victories to the accommodationists in the Religious Right during this time. In two different cases (*Zobrest v. Catalina Foothills* and *Agostini v. Felton*), the Court moved away from its previous precedent and allowed greater cooperation between state governments and private religious schools. The Court also required public post-secondary educational institutions to provide similar accommodations to religious and nonreligious student organizations (*Rosenberger v. Rectors of the University of Virginia*). But in *Lee v. Weisman*, the Court invalidated the practice of allowing religious invocations at public high school commencement ceremonies. It was also during Clinton's presidency that the Supreme Court invalidated the Religious Freedom Restoration Act as it applied to the states (*City of Boerne v. Flores*).

During his presidency, Clinton's Department of Education authored several versions of a document called "Guidelines on Religious Expression in Public Schools." These documents focused on the need to find ways for faith-based organizations to be involved in public schools. They proscribed any secular activities, but encouraged cooperation in the areas of tutoring, after-school programs, and more. Although this may have been a rhetorical win for religious affinity groups, the guidelines were mostly ignored (Marus 2003).

One of the most important issues to religious affinity groups is abortion, and President Clinton's appointees and policies reflected his pro-choice position. At the beginning of his term, a plurality of the Supreme Court reaffirmed the right to privacy, but opened the door for more restrictions on access to abortion (*Planned Parenthood v. Casey*). But this limited win for conservative Christians failed to translate into changes in national abortion policy; Clinton twice vetoed bans on partial birth abortions, once in 1995 and again in 1997. He did, however, sign an appropriations bill in 1995 that contained a rider prohibiting the Department of Health and Human Services from providing federal funding for research that resulted in the destruction of a human embryo. But after the successful isolation of human embryonic stem cells by researchers in 1998, Clinton's National Institutes of Health issued guidelines that provided federal funding to embryonic stem cell research.

Real policy victories for the Religious Right came with the election of President George W. Bush in 2000. The second President Bush was a professed evangelical Christian. The ballots cast by "moral values" voters most certainly pushed President Bush over the top in the very close election; the work of the Religious Right increased conservative turnout by as much as 4 million votes (Kaplan 2005). President Bush made a point to include evangelical Christians as a substantial part of his administration (Lindsay 2007).

Unlike their previous electoral successes, the election of George W. Bush led to some real, tangible policy changes that religious groups favored. Bush's brand of "compassionate conservatism" was in line with both their faith and their political philosophy (Balmer 2008). His was the first presidency since the Warren Court to create national policy that accommodated religious interests and cooperated directly with religious entities. Bush's first executive order created the Office of Faith-Based and Community Initiatives, which enhanced the cooperation between the federal government and the non-proselytizing components

of religious charitable entities, and it was seen as a major win for religious organizations (Martin 2012). Throughout his administration, Bush sought to further such cooperation while protecting the rights of religious institutions to maintain their religious principles. Bush's policies were successful inasmuch as they could be accomplished through executive actions. He had no real legislative success in this arena, though; this failure was largely due to the controversy over whether religious groups involved in these partnerships could continue to discriminate on the basis of religion in their hiring practices (Daly 2009).

The accommodationism of Bush's presidency extended to public schools as well. Bush's No Child Left Behind Act provided a federal funding mechanism for local schools. The Bush administration's version of the Clinton-era guidelines, now called "Guidance on Constitutionally Protected Prayer in Public Elementary

President George W. Bush signs executive orders to advance his "faith-based initiative" at a meeting of religious and charitable leaders in Philadelphia, December 2002. (AP Photo/Pablo Martinez Monsivais)

and Secondary Schools," focused on protecting the free exercise rights of students and teachers in the public school setting (Marus 2003). Efforts to protect the free exercise claims of students and teachers to engage in religious activities in public schools, however, continued to be stymied by the Supreme Court (*Santa Fe ISD v. Doe*).

The Supreme Court at this time was willing to allow a significant amount of cooperation between government and faith-based private schools. A federal program facilitating the lending of educational material to public and private schools was upheld in 2000 (*Mitchell v. Helms*). It also allowed a state voucher program that gave parents financial support to send their children to parochial schools (*Zelman v. Simmons-Harris*).

The Religious Right was also able to secure a win in the realm of free exercise of religion. At the beginning of Bush's first term, he signed the Religious Land Use and Institutionalized Persons Act. This legislation essentially revisited the Religious Freedom Restoration Act that had been partially invalidated in *City of Boerne v. Flores*. It relied on specific constitutional provisions to justify the use of federal power to bind states to a higher level of scrutiny for certain free exercise claims. The Supreme Court upheld this legislation in *Cutter v. Wilkinson*.

The Religious Right also saw significant progress in right-to-life issues during the George W. Bush administration. President Bush signed the Partial-Birth Abortion Ban Act of 2003, and his appointees to the Supreme Court voted to uphold the constitutionality of the law (*Gonzales v. Carhart*). He also reinstituted the Mexico City Policy. He placed strict limitations on the number of embryonic stem cell lines available for federal funding. In his first use of the veto power, Bush vetoed a bill that would have expanded federal funding for such research; he vetoed a similar bill a year later.

Contemporary Developments

The Religious Right suffered its first major electoral defeat in years with the election of President Barack Obama in 2008. Although the traditional Christian conservative voters continued to turn out for the Republican candidate, members of minority religious groups shifted to the Democrats. At the time of his election, he had long been a member of the United Church of Christ, which is a mainstream branch of Protestant Christianity. He made a concerted effort during his campaign to reach out actively to religious voters, both in his use of religious rhetoric in his speeches and in his public appearances before religious congregations (Guth 2011). He also promised to support faith-based initiatives if elected (Daly 2009). But some unique features of his personal religious history worked against him in the campaign, including his association with adherents to black liberation theology and his father's and step-father's Muslim faiths (Rennick 2010).

Obama took up policy matters of interest to the Religious Right almost immediately upon taking office. The Obama administration has essentially consolidated the Bush administration's faith-based initiatives policy through his creation of the White House Office of Faith-Based and Neighborhood Partnerships. Although he pledged to "change how decisions on funding practices are made" (Martin 2012, 62), this move concedes the basic assumption that the federal government can and should partner with religious groups to provide needed services and secular outreach in underserved communities. During his term, the Supreme Court weighed in on the issue of religious employment discrimination in an opinion that solidified the "ministerial exception" allowing churches to discriminate based on religion when hiring people to fill ministerial roles (*Hosanna-Tabor*).

Aside from his support of faith-based initiatives, the conservative Christian movement has found very little to like about President Obama's policies. Obama has long been a supporter of access to abortion and contraception. His signature health care reform measure, the Patient Protection and Affordable Health Care Act of 2010, requires the provision of free contraception—including emergency contraception—by private insurance companies. Despite the narrow exception granted to houses of worship, critics argue that it essentially forces other religious institutions to pay for the provision of services and medications against their religious beliefs. There are several lawsuits challenging the constitutionality of this contraceptive mandate at various stages in the federal courts. It is likely that one or more of these cases will reach the Supreme

Court in the next year or so. The final bill did include the Stupak Amendment, which prohibits any federal funding of abortion, but this was included only as a way to shore up support from wavering pro-life legislators. Obama also reversed the "conscience clause," which had allowed protection for medical professionals who refused to perform procedures that violated their religious beliefs (Guth 2011).

Despite the president's support for access to abortion, the overall policy trend nationwide during his tenure has been toward increasing restrictions on abortion. Aside from the contraception mandate, the only other major national policy change involving right-to-life issues has been Obama's overturning the Mexico City Policy and his reinstatement of federal funding for embryonic stem cell research. The Supreme Court's apparent willingness to allow more restrictions on abortions has emboldened pro-life activists and lawmakers alike. In the time since the Court's decision in *Gonzales v. Carhart*, states have increased legislation restricting abortion. These new restrictions include mandatory ultrasounds and "fetal pain" laws that ban abortions after 20 weeks' gestation.

The Obama administration's record on other social issues of concern to the Religious Right represents a significant defeat for Christian conservatives. Obama was a vocal critic of the Clinton-era Don't Ask, Don't Tell policy and the Defense of Marriage Act. During his campaign, he stopped short of supporting same-sex marriage—perhaps for fear of alienating the religious members of his coalition (Guth 2011)—although he would announce a change of heart on the matter in the run-up to the 2012 presidential campaign. He signed the Don't Ask, Don't Tell Repeal Act in 2010. In 2011, his administration announced that it would not defend the Defense of Marriage Act in Court, citing the administration's view that the law was unconstitutional. A legal challenge to the Defense of Marriage Act was heard by the Supreme Court in March 2013, and a ruling on its constitutionality is expected in June. The Obama administration also set out an immigration proposal in 2013 that would treat same-sex partnerships the same as married partnerships for the purposes of determining eligibility.

Although President Obama won reelection in 2012, it is too early to declare the end of the electoral power of religious affinity groups. Just two years after Obama's win in 2008, the Religious Right partnered with the fledgling "Tea Party" movement to deliver a sound defeat to the president's party in the midterm elections. It is not clear that the alliance of religious affinity groups and the Republican party was driving the successes of the Tea Party success in 2010; the 2010 election seemed to be lacking in the religious messaging and outreach (Guth 2011) that characterized both the 2008 and 2012 elections. Of course, the relationship between church and state is only partly determined by the electoral successes or defeats of the Religious Right. First, it is important to consider the shifting demographics and policy goals that are happening both among the public at large and within the various religious affinity groups. While support of same-sex marriage among the American public seems to be increasing, the public is less supportive of abortion than it has been in recent past (Rozell and Wilcox 2012). This is so both in the general public and in the newer generation of Christian conservatives. This is also reflected in the recent state-level policy successes of same-sex marriage proposals as well as the increasingly restrictive abortion policies that have been enacted by state legislatures. But the Supreme Court will continue to play an important role in determining the boundaries of church–state relations in America, despite the electoral fate of religious groups.

See also Abortion and Politics; Biotechnology and Politics; Culture Wars; Evolution, Creationism, and Politics; Gay and Lesbian Culture and Politics; Prayer and Religious Symbols in Public Places; Protestants, Evangelicals, and Politics; Religion and Politics.

Rebecca Gill and Jonathan Doc Bradley

Bibliography

Baer, Judith. 2005. "Abortion." In K.L. Hall, ed. *The Oxford Companion to the Supreme Court of the United States.* New York: Oxford University Press.

Balmer, Randall. 2006. *Thy Kingdom Come: How the Religious Right Disports the Faith and Threatens America: An Evangelical's Lament.* New York: Basic Books.

Balmer, Randall. 2008. *God in the White House: A History 1960–2004.* New York: HarperCollins.

Bivins, Jason C. 2003. *The Fracture of Good Order.* Raleigh: The University of North Carolina Press.

Canon, Bradley C., and Charles A. Johnson. 1999. *Judicial Policies: Implementation and Impact.* 2nd ed. Washington, DC: CQ Press.

Daly, Lew. 2009. *God's Economy: Faith-Based Initiatives and the Caring State.* Chicago: University of Chicago Press.

Guth, James L. 2011. "Obama, Religious Politics, and the Culture Wars." In S. E. Schier, ed. *Transforming America: Barack Obama in the White House.* New York: Rowman & Littlefield.

Hood, M. V., III, Quentin Kidd, and Irwin L. Morris. 2011. "The Reintroduction of the Elephas Maximus to the Southern United States." In R. Niemi, H. Weisberg, and D. Kimball. *Controversies in Voting Behavior.* Washington, DC: CQ Press.

Jefferson, Thomas. 1998. "Jefferson's Letter to the Danbury Baptists: The Final Letter, as Sent." In *Information Bulletin.* Washington, DC: Library of Congress.

Jelen, Ted G. 2010. *To Serve God and Mammon: Church–State Relations in American Politics,* 2nd ed. Washington, DC: Georgetown University Press.

Kaplan, Esther. 2005. *With God on Their Side: George W. Bush and the Christian Right.* New York: New Press.

Lindsay, D. Michael. 2007. "Ties That Bind and Divisions That Persist: Evangelical Faith and the Political Spectrum." *American Quarterly* 59, no. 3: 883–909.

Lopez, Mark H., and Ana Gonzalez-Barrera. 2012. "'Nones' on the Rise: One-in-Five Adults Have No Religious Affiliation." Washington, DC: Pew Research Center.

Martin, Michelle E. 2012. "Philosophical and Religious Influences on Social Welfare Policy in the United States: The Ongoing Effect of Reformed Theology and Social Darwinism on Attitudes toward the Poor and Social Welfare Policy and Practice." *Journal of Social Work* 12, no. 1: 51.

Martin, William. 1996. *With God on Our Side: The Rise of the Religious Right in America.* New York: Broadway Books.

Marus, Robert. 2003. "White House Guidelines Go Where Courts Fear to Tread." *Baptist Standard* (February 17).

Moss, J. Jennings. 1996. "Bill Clinton Interview." *The Advocate* (June 25).

Rennick, David. 2010. *The Bridge: The Life and Rise of Barack Obama.* New York: Alfred A. Knopf.

Rozell, Mark J., and Clyde Wilcox. 1995. *God at the Grass Roots: The Christian Right in the 1994 Elections.* Lanham, MD: Rowman & Littlefield.

Rozell, Mark J., and Clyde Wilcox. 2012. "Do Elections Indicate the Death of the Christian Right? Not So Fast." *Washington Post* (November 15).

Wilcox, Clyde. 1989. "The New Christian Right and the Mobilization of the Evangelicals." In T. G. Jelen, ed. *Religion and Political Behavior in the United States.* New York: Praeger.

Wilcox, Clyde. 2010. *Onward Christian Soldiers? The Religious Right in American Politics.* 4th ed. Boulder, CO: Westview Press.

Wills, Gary. 1990. *Under God.* New York: Simon & Schuster Paperbacks.

Cases
Agostini v. Felton, 521 U.S. 203 (1997).
Board of Education v. Mergens, 496 U.S. 226 (1990).
Bob Jones University v. Simon, 416 U.S. 725 (1974).
Bowen v. Kendrick, 487 U.S. 589 (1988).
City of Boerne v. Flores, 521 U.S. 507 (1997).
Cutter v. Wilkinson, 544 U.S. 709 (2005).
Edwards v. Aguillard, 482 U.S. 578 (1987).
Employment Division v. Smith, 494 U.S. 872 (1990).
Engel v. Vitale, 370 U.S. 421 (1962).
Gonzales v. Carhart, 550 U.S. 124 (2007).
Hosanna-Tabor Lutheran v. Equal Employment Opportunity Comm., 565 U.S. ___ (2012).
Lee v. Weisman, 505 U.S. 577 (1992).
Mitchell v. Helms, 530 U.S. 793 (2000).
Muller v. Allen, 463 U.S. 388 (1983).
Planned Parenthood v. Casey, 505 U.S. 833 (1992).
Reynolds v. U.S., 98 U.S. (8 Otto.) 145 (1879).
Roe v. Wade, 410 U.S. 113 (1973).
Rosenberger v. Rectors of the University of Virginia, 515 U.S. 819 (1995).
Santa Fe Independent School District v. Doe, 530 U.S. 290 (2000).
Wallace v. Jaffree, 472 U.S. 38 (1985).
Webster v. Reproductive Health Services, 492 U.S. 490 (1989).

Widmar v. Vincent, 454 U.S. 263 (1981).
Zelman v. Simmons-Harris, 536 U.S. 639 (2002).
Zobrest v. Catalina Foothills School District, 509 U.S. 1 (1993).

CITIES AND POLITICS

The promise of democracy in the United States is arguably best realized in cities. It is at the metropolitan level that many of the structures that frame people's lives are governed. Indeed, under federalism, most policies concerning transportation, economic development, education, the development of housing, and so on, take their ultimate shape in metropolitan areas, even if the policies receive support from higher levels of government. In the end, local governments implement policy and must do so in ways that resonate with citizen preferences, stakeholder interests, and governing practices. Consequently, there is widespread agreement that government in cities is distinct from how government operates at other levels; however, there is also robust debate about the foundations that underlie how to study urban politics. The different positions in this debate are explored through specific consideration of the politics surrounding urbanization. These politics take multiple forms, and two are considered herein: highly public and direct attempts to influence growth and development, and less direct ways that attempt to define what is desirable in growth and steer development toward specific ends. Consideration begins with established perspectives on how governments interface the politics of urbanization. Subsequent discussion considers more recent and less settled perspectives on the study of cities and politics.

From Pluralism to Political Economy

Dahl's (1961) landmark study of government decision making in New Haven, Connecticut, articulates one of the foundational theories of urban politics. This study is based on a two centuries–long look at the individuals and institutions that shaped the development of New Haven through making decisions concerning several issue areas: urban renewal, public education, and nominees for political office. Dahl's study found

that influence in the decisions about how and where to develop in New Haven was dispersed among stakeholders, highly competitive, and changed over time according to local elections. Dahl's study emerged as one of the principal references for the theory of urban pluralism. Pluralism assumes different interests within a society exist and compete in a marketplace of ideas. Further, government essentially functions to negotiate these divergent interests. Power in this theory is understood as the ability to affect decisions that local governments make about policies concerning urbanization and how people will live together. Urban pluralism offers a state-centered analysis and maintains that the authority provided to local government is subject to popular control through free, open, and regular elections. Authority in this view is exercised primarily through setting agendas for government decision making, noting that some issues are privileged and others marginalized. Control over government authority is further conceptualized as competitive. At the same time, authority can be unequally distributed across different interest groups when one is able to bring more resources to bear. Nevertheless, studies like Dahl's found that no one interest group exerted authority across all issue areas and thus maintains that power is dispersed throughout a community. Two distinct critiques of urban pluralism have emerged to advance the study of urban politics in important ways.

In contrast to pluralism's notion that harnessing governmental authority is competitive, elite theory stresses that elites in the private economic sector ultimately limit or constrain governmental authority if they do not appropriate it to serve their own interests. Elite theory emphasizes the importance of class dynamics in explaining how members of the upper class coordinate to dominate urban politics. Importantly, this theory focuses on how elites shape policy from outside of government. This may of course be accomplished through patronage. But elite theory draws attention to two strategies of indirect influence. On the one hand, corporate and business communities labor to create a "policy-planning network" that is receptive to their interests (Domhoff 2013). These communities manage this by populating the boards of organizations in the nonprofit sector (including civic organizations, universities, philanthropic foundations, and cultural organizations), which in turn cultivate a business-friendly political climate in a locality. On the other hand, economic elites are also able to shape urban policy by forming "growth coalitions" that seek to increase the profits that can be extracted from intensifying land uses (i.e., growth). Growth coalitions include a diverse array of entities, from utility companies and newspapers to real estate developers and banks, which are ultimately united in their pursuit of growth. Furthermore, these coalitions frame growth as unquestionably beneficial to the local economy by creating jobs and bringing investment to a place, which can have multiplier effects and encourage ancillary growth (Logan and Molotch 1987). Both of these strategies combine to give growth coalitions leverage over local governments that simultaneously operate in specific policy-planning environments that may also be shaped in ways that favor growth. To be sure, dominance does not connote complete control over government. Further, elite theory allows for influence of working- and middle-class interests in shaping urbanization. At the same time, elite theory is decidedly clear about the hierarchical social arrangements through which urban politics operate.

Where elite theory emphasizes the constraints that the private economic sector places on local government, urban regime theory focuses on the ways in which elected officials enroll private sector actors into a "governing coalition." Regime theory insists that controlling government through an election is a necessary but insufficient component for governing. Rather, in addition to winning elections, public officials must build partnerships with nongovernmental actors. These partnerships can be formed for a variety of purposes, but are ultimately contingent upon the fact that private sector actors must continue to be profitable, to lesser or greater degrees. Nevertheless, the formation of these partnerships is understood to be the result of long-term collaborations between partners, which involve processes of learning about one another, sharing resources, and crafting strategies to accomplish goals that are mutually beneficial. At their peak, these coalitions persist through several elections and thus come to establish a regime. Regimes can break apart when there is conflict among partners, which can result from misunderstandings among coalition partners as much as from the pursuit of purposes that pose contradictions for specific coalition members. Governing coalitions are thus delicate arrangements that take constant investment and work to maintain cohesion. When cohesion can be maintained, however, regime theory posits that governing coalitions can mobilize resources to pursue decidedly progressive purposes (Stone 2005).

Elite theory and urban regime theory are ultimately complementary frameworks that, respectively, answer the questions of who governs and through what institutional channels. These theories offer important counterarguments to pluralism, which serves as the prevailing mythos about how American urban politics operate. At the same time, elite theory and regime theory focus on the indirect ways in which actors influence governing by setting agendas for decision making. There are other equally important perspectives that bring into consideration how certain ideas and ideologies come to influence notions of what is desirable or even possible in cities.

Analyzing Urban Politics from Network Perspectives

The theory of governmentality holds that governing is inextricably bound up with thought and ways of thinking. Governing is both made possible and constrained by what can be thought at particular moments in history. This theory gives attention to the hegemonic ways in which power is exercised through consent and common sense and thus takes a different approach to studying politics than elite theory and regime theory. One key difference is that governmentality approaches the social world as a network, rather than a hierarchy. The significance of this is summarized in a RSA Animate (2012) feature on networks. Governmentality is no less focused on institutions, though.

Foucault (1979) describes governmentality as a project to interrogate the taken-for-granted assumptions that undergird how political processes work to achieve certain ends, reify certain values, and establish truths. The purpose of this theory is to analyze governing institutions and reveal the manner through which domination works so that it may be effectively contested. Analysis proceeds by examining several interconnected ways in which governing works: particular ways of knowing the world are privileged, these in turn legitimize certain forms of knowledge and claims to truth, which are consequently reproduced through programs and practices that circulate particular ways of seeing and knowing. Finally, citizens are also socialized as political subjects who support and reproduce the particular ways of knowing and operating in the world. Studies of citizen participation in neighborhood planning provide an illustrative example as they show how local governments make plans in ways that naturalize a Cartesian view of the world and privilege quantifiable information. In their work, Elwood and Leitner (2003) show that local governments reproduce these views through technocratic processes of neighborhood planning that allow citizen input on maps and planning documents in ways that reinforce the primacy of Cartesian views and positivist understanding. Citizens are simultaneously disciplined to work in these ways by translating local knowledge through mapping processes, which marginalizes some ways of knowing and reinforces technocratic ways of thinking. Foucault's theory notwithstanding, the topic of citizen involvement in planning processes is discussed substantively in the final section. Concurrent with governmentality perspectives, there is another method and form of theorizing the politics of urbanization that emphasizes networks and assemblages, hereafter "Actor-Network-Theory" (ANT).

Born from science and technology studies (Latour and Woolgar [1979] 1986), and influenced by Deleuzian conceptions of assemblage, ANT is now finding expression in a variety of subfields of urban studies (e.g., Cronon 1991; Farias and Bender 2010). These works exemplify or explore the major tenets of ANT, specifically that abstract categories that are given causal primacy for understanding phenomena should be replaced by a strong empiricism that traces ties and associations between actors. Such associations, extended, form networks. However, networks only exist as they are produced. When not in formation, they decline.

In opposition to structural perspectives, like elite theory and regime theory, ANT rejects the reliance on and imposition of transcendental-metaphysical entities—"social class," "society"—as causal agents, unless such abstractions are mobilized by actors themselves. ANT's focus on trace association and networks is a radical ontological challenge because it flattens accounts of being by removing vertical schema (e.g., local, state, regional, national, international) in favor of horizontal, rhizomatic relations. This poses a challenge to conceptions like community, neighborhood, and city as abstractions posited a priori and as totalities over and above action.

Urbanists see the appeal of ANT as it seems to confirm observations of the heterogeneous complexity of cities. The city, from an ANT account, appears far more contingent, active, and porous than the static and bounded conceptions of the city presented by the Chicago School or urban political economy. Indeed, according to ANT, the city is an active "assemblage of assemblages," a multiplicity that is never fixed (Bender 2010). Patterns of organization and practice confound scalar schemas due to their character as imbroglios. For instance, inter-urban influences on the sustainability model of Whistler, British Columbia, pose an assemblage challenge to traditional-bounded conceptions of urbanism (Temenos and McCann 2012).

There are two ways in which ANT theorizing and methodology relate to the politics of urbanization. First, by emphasizing networks of relations, a different image of political power emerges, one that is far more specific and less geographically arbitrary. As with all politics, such a conceptualization of urban formation is an opportunity for both exploitative and liberationist politics. A new urban development may be understood not as the relation of abstract categories but as specific actors and can therefore be contested in a much more precise way. Second, as Bender (2010) points out, the politics of urbanization implied in ANT maintain that publics are formations in response to problems. Hence, politicized practices must be formed and performed; in the absence of such performance, political interventions or challenges fade.

Urban political economy theory has begun wrestling with ANT's challenges. Brenner, Madden, and Wachsmuth (2011) identify three levels (articulations) of assemblage analysis: (1) empirical—assemblages as research objects that may be studied from an urban political economy perspective; (2) methodological—assemblages conceptualized as a metabolic process, thereby allowing urban political economy to extend inquiry to new foci; and (3) ontological—assemblages as an entirely new depiction of reality. Brenner, Madden, and Wachsmuth (2011, 233) argue that "the merits of levels 1 and 2 . . . have been theoretically and substantively demonstrated in the urban studies literature . . . (but) we are much more skeptical regarding the possible contributions of analyses conducted on level 3."

On the third level, Brenner, Madden, and Wachsmuth (2011, 231) purport it as "displac(ing) the investigation of capitalist urban development and the core concerns of urban political economy." They further argue that "without recourse to political economy or to another theoretical framework attuned to the structuration of urban processes . . . , an ontologically inflected appropriation of assemblage analysis confronts serious difficulties as a basis for illuminating the contemporary urban condition" (Brenner, Madden, and Wachsmuth 2011, 233). Important tools of urban political economy, such as capital investment and disinvestment, state formation, the activities of global powers such as the World Bank and International Monetary Fund, are rendered far more impotent in ANT's politics of urbanization than they really are (Brenner, Madden, and Wachsmuth 2011, 234). Moreover, they argue that by ignoring structuration processes a "passive voice politics prevails" rendering ANT's approach far less powerful as a normative project than urban political economy.

Alongside the rise of ANT over the past two decades, American cities have also experienced increases in the private control of urban development. This phenomena is punctuated by the 2005 Supreme Court Decision in *Kelo v. The City of New London*, which allows cities to use their power of eminent domain to transfer property from one private owner to another to enable economic development that has a community benefit. But even before this moment, local governments have applied public investment to spur private market gentrification, and at the same time, governments have been ceding control of public spaces and parks to the private sector. This trend is significant for cities and politics precisely because economic elites have been garnering more influence over how cities develop and where investment flows.

At the same time, the privileging of market rule and the ascendency of the logic of privatization through neoliberalism naturalizes this trend. Governmentality, ANT, elite theory, and regime theory can all help examine why and how private influence over cities and politics is on the rise. Yet, the excesses of privatization have also provoked public protest, which takes multiple forms. Such protests are uniform, however, in their goal to give common people voice in the struggle over how urban development ought to proceed and whom it should benefit. New ways of studying these politics of urbanization have also emerged and are discussed next.

The Practice of Urban Politics within and Beyond Government

The notion of open government and the opportunity for public comment are built into city planning processes in the United States. The history of public involvement in urban planning processes in the United States, prior to World War II, was characterized by the battle between machine politics and reformers. Powerful interests controlled urban planning and construction processes without significant, or at least patterned, *successful* involvement of citizens *qua* citizens. Of course, this broad generalization is complicated by moments of organized resistance that manage to pierce the fortress of exclusion.

This situation began to change in the 1960s, with the most famous example of organized resistance to urban planning processes coming from a group of residents in Greenwich Village led by the legendary urbanist Jane Jacobs. Urban planning began to democratize its processes, involving citizens at a local level. This was formalized through the creation of Community Action Planning, Model Cities programs, and Community Development Corporations. Such organizations exist to this day to various degrees, city to city. Beyond these programs, city governments also mandate public commentary in planning processes, but in widely varying ways. Common methods deployed include public meetings, public hearings, open houses, and public commentary opportunities. Typical venues include neighborhood community centers, planning commissions, city councils, and online forums.

Concurrent with the development of organizations whose purpose is to provide material support for organizing residents to participate in planning communities and cities, urban planning theorists began to theorize about the challenge and possibilities of citizen involvement in planning processes, Arnstein's (1969) "ladder of citizen involvement" being an early exemplar. The importance of this work was its elucidation of degrees of participation, from disingenuous invitations by decision makers to include people in planning processes to citizen control over such processes. Over the past more than 40 years, many scholars have built on that foundation, elaborating new criteria that recognize similar variation of possible citizen involvement in planning processes, or raising new questions about theories of practices of participatory and inclusive planning.

One of the difficulties in achieving inclusion of publics in planning processes is the differential in knowledge between those trained as experts in the formation of urban spaces and institutions and citizens without such formal education. Reconciling the tension between a specialized or systems perspective on urban structures and the everyday experiences of people who live the consequences of planning has been a theme in studies of cities and politics for decades. Particularly important in the literature on this divergence has been what is referred to as the "communicative turn" in urban planning theory. Widely influenced by Habermas (1985), this line of inquiry has analyzed planners' discursive practices as well as the achievement of dialogue whereby municipalities learn to listen more effectively and take seriously lay knowledge as its own expertise cultivated through the trials of daily life and lived experience.

Another perennial issue that practitioners and scholars have wrestled with regarding public involvement in urban planning processes is the genuine achievement of a diversity of voices. That this remains a challenge reflects centuries' old patterns of inequality, disenfranchisement, and disempowerment. Simply, how can planning process include the voices of those most directly affected by such decisions, as well as those more distant geographically and temporally, but who still have a stake in the plan being proposed? How do municipalities involve persons in the neighborhood, city, and region, and how are they to account for future stakeholders? Moreover, given the diversities that characterize cities, how are planners and decision makers able to avoid generalizing the interests of the public or community in the face of unassimilable difference (Young 1990)? This is an increasing challenge as cities the world over become more diverse along every conceivable axis of sociality (race, ethnicity, gender, religion, sexuality, socioeconomic status, etc.). Achieving a diversity of voices in urban planning is also hampered by the notion of "the public" as an a priori formation. Challenges to this notion have been a theme in theories of urban planning, built on planning's Pragmatist legacy that emphasizes the formation of publics as responses to problems (Dewey 1927).

The last decade and a half has witnessed increasing attention to case study research on strategies to address these and other challenges of fulfilling democratic promises in relation to urbanization. These include evaluations and critiques of formal municipal practices, focusing on the limits of planners' capacity (in terms of both resources and training) for effective outreach and inclusion of publics, as well as the acknowledgment of municipal adoption of methods that have proven more effective at public engagement.

While the previous discussion implies that democratic participation in urban planning appears to be increasing over a long historical span, there is still a reasonable critique of such practices as actions by the state to satiate and co-opt people in the achievement of elite urban aims. Moreover, even when the state enacts methods of public participation, they may fail, leaving people no other means than to engage more contentious challenges to elites. Indeed, one of the few axioms of social science is that when formal and legitimate political processes fail, publics will turn to extra-institutional ways of expressing grievances and informing politics (Tarrow 1994). So it is with urbanization, and in a wide array of forms.

One such form is social movements' responses to changes in urban spaces and practices. When confronted with existing or changing urban developments, people who feel their voices are ignored or suppressed may form social movement organizations and engage in confrontational actions to resist such developments. Moreover, social movements may make use of urban spaces as arenas of contention, from sit-ins at quasi-public establishments, marching and rallying in symbolically meaningful urban locations, blockading access to meetings of elites, occupying public plazas and squares, and, in rare instances, expressing the "voice of the unheard" through rioting. Responses by elites to such movements has included declarations of martial law, preemptive curfews, fencing of substantial portions of an urban center, and raids on convergence centers where activists plan protests.

Another form of political expression outside legitimate channels is the practice of popular critique that draws attention to exclusionary developments in urbanization, including the privatization and commercialization of public spaces and gentrification of neighborhoods. The emergence of uncommissioned arts—streets art, music festivals, spontaneous theater performances, critical mass bicycle rides, and the like—is understood as political expressions and critical commentary on urban spaces. Such a form of urban politics runs parallel with the formation of urbanity and creation of urban culture independent of and autonomous from urban planning.

Conclusion

While framed as part of a debate, it is clear that the perspectives on pluralism, political economy, networks, and the practice of urban politics beyond government make distinct contributions to the study of cities and politics. To be sure, one perspective emerges from the critique of another. Yet, it is possible to employ multiple perspectives in complementary ways, depending on one's line of inquiry. Indeed, recent discussion in urban studies has highlighted the importance of both political economy and ANT perspectives to gain critical perspectives on the ordering of urban life. In studying such a phenomenon, the perspectives considered herein point to two fundamental tensions that must be apprehended in moving toward a comprehensive understanding of cities. On the one hand, there is the tension between the institutional life of government, with its intentional strategies and formal procedures, and everyday life of people, which reflects creative capacities that are often ad hoc, spontaneous, or reactive. On the other hand, these perspectives highlight how to conceptualize power, its distribution, and application. Understanding these tensions is certainly important for any theory of cities and politics and absolutely necessary for efforts seeking pragmatic intervention into the American democratic experiment.

See also Citizenship and Politics; Cultural Pluralism; Housing Policy and Politics; Immigration and Politics; Infrastructure and Politics; Public–Private Partnerships; Regions and Regionalism: The Midwest; Regions and Regionalism: The Northeast; Regions and Regionalism: The South; Regions and Regionalism: The West; State and Local Politics.

Daniel Trudeau and Lars Christiansen

Bibliography

Arnstein, S. R. 1969. "A Ladder of Citizen Participation." *Journal of the American Planning Association* 35, no. 4: 216–24.

Bender, T. 2011. "Postscript: Reassembling the City: Networks and Urban Imaginaries." In I. Farias and T. Bender, eds. *Urban Assemblages: How Actor-Network Theory Changes Urban Studies*. London: Routledge, pp. 303–24.

Brenner, N., D. Madden, and D. Wachsmuth. 2011. "Assemblage Urbanism and the Challenges of Critical Urban Theory." *City* 15, no. 2: 225–40.

Briggs, X. S. 2008. *Democracy as Problem Solving: Civic Capacity in Communities across the Globe*. Cambridge, MA: MIT Press.

Caro, R. 1974. *The Power Broker: Robert Moses and the Fall of New York*. New York: Vintage.

Cronon, W. 1991. *Nature's Metropolis: Chicago and the Great West*. New York: W.W. Norton.

Dahl, R. 1961. *Who Governs? Democracy and Power in an American City*. New Haven, CT: Yale University Press.

Dewey, J. 1927. *The Public and Its Problems*. Athens, OH: Swallow Press.

Domhoff, G. 2013. *Who Rules America? The Triumph of the Corporate Rich*. 7th ed. New York: McGraw-Hill.

Elwood, S., and H. Leitner. 2003. "GIS and Spatial Knowledge Production for Neighborhood Revitalization: Negotiating State Priorities and

Neighborhood Visions." *Journal of Urban Affairs* 35: 139–57.

Farias, I., and T. Bender, eds. 2011. *Urban Assemblages: How Actor-Network Theory Changes Urban Studies*. London: Routledge.

Foucault, M. 1979. *The History of Sexuality, Volume 1. An Introduction*. London: Allen Lane.

Habermas, Jurgen. 1985. *The Theory of Communicative Action*. Boston, MA: Beacon Press.

Harvey, D. 2012. *Rebel Cities: From the Right to the City to the Urban Revolution*. London: Verso.

Latour, B., and S. Woolgar. [1979] 1986. *Laboratory Life: The Construction of Scientific Facts*. Princeton, NJ: Princeton University Press.

Logan, J., and H. Molotch. 1987. *Urban Fortunes: The Political Economy of Place*. Berkeley: University of California Press.

Mills, C. W. 1956. *The Power Elite*. Oxford: Oxford University Press.

Rohe, W. 2009. "From Local to Global: 100 Years of Neighborhood Planning." *Journal of the American Planning Association* 75, no. 2: 209–30.

Rose, N. 1999. *Powers of Freedom: Reframing Political Thought*. Cambridge: Cambridge University Press.

RSA Animate. 2012. "The Power of Networks." http://www.thersa.org/events/rsaanimate/animate/rsa-animate-the-power-of-networks. Accessed May 16, 2014.

Sandercock, L. 1997. *Towards Cosmopolis: Planning for Multicultural Cities*. Chichester, England: John Wiley and Sons.

Stone, C. 2005. "Looking Back to Look Forward: Reflections on Urban Regime Analysis." *Urban Affairs Review* 40: 309–41.

Tarrow, S. 1994. *Power in Movement: Social Movements and Contentious Politics*. Cambridge: Cambridge University Press.

Temenos C., and E. McCann. 2012. "The Local Politics of Policy Mobility: Learning, Persuasion, and the Production of a Municipal Sustainability Fix." *Environment and Planning A*44, no. 6: 1389–406.

Young, I. M. 1990. *Justice and the Politics of Difference*. Princeton, NJ: Princeton University Press.

CITIZENSHIP AND POLITICS

Figures on both the political right and the political left are increasingly concerned with the state of American citizenship, or what it is to be an American. On the right, critics working from a variety of conservative perspectives worry about America's excessive concern with material wealth and narrow egoism (as opposed, e.g., to traditional family values). This narrow focus is regarded as problematic in that it undermines the universal political principles that serve as the foundation of the American way of life, principles that are held to unify all Americans. On the left, critics argue that Americans do not participate enough politically. For these critics, political participation and consequently American citizenship have been reduced to mere symbolic behavior. Whether on the political right or the left, nearly all observers argue that increasing alienation from the political process and the breakdown of community are causes for concern.

Making use of the concept of nationalism, defined as the cultural, linguistic, economic, and political dimensions of identity that allow members of society to feel that they belong, the present entry provides an overview of four competing understandings of what it means to be an American along with challenges to these interpretations (King 2005, 4). As will be discussed, the four perspectives are (1) universal nationalism, or the universalist perspective, which emphasizes acceptance of the liberal, universal political principles embedded in the American Creed; (2) cultural nationalism, or the cultural perspective, which defines American-ness in terms of an Anglo-Protestant cultural heritage; (3) civic nationalism, or the civic perspective, which finds meaning in the social and political practices that encourage the development of civic capacities identified with good citizenship; and (4) commercial nationalism, or the commercial perspective, which focuses on the productive capacities—the industriousness—of Americans as the key to understanding the flourishing commercial empire that is the United States. After laying out each of these four perspectives and considering criticisms of each in turn, the entry concludes by looking at how each perspective informs the current immigration debate.

Universal Nationalism

The universalist understanding of American citizenship sees America as a nation founded on universal political principles. These universal principles are expressed in the form of a political tradition, the American Creed. Initially articulated in Alexis De Tocqueville's *Democracy in America*, the American Creed emphasizes principles consisting of universal rights and of political structures that both secure and advance personal freedom, minority rights, and the development of civic involvement (Fuchs 1990, 4–6). The clearest expression of these principles is found in *The Declaration of Independence*, where it is written "that all men are created equal, that they are endowed by their Creator with certain unalienable Rights, that among these are Life, Liberty, and the pursuit of Happiness." The creed's emphasis on freedom, rights, and participation suggests that the creed is inherently individualistic. The American Creed argument assumes, then, a progressive elimination over time of group distinctions as individualism absorbs and displaces group distinctions (King 2005, 6–7). With group distinctions lessened or removed, America, on this view, can move from an imperfect liberalism to a form in which the equal rights of all individuals prevail.

According to the universalist perspective, key figures and texts from classic liberalism are essential to any understanding of American political thinking (Sinopoli 1992). That is, the universalist perspective is informed by the liberal political tradition and its recognition that certain character traits are an inherent part of being a good citizen. These traits include self-denial, civility, liberality, justice, courage, endurance, humanity, curiosity, industry, truthfulness, vigilance, prudence, and love of liberty (Berkowitz 1999). The liberal tradition employed by universalists, moreover, rejects the proposition that protecting individual rights and achieving social solidarity are necessarily antagonistic; rather, it sees each as potentially complementing the other.

Critics of the universalist account of American citizenship make three arguments in response. First, they challenge the notion of a gradual unfolding and expanding of that citizenship. Instead, citizenship in the United States can and should be understood in terms of the persistent restriction and denial of the

rights, privileges, and immunities of citizenship. In other words, scholars argue that American citizenship is characterized by the recurring use of a set of ideas that attempt to justify inequality based on characteristics such as race, ethnicity, and gender (Smith 1997). Second, critics take issue with the focus on individualism. Analysis of citizenship in the United States in the 19th and 20th centuries, for example, shows that proponents of the universalist perspective underestimate the endurance of group-based distinctions in American social and economic life (King 2005). Finally, critics offer two arguments against the universalists' emphasis on attachment to abstract political principles. Proponents of cultural nationalism, for example, maintain that such universal principles cannot provide the requisite homogeneity or "esprit de corps" needed to sustain a sense of what it means to be an American. Civic nationalists, too, argue that the universalist, rights-based account of citizenship ignores the importance of citizenship *as an activity*; in other words, the universalists' emphasis on rights and their protection does not actually facilitate self-government.

Cultural Nationalism

Cultural nationalism, as a perspective on citizenship, affirms the United States' distinctive Anglo-Protestant cultural heritage. Of critical importance here are the English language, Protestant Christianity, and British political traditions (Huntington 2004). American citizenship so understood is said to have three primary sociopolitical consequences. First, an appreciation of American culture and history is central to American national identity, even though the salience of that identity may vary over time. Second, elements of the common heritage are believed to unify Americans to a unique degree or in a unique manner, creating, in fact, a sense of American "exceptionalism"—a sense that Americans have a special place or a special destiny in the world order. Together, these two aspects or consequences of cultural nationalism are thought to have the effect of creating sufficient homogeneity or emotional political attachment as to make free government possible (Pickus 2005, 142).

Cultural nationalists do not believe, as do their universalist counterparts, that shared political principles can manage the conflict invited by a multiethnic society. Instead, proponents of cultural nationalism argue that it is the role of religious, familial, social, and governmental forces to manage conflict. Of central importance is the role of religion. Cultural nationalists generally equate good citizenship with being a good Christian (see Shain 1994). This means, essentially, that all Americans ought to imitate the life of Christ by walking in the path of the Lord. (According to Scripture, walking in the path of the Lord is a continuous process and a habitual lifestyle.) Thus, progress is defined by many cultural nationalists not in terms of the development of shared, universal rights, or civic participation, or commercial prosperity and increased enjoyment of private property, but rather in terms of the community's and the individual's religious faith and aptitude.

The Anglo-Protestant cultural perspective, it may be argued, involves several controversial precepts. Critics have challenged the proposition that a national culture, in the ethno-linguistic and religious sense, is necessary for the formation of a successful democratic polity (Fraga and Segura 2006, 281). Indeed, critics have suggested that cultural nationalism ultimately makes the problem of alienation from society even greater—because its emphasis on national identity threatens the intermediate institutions of civil society that serve to keep individuals engaged and the polity operating (Pickus 2005, 157). In addition, critics have doubted that the religious emphasis is a genuinely positive force in American national life. Instead of being a source of inclusion, it is argued, religion has been used to justify unequal treatment under the law and exclusionary policies against immigrants and those of other faiths (Smith 1997). Such critics contend that closer inspection of these arguments and a more accurate reading of American history undermine the idea that American democracy owes its existence to its Anglo-historic and religious traditions.

Civic Nationalism

Civic nationalism holds out an alternative means for understanding American citizenship, one that bypasses the ethnocultural and linguistic unity portrayed by the cultural nationalists and looks instead to civic participation. A focus on the capacity for civic deliberation, self-criticism, and democratic change, the civic nationalists suggest, better explains the longevity of the American republic than does attachment to abstract political principles or a dominant Anglo-Protestant culture. Civic nationalism, in other words, maintains that progressive engagement in the public sphere is what defines American citizenship and largely shapes American national identity (Pickus 2005; Sandel 1998). This is not to be interpreted as meaning that civic involvement is an end in itself; rather, civic nationalism requires Americans, through ongoing civic participation, to actively shape their own national identity. Such a process ensures that Americans will defend what they collectively value against the cultural, political, and economic forces thought to undermine these values.

The emphasis on civic participation, or self-governance, requires citizens to understand the political principles that make free government possible. In short, civic nationalism requires civic *virtue*, a term that suggests civic nationalism's link with classical republican political thought. Republicanism is characterized by the themes of mixed government and, more important, active citizen participation (by equal and independent citizens). Proponents of the civic understanding of American citizenship and national identity argue, after Aristotle, that it is possible to fully develop as a person only through political participation. This generally leads proponents of this perspective to find the fundamental meaning of what it is to be an American in a particular interpretation of a key event in the nation's history, the American Revolution. The revolution, on this view, is seen as a supreme act of civic participation, one that kept the American colonies from being corrupted. Pointing backward to classical republicanism and its commitment to public liberty and virtue, civic nationalism serves as the most politically focused understanding of American national identity.

It is, however, an open question whether the nation's founders were committed to an active theory of citizenship centered on fostering civic virtue. The founders did not refer to government created by the U.S. Constitution as a civic republic; rather, they referred to it as a commercial republic (Hamilton,

Madison, and Jay 2001, 66). As Zolberg (2006) has shown, commercial considerations have and continue to be central to the debate over what it means to be an American citizen and what it means, as well, to immigrate to this country.

Commercial Nationalism

None of the three perspectives discussed so far consider the commercial aspects of American national identity, and, to the extent that they do, they relegate such considerations to a relatively minor role. Commercial nationalism, as a perspective on citizenship, holds that industry and the individual's capacity to contribute to a flourishing, commercial empire are key to understanding citizenship in the United States. It proposes that Americans are held together as a people by the spirit of commerce. Guided by a belief in the value of receiving rewards for one's toils, commercial nationalists maintain that it is the responsibility of government—to the extent that government plays a role—to pursue policies that multiply the means of gratification available to Americans. Freed from the rigorous political responsibilities of civic nationalism and from the social, cultural, and religious restrictions of cultural nationalism, commercial nationalists conclude that the defining characteristic of American citizenship is the pursuit of gain, in part as an expression of liberty.

Commercial nationalism's emphasis on the pursuit of gain distinguishes the liberalism informing its understanding of what it means to be an American from the liberalism informing universalist nationalism. Commercial nationalism draws on a form of liberalism focusing on self-preservation and prosperity. The liberalism of the commercial perspective, that is, is indifferent to the cultivation of character, relatively hostile to the human bonds holding societies together, and antagonistic to human excellence (viewed as the pursuit of perfection; Macpherson 2011). For commercial nationalists, it is not the place of the state to cultivate character traits held to make self-government possible. Instead, the state is to remain neutral on questions of how one ought to live because these are questions that every individual must ask and answer for himself or herself.

Following Tocqueville (2000, 661–65), the most common criticism of commercial nationalism is that its emphasis on commercial activity focuses too narrowly on the small and vulgar pleasures of life. To prevent citizens from becoming absorbed in the pursuits of gain, something more is required. Civic nationalists, in fact, argue that this "something more" is provided by civic engagement wherein citizens come to learn that their self-interest coincides with the public interest, thereby potentially advancing the public good. Universalist nationalists, for their part, offer a similar argument, but instead of emphasizing the cultivation of civic virtue, they argue that citizens will vigilantly seek to protect the rights that define what it means to be an American. Cultural nationalists, also contributing to the debate, follow Tocqueville in emphasizing the important role played by religion in transforming selfishness into self-interest, broadly understood (Tocqueville 2000, 504–5). All three lines of criticism argue for an individual who is willing to engage in "little sacrifices each day" and to cultivate the disciplined habits of regularity, temperance, moderation, foresight, and self-command (Tocqueville 2000, 502).

Citizenship Challenges Today

Arguably, the most contentious area of public policy relating to what it means to be an American citizen is immigration policy. In addressing arguments over immigration, it is important to draw a distinction between the concepts of assimilation and acculturation. The former involves identifying with the nation's ideals and incorporating them as one's own, while the latter involves identifying with a particular culture and seeking to learn its ways (Pickus 2005, 144–45). The two concepts are closely related yet distinct. Of the four perspectives on citizenship discussed earlier, three (universalist, civic, and commercial nationalism) primarily involve assimilation, and one (cultural nationalism) primarily involves acculturation.

Universalist nationalism, as a matter of practice, requires immigrants to attach themselves to the liberal principles of the American Creed. The universal quality of these principles serves as an inducement to immigration insofar as the United States is seen as obligated to protect the rights of all human beings in the

Citizenship and Legal Status

Citizenship in the United States (and other democracies) confers the right to political participation. It affords the individual full integration into the political system and allows him or her to hold the government—its representatives, its policies, and its actions—accountable. In turn, the citizen is invested with certain responsibilities, including obedience to the law and the payment of taxes. Ultimately, it is incumbent upon the citizen to express his or her wishes to government officers (through voting or other means) if the democratic process is to function as intended.

According to the U.S. Citizenship and Immigration Service, the agency that oversees lawful immigration to the United States (and which is part of the Department of Homeland Security), one may become a U.S. citizen either at birth or after birth, upon meeting certain requirements.

To become a citizen at birth, one must

- have been born in the United States or certain territories or outlying possessions of the United States, and be subject to the jurisdiction of the United States, *or*
- have a parent or parents who were citizens at the time of one's birth (if one was born abroad) and meet other requirements.

To become a citizen after birth, one must

- apply for "derived" or "acquired" citizenship through parents, *or*
- apply for naturalization.

Varieties of Citizenship

Naturalization

In most cases, a person who wants to become a naturalized citizen must first be a permanent resident. By becoming a U.S. citizen, one gains many rights that permanent residents or others do not have, including the right to vote. To be eligible for naturalization, one must first meet certain requirements set by U.S. law, specifically:

- be age 18 or older
- be a permanent resident for a certain amount of time (usually 5 years or, in some cases, 3 years)
- be a person of "good moral character" (no outstanding warrants, etc.)
- have a basic knowledge of U.S. government (as determined by test)
- have a period of continuous residence and physical presence in the United States
- be able to read, write, and speak basic English (as determined by test).

Citizenship for Military Members and Dependents

Non-citizen members and veterans of the U.S. armed forces and their dependents (spouses and children) may be eligible for special naturalization provisions under the Immigration and Nationality Act (INA).

Dual Citizenship

The concept of dual nationality means that a person is a citizen of two countries at the same time. Each country has its own citizenship laws based on its own policy. Persons may have dual nationality by automatic operation of different laws rather than by choice. For example, a child born in a foreign country to U.S. citizen parents may be both a U.S. citizen and a citizen of the country of birth. Dual nationals, however, owe allegiance to both the United States and the foreign country. They are required to obey the laws of both countries.

Source: U.S. Citizenship and Immigration Service. http://www.uscis.gov/portal/site/uscis.

country, whether one is a national or not. In addition, the universalist understanding does not require immigrants to give up their cultural identity as required, for example, by cultural nationalism.

Civic nationalism, similarly, stresses the belief that immigrants can become good citizens as long as

A woman receives her certificate of naturalization during a special naturalization ceremony for 118 new citizens at the U.S. Citizenship and Immigration Services in Irving, Texas, 2010. (AP Photo/Cody Duty)

the nation is committed to a strong form of civic education. Civic nationalism thus differs from universal nationalism in one important respect. Whereas universalist nationalists make no distinction between citizen and alien, civic nationalists hold that Americans have special obligations to one another as members of a self-governing community. Consequently, civic nationalists prioritize the needs of Americans (especially the poorest) over those of prospective Americans. In practical terms, this means that if immigration policies adversely affect American citizens (see Borjas 1990), more restrictive policies are justified.

The perspective of commercial nationalism requires the state to secure commercial rights and freedoms to all persons. Unlike the universal and civic views of assimilation that view the naturalization process as a means to a larger, political vision of what it means to be an American, commercial nationalism views immigration and the naturalization process as an opportunity to return America to its first commercial principles. Bonnie Honig (2001, 74), for example, argues that immigration reminds all Americans of their fundamental economic principles: (1) the possibility of upward economic mobility and (2) the economic rewards stemming from dedication to hard work. While this may be true as far as it goes, it presents only part of the picture. By emphasizing industriousness as the defining characteristic of all Americans, commercial nationalism views immigration as a dynamic force that "sets and keeps the capitalist engine in motion" by bringing in new goods, ideas, and markets (Schumpeter 1975, 82).

For its part, cultural naturalism, as noted, emphasizes acculturation. According to this perspective,

Noncitizen Categories

Permanent Resident

Permanent residency applies to any person who is not a citizen of the United States but is residing in the country under legally recognized and lawfully recorded permanent resident status as an immigrant. The status is also known as "Permanent Resident Alien," "Lawful Permanent Resident," "Resident Alien Permit Holder," and "Green Card Holder" (because of the type of identification card issued).

Other Statuses

Additional lawful statuses include 1) Temporary Worker, or persons permitted to stay in the country on a temporary basis and who are restricted to the activity or reason for which their nonimmigrant visa was issued; and 2) Student and Exchange Workers, or those allowed to work in the United States upon obtaining permission from an authorized official at their U.S. school.

Source: U.S. Citizenship and Immigration Service. http://www.uscis.gov/portal/site/uscis.

to become Americans immigrants and their children must divest themselves of the culture of their country of origin. Cultural nationalism thus permits government to restrict or prohibit immigration from countries deemed to have cultural, political, and religious practices incompatible with American society. It is a view that generates the most restrictive immigration policies. Under it, arguments have been advanced to lengthen the residency requirement for achieving citizenship, enforce English-only language provisions, and reduce the scope of immigrant rights generally.

Conclusion

The four models of American nationalism described here provide four distinct visions of what it means to be an American citizen and four different perspectives on the immigration debate. Citizenship, construed in this way, serves as a valuable lens through which to view not only American identity and immigration issues but also public policy in areas as diverse as welfare, education, labor markets, and international relations. In each such area, citizenship addresses two questions that virtually all public policy must take up in one form or another: (1) what are the boundaries of citizenship and how are these boundaries set up? and (2) what are the benefits and burdens associated with citizenship and how are they to be distributed? The first question identifies who is and who is not a member of the polity, and the second speaks to the privileges and responsibilities of community membership. As the example of immigration shows, different perspectives on American citizenship answer these questions in different ways, and these differences can and do fundamentally affect the shape of public policy.

How we answer the question of what it means to be an American citizen does more than inform public policy. It also addresses the prospect of sustaining democracy in America. Civic and universalist nationalists, for example, worry that American citizenship and society no longer emphasize the development or protection of a public morality that makes self-government possible. They worry, at the same time, that commercial nationalism holds sway and that American citizenship has been reduced to the rampant pursuit of personal gratification (Callan 1997, 3). Similarly, cultural nationalists worry that too much concern with commerce undermines the cultural foundations that make American democracy possible. In short, Americans' willingness to forego public concerns in favor of private satisfaction suggests that the economic threats to citizenship have succeeded in undermining the conditions that make self-government possible (Sandel 1998). Meanwhile, commercial nationalists argue that extra-commercial considerations hinder continued progress. These are all important concerns that speak to who we are as a people and who we will be in the future.

See also American Dream; American "Exceptionalism"; Civil Liberties; Cultural Pluralism; Immigration and Politics; Individualism; Liberals and Liberalism; National Identity; Nationalism.

Jordon Barkalow

Bibliography

Berkowitz, Peter. 1999. *Virtue and the Making of Modern Liberalism*. Princeton, NJ: Princeton University Press.

Borjas, George. 1990. *Friends or Strangers: The Impact of Immigration on the U.S. Economy*. New York: Basic Books.

Callan, Eamonn. 1997. *Creating Citizens: Political Education and Liberal Democracy*. New York: Oxford University Press.

Fraga, Luis R., and Segura, Gary M. 2006. "Culture Clash? Contesting Notions of American Identity and the Effects of Latin American Immigration." *Perspectives of Politics* 4: 279–87.

Fuchs, Lawrence H. 1990. *The American Kaleidoscope: Race, Ethnicity, and the Civic Culture*. Hanover, NH: University Press of New England.

Hamilton, Alexander, James Madison, and John Jay. 2001 [1788]. *The Federalist*. Edited by George W. Carey and James McClellan. Indianapolis: Liberty Fund.

Honig, Bonnie. 2001. *Democracy and the Foreigner*. Princeton, NJ: Princeton University Press.

Huntington, Samuel P. 2004. *Who Are We? The Challenges to America's National Identity*. New York: Simon and Schuster Paperbacks.

King, Desmond. 2005. *The Liberty of Strangers: Making the American Nation*. New York: Oxford University Press.

Macpherson, C. B. 2011. *The Theory of Possessive Individualism: From Hobbes to Locke*. New York: Oxford University Press.

Pickus, Noah. 2005. *True Faith and Allegiance: Immigration and American Civic Nationalism*. Princeton, NJ: Princeton University Press.

Sandel, Michael J. 1998. *Democracy's Discontent: America in Search of a Public Philosophy*. Cambridge, MA: The Belknap Press of Harvard University Press.

Schumpeter, Joseph A. 1975. *Capitalism, Socialism, and Democracy*. New York: Harper.

Shain, Barry A. 1994. *The Myth of American Individualism: The Protestant Origins of American Political Thought*. New Haven, CT: Yale University Press.

Sinopoli, Richard. 1992. *The Foundations of American Citizenship*. New York: Oxford University Press.

Smith, Rogers M. 1997. *Civic Ideals: Conflicting Visions of Citizenship in U.S. History*. New Haven, CT: Yale University Press.

Tocqueville, Alexis de. 2000 [1835]. *Democracy in America*. Edited by Harvey Mansfield and Delba Winthrop. Chicago: University of Chicago Press.

Zolberg, Aristide. 2006. *A Nation by Design: Immigration Policy and the Founding of America*. Cambridge, MA: Harvard University Press.

CIVIL LIBERTIES

The term "civil liberties" refers to freedoms that individual citizens enjoy due to restraints on governmental power. Though the terms "liberties" and "rights" are often used interchangeably, scholars usually distinguish between *civil liberties* and *civil rights*. Civil liberties concern realms into which government cannot intrude (e.g., the free exercise of religion), while civil rights focus on claims that citizens make on the government for equal treatment (e.g., the right to vote). Civil liberties put limitations on government, while civil rights demand governmental action.

In a democratic republic such as the United States, the government—when it is operating properly—is composed of representatives who rule according to the will of the majority of the citizens. Civil liberties can therefore be seen as restraints upon the will of the majority. For example, even though three-quarters of U.S. citizens support a ban on burning the American flag, the Supreme Court has ruled that an individual has a right to express his political opinion through flag burning (*Texas v. O'Brien*, 1989). Thus, civil liberties protect individuals from the "tyranny of the majority": there are some actions the majority cannot lawfully take against individuals. In the United States, the limitations on the majority that protect individuals can be found primarily within the U.S. Constitution.

Types of Limitations on Governmental Power

Liberties protected through constraints on the government are often divided into two categories: *substantive* and *procedural*. *Substantive* limitations on governmental power are limitations based on the content (or substance) of the liberty. Within the U.S. Constitution, these liberties are primarily found in the First Amendment. For example, laws or governmental practices that restrict speech, the press, or religious practices are substantive limitations on an individual's liberty. *Procedural* limitations on governmental power relate to the processes the government must follow when seeking to punish a citizen. The government cannot simply throw a citizen in prison: it is restrained by certain rules. For example, officials must have a warrant before searching a home, cannot force a person to testify against himself, and must provide an impartial jury. Procedural protections can be found in the Fourth, Fifth, Sixth, Seventh, and Eight Amendments, all of which put restrictions on the procedures government must follow in prosecuting and punishing its citizens.

Liberty versus Equality

We often equate *liberties* and *rights*, but civil liberties and civil rights are often in conflict. Civil liberties are protections against governmental power, while civil rights are guarantees of equal treatment. Sometimes, if government is to ensure that all citizens are treated equally, individuals' liberties will be limited. And if liberties are to be given maximum protection, equality may be sacrificed.

Examples of this involve laws protecting people from discrimination. The Civil Rights Act of 1964 prohibits employers from hiring—or refusing to hire—individuals based on race, color, religion, sex, or national origin. This law has increased equality in the workplace. But the liberty of individual employers is now limited; they cannot legally choose only members of their religion or nationality for their workforce. Recently, this clash between liberty and equality has appeared in the increase of local and state statutes protecting gays and lesbians from discrimination. Illinois, for example, prohibits discrimination based on sexual orientation. Same-sex couples therefore have the same right to rent facilities for wedding celebrations as do opposite-sex couples. But some hotel and restaurant owners say this law violates their free exercise of religion. Because these owners believe homosexuality is a sin, they argue that being required to host same-sex celebrations violates their free practice of religion.

The liberty versus equality conflict also manifests itself in elections. Some candidates have large amounts of money to spend on campaign ads, giving them an enormous advantage. State legislatures and Congress have enacted statutes putting limits on campaign spending to equalize candidates' chances of being elected. But doing so intrudes on individuals' liberty to spend their own money to present their candidacy to the public.

Americans value both liberty and equality; citizens must realize that sometimes one value must give way to the other.

British Roots

The concept of individual rights did not originate with the Constitution, or even in America. While in a contemporary democracy civil liberties act as restraints on the popular will, they began as restraints upon the power of the monarchy. Some important procedural liberties, such as writs of habeas corpus (legal documents preventing unlawful imprisonment) and trial by jury, existed in some form from the time of Anglo-Saxon England in the early middle ages. But Anglo-American historians tend to point to the *Charter of Liberties*, proclaimed by King Henry I of England in 1100, as one of the first documents limiting the power of the monarch and promising the nobility certain customary rights involving property, taxation, and inheritance. A century later, Magna Carta, sealed by King John of England in 1215, repeated similar restraints on the monarch's power over individuals. English nobles forced John to agree to "the Great Charter," which included rights of inheritance and the promise of treatment for all according to the rule of law. It also affirmed that free men should not be imprisoned except by "judgment of his peers or the law of the land"—indicating a right to trial by jury and an assumption that even the king must follow the law when punishing individuals. Neither charter actually established civil liberties for the general populace in England (and Magna Carta was quickly repudiated by King John), but to later generations they became important symbols of legal restraints on the arbitrary power of kings. Magna Carta in particular has been mythologized as the document first defending the rights of individuals (Holt 1991, 1–4).

In the 1600s, the British Parliament put additional restraints (both procedural and substantive) on the monarch's authority through two important pieces of legislation. The *Petition of Right* of 1628 and the *Bill of Rights* of 1689 were influential in establishing civil liberties in England, and important aspects of these statutes remain in effect to this day. Included in the *Petition* were limitations on the monarch's powers to tax without the consent of Parliament, to quarter soldiers in people's homes without permission, and to imprison citizens without cause. Among other provisions, the *Bill of Rights* prohibited excessive bail and

"cruel and inhuman" punishment, returned to Protestants their right to bear arms, and allowed citizens to petition the monarch without fear of retribution. This act was passed after Britain's "Glorious Revolution" of 1688, which removed King James I from the throne and permanently ensured the existence of a monarchy constrained by law and by the Parliament. The *Bill of Rights* also reinvigorated the notion of an independent judiciary by prohibiting the monarch from unilaterally creating new courts or acting as a judge. It reaffirmed the necessity of Parliament's consent in levying taxes and stated that the king could not interfere in parliamentary elections nor deprive members of Parliament of freedom of speech during debates. Thus, these two documents demonstrated a gradual move toward restraining the monarch in favor of the power of Parliament and toward restraining the power of government itself over its citizens. This is not to say that the existence of these documents actually guaranteed that the British populace automatically enjoyed all of the liberties listed. But the formal enactment of certain "rights of Englishmen" gave weight to the movement toward democratization and protection against arbitrary governmental actions.

Liberties in Early America

American mythology often paints the early colonists of the 17th and 18th centuries as seekers of liberty and defenders of individual rights. It is certainly true that many of the early settlers came to the "New World" to escape religious persecution in England and Europe. However, many of the communities formed by the new Americans had official, state-supported churches and denied religious liberty to dissenters. In the 13 colonies as a whole, numerous Protestant denominations did coexist peacefully, but this religious pluralism was partly due to the size of America and its decentralized system of government. This approach allowed different faith groups to segregate into separate neighborhoods, cities, and colonies. Nonetheless, as notions of individual liberties slowly gathered strength in early modern England, the colonists followed the events from afar and voiced similar views. Many colonists looked favorably on England's Glorious Revolution, adopting the language of rebellion and hoping to gain equal representation in Parliament (Lovejoy 1980). The idea that there existed ancient and customary "rights of Englishmen"—supposedly stretching back to Magna Carta—gained traction among Americans.

The works of English philosopher John Locke gained influence as the 1700s wore on. During the struggles of the 1600s between Parliament and the monarchy, Locke wrote both about consent of the governed and about civil liberties. In *A Letter Concerning Toleration*, he supported religious pluralism (with the exception of atheists and Roman Catholics), arguing that civil authorities should not try to enforce particular spiritual beliefs through violence. Even more well known is his *Second Treatise on Government*, in which Locke argued that political communities were formed through a "social contract" among free individuals. Stating that "life, liberty, and property" were inalienable human rights, Locke maintained that government was formed to protect these rights, and any government violating this social compact had lost legitimacy. Locke's works were well known by learned American colonists of the 1700s and even referenced by clergy from the pulpit. Most famously, Thomas Jefferson used Locke's reasoning in drafting the *Declaration of Independence*, as discussed later.

By well into the 1700s, American colonists engaged in frequent talk about rights and liberties, particularly in regard to the ways in which they thought England intruded upon them. Scholars agree that much of this discussion of rights was not precise or well considered. The average colonist agitating for the protection of his rights apparently had little understanding of political theory, the law, or the specific rights protected under British law (Hutson 1991, 63). Nonetheless, this "rights talk" escalated as Parliament imposed more direct taxes, stationed British troops in private homes, limited self-government in Massachusetts, and interfered with the colonists' administration of their courts. Because the colonists had no representatives in Parliament, they perceived the taxes as particularly grievous. "No taxation without representation!" was a common slogan, and colonists pointed to Magna Carta and the *Petition of Right* to support their claims. When war finally broke out between the colonies and England, the Americans framed the rebellion as the logical outcome of a distant, repressive government systematically denying the colonists of their rights as British citizens.

The Declaration of Independence, signed in 1776 as the revolution entered its second year, begins with language taken straight from Locke's *Second Treatise*. It asserted all men enjoy the inalienable rights of "life, liberty, and the pursuit of happiness," and that when a government violates these rights, citizens are justified in dissolving their compact with the government. The remainder of the *Declaration* read like a legal brief: it systematically listed the various ways in which King George III has intruded on the customary rights of Englishmen. This list of accusations included the Crown's interference in the judicial system and dissolution of colonial legislatures. In many ways, the *Declaration* read as a somewhat conservative document: the Americans were not demanding an entirely new type of government but rather were separating from Great Britain because it had broken with traditional understandings of what a government does and does not have the authority to do. The document did not state that the very existence of a monarchy was intolerable. Instead the *Declaration* said that because this particular monarch violated the colonists' inherent rights and liberties, he had broken the social compact and made rebellion inevitable.

After the Revolutionary War began, the colonies organized themselves into independent states, with new state charters and constitutions. These new documents contained protections of liberties, though the specific rights enumerated differed from state to state. All contained some type of guarantee to free exercise of conscience/religion; a local, impartial jury; and the use of common law with a jury trial. Also frequently mentioned were the right to petition for redress of grievances, freedom of the press, no excessive bails and fines, and due process of law. Notably missing from several of these, however, were provisions banning an official state religion (such as the one held by Massachusetts until 1833). And perhaps most surprising is the fact that only Pennsylvania guaranteed freedom of speech.

Therefore, by the time the Constitution was framed and sent to the states for ratification, American citizens were well acquainted with documents spelling out specific limitations on the powers of government, and many expected this new charter to contain them as well.

Liberties within the Constitution

The original Constitution adopted in 1789 offered little protection for civil liberties, though it did contain a few limitations on the majority's power over individual citizens. The original Constitution prohibited ex post facto laws (laws that apply retroactively), protected writs of habeas corpus, prohibited bills of attainder (legislation declaring an individual guilty of a crime), and guaranteed trial by jury in criminal cases. But primarily, the 1789 Constitution set up the structures of the federal government and the rules for operation, defining the ways in which the majority would govern in a representative republic. Most delegates at the convention assumed that protection of liberties would lie within state constitutions and state legislation.

As the states debated whether to ratify the Constitution, a number of citizens expressed concerns that it did not sufficiently protect individual liberties from intrusion by the federal government. Thomas Jefferson, who did not attend the Constitutional Convention, argued that a Bill of Rights was necessary to protect individuals from "the tyranny of legislatures." Alexander Hamilton disagreed: in *Federalist* #84 he maintained such written protections were not necessary in a representative republic where the people, and not monarchs, formulate the laws. He pointed out that previous documents protecting civil liberties, such as Magna Carta, were concerned with limiting the powers of kings. James Madison's views lie between the two, for he believed a Bill of Rights would be a welcome addition to the document but that its omission should not prevent ratification.

Accordingly, after the Constitution was ratified, James Madison introduced a Bill of Rights to the House of Representatives. He presented them as possible amendments to the new Constitution. Madison's original bill included 19 proposals. The House and the Senate modified and reorganized them into 12 amendments that were sent to the states for ratification. Two of them, which related to congressional apportionment and salaries, and not civil liberties, were not ratified. The remaining 10 amendments—the Bill of Rights—were formally added to the Constitution in 1791. Within these 10 amendments lie 26 separate guarantees of liberty, containing both substantive and procedural limitations on the new U.S. government.

Applying the Bill of Rights to the States

The Bill of Rights did not originally protect citizens from the power of state and local governments. In the 20th century, the Supreme Court applied the Bill of Rights to the states through a process called "selective incorporation."

Because the First Amendment starts with "Congress shall make no law," it implies that the guarantees of speech, press, religion, and assembly are guarantees against intrusion by the *federal* government. It says that *Congress* may not invade these liberties; it says nothing about whether state or local officials are also constrained by its language. In the early 19th century, Chief Justice John Marshall ruled the entire Bill of Rights applied only to actions taken by the federal government (*Barron v. Baltimore*, 1833). This ruling meant that state and local governments were not obligated to follow the Fourth, Fifth, or Sixth Amendment when prosecuting citizens, nor need they respect citizen's rights to freedom of speech or press. Though as discussed earlier, state constitutions contained their own bills of rights, these were not necessarily identical to the federal Bill of Rights and frequently contained fewer protections.

Following the Civil War, the Fourteenth Amendment was added to the Constitution, containing the famous "Due Process" Clause: "[N]or shall any state deprive any person of life, liberty, or property without due process of law." For decades, this new phrase had no effect on Marshall's ruling that the Bill of Rights applied only to the federal government. But starting in 1925, the Supreme Court ruled that the "liberty" mentioned in the Fourteenth Amendment's Due Process clause included the fundamental freedom of speech (*Gitlow v. New York*). Therefore, the liberty of free speech protected by the First Amendment was now applied to actions taken by *state* governments through the Due Process clause of the Fourteenth Amendment. In 1931, the Court added freedom of the press to the restraints on state governments (*Near v. Minnesota*); free exercise of religion followed in 1940 (*Cantwell v. Connecticut*). Over the course of the next few decades, the Court slowly incorporated pieces of the Bill of Rights into the liberty of the Fourteenth Amendment's Due Process clause. This process was called the selective incorporation, or the "nationalization" of the Bill of Rights, with the result being the expansion of civil liberties across the nation, into each state and locale.

The procedural limitations on governmental power addressed in the Fourth, Fifth, Sixth, and Eight Amendments were incorporated at a rapid pace during the 1960s. Under Chief Justice Earl Warren, the Supreme Court ruled that protections such as the right to counsel when accused of a crime (*Gideon v. Wainwright*, 1963), the right against self-incrimination (*Miranda v. Arizona*, 1966), and the right to an impartial jury (*Parker v. Gladden*, 1966) restrained the powers of state and local police forces in their attempts to prosecute criminals. This created considerable controversy, especially given the general social turbulence of the time. The Court was sharply criticized for its rulings, as many conservative politicians claimed it had undermined law enforcement and allowed criminals to escape prosecution on legal technicalities. Though some scholars have argued that the public was not as upset about street crime as the media of the time projected (Loo and Grimes 2004), it is indisputable that conservative politicians adopted "law and order" platforms in everything from local elections to presidential races. Richard Nixon's 1968 presidential campaign dwelled on fears of crime and denounced the Warren Court's decisions in this area. He pledged to appoint conservative Supreme Court justices, and during his presidency, Nixon chose three associate justices and a chief justice whom he hoped would change the direction of the Court. For the most part, however, the work of the Warren Court in the area of criminal justice remained undisturbed, though there was little more expansion of procedural liberties under the next chief justice.

By the end of the 1960s, incorporation drew to an end. One additional incorporation occurred in the 21st century when the Supreme Court applied the Second Amendment's "right to keep and bear arms" to the states in 2010 (*McDonald v. Chicago*). Today, only a few parts of the Bill of Rights remain unincorporated. The Ninth Amendment, stating that rights beyond those enumerated exist, and the Tenth Amendment, which reserves powers to the states, do not contain specific liberties to incorporate. The Third Amendment (prohibiting the quartering of troops in private homes) and the Seventh Amendment (guaranteeing jury trials for civil cases) are also unincorporated. Finally, the Fifth Amendment's right to presentment by a grand jury and the Eight Amendment's protection against excessive bail and fines are not incorporated, but all of the states have due process guarantees that make incorporation of these provisions unnecessary.

The Bill of Rights is now accepted as a protection of civil liberties that binds *all* levels of governments in America: federal, state, and local.

Public Attitudes toward Civil Liberties

American citizens overwhelmingly support the concept of civil liberties in the abstract, but express far more ambivalence when confronted with actual controversies. This behavior is probably to be expected, when one remembers that protecting these liberties often thwarts governmental policies supported by the majority. Speech is more likely to be repressed when it expresses unpopular views, and procedural protections for those accused of crimes frustrate citizens who fear for their own safety. But beyond this generalization, public support for specific civil liberties varies widely depending on a variety of variables, including the historical context, and the ideology and political knowledge of the individual citizen.

As the Supreme Court applied the Bill of Rights to the states in the mid-20th century, political scientists began to study the extent to which Americans support civil liberties. More specifically, scholars focused on how much tolerance citizens have for those whose opinions differ from their own. This question arose with particular importance when the "Red Scare" took hold after World War II, and those with leftist political views were frequently seen as communists. A study conducted in the early 1950s, based on surveys and interviews of a wide variety of citizens, found that community leaders (so-called elites) were more likely to be tolerant of free speech for dissenters than ordinary citizens (the "masses") (Stouffer 1992). This finding was repeated in other studies, a number of which considered liberties beyond free speech (e.g., McCloskey and Brill-Scheuer 1983). These results led to a troubling conclusion: if elites are more tolerant of civil liberties than are the masses, and civil liberties are necessary for democracy, then, ironically, elites—and not ordinary people—are the preservers of democracy. This spawned a theory called "democratic elitism": a theory that the elites, rather than the masses, are actually responsible for upholding the liberties sacred to a functioning democracy (Dye, Ziegler, and Schubert 2012).

Later research demonstrated that public attitudes toward civil liberties are more complex than originally thought. Some found that the gap between the tolerance levels of the masses and the elite is less dramatic than earlier studies maintained (Lock 1999) and that the media have a crucial role in influencing people's support for liberties (Nelson, Clawson, and Oxley 1997). Others found that levels of support for civil liberties vary more widely among members of the elite than between elites and common folk (Sniderman et al. 1991). Among many studies there is a common finding that intolerance for dissenting political views increases when people feel their security is threatened, such as during the Cold War and after the attacks on 9/11 (Gibson 2006, 23). Therefore, an individual's support for civil liberties may wax and wane over time, depending on current events.

Support for specific liberties is also a function of a citizen's political ideology and partisan affiliation. Since the Supreme Court began applying the Bill of Rights to the states during the 20th century, support for these liberties has usually been strongest among self-identified liberals and within the Democratic Party. Liberals have been more likely to endorse the free speech rights of political dissidents, the free exercise liberties of religious minorities, and the procedural rights of those accused of crimes. However, conservatives and Republicans are strong defenders of the right to bear arms, property rights, and the free exercise rights of Christians. Furthermore, conservatives have become increasingly concerned about government becoming too powerful and intruding on privacy.

For example, Republicans have protested the government's use of the Census to gather citizens' personal information, as well as the Internal Revenue Service's close examination of conservative nonprofit organizations. So an individual's defense of civil liberties, while more prominent among liberals, is somewhat dependent on the liberty in question.

Conclusion

Civil liberties are a collection of protections against arbitrary governmental power. Americans' understanding of these rights can be traced to England's struggles between the monarchy and the nobility, and extended to the colonists' desire for independence. Specific protections for liberties can be found within the federal Bill of Rights, as well as in state constitutions. While Americans defend the notion of freedom in the abstract, a citizen's support for specific liberties is dependent on historical context, level of education, and political ideology.

See also Civil Rights; Constitution and Constitutionalism; Democracy; Liberty; Privacy Rights and Politics; States' Rights; Supreme Court, United States.

Gwyneth I. Williams

Bibliography

Dye, Thomas, Harmon Ziegler, and Louis Schubert. 2012. *The Irony of Democracy*. 15th ed. Boston: Wadsworth.

Gibson, James L. 2006. "Enigmas of Intolerance: Fifty Years after Stouffer's Communism, Conformity, and Civil Liberties." *Perspectives on Politics* 4: 21–34.

Holt, James Clarke. 1991. *Magna Carta*. 2nd ed. Cambridge: Cambridge University Press.

Hutson, James H. 1991. "The Bill of Rights and the American Revolutionary Experience." In Michael J. Lacey and Knud Haakonssen, eds. *A Culture of Rights: The Bill of Rights in Philosophy, Politics, and Law, 1791 and 1991*. New York: Press Syndicate of University of Cambridge, pp. 62–97.

Lock, Shmuel, 1999. *Crime, Public Opinion, and Civil Liberties: The Tolerant Public*. Westport, CT: Praeger Publishers.

Loo, Dennis D., and Ruth-Ellen M. Grimes. 2004. "Polls, Politics, and Crime: The 'Law and Order' Issue of the 1960s." *Western Criminology Review* 5: 50–67.

Lovejoy, David S. 1980. "Two American Revolutions, 1689 and 1776." In J. G. A. Pocock, ed. *Three British Revolutions: 1641, 1688, 1776.* Princeton, NJ: Princeton University Press, pp. 244–62.

McCloskey, Herbert, and Alida Brill-Scheuer, 1983. *Dimensions of Tolerance: What Americans Believe about Civil Liberties.* New York City: Russell Sage Foundation.

Nelson, Thomas E., Rosalee A. Clawson, and Zoe M. Oxley. 1997. "Media Framing of a Civil Liberties Conflict and Its Effect on Tolerance." *The American Political Science Review* 91: 567–83.

Sniderman, Paul M., et al. 1991. "The Fallacy of Democratic Elitism: Elite Competition and Commitment to Civil Liberties." *British Journal of Political Science* 21: 349–70. Doi: 10.1017/S0007123400006190.

Stouffer, Samuel Andrew. 1992. *Communism, Conformity and Civil Liberties: A Cross-section of the Nation.* New Brunswick, NJ: Transaction Publishers. First published 1955 by Doubleday Co.

Cases

Barron v. Baltimore, 32 U.S. 243 (1833).
Cantwell v. Connecticut, 310 U.S. (1940).
Gideon v. Wainwright, 372 U.S. 335 (1963).
Gitlow v. New York, 268 U.S. 652 (1925).
McDonald v. Chicago, 561 U.S. 3025 (2010).
Miranda v. Arizona, 384 U.S. 436 (1966).
Near v. Minnesota, 283 U.S. 697 (1931).
Parker v. Gladden, 385 U.S. 363 (1966).
Texas v. Johnson, 491 U.S. 397 (1989).

CIVIL RELIGION

The historical often influences the historiographical (or, put differently, historic events often alter one's perspective—including one's perspective on history). Such was clearly the case with civil religion in the wake of the terrorist attacks launched on the United States on September 11, 2001. 9/11 and the wars that followed placed the idea of civil religion in the spotlight once again. A hotly contested term since at least the mid-1960s, it captured the kind of moral appeal President George W. Bush made to the nation at the National Cathedral on the National Day of Prayer and Remembrance three days after the terrorist attacks. Standing before an audience of religious leaders, government, and military officials who all sat in pews, Bush told the nation, while "[God's] purposes are not always our own . . . our responsibility to history is already clear. To answer these attacks and rid the world of evil" (Bush 2001). As the United States went back to war, the president and many Americans hoped that in such action the nation would affirm its historical morality.

This conflation of religion and the nation, while not necessarily unusual in American history, prompted the American press to look for comment from Robert Bellah, an American sociologist who did more than almost anyone else to define civil religion in its American context. While Bellah built his scholarly career as a sociologist of religion, he became closely, and it seems permanently, associated with the term "civil religion" because of a 1967 essay he wrote entitled "Civil Religion in America." In light of the political–religious mission that President Bush had apparently announced at the National Cathedral, Bellah told reporters that he found Bush's address "stunningly inappropriate." Bellah caustically observed that the president had "invoked civil religion to make the case for war" (Silk 2001). That reaction struck religious scholar Mark Silk as surprisingly odd, for as he said, "if civil religion is about anything, it's about war and those who die in it" (Silk 2001). Silk too has written about civil religion, and these different takes on Bush's speech were revealing: Bellah rejected Bush's invocation of civil religion because the president had used a normative understanding of the term to justify a war not yet waged. Silk observed that the terrorist attacks had made the need for civil religion grow more apparent, perhaps even evident, as Americans sought to understand the period they had now entered. Both agreed that civil religion had once again entered the public debate in a time of war; the moral stakes of going to war force people to consider the faith and judgment they invest in their nation.

President George W. Bush speaks during a national day of prayer and remembrance service at the National Cathedral in Washington, D.C., September 14, 2001. (AP Photo/J. Scott Applewhite)

Defining Civil Religion

The intellectual historian Wilfred McClay observed that while civil religion might describe the social reality of conflating religion and politics, it is "admittedly very much a scholar's term, rather than a term arising out of general parlance. . . . Civil religion is a means of investing a particular set of political and social arrangements with an aura of the sacred, thereby elevating their stature and enhancing their stability. It can serve as a point of reference for the shared faith of an entire nation" (McClay 2004).

Political theorist Ronald Beiner points out that "civil religion is the appropriation of religion by politics for its own purposes" (Beiner 2011, 2). Beiner's book-length study of civil religion serves as a kind of extended etymology of the term as applied to political thinkers from Machiavelli and Rousseau to Nietzsche

and Heidegger. Beiner notes that even though the philosophers he profiles all contributed to the "radical secularization of modern politics," all also expressed "not a little sympathy for some manner of theocracy" (Beiner 2011, 3). Such tension brings the constructive paradox of civil religion into greater relief—societies as different as Iran and the United States can seek ways to appropriate religion by politics for their own purposes. As Beiner explains: "Civil religion is the empowerment of religion, not for the sake of religion, but for the sake of enhanced citizenship—of making members of the political community better citizens, in accordance with whatever conception one holds of what constitutes being a good citizen" (Beiner 2011, 12).

For example, the originator of the term, Jean Jacques Rousseau, the 18th-century French philosopher, believed "a state has never been founded without religion serving as its base" (Rousseau 1762). For

Rousseau, civil religion had to exist for a modern state to survive but a state's civil religion had to cut two different ways: first, as a set of dogmas "without which a man cannot be a good citizen or a faithful subject," and second, as a point of reference for the many faiths professed by people living under a single sovereign. To Beiner, it is Rousseau's inability to resolve a tension between politics and religion that demonstrates both the philosophical allure of civil religion and the many unsatisfying versions of it. The tension is unresolvable and therefore the term, while relatively easy to define, is frustrating to realize in practice. In Rousseau's mind, a "real" civil religion would require the practical application of a transcendent politics. Beiner points out the obvious contradiction: "we are left with two unhappy alternatives of a morally true religion that is in its essence subversive to politics, and a sound civil religion that is both morally unattractive and, historically, an anachronism" (Beiner 2011, 14).

The version of civil religion proposed by Rousseau and other political theorists was heavy-handed and top-down, suggesting that civil religion is implicitly hegemonic if it is going to work, but also conceding that civil religion cannot exist without popular belief in religion.

American Civil Religion

The relationship between religion (or those who are religious) and civil religion has another side to it, one that sees civil religion as a force growing somewhat organically within a modern nation-state. Rather than imagine civil religion as a product solely of a hegemonic ruler or ruling class, a pair of Frenchmen writing at different ends of the 19th century argued that civil religion emerged as a way to square devotion to God and nation. Alexis de Tocqueville and Émile Durkheim provided what might be considered a "bottom up" view of civil religion. While neither used the term "civil religion" (perhaps to distinguish their observations from Rousseau), their insights primarily influenced what became the dominant view of civil religion in America.

In his landmark work of social observation and political analysis *Democracy in America*, Tocqueville wrote that "the greatest advantage of religion is to inspire diametrically contrary principles. There is no religion that does not place the object of man's desires above and beyond the treasures of earth and that does not naturally raise his soul to regions far above those of the senses. Nor is there any which does not impose on man some duties towards his kind and thus draw him at times from the contemplation of himself. This is found in the most false and dangerous religions" (Tocqueville 1840). And therefore religion served as a source of both inspiration and self-control in ways that help a nation if it hopes to command not merely its citizens' respect of law but their devotion to the existential existence of the nation. In other words, Tocqueville argued that democracies in particular needed a way to pull people together because political forces in a democracy naturally pushed them toward independence from almost all forms of control.

Durkheim did not write specifically about the American experience with religion, but he did comment on the significance of social cohesion in all kinds of societies. As he saw it, everything from primitive societies to modern, pluralistic societies had religious qualities. In *The Elementary Forms of the Religious Life*, Durkheim observed: "Men who feel themselves united, partially by bonds of blood, but still more by a community of interest and tradition, assemble and become conscious of their moral unity"; and, significantly, that moral unity gets expressed in ways that they can observe and honor: "They are led to represent this unity" (quoted in Bellah and Hammond 1980).

The United States that Tocqueville wrote about had developed traditions and expressions that promulgated popular obedience. While any state has direct interest in promoting ceremonies that affirm faith in the nation it governs, such faith had legitimacy because generations of citizens practice and legitimize such ceremonies. Robert Bellah and his coauthor Phillip Hammond in *Varieties of Civil Religion*, explained: "it is the fact of unity more than the fact of religion with which Durkheim begins. Religion is more the *expression* of an integrated society than it is the *source* of a society's integration" (Bellah and Hammond 1980). The point that Bellah and Hammond wanted to emphasize was that social cohesion could manifest itself in actions that looked religious but which, importantly, did not require faith in a single religion to be effective.

In other words, a people could express faith in a nation through a civil religion without reifying themselves or believing that the nation was somehow transcendent. Certainly nothing tests the faith in one's nation quite like the moral catastrophe of war—for it is in war that a people affirms a nation's power to command control over the fate of people in absolute terms.

Robert Bellah and American Civil Religion

It was not surprising, then, that Bellah developed his complex reading of civil religion in the middle of the Vietnam War. During that period, he witnessed his nation struggle with the moral consequences of fighting a war that not had only grown increasingly popular but appeared to be the antithesis of the civil rights movement—a moral movement that had united and inspired many Americans. In the winter of 1967, Bellah contributed his essay to the academic journal *Daedelus*, expressing a qualified optimism about the fate of the United States in the midst of the Vietnam War.

Bellah chose to begin his analysis by acknowledging the power presidents often extended through moral appeals. Specifically, he referred to the inaugural address by John F. Kennedy, the nation's first Catholic president, and his use of references to God to compel Americans to act. Given the controversy surrounding Kennedy's religion, the president did not admonish Americans to be better Catholics or better Christians or even God-fearing people. Rather, he employed the widely shared assumption that the United States was a nation under God and had an obligation to do good. Bellah argued that Kennedy, like many presidents before him, appealed to the "religious dimension" of American life. "This public religious dimension is expressed in a set of beliefs, symbols, and rituals that I am calling the American civil religion," Bellah explained. The presidential inauguration was one of these rituals that affirmed "the religious legitimation of the highest political authority" (Bellah 1967, 22).

The postwar period had seen the development of increasingly overt expressions of civil religion. The Cold War prompted the institutionalization of civil religion, particularly in such acts as adding "under God" to the pledge of allegiance and "In God we trust" to the currency. The apparent willingness of Americans to accept that "ultimate sovereignty has been attributed to God" led not to a theocracy but to a sense that "the will of the people is not itself the criterion of right and wrong. There is a higher criterion in terms of which this will can be judged; it is possible that the people may be wrong." Bellah concluded that Kennedy's appeal to God was not unique but "only the most recent statement of a theme that lies very deep in the American tradition, namely the obligation, both collective and individual, to carry out God's will on earth." Rather than see that mission as either providential or over, Bellah regarded the crisis sparked by the Vietnam War to be one of those critical periods that shaped how Americans understood the religious dimension to their political life (Bellah 1967, 23).

Bellah was far from the first scholar to observe the religious quality of American life. But he was especially astute at illustrating why civil religion made sense as way to comprehend the American experience in a time of crisis. His argument was fairly straightforward: civil religion was and would continue to be a tangible source for judgment as well as inspiration based on historical experience. Such experiences were not random but were widely considered by generations of Americans to be foundational—they included the Puritan covenant in the new world, the writing of the Declaration of Independence and the Constitution, Lincoln's magnanimity during the Civil War, and the sacrifices made in World War II. Thus, the collective power of such experiences provided a moral standard by which to measure the actions of the United States. He explained that over time Americans had come to accept a common moral purpose of their nation. He described this collective faith as "an understanding of the American experience in the light of ultimate and universal reality . . . [and] at its best [it] is a genuine apprehension of universal and transcendent religious reality as seen in or one could almost say, as revealed through the experience of the American people" (Bellah 1967, 33).

Bellah's was a chastened civil religion, born from the theological crisis precipitated by the Cold War and made acute by Vietnam. The key for him was to extend the appeals to moral authority made during struggle for civil rights to foreign policy. Yet that would require a sense of judgment that Bellah feared was fading from American life just at the moment when the nation needed a renewed sense of morality. In short, the nation needed a judgmental God. "But today," he observed in 1966, "as even *Time* has recognized, the meaning of the word *God* is by no means . . . clear or obvious. There is no formal creed in the civil religion," Bellah lamented. Thus, he implored, "it is not [too] soon to consider how [this] deepening theological crisis may affect the future of [civil religion's] articulation" (Bellah 1967, 37).

Like Tocqueville, Bellah's notion of a civil religion suggested that the American experiment with democracy had a faith dimension. However, he did not believe that an American experience made the nation exceptional in a normative way. Other countries also gained existential understanding of themselves from their experiences. Bellah had merely applied an approach of identifying the religious dimension of any society to the specific experiences of the United States. Thus, he argued, while we can study civil religion in the United States, scholarship did not somehow prove that the nation stood apart from all other nations or closer to God. In fact, Bellah ended his famous essay suggesting that the ultimate result of the American war in Vietnam might be the rise of a global civil religion (something Durkheim also predicted) under which the actions of the many nations struggling to figure out a period of revolution could be both guided and judged.

Somewhat surprising to him, Bellah's essay remained a touchstone for studies that attempted to parse out different aspects of American civil religion, from the role of presidents and public ceremonies to finding statistical evidence of the existence and strength of civil religion in a society. Over that same period, civil religion was also defended as a positive force to reunify a nation torn apart by war, economic hardship, and cultural changes and derided as either an illegitimate alternative to theistic religions or "an ideological campaign masquerading as an analytical category" (Chernus 2010, 63). Acutely aware of the debates swirling around the term, Bellah actively tried to disassociate himself from civil religion.

Bellah's strained relationship to the term came through in a book of essays compiled from lectures he gave in the early 1970s. Anticipating scholarly interest in the fracturing of American intellectual life during the developing culture wars, Bellah wrote in *The Broken Covenant*:

> The erosion of language . . . is a symptom of the erosion of common meanings, of which there is a great deal of evidence in our society. This takes the form, which is by now statistically well documented, of a decline of belief in all forms of obligation: to one's occupation, one's family, and one's country. A tendency to rank personal gratification above obligation to others correlates with a deepening cynicism about the established social, economic, and political institutions of society. A sense that the basic institutions of society are unjust and serve the interests of a few at the expense of the many, is used to justify the inapplicability of moral obligations to one's self. (Bellah 1975, preface)

With this tone, Bellah also anticipated the growing consensus among a generation of scholars that civil religion appeared dangerously affirmational rather than analytical. Yet at the same time, Bellah had not argued for a civil religion as a normative construct of sacred American beliefs, but rather as a social and rhetorical construct that required genuine civic participation to make apparent. Indeed, to accept the reality of the culture wars also meant entertaining the notion that the stakes in that struggle had something to do with the fate of the United States.

American Civil Religion and 9/11

To observers such as Wilfred McClay, the popular response to 9/11 served as a profound counterpoint to the culture wars. McClay remarked that one might not have been surprised, given the religious motivations of the terrorists, if 9/11 had only have confirmed the need to marginalize religion in the public square. Yet the exact opposite happened. McClay noted, "The more common public reaction was something much simpler and more primal. Millions of Americans went to church in search of reassurance, comfort, solace, strength, and some semblance of redemptive meaning in the act of sharing their grief and confusion in the presence of the transcendent" (McClay 2004, 2). The collective reaction of millions of Americans indicated to McClay that American civil religion had historical resonance within the United States.

McClay's reaction to the popular expression of civil religion reflected a broader hope among many intellectuals that the nation had found its way out of the culture wars and to a traditional and more authentically American moral authority. While he acknowledged that civil religion had the capacity to grow intolerable in its most extreme forms, he also defended the tradition in the United States "to conflate the realms of the religious and the political" to affirm a higher set of ideals to guide and judge the nation. "Religion and the nation are inevitably entwined," McClay noted, "and some degree of entwining is a good thing. After all, the self-regulative pluralism of American culture cannot work without the ballast of certain elements of deep commonality" (McClay 2004, 5). Yet McClay also recognized that the diversity of American culture did not operate in a religious vacuum; there was a dominant tradition, and it exercised considerable influence in the aftermath of 9/11.

For example, among the most evocative examples of the Christian dominance of American civil religion was the discovery of cross-shaped girders in the wreckage of the Twin Towers. Ground zero in Manhattan had quickly become a kind of holy site for the nation's reformed civil religion. "What," McClay wondered, "does this object mean to the people viewing it, many of whom are not Christian and not even Americans?" There was little ambiguity in the "discovery" of the cross at ground zero—it emerged as a clear symbol of a Christian-dominated civil religion—civil religion in America reflects the dominance of a history in which Christianity has been intertwined with the fate of the nation. Indeed, for better or worse, McClay noted that the "September 11 attacks reminded us . . . that the impulse to create and live inside of a civil religion is an irrepressible human impulse" (McClay 2004, 6).

American Civil Religion and War

It seems to me that we can accept McClay's observation that there exists an impulse to "live inside of a civil religion" while also interrogating why that impulse persists and how it manifests itself in certain ways. Since 9/11, scholars have employed the term to describe historical narratives as well as to analyze them. For example, scholars of religion have used civil religion to explain American experience in wars: Mark Noll, Harry S. Stout, and George Rable have done this in regard to the Civil War; William Inboden, Jeremy Gunn, and Raymond Haberski find civil religion useful to explain the cold war, while Andrew Preston locates it in the long-term mixing of religion and American foreign relations. Arthur Remillard and other scholars have prodded us to speak in terms of many different civil religions, rather than any unified and ubiquitous version.

One can understand Robert Bellah's lament about being associated so closely with civil religion: over time the term sometimes seemed to be little more than a parody of itself. And yet, Bellah's 1967 essay remains evocative not because he proposed reifying the United States (in a way akin to American "exceptionalism") but because he identified a tradition that exists within many societies. As Robert Beiner has demonstrated, civil religion exists as a political theory, but debates such as the one Robert Bellah instigated in 1967 tell us a great deal about the society that continues to use varieties of it.

See also American "Exceptionalism"; American Flag; Citizenship and Politics; Monuments, Memorials, and Public History; National Identity; Political Communications; Prayer and Religious Symbols in Public Places; Theater and Ritual in American Politics; War and Politics.

Raymond Haberski Jr.

Bibliography

Beiner, Ronald. 2011. *Civil Religion: A Dialogue in the History of Political Philosophy*. Cambridge: Cambridge University Press.

Bellah, Robert N. 1967. "Civil Religion in America." *Daedalus* 96 (Winter); reprinted in Russell E. Richey and Donald G. Jones, eds. *American Civil Religion*. New York: Harper & Row, 1974.

Bellah, Robert N. 1975. *The Broken Covenant*. New York: Seabury Press.

Bellah, Robert N., and Phillip Hammond. 1980. *The Varieties of Civil Religion*. San Francisco: Harper & Row.

Bush, George W. 2001. "9/11 Remembrance: Remarks by the President." National Cathedral Digital Archives. www.nationalcathedral.org/worship/sermonTexts/gwb20010914.shtml. Accessed April 21, 2014.

Chernus, Ira. 2010. "Civil Religion." In Philip Goff, ed. *The Blackwell Companion to Religion in America*. Hoboken, NJ: Wiley-Blackwell.

De Tocqueville, Alexis. 1840. "How Religion in the United States Avails Itself of Democratic Tendencies." *Democracy in American*, Chapter V, Section I, Volume II. Available at xroads.virginia.edu/~HYPER/DETOC/ch1_05.htm. Accessed April 19, 2014.

Gunn, Jeremy. 2008. *Spiritual Weapons: The Cold War and the Forging of an American National Religion*. Westport, CT: Praeger Publishing.

Haberski, Raymond, Jr. 2012. *God and War: American Civil Religion since 1945*. New Brunswick, NJ: Rutgers University Press.

Hughes, Richard T. 2004. *Myths America Lives By*. Champaign: University of Illinois Press.

Inboden, William. 2010. *Religion and American Foreign Policy, 1945–1960: The Soul of Containment*. New York: Cambridge University Press.

McClay, Wilfred M. 2004. "The Soul of a Nation." *Public Interest* 155 (Spring): 4–19.

Noll, Mark. 2006. *Civil War as a Theological Crisis*. Chapel Hill: University of North Carolina Press.

Rodgers, Daniel T. 2011. *The Age of Fracture*. Cambridge, MA: Harvard University Press, 2011.

Rousseau, Jean Jacques. 1762. "Civil Religion." *Social Contract*, Book IV. Available at www.constitution.org/jjr/socon_04.htm. Accessed April 15, 2014.

Silk, Mark. 2001. "The Civil Religion Goes to War." *Religion in the News* 4, no. 3. Available at www.trincoll.edu/depts/csrpl/RINVol4No3/civil%20religion.htm. Accessed April 15, 2014.

Stout, Harry S. 2006. *Upon the Altar of the Nation: A Moral History of the Civil War*. New York: Viking Press.

Wimberley, Ronald C., and William H. Swatos Jr. 1998. "Civil Religion." In William H. Swatos Jr., ed. *Encyclopedia of Religion and Society*. Walnut Creek, CA: Alta Mira Press, pp. 94–96.

CIVIL RIGHTS

Civil rights is as old as Western civilization. When an Athenian jury convicted Socrates for making "the worse appear the better cause," he was fighting a civil rights struggle for "philosophy," or the right to study reason over superstition (Plato 1992, 20). When given the chance to escape the death penalty for engaging in what would be called *free speech* today (as guaranteed by the First Amendment to the U.S. Constitution), Socrates refused to disobey the clearly unjust verdict against him, citing the struggle of the philosopher: "I am and always have been one of those natures who must be guided by reason, whatever reason may be which upon reflection appears to me to be the best" (Plato 1992, 46). Socrates lived and died fighting for the right to philosophize. In a sense, the cause of Socrates, like the "cause of America," according to Thomas Paine (1997, 2), "is in a great measure the cause of all mankind."

The American founding points to Socrates and to philosophy:

> James Madison had the Socratic tradition in mind when he wrote that "A government deriving its energy from the will of the society, and operating, by the reason of its measures, on the understanding and interest of the society . . . is the government for which philosophy has been searching and humanity been fighting from the most remote ages." (Jaffa 2000, 121)

The Declaration of Independence calls for a government that exercises power in the interests of all of humanity, not just the majority or a powerful few. It reads: "That to secure these rights, Governments are instituted among Men, deriving their just powers from the consent of the governed." Ideally, the American founders were involved in a Socratic struggle for individual liberty, for freedom from the arbitrary exercise of government power and the right to autonomy.

A lesser view is that the founders were determined to maintain their own property at the expense of others. As Charles A. Beard (2009, 1018) argued in 1922, although the Constitution of the United States "nowhere takes into account the existence of economic divisions" between the rich and poor, the founders created a Constitution that, in practice, primarily protected only white, male property owners. According to Beard (2009, 1021), the founders could have said:

> "We are fighting for the plantation owners of the South, the merchants and landed gentry of the North, and the free farmers in both sections, in order that they may govern themselves" . . . [although] such a chilly description of fact would not have thrilled the masses . . . who enjoyed no political rights under either system.

It is tragic irony that the language of the Declaration of Independence sets forth that "all Men are created equal" even though some of its signers held slaves. Beard (2009, 1021) notes the irony and points out that "these high principles did not square with slavery, indentured servitude, and political disenfranchisement." Though a critic of the application of the words of the Declaration of Independence, Beard acknowledges that "the grand words stood for all time, and advocates of manhood suffrage and woman suffrage afterward appealed to them with great effect in attacking property and sex qualifications on the right to vote" (Beard 2009, 1021).

Here, then, are the ingredients of civil rights: an identifiable group and the unjust denial of their fundamental rights—or, stated differently, unequal or unfair treatment. Civil rights exists whenever individual members of an identifiable (unpopular) group struggle to be free from an oppressor(s) that denies them their basic individual rights.

The struggle for the equal enjoyment of civil liberties by disenfranchised groups is the definition of "civil rights." As Thomas E. Patterson (2011, 150) puts it: civil rights refers "to the right of every person to equal protection under the laws and equal access to society's opportunities and public facilities"; it is "a question of whether individual members of differing *groups*, such as racial, gender, and ethnic groups, are treated equally by government and, in some instances, private parties." According to Brooks, Carrasco, and Selmi (2000, 3–4) civil rights is primarily about "society's longest running social and moral dilemma" between the treatment of two groups, "one white, the other black"—although we may have "reached a point in our culture where the concept of 'race' must be viewed as a metaphor for 'otherness,'" which includes the "experiences of African Americans, women, disabled Americans, gays and lesbians and other 'culturally oppressed,' or 'outsider,' groups." Put simply, civil rights refers to the struggle by outsider groups to be free from unjust oppression.

History and Scope

The struggle of philosophy led by Socrates in ancient Athens was the first civil rights movement (as far as we know) in human history. In America, the founders led by George Washington struggled against King George II in the 1770s; abolitionists led by Abraham Lincoln struggled in the antebellum south for the end of slavery in the 1860s; Dr. Martin Luther King Jr. led a movement to end segregation in the 1950s–1960s, and so on. If, as one might argue, the American Revolution was the first civil rights movement, then that was followed by the question of whether Federalists or anti-Federalists would rule by a Constitution or by the Articles of Confederation. That early struggle at the Constitutional Convention was followed by a struggle over whether to add a Bill of Rights to the new Constitution. The history of civil rights has been one struggle after another by members of unpopular groups who seek to exercise their fundamental rights.

Note that these early struggles in American history were fought largely over economic interests by different groups (farmers vs. merchants vs. manufacturers vs. financiers), and they all involved (primarily) white men. All others were denied political equality in different ways. Poor, white males fought for suffrage all the way into the 1930s, and, today, same-sex couples struggle for the right to marry. Perhaps the most enduring civil rights struggle is about race. The Declaration of Independence refers to Native Americans as "savages" and, of course, there was chattel slavery in the United States for anyone of African ancestry up until the Civil War, which itself was followed by racial segregation.

Race is an ascribed status; people do not choose their skin hue by nature. Therefore, race is an arbitrary basis by which to discriminate against people. In *Dred Scott v. Sandford* (1856), the Supreme Court held that slaves were not "persons" and, therefore, they were not entitled to "due process." The Court also ruled that the Missouri Compromise, which prevented slavery from encroaching north of the southern border of Missouri, was unconstitutional (a major cause of the Civil War). The struggle for the end of slavery was a civil rights struggle to end the servitude of African Americans, which resulted in a Civil War and President Lincoln's Emancipation Proclamation of 1863, as well as the passage of the Thirteenth (end of slavery), Fourteenth (guarantee of due process and equal protection at the State level), and Fifteenth (right to vote without regard to "race, color, or previous condition of servitude") Amendments (Bardes, Shelley, and Schmidt 2009, 148).

Though Congress, from 1865 to 1875, "passed a series of civil rights acts . . . aimed at enforcing these amendments . . . [they] ultimately did little to secure equality for African-Americans" (Bardes, Shelley, and Schmidt 2009, 148). The Supreme Court upheld Jim Crow segregation (i.e., the separate-but-equal doctrine) in *Plessy v. Ferguson* (1896), a case about a Louisiana statute that made it a criminal offense for nonwhites to ride in whites-only railcars. The Court considered the segregation fair because the law made it a crime for both races to mix (the discrimination was *equal*). The *Plessy* decision resulted in segregated public schools and private discriminatory practices in businesses nationwide. African Americans had won their freedom in the Civil War, but they did not yet enjoy full equality under the law.

The Supreme Court in *Brown v. Board of Education of Topeka* (1954) struck down Jim Crow segregation on the basis that the separate-but-equal doctrine was inherently unequal and violated the equal protection clause of the Fourteenth Amendment. The Court's decision in a second *Brown* decision (decided the following year) came with a proviso that segregated schools must be integrated "with all deliberate speed." This command, along with the actions of people such

as Rosa Parks, a 43-year-old African American woman who refused to sit in the "colored" section of a city bus and consequently was arrested for it, led to a new civil rights movement. "For an entire year, African-Americans boycotted the Montgomery bus line," and their leader was "a twenty-seven-year-old Baptist minister, Dr. Martin Luther King, Jr." (Bardes, Shelley, and Schmidt 2009, 253).

Dr. King led a civil rights struggle that is epitomized in his "I Have a Dream" speech, delivered on the steps of the Lincoln Memorial on August 28, 1963. In that speech, Dr. King (2006, 111) lamented that "the life of the Negro is still sadly crippled by the manacles of segregation and the chains of discrimination." Dr. King (2006, 111–12) said that he came to Washington, DC, "to cash a check," because when "the architects of our republic wrote the magnificent words of the Constitution and the Declaration of Independence,

Martin Luther King Jr. waves to the crowd at the Lincoln Memorial after his "I Have a Dream" speech in Washington, D.C., August 28, 1963. (AP Photo)

they were signing a promissory note to which every American was to fall heir . . . that all men would be guaranteed the unalienable rights of life, liberty, and the pursuit of happiness." Note the way Dr. King references the American founding, thus connecting the struggle to end segregation with a struggle for justice that goes back as far as Socrates.

The struggle for civil rights led by Dr. King culminated with civil rights legislation that guarantees against discrimination on the basis of race, color, religion, gender, and national origin when it comes to voter registration, service at public accommodations—for example, hotels and restaurants—public education, and employment (Bardes, Shelley, and Schmidt 2009, 155). The 1964 Civil Rights Act also created a five-member commission called the Equal Employment Opportunity Commission (EEOC) whose charge is to issue guidelines and regulations on discrimination, as well as investigate discriminatory claims. The EEOC has the power of subpoena and can require witnesses to testify under the penalty of perjury.

Women have also had to struggle for the equal enjoyment of their liberties. There were no women at the Constitutional Convention, though women were politically active through letters and private discourse. Abigail Adams (2009, 506), for example, wrote to her husband John Adams in 1776 demanding better treatment for women in a new republic:

> [T]he passion for Liberty cannot be Equally Strong in the Breasts of those who have been accustomed to deprive their fellow Creatures of theirs. I long to hear that you have declared an independency—and by the way in the new Code of Laws which I suppose it will be necessary for you to make I desire you would Remember the Ladies, and be more generous and favourable to them than your ancestors. Do not put such unlimited power into the hands of the Husbands . . . all Men would be tyrants if they could.

Women would have to wait until August 18, 1920, for the right to vote when the Nineteenth Amendment was ratified. Female suffrage was the product of a long battle for equality. In 1837, Sarah M. Grimké (2009,

515), a Quaker abolitionist, fought for equal rights for women by claiming that women have moral "duties" that are "private, but the sources of *mighty power*," such that when the "influence of woman upon the sternness of man's opinions is fully exercised, society feels the effects of it in a thousand ways." Grimké (2009, 517), like Socrates, wanted simply the basic right of the freedom of conscience—that is, to study and to speak on morality, and she argued for full equality between the sexes in this regard, saying that there is "no distinction between us, as moral and intelligent beings."

When Socrates fought for the right to think, he was engaged in civil rights. When abolitionists struggled to end slavery, they were engaged in civil rights. When women fought for political equality at the ballot box, they were engaged in civil rights. Unfortunately, segregation followed slavery and women still earn less than their male counterparts for the same job. The discrimination continues and so too does the struggle for fairness. African Americans and women are still engaged in a civil rights struggle, as are other groups. The whole history of America is a struggle for civil rights: "Every generation blames a slack-virtued, un-American 'them' " (Morone 2003, 3). Thus, every generation potentially witnesses a *them* who will rise up and demand equality.

Other and Ongoing Struggles for Civil Rights

The history of civil rights involves any group of subordinated outsiders who struggle for the equal enjoyment of their individual liberties. Whenever those in power abuse their authority by systematically singling out a distinct group of people either expressly by law (de jure) or implicitly (de facto) through hidden interactions or unconscious bias, the stage is set for *them* to fight for justice and fair treatment. The scope of civil rights is quite broad.

Immigrants, for example, have been and currently are struggling for equal rights. For the first 100 years of the United States, there was an "open-door immigration policy" (Greenblatt 2008, 201). America in theory is universal; not a matter of breed or skin hue, nor a geography or religion: "an American may belong to any ethnic group" (Fiorina 2006, 67). In the late 1800s, however, immigrants from China were excluded via the Chinese Exclusion Act of 1882. In 1917, "zones" were created for Asian immigrants dictating where people could (or could not) live and work (Greenblatt 2008, 201). Drug laws were used to target immigrants, too. "Some of the Chinese workers who built the railroads also built opium dens, which became a 'visible symbol of the Chinese presence . . . and as such became the target of anti-Chinese sentiment" leading to legislation such as the Opium Exclusion Act of 1909 (White 2004, 21–21).

Other early drug laws are connected to civil rights for immigrants, too. In listing the reasons why the war for independence was winnable in 1776, Thomas Paine (1997, 39) observed: "Hemp flourishes even to rankness, so that we need not want cordage." Over 100 years later, hemp (the name for the industrial use of marijuana) had transformed into something evil. In the early 1900s, Hispanic immigrants were being targeted via drug laws such as the Marihuana Tax Act of 1937, which prohibited marijuana at the federal level (something many states had already done) (White 2004). In testimony on the act, Congress heard appeals to gross racial animus on the "scourge" of what is known today as *reefer madness*:

> The people and the officials here want to know why something can't be done about marihuana. . . . I wish I could show you what a small marihuana cigarette can do to one of our degenerate Spanish-speaking residents. That's why our problem is so great; the greatest percentage of our population is composed of Spanish-speaking persons, most of whom are low mentally, because of social and racial conditions. (quoted in White 2004, 22)

The beginning of drug prohibition in the United States is mired in racism, and the current effects of prohibition not surprisingly point toward a disparate impact on race. In fact, the war on drugs has been called "the new Jim Crow" (Alexander 2012). There is a current struggle to end marijuana prohibition that has achieved a measure of success. To date, 18 states have passed medical marijuana laws and two states

(Colorado and Washington) have passed marijuana legalization. The trend of relaxing marijuana laws since California passed the nation's first medical marijuana law (the Compassionate Use Act) in 1996 has shifted the debate on drug policy. "Moral bans lose power as the dangerous villains fade" (Morone 2003, 473). The nation may no longer be afraid of marijuana users, especially when they include the past three presidents of the United States or cancer patients, but the struggle to end the prohibition of a plant Thomas Paine once considered essential to the success of the union continues.

The struggle for fair treatment also continues for members of the gay and lesbian community. "In less than 30 years, the gay and lesbian movement has become one of the largest civil rights movements in contemporary America" (Ginsberg et al. 2009, 127). The Supreme Court had never ruled on a case involving discrimination based on sexual orientation until 1986 in *Bowers v. Hardwick*, where the Court ruled that sodomy is not a fundamental right protected by the Constitution. In 2003, the Court distinguished *Bowers v. Hardwick* in *Lawrence v. Texas* when it held that there is no rational basis to criminalize the private sexual practices of consenting adults. The laws that prohibit same-sex activities are unconstitutional as a result of *Lawrence v. Texas*, but what about the right to marry and other considerations such as hospital visitation, taxes, and death and estate issues for same-sex couples? These questions remain unanswered. The Supreme Court is currently considering whether California's 2008 ban on same-sex marriage is constitutional. This case will likely shape the future parameters of debate over civil rights in this area for years to come.

The start of the fight for civil rights in the modern era for the gay and lesbian community, which also includes transgender persons and bisexual persons, happened on June 27, 1969, when patrons at the Stonewall Inn staged an impromptu protest over police harassment. The standoff lasted two nights, and it led to a "gay power" movement where people felt empowered to demand equal treatment. Stonewall has been called "the shot heard round the homosexual world" (Bardes, Shelley, and Schmidt 2009, 174). Because one's sexual orientation is a private matter, and because laws prohibiting same-sex behaviors were based on passionate appeals against *them* without evidence of any threat to *us*, the struggle for the gay and lesbian community to enjoy equal rights is unquestionably part of the history and current landscape of civil rights that will continue into the future.

Issues that raise the specter of civil rights abound in American politics. They include discrimination based on race, gender, country of origin, religion, sexual orientation, voting rights, boundaries of political representation, hate crime legislation, affirmative action policies, disability rights, age discrimination, criminal justice, and the war on terror. These issues raise a philosophic question, which is as old as Socrates and the American founding—that is, when should the rights of the individual trump the desires of the majority, and/ or when should the rights of the majority trump the desires of the individual?

Conclusion

Civil rights refers to the struggle by subordinated groups for fair treatment or, "the protection of the individual from arbitrary or discriminatory acts by government or by individuals based on that person's groups status, such as race and gender" (Tannahill 2010, 365). The subordination of these groups is unjust. It is right to punish criminals for harming their fellow human beings, but being born a certain skin hue or gender is no crime. The sick patients who could benefit from medical marijuana do not deserve to be arrested for following the advice of their respective doctor. The children of immigrant parents who were brought to the United States by their parents did not choose to violate federal immigration statutes, so why punish them? There are many civil rights struggles, but they all have in common the ingredients of a powerful group unjustly denying basic rights (such as the right to marry, to food and medicine, and the franchise) to members of a distinct minority group whose identity is tied to something that they cannot control—skin hue, gender, or sickness—by nature. Wherever there is a group of people who want freedom from oppression to enjoy basic human rights to liberty, medicine, and so on, the stage is set for a civil rights struggle. Consider this mantra of civil rights: *we* may not like *them*, but unless *they* pose actual harm to *us*, then there is no justification for denying *them* the liberties *we* hold dear.

See also Affirmative Action; African Americans and Politics; American Indian Politics; Asian Americans and Politics; Catholics and Politics; Civil Liberties; Cultural Pluralism; Disability and Politics; Free Speech; Gay and Lesbian Culture and Politics; Immigration and Politics; Inequality and Politics; Jews and Politics; Latinos and Politics; Mormons and Politics; Muslims, Arab Americans, and Politics.

Kenneth Michael White

Bibliography

Adams, Abigail. 2009. "Letter to John Adams (1776)." In Isaac Kramnick and Theodore J. Lowi, eds. *American Political Thought.* New York: Norton.

Alexander, Michelle. 2012. *The New Jim Crow.* New York: The New Press.

Bardes, Barbara, Mack Shelley, and Steffen Schmidt. 2009. *American Government and Politics Today: The Essentials.* Belmont, CA: Thomson Wadsworth.

Beard, Charles A. 2009. "The Economic Basis of Politics." In Isaac Kramnick and Theodore J. Lowi, eds. *American Political Thought.* New York: Norton.

Bell, Derek. 1992. *Race, Racism and American Law.* Boston: Little Brown.

Brooks, Roy L. 1993. "A Critical Race Theory Critique of the Right to a Jury Trial under Title VII." *Journal of Law & Public Policy* 5: 159–466.

Brooks, Roy L., Gilbert Paul Carrasco, and Michael Selmi. 2000. *Civil Rights Litigation.* Durham, NC: Carolina Academic Press.

Fiorina, Morris. 2006. *Culture War? The Myth of a Polarized America.* New York: Pearson Longman.

Ginsberg, Benjamin, Theodore J. Lowi, and Margaret Weir. 2009. *We the People: An Introduction to American Politics*, 6th ed. New York: W.W. Norton.

Greenblatt, Alan. 2008. "Immigration Debate." *Issues in Race and Ethnicity.* Washington, DC: CQ Press.

Grimké, Sarah M. 2009. "Letters on the Equality of the Sexes and the Condition of Women (1837)." In Isaac Kramnick and Theodore J. Lowi, eds. *American Political Thought.* New York: Norton.

Jaffa, Harry V. 2000. *A New Birth of Freedom: Abraham Lincoln and the Coming of the Civil War.* Lanham, MD: Rowman & Littlefield.

King, Martin Luther, Jr. 2006. "I Have a Dream." In James Daley, ed. *Great Speeches by African Americans*. Mineola, NY: Dover.

Morone, James A. 2003. *Hellfire Nation: The Politics of Sin in American History*. New Haven, CT: Yale University Press.

Paine, Thomas. 1997. *Common Sense*. Mineola, NY: Dover.

Patterson, Thomas E. 2011. *We the People: A Concise Introduction to American Politics*. New York: McGraw-Hill.

Plato. 1992. *The Trial and Death of Socrates: Four Dialogues*. Baltimore: Dover.

Tannahill, Neal. 2010. *Think: American Government*. New York: Longman.

West, Cornel. 1993. *Race Matters*. Boston: Beacon Press.

White, Kenneth Michael. 2004. *The Beginning of Today: The Marihuana Tax Act of 1937*. Baltimore: PublishAmerica.

Cases

Bowers v. Hardwick, 478 U.S. 186 (1986).

Brown v. Board of Education, 1954. 347 U.S. 483; 349 U.S. 294.

Buchanan v. Warley, 245 U.S. 60 (1917).

Dred Scott v. Sandford, 60 U.S. 393 (1856).

Griswold v. Connecticut, 381 U.S. 479 (1965).

Korematsu v. United States, 323 U.S. 214 (1944).

Lawrence v. Texas, 539 U.S. 558 (2003).

Loving v. Virginia, 388 U.S. 1 (1967).

Plessy v. Ferguson, 169 U.S. 537 (1896).

Plyler v. Doe, 457 U.S. 202 (1982).

Regents of the University of California v. Bakke, 438 U.S. 265 (1978).

Roe v. Wade, 410 U.S. 113 (1973).

United States v. Virginia, 518 U.S. 515 (1996).

CIVIL WAR (1861–1865) AND MODERN MEMORY

Organized efforts to craft the "memory," or, more accurately, "memories" of the Civil War began as the last of that war's smoke still cleared from the battlefield. In April 1865, northern officers joined together with the specific intention to remember the causes and sacrifices of loyal Unionists. Soon, other Union veterans'

groups added to the growing efforts to maintain a northern memory of the war. In the South, women took up the mantle of war memory before former Confederate soldiers organized such efforts officially later in the 19th century. Ex-rebels proceeded to author a distinctive memory of the war in response to their northern counterparts. Over the course of the next several decades, both sides battled to dominate national Civil War memory through commemorations on very sectional terms. By the 1930s, the generation that had survived the war had lived on to enshrine two very different versions of Civil War memory in the national vernacular. While veterans lived, consensus in regard to a truly unified national memory never emerged.

There was, however, a national Civil War memory that existed apart from the memories of those who had fought in and survived the Civil War. This highly scripted memory reflected the wishes of those interested, on the one hand, in political and economic expediency and, on the other, in the national image of a unified—and thus reconciled—United States during the latter third of the 19th century and the first part of the 20th century. As American prowess grew in relation to the rest of the world, politicians and others deemed paramount a reconciled and unified national image free from contention. Civil War veterans could be and often were caught up in this very particular strand of memory. The Fiftieth Anniversary Reunion at Gettysburg in 1913, commemorating the battle, epitomizes the benign national memory of the war. At this blue-gray "love fest," former enemies came together in the spirit of peace and reconciliation. The focus on the reunion's activities, including a speech by President Woodrow Wilson and an epic recreation of the Pickett-Pettigrew assault, focused on the shared American virtues of bravery, fortitude, and commitment to cause. Memories of wartime issues such as slavery, tyranny, states' rights, and treason were conspicuously absent.

Though images of former enemies shaking hands across a stone wall as a gesture of forgiveness and reconciliation did not accurately reflect the sentiments of most Civil War veterans, they did capture the nation's imagination, especially the postwar generations who had not lived through the conflagration of the 1860s. These images of a reconciled Civil War memory held sway for decades as the nation put distance between the issues of the 20th century and the conflicts of the 19th century.

During the mid-20th century conflicting memories shifted from a geographic to a racial axis. Many white southerners, particularly in response to the civil rights movement of the 1950s and 1960s, organized along the line of massive resistance and harnessed not only the Confederate images of their ancestors but also memories of states standing up against the tyranny of the federal government during the secession winter of 1860–1861. Massive resistance protests often used the language of the past to support distinctly racist motives of segregation and the limitation of basic citizenship rights for black people in the present. These protests reflected the many ways in which people select specific memories for political purposes. Civil rights leaders responded by conjuring Civil War memories of their own, seeking to illustrate the shortcomings of emancipation and to demand the rights promised in the postwar constitutional amendments. The centennial Civil War celebrations (1960–1965) were very much at odds with various antagonistic memories circulating during the mid-20th century and much more representative of a pleasantly scripted national memory of the war devoid of controversy. Commemorations during this period were thus descendent from the 1913 and 1938 anniversaries at Gettysburg and featured benign monument rededications, reenactments, and public displays of reconciliation free from contentious issues.

Thus, the mid-twentieth century witnessed significant changes in Civil War memory. As time grew distant from the war and the children, grandchildren, and great-grandchildren of the Civil War generation came of age, a reconciled and mostly benign version of Civil War memory dominated the national commemorative landscape. Especially in the wake of World War II through the centennial years and well beyond, a national recollection of fortitude, bravery, and commitment to cause offered white Americans a memory of the Civil War relatively free from controversial issues such as the fight over slavery and the cause of emancipation.

During the latter third of the 20th century, scholars began to assess and analyze the decades of reflection after the Civil War and developed Memory Studies as a cottage industry within the field of American History and American Studies. By the beginning of the 21st century, a consensus formed whereby scholars concluded that national reconciliation was a reflection of white America's mutual acceptance of racism that stemmed directly from the activities of the Civil War generation. Together, this "reconciliation premise" suggests white supremacists and reconciliationists "locked arms" and created a Civil War memory on southern terms. In recent years, scholars have begun to challenge this premise by noting the truly exceptional nature of commemorative events that, while conspicuous, were free from controversy. More recent conclusions have noted that the overwhelming majority of the commemorative events and other vehicles for memory (books, articles, speeches, etc.) authored by the generation that fought and survived the war emphasized controversial issues. Only after the last of that generation passed did the benign national Civil War memory take hold. Even then, this memory was not intentionally racist, just devoid of controversy.

The Shepherds of Modern Civil War Memory

There are many facets of modern Civil War memory. While in some ways disparate, they can all be placed under the general memory umbrella. The categories of those involved with the perpetuation of modern memory range from active participation to mere observation. All reflect how people affect, and are thus affected by, modern Civil War memory. Of those that consider themselves the keepers of Civil War memory, heritage organizations, reenactors, and round table groups constitute the majority. How people use Civil War memory is varied and can range from the social to the political. It is often, though not always, a reflection of the Civil War generation's memories.

Heritage organizations including Sons and Daughters groups are a primary contributing force to modern Civil War memory. This is both the likely and logical succession in regard to who might watch over and act as the shepherds of veterans' memories. In the decades following the war, surviving veterans commented that it left to posterity to ensure that the old soldiers' memories did not fade with time. Heritage groups have taken up this mantle with great fervor. Membership in such groups generally requires a verifiable ancestral connection to a Civil War soldier, but one can also join as an auxiliary member through a process of approval by group leadership. While preservation of memory is these groups' main concern, they vary with intensity when it comes to controversial issues.

Confederate heritage groups, in particular the Sons of Confederate Veterans, seem to shoulder the most burden. In the recent decades and especially the 21st century, Civil War memories broadly defined have fallen more closely in line with the sweeping understanding—prevalent in school textbooks throughout the nation—that slavery was central to secession and war. Confederate heritage groups consider this assertion at best misleading and at worst an outrageous lie perpetrated by "revisionist" Yankee historians. Such memories, Confederate heritage groups assert, are not those of their ancestors who fought to preserve state rights and the virtues of the founding generation. Many, though certainly not all, have modified their stance on race since the tumultuous racially charged days of the late 19th and early 20th centuries. They have insisted that while the war was not fought over slavery (rather it was the "occasion" of the war), emancipation was ultimately a positive event—one that white southern slaveholders would have eventually undertaken themselves. Thus, modern commemorations of the Confederate war effort celebrate the virtues of the southern fighting spirit and reflect "heritage not hate."

The commemorative activities of Union heritage groups are generally less controversial, though they can also invoke the memories of their veteran ancestors with regard to controversial issues from the war years. The reasons for this are simple: national Civil War memory—especially the Union memory of the cause of slavery and the fight for emancipation—is generally accepted throughout the country, even (to a lesser degree) in the states of the former Confederacy. Thus, in some ways, the memory of Union veterans has triumphed in the 21st century. One aspect of Union Civil War memory has, however, faded from the most prominent position among the general public. Supplanted by the memories of slavery and emancipation, the fight to preserve the Union is less frequently emphasized in public discourse. Union heritage groups, such as the Sons of Union Veterans, have worked to preserve the memory of the preservation of Union—but with only minimal success. This cause, fundamental in 1861–1865, may be less acknowledged now because so many Americans currently residing in the states loyal to the Union in the 1860s—their ancestors immigrating to the United States in the late 19th and early 20th centuries—have little or no connection to the war.

Civil War roundtables also function in ways that connect modern Civil War memory to those of the Civil War generation. Round tables—groups of people ranging from large to small and sharing an interest in Civil War history—meet regularly across the nation and the world to discuss issues relevant to the war as well as the antebellum and Reconstruction years. A typical meeting will consist of one speaker or more offering a talk on a particular subject followed by discussion with the audience. The subjects are often on a military nature but can cover other topics as well. Here again, depending of the demographic makeup of the participants, various wartime memories can and often do emerge. Many of those who participate in roundtable groups work to ensure that particular memories survive as fact while others are deemed myth.

A vibrant subculture exists among Civil War enthusiasts known as living historians. One should also consider living historians—or on more recognizable terms, reenactors—as shepherds of Civil War memory. Living historians span gender and socioeconomic demographic, though generally speaking, reenactors are men and have disposable income—reenacting soldier life is predominantly a male pursuit and can be a costly endeavor. They strive to recreate, as best as possible, the feeling, both visually and emotionally, of Civil War camp life and battle. There are also those who reenact life on the home front as well as particular civilian activities such as significant political events. Some of those outside of this culture dismiss living historians as "fans" of war participating in a perverse hobby where death and suffering is reduced to a weekend game. However, the reenactors themselves consider this highly performative activity an important aspect of the preservation of Civil War memory. Living historians educate visitors (their audience) about soldiers' camps and battle, often taking up the persona of specific individuals or common soldiers. As such, they perpetuate the memories of those they portray. In addition, a significant feature of living historians' work is battlefield preservation. Their work in this arena is absolutely crucial to the preservation of the commemorative landscape and, thus, Civil War memory.

The Politics of Modern Civil War Memory

Despite claims that their commemorative activities are geared specifically to emphasize heritage while shying away from politics and wartime issues, Confederate heritage groups—their words and actions—are often steeped in controversy. For example, dedication ceremonies for the Abraham Lincoln monument at the former Tredegar Iron Works in Richmond, Virginia, in April 2003 reveal the animus harbored by so many supporters of Confederate heritage groups and illustrate how the issues of the war resonate today. Confederate heritage groups suggested that placing a monument to Lincoln in the former Confederate capital was tantamount to blasphemy. Politicians in support of the heritage protests such as conservative Virginia legislator Virgil Goode challenged the legality of the statue and worked diligently to block the dedication—but to no avail. The statue stands today as a reminder of Lincoln's efforts to reconcile the country. But that notwithstanding, the episode at Tredegar reveals the deep divisiveness over who should control Civil War memory in the public arena.

One of the primary contentions in the realm of modern Civil War memory concerns the display of the Confederate Battle Flag (the Saint Andrew's Cross) at schools and at public buildings. Confederate heritage groups consider the display of the banner protected under the First Amendment right to free speech. Those who wear battle flag tee shirts or belt buckles, heritage groups insist, are merely exercising that right and should be left alone. Demands to fly the flag over public buildings reflect precisely the same argument taken to its logical next step. This battle most clearly shows the intersection of politics and modern Civil War memory. One on hand, flag advocates claim that the display is a First Amendment right guaranteed by the Constitution. But the argument really distills down

to what the flag means and to whom. Flag supporters state that the symbol is entirely innocuous and represents only the struggles and virtues of the common fighting man—it is an American symbol of dedication and bravery and a part of U.S. history that all can respect and appreciate. Others claim that it is a vile symbol of racism—used by a section of the country that sought independence to protect the institution of slavery that was subsequently adopted by racist hate groups across the country and around the world. Regardless of the intention of the flag's display, flag detractors insist that it conjures up the most negative memories of the nation's past. The battle rages over flag interpretation, and the issue does not seem ready to die anytime soon. Confederate imagery in such places as public schools and public buildings and on government-issued license plates continues to stir the ire of those interested in such things today. Heated exchanges in the press, on the Internet, and at staged public protests clearly indicate that the battle over Civil War memory is as hot as ever.

Commemoration and interpretation at National parks and other public venues also serve to connect politics to modern Civil War memory. Recent efforts by the National Park Service to provide contextual information on battlefield placards and at battlefield visitor centers have caused rifts among many visitors along both a sectional and racial axis. Particularly concerning the issue of slavery and the fight for emancipation, but also the conflicting issues of treason and state rights, many Civil War enthusiasts see such battlefield interpretative markers and displays as a government intrusion and the promotion of one side of the story at the expense of the other. Other problems with memory and public monuments have stirred the flames of contentions as well. Especially in the South, movements are under way to change the name of roads and schools named for famous Confederates and, in some cases, to remove monuments to such individuals as Nathan Bedford Forrest—a Confederate hero but a notorious antebellum slave trader and postwar leader of the Ku Klux Klan. Shifting memories and demographic changes in certain areas indicate that many are favoring a change in the commemorative landscape.

Sesquicentennial activities beginning in 2010 served to illuminate conflicting Civil War memories

A group called Virginia Flaggers raises the Confederate battle flag on a pole near Interstate 95 in Chester, Virginia, September 28, 2013. Hundreds gathered to celebrate the raising of the Confederate battle flag, an event that stirred strong feelings among those who view it as a symbol of division. (AP Photo/Steve Helber)

in various ways. Celebrations and commemorations, many funded at both the state and national levels, caused some to question why one would honor such a war at all. Representatives of the National Association for the Advancement of Colored People, for example, rejected the celebration of an event that left black Americans as second-class citizens with little or no rights. Privately arranged events further pushed conflicting memories into battle. For example, South Carolina's Secession Ball in Charleston and the reenactment of the swearing in of Jefferson Davis in Montgomery, Alabama, aroused protests from many sectors of the country and reminded Americans that sectional memories were alive and well in the 21st century.

From the extremist fringe to the moderate romantic, those who partake in modern Civil War memory continue to be a vociferous lot. The blogosphere and social media platforms are hot with action and marked with conflict. Participants both on the web and in public create new memories that challenge and direct the politics of the 21st century. In addition, they preserve historic memories through myth and ceremony. Thus, in many ways, modern Civil War memories are direct descendants of their war generation predecessors.

M. Keith Harris

Bibliography

Blight, David W. 2001. *Race and Reunion: The Civil War in American Memory.* Cambridge, MA: Harvard University Press.

Bodnar, John. 1992. *Remaking America: Public Memory, Commemoration, and Patriotism in the Twentieth Century.* Princeton, NJ: Princeton University Press.

Coski, John M. 2005. *The Confederate Battle Flag: America's Most Embattled Emblem*. Cambridge, MA: Harvard University Press.

Fahs, Alice, and Joan Waugh. 2004. *The Memory of the Civil War in American Culture*. Chapel Hill: University of North Carolina Press.

Foster, Gaines M. 1985. *Ghosts of the Confederacy: Defeat, the Lost Cause, and the Emergence of the New South*. New York: Oxford University Press.

Gallagher, Gary W. 2008. *Causes Won, Lost, & Forgotten: How Hollywood and Popular Art Shape What We Know about the Civil War*. Chapel Hill: University of North Carolina Press.

Gannon, Barbara A. 2011. *The Won Cause: Black and White Comradeship in the Grand Army of the Republic*. Chapel Hill: University of North Carolina Press.

Grant, Susan-Mary, and Peter J. Parish, eds. 2003. *Legacy of Disunion: The Enduring Significance of the Civil War*. Baton Rouge: Louisiana State University Press.

Harris, M. Keith. 2014. *Across the Bloody Chasm: The Culture of Commemoration among Civil War Veterans*. Baton Rouge: Louisiana State University Press.

Janney, Caroline E. 2008. *Burying the Dead but Not the Past: Ladies' Memorial Associations and the Lost Cause*. Chapel Hill: University of North Carolina Press.

Janney, Caroline E. 2013. *Remembering the Civil War: Reunion and the Limits of Reconciliation*. Chapel Hill: University of North Carolina Press.

CLASS AND POLITICS

In the mid-20th century, the dominant paradigm about politics in advanced industrial societies was that it was, in the famous statement of political sociologist Seymour Martin Lipset, "the democratic translation of the class struggle." The less affluent and those with lower social status voted for parties of the left, while more affluent higher-status people voted for parties of the right. This, according to Lipset, was a "response to group needs." Low-status people were likely to face economic stress (thus needing the "social safety net" of the welfare state) and to benefit from redistribution of income. More affluent people had very different interests.

Of course, as Lipset readily acknowledged, other cleavages—based on religion, regionalism, race, and ethnicity—could complicate and even overshadow this dynamic, but the general tendency would usually reassert itself, like a gyroscope righting itself.

Further, as other essays in the volume explain, various features of the American political culture have led to a politics that is less class oriented than the politics of other industrial democracies.

Political scientist V.O. Key demonstrated how Franklin Roosevelt's New Deal led to a sorting out of lower-status blue-collar workers and higher-status white-collar workers, with the critical election of 1936 beginning an era when the politics of class rose to a new importance, and the party system realigned in a way consistent with Lipset's description. Like 1936, 1948 was an election in which a sharp class cleavage in voting was apparent.

As history moved into the 1950s and 1960s, many commentators claimed to see a decline in the importance of social class. The administration of Dwight Eisenhower saw the assimilation of the New Deal expansion of the welfare state into the body politic, but no large expansion of social welfare programs. Economic growth in the 1950s and 1960s seemed to soften the potential for class conflict that had existed in the 1930s, or even in the contentious and highly class-polarized election of 1948. Lyndon Johnson's Great Society programs were targeted, not toward the blue-collar working class that had been the core of the New Deal coalition, but toward the poor and (in the case of Medicare) the elderly.

But perhaps more importantly, what historian James Sundquist called "crosscutting issues"—issues that cleaved the citizenry in a way that cut across traditional lines of cleavage—rose to prominence.

But has class polarization in fact decreased, or is it the case that in spite of appearances, social class continues to have a robust effect? Figure 1 shows the correlation of party identification (Democrat, Independent, or Republican) with two key social class variables: income and blue versus white-collar status.

SOCIAL CLASS POLARIZATION OF PARTY IDENTIFICATION BY INCOME AND OCCUPATION

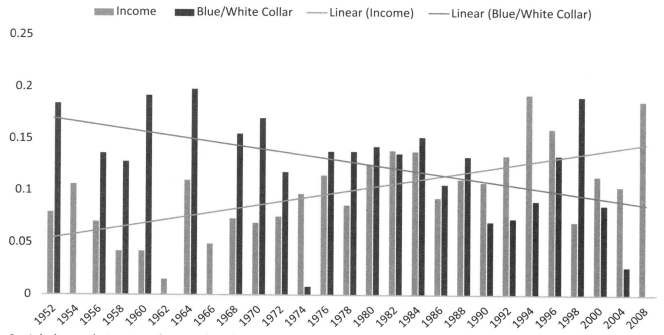

Social class polarization of party identification by income and occupation. Albeit a complicated picture, the data show the effect of social class declining and the effect of income increasing.

The first thing one notices is that contextual factors related to particular political eras or seasons, and indeed to individual elections, influence the level of class polarization. However, trying to interpret all the ups and downs in the data approaches the reading of tea leaves in terms of making reliable interpretations. But two clear trends exist in the data. The effect of social class, defined as white-collar versus blue-collar employment, has been trending downward, and the effect of income has been trending upward.

The full explanation for this pattern is beyond the scope of this essay (even if there were a single clear explanation supported by the data), but an explanation for the decreasing effect of the collar line will be offered later. As for the increasing polarization of income, perhaps the size and scope of the U.S. government (which currently spends over $2 trillion on social welfare programs) has rendered citizens more aware of their role as either the recipients of government redistribution or alternatively those who pay the costs of redistributive programs.

Crosscutting Issues

Since the 1960s, various "crosscutting issues" have continued to affect American politics. Abortion has continued to divide Americans, and in spite of the *Roe v. Wade* decision, continuing conflict over whether taxpayers should pay for some abortions, partial birth abortion, and various restrictions on abortion short of a ban have continued to roil politics. Gay marriage, which came to the forefront when the Massachusetts Supreme Court legalized it in that state in a 2003 decision, has cleaved the public in a similar way, pitting more religious against more secular people. Affirmative action racial preferences have continued to be quite controversial, and conflict over gun control ebbs and flows. All of this is subsumed under the rubric "the culture wars."

On many of these issues, less affluent people hold more conservative positions and thus might desert the Democratic Party if the issues receive sufficient salience. Thus, pundits have talked about "Reagan Democrats" in the 1980s and "values voters" in the 2004 election. But the most famous statement of this theme came from author Thomas Frank in a 2004 book *What's the Matter with Kansas?* Frank's thesis was that social issues had caused working-class and poorer citizens of Kansas to desert the Democratic Party and vote Republican, which Frank believed was against their interests.

The book was highly controversial, and drew rejoinders such as an essay titled "What's the Matter with *What's the Matter with Kansas?*" by political scientist Larry Bartels (2005). Bartels conceded that the salience of social issues had increased in the previous 20 years, but found that this increase was mostly among highly educated voters, rather than less educated and affluent voters. Finally, Bartels found that while less-educated voters had moved in a Republican direction, the movement was almost entirely in the South, which had had inflated levels of Democratic identification as a one-party region since Reconstruction.

Debate on these issues continues, and the most reasonable conclusion is that sometimes, where some issues are concerned, working-class and poorer voters do defect from the Democratic coalition because of their conservative views on social issues. As is the case with the six blind men and the elephant, what one finds on this issue depends upon exactly where one looks.

The New Class

Since the 1960s, the existence of highly liberal and Democratic groups with elite status has become increasingly obvious. Highly educated people, with comfortable incomes, have been the core of the anti-Vietnam War movement, the environmental movement, the feminist movement, the gay rights movement, down to the more recent "Occupy" movement.

This phenomenon has led some analysts to posit that there has arisen a New Class of affluent liberals. To be a class in a Marxist (or indeed any serious theoretical sense) such people would need to have class interests that incline them toward a "liberal" (in the U.S. sense) or leftist political agenda. More specifically, they would need to possess the sorts of human capital that would give them a *comparative* advantage in politics, as opposed to economic markets. This would put them at odds with the traditional business-oriented elite, which enjoys high income, social prestige, and so on because of its ability to function in economic markets.

What sorts of groups might this be? One group would be those with professional occupations. While they have traditionally occupied the same neighborhoods, churches, country clubs as the business elite, some analysts have noted a clear difference in the orientation inherent in professionalism. As Everett C. Hughes put it "Professionals profess. They profess to know better than others the nature of certain matters, and to know better than their clients what ails them or their affairs." Thus, professionals are likely to be frustrated with economic markets, in which people can buy whatever they want, regardless of what professionals think they ought to be consuming.

The market-oriented business class, in contrast, is generally happy to provide whatever goods and services the consumer wants.

Further, when the market handles the allocation of goods and services, it automatically answers certain questions: what is to be produced, and in what quantity, and with what inputs. When government allocates resources, on the other hand, it requires professional expertise to decide on allocation decisions. The expansion of government typically involves the increased regulation of specialized and technical matters, which in turn requires the increasing technical expertise of professionals.

Of course, one would expect that an ideology would be created to legitimate professionalism and perhaps also delegitimize the market orientation of the business class. As Alvin C. Gouldner (1979) has observed:

Professionalism is one of the public ideologies of the New Class. . . . and is the genteel subversion of the old class by the new. . . . While not overtly a critique of the old class, professionalism is a tacit claim by the New Class to technical and moral superiority over the old class, implying that the latter lack technical credentials and are guided by motives of commercial venality. Professionalism silently installs the New Class as the paradigm of virtuous and legitimate authority, performing with technical skill and with dedicated concern for the society-at-large.

The business manager, as an ideal type, is happy to accept as given the preferences of customers and prospers by catering to those preferences. The professional, as we have discussed, is likely to believe those preferences are the problem.

If professional training gives certain groups in society class interests in the expansion of government, so does education—which of course overlaps with professionalism. As John Kenneth Galbraith has claimed: "The New Class is not exclusive. While virtually no one leaves it, thousands join it every year. Overwhelmingly, the qualification is education." The highly educated tend to be symbol specialists; they are trained to produce technical analyses, but also more widely accessible products such as compelling rhetoric and appealing images. The latter are likely to be highly important in politics. Of course, the market rewards these skills too, but not always or consistently, and we are indeed talking about *comparative* advantage here.

Testing the Theory

In any class theory, there must be some critical juncture at which people with certain resources that give them certain interests (whether it be the control of physical capital—as with the bourgeoisie—or the distinctive human capital of the New Class) come together and begin to form a distinctive class consciousness. For the industrial proletariat, Marx believed it was when workers were brought together in large factories as part of the industrial revolution. For the New Class, the dividing line might be expected to be the 1960s, when the coming of age of the baby boom generation produced a large increase in the college cohort, and a concomitant increase in higher education. Other critical events—the Vietnam War, the civil rights movement, the rise of feminism, and so on—would be both a product of this and a spur to a distinctive class outlook.

Figure 2 shows the development of the New Class as a force different than, and indeed in opposition to, the traditional business class. In a model that controls for region (South), gender, and income (and excludes blacks), we compare the party identification of those with a professional occupation with that of persons with those who are managers, proprietors, and officials. We also compare (in a model with the same controls) those who have some graduate education with

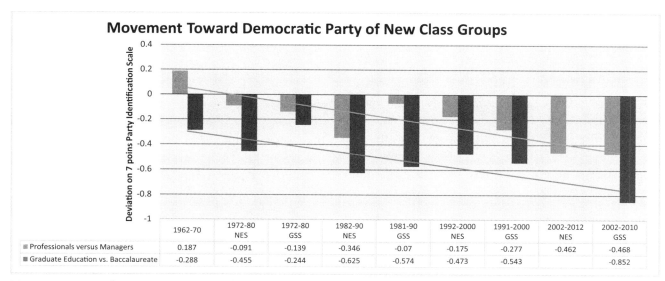

Movement toward Democratic Party of new class groups. The data show that professionals and those with graduate education are moving in the direction of the Democratic Party.

those who have only a baccalaureate degree. The trend lines are clear. Both professionals and those with graduate education are moving in a Democratic direction.

This divergence of professional and managerial workers explains, to a substantial degree, the declining importance of the "collar line" separating white- and blue-collar workers. Increasingly, the ranks of white-collar workers contain substantial numbers of left-leaning (and Democratic leaning) professionals, and those with graduate education.

A Three-Front Class Conflict

All of this suggests a three-front class conflict. On social issues (those underlying the "culture wars"), the main axis of conflict is between the liberal New Class and the conservative working class. On economic issues, the conflict is between both the New Class and the working class as opposed to the traditionally conservative business class. Thus, much depends on the salience of social issues. Where social issues are important, the business class can often ally with the working class and often win elections. Where economic issues are concerned, the New Class can often ally with the working class (and minorities that identify with their racial or ethnic group more than with a particular social class) and often win elections.

Of course, factors such as the quality of the candidates, the flow of events, and the state of the economy make elections far from a "lock" in any circumstances and make politics one of the top spectator sports in this republic.

See also Corporate Behavior and Politics; Economic Policy and Politics; Labor and Politics; Race, Ethnicity, and Politics; Regions and Regionalism: The Midwest; Regions and Regionalism: The Northeast; Regions and Regionalism: The South; Regions and Regionalism: The West; Religion and Politics.

John McAdams

Bibliography

Bartels, Larry. 2005. "What's the Matter with What's the Matter with Kansas?" *Quarterly Journal of Political Science* 1: 201–26.

Bruce-Briggs, B. 1979. *The New Class?* New Brunswick, NJ: Transaction Books.

Frank, Thomas. 2004. *What's the Matter with Kansas?* New York: Henry Holt and Company.

Galbraith, John Kenneth. 1984. *The Affluent Society.* 4th ed. Boston: Houghton Mifflin.

Gouldner, Alvin W. 1979. *The Future of Intellectuals and the Rise of the New Class.* New York: Seabury.

Key, V. O. 1966. *The Responsible Electorate.* Cambridge, MA: Harvard University Press.

Lipset, Seymour Martin. 1981. *Political Man.* Expanded and updated edition. Baltimore: Johns Hopkins University Press.

McAdams, John. 1987. "Testing the Theory of the New Class." *The Sociological Quarterly* 28, no. 1: 23–49.

Sundquist, James. 1973. *Dynamics of the Party System.* Washington, DC: The Brookings Institution.

CLIMATE CHANGE AND POLITICS

As the U.S. environmental movement passes 40 years and enters middle age, the issue of climate change has matured into one of the nation's most polarizing, contested disputes. Debate mounts today over whether climate change is real; if so, whether it is accelerating; and whether it is caused by humans or not. Experts say droughts and wildfires, floods, seasonal anomalies, melting ice, disappearing species, and more intense storms demonstrate the reality that climate change is under way. However, the American public has been increasingly divided on this issue.

Some naysayers claim that fearmongers and scam artists hawking worthless tonics are looking to profit from an emergent green industry. Far-right conservatives suggest that democracy itself is at stake, as they accuse liberal left extremists of using climate change as the ultimate socialist tool to rein in capitalist growth. Those on the far left worry that organized climate change reform could lead to global governance and the emergence of a "New World Order" that will threaten national sovereignty. Yet, for the rest—nearly 60 percent of all Americans—the symptoms of climate change are real enough for them to believe that global warming is occurring and to accept that there is a need to offset or counter the negative impacts of human activity (Saad 2013a).

Such divisiveness raises three key questions: What accounts for these vastly different perceptions across America's cultural, ideological, and political landscape? How strong or debilitating are these cleavages? Finally, amid this contentiousness, what actual progress, if any, has there been to American understanding, preparation, and response to climate change? Exploring these three primary areas of concern reveals a dynamic, complex terrain that shapes a varied landscape of American public perception and response around climate change today.

America's Attitudinal Shifts on Climate Change: Tracing the Boundaries

Paradoxically, from 2000 to 2010, the United States experienced one of its most acute decades in terms of climate variations and extremes, but overall concern over climate change in 2010 recorded a 20-year low. Some analysts suggest that in the United States, climate concern has been eclipsed by the public's worries over the economy and over finite energy supplies and rising energy costs. Waning focus on climate change may also be due to public irritability (if not exhaustion) from attempts to read between the lines of climate science discourse or terrifying climate "catastrophism," as well as from competing political interests in the climate change debate. While the latter has become increasingly bitter, the dissemination of scientific information has not managed to alleviate the situation.

Blinded by Science—and Politics

Consensus has grown over the past decade among leading scientific experts worldwide on the realities and consequences of climate change (National Research Council 2010; Revkin 2013). According to a recent survey of scientific papers on climate science, approximately 97 percent of the expert literature states that climate change is real and is primarily due to anthropogenic (human) causes (Schuetze 2013). Yet this degree of confidence has been waning in recent years for the American public.

Since 2002, when the Intergovernmental Panel on Climate Change (IPCC) issued a report on the potential impacts facing the planet, an often-mistaken assumption and practice by scientists has been

that providing more and more information about climate change would lead to better public knowledge on the topic, which in turn would categorically produce greater concern by the masses. Simultaneously, a very vocal, but powerful and industry-funded minority of climate change contrarians has also persistently contested mainstream scientists. These conservative skeptics, often supported by wealthy and powerful fossil-fuel interests, receive considerable media coverage and have repeatedly challenged the credibility of independent and objective climate science (Boycoff and Boycoff 2004; Jacques et al. 2008; Malka et al. 2009; McCright and Dunlap 2003).

For the American public, the technical complexity of climate science does not lend itself to robust understanding and decision making on this controversial issue (Marquart-Pyatt et al. 2011; Schneider 2009). The challenges of weighing the costs and benefits from various greenhouse gas emissions that are accumulated over the short term and long term in the atmosphere, recognizing and understanding the signs of climate change versus ambient weather variability, evaluating and assessing scientific models of probability and uncertainty, and considering the varied environmental, social, and economic implications of climate may not be common skill sets for the U.S. vernacular. However, climate scientists have often implicitly assumed that the public makes rational choices and calculated decisions equipped with this complex knowledge and understanding (Moser 2011; Pidgeon and Fischoff 2011).

Faced with this daunting science and the purported future of the planet and humanity at stake, Americans more than likely rely on the resources they typically turn to for such profound or complicated decisions. These resources are the veritable wellsprings that consistently nurture Americans' beliefs, values, ideologies, and worldviews (Leiserowitz 2005; Marquart-Pyatt et al. 2011; Nisbet 2009). Whether religious, political, or cultural, the overarching doctrines of these resources are capable of aggregating, translating, and framing the issue of climate change on behalf of their followers, according to fundamental sets of standards, norms, and objectives that are familiar to and resound well with their followers.

Recent research also suggests that while there is a positive relationship between education and understanding of climate change for some Americans, for others there is an inverse relationship between these two variables. Specifically, the more U.S. liberals/Democrats know and understand climate change, the more likely they are to believe it is real and to be concerned about it. Conversely, the more that U.S. conservatives/Republicans know and understand climate change, the less likely they are to believe in it and the less likely they are to support climate change reform, although there are signs that this may be changing (Malka et al. 2009, 38; McCright and Dunlap 2003, 28; Saad 2013b). Overall, political ideology appears to be the most significant factor framing American perceptions and actions on climate change.

In fact, a 2011 Gallup poll survey found that while 72 percent of Democrats worried about climate change, only 31 percent of Republicans expressed this same concern. Moreover, while 62 percent of Democrats agreed that climate change was already under

Demonstrators question the scientific evidence surrounding global warming at the Live Earth concert in Washington, D.C., in July 2007. (Joshua Davis)

way, only 32 percent of Republicans believed that to be the case. In terms of what is causing climate change, 71 percent of Democrats in 2011 cited human impact on the environment, but only 36 percent of Republicans attributed climate change to human causes. A significant gap also existed in 2011 between these two political ideologies and perceptions of media exaggeration of climate change. Though only 22 percent of Democrats believed the media was sensationalizing climate change, 67 percent of Republicans agreed that the news exaggerated the effects of climate change (Jones 2011). Two years later the numbers showed only a slight convergence of opinion (Saad 2013a, 2013b).

Overall, these data, which are part of the Gallup's Annual Social Services Environmental Poll, indicate only a modest increase in concern by the American public over climate change in the past few years (and less concern, overall, than in early 2008, a high point). Related trends observed in Gallup poll research demonstrate that in general, Americans worry less about the environment when the nation is led by a Democratic president than they do when a Republican is in charge of the White House (Jones 2011). While these trends are supported by data from 1987 to 2008, a significant deviation from this norm began in 2008 (or slightly earlier). The nation's economic slowdown, which began about the same time, may have at least temporarily trumped U.S. concerns over climate change. Gallup poll findings demonstrate as much. In fact, a Gallup poll conducted in 2009 showed that for the first time in 25 years, a majority of Americans surveyed stated that if it came down to a trade-off, they were willing to sacrifice the environment to some degree in favor of economic growth (Newport 2009).

Trade-Offs between the Economy and the Environment

Gallup poll researchers began a long-term inquiry into the perceptions of Americans over potential trade-offs between the economy and the environment in 1984. At that time, 6 of 10 Americans surveyed believed that the environment should be given priority, even if it threatened economic growth (Newport 2009). As U.S. support of the environment over economic growth grew from 1987 to 1991, the percentage of

Americans willing to trade environmental well-being in favor of economic growth dipped to 19 percent during this same period. By 1990–1991, 71 percent of Americans surveyed supported the environment over the economy. Though support for the environment over the economy dropped to 58 percent in 1992, it rebounded to 70 percent in the late 1990s–2000 alongside an economic upswing.

The first persistent decline in Americans' support for the environment can be traced to 2000–2001, when Republicans held sway in the White House. By 2003, for the first time since the Gallup survey was conducted, fewer than 50 percent of Americans surveyed favored environmental preservation over economic growth. Economic growth at the expense of the environment dipped again in 2005 but has steadily risen since then, from 37 percent in 2007 to 51 percent in 2009 (Newport 2009). Today, Americans appear to be more divided over economic versus environmental trade-offs than they have ever been. For the first time, those willing to sacrifice the environment over the economy represented a solid majority, and under a Democratic president no less. These findings suggest that in addition to partisan shifts in political power in the United States, American perceptions and actions on the environment and climate change may be even more profoundly affected by economic pressure and strain.

As a reverberating impact of the U.S. economic recession, unemployment swiftly rose in the United States from 6.6 percent in 2008 to 10 percent of the population in 2010, falling to 7.5 percent by 2013. When the Pew Research Center for People and the Press conducted a poll in 2012 on issue priorities, only 25 percent of Americans designated global warming as a top concern. This marked a 13 percent decline from Pew's 2007 data on American support for climate change reform. Overall, the Pew Report found that not only had the economy, jobs, and terrorism topped the list of Americans' concerns in 2012, but that as these priorities rose, public priority levels simultaneously declined for the environment, illegal immigration, energy, and domestic crime (Pew Research Center 2012). This is not the first time this anomaly has occurred. In 2000, of a list of 13 environmental problems facing the nation, Americans rated global warming as the second

least important issue. Moreover, Americans also listed the environment as a whole as 16th on a list of the nation's most pressing problems (Leiserowitz 2006, 46).

These findings may support previous research on the limits of the American psyche, particularly in terms of how many diverse challenges and degrees of threat the public can simultaneously absorb and manage (Linville and Fisher 1991; Weber 2006). In other words, as new stressors emerge or ongoing stressors intensify, Americans are most likely to suppress or table their concerns over other issues, particularly if the latter pose longer-term risks or if uncertainty heightens over how to resolve these concerns (Swim et al. 2009). Alongside continued (though lessened) worries over terrorism, war and conflict in the Mideast and elsewhere, the lingering effects of economic recession, and concerns about health care costs and retirement security, the amount of attention that Americans focused on climate change has diminished. Uncertainty over climate change also intensified in the American public mind in 2009, amid a brouhaha known as "Climate-gate."

"Climate-Gate": A Test of American Trust

A controversy that challenged the integrity and honesty of key climate scientists surfaced in 2009 on the Internet, went viral in the "blogosphere," grabbed the attention of national news, and caused international political reverberations. This scandal, which became known as Climate-gate, triggered independent investigations by the United Nations, the United Kingdom's Information Commissioner, and the U.S. Senate (Black 2010; Dunlap and McCright 2010). Climate-gate stemmed from two massive, unauthorized releases on the Internet in 2009 and 2011 of private e-mails primarily between two key scientists in England and the United States who had helped to shape historic and Nobel-renowned global assessments completed by the IPCC. These breached communiqués centered on the defensive strategies that these scientists considered and employed to guard their data, preserve their findings, and prevent publication of competing climate change findings they believed originated from well-funded critics' attacks against them.

It is relevant to point out that as a matter of course in the scientific community, new findings—especially those that affect the body of known knowledge—must be vetted by peer review processes prior to publication and acceptance by the overarching scientific community. However, a number of the private e-mails hacked and published online seemed to indicate that in some instances, the climate scientists involved attempted to block access to their data by those they viewed as adversaries and were reluctant to accommodate the publication of other papers critical of their findings (Carrington 2011, para. 5–6). The IPCC has vehemently denied any role in the suppression of countervailing data or findings.

Regardless, amid the ensuing uproar caused by Climate-gate, the American public, politicians, and even others in the scientific community wondered at the wisdom of allowing such important data to be controlled by an elite group of researchers and began to demand greater transparency. In fact, Climate-gate has been referred to as a "game-changer" that has since compelled climate scientists to be more direct and frank about their own reservations, doubts, and uncertainties (Pearce 2010, para. 5–8). Some Americans have since questioned the climate science community's integrity, motives, capacity, and willingness to manipulate the public through the selective use of already confounding data. Initially, the fallout from this controversy injured public trust among Americans over the climate change question. By 2013, however, confidence in the science behind climate change was on the rise (Saad 2013a; Schuetze 2013).

Speaking Power to Power

The Climate-gate scandal also represented a fortuitous political boost and good timing for libertarian and conservative climate change contrarians, as well as for powerful special-interest groups that stood to benefit from casting suspicion on climate change science and the extent of potential human impact as the chief cause of climate change (Dunlap and McCright 2010; McCright and Dunlap 2010; Oreskes and Conway 2010). As a case in point, though climate change advocates and Democrats experienced early successes in the Obama administration in 2009 with passage in the U.S. House of Representatives of major federal cap-and-trade climate legislation to limit carbon emissions, this historic measure subsequently died in the U.S. Senate, along with hopes for other stronger domestic climate reform policies.

Amid the storm of Climate-gate and alongside the nation's continuing economic recession, conservative Republicans in November 2010 won control of the U.S. House and secured additional seats in the U.S. Senate (Carson and Hellberg 2010). This political paradigm shift served the interests of well-funded climate contrarians and amplified their long-term crusade against climate change reform platforms. These political groups find powerful support from economic interests in the United States that are heavily connected to fossil-fuel industries, including oil, coal, gas, and mining; fossil-fuel-dependent activities, including agriculture, transportation, and electricity production sectors; and the regionally concentrated constituencies that economically rely upon these initiatives.

Collectively, these forces spend considerable dollars to fund climate "debunking" research and to promote negative media press on climate change and climate change reform (Carson and Hellberg 2010, 2). These efforts have especially resonated among Americans who reside in geographic regions where this interdependent, fossil-fuel infrastructure would be most affected by such climate change reforms as carbon emission–limiting cap-and-trade legislation. In fact, the well-funded launch of the Tea Party as a right-wing libertarian movement has gained popular momentum and public support by, among other things, denouncing cap-and-trade legislation and calling climate change a hoax (Carson and Hellberg 2010).

Especially amid the U.S. economic downturn, the power of the dollar has also played a supporting role in the shaping of American perceptions, priorities, and actions related to climate change. Coal, a significant contributor to global warming, has remained a significant source of energy production and consumption in the United States. In 2012, coal mined and transported across the country produced about 36 percent of the U.S. electricity and nearly 20 percent of all U.S. energy. Moreover, while many outdated production plants and electrical transmission grids have contributed significant pollution from carbon emissions, the cost of coal-produced electricity has also remained fairly inexpensive for consumers who have often been among the least able to pay for energy-efficient improvements (Carson and Hellberg 2010; Lacey 2012). The trade-off between the environment and the economy is much more than perceptual in these instances.

American Perceptions of Risk from Climate Change: An Experiential Paradox

The weather in the United States has been particularly "noisy" of late, in terms of making the presence of its anomalies and extremes known in certain regions of the nation. Before Hurricane Sandy devastated the northeast in October 2012, record-setting snows were noted in the midsection and eastern region of the United States (during the winters of 2010 and 2011). Global warming skeptics took advantage of the latter to mock climate change scientists and to claim instead that, if anything, the climate was cooling. Termed "Snowmageddon," these frigid weather events may very well have temporarily eased Americans' concerns over climate change (Broder 2010). Moisture produced by massive snow melt along with spring and summer rains greatly reduced the size and extent of summer drought. For the second year in a row, the United States also remained hurricane free. Even though record heat hit the southern and eastern United States hard in the summer of 2010 and the northern plains and Midwest experienced heavy rains and the sixth busiest summer tornado season in six decades, the general perception of risk from climate change seemed further removed for many Americans (Broder 2010). These perceptions were not unexpected. After all, the public perception of risk is a complex affair that derives not only from information provided by experts but also from cultural worldviews, political orientations, trust, and personal experience (Leiserowitz 2005, 1434). Because of these differences and these different experiences, people are bound to hold different ideas about what constitutes a "dangerous" climate.

Perception of risk from climate change, then, is not particularly strong in the minds of Americans. In 2013, approximately 57 percent of all Americans worried a great deal or a fair amount about climate change. While this outcome does represent a majority of the U.S. population (as statistically sampled), it still marks a decline compared to Gallup poll data for 2008, when two-thirds (66 percent) of the American public voiced this same concern. The percentage of Americans who doubt that climate change will ever happen also continues to remain more or less steady, having risen from 7 percent in 2001 to 19 percent in 2010 and holding at 15 percent in 2012 and 2013 (Saad 2013a). Among those affected by Hurricane Sandy, at least, there has

The Physics of 1°

In his June 20, 2013, *New York Review of Books* article "Collapse and Crash," noted environmentalist Bill McKibben points out how a 1° rise in global temperature, which he says has already occurred, can have a serious multiplier effect and greatly impact government policies. Reminding us that warm air holds more moisture than cold air, McKibben observes that by virtue of the increased average global temperature there is now about 4 percent more water vapor in the atmosphere. This, in turn, heightens the likelihood of drought (less surface water being available) as well as flooding, because the atmospheric moisture eventually must return to the surface in the form of rain. In McKibben's view, this change partly explains some of the extreme weather events the nation has seen in recent years. It also explains the scrambling of policy priorities in Washington, DC. "The federal government," McKibben writes, "spent more money last year [i.e., 2012] repairing the damage from extreme weather than it did on education" (pp. 53–54).

been a change in perception regarding risk, even while few such people are willing to pay for the steps necessary to reduce the risk (Watson 2013).

Conclusion

Despite setbacks at the national level on climate change policy, less than universal trust in the climate change science sector, and widening cleavages in worldviews and political ideologies over climate change, Americans are, to some extent, taking actions on their own to reduce greenhouse gas emissions and to shrink the nation's ecological footprint. Progress can be observed at the regional and state levels, as well as in the individual households of Americans themselves. By mid-2013, 36 of the nation's 50 states had developed or enacted climate change action plans (with two more in progress) and 42 states had instituted emission registries for greenhouse gases and data architecture required for tracking (and perhaps in the future, limiting) these emissions. Twenty states have established lower greenhouse gas emission goals (Center for Climate and Energy Solutions 2013).

Two states, New York and California, have taken this one step further by placing mandatory limits on greenhouse gas emissions and putting mandatory cap-and-trade programs into effect. Regional initiatives are also on the rise. One of the most significant actions has included the creation of three regional initiatives in the United States to voluntarily cap greenhouse gas emissions. More than 30 states are taking part in these efforts, coordinated by the Midwestern Greenhouse Gas Reduction Accord, the Regional Greenhouse Gas Initiative, and the Western Climate Initiative. Each of these three regions has experienced a different range of extreme weather and climate events, including flooding, drought, devastating tornado outbreaks, and record snows (Center for Climate and Energy Solutions 2013; *State of the Climate National Overview* 2011). However, the shared intensity of these unique experiences has produced unprecedented alliances. Though limited in terms of geographic scale and individual emission targets, the collective impact of these three initiatives represents an aggressive and substantial potential target reduction in global greenhouse gas emissions. The tabling of national cap-and-trade legislation

has not prevented these three collectives from forging plans to tie their own separate initiatives together and to also synchronize data collection procedures with the federal Environmental Protection Agency's regulations. On the other hand, a Republican congressional majority (arising from the 2014 midterm elections) remains committed to rolling back federal environmental regulations.

See also Biotechnology and Politics; Energy Policy and Politics; Environmental Policy and Politics; Green Movement and Politics.

Kathleen O'Halleran

Bibliography

Black, Richard. 2010. "Scientists to Review Climate Body." *BBC* (March 10). http://news.bbc.co.uk/2/hi/8561004.stm. Accessed May 27, 2014.

Boykoff, M.T., and J.M. Boykoff. 2004. "Balance as Bias: Global Warming and the U.S. Prestige Press." *Global Environmental Change* 14: 125–36.

Broder, John M. 2010. "Climate Change Debate Is Heating Up in Deep Freeze." *New York Times* (February 10). http://www.nytimes.com/2010/02/11/science/earth/11climate.html?hp. Accessed May 27, 2014.

Carrington, Damien. 2011. "Q and A Climategate." *The Guardian* (November 22). http://www.guardian.co.uk/environment/2010/jul/07/climate-emails-question-answer. Accessed May 27, 2014.

Carson, Marcus, and Joakim Hellberg. 2010. *Washington Descends Deeper into Climate Gridlock: California and the States Creep Forward*. Stockholm: Stockholm Environment Institute. http://www.sei-international.org/mediamanager/documents/Publications/Climate-mitigation-adaptation/Carson%20-%20US%20PB%20101122c%20web.pdf. Accessed May 27, 2014.

Center for Climate and Energy Solutions. 2013. "U.S. Climate Policy Maps." http://www.c2es.org/us-states-regions/policy-maps. Accessed May 27, 2014.

Dunlap, R.E., and A.M. McCright. 2010. "Climate Change Denial: Sources, Actors and Strategies." In C. Lever-Tracy, ed. *The Routledge International Handbook of Climate Change and Society*. New York: Routledge Press, pp. 240–59.

Jacques, P.J., R.E. Dunlop, and M. Freeman. 2008. "The Organization of Denial: Conservative Think Tanks and Environmental Skepticism." *Environmental Politics* 17(3): 349–85.

Jones, Jeffrey. 2011. "In U.S., Concerns about Global Warming Stable at Lower Levels." *Gallup Politics* (March 11). http://www.gallup.com/poll/146606/concerns-global-warming-stable-lower-levels.aspx. Accessed May 27, 2014.

Lacey, Stephen. 2012. "U.S. Coal Generation Drops 19 Percent in One Year." *Climate Progress* (May 14). http://thinkprogress.org/climate/2012/05/14/483432/us-coal-generation-drops-19-percent-in-one-year-leaving-coal-with-36-percent-share-of-electricity/?mobile=nc. Accessed May 27, 2014.

Leiserowitz, Anthony A. 2005. "American Risk Perceptions: Is Climate Change Dangerous." *Risk Analysis* 25, no. 6: 1433–42.

Leiserowitz, Anthony A. 2006. "Climate Change Risk Perception and Policy Preferences: The Role of Affect, Imagery, and Values." *Climatic Change* 77: 45–72.

Linville, P.W., and G.W. Fischer. 1991. "Preferences for Separating and Combining Events: A Social Application of Prospect Theory and the Mental Accounting Model." *Journal of Personal and Social* Psychology 60: 5–23.

Malka, A., et al. 2009. "Featuring Skeptics in News Media Stories about Global Warming Reduces Public Beliefs in the Seriousness of Global Warming." Woods Institute for the Environment, Stanford University, Technical Paper. http://woods.stanford.edu/research/global-warming-skeptics.html. Accessed May 27, 2014.

Marquart-Pyatt, Sandra T., et al. 2011. "Understanding Public Opinion on Climate Change: A Call for Research." *Environment: Science and Policy for Sustainable Development* 53, no. 4: 38–42.

McCright, A.M., and R.E. Dunlap. 2003. "Defeating Kyoto: The Conservative Movement's Impact on US Climate Change Policy." *Social Problems* 50: 348–73.

McCright, A.M., and R.E. Dunlap. 2010. "Anti-Reflexivity: The American Conservative Movement's Success in Undermining Climate Science

and Policy." *Theory, Culture, and Society* 27, no. 2/3: 100–133.

Moser, S.C. 2011. "Communicating Climate Change: History, Challenges, Process, and Future Directions." *Wiley Interdisciplinary Reviews: Climate Change* 1, no. 1: 31–53.

National Research Council. 2010. *Advancing the Science of Climate Change.* Washington, DC: National Academies Press.

Newport, Frank. 2009. "Americans: Economy Takes Precedence over Environment." *Gallup Economy* (March 19). http://www.gallup.com/poll/116962/Americans-Economy-Takes-Precedence-Environment.aspx. Accessed May 27, 2014.

Nisbet, M. 2009. "Communicating Climate Change: Why Frames Matter for Public Engagement." *Environment* 51, no. 2: 12–23.

Oreskes, N., and E.M. Conway. 2010. *Merchants of Doubt.* New York: Bloomsbury Press.

Pearce, Fred. 2010. "How the 'Climate-gate' Scandal Is Bogus and Based on Climate Skeptics' Lies." *The Guardian*, Feb. 10.

Pew Research Center. 2012. *Public Priorities: Deficit Rising, Terrorism Slipping.* January 23. http://www.people-press.org/2012/01/23/public-priorities-deficit-rising-terrorism-slipping/. Accessed May 27, 2014.

Pidgeon, N., and B. Fischoff. 2011. "The Role of Social and Decision Sciences in Communicating Uncertain Climate Risks." *Nature Climate Change* 1: 35–41.

Pooley, E. 2010. *The Climate Wars.* New York: Hyperion.

Revkin, Andrew. 2013. "Science Group Criticizes Politicians for Global Warming Distortions." *New York Times* (May 23). http://dotearth.blogs.nytimes.com/2013/05/23/science-group-criticizes-politicians-for-global-warming-distortions/?ref=globalwarming. Accessed May 27, 2014.

Saad, Lydia. 2013a. "Americans' Concern about Global Warming on the Rise." *Gallup Politics* (April 8). http://www.gallup.com/poll/161645/americans-concerns-global-warming-rise.aspx. Accessed May 27, 2014.

Saad, Lydia. 2013b. "Republican Skepticism toward Global Warming Eases." *Gallup Politics* (April 9).

http://www.gallup.com/poll/161714/Republican-skepticism-global-warming-eases.aspx. Accessed May 27, 2014.

Schneider, S.H. 2009. *Science as a Contact Sport.* Washington, DC: National Geographic Society.

Schuetze, Christopher S. 2013. "Scientists Agree Overwhelmingly on Global Warming." *New York Times* (May 16). http://rendezvous.blogs.nytimes.com/2013/05/16/scientists-agree-overwhelmingly-on-global-warming-why-doesnt-the-public-know-that/?_r=0. Accessed May 27, 2014.

State of the Climate National Overview: Annual 2011. 2011. National Oceanic and Atmospheric Administration: National Climate Data Center. http://www.ncdc.noaa.gov/sotc/national/. Accessed May 27, 2014.

Swim, Janet, et al. 2009. "Psychology and Global Climate Change: Addressing a Multi-faceted Phenomenon and Set of Challenges." American Psychological Association's Task Force on the Interface Between Psychology and Global Climate Change. http://www.apa.org/science/climate-change. Accessed May 27, 2014.

Watson, Sarah. 2013. "New Jerseyans Say Hurricane Sandy Changed Their Views on Climate Change." *Press of Atlantic City* (May 22). http://www.pressofatlanticcity.com/news/breaking/new-jerseyans-sayd-hurricane-sandy-changed-their-views-on-climate/article_b01a6002-c2ef-11e2-9d52-001a4bcf887a.html?mode=jqm. Accessed May 27, 2014.

Weber, E.U. 2006. "Experience-Based and Description-Based Perceptions of Long-Term Risk: Why Global Warming Does Not Scare Us (Yet)." *Climate Change* 77, no. 1/2: 103–20.

COASTAL ZONES, ECONOMICS, AND POLITICS

Existing at the interface of land and sea, the coastal zone includes coastal waters and adjacent shore lands. The geographic scope of the coastal zone has been defined to extend seaward to the continental shelf and landward to 100 kilometers of the shoreline. Coastal zones are home to a diverse array of ecosystems, including beaches, wetlands, marshlands, estuaries, mangroves, and reefs. These ecosystems provide a range of valuable services, including provisioning services such as production of food, medicine, and materials, cultural services such as opportunities for recreation, leisure, and tourism, regulating services such as pollution filtration and shoreline protection, and supporting services such as waste removal and habitat provision.

Marine and Coastal Resources

Marine systems have served as the primary means for regional trade throughout human history; hence, coastal zones also serve as centers of commerce. Because people are attracted to the coastal zone for these benefits and the esthetic appeal of the land and water nexus, coastal zones are densely inhabited, being home to between 23 percent and 39 percent of the world's population. Twenty-one of the world's 33 megacities, nearly all of which are growing, are located within 100 kilometers of the coast. Concentrations of human activity around coasts result in numerous anthropogenic stressors on coastal ecosystems, including direct habitat alteration, overharvest of marine species, pollution runoff, nutrient loading, sedimentation, and the introduction of nonnative species. Because these impacts may affect the ability of coastal ecosystems to continue producing ecosystem services, effective management of coastal resources is therefore of great importance to human well-being. The objective of coastal resource management can be viewed as achieving sustainable stocks and flows of coastal and marine resource goods and services, in combination with a socially acceptable distribution of welfare gains and losses.

Sustainable management of coastal resources presents a unique set of challenges and trade-offs. Coastal zones often include private property on the landward side and open access or common property resources on the seaward side. Potential uses of these common property resources are often conflicting (e.g., commercial vs. recreational fishing, dredging vs. habitat provision). Moreover, markets and behaviors on the landward side directly impact the quality of nonmarket goods and services on the seaward side and vice versa. Human populations and physical capital in the coastal zone are also at risk of coastal hazards such as flooding and storms.

Attempts to mitigate the risks of such hazards via habitat modification may reduce the natural resiliency of coastal ecosystems and increase susceptibility to damage. Further, the natural dynamics of coastlines may cause actions in one coastal area to impact flows of goods and services in adjacent or proximate areas.

Overcoming these challenges requires an understanding of the biological and physical processes that provide coastal ecosystem services, as well as the determinants of human behavior and well-being. As such, economic theory and analysis can contribute to coastal resource management in a variety of ways, including modeling how individuals and markets behave in response to changes in resource quality, designing policy instruments that are consistent with the economic incentives faced by resource users, and understanding the range of economic values associated with coastal resources.

The process of resource valuation can play an important role in all of the earlier-mentioned areas. By monetizing the costs associated with habitat loss, the benefits of conservation and restoration efforts, or the economic dependence on coastal ecosystems, valuation can assist policy makers in making difficult decisions regarding the allocation of scarce resources among competing demands. To date, coastal resources in the United States have been the subject of considerable attention by resource economists compared to other regions of the world. Economic valuation studies have focused largely on measuring benefits from coastal resources that are more apparent and observable, such as those from provisioning and cultural ecosystem services like fisheries production, recreation, and tourism. While the value of shoreline protection services has received some attention by economists, relatively little is known regarding the economic value of the regulating and supportive services provided by coastal ecosystems. For example, the contribution of coastal ecosystems to fisheries production, pollution filtration, climate regulation, and habitat provision, while recognized as economically valuable, is rarely the subject of economic valuation. This is likely due to the difficulty associated with modeling linkages between changes in the quality of these ecosystem services and well-being.

Fisheries Management

The history of fisheries management is a history of successes and failures in addressing what economists call the open access problem (a resource to which all have access). There was a time when even many scientists believed that fishery resources were effectively limitless. Well into the 20th century, fisheries management was aimed primarily at promoting and developing fisheries without recognition of the capacity of humans to affect the availability of fish in the future and with little regard for the problem of open access. By the 1950s, scientific awareness of the finite nature of fishery resources had grown, and the problem of open access was well understood by economists. But the most significant breakthrough in solving the exclusion problem did not come until 1976, when nations agreed to define 200-mile exclusive economic zones (EEZ), which were formally adopted by the UN Convention on the Law of the Sea in 1982. Because the majority of fishery resources exist above continental shelves and in other nearshore environments, the 200-mile EEZ creates the potential for nations to exclude users and manage their fishery resources to sustain the biological resource and generate economic rents. However, to date there is considerable variation in the extent to which nations have addressed excludability within their EEZs. For resources outside of EEZs (ones that are only on the high seas or highly migratory fish that move through the high seas), excludability is limited because it requires an international agreement. For resources that span multiple EEZs (known as straddling stocks), bilateral or multilateral agreements are necessary to address open access.

In the United States, the centerpiece of fisheries law is the Magnuson-Stevens Fishery Conservation and Management Act. At its core is a mandate to end overfishing by setting catch limits in federally managed fisheries. Historically, this mandate has focused on the symptom of the problem, namely biological overfishing, without addressing the cause of the problem. By setting catch limits without addressing the exclusion problem, managers began to control biological overfishing but inadvertently worsened the race to fish. This regulatory approach is known as regulated open access: aggregate catch limits can maintain a biologically healthy stock; fishermen have incentives to build more and bigger vessels to catch fish before their competitors; and managers respond by shortening season lengths, forcing unsafe fishing conditions, gluts of product onto the market, and the need to sell fish frozen rather than fresh. Because the stock of fish is maintained at a healthy level, regulated open access can lead to even more excess fishing capacity and associated economic waste than pure open access. Most notoriously, an economically wasteful derby in the Pacific halibut fishery of Alaska shrunk the season length to less than three days by 1994. In 1995, a solution to address the cause of this problem was introduced: an individually transferable quota program that set the total catch based on biological assessment and divided the catch between resource users into shares that could be traded. Individually transferable quotas were used in only a handful of other U.S. fisheries but appeared to be successful in managing larger numbers of fisheries

in Iceland and New Zealand. With the new policy, the Pacific halibut fishery was transformed overnight from a source of tremendous economic waste to one of the great success stories in fisheries management with a season lasting 245 days and a steady flow of fresh high-value product to the market.

The 2006 reauthorization of the Magnuson-Stevens Act provided a means to use new tools like the halibut program in federal fisheries management. These tools are broadly defined as Limited Access Privilege Programs (LAPPs) and include individual fishing quotas (both tradable like in halibut and nontradable) and territorial use rights in fisheries. In policy circles, individual fishing quotas have now been renamed catch shares. LAPPs address the cause of overfishing and not just the symptoms by solving the exclusion problem, thus aligning the incentives of individual fishermen with the objectives of fisheries management.

Deepwater Horizon Oil Spill

On April 20, 2010, an exploratory oil drilling operation located in the northern Gulf of Mexico (approximately 40 miles off the Louisiana coast) exploded. The drilling platform, known as the *Deepwater Horizon* (DWH), was owned by Transocean but leased by BP (formerly British Petroleum). At the time of the explosion, the production casing was being cemented at 18,360 feet (5,600 m) below sea level. The explosion was caused by a combination of factors including flaws in the design of the drilling equipment, equipment that malfunctioned, and human error.

On April 22, 2010, the DWH sank and crude oil was first observed. An oil leak was not immediately determined because the leak occurred on the sea floor, which complicated the estimation of the flow and the ability to stop it. The primary leak was contained on July 15, 2010. During the 87 days, at least 4.9 million barrels of crude oil (approximately 205 million gallons) had been spilled, making the DWH the largest accidental marine oil spill in history.

The spilled oil caused visible damage to marine and wildlife habitats, killed marine animals, and by extension caused economic damage to the Gulf's fishing and tourism industries. Also, BP used approximately 1.9 million gallons of Corexit, an oil dispersant with an unknown environmental impact, to aid the biodegradation of oil.

Although long-term effects of the DWH oil spill are unknown, past oil spills provide some insights. For example, with the Exxon *Valdez* oil spill, some fish populations did not start to decline until four to six years after the spill. Long-term threats of the DWH spill could include erosion of coastal marshes due to affected vegetation, the potential existence of plumes of suspended oil in relation to marine habitats, and implications for the sea floor since natural assimilation works best on surface oil.

—*Sherry L. Larkin*

Economists have shown that problem of open access applies to a broader definition of marine resources than just a single targeted fish stock. A number of innovations have examined spatial heterogeneity of fish stocks and fishing fleets and the potential for closing fishing grounds to increase yields and profits. Here the issue is whether to exclude access to a spatially delineated portion of the stock rather than to the stock as a whole. To some extent, regulators are repeating their mistakes of regulated open access in attempts to control bycatch, the unintentional catch of nontarget species. By setting industry-wide caps rather than individual vessel quotas, regulations create the potential for a race to bycatch. Similar issues arise in the protection of critical habitat and other marine ecosystem services. Proposed solutions to these problems require aligning incentives of individuals with the objectives of management, including spatially delineated management, individual bycatch quotas, and individual habitat quotas.

Sea Level Rise

Global sea levels have risen by more than 2 millimeters per year on average since the late 19th century. Climate change and higher global temperatures are likely to accelerate the historical rate of sea level rise over the next century through the melting of ice masses and thermal expansion of the oceans. There are significant uncertainties about the magnitude and speed of future sea level rises given the uncertainty of future greenhouse gas emissions and the human response to changing natural conditions. The IPCC estimates that the global average sea level will rise by 18 to 59 centimeters by 2100 if nothing changes.

Sea level rise projections indicate substantial variability at different locations. Some locations could experience sea level rises higher than the global average, while others could have a fall in sea levels, depending upon the effects of local land subsidence or uplift. For areas experiencing a significant rate of subsidence such as the mid-Atlantic and Gulf Coast, relative sea level is increasing at a more rapid rate than in other areas. For areas in which uplift is taking place, such as portions of the Alaskan coastline and in parts of the Pacific Northwest, relative sea level has been decreasing.

Changes in atmospheric winds and ocean currents also affect regional variations in sea level rises, although these variations cannot be predicted reliably.

Coastal areas in the United States include some of the most developed land and represent a significant wealth of natural and economic resources. Fueled by preferences for coastal locations, the population of U.S. coastal counties has exploded over the last several decades, with a growth rate more than double the national average. According to the National Oceanic and Atmospheric Administration, more than 50 percent of the nation's population lived in a coastal zone in 2010, which accounts for less than 20 percent of U.S. land area (excluding Alaska). Population growth in coastal zones has been accompanied by economic development which produced numerous benefits, including employment, recreation and tourism, and nature-based commerce and energy.

As the coastal population continues to grow, the relatively dense populations and valuable economic developments have become more vulnerable to risks associated with climate change and sea level rises. Sea level rise affects coastal areas that already face a wide range of natural and human-induced stresses. Long-term sea level rise can cause inundation of low-lying areas, erosion of beaches and shorelines, and increased flooding and storm damage. This combination of population growth and increased vulnerability has been seen as an explanation for the trend of rising insured disaster losses along the U.S. coast.

Given the potentially severe impact on the natural environment and human systems, it is important to understand the implications of higher sea levels for the United States. For example, what are the estimated rates of sea level rise along the U.S. coast, and which ecosystems or economic sectors are most vulnerable to rising sea levels? Are certain regions more likely to experience higher damage than others? How well can we cope with sea level rises, and is there a threshold beyond which certain regions can no longer effectively adapt? Under what conditions could adaptation and mitigation be realized? These are critical questions for decision makers as they assess the implications of sea level rises.

National assessments suggest that the expected rise in global sea levels could have significant impacts for the United States. In general, the Southeast and mid-Atlantic coasts are most vulnerable because of their low-lying topography, high economic value, and rapid land subsidence. Parts of the Northeast, particularly coastal islands in southern New England, are also vulnerable to inundation because of their low-lying and heavily developed land. The West Coast, with the exception of San Francisco Bay and Puget Sound, is generally at lower risk as a large portion of the area is made up of rocks or cliffs.

An economically efficient response to sea level rises suggests that areas should be protected when the value at risk exceeds the costs of protection. A policy that requires all developed areas to be protected is likely to result in negative net benefits. The adaptation strategies will determine building coastal defenses to protect high-value areas and abandoning property and assets in low-value areas. Nevertheless, sea level rises will result in higher infrastructure costs for some coastal development and the inundation of many unprotected coastal areas. A review of the existing literature indicates that estimates of the cumulative impact of a 50-centimeter sea level rise by 2100 on coastal property range from $20 to $150 billion.

These estimates do not reflect the potentially large effect on coastal wetlands, which provide a wide range of services such as habitat for fish and wildlife, opportunities for recreation education and research, and esthetic values. These functions and services are economically and ecologically valuable. As such, the estimated impact shown earlier provides only a limited measure of total economic costs associated with sea level rises. Improving comprehensiveness and accuracy for various policy options is essential for future impact assessments. A comprehensive benefit–cost analysis should inform decision makers if such policy options are justified from an economic efficiency perspective.

See also Climate Change and Politics; Disasters and Politics; Endangered Species Act, Habitat Loss, and Politics; Oil, Natural Gas, and Politics; Water Policy and Politics.

Peter W. Schuhmann, Martin D. Smith,
and Okmyung Bin

Bibliography

Homans, F.R., and J.E. Wilen. 1997. "A Model of Regulated Open Access Resource Use." *Journal of Environmental Economics and Management* 32, no. 1: 1–21.

Intergovernmental Panel on Climate Change. 2007. *Climate Change 2007: The Physical Science Basis Contribution of Working Group I to the Fourth Assessment Report of the Intergovernmental Panel on Climate Change.*

Ledoux, L., and R.K. Turner. 2002. "Valuing Ocean and Coastal Resources: A Review of Practical Examples and Issues for Further Action." *Ocean and Coastal Management* 45, nos. 9–10: 583–616.

Martínez, M.L., et al. 2007. "The Coasts of Our World: Ecological, Economic and Social Importance." *Ecological Economics* 63, nos. 2–3: 254–72.

National Commission on the BP Deepwater Horizon Oil Spill and Offshore Drilling. January 2011. Deep Water: The Gulf Oil Disaster and the Future of Offshore Drilling. Report to the President, p. 379.

National Oceanic and Atmospheric Administration. 2012. *The Economic Value of Resilient Coastal Communities.* http://www.ppi.noaa.gov /wp-content/uploads/PPI_Ocean_Econ_Stats_re vised_031912.pdf. Accessed May 18, 2014.

Neumann, J.E., et al. 2000. *Sea-Level Rise and Global Climate Change: A Review of Impacts to U.S. Coasts.* Arlington, VA: Pew Center on Global Climate Change.

NOAA Restoration Center. 2012. Natural Resource Damage Assessment Status Update for the *Deepwater Horizon* Oil Spill. Silver Spring: NOAA's Damage Assessment, Remediation, and Restoration Program (DARRP). April, p. 91. http://www.gulf spillrestoration.noaa.gov/. Accessed May 18. 2014.

Ostrom, E. 1990. *Governing the Commons: The Evolution of Institutions for Collective Action.* Cambridge: Cambridge University Press.

Smith, M.D. 2012. "The New Fisheries Economics: Incentives across Many Margins." *Annual Review of Resource Economics* 4: 379–402.

Turner, R.K., et al. 2003. "Valuing Nature: Lessons Learned and Future Research Directions." *Ecological Economics* 46, no. 3: 493–510.

Wilen, J. E., 2006. "Why Fisheries Management Fails: Treating Symptoms Rather Than Causes." *Bulletin of Marine Science* 78, no. 3: 529–46.

Wilson, M. A., and S. Farber. 2008. "Accounting for Ecosystem Goods and Services in Coastal Estuaries." In Linwood Pendleton, ed. *The Economic and Market Value of Coasts and Estuaries: What's at Stake?* Report for Restore America's Estuaries. Washington, DC: NOAA.

COLD WAR POLITICAL CULTURE

The Cold War refers to a period of time, roughly 1946–1991, in which global politics was dominated by a fierce competition between the United States and the Soviet Union. During the Cold War, international relations, and particularly American foreign policy, was marked by animosity, suspicion, and even paranoia between the two major global powers. In the immediate aftermath of World War II, as both powers sought to promote their own security and interest, each side attempted to expand its own influences to meet and satisfy its needs and interests, especially security. Seemingly inevitable, interests overlapped and competition between the two countries became more pronounced and difficult. The United States considered itself as the beacon of democracy and free market (capitalist) economics, while characterizing the Soviet Union, on the other hand, as dictatorially Marxist-Leninist in its politics and a planned socialist economy. While the exact cause of the Cold War (ideology, history, security, misperception, or the nature of international relations) remains a matter for academic debate, the introduction of atomic and nuclear weapons into the competition meant that the potential for a military confrontation between the United States and the Soviet Union had dire implications.

Because there was never actually a war between the two countries, competition was often accomplished through other means. Both countries militarily and economically supported regimes and allies and used rhetoric to bolster their claims for a better and appropriate political and economic model. There was an emphasis on technology (especially in space exploration,

which was a proxy for military proficiency) as a measure of which country was doing better. As such, the competition hinged on the ability of both countries to make claims, and thus there was a competition over discourse (Appy 2000, 3).

The Cold War competition had ramifications for American politics as well as for American popular culture. There was a general understanding that the Soviet Union and the international communist effort represented an existential threat to American values and interests, which in turn precipitated some highly extraordinary incidents that would change politics for future generations. As Dickstein (1993, 534) has pointed out, the Cold War created a sense that a threat from abroad existed (as in a war, hence the term "Cold War"); however, the idea that there was a single set of values with which to comprehend and deal with this threat served to stifle dissent and suppress diversity. Much of what marked American politics during the Cold War was based on adherence to a common political frame of reference and an attempt to build and justify conformity.

Aspects of Cold War Political Culture

Because of the specter of external domination, of changes to the constitutional framework, and of annihilation from nuclear weapons, certain core aspects of American political culture were transformed under the political lens of the Cold War. Christian Thorne (1992), for example, has noted that many long-term trends in American political culture were augmented or changed as a result of the focus on and interaction with the Soviet Union. Americans traditionally have a certain ambivalence toward power; however, during the Cold War, this attribute diminished because of the security threat the Soviets posed. Further, most Americans traditionally believe that progress is essentially good and that progress, in all forms, is a mark of a dynamic and prosperous society (Lynd and Lynd 1937; McDougall 1985). But the Soviet Union and other communist states had their own version of progress, one that came to be seriously questioned by most Americans even as they bolstered their own efforts to move forward.

During the Cold War, there was increased pressure for those in the United States "to belong" to American society. This generally meant an acceptance of common cultural, linguistic, and social norms. Those who were perceived as not belonging were regarded as "the other" and viewed with suspicion or even considered a threat. Politics, along with societal perceptions, was reduced to a simple dichotomy defined by an "us versus them" mentality. Communism and communists represented "the other" and were held to be antithetical to the United States. Often, whatever did not fit or seemed to run counter to expectations was termed "un-American" or "anti-American." The word "communist" itself took on greater meaning and was applied to anything or anyone who appeared to stand outside the realm of American political thought, as conventionally understood.

Writers employing feminist perspectives have also taken note of this tendency. The popular culture of the 1950s was predicated on a strong form of masculinity and on females who were generally submissive (Cuordileone 2000, 2005). Thus, there was a kind of masculinization of American political rhetoric. As Elaine Tyler May (1988) has suggested, the all-important term "containment," which was a military and political strategy aimed at hemming in the Soviet Union, applied domestically as well. The roles of men and women were defined relatively narrowly according to permissible standards of thought and behavior; changes in those roles were viewed as a threat, a foreign undertaking. Cold War authors such as Arthur M. Schlesinger Jr. (1949) posited that Communism perverted and emasculated politics. Consequently, communists were often portrayed as effeminate and indecisive. By contrast, the democratic society, said Schlesinger, was one marked by people who were "doers" and had an appetite for tough decisions and serious responsibility. Although nowadays we tend to be skeptical of such characterizations, they were pervasive at the time.

With American politics being filtered through the lens of the global competition that was the Cold War, the rhetoric of American politicians, too, came to center on a split vision of world politics in which the free democratic world struggled against the slavish world of the communists (Appy 2000, 2–3). And yet, as some critics have reminded us, the emphasis on belonging in the United States resulted in an enforced conformity in which people or actions that veered away from accepted political guidelines were subject to charges of anti-Americanism or of harboring communist sympathies. The sense of ideological certitude in mainstream political circles meant that ideas that were counter to such certitude represented a threat to American values and the American way of life. For instance, when Rachel Carson (1962) published *Silent Spring*, a critique of the widespread use of pesticides and the damage it caused in the environment, the book was viewed by some as contrary to the basic precepts of capitalism, as an excuse for government regulation, and as veiled advocacy of a socialist economy (Meiners, Desrocher and Morriss 2012). Similarly, desegregation and civil rights leaders were often castigated as potential subversives or communist agents (Branch 2006). The tradition of collective bargaining in American labor, which had begun in the late 19th century and continued into World War II, was dramatically altered by the politics of anticommunism. Because communist parties and officials targeted the same segment of society as labor advocates did—namely, the working-class—opponents of organized labor found a ready-made weapon through the labeling of all who sought labor rights as communists. Even after the Cold War, as Schrecker (2004, 8) points out, the demonization of communism, and the linking of it to left-leaning labor groups, meant that labor advocates found it difficult to overcome a lingering stigma.

Many American politicians, notably Presidents Nixon and Reagan, built their careers and their political reputations on their anticommunist activities. Both political parties, Republican and Democratic, during the Cold War engaged in electoral campaigns that sought to highlight their pursuit of American ideals and their opposition to the principles of communism. This trend was reinforced by how campaigns were conducted. A candidate who was perceived as "soft on communism" was not only in danger of losing his or her electoral bid but of harming his or her future career outside of politics. In some cases, if one were perceived as sympathetic toward communism one could, unofficially, be excluded from public office or government contract work (Fariello 1995, 127–74; Steinberg 1984, 35–49).

Policies and Politics

The framing of world politics in terms of a dichotomy and the fear and suspicion of "the other," created a new form of politics that dramatically altered American domestic and foreign policy. Among the strongest criticisms of the United States and its policies during the Cold War (and after) was that the nation had become imperialist. Whereas the dominant foreign-policy tendency before World War II was isolationism, the potential threat of the Soviet Union led the United States to consider foreign intervention more readily. Ideological certitude and believing that the struggle was one of "us versus them" created a made-to-order justification for military interventions around the world, particularly where communist governments or movements were taking hold or where communist "threats" were perceived. The American tendency to conceptualize the world as a dichotomous battle resulted in the United States, according to many observers, treating other countries unjustly. Political leaders, scholars, journalists, and many in the general public felt it necessary that the United States "protect" supposedly naïve, less developed countries that did not necessarily know or appreciate their own best interests. This line of thought echoed an older argument made by European imperialists that some peoples and societies were ill-equipped for self-government (Bradley 2000). In the case of the United States, throughout the Cold War it became embroiled in military conflicts in countries such as Korea, Vietnam, Angola, Afghanistan, Nicaragua, and Grenada in the name of countering a communist threat. The United States also became involved in the domestic politics of many countries. Policies, programs, and organizations were developed to help prevent countries from considering adopting leftist politics and possibly joining the Soviet camp. In many cases, however, conflicts and controversies had more to do with local politics and grievances than an ideological battle between democracy and communism.

Domestically, several incidents took place that pitted concerns about security and espionage during the Cold War against traditional political values such as freedom of conscience and the right to free political expression. Among the high-profile cases early during the Cold War period was the trial of Julius and Ethel

Rosenberg, who were tried and executed for passing atomic secrets to the Soviet Union. The Rosenberg case was particularly controversial because of the paucity of evidence against Ethel Rosenberg and the imposition, in the end, of the death penalty against two American citizens. Julius Rosenberg claimed that the trial was nothing more than a politically staged event to justify American intervention in Korea. There was a great deal of outrage against the death sentence and, despite pleas and protests, both Rosenbergs were executed in June 1953.

Even more infamous were the hearings before the House Un-American Activities Committee (HUAC) during the early phases of the Cold War. In 1947, HUAC began a series of hearings to investigate Communist

Ethel and Julius Rosenberg ride to separate prisons following their espionage convictions on March 29, 1951. The Rosenbergs' trial for conspiracy to commit espionage took place in New York City during the height of the Red Scare. (Library of Congress)

influence and infiltration into the film industry in Hollywood. A number of high-profile people, including actors, writers, technicians, and directors, were called to testify. Although there was a series of individuals who admitted to being members of the Communist Party of the United States (particularly during the Great Depression), and testimonies against other people accused of being communists, several people refused to testify based on their Fifth Amendment right against self-incrimination. As a result, the industry unofficially blacklisted 10 people whose careers were effectively over. The group, collectively known as the "Hollywood Ten," became a symbol of Cold War hysteria for many.

The other, perhaps best-known example of hearings regarding communist infiltration and un-American activities were those held by Sen. Joseph McCarthy. The senator lent his name, McCarthyism, to a new term that indicated a process by which unsubstantiated accusations and questions about a person's loyalty were used to smear the person's reputation, prop up one's own sense of patriotism, and stifle political dissent. With little or no evidence McCarthy claimed that he had a list of employees in the U.S. State Department who were communist, disloyal, or homosexual. In 1953–1954, to the consternation of many observers, McCarthy turned his attention to the army, which he said similarly harbored communists. The hearings, which came to be known as the Army-McCarthy hearings, were broadcast on national television and the result, counter to the senator's own expectations, substantially damaged McCarthy's reputation. It was during these hearings that the famous lament directed at McCarthy by Army counsel Joseph Welch was uttered: "Have you no sense of decency, sir? At long last, have you left no sense of decency?"

As many would point out, however, by no means were the fears of the anticommunists without some justification. There were in fact a number of Soviet spies and sympathizers who infiltrated various scientific organizations (Sibley 2004). The claims by McCarthy, however, about the mass infiltration of the State Department, the army, and other government institutions by communist spies have been discredited.

Events in the 1960s, most notably (1) the American-organized operation against Cuba at the Bay of Pigs in 1961 and (2) the increasing U.S. military involvement in the conflict in Vietnam (1961–1973), began to shake public confidence in the validity of anticommunism as a policy principle. After the Bay of Pigs and the narrowly avoided military confrontation during the Cuban Missile Crisis (1962), the United States and the Soviet Union began to cooperate to the extent that both sides sought to evade a direct military confrontation. During the 1970s, both countries entered a period of time known as détente, a relaxing of tensions between the two. After the Soviet invasion of Afghanistan in 1979, however, there was a brief return to anticommunist rhetoric in the United States, especially with the election of Ronald Reagan to the presidency in 1980. Even so, by the middle of the decade, with the appointment of Mikhail Gorbachev as leader of the Soviet Union and with progress on nuclear arms control, tensions began to permanently subside. By the late 1980s, Communist regimes in Eastern Europe began to collapse, replaced by Western-style multiparty, parliamentary democracies. Finally in 1991 the Soviet Union itself was dissolved with the collapse of communism and the resignation of Gorbachev. Increasingly, anticommunist rhetoric became anachronistic.

In the aftermath of the Cold War, there was a sense that the United States had "won" and that communism, as an alternative to capitalism, had largely been discredited. Some even claimed the "end of history" as we knew it (Fukuyama 1989). This had the effect of reinforcing a "triumphalist" ideology. Despite the continuing presence of a few communist governments around the world, many of the more egregious excesses of the period dissipated. Yet the legacy of Cold War–period political culture remains strong; many of the perspectives, policies, and approaches developed during the Cold War continue today. Appy (2000, 8), for example, has argued that despite the change in the structure of global politics at the end of the Cold War, because many American leaders came of age during the heyday of Cold War political culture, their understandings and actions are shaped by that period.

Popular Culture and the Cold War

The political culture of the Cold War was, and is, readily observable in the popular culture of the time. Films, television shows, radio programs, and novels of the period either reflect the values expressed during the era or to some extent aimed to be critiques of the prevailing trends. Cuordileone (2005, xiii–xiv) notes, for example, that the fictional detective Mike Hammer, created by novelist Mickey Spillane, might be the archetypical symbol of anticommunist machismo of the late 1950s. Hammer was a hard-nosed, tough private investigator who had a grudge against the effete aspects of society. He had no time or patience for intellectuals, homosexuals, or those who were hampered by rules and regulations in the pursuit of law and order. Many of the male heroes of popular culture exhibited similar characteristics.

Films and other forms of media also helped to reinforce the conceptions and trends found in the political culture of the Cold War. Popular films such as *The Red Menace* (1949), *I Was a Communist for the FBI* (1951), *Big Jim McLain* (1952), *Red Dawn* (1984), and *Rocky IV* (1985) utilized many of the cultural attributes that were prevalent at the time, including dichotomous arguments, machismo, suspicion of unassimilated individuals, and highly specific gender roles. Particularly in the 1960s, however, films began to challenge the prevailing views. *Dr. Strangelove or: How I Learn to Stop Worrying and Love the Bomb* (1964), *Fail-Safe* (1964), and *The Russians Are Coming, the Russians Are Coming* (1966), for example, humanized the Soviets, suggested that an "us versus them" mentality oversimplified a complex world order, and lampooned bravado and overblown masculinity (Sachleben and Yenerall 2012, 65–68). As other critiques and counter-visions emerged in later periods, and as artists, thinkers, and ordinary citizens from formerly communist countries themselves began to contribute to the dialogue, it became apparent that traditional Cold War frames of reference were passé.

See also Conspiracy Theory and the "Paranoid Style"; Disinformation, Deception, and Politics; Fear Tactics in Politics; Nationalism; Nuclear Weapons and Politics; Popular Culture and Politics; Surveillance, Society, and Politics.

Mark Sachleben

Bibliography

Appy, Christian G. 2000. "Introduction: Struggling for the World." In Christian G. Appy, ed. *Cold War Construction: The Political Culture of United States Imperialism, 1945–1966*. Amherst: University of Massachusetts Press.

Bradley, Mark. 2000. "Slouching toward Bethlehem: Culture, Diplomacy, and the Origins of the Cold War in Vietnam." In Christian G. Appy, ed. *Cold War Construction: The Political Culture of United States Imperialism, 1945–1966*. Amherst: University of Massachusetts Press.

Branch, Taylor. 2006. *Canaan's Edge: America in the King Years 1965–68*. New York: Simon and Schuster.

Carson, Rachel Louise. 1962. *Silent Spring*. Cambridge, MA: Riverside Press.

Cuordileone, K. A. 2000. "Politics in an Age of Anxiety": Cold War Political Culture and the Crisis in American Masculinity, 1949–1960. *The Journal of American History* 87, no. 2: 515–45.

Cuordileone, K. A. 2005. *Manhood and American Political Culture in the Cold War*. New York: Routledge.

Dickstein, Morris. 1993. "After the Cold War: Culture as Politics, Politics as Culture." *Social Research* 60, no. 3: 531–44.

Fariello, Griffin. 1995. *Red Scare: Memoirs of the American Inquisition: An Oral History*. New York: W.W. Norton.

Fukuyama, Francis. 1989. "The End of History." *The National Interest* 16: 1–31.

Gaddis, John Lewis. 2005. *The Cold War: A New History*. New York: Penguin Press.

Giglio, Ernest. 2000. *Here's Looking at You: Hollywood, Film and Politics*. New York: Peter Lang.

Griffin, Robert. 1970. *The Politics of Fear: Joseph McCarthy and the Senate*. Lexington: University Press of Kentucky.

Honey, Michael K. 2004. "Operation Dixie, the Red Scare, and the Defeat of Southern Labor Organizing." In Robert W. Cherney, William Issel, and Kieran Walsh Taylor, eds. *American Labor and the Cold War: Grassroots Politics and Postwar Political Culture*. New Brunswick, NJ: Rutgers University Press.

Lerner, Max. 1957. *American as a Civilization: Life and Thought in the United States Today*. New York: Simon and Schuster.

Lynd, Robert Staughton, and Helen Merrell Lynd. 1937. *Middletown in Transition: A Study in Cultural Conflict*. New York: Harcourt, Brace and Company.

May, Elaine Tyler. 1988. *Homeward Bound: American Families in the Cold War Era*. New York: Basic Books.

McDougall, Walter A. 1985. *The Heavens and the Earth: A Political History of the Space Age*. New York: Basic Books.

Meiners, Roger E., Pierre Desrochers, and Andrew P. Morriss, eds. 2012. *Silent Spring at 50: The False Crises of Rachel Carson*. Washington, DC: Cato Institute.

Sachleben, Mark, and Kevan M. Yenerall. 2012. *Seeing the Bigger Picture: American and International Politics in Film and Popular Culture*. 2nd ed. New York: Peter Lang.

Schlesinger, Arthur M., Jr. 1967. "Origins of the Cold War." *Foreign Affairs* 46, no. 1 (October): 22–52.

Schlesinger, Arthur M., Jr. 1949. *The Vital Center: Our Purposes and Perils on the Tightrope of American Liberalism*. Boston: Houghton Mifflin.

Schneir, Walter, and Miriam Schneir. 2010. *Final Verdict: What Really Happened in the Rosenberg Case*. Brooklyn, NY: Melville House.

Schrecker, Ellen. 2004. "Labor and the Cold War: The Legacy of McCarthyism." In Robert W. Cherney, William Issel, and Kieran Walsh Taylor, eds. *American Labor and the Cold War: Grassroots Politics and Postwar Political Culture*. New Brunswick, NJ: Rutgers University Press.

Sibley, Katherine. 2004. *Red Spies in America: Stolen Secrets and the Dawn of the Cold War*. Lawrence, KS: University Press of Kansas.

Steinberg, Peter L. 1984. *The Great "Red Menace": United States Prosecution of American Communists, 1947–1952*. Westport, CT: Greenwood Press.

Thorne, Christian. 1992. "American Political Culture and the End of the Cold War." *Journal of American Studies* 26, no. 3: 303–30.

X (George F. Kennan). 1947. "The Sources of Soviet Conduct." *Foreign Affairs* 25, no. 4: 566–82.

Communications. *See* Political Communications

CONGRESS AND CONGRESSIONAL POLITICS

Certain features of the U.S. Congress are enduring. Its members serve in a bicameral institution representing both citizens and states, for instance, and the two chambers have different terms of office. The Constitution's framers adopted such features to enhance the institution's representative and deliberative capacities. Since they are sensitive to different time-pressures and responsive to diverse constituencies and interests, legislators are provided the chance to entertain and evaluate each other's concerns as they deliberate about national policies. While these constitutional features endure, and deliberation is still considered to be one of the institution's central responsibilities, many of the ways in which Congress tries to meet this distinctive responsibility have changed, and the alterations in its internal procedures over the past 50 years have been so dramatic that scholars frequently compare and contrast today's Congress to its mid-20th-century counterpart.

The older Congress is frequently referred to as the "textbook Congress" (Shepsle 1989). Its parties were neither cohesive nor polarized, for in both chambers the two parties included liberal and conservative wings. These four groups "moved like planets that traveled along distinct orbits: They would briefly align, then drift apart" (Brownstein 2007, 65). To shape policy in this environment, members had to be able to forge a consensus among ideologically diverse members and be willing to compromise and cut deals with their colleagues across the aisle. It was a committee-centric body that generally adhered to regular order (i.e., standard procedure). Thus, bills usually originated in committees, moved to a floor vote, and if they passed the House and the Senate in different forms, those differences were resolved by a conference committee composed of members who sat on the committees that initiated the proposal. Committee chairs were the most powerful legislators and the institution rewarded members who developed policy expertise, shunned the media spotlight, and spoke in a collegial manner (Asher 1973; Matthews 1960).

The "modern Congress," by contrast, is a more partisan legislative body. Today, both chambers' parties are more ideologically monolithic and polarized than they have been at any point in the past 60 years (CQ Roll Call's Vote Studies—2013 In Review 2014). As a result, members expect their leaders to use their powers to advance their party's preferences. This is especially true in the House, where power is more centralized than in the Senate, which as a body is more inclined to protect the prerogatives of its individual members. In this more partisan environment, committees are frequently enlisted to serve the party's programmatic goals, compromise between parties is discouraged, Senate filibusters are more common, and regular order is frequently sacrificed for narrower partisan ends (Mann and Ornstein 2012). While committees and their chairs dominated legislative deliberation in the textbook Congress, today those panels are less likely to be "the originators of important bills" and members most interested in shaping legislation know that "committees are no longer the place to be" (Stewart 2011, 107, 106). Contemporary members also routinely take their cases outside their chambers, employing a wide range of media outlets as they battle their opponents over legislation in spirited public relations campaigns (Malecha and Reagan 2012, Chapter 3).

Comparing how these two Congresses handled similar policies illustrates the different ways that the institution has tried to fulfill its deliberative responsibilities. To that end, we compare the internal processes Congress followed to pass the Medicare and Medicaid Act of 1965 and the Patient Protection and Affordable Care Act (Obamacare) of 2010, two policies that share a number of similarities. Both mark dramatic change in the American health care system. Both were passed by Democratic administrations working with substantial majorities in Congress. Finally, both policies ignited a divisive public argument about the government's role in American life that, for the past 50 years, has been characterized by predictable alarmist narratives made by groups who distrust each other (Marmor 2000, 68).

Medicare and Medicaid Act of 1965

Lyndon Johnson made Medicare a defining issue in the 1964 election. Of all the positions he took in that campaign, none were taken "as often or as fervently" as his support for Medicare (Blumenthal and Morone 2010, 186). Voters gave the president and his party a "landslide" victory, and Democratic majorities swelled to virtually unstoppable margins in both chambers. This convinced long-time Medicare opponent, Rep. Wilbur Mills (D-AR), who chaired the House Ways and Means Committee that would hear the bill, to change his position and announce the day after the election that he was now "receptive to a Medicare proposal" (Wolfensberger 2009). The election's outcome was so decisive that passage of some kind of health reform bill was "a statutory certainty. The only question remaining was the precise form the health insurance legislation would take" (Marmor 2000, 45).

The House and Medicare

Ways and Means was the key arena for Medicare's passage. It took up the president's bill, which aimed to cover hospital costs for the elderly, shortly after the start of the session. Chairman Mills led the committee to hear two alternative proposals. The first, "Eldercare," was supported by the American Medical Association, an interest group fiercely opposed to the Johnson's initiative; it sought a modest extension of existing state-run plans to help the elderly pay their medical bills. The committee's ranking minority member drafted the other alternative, "Bettercare"; it promised to cover doctors' bills and selected patient services. Initially, then, Ways and Means had three different and apparently "mutually exclusive alternatives" to consider, two of which were supported by the administration's opponents (Oberlander 2003, 30).

Mills subsequently invited members of the administration to meet with his committee in a closed executive session to explain what they thought was wrong with the "Bettercare" plan. They had a difficult time convincing attendees that the proposal was seriously flawed, and after an extensive back-and-forth, Mills concluded that it might "be a good idea if we put all three of these bills together" (Zelizer 1998, 240–41).

By incorporating the two alternatives with the administration's proposal into a "three-layer cake" plan, Mills accommodated Republicans and defused the most serious attempts by Medicare's congressional opponents to derail health care reform. As a colleague later recalled, "[i]t was Wilbur Mills at his best. His maneuvering was beautiful, and I don't mean maneuvering in a bad sense. Right then . . . everyone in the room knew that it was all over. The rest would be details. In thirty seconds . . . the greatest departure in the social security laws in thirty years was brought about" (Zelizer 1998, 241).

While all three "layers" were modified as the bill made its way out of Ways and Means and over to the Senate and back to a conference committee, the "three-layer cake" structure remained intact and wound up in the final bill. The administration's bill effectively became Medicare's Part A and covered hospital costs, "Bettercare" became Part B and covered physician services for the elderly, while "Eldercare" became Medicaid and covered health care costs for the poor.

To ensure that the bill was technically sound, the committee met privately and regularly with administrative experts to fine-tune the bill. Their deliberations were not "filled with dramatic debates about the rights of the elderly . . . or about the threats of socialized medicine." Instead, talks focused on a list of technical items that needed to be addressed if Medicare were to work as intended. This group's focus was to "reexamine the actuarial assumptions, reassess cost estimates, and review cost-control devices." Policy makers painstakingly evaluated the bill, reviewing it "line-by-line. . . . During these final sessions, the discussion was filled with actuarial jargon that few of the representatives could understand without expert help . . . [Mills] dazzled his colleagues with his mastery of the data, as one Democrat recalled, 'You should have seen him when we had the executive people in on Medicare. He just knew so much more than they did that it wasn't even funny'" (Blumenthal and Morone 2010, 245).

The House took up the bill under a closed rule, which prohibited any amendments and forced legislators to either support or oppose the bill as the committee wrote it. This reflected the deference Mills's

colleagues had for the chairman's policy expertise and his willingness to include Republican alternatives in the final bill (Stewart 2011, 104). Later, when Mills rose to support the bill on the floor, he "received a standing ovation from *both* sides of the aisle" and as he explained the measure "he quickly justified the reputation he had acquired for always being in command of his material. [R]arely referring to notes, he outlined provisions of the [296 page long] bill" (emphasis added) (Zelizer 1998, 250).

The House passed Medicare on a bipartisan vote by a wide 313 to 115 margin. Of the 138 Republican representatives who voted that day, nearly half voted for Medicare and they accounted for close to one-fifth of the majority's vote. Slightly less than 10 percent of the Democrats opposed the bill, and they accounted for slightly more than a third of all the no votes cast in that chamber.

Bipartisan to the End—Congress Passes Medicare

This bipartisan voting pattern occurred repeatedly as Medicare moved to the Senate, then to a conference committee, and back for a last floor vote in each chamber. Significant blocs of Republicans supported Medicare at every stage of the process, and a persistent number of Democrats opposed it. For instance, 41 percent of the GOP senators voted for the initiative when it first passed the Senate (Wolfensberger 2009). And when the Senate adopted the conference report creating Medicare, 43 percent of the voting Republican senators voted yea, accounting for approximately 19 percent of the majority vote. The GOP support for the final Medicare vote was even stronger in the House: slightly more than half of voting Republicans supported it. Democrats were also found on both sides of these votes. Eleven percent of Senate Democrats voted to reject the conference committee's report creating Medicare, accounting for almost a third of the Senate's no votes, while on the House side 17 percent of Democratic representatives voted against the final report, accounting for 41 percent of all the nay votes (Legislative History 1965).

In signing Medicare and Medicaid into law, President Johnson praised the many members of Congress on both sides of the aisle who had contributed to making the legislation a reality. He also singled out "the legislative genius of the Chairman of the Ways and Means Committee, Congressman Wilbur Mills" (Remarks with President Truman 1965).

Patient Protection and Affordable Care Act

Although President Barack Obama campaigned on health care reform and made it an important part of his agenda, he decided to let Congress, which Democrats controlled by healthy margins, take charge of writing a bill. He opted to use his office to focus the spotlight on health care reform and to take the lead in negotiating deals that would lead to its enactment into law (Connolly 2009; Edwards 2012).

The Committees Take Up Reform

Five congressional committees—three in the House, two in the Senate—took up the job of drafting a bill. In the House, party leaders intervened to guide their chamber's committee processes. Speaker Nancy Pelosi (D-CA) and Majority Leader Steny Hoyer (D-MD) directed the chairs of three committees with jurisdiction over the legislation—Education and Labor, Energy and Commerce, and Ways and Means—to work together to introduce a single measure for their committees' consideration (Pear 2009). The two leaders also frequently injected themselves in the process to ensure that any legislation this group introduced would reflect the preferences of their party's caucus. Chairs of the three committees huddled in closed-door sessions with a handful of Democratic legislators, key aides, and members from the administration over the course of three months to draft a proposal (Cohen 2009; Soraghan 2009). Although the panel heads held open discussions on their initiative shortly after they released their plan, Republicans generally remained on the sidelines. Some in the GOP frankly acknowledged that they intended to try to delay the legislation and concentrate their energies on whipping up popular sentiment in opposition to it (Smith 2009).

Democratic members of Education and Labor and Ways and Means quickly voted the legislation out of their committees. Education and Labor took it up one day and approved it the next, with all Republicans voting against it. Ways and Means dispatched the legislation in a single day with no GOP support (Armstrong and Clarke 2009). At Energy and Commerce the legislation met some resistance from moderate Blue Dog Democrats, but Speaker Pelosi and the White House intervened to broker a compromise to bring enough Democrats on board to vote a bill out of committee without any Republican support (Armstrong and Wayne 2009; Kane and Murray 2009; O'Connor 2003; Sinclair 2012).

In the Senate, the Democrats on the Committee on Health, Education, Labor and Pensions (HELP) worked in closed sessions with key aides and policy experts and no Republicans to craft a bill to be sent to the full committee for markup. After slightly more than a month of committee hearings and deliberations, HELP voted out a bill on a strict party line vote. The other Senate panel to consider the legislation, the Finance Committee, initially tried to produce a bipartisan accord. Chairman Max Baucus (D-MT) brought together a select "gang" of senators from both sides of the aisle for private meetings. Eventually, members of the gang gave in to pressure from their partisan colleagues to stop these across-the-aisle negotiations. This prompted Baucus to have the full panel commence working on his own draft. The committee eventually reported out a bill, and despite weeks of efforts trying to reach a bipartisan agreement, only one Republican, Sen. Olympia Snowe (D-ME), voted to move the measure to the floor (Bolton 2009b; see also Reagan and Malecha 2013).

Oppositional Moves and Party Leader Actions

With Democratic leaders working out legislative adjustments that could be put together in a bill that would pass their chambers, Republicans mounted a public relations campaign to shape popular sentiment in opposition to any health care reform measure. Even before the summer recess, Republican senators and representatives had been meeting with pollsters, public relations consultants, and experts from think tanks to map out their communications strategy. They had been holding town hall meetings and teleconferences and engaging a variety of media outlets and platforms to frame the debate and to shape the public's perception on the legislation Democrats were writing. Some even joined high-profile Capitol Hill rallies to make their case (Reagan and Malecha 2013).

While Republicans continued their public relations assault on the Democrats' reform efforts, Speaker Pelosi convened meetings in her Capitol Hill conference room to blend, in a single measure that could be brought to the floor, the bills her party had marked up and voted out of the three different House panels. Over the course of several weeks, she met and negotiated with different groups of the Democratic caucus and members of the administration. She responded to many of their concerns and continued to make adjustments to the legislation until she felt confident that she had obtained the 218 Democratic votes that she knew she needed to pass the bill. Working closely with the Rules Committee, she arranged to bring the legislation to the floor under a modified closed rule. The Speaker eventually prevailed when House passed the measure in a highly partisan 220 to 215 vote. Overall, she lost 39 Democrats and gained only a single Republican vote.

In the Senate, Majority Leader Harry Reid (D-NV) personally conducted behind-the-scenes negotiations with individual senators and different groups to merge the two bills produced by his chamber's committees. As a result of these meetings, he made major adjustments to the legislation. He worked to keep together all 58 Democrats and the two Independents who caucused with them. That would be enough to prevent the minority's strategic use of the filibuster, which is now routinely used. In carrying out his task, Majority Leader Reid disclosed little information on the measure he was crafting; indeed, just two days before he presented his plan to the caucus neither of the chairs of the committees that had marked up a bill had yet seen his plan.

Shortly after he unveiled his plan to his caucus, Reid quickly moved to have it considered by the full Senate. After sustaining cloture in a highly partisan 60 to 39 vote, he brought up his plan and employed a parliamentary tactic—"filling the amendment tree"—to prevent Republicans from offering any amendments. Both parties organized themselves to manage floor operations and to choreograph their statements and their publicity activities. The chamber then moved to a series of partisan votes, all of which the Democrats won. Finally, in another partisan vote taken shortly before the Christmas recess, the Senate passed the legislation, with not a single Republican crossing the aisle to support the bill.

The Final Act

Democrats returned from their holiday break determined to resolve, without delay, the differences between the House and Senate bills. Instead of going through the conference process, they opted to resolve their differences without any Republican input. Democratic leaders, heads of relevant committees, congressional staffers, members of the White House, and occasionally even the president held a series of private meetings to work out a deal that could be endorsed and passed by both chambers. As they were working toward their goal, however, Senate Democrats were dealt a major setback when their party lost a special election to fill a Senate seat once held by Sen. Edward Kennedy (D-MA). The victory by Scott Brown, the Republican candidate, meant the Democrats no longer had a filibuster proof majority that they would likely need to pass legislation that reconciled differences between the bills the two chambers had already passed.

As President Obama publicly battled with Republicans over health care reform (Reagan and Malecha 2013), Democratic leaders prepared the way to use a special procedure, reconciliation, to surmount a potential filibuster and complete their work. Since reconciliation required only a simple majority vote, Democrats could use it to make changes to the policy the House wanted once that chamber passed the legislation that had already cleared the Senate before the start of the holiday recess. After the Democratic leaders of the two chambers reached an agreement on how to proceed, the House passed the Senate's version of the legislation by a vote of 219 to 212. Not a single Republican lent his or her support to that bill. After the president gave his approval, the House then made the legislative changes it initially wanted to make in the bill cleared by the Senate by passing a reconciliation bill by a vote of 220 to 211. Not a single Republican supported the reconciliation measure. The Senate quickly passed that reconciliation bill by a vote of 56 to 43, with all Republicans voting against it. Because the Senate slightly modified the reconciliation measure, they sent it back to the House, which promptly passed it without any Republican support by a vote of 220 to 207. Democrats then sent the legislation to the White House for President Obama to sign.

Conclusion

Forty-five years separated the passage of Medicare and Obamacare. While both bills brought important changes to American health care, the ways in which Congress passed these measures were dramatically different. Assessing these institutional differences illuminates both the nature of these changes and the constellation of forces that combine to drive congressional politics in other policy domains.

The "Medicare Congress" was composed of ideologically diverse parties. Since Republicans and Democrats both counted liberals and conservatives in their ranks, chamber leaders were reluctant to support ideologically divisive policies that could divide their members and instead favored moderate proposals capable of attracting bipartisan majorities. In this setting, committee leaders enjoyed a privileged position. Due, in part, to the policy expertise they possessed from long committee service, the Senate and especially the House regularly deferred to committee chairs' policy recommendations. And these recommendations emerged from regular order—bills were sent to committees, where they were carefully examined and often extensively rewritten, and reported back to the floor where the panel's recommendation was rubber-stamped. If the chambers passed different versions of the same bill, a conference committee composed of representatives and senators from the original committees met to reconcile these differences and, as before, the floors tended to support these conference committee reports. The substantive details of policies were decisively shaped by legislators who, because of their committee work, were policy experts and whose collegial demeanor invited cooperation with colleagues across the aisle.

The "Obamacare Congress" could hardly be more different. Its parties are ideologically homogeneous, and most of the older incentives supporting bipartisanship have long disappeared. Chamber leaders, chosen by members who share a similar philosophical orientation, are today expected to use their powers to advance policy positions that appeal to the party's base of electoral and financial supporters. In this more partisan setting, power over policy has in the House shifted from committee chairs to the Speaker's office. Meanwhile, in the Senate, the majority leader has come to play a more active role in shaping policy outcomes. Instead of being arenas where vital substantive policy decisions are made, committees' decisions are frequently and substantially modified by the chambers' party leaders (Sinclair 2012). In both legislative chambers, regular order is routinely abandoned in an effort to secure party policy objectives. This more doctrinaire environment attracts members who enjoy waging battles with those who disagree with them ideologically and tends to frustrate legislators more interested in finding common ground with their opponents.

The larger ways that the Congress has changed over the past half-century are thus captured by the different processes by which these two landmark health care bills were passed. Legislators yearning for influence in the Medicare Congress took their bearings from Wilbur Mills, who "above all believed passionately in the value of political and intellectual compromise" (Zelizer 1998, 281). Members of the contemporary Congress tend to be a different sort, a "more ideological species of elected politician": when asked to moderate ideological principles to pass policies required for the "government to work," today's legislators "are quite likely to refuse" (Nesmith and Quirk 2013, 196).

See also Factions and Intra-party Conflict; Health Care and Politics; House of Representatives, United States; Partisanship and Polarization; Presidency and Presidential Politics; Senate, United States; Separation of Powers.

Daniel J. Reagan and Gary Lee Malecha

Bibliography

Altman, Stuart, and David Shactman. 2011. *Power, Politics, and Universal Health Care: The Inside Story of a Century-Long Battle.* Amherst, NY: Prometheus Books.

Armstrong, David, and David Clarke. 2009. "Panels Advance Health Overhaul." *CQ Weekly Report* (July 20): 1708–10.

Armstrong, Drew, and Alex Wayne. 2009. "Majority Forced by Its Own to Go Slow." *CQ Weekly* (July 27): 1778–80.

Asher, Herbert. 1973. "The Learning of Legislative Norms." *American Political Science Review* 67: 499–513.

Bessette, Joseph M. 1994. *The Mild Voice of Reason: Deliberative Democracy and American National Government.* Chicago: University of Chicago Press.

Blumenthal, David, and James A. Morone. 2010. *The Heart of Power: Health and Politics in the Oval Office.* Berkeley: University of California Press.

Bolton, Alexander. 2009a. "Dems Warn Baucus with Gavel Threat." *The Hill* (July 30). http://thehill .com/homenews/senate/52699-dems-warn-bau cus-with-gavel-threat. Accessed May 19, 2014.

Bolton, Alexander. 2009b. "Gang of Six Healthcare Reform Negotiations on Verge of Collapse." *The Hill* (September 4). http://thehill.com/homenews /senate/57285-gang-of-six-negotiations-on-verge- of-collapse. Accessed May 19, 2014.

Brownstein, Ronald. 2007. *The Second Civil War: How Extreme Partisanship Has Paralyzed Washington and Polarized America.* New York: The Penguin Press.

Cohen, Richard. 2009. "Can the Committee System Handle Obama's Ambitious Agenda?" *National Journal* (May 1): 17.

Connolly, Ceci. 2009. "On Health-Care Reform, Obama Looks to the LBJ Model; President Urges Lawmakers to Act." *Washington Post* (July 14).

Cooper, Joseph. 2013. "The Modern Congress." In Lawrence C. Dodd and Bruce I. Oppenheimer, eds. *Congress Reconsidered.* 10th ed. Washington, DC: CQ Press, pp. 401–36.

"CQ Roll Call's Vote Studies—2013 in Review." February 4, 2014. http://media.cq.com/votestudies/. Accessed May 19, 2014.

Edwards, George. 2012. *Overreach: Leadership in the Obama Presidency.* Princeton, NJ: Princeton University Press.

Jacobs, Lawrence R., and Theda Skocpol. 2012. *Health Care Reform and American Politics: What Everyone Needs to Know.* New York: Oxford University Press.

Kane, Paul, and Shailagh Murray. 2009. "Lawmakers Cut Health Bill's Price Tag: Negotiators in House and Senate Move toward Compromises on Reform Packages." *Washington Post* (July 30).

Loomis, Burdett A., ed. 2012. *The U.S. Senate: From Deliberation to Dysfunction.* Washington, DC: CQ Press.

Malecha, Gary Lee, and Daniel J. Reagan. 2012. *The Public Congress: Congressional Deliberation in a New Media Age.* New York: Routledge Press.

Mann, Thomas, and Norman Ornstein. 2012. *It's Even Worse Than It Looks: How the American Constitutional System Collided with the New Politics of Extremism.* New York: Basic Books.

Marmor, Theodore R. 2000. *The Politics of Medicare.* 2nd ed. New York: Aldine De Gruyter.

Matthews, Donald R. 1960. *U.S. Senators and Their World.* New York: Vintage Books.

McDonough, John E. 2011. *Inside National Health Reform.* Berkeley: University of California Press.

Mucciaroni, Gary, and Paul J. Quirk. 2006. *Deliberative Choices: Debating Public Policy in Congress.* Chicago: University of Chicago Press.

Nesmith, Bruce, and Paul J. Quirk. 2013. "No Exit from Deadlock." In Michael Nelson, ed. *The Election of 2012.* Washington, DC: CQ Press, pp. 175–202.

Oberlander, Jonathan. 2003. *The Political Life of Medicare.* Chicago: The University of Chicago Press.

Oleszek, Mark, and Walter J. Oleszek. 2012. "Legislative Sausage-Making: Health Care Reform in the 111th Congress." In Jacob R. Straus, ed. *Party and Procedure in the United States Congress.* Lanham, MD: Rowman and Littlefield Publishers, Inc., pp. 253–85.

Pear, Robert. 2009. "Team Effort in the House to Overhaul Health Care." *The New York Times* (March 18).

Peters, Ronald M., and Cindy Simon Rosenthal. 2010. *Speaker Pelosi and the New American Politics.* New York: Oxford University Press.

Quirk, Paul J., and William Bendix. 2013. "Deliberation in Congress." In Eric Schickler and Frances E. Lee, eds. *The Oxford Handbook of the American Congress.* Oxford: Oxford University Press, pp. 550–74.

Reagan, Daniel J., and Gary Lee Malecha. 2013. "Institutional Setting and Deliberation: The 'Old' and 'New' Congress." Paper prepared for delivery at the 2013 Annual Meeting of the American Political Science Association, Chicago, August 29–September 1.

"Remarks with President Truman at the Signing in Independence of the Medicare Bill." July 30, 1965. http://www.presidency.ucsb.edu/ws/?pid=27123 . Accessed May 19, 2014.

Shepsle, Kenneth A. 1989. "The Changing Textbook Congress." In John E. Chubb and Paul E. Peterson, eds. *Can the Government Govern?* Washington, DC: The Brookings Institution, pp. 238–66.

Sinclair, Barbara. 2006. *Party Wars: Polarization and the Politics of National Policy Making.* Norman: University of Oklahoma Press.

Sinclair, Barbara. 2012. *Unorthodox Lawmaking: New Legislative Processes in the U.S. Congress.* Washington, DC: CQ Press.

Smith, Ben. 2009. "Health Reform Foes Plan Obama's Waterloo." *Politico* (July 17). http://www.politico .com/blogs/bensmith/0709/Health_reform_foes_ plan_Obamas_Waterloo.html. Accessed May 19, 2014.

Soraghan, Mike. 2009. "Hoyer Aim: Old Bulls Running Together." *The Hill* (April 24).

Stewart, Charles, III. 2011. "Congressional Committees in a Partisan Era." In Jamie L. Carson, ed. *New Direction in Congressional Politics.* New York: Routledge, pp. 85–110.

Wolfensberger, Don. 2009. "Health Care Reform and the Medicare Analogy: An Introductory Essay," for the Seminar on Universal Health Care, Woodrow Wilson International Center for Scholars, September 9.

Zelizer, Julian E. 1998. *Taxing America: Wilber D. Mills, Congress, and the State, 1945–1975.* Cambridge: Cambridge University Press.

CONSERVATIVES AND CONSERVATISM

In a November 1963 interview with *The New York Times*, Sen. Barry Goldwater (R-AZ) defined a conservative as someone who "has a philosophy based upon the proven values of the past." Though those values were not as immutable as Goldwater supposed, he was correct that conservatives often invoked tradition to formulate and defend their positions on the regulation of morality, the maintenance of ethnic and cultural hierarchies, the government's role in the economy, and foreign policy. Yet, to a surprising degree, conservative values and priorities in these four arenas conflicted, notwithstanding the efforts of coalition-conscious Republican politicians and activists to fashion a "big-tent" movement. These conflicts help to explain why modern conservatism has had such a checkered political and cultural record: it was never internally consistent.

The American Conservative Worldview

American conservatism has long had a strong moral component, notably with regard to the suppression of obscenity, deviant sexuality, and vice enterprises like gambling houses and saloons. Moral conservatives, particularly rural, native-born evangelical Protestants, supported state prohibition laws and the national experiment with alcohol prohibition that ran its course from 1920 to 1933. Other conservative religious groups, such as the Catholic Church, championed censorship, including the Motion Picture Production Code that spelled out the moral dos and don'ts for Hollywood filmmakers from 1930 to 1968. And religious conservatives of all stripes challenged the relaxed sexual mores ushered in by the long 1960s, focusing particular fury on the 1973 *Roe v. Wade* decision that legalized abortion. Yet the persistent attempts of moral conservatives to recriminalize abortion have sometimes clashed with other commitments, notably the libertarian preference for less intrusive government in all realms of life.

American conservatism has also had an ethnocultural tradition, which featured transparent (and not-so-transparent) attempts to preserve a racial and ethnic hierarchy dominated by white, Protestant men. During the 19th century and much of the 20th century, social and religious thought, the force of written and interpreted law, and social custom all helped to justify a racial hierarchy that most conservatives favored. The most obvious instances of this strain of conservatism involved Jim Crow, the system of legal and extralegal exclusions that evolved after Reconstruction, and the revitalized nativist movement that led to adoption of more restrictive immigration laws in the early 1920s.

Historically, ethnocultural conservatives could be found in both major political parties. Southern Democrats fought well into the 1960s to preserve the racial caste system. The 1956 Southern Manifesto, a defiant declaration of resistance to school desegregation, blended two venerable southern conservative themes, defiance of integration and contempt for the coercive power of the federal government. Yet the latter-day descendants of these ethnocultural conservatives have embraced a demand for greater federal coercion and regulation, as in calls for intensified border security or demands to limit official communications to the English language.

Rhetorically, conservatives have been most consistently libertarian in economic policy. They have opposed steeply progressive taxation, most corporate regulation, and government management of the economy through fiscal or monetary means. In what became the most sustained economic downturn in American history, President Herbert Hoover's secretary of the treasury, Andrew Mellon, proposed that the business community tighten up, sell off assets, cut back output, and allow the economy to recover on its own. "Liquidate labor, liquidate stocks, liquidate the farmers, liquidate real estate," Mellon allegedly told Hoover. Mellon and other economic conservatives trusted that sound money, budgetary restraint, and unimpeded markets would soon restore prosperity.

Hoover's successor, the Democrat Franklin D. Roosevelt, had other ideas. After a period of experimentation in 1933 and 1934, Roosevelt's New Deal established the basis for a permanent, if initially modest, regulatory and welfare state centered on the federal government. That state oversaw a variety of programs aimed at economic relief, recovery, and reform, including the reform of making organized labor more nearly equal to big business. Though most historians viewed these measures as having saved capitalism and provided a foundation for its future growth, orthodox libertarians regarded the New Deal as unprecedented intrusion on free markets and individual economic freedom. The libertarian counteroffensive assumed many forms, from state right-to-work legislation to limits on unemployment insurance and other federally financed welfare benefits. However, many conservatives, less pure in their libertarian ardor, contentedly harvested

their share of personal and corporate benefits provided by the expanded federal government. They believed, as historian Ronald P. Formisano put it, in "libertarianism with benefits" (Formisano 2012, 87).

U.S. foreign policy presented conservatives with similar conundrums and temptations. Though early 20th-century conservatives supported military preparedness and voiced nationalistic sentiments about America's special place in history, they did not necessarily believe in an active role in world affairs. They feared foreign entanglements, above all in European wars, and believed their country safe behind two great oceans. Conservative wariness of international involvement was most apparent in the successful struggle to keep America out of the League of Nations in 1919 and 1920 and in the several Neutrality Acts passed during the 1930s. However, the American triumph in World War II, the emergence of a nuclear-armed Soviet Union, the communization of China, and a wave of decolonization that put the allegiances of newly independent nations into play forced a rethinking of conservative foreign-policy views. Champions of the Old Guard, such as U.S. senators William Borah (R-ID) and Robert A. Taft (R-OH), gave way to a rising generation of conservatives who accepted an active containment policy, heavy defense spending, and America's role as an international policeman—not only in the Western Hemisphere, but everywhere in the world.

The Cold War marked a turning point in the history of modern American conservatism. "Fusionist" conservative writers such as Frank Meyer made preoccupation with national security a permanent part of the conservative worldview. Indeed, if there has been one overarching victory for conservatism since World War II, it would be in the ability of conservative political actors and voices to project this guardian role as a core component of conservatism, creating a reflexive defensiveness in liberals reluctant to be cast as national-security weaklings. Even so, conservative skepticism over interventionism has never entirely disappeared. In 2007 and 2008, Rep. Ron Paul (R-TX) made a run for the presidency—one of several in his gadfly career—that confronted President George W. Bush's overreaching in Iraq and other fronts in the war on terror, which Paul dismissed as a pretext for an engorged post–Cold War security state. Yet Paul departed from the libertarian ethos, notably in his staunchly pro-life views. He ran, quipped one *New York Times* correspondent, an "antiwar, anti-abortion, anti-Drug-Enforcement-Administration, anti-Medicare candidacy" (Caldwell 2007).

To what extent did the mishmash of conservative values, policy preferences, and personalities affect American politics and culture after World War II? Similarly, where did conservatives gain ground and where did they lose it? To answer these questions, we will look first at conservative fortunes from the end of World War II until the late 1960s, when liberals finally began to lose their political grip. Then we will examine 1966 to 2008, a period of transition and ascendancy for conservatives in national political affairs—though not, as it turned out, in cultural disputes. Finally, we will consider the ways in which conservative activists and ideas have affected state politics in the early 21st century.

Mid-20th-Century Conservatism

If the New Deal and the growth of the federal government during and after World War II represented historic defeats for libertarians, and if the Cold War provoked a crisis among conservative isolationists, ethnocultural conservatives at least managed to fight a successful delaying action. Still influential in the Democratic Party (one celebrated conservative politician, South Carolina's Strom Thurmond did not think it necessary to switch his party membership from Democrat to Republican until as late as 1964), conservatives used their strength in the South to block desegregation and other extensions of federal power into the region, save those that funded highways, public buildings, and military bases. But the racism behind the defense of the segregationist status quo proved an embarrassment and an impediment to a broader national conservative movement, as many conservative thinkers recognized during the 1950s and 1960s.

Conservatives achieved another victory of sorts during the late 1940s and early 1950s, when they backed efforts, led by Sen. Joseph McCarthy (R-WI) and other headline-hunting politicians, to root out domestic subversives. The movement eventually targeted not only communists in the government and Hollywood but homosexuals whose sexual deviancy allegedly made them susceptible to blackmail and hence security risks. In matters of sex and gender, postwar America remained a place where any nails found sticking up were promptly hammered down. Though the Victorian façade was visibly cracking—Hugh Hefner launched *Playboy* in late 1953, Allen Ginsberg composed his beat epic "Howl" in 1955—most middle- and working-class Americans remained morally conservative and family centered. During the 1950s, couples married young and stayed married; rates of divorce and out-of-wedlock births remained low throughout the decade. In later years, moral conservatives celebrated the 1950s as a golden age against which they measured the decline of family life during the last third of the 20th century—ironically, the very years of conservative Republican political ascendancy.

If conservatives looked back with nostalgia at the sexual mores of the 1950s, the same cannot necessarily be said of the two-term presidency of Dwight D. Eisenhower (1953–1961). Conservative discontent with Eisenhower's domestic policies surfaced quickly. Free-market advocates such as William Rusher, the publisher of the *National Review*, professed themselves disenchanted with the president's failure to roll back the New Deal. The administration's handling of the Cold War was another matter, however. Secretary of State John Foster Dulles and other key cabinet members were reliably hawkish and, though Eisenhower came to entertain doubts about the influence and fiscal burden of the military-industrial complex, defense spending as a percentage of the nation's economic output remained far higher, during his two terms, than it had been in the interwar years. The president and Congress also used national security to justify increased federal spending on transportation infrastructure and education. The defense expenditures and the growing U.S. role as world policeman dismayed old-school foreign-policy conservatives. But, as if on cue, Robert Taft, the leading representative of that worldview, died in 1953, clearing the field for a new generation of conservatives who countenanced federal growth and spending to compete with the Soviet Union.

Conservatives new and old found an intellectual home in the *National Review*, which commenced publication in 1955. Its editor, William F. Buckley Jr., assumed a unique role as American conservatism's charismatic high priest, intellectual arbiter, erudite wit, and sometime enfant terrible. A Catholic and traditional moralist who harbored a streak of ideological and personal libertarianism—Buckley liked good wine and cigars and high living—he could not resist lobbing the occasional verbal bomb. He spared neither the cranks to his right nor the do-gooders to his left. His great mission was to bring conservatives together around a respectable, consensual, and coherent program that he and a stable of talented writers laid out in the pages of the *National Review*. His success in achieving that goal made him an icon—his apostles said *the* icon—of American conservatism in the second half of the 20th century.

Grassroots actors participated in "massive resistance" campaigns, distributed pamphlets, and fired off letters excoriating the Supreme Court for its *Engel v. Vitale* (1962) and *Abington v. Schempp* (1963) school-prayer decisions. They joined anticommunist and anti-integrationist organizations like the John Birch Society, founded in 1958 by retired candy manufacturer Robert W. Welch Jr. And they turned out to vote, though often for what seemed the lesser of two evils. For all of their determination, American conservatives still lacked what mattered most in national politics: control of one of the two major parties.

That deficiency was apparent during the 1960 presidential campaign. The Democrats nominated Sen. John Kennedy, a Cold War liberal who promised renewed application of federal power to "get the country moving again." The Republicans nominated Vice President Richard Nixon, a politician of impeccable anticommunist credentials but flexible ideology who flustered conservatives with his willingness to reach out to New York governor Nelson Rockefeller and other establishment moderates. Things went from bad to worse when Nixon narrowly lost the 1960 election and Kennedy fell to assassination in November 1963. Kennedy's death gave Vice President Lyndon Johnson, his legislatively savvy successor, an opening to pursue the stalled liberal agenda. In 1964 and 1965 Johnson succeeded in enacting landmark federal civil rights laws and big-ticket social welfare programs such as Medicare and Medicaid. To these conservative injuries Johnson added the insult of an electoral thrashing. In 1964 Johnson sought, and decisively won, the presidency in his own right.

Yet the 1964 election also marked a turning point for conservatives, who could finally vote for a major-party nominee who unabashedly advocated their core values and traditions. That champion was Barry Goldwater. In 1952 and 1958 the Arizonan had won election to the U.S. Senate; in 1960 he attached his name to *The Conscience of a Conservative*, a book ghostwritten by speechwriter L. Brent Bozell Jr., Buckley's brother-in-law and former Yale debate partner. The book staked out positions that meshed comfortably with both the ethnocultural and libertarian traditions. In the pages of his book and on the stump, Goldwater seemed to speak his mind, unfettered by the tactical accommodations of more mainstream Republicans. Goldwater condemned moral rot, upbraided the Supreme Court for exiling Christianity from the public schools, stressed the need to confront communism across the globe, and decried federal regulation in all walks of life, including integrated public accommodations. Though Goldwater justified his opposition to the 1964 Civil Rights Act in libertarian, rather than racial, terms, his stance appealed strongly to ethnocultural conservatives. They rewarded him with the electoral votes of five states in the Deep South.

Everywhere else, save in his native Arizona, Goldwater lost badly. Yet his historic campaign convinced conservatives that their future lay with the Republican Party. Their enthusiasm, ideas, and money would ultimately transform the party, making it both more competitive in national politics and more ideologically exclusive. Between 1980 and 2012 no Republican candidate who called himself moderate or liberal won his party's presidential nomination. During the same span, Republican candidates who called themselves conservative (whatever their private convictions) won the White House in five presidential elections out of nine.

Republican conservatives also became more competitive in congressional and state races, particularly in the South, which moved decisively into the GOP camp during the historic presidency of Ronald Reagan (1981–1989). It was, in fact, Reagan who completed the regional realignment process that Goldwater had begun. A Hollywood actor and conservative convert who became Goldwater's most effective spokesman during the 1964 campaign, Reagan positioned himself as a smoother and more telegenic version of the combative Arizona senator. "He believed basically what Barry believed," Reagan campaign strategist Stuart Spencer remembered in an oral history interview. "He said a lot of things that Barry said, but he said them differently. He said them in a soft way, in a more forgiving way. Style was the difference" (Miller Center, Spencer Interview, 2001).

Years of Transition and Political Ascendancy

Though Reagan's masterful style enabled conservatives to grasp the presidential prize that had so long eluded them, they first had to endure a difficult period of transition during the late 1960s and 1970s. Their biggest problem was institutional. Despite the creation of new activist organizations, such as the Young Americans for Freedom (est. 1960), the American Conservative Union (est. 1964), the Heritage Foundation (est. 1973), and the Moral Majority (est. 1979), conservatives remained outgunned in the national media, the universities, the think tanks, the federal judiciary, and other elite opinion-shaping institutions. If the franchise had been limited to college graduates and *New York Times* readers, conservatives would never have achieved power.

Yet populist forces more than offset this institutional and media handicap. As early as 1966, disenchanted voters, upset by rising crime and racial disorder, accelerating inflation, a costly and prolonged war in Vietnam, and violent protest on college campuses, punished liberal candidates in the congressional and gubernatorial elections. The growing perception of liberal mismanagement and overreach, combined with Johnson's decision not to seek a second term, Robert F. Kennedy's stunning assassination, and a chaotic Democratic Convention, opened a door to the White House in 1968.

The candidate who walked through that door was Richard Nixon. During the campaign he attacked liberalism, lax criminal-procedure doctrines imposed by activist judges, and the absence of law and order in American cities. His coded racial appeals were more effective than those of Alabama governor George Wallace, a third-party candidate of popular illiberalism who preferred a demagogic style. Nixon stuck to a safer conservative script. Once in office, though, he proposed policy experiments that alarmed the GOP's activist base, going so far as to propose welfare reform by way of a guaranteed income for poor Americans. His conservatism seemed opportunistic, anything but libertarian. Even on matters of foreign policy, Nixon dismayed conservatives. He widened the war in Vietnam to end it, but elsewhere departed from the rigid anticommunism that had become conservative gospel. Nixon and his national security advisor Henry Kissinger established, through back-channel negotiations, a dialogue with the leadership of the People's Republic of China. This dialogue helped to pave the way for Nixon's February 1972 visit to that country, and the formal reestablishment of diplomatic relations in 1979.

Apart from the successful campaign to derail the Equal Rights Amendment, led by activist Phyllis Schlafly, moral traditionalists also suffered setbacks in the early 1970s. Their most notable defeat came from a familiar quarter, the Supreme Court, which in 1973 legalized abortion. However, the *Roe* decision energized grassroots and religious conservatives. It gave rise to a sustained pro-life movement, a politically re-energized Christianity, and alliance building among conservative Protestants and Catholics. One of the pro-life movement's early achievements was the 1976 Hyde Amendment, which curtailed Medicaid funding for abortions.

Nixon's Watergate disgrace and August 1974 resignation—urged by none other than Barry Goldwater—also provided a peculiar sort of victory for conservatism. As Nixon was not really one of them, principled conservatives did not have to share the blame for his downfall. More importantly, in the aftermath of Watergate government seemed even more sinister and less reliable. The weakened and embattled presidencies of Gerald Ford and Jimmy Carter did little to restore confidence. Americans, it seemed, had every reason to doubt government.

The economic woes of the 1970s further validated these doubts. Liberal commitments and policies seemed outdated, if not actually to blame. The near default of New York City in 1975 provided conservatives with a dramatic example of the need to scale back public spending. In June 1978 Californians staged their own revolt by passing Proposition 13, which reduced and limited the future growth of property taxes in the nation's most populous state. Meanwhile, in Washington, DC, an alliance of free-market conservatives and consumer advocates managed to enact legislation to deregulate important industries like air transport (1978) and trucking (1980). Even before Reagan's election in November 1980, public opinion was swinging toward economic conservatism.

In 1976 Reagan, conservatism's late-rising star, tried and failed to wrest the GOP presidential nomination from incumbent Gerald Ford. In 1980, though, he won both the nomination and the election, thanks to lingering stagflation, the ongoing national humiliation of the Iranian hostage crisis, and the fecklessness of the Carter administration. Reagan also had a positive message, polished by years of reading from conservative scripts. His upbeat, sincere, telegenic style made conservatism seem enlightened and optimistic, the proper political worldview to promote long-overdue change. He seemed to speak for, as much as to, Americans in his 1981 inaugural address, when he famously declared that "government is not the solution to our problem; government is the problem."

Reagan and his supporters embraced supply-side economics, which made tax cuts the key to renewed growth. The Economic Recovery Tax Act of 1981, which lowered the top marginal income tax rate from 70 percent to 50 percent, was an important early victory. But between 1982 and 1986 a series of hard-fought tax battles with Congress returned the overall level of federal taxation to roughly where it had been in 1980. Meanwhile, the Reagan administration's defense buildup, lack of domestic-spending discipline, and ongoing growth in politically sacrosanct entitlement programs drove the annual federal deficit to over $200 billion. In 1990 the accumulated deficits undermined the political fortunes of Reagan's presidential successor, George H.W. Bush, who incurred the wrath of economic conservatives by abandoning his "no new taxes" campaign pledge. Their disenchantment contributed to his defeat in the 1992 election.

Reagan was also something of a disappointment to moral conservatives. He spoke to their concerns, made war on crime and drugs, and named conservatives to the federal bench. Or he tried to name them, as in his 1986 Supreme Court nomination of Robert Bork, whom the Senate refused to confirm. But Reagan delivered no measures on school prayer or abortion as substantial as the Hyde Amendment, which was already on the books. Culturally, Madonna had as good a claim to the 1980s as Reagan. Pop culture and mass media continued their erotic drift.

Reagan's administration did reprise the firm anti-communism that conservatives had endorsed since the outset of the Cold War. The administration negotiated with the Soviet Union over nuclear armaments from a position of heightened American military spending and calls for a Strategic Defense Initiative designed to render the United States less susceptible to Soviet nuclear attack. Historians and partisans still debate the role of these spending gambits in bringing about the demise of the sclerotic Soviet empire. What is less open to debate is that Reagan-era "neoconservatives," keen on punishing their foreign enemies and supporting their foreign friends, were willing to tolerate deficits, government growth, and counterrevolutionary intrigues that would have been unimaginable to conservatives of the Taft generation.

Reagan and George H.W. Bush, whose 1989–1993 presidency was in some respects a third Reagan term, also helped bring about the final political collapse of Great Society liberalism. Bush, in fact, used "liberal" as a political epithet during his aggressive 1988 presidential campaign against Massachusetts governor Michael Dukakis. He and his advisors knew that Dukakis and other liberals were vulnerable on crime and welfare issues that had an implicit racial edge. "New Democrats," led by Arkansas governor Bill Clinton, recognized these vulnerabilities. They vowed to move the party back toward the center on domestic policy. In 1992 their maneuvering paid off when Clinton, aided by a sour economy and the third-party candidacy of H. Ross Perot, captured the White House with 43 percent of the popular vote.

In office, Clinton tried to govern too far to the left, suffering a sharp rebuke in the 1994 congressional elections. He survived by tacking to the right. In 1996 he signed the Personal Responsibility and Work Opportunity Act, fulfilling his promise "to end welfare as we have come to know it." That same year he remarked, in his State of the Union Address, that "the era of big government is over." In fact it was not over, though the era of union power and blue-collar prosperity was waning in the face of globalization, a trend accelerated by the 1994 North American Free Trade Agreement (NAFTA).

Clinton's support of NAFTA—and welfare reform, and the 1996 Defense of Marriage Act, and a balanced budget—won him few points with conservatives. They still regarded him as a closet liberal and a draft-dodger and a libertine. The latter charge was borne out by the 1998 revelation of an affair with White House intern Monica Lewinsky. Hard-liners like House Majority whip Tom DeLay (R-TX) used new media—blast faxes, the Internet, conservative talk radio, and the Fox News Network (est. 1996)—to fire up the GOP's anti-Clinton base and to keep pressure on House Republicans to vote for impeachment. Impeach Clinton they did, though the Senate acquitted him in a 1999 trial that did nothing to hurt his approval ratings, which remained in the 60 percent range for the remainder of his term.

Clinton's successor as president, Texas Republican governor George W. Bush, understood that DeLay's brand of sexual McCarthyism was political poison. In the 2000 presidential campaign against Vice President Al Gore, Bush ran as a "compassionate conservative," emphasizing tax cuts and a limited role for the United States abroad. With an assist from third-party candidate Ralph Nader, confused Florida voters, and the U.S. Supreme Court, whose five Republican appointees all voted in his favor, Bush won the disputed 2000 election. He seemed to be settling into a moderate caretaker presidency not unlike Eisenhower's when the September 11, 2001, terrorist attacks unbalanced the political equation, boosting Bush's political popularity and handing his party a powerful security issue.

What happened next revealed, yet again, the fault lines within American conservatism. In addition to launching preemptive wars against terrorism in Afghanistan and Iraq, Bush and his neoconservative advisors rushed through omnibus legislation, the 2001 Patriot Act, that greatly expanded the federal government's powers of domestic surveillance. Fiscal

conservatives (who had been cheerfully silent in June 2001, when Bush signed legislation cutting federal income tax rates and revenues) began to worry about the cost of an open-ended war, while libertarians feared the open-ended privacy intrusions. Small-government conservatives of all stripes disliked Bush's signature domestic legislation, the No Child Left Behind Act, signed in early 2002, and the generous expansion of Medicare prescription benefits enacted in 2003. Security- and benefits-conscious voters were more enthusiastic, rewarding Republicans with control of both houses of Congress in the 2002 and 2004 elections and returning Bush for a second term.

Bush's second term proved a watershed for modern conservatism. The rising tide of red ink, the mounting casualties in Iraq, charges of crony capitalism, and the massive 2008 federal bailout of the financial industry provoked open rebellion. Conservative luminaries such as radio talk-show host Rush Limbaugh, libertarian guru Lew Rockwell, and Buckley himself, then in the twilight of his long and influential life, denounced Bush as a phony conservative. Restive voters were more inclined to regard him as a failed president. In 2006 they restored Democratic control of the House and Senate and in 2008 elected a black liberal Democrat, Illinois senator Barack Obama, to the White House.

Conservative activists retreated to the redoubt of the Tea Party. Nominally a grassroots movement, but actually a well-financed and carefully orchestrated party within a party, it sought to ensure that GOP candidates toed a hard conservative line. Tea Party operatives threatened Republican incumbents with primary challenges from the right if they strayed from rigid adherence to conservative principles, particularly on taxes and spending—the key issues as the federal debt continued to mount during the Obama presidency. Though the Tea Party and its media affiliates accused Obama of reckless spending, notably by expanding subsidized health insurance through the Affordable Care Act (2010), the deeper truth was that the nation's fiscal crisis had originated during the years of conservative ascendancy. National debt as a percentage of the gross domestic product declined under every Democratic president from Truman through Clinton. Eisenhower and Nixon managed the same feat. But every

Republican president from Ford on left office with the debt percentage higher. The fondness for big government and the political dividends it paid to incumbents plainly extended beyond Democrats, which was why Tea Party activists were determined to purge "RINOs" (Republicans in Name Only) from the ranks of the GOP. Only the pure could make the real revolution.

Red-State Conservatism

This judgment about *national* politics and culture—that American conservatives failed to reconcile their internal contradictions and divisions, that conservative officeholders often disappointed conservative activists, and that no conservative movement or faction succeeded in reversing long-term trends toward secularization and sexual liberalization—requires one important qualification. It is that, in a religiously and culturally diverse nation with a federal constitution, conservative prospects and legislative accomplishments varied greatly from state to state.

One of the first to recognize this was the journalist and historian Thomas Frank. Not long after the bitterly contested election of 2000 seared a map of conservative "red" and liberal "blue" states into the national consciousness, Frank published *What's the Matter with Kansas? How Conservatives Won the Heart of America* (2004). He argued that cultural wedge issues had become so dominant in one red state, Kansas, that many of its citizens had begun voting against their own economic self-interest. Moral issues, especially abortion, and populist jeremiads against liberal coastal elites had prompted mad-as-hell voters to elect "social" conservatives who, once in office, pursued a corporate agenda of deregulation, tax cuts, and a weakening of the public sector that economically undercut the very voters who had given them power.

In the decade following the publication of Frank's book, it became apparent that similar dynamics were at play in many red states. An influx of conservative money, most of which had previously gone into national politics, helped state conservative candidates exploit cultural issues and populist resentments. New conservative special-interest groups, state policy networks, Astroturf watchdog entities, think tanks, and even faux news organizations began appearing in state capitals in the early 2000s. Often exempt from tax laws

and backed by wealthy industrialists, these groups provided an infrastructure of support for right-wing candidates running for state and local office, enabling them to sweep aside moderates in the Republican primaries and then defeat Democrats in the general election.

After Obama's 2012 reelection, red-state governments and their financiers became even more aggressive. Some began asserting anew the "nullification" doctrine, the premise that certain aspects of federal health reform, voter registration, and even gun laws did not necessarily control over more narrowly drawn and specific state initiatives. In a 2013 episode that recalled antebellum constitutional battles and segregationists' assertions of states' rights, Kansas (among other red states) enacted a measure designed to nullify federal law for firearms manufactured in the state and even authorize the filing of charges against federal officials performing their duties. U.S. attorney general Eric Holder felt it necessary to send a letter reminding Kansas officials that "the United States will take all appropriate action" to prevent interference with federal officials seeking to enforce federal law.

Elsewhere state and local conservatives pursued a variety of antigovernment and antiwelfare measures, including increased privatization of corrections and other public services; weakened commitments to public pensions; prohibition of collective bargaining by teachers; efforts to remove civil service protection; drug testing for recipients of assistance programs; subsidies for private schools; and enactment of further tax cuts to curtail spending. Red states, in short, became laboratories for conservative policies not likely to have a chance of passage in Congress, and a proving ground for candidates to test their mettle before moving onto the national stage. After the Democrats suffered reversals in many gubernatorial and state legislative elections in 2010, conservatives used their control of state governments for a new round of gerrymandering, enabling the GOP to maintain control of the U.S. House of Representatives after the 2012 elections, notwithstanding the fact that Democratic candidates received 1.4 million more votes nationwide. The GOP did even better in 2014, when gerrymandered districts, Obama's flagging popularity, abundant campaign donations, and the low voter turnout typical of midterm elections enabled conservative candidates to make additional gains in state legislatures, in the U.S. House, and in the U.S. Senate, which swung from Democratic to Republican control. However, as in 1952, 1994, and 2002, there remained a difference between securing Republican majorities and assuring unity among the party's conservative factions, whose tensions had proved more durable than any particular election cycle.

See also Culture Wars; Far-Right Parties and Organizations; Libertarians and Libertarianism; Privatization and Deregulation; Republican Party; States' Rights; Tea Party.

Christopher Hickman, Chris W. Courtwright, and David T. Courtwright

Bibliography

Berman, William C. 1998. *America's Right Turn: From Nixon to Clinton*. 2nd ed. Baltimore: Johns Hopkins University Press.

Brennan, Mary C. 1995. *Turning Right in the Sixties: The Conservative Capture of the GOP*. Chapel Hill: University of North Carolina Press.

Caldwell, Christopher. 2007. "The Antiwar, Anti-Abortion, Anti-Drug-Enforcement Administration, Anti-Medicare candidacy of Dr. Ron Paul." *New York Times Magazine* (July 22), E26.

Critchlow, Donald T. 2005. *Phyllis Schlafly and Grassroots Conservatism: A Woman's Crusade*. Princeton, NJ: Princeton University Press.

Courtwright, David T. 2010. *No Right Turn: Conservative Politics in a Liberal America*. Cambridge, MA: Harvard University Press.

Flamm, Michael W. 2005. *Law and Order: Street Crime, Civil Unrest, and the Crisis of Liberalism in the 1960s*. New York: Columbia University Press.

Formisano, Ronald P. 2012. *The Tea Party: A Brief History*. Baltimore: Johns Hopkins University Press.

Frank, Thomas. 2004. *What's the Matter with Kansas? How Conservatives Won the Heart of America*. New York: Metropolitan Books.

Horowitz, David A. 1997. *Beyond Left and Right: Insurgency and the Establishment*. Urbana: University of Illinois Press.

Lassiter, Matthew D. 2006. *The Silent Majority: Suburban Politics in the Sunbelt South*. Princeton, NJ: Princeton University Press.

Lewis, Hyrum. 2012. "Historians and the Myth of American Conservatism." *Journal of the Historical Society* 12: 27–45.

Lilla, Mark. 1998. "A Tale of Two Reactions." *New York Review of Books* (May 14), 4–7.

McGirr, Lisa. 2001. *Suburban Warriors: The Origins of the New American Right*. Princeton, NJ: Princeton University Press.

Mergel, Sarah Katherine. 2010. *Conservative Intellectuals and Richard Nixon: Rethinking the Rise of the Right*. New York: Palgrave Macmillan.

Miller Center. 2001. "Interview with Stuart Spencer." University of Virginia. November 15–16. http://millercenter.org/president/reagan/oralhistory/stuart-spencer. Accessed February 4, 2014.

Nash, George H. 2006. *The Conservative Intellectual Movement in America since 1945*. 30th Anniversary edition. Wilmington, DE: Intercollegiate Studies Institute.

Perlstein, Rick. 2001. *Before the Storm: Barry Goldwater and the Unmaking of the American Consensus*. New York: Hill and Wang.

Phillips-Fine, Kim. 2011. "Conservatism: A State of the Field." *Journal of American History* 98: 723–43.

Ribuffo, Leo P. 1994. "Why Is There So Much Conservatism in the United States and Why Do So Few Historians Know Anything about It?" *American Historical Review* 99: 438–49.

Schulman, Bruce J., and Julian E. Zelizer, eds. 2008. *Rightward Bound: Making America Conservative in the 1970s*. Cambridge, MA: Harvard University Press.

Skocpol, Theda, and Vanessa Williamson. 2012. *The Tea Party and the Remaking of Republican Conservatism*. New York: Oxford University Press.

Zelizer, Julian E. 2010. "Reflections: Rethinking the History of American Conservatism." *Reviews in American History* 38: 367–92.

CONSPIRACY THEORY AND THE "PARANOID STYLE"

"Conspiracy theory"—or, as it is also called, conspiracism—refers to a worldview in which the causes of important events and historical trends are attributed to the secret machinations of cabals of elites or subversive forces. Conspiracists advance "conspiracy theories," what one commentator has called "the poor man's cognitive mapping" (meaning that such theories are often rather simple-minded; Jameson 1988, 356). Ever since the publication of Richard Hofstadter's seminal essay "The Paranoid Style in American Politics," published in *Harper's Magazine* in 1964 (later expanded into a book; 1965), most ruminations on conspiracism treat the phenomenon as a form of mass pathology, or delusion. In the last two decades, however, scholars have begun to question whether such theories are always primitive, dangerous, or disempowering.

Conspiracism and Paranoia

The forerunner of Hofstadter's essay was Harold Lasswell's pioneering book *Psychopathology and Politics* (1930), which was written in the context of the long shadow cast by totalitarian dictatorship and sought to identify the personal motivation of those who agitate politically by accusing others of base motives, especially agitators who traffic in hate. Lasswell's subsequent book *Power and Personality* (1948) warned that irrational, pathological tendencies within the public must be curtailed before they pose a danger to the body politic—a theme recurrent in many later studies of conspiracism.

Hofstadter's "Paranoid Style" does not directly reference Lasswell, but it similarly raises concern about antirational tendencies in politics and was inspired by concern over McCarthyism and the anticommunist witch hunts of the early Cold War era. A liberal historian, Hofstadter was immediately alarmed by Barry Goldwater's presidential campaign of 1964 and the nominee's declaration, in his acceptance speech, that "extremism in the defense of liberty is no vice."

In his book, Hofstadter claims to use "paranoid" in a broad, metaphorical sense rather than in the clinical or medical sense, applying it to a style of discourse that is "overheated, oversuspicious, overaggressive, grandiose, and apocalyptic" (1965, 4). And, for Hofstadter, style matters: even legitimate discourse can be cloaked in paranoid rhetoric. Hofstadter cites in this respect the example of those who might legitimately oppose gun control but go so far as to characterize it as an "attempt

by a subversive power to make us part of one world socialist government" (1965, 5).

Daniel Pipes elaborates on the Hofstadter thesis in *Conspiracy: How the Paranoid Style Flourishes and Where It Comes From* (1997), arguing that conspiracism constitutes a reactionary critique of Enlightenment thought and rationality. For Pipes, conspiracy theory refers to "fears of non-existent conspiracy." Those most likely to believe are the disaffected and the "culturally suspicious." He acknowledges that past injustices or mistreatment might spawn cultural suspicion in some groups, but says that these past events do not make a conspiracy theory any more credible.

One of Pipe's examples involves findings that African Americans, on the whole, are more likely than whites to believe that the CIA deliberately introduced crack cocaine into black communities in the 1980s. Pipes recognizes that the Tuskegee experiments of 1932–1972, when a group of African American farmers were deceived into thinking they were receiving free government medical care but instead were being used as test subjects to study the progression of syphilis, might incline members of the African American community to believe the worst; but he rejects any serious truth value in the CIA-cocaine theory itself. Yet, there is no absolute consensus among researchers and commentators on this last point; indeed, there is some evidence in support of conspiracy.

Allegations of CIA complicity in the drug trade were brought to light by Gary Webb, a reporter for the *San José Mercury News*, whose investigative reporting exposed ties between drug traffickers, the introduction of cocaine into black communities in Los Angeles and other cities, and the Nicaraguan contras, who were being backed by the CIA. The stories, later published as a book (1999), gained traction because of the reaction of African American leaders, including Rep. Maxine Waters, who forced the CIA to respond and to apologize (without acknowledging direct complicity), and because of increased circulation of the stories over the Internet.

The mainstream media, especially *The Washington Post* and *The New York Times*, went to extraordinary lengths to discredit Webb's account, contributing ultimately to the reporter's ostracism and suicide. Jack Bratich, a professor of journalism, contends that

Webb's stories were well researched, flawed only by some relatively minor errors. He argues that when discontented and aggrieved citizens reach an audience in the mainstream, authorities often respond with "conspiracy panic." In other words, institutional mechanisms, both private and public, go into action to close down the space for dissent. Such a reaction, says Bratich (2008), is typical of how official guardians of knowledge attempt to limit intruders who threaten their authoritative, gate-keeping roles. It may be argued, further, that this process is abetted by mainstream intellectuals trained in positivist traditions of social science and biased against explanations that introduce elements of uncertainty into the understanding of history and social life (Hellinger 2003).

Rejection of conspiracy theory is not limited to liberal and conservative intellectuals. Noam Chomsky, for example, whose radical views on American foreign policy are often labeled "conspiracy theory," rejects the term outright. His outlook, he says, is "precisely the opposite of conspiracy theory" (2007, 243). Noting that mainstream media stories are typically skewed to favor vested interests by means of reporters quoting establishment representatives at length while neglecting to quote critics of the establishment, Chomsky remarks that it is not conspiracy theory to point this out and to recognize that "institutional factors . . . set boundaries for reporting and interpretation in ideological institutions." For Chomsky, labeling something as "'conspiracy theory' is part of the effort to prevent an understanding of how the world works."

Evolution of Conspiracism in America since 1930

In the contemporary era, among many different conspiracy theories, the two most influential and persistent are (1) the theory that Lee Harvey Oswald did not act alone in the assassination of President John F. Kennedy (henceforth "JFK") and (2) theories that implicate the administration of President George W. Bush in the attacks upon the World Trade Center and the Pentagon on September 11, 2001 (henceforth "9/11").

Kathryn Olmsted (2009) has argued that these conspiracy theories are emblematic of a shift in American conspiracism during the 20th century. Before World War II conspiracism tended to focus on private concentrations of economic and political power; by mid-century, however, the "real enemy" in conspiracist thought had shifted to government, which had increased in size and power in response to the Great Depression and World War II. Emblematic of this shift is the charge that President Franklin Roosevelt deliberately allowed the Japanese to attack Pearl Harbor to facilitate America's entrance into the war, which bears similarity to one version of 9/11 conspiracism that contends the Bush administration let 9/11 happen on purpose to facilitate its plans for a wider war in the Middle East.

In the case of JFK, the official Warren Commission conclusion that Oswald acted alone (the "lone shooter" thesis) was initially widely accepted by the public. By the 1970s, after the release of the Zapruder film (which raised several questions about the number and origin of shots), skepticism about the lone shooter theory mounted, fed in part by a number of scandals and tragedies that undermined trust in government. These events included the release of the Pentagon Papers, which uncovered government deceptions about the Vietnam War; the assassinations of Martin Luther King Jr., Malcolm X, and Robert Kennedy; the Watergate scandal, which forced President Nixon's resignation; and the Iran-Contra scandal involving the Reagan administration's sales of arms to Iran and the transfer of illegal funds to the contras fighting the Sandinista government in Nicaragua.

In 1964, 87 percent of respondents told Gallop researchers that they believed the Warren Commission's version of events to be true. Thirty-seven years later, the tables had turned and 81 percent said that they believed there had been a conspiracy (Gallop 2003). By 2013, the passage of time had somewhat eroded belief in JFK conspiracy theories; nonetheless, 59 percent told Gallop (2013) that they rejected the Warren Commission's conclusion (see also Boardman 2013).

That Osama Bin Laden and Al Qaeda were the authors of 9/11, similar to the lone gunman theory, initially generated little dissent in public circles. By 2004, however, skepticism had begun to mount, encouraged by revelations that the Bush administration had lied about the presence of weapons of mass destruction in Iraq and about the alleged complicity of

U.S. president John F. Kennedy, Governor John Connally of Texas, and First Lady Jacqueline Kennedy ride through Dallas, Texas, on November 22, 1963, moments before the president is killed by an assassin. The event has spawned numerous conspiracy theories. (Library of Congress)

Saddam Hussein in the 9/11 attacks. In October 2006, a *New York Times*/CBS poll found that only 16 percent of those surveyed believed that the government was "telling the truth" about the attacks; a full 53 percent said that it was "mostly telling the truth but hiding something"; and a sizeable 28 percent said that it was "mostly lying."

Public skepticism about an "official story" does not necessarily translate into full-blown belief in a particular conspiracy theory. For example, an Angus-Reid Public Opinion Poll (2010) found that overwhelming majorities view as "not credible" four specific 9/11 theories widely disseminated by the so-called Truthers, the community of skeptics actively researching and promoting alternative interpretations of 9/11 and other historical events. Among the 9/11 theories doubted by the public were the "Let It Happen on

Purpose" theory and the "Made It Happen on Purpose" theory, both of which lay blame with the U.S. government for being directly involved. The Reid poll found, for example, that no more than 15 percent of the public believes that the Twin Towers were brought down by a controlled demolition—a percentage which might be regarded as still surprisingly high.

Certainly many conspiracists hold their views with an unbreakable faith, reject any contrary evidence as fabricated, and equate possible motivation for carrying out an act with actual guilt. Some such individuals are indeed pathological—to the point, even, of being criminally dangerous. However, conspiracy theories about JFK and 9/11, among others, also garner respected public intellectuals. Two examples of such scholars are (1) Peter Dale Scott, a retired professor of literature and former Canadian diplomat, who served as an advisor to director Oliver Stone for the film *JFK*; and (2) David Ray Griffin (2008), a prominent theologian, who has written and lectured widely in connection with the 9/11 "truth movement."

In *Deep Politics* (1996), Scott contends that the recurrence of major scandals and violence in American politics since World War II is symptomatic of a seamy side of politics—"deep politics" or "parapolitics." As paramilitaries are to official militaries, so para-politics are to politics, he argues. One particularly conducive hothouse for conspiracies in this dark political realm is the place where security agencies—police, military, intelligence agencies, and so on—interact with unsavory criminal elements, such as the drug lords whose profits have benefitted paramilitary groups (in Laos, Afghanistan, Central America, etc.) aligned with American foreign-policy objectives. Although the scandals are on the record, as with many such theories it can be difficult to entirely prove or disprove them.

The most widely read rebuttal of JFK conspiracism is Gerald Posner's *Case Closed* (1984), which concluded that despite a highly flawed investigation, the Warren Commission was right: Lee Harvey Oswald acted alone. The book was hailed by the mainstream press as the final word on the Kennedy assassination—but that hardly proved to be the case. Posner shows how one man could have killed Kennedy, and he provides plausible explanations for many anomalies raised by Scott and others. His own account, however, still asks us to believe a strange tale about how Oswald, a misfit who repeatedly crossed paths with security agencies, managed to kill the president and subsequently fall victim to a nationally broadcast murder (by Jack Ruby). Taken one at a time, Posner's explanations are plausible; taken together, they are less parsimonious, less compelling than the theory that Oswald acted in concert with others.

The Internet, Globalization, Agency Panic, and Fusion

One common strain of conspiracism in American life consists of various communities and subcultures adopting world conspiracy theories about globalization, often portraying themselves as defenders of national sovereignty, truth, and democracy in a Manichean ("good vs. evil") struggle against a grim New World Order. This type of conspiracism attracts, among others, fervent right-wing populists and radical fundamentalist Christians who believe in the "end time," or the imminent appearance of an anti-Christ prior to the expiration of earthly existence, as described in the biblical book of Revelations.

At times such skeptics have "fused" ideologically with leftist antiglobalization activists (Barkun 2003). These uneasy and unlikely bedfellows share suspicions about secret negotiations of free trade agreements, about the role of secretive and closed world conferences (held annually, at Bilderberg and Davos, Switzerland), and about various organizations of elites, such as the Trilateral Commission. Michael Kelly (1995) and Chris Berlet (Berlet and Lyons 2000), among others, view this fusion with alarm, warning that liberals who adopt conspiracy theories risk empowering the right and muddying their own political identity.

Olmsted (2009, 202) sees fusion, for example, in the convergence of the seemingly disparate writings of Ted Kaczynaki (the Unibomber), Timothy McVeigh (convicted of bombing the Federal Building in Oklahoma City), and Ramzi Yousef (a main perpetrator of 1993 bombing of the World Trade Center). All three individuals have expounded ideas that converge around the notion that the American government is in collusion with global elites to dominate the world.

The radio/Internet programs of Alex Jones, which have attracted hundreds of millions of views (not necessarily "viewers") have provided a forum for fusion. Jones claims to be a libertarian and is militantly opposed to gun-control but nurtures the "Birther" movement's contention that President Barrack Obama is not a natural-born American, as the Constitution requires. At the same time, he has provided an opportunity for figures like Griffin and Scott to reach a wide audience usually denied them by the mainstream media.

Almost all observers of contemporary conspiracism see the emergence of the Internet and social media as giving new impulse to the phenomenon, though no one has clearly documented this claim empirically. The Internet has facilitated the formation of communities of amateur researchers who can readily exchange views and disseminate analyses at odds with mainstream intellectuals and journalists. High-speed travel has augmented the communications revolution, allowing regular conferences—a tendency that seems pronounced among those focused on JFK, 9/11, and economic globalization.

Revisionist Views on Conspiracism

Recent years have seen some reconsideration of the idea that conspiracy theories are always disempowering and counterproductive. From this perspective, contemporary conspiracy is a product of "agency panic" (Knight 2000; Melley 2000) and lack of transparency (West and Sanders 2003) in an increasingly globalized world. "Agency panic" refers to a sense of loss of control and victimization in relation to social and economic forces (where an individual actor has "agency," or the ability to choose).

As Fenster (1999, xiii) characterizes it, conspiracy theory "draws on the most simplistic, disabling and dangerous interpretations of political order, including fascism, totalitarianism, racism, and anti-Semitism—yet also represents a populist possibility, a resistance to power that implicitly imagines a better future." Melley (2000, 3) admits that whether or not conspiracism is more widespread in the current epoch is difficult to discern, but it is certainly perceived to be: "Conspiratorial explanations have become a central feature of American political discourse, a way of understanding power that appeals to both marginalized groups and the power elite." The evidence is all around us in popular culture (see sidebar).

Treating conspiracy theory as mass pathology, as deluded thinking, leaves us with little to say about what role conspiracies play as forms of political behavior. Pipes attempts to account for this problem by distinguishing "petty conspiracies" (e.g., ordinary criminal activities, lesser abuses of power, bribes to secure a political favor) from "world" or "global conspiracies" (e.g., positing cabals of elites building a new

Conspiracism in Popular Culture and Literature

"The truth is out there" was featured prominently in *The X-Files*, the highly popular TV show that ran from 1993 to 2002. The program in many ways expressed paranoia and cultural fusion as FBI agents Scully and Mulder were weekly frustrated and threatened as they tried to get to the bottom of signs that the government was, among other things, under the control of aliens and covering up its involvement in the assassination of JFK.

Director Oliver Stone's film, *JFK* (1991), revived interest in JFK conspiracy theories. It was nominated for eight Academy Awards (winning two) and featured some of Hollywood's most prominent actors. Stone fused documentary film with fictional scenes virtually indistinguishable from documentary footage. Stone contended that his goal in producing JFK was to reopen the case, and he had some success. The government released thousands of additional documents and collected new testimony from surviving witnesses.

Before Stone, John Frankenheimer directed a film version (1962) of Richard Condon's *The Manchurian Candidate*. A parody of McCarthyism, the film gained notoriety because of some parallels to the subsequent Kennedy assassination. The would-be assassin was an apparent Korean War hero brainwashed by International Communists so that he would, on queue, lose his own will.

Conspiracism in more rarified realms of American literature includes Joan Didion's (nonfiction) *The White Album* depicting an America resigned to decay and increasingly paranoid; Thomas Pychon's *The Crying of Lot 49* involving conflict among cartels dating back to the Middle Ages; Don Delillo's *Libra* which follows Lee Harvey Oswald to his date with destiny; and David Clewell's poems *The Conspiracy Quartet* and *Jack Ruby's America*, which explore ordinary lives in the crevices of what Scott would call "deep politics."

world order in secret). Between these two extremes exist conspiracies (e.g., an assassination, a secretly negotiated alliance, or a terrorist attack) that have significant global and national consequences. Pipes himself calls such instances "operational conspiracies" (1996, 26) and even acknowledges that revolutions seem to require them.

Hellinger (2003) argues that operational conspiracies undertaken in the name of "national security," or to block public debate about economic globalization (e.g., free trade agreements), have introduced persistent tension between American democratic principles and the maintenance of U.S. power or hegemony. American hegemony is closely linked to promoting capitalist economic globalization—the process of freeing the movement of capital, goods, and services (but not people) across international borders. It is no wonder that, as this process proceeds, ordinary people on both the left and the right have come to sense a lack of control over their life's fortunes and to see global elites as operating in a conspiracy to advance abstract global goals at the expense of national sovereignty and more traditional values.

Conclusion

Hofstadter's seminal essay remains a touchstone for observers within the mainstream media of conspiracism in American political culture. For many, conspiracy theorists are all "just crazy." However, recent studies open debate about whether all forms of conspiracism are antirational and dangerous. Both camps agree that lack of transparency in national and global governance ensures that conspiracism will remain a feature of American popular culture.

See also Anti-intellectualism in American Life; Cold War Political Culture; Fear Tactics in Politics; Globalization; Popular Culture and Politics; Talk Radio and Politics.

Daniel Hellinger

Bibliography

Angus-Reid. 2010. "Most Americans Reject 9/11 Conspiracy Theories." *Angus-Reid Public Opinion* (March 21). http://www.angus-reid.com/polls /38598/most_americans_reject_9_11_conspiracy_ theories/. Accessed May 22, 2014.

Barkun, Michael. 2003. *A Culture of Conspiracy: Apocalyptic Visions in Contemporary America.* Berkeley: University of California Press.

Berlet, Chip, and Matthew Lyons. 2000. *Right-Wing Populism in America: Too Close for Comfort.* New York: The Guilford Press.

Boardman, William. 2013. "Kennedy Assassination. 50th Anniversary Commemoration." *Global Research* (June 1). http://www.globalresearch.ca /kennedy-assassinationm-50th-anniversary-comme moration-no-one-knows-the-full-story-of-what-happened/5337185. Accessed May 22, 2014.

Bratich, Jack A. 2008. *Conspiracy Panics: Political Rationality and Popular Culture.* Albany: State University of New York Press.

Carlson, Darren. 2001. "Most Americans Believe Oswald Conspired with Others to Kill JFK." Gallup News Service (April 11). http://www.gallup.com /poll/1813/most-americans-believe-oswald-con spired-others-kill-jfk.aspx. Accessed May 22, 2014.

Chomsky, Noam. 2002. *Understanding Power: The Indispensable Chomsky.* Peter R. Mitchell and John Schoeffel, eds. New York: The New Press.

Chomsky, Noam. 2007. *What We Say Goes.* London: Allen & Unwin.

Fenster, Mark. 1999. *Conspiracy Theories: Secrecy and Power in American Culture.* Minneapolis: University of Minnesota Press.

Gallup. 2003. "Americans: Kennedy Assassination a Conspiracy." November 21. http://www.gallup .com/poll/9751/americans-kennedy-assassination-conspiracy.aspx. Accessed October 31, 2014.

Gray, Matthew. 2010. *Conspiracy Theories in the Arab World: Sources and Politics.* New York: Routledge.

Griffin, David Ray. 2008. *The New Pearl Harbor Revisited: 9/11, the Cover-Up and the Exposé.* Disturbing Questions. Ithaca, NY: Olive Branch Press.

Hellinger, Daniel. 2003. "Paranoia, Conspiracy, and Hegemony." In Harry G. West and Todd Sanders, eds. *Transparency and Conspiracy: Ethnographies of Suspicion in the New World Order.* Durham, NC: Duke University Press, pp. 204–32.

Hofstadter, Richard. 1965. *The Paranoid Style in American Politics and Other Essays*. Cambridge MA: Harvard University Press.

Jameson, Fredric. 1988. "Cognitive Mapping." In Cary Nelson and Lawrence Grossberg, eds. *Marxism and Interpretation of Culture*. London: MacMillan, pp. 347–60.

Kay, Jonathan. 2011. *Among the Truthers: A Journey through America's Growing Conspiracist Underground*. New York: Harper Publishing.

Kelly, Michael. 1995. "The Road to Paranoia." *The New Yorker* (June 19), 60+.

Knight, Peter. 2000. *Conspiracy Culture: From Kennedy to The X-Files*. New York: Routledge.

Lasswell, Harold. 1930. *Psychopathology and Politics*. Chicago: University of Chicago Press.

Lasswell, Harold. 1948. *Power and Personality*. Chicago: University of Chicago Press.

Melley, Timothy. 2000. *Empire of Conspiracy: The Culture of Paranoia in Postwar America*. Ithaca, NY: Cornell University Press.

Olmsted, Kathryn. 2009. *Real Enemies: Conspiracy Theories and American Democracy: World War I to 9/11*. New York: Oxford University Press.

Pipes, Daniel. 1996. *The Hidden Hand: Middle East Fears of Conspiracy*. New York: St. Martin's Press.

Pipes, Daniel. 1997. *Conspiracy: How the Paranoid Style Flourishes and Where It Comes From*. New York: Free Press.

Popular Mechanics Magazine. 2006. *Debunking 9/11 Myths: Why Conspiracy Theories Can't Stand Up to the Facts*. New York: Hearst Publications.

Posner, Gerald. 1984. *Case Closed: Lee Harvey Oswald and the Assassination of JFK*. New York: Random House.

Scott, Peter Dale. 1996. *Deep Politics and the Death of JFK*. Berkeley: University of California Press.

Scott, Peter Dale. 2007. *The Road to 9/11: Wealth, Empire, and the Future of America*. Berkeley: University of California Press.

Shehan, Daniel. n.d. *Iran-Contra Scandal*. Speech on YouTube. http://www.youtube.com/watch?v=Rg YFD8_jmQY. Accessed June 25, 2013.

USA Today. 2013. "Poll: Belief in JFK Conspiracy Slipping Slightly." *USA Today* (May 11). http://www .usatoday.com/story/news/nation/2013/05/11 /poll-jfk-conspiracy/2152665/. Accessed May 22, 2014.

Webb, Gary. 1999. *Dark Alliance: The CIA, the Contras, and the Crack Cocaine Explosion*. New York: Seven Stories Press.

West, Harry G., and Todd Sanders, eds. (2003). *Transparency and Conspiracy: Ethnographies of Suspicion in the New World Order*. Durham, NC: Duke University Press.

CONSTITUTION AND CONSTITUTIONALISM

The term "constitution" generally refers to a written document that defines the powers of government and the rights of individuals. Most nations and states have a single document. It is said that England has an "unwritten constitution," but in fact it is guided by a series of statutes adopted over the years that set forth the structure, principles, and processes of government (Jennings 1962). Among the important written documents are the Magna Carta, the Habeas Corpus Act, the Petition of Right, and the Act of Settlement (Greaves 1955). The existence of a constitution need not offer any protections for individual rights and liberties. Authoritarian and totalitarian states may print a document called a constitution, but power is placed in one or a few persons. In such countries, express provisions for religious liberty, free speech, free press, and other safeguards for individual rights have no meaning. Self-government does not exist. Individuals have whatever freedoms the rulers decide to extend.

The term "constitutionalism" presents a larger concept. It stands for a form of government where the principles expressed in a constitution have real force. People are allowed to meet together, offer their opinions individually and through associations, and participate in free elections to determine their political leaders. Constitutions that merely sanction the use of governmental power without limiting it are hostile to constitutionalism.

Some principal elements of constitutionalism were identified by Lord Bolingbroke in 1733: "By constitution we mean, whenever we speak with propriety and exactness, that assemblage of laws, institutions and customs, derived from certain fixed principles of reason, directed to certain fixed objects of public good, that compose the general system, according to which the community hath agreed to be governed" (McIlwain 1947, 3). Constitutionalism imposes a legal limitation on government. Without that understanding, governments may function in an arbitrary and despotic manner, acting not by law but by will.

Origins of Constitutionalism

Scholars trace the tradition of constitutionalism to ancient Athens. Legislation by Solon proposed "to give the common people a share in the rest of the government, of which they had hitherto been deprived" (Wormuth 1949, 5). In the second century BC, the Greek historian Polybius described the Roman government as being divided on the basis of social status among the monarchy, the aristocracy, and the people, developing an early system of separation of powers with checks and balances. Whenever either of the separate parts of government "attempts to exceed its proper limits," the other powers respond to exert reciprocal control to reduce the aggressor to its "own just bounds" (Harriger 2003, 183).

John Locke's form of government, published in 1690, contemplated separate executive and legislative branches. Under his theory, "there can be but one supreme power, which is the legislative, to which all the rest are and must be subordinate" (Harriger 2003, 188). However, the power he called "federative," which for us would be foreign policy and the war power, he placed solely in the executive. In case the executive used force against the people without authority, Locke answered that "the true remedy of force without authority, is to oppose force to it" (Harriger 2003, 189). Montesquieu, in his *Spirit of the Laws* (1748), concluded that whenever "the legislative and executive powers are united in the same person, or in the same body of magistrates, there can be no liberty" (Harriger 2003, 189).

Separated Powers in the United States

The principle of separation of powers in the U.S. Constitution is highly complex. There was never an effort to establish a pure separation of powers. To allow for checks and balances, the branches of government had to overlap. It is often said that powers are separated to preserve liberty. It is equally true that a rigid, or pure, separation can destroy liberties. The historic swings in France between executive and legislative powers illustrate the danger of extreme separation. The French constitutions of 1791 and 1848, based on a pure separation of powers, led to absolutism and reaction (Vile 1967, 176–211). The American framers wanted to avoid political fragmentation and paralysis of power. As Joseph Story noted, they knew that a rigid adherence to separated powers "in all cases would be subversive of the efficiency of the government and result in the destruction of the public liberties" (Story 1970, 2, 12).

When America declared its independence from England, the national government had only one branch: the Continental Congress. There was no separate executive or judiciary. Members of the Congress had to legislate and also sit on committees to handle administrative and adjudicative matters. Single executives were created in 1781 to improve efficiency, but they functioned as agents of Congress. In 1780, Congress created a Court of Appeals in Cases of Capture, but it too served as an agent of Congress.

The separation of legislative, executive, and judicial functions incorporated in the U.S. Constitution reflects the framers' search for a form of government more efficient than the Continental Congress. The nature of this separation was driven principally by events, not theory. In a striking phrase, the historian Francis Wharton said that the Constitution "did not make this distribution of power. It would be more proper to say that this distribution of power made the Constitution of the United States" (Wharton 1889, 1, 663). In *Myers v. United States* (1926), a dissent by Justice Louis Brandeis spoke a half-truth when he claimed that the doctrine of separated powers was "adopted by the Constitution of 1787, not to promote efficiency but to preclude the exercise of arbitrary power." A more efficient national government was a key objective.

A thoughtful concurrence by Justice Robert Jackson in *Youngstown Co. v. Sawyer* (1952) describes the complex and sometimes conflicting elements that co-exist in America's separation doctrine. For checks and balances to operate, the branches must be separate. If they are too separate they cannot check. Jackson offered this account:

> The actual art of governing under our Constitution does not and cannot conform to judicial definitions of the power of any of its branches based on isolated clauses or even single Articles torn from context. While the Constitution diffuses power the better to secure liberty, it also contemplates that practice will integrate the dispersed powers into a workable government. It enjoins upon its branches separateness but interdependence, autonomy but reciprocity. Presidential powers are not fixed but fluctuate, depending upon their disjunction or conjunction with those of Congress. . . .
>
> . . . With all its defects, delays and inconveniences, men have discovered no technique for long preserving free government except that the Executive be under the law, and that the law be made by parliamentary deliberations.

Several delegates at the state ratifying conventions objected to the draft Constitution. Instead of the three branches being kept separate, they had been intermingled. "How is the executive?" demanded one irate delegate at Virginia's ratifying convention. "Contrary to the opinion of all the best writers, blended with the legislature. We have asked for bread, and they have given us a stone" (Elliot 1836–1845, 3, 280). This outcry attracted some support, but not much. By the time of the Philadelphia Convention, the rigid doctrine of separated powers had been replaced by a system of checks and balances. One contemporary pamphleteer called the separation of powers, in its pure form, a "hackneyed principle" and a "trite maxim" (Vile 1967, 153).

Alexander Hamilton, John Jay, and James Madison wrote a number of essays to defend the draft Constitution. The collected set is called the *Federalist Papers*. Hamilton and Madison explained the need for overlapping powers and why it was superior to the impracticable partitioning of powers demanded by some anti-Federalists. It was necessary, Madison argued in *Federalist* #51: "Ambition must be made to counteract ambition" (Wright 2002, 356). In *Federalist* #48 he warned that "unless these departments be so far

connected and blended as to give to each a constitutional control over the others, the degree of separation which the maxim requires, as essential to a free government, can never in practice be duly maintained" (Wright 2002, 343). In *Federalist* #75, Hamilton responded to critics who objected to the president and the Senate sharing the treaty power. He bristled about "the trite topic of the intermixture of powers" (Wright 2002, 475).

The case for a strict separation of powers was presented by three states: Virginia, North Carolina, and Pennsylvania. They proposed a separation clause to be added to the Bill of Rights (Elliot 1836–1845, 3, 280, and 4, 116, 121; McMaster and Stone 1888, 475–77). The recommended language: "The powers delegated by this constitution are appropriated to the departments to which they are respectively distributed: so that the legislative department shall never exercise the powers vested in the executive or judicial [,] nor the executive exercise the powers vested in the legislative or judicial, nor the judicial exercise the powers vested in the legislative and or executive departments" (Dumbauld 1957, 174–75, 183, 199). Congress rejected this proposal, as well as a substitute amendment to make the three departments "separate and distinct" (Annals of Congress 1789, 453–54, 789–90).

The separation of power doctrine, subjected to ridicule for much of the 20th century as an anachronous, inefficient theory, retains its vitality. The framers relied on separation of powers to avoid the abuse and illegality of concentrated power. Human nature of 1787 has not improved by 2013. People in political positions abuse power. Checks are needed. Sen. George Wharton Pepper offered this perspective in 1931: "if the geometers of 1787 hoped for perfect peace and if the psychologists of that day feared disastrous conflicts, history, as so often happens, has proved that hopes were dupes and fears were liars. There has not been perfect peace; but the conflicts have not proved disastrous" (Pepper 1931, viii).

Judicial Review

Part of the checks of the American political system come from the authority of courts to exercise judicial review: striking down as void actions by the legislative and executive branches. An early precedent comes from an English opinion by Chief Justice Coke in *Dr. Bonham's Case* (1610). He said that when an act of Parliament "is against common right and reason, or repugnant, or impossible to be performed, the common law will control it, and adjudge such Act to be void." A few British judges in the 17th and 18th centuries cited Coke's argument, but the principle of judicial review never took root on English soil. In *Hurtado v. California* (1884), the Supreme Court noted: "notwithstanding what was attributed to Lord Coke in Bonham's Case . . . the omnipotence of Parliament over the common law was absolute, even against common right and reason."

There should be little doubt that the basic principle of judicial review is implied in the U.S. Constitution. For example, Article I, Section 9, states that Congress shall not pass a bill of attainder (legislative punishment without judicial trial). Were Congress to enact such a bill, the federal courts would have authority to declare it unconstitutional. In *Calder v. Bull* (1798), Justices Chase and Iredell agreed that if Congress in a "clear case" passed a bill in violation of the Constitution, the Supreme Court would be empowered to declare it void. Two years earlier, in *Hylton v. United States*, the Court upheld a congressional statute that imposed a tax on carriages. If the Court possessed authority to uphold legislation, presumably it had authority to strike one down.

The first time the Court invalidated a congressional statute was *Marbury v. Madison* (1803), when it held that Section 13 of the Judiciary Act of 1789 was unconstitutional by expanding the original jurisdiction of the Court. This is the first example of judicial review by the Court, in terms of nullifying congressional legislation, but judicial review is not judicial supremacy. Chief Justice John Marshall, who wrote the opinion, recognized that it would have been institutionally foolhardy for the Court to try to elevate itself above the elected branches. In a letter to Justice Samuel Chase, he wrote that if Congress did not like a Supreme Court decision there was no need to resort to impeachment. Congress could simply pass legislation to override a judicial ruling it objected to (Fisher 2011, 37).

Language in *Marbury* is presented as evidence that the Court has the last word on the meaning of the Constitution. Marshall stated that it is "emphatically the province and duty of the judicial department to say what the law is." So it is, but the same can be said of Congress. Certainly it is the province and duty of the legislative department to say what the law is. Marshall knew in 1803 that he lacked the power to command President Thomas Jefferson or Secretary of State James Madison to deliver commissions to William Marbury and other individuals whose appointments to judicial positions had been confirmed by the Senate but the commissions had never been delivered to them.

The Supreme Court has never maintained a monopoly in determining the meaning of the Constitution. Throughout more than two centuries that task has been shared with Congress, the president, the 50 states, and the general public. For example, in *Minersville School District v. Gotibis* (1940), a commanding 8–1 majority of the Supreme Court upheld a compulsory flag salute that violated the religious beliefs of two public school children who belonged to the Jehovah's Witnesses. They interpreted the Bible literally: "Thou shalt not make unto thee any graven image, or any likeness of any thing that is in heaven above, or that is in the earth beneath, or that is in the water under the earth. Thou shalt not bow down thyself to them, nor serve unto them" (Exodus 20:4–5). Lower courts defended their refusal to salute the flag on the ground of religious conscience. The Court's opinion in 1940 triggered widespread opposition in newspapers, law reviews, and the public, leading the Court three years later in *West Virginia State Board of Education v. Barnette* to reverse its ruling (Fisher 2011, 146–52).

Another case of religious liberty illustrates why judicial supremacy does not exist. In the 1980s, the Air Force told Captain Simcha Goldman, an orthodox Jew, that he could not wear his yarmulke indoors while on duty. The Supreme Court in 1986, in *Goldman v. Weinberger*, agreed that the military had constitutional authority to require Goldman and other members of the military to conform to standards of uniformity, hierarchy, unity, discipline, and obedience to ensure military effectiveness. That was not the last word. Article I, Section 8, of the Constitution gives to Congress, not the Court, authority to make rules for "the land and naval Forces." Within one year Congress passed legislation ordering the military to change its regulations to permit military personnel to wear religious apparel unless it interferes with military duties (101 Stat. 1086–87, sec. 508 (1987)).

A Continuing Dialogue

The historical record is clear that all three branches and the states participate in shaping constitutional values (Fisher 1988). However, in a religious liberties case in 1997, the Supreme Court in *Boerne v. Flores* announced that if a conflict occurs between a Court precedent and a congressional statute, the Court's ruling "must control." The Court defended that position by pointing to "our national experience." There is nothing in the framers' intent or our national experience to justify the claim that when the Supreme Court decides a constitutional issue, its ruling is binding and final on the elected branches.

Dred Scott in 1857 helped precipitate the Civil War. *Plessy*'s "separate but equal" doctrine in 1896 met increasing resistance from Americans, leading to lawsuits that chipped away at its foundation until federal courts from 1954 to 1963 rejected the doctrine. The Court in the *Civil Rights Cases* of 1883 struck down congressional legislation that provided blacks with equal access to public accommodations. In the Civil Rights Act of 1964, Congress included a section on public accommodations and the Supreme Court upheld it. The Court in *Lochner* (1905) invented a "liberty of contract" doctrine to strike down federal and state efforts to regulate economic conditions. By the late 1930s, the Court abandoned the doctrine.

The Supreme Court's trimester framework in *Roe v. Wade* (1973) encountered strong critiques from scholars and the public, resulting in a 1992 decision (*Planned Parenthood v. Casey*) that jettisoned the framework. The Court's school busing decisions from 1971 into the early 1980s provoked such intense congressional and public opposition that the Court abandoned its policy. In *Bowers v. Hardwick* (1986), the Court upheld a sodomy statute in Georgia. Public attitudes about punishing gays for private sexual activity were rapidly changing. In *Lawrence v. Texas* (2003), the Court struck down a Texas sodomy statute. Currently, there is substantial opposition to the Court's

2010 ruling in *Citizens United*, which declared—without any supporting evidence—that unlimited campaign contributions by corporations and labor union do not result in corruption or even in the appearance of corruption.

In her book, *The Majesty of the Law*, Justice Sandra Day O'Connor offered conflicting positions on judicial finality. At times she described the judiciary as "the final arbiters of the constitutionality of all acts of government," even citing language in *Marbury* on the Court's authority "to say what the law is" (O'Connor 2003, 243). Elsewhere she showed an appreciation for the mix of judicial and nonjudicial forces that constantly shape the Constitution. She spoke of the "dynamic dialogue between the Court and the American public" and understood that no one could consider *Roe v. Wade* as settling "the issue for all time" (O'Connor 2003, 45). More generally, she said that a nation "that docilely and unthinkingly approved every Supreme Court decision as infallible and immutable would, I believe, have severely disappointed our founders" (O'Connor 2003, 45).

A judicial ruling is not fixed and binding simply because it has been issued. It is controlling if sound in substance and reasoning. In 1832, Congress decided to reauthorize the U.S. Bank. President Andrew Jackson was urged to sign the bill because the bank had been endorsed by previous Congress, previous presidents, and the Supreme Court in *McCulloch v. Maryland* (1819). Supposedly he was duty bound to sign the bill. In issuing a veto, Jackson rejected that advice. He considered "mere precedent" a "dangerous source of authority, and should not be regarded as deciding questions of constitutional power except where the acquiescence of the people and the States can be considered as well settled" (Harriger 2003, 288). He reviewed the checkered history of the bank. The elected branches favored a national bank in 1791, decided against it in 1811 and 1815, and returned their support in 1816. At the state level, legislative, executive, and judicial opinions on the constitutionality of the bank were mixed. He found nothing in the record persuasive or decisive. Congress sustained his veto.

To Jackson, even if Chief Justice Marshall's opinion on the bank in *McCulloch* "covered the whole ground of this act, it ought not to control the coordinate authorities of this Government." All three branches, he said, "must each for itself be guided by its own opinion of the Constitution." Each public official takes an oath to support the Constitution "as he understands it, and not as it is understood by others" (Harriger 2003, 288). It is as much the duty of the House, the Senate, and the president to decide upon the constitutionality of legislation as it is of judges. The opinion of courts "has no more authority over Congress than the opinion of Congress has over the judges, and on that point the President is independent of both." Decisions by the Supreme Court must not be permitted to control the elected branches when acting in their legislative capacities, "but to have only such influence as the force of their reasoning may deserve" (Harriger 2003, 288).

In 1849, a dissent by Chief Justice Taney in the *Passenger Cases* urged the Court to keep an open mind. In his view, an opinion by the Court "is always open to discussion when it is supposed to have been founded in error, and . . . its judicial authority should hereafter depend altogether on the force of the reasoning by which it is supported." Also in dissent, Justice Brandeis in *Burnet v. Coronado Oil & Gas Co.* (1932) observed: "The Court bows to the lessons of experience and the force of better reasoning, recognizing that the process of trial and error, so fruitful in the physical sciences, is appropriate also in the judicial function." The Court, as a creature of the Constitution as well, to be judged on the basis of its performance and respect for self-government, not on some abstract theory of judicial finality.

See also Church–State Relations; Civil Liberties; Democracy; Federalism; Separation of Powers.

Louis Fisher

Bibliography

Annals of Congress. 1789. This series covers congressional debates from 1789 to 1824. The discussion on the separation of power amendment occurred on June 8 and August 18, 1789.

Dumbauld, Edward. 1957. *The Bill of Rights and What It Means Today.* Norman: University of Oklahoma Press.

Elliot, Jonathan, ed. 1836–1845. *The Debates in the Several State Conventions, on the Adoption of the Federal Constitution.* 5 vols. Washington, DC: Printed for the Editor.

Fisher, Louis. 1988. *Constitutional Dialogues: Interpretation as Political Process.* Princeton, NJ: Princeton University Press.

Fisher, Louis. 2011. *Defending Congress and the Constitution.* Lawrence: University Press of Kansas.

Greaves, H. R. G. 1955. *The British Constitution.* London: Allen & Unwin.

Harriger, Katy J., ed. 2003. *Separation of Powers: Documents and Commentary.* Washington, DC: CQ Press.

Jennings, W. Ivor. 1962. *The British Constitution.* London: Cambridge University Press.

McIlwain, Charles Howard. 1947. *Constitutionalism: Ancient and Modern.* Ithaca, NY: Cornell University Press.

McMaster, John Bach, and Frederick D. Stone, eds. 1888. *Pennsylvania and the Federal Constitution.* Lancaster, PA: Historical Society of Pennsylvania.

O'Connor, Sandra Day. 2003. *The Majesty of the Law: Reflections of a Supreme Court Justice.* New York: Random House, 2003.

Pepper, George Wharton. 1931. *Family Quarrels: The President, the Senate, the House.* New York: Baker, Voorhis & Company.

Story, Joseph. 1970. *Commentaries on the Constitution of the United States.* 3 vols. New York: Da Capo Press.

Vile, M. J. C. 1967. *Constitutionalism and the Separation of Powers.* London: Oxford University Press.

Wharton, Francis. 1889. *The Revolutionary Diplomatic Correspondence of the United States.* 6 vols. Washington, DC: Government Printing Office.

Wormuth, Francis D. 1949. *The Origins of Modern Constitutionalism.* New York: Harper & Brothers.

Wright, Benjamin F., ed. 2002. *The Federalist.* New York: MetroBooks.

Youngstown Co. v. Sawyer, 343 U.S. 549 (1952).

Consultants. See Political Consultants and Campaign Managers

CONSUMER CULTURE AND POLITICS

Since before the founding of the United States, Americans have used consumer goods in ways that have had diverse effects in politics, society, and culture. Though historians disagree about exactly when it happened, many find it fair to say that the 20th-century United States can be characterized as a "consumer society," a society in which the accumulation of possessions serves to foster identities and community and in which the possessions themselves are imbued with symbolic and cultural value. The present entry will examine the political and social developments surrounding the American transfiguration into a consumer society. By examining the consumer culture of the United States, we can see how Americans used and continue to use consumer goods for symbolic or political purposes. Despite this, Americans have reacted in varied ways to the rise of what Lizabeth Cohen has called the "Consumers' Republic"; while some have embraced consumerism, others have been deeply critical of the cultural significance of consumer goods in American life. As a result, Americans have a long history of mobilizing consumer goods for political purposes, even if they often feel anxiety over the ways in which consumerism has transformed American culture.

Origins

As early as the American Revolution, Americans politicized the act of consumption. In the process of creating an oppositional movement, colonial Americans stigmatized the consumption of exported British goods, uniting geographically separated Americans in a shared boycott. This served a key role in creating American identity, historians such as T.H. Breen have argued, ultimately contributing to the success of the rebellion (Breen 2004, 1–29). Throughout the 19th century, Americans continued to use consumer movements for political means. Two notable instances were the "free produce" movement, an act of consumer activism by abolitionists who tried to encourage Northerners to only buy produce made without slave labor, and the "non-intercourse" movement, a Southern counter-boycott which encouraged Southerners to avoid buying from the North. By the 1880s, boycotts were often used by Americans to protest poor work conditions or unfair business practices. By the turn of the century, boycotts had gained notoriety as a dangerous political tool (Glickman 2009, 61–89, 94–96, 131–42).

The Creation of a Consumer

The end of the 19th century saw a consumer revolution that changed American habits of buying and selling. Department stores became hubs of commerce even in middle-sized cities, and by 1895 they dominated merchandising. Not only did these large stores collect different types of goods under one roof to make buying more convenient, but they also stimulated demand for new types of consumer purchases, such as ready-made clothing. More importantly, these stores changed how goods were sold. Business increasingly began to rely on spectacle to attract customers, eventually transforming shopping from a chore into a leisure activity that satisfied consumer desires as much as it incited the need for more. The invention of large plate glass windows, to take one example, allowed stores to display their goods to the outside public, and these displays often became a form of advertising, showing shoppers exciting examples of carefully arrayed new fashions or toys (Leach 1993, 20–26, 49–67). At the same time, merchandisers discovered the power of advertising, which developed images of pastoral landscapes and promises of abundance to sell goods by appeals to emotion (Lears 1994, 102–13).

Early progressive reformers were often spurred to action by these changes: as consumption became a greater part of each American's life, potential for abuse by business was rampant. Because shopping was considered to be a domestic responsibility, women often took the lead in consumer advocacy; the National Consumers' League, which advocated that women use their buying power to promote "ethical consumption," was one of the most prominent organizations of the time. But it was not until the 1930s when the consumer movement gained momentum. The Roosevelt administration was sympathetic to consumer concerns, and New Deal agencies often had offices that dealt with issues relating to consumer goods. But even more importantly, existing women's organizations took up the cause of consumer advocacy. Groups like the National League of Women Shoppers used boycotting to support striking workers and eventually used their political power to fight for other reforms. These organizations were especially effective at creating grassroots support; a boycott of meat in 1935 as a reaction against high prices got so much popular support the organizations nearly shut down the retail meat industry. When the United States entered World War II, these women's organization rallied around rationing, defining patriotic support of the war through proper consumerism that supported American troops (Cohen 2003, 20–37).

This idea of the "citizen consumer"—the belief that Americans (in particular women) could perform their citizenship through the conscientious buying of consumer items, was short lived. Though the war ended the Depression, it also convinced the government that consumer protection did not guarantee economic prosperity. Instead, the government began to pursue policies that would incentivize continued economic growth. Moreover, the ensuing anticommunism in the postwar United States connected consumer advocacy groups and communism, weakening their postwar influence. Both factors led to a postwar America that focused on consumption as an economic good, but that often ignored consumer protection as unnecessary (Cohen 2003, 112–18, 129–33).

Postwar Consumer Politics

Promoting consumption became one of the American government's primary goals during the 1950s, and this focus, combined with the unprecedented prosperity of the decade, created an environment in which businesses were able to reshape the American landscape. The proliferation of shopping malls was one visible example of how private institutions became central to American life. Introduced primarily in the 1950s and prolific by the 1970s, malls replaced old public areas such as community centers and shifted shopping into the suburbs and out of downtown areas in cities. Suburban malls took on cultural importance as people spent more time in them: some offered day cares and amusements parks, while a few, such as Minneapolis's

Mall of America, attracted tourists to a huge spectacle devoted to consumption (Blaszczyk 2009, 207–10).

The rise of malls had important effects on American society. First, large retailers could offer lower prices and longer hours than smaller stores in the cities. This, at best, exasperated price discrimination between the urban poor and those who lived in suburbs and, at worst, led to urban decay as smaller businesses were forced to close. The Consumer Goods Pricing Act of 1975, signed into law by President Gerald Ford with the intention of encouraging low prices for the good of the consumer, furthered this process by repealing New Deal–era laws that forced larger retailers to abide by pricing restrictions (Blaszczyk 2009, 211–14). Second, the privatization of American life posed dangers for democratic institutions, most notably free speech. While city centers used to be a place in which protestors could disseminate ideas to large crowds, newer privately owned malls could refuse to allow speech they disagreed with. In the Supreme Court's 1976 decision *Lloyd v. Tanner*, the court upheld the ability of private owners to not allow protestors onto the premises, although further rulings have left it up to states to decide how much power private institutions have in silencing speech (Cohen 2003, 274–75).

The way people used consumer goods also changed. Fashion, for instance, became less about demonstrating class standing, but instead reflected individual identities through style choices. The youth of the 1950s used blue jeans as a symbol of rebellion, and in the 1960s members of the counterculture wore homemade clothes or casual styles specifically intended to challenge the mainstream. Clothing-as-rebellion was short lived, however, in both cases. Like rock 'n' roll, another postwar consumer product, the rebellious nature of these products made them all the more marketable and turned into an identity that can be bought and sold. Today, stores like Hot Topic and Old Navy use advertising to promote the idea that their clothing offers an identity along with the brand (Blaszczyk 2009, 194–95, 217–22).

Politically, the 1960s marked the high point of the consumer movement. John F. Kennedy once proclaimed that "the consumer is the only man in our economy without a high-powered lobbyist—I intend to be that lobbyist," and in 1962 called for a Consumer

Bill of Rights that would protect consumers through legislation. Between 1967 and 1973—what Lizabeth Cohen has termed the "third consumer movement"—Congress passed more than 25 consumer protection laws and regulated many more industries. Among those laws were the Consumer Credit Protection Act (1968), the Child Protection and Toy Safety Act (1969), and the Consumer Product Safety Act (1970). By the 1970s, consumer advocacy was an important plank of the Democratic Party and key to liberal reform (Cohen 2003, 345–61).

But these reforms in the 1960s proved to be the high-water mark of consumer legislation. As conservatives focused on dismantling the liberal state of the 1960s, they targeted consumer protection as one of the key pieces of liberalism. Arguing that consumer protection laws were prime examples of liberal "nannying," conservatives created a backlash against consumer protection laws and against the regulation of businesses. The case of the Consumer Protection Agency is a prime example of fading support for consumer advocacy. Assumed to be without opposition in the 1960s, legislation to set up this agency failed 15 times before eventually being abandoned (Glickman 2009, 275–94). It took until 2010, in the wake of the 2008 financial crisis, for the Obama administration to pass similar legislation for the Consumer Protection and Finance Bureau, which finally served as a federal agency overseeing consumer issues. This has still proven controversial; Republican representatives in the House of Representatives stalled the appointment of its director hoping to stymie any effect the agency may have had (Wyatt and Protess 2011).

Despite the federal government's retreating in its commitments to consumer advocacy, consumerism continues to shape American politics. First, political campaigns have increasingly used the strategies developed by advertisers to market their candidates. Though candidates have been advertised since the turn of the century, postwar campaign managers became convinced that, in the words of 1952 Republican Party chairman Leonard Hall, "you sell your candidates and your programs the way business sells its products." In that election, Republicans hired three ad agencies to market Eisenhower on television, leaving the Democrats at a disadvantage. By the election of 1968, these

techniques had been further refined: Richard Nixon, for example, commissioned musical artists to craft campaign songs with stanzas about different issues that could be added or discarded to the songs depending on whether that particular issue polled well in a particular area (Cohen 2003, 331–44).

Second, despite a lack of support for consumer advocacy, the idea that consumption is the key to American prosperity has never left the American political sphere. On September 27, 2001, in the wake of 9/11, President George W. Bush gave a speech demonstrating the depth to which consumerism is ingrained in the political discourse. In this speech, directed to airline workers at Chicago O'Hare Airport, Bush explained that "one of the great goals" of the war on terrorism, was to "restore public confidence in the airline industry. It's to tell the traveling public: Get on board. Do your business around the country. Fly and enjoy America's great destination spots. Get down to Disney World in Florida. Take your families and enjoy life, the way we want it to be enjoyed." Though much was made of Bush's alleged requests for Americans to "go shopping" to fight terrorism, much of it exaggerating or misquoting Bush's actual rhetoric, statements like this illustrate the degree to which in American politics it is assumed that consumption and freedom are intimately linked (Bush 2003).

Boycotts and Occupy Protests

Even though governmental support for consumer protection waned in the late 1970s, grassroots politicization of consumer goods made a resurgence in the 1990s and 2000s. *The Wall Street Journal* declared 1990 as "the year of the boycott," and since then the use of boycotts, and their media visibility, has only risen (Glickman 2009, 304–7). High-profile boycotts, such as one led against Cracker Barrel in 1991 and against Chick-fil-A in 2012, both spurred by each company's hostility to gay rights, were heavily publicized by the media and served to use consumer activism to take sides in America's culture war (Noble 1992). In the latter case, while liberal activists organized a same-sex "kiss-in" to protest antihomosexual comments by Chick-fil-A's owner, far more conservative activists rallied to defend the company, buying sandwiches to show their opposition to same-sex marriage and highlighting how consumerism could be used by both the left and the right (Hsu, Hautala, and D'Urso 2012).

Most recently, dissatisfaction with consumerism, and in general with American capitalism, crystallized into the Occupy Wall Street protest in late 2011. Occupy Wall Street originated from a call for protest from Adbusters, a Canadian group responsible for popularizing the idea of "Buy Nothing Days," in which Americans concerned about consumerism abstain from buying on high shopping days (Sommer, 2012). However, the movement soon organized into a much larger protest as liberal Americans converged on Zuccotti Park in New York City. Though protestors often had conflicting goals or even understood the meaning of the protest in very different ways, in general they cited anger at corporate greed and a capitalist system that allowed a small fraction to grow extremely wealthy while the rest of the America suffered in the economic recession (Gitlin 2012, 105–10).

Until they were evicted from the park, the Occupy protesters caught media attention, focusing the country's attention to their critiques of American society. Despite the initial attention however, Occupy Wall Street fizzled out without affecting any sort of real reforms. Partly this was because of their inability to create a clear message due to their philosophical belief in complete democracy, which prevented any single leader from taking charge and demanding reform (Gitlin 2012, 92–104). But it also demonstrated how difficult it is to create a viable alternative to American capitalism and consumerism. Occupy Wall Street tried to present a revolutionary vision to American society, one that was vague but was, in the minds of many protestors, fundamentally opposed to consumerism. However, the greater American public was unlikely to be swayed by this radical agenda: while Americans might be uncomfortable with a capitalist system that allows for drastic income inequality, they also appreciate the pleasures that consumer goods bring them. In fact, as the 20th century demonstrates, consumer goods have occupied an important place in American political expression, and whether Americans find consumption immoral or not, they often use it to wage political battles. A movement like Occupy Wall Street, then, advocated a break with American political traditions, a position unlikely to succeed.

Moreover, as if to stress the precariousness of an anti-consumerist position in American politics, the movement was continually in danger of being co-opted and transformed into a consumer slogan. Among other instances, a pizza restaurant in New York offered the OccuPie and Snoringcenter.com bought billboard space for the slogan, "Occupy your bedroom: don't let snoring keep you apart." Most controversially, the rapper Jay-Z tried to market Occupy t-shirts before his company met heavy opposition from Occupy protesters. Anti-consumerist or not, Occupy Wall Street faced problems not only in trying to advocate a new type of American society but also in trying to escape consumerist assumptions (Gitlin 2012, 51–52, 153–54).

Meanings of Consumption

The Occupy Wall Street movement demonstrates the conflicted relationship Americans have always had with the consumer society. While on the one hand, Americans are often dissatisfied with the problems that consumerism brings into their lives, it is nearly impossible to escape from the assumptions of consumerism, or to argue for anything but a reform of the current system. Just focusing on the period after World War II demonstrates how Americans have debated and resisted consumerism just as much as they have used consumer culture for their own ends.

Postwar Americans bothered by consumerism have often tried to fashion lifestyles or ideologies that function as alternatives to consumer culture. Some of these, like the communes made by the 1970s' counterculture or the Diggers of Haight-Ashbury that declared all food free and staged performances against consumerism, were as theatrical as they were often short lived. But ambivalence over consumerism was more widespread than these small examples: by the 1990s, around 75 percent of Americans felt that the country had become too materialistic, and between 1990 and 1996, 19 percent of Americans had made a voluntary lifestyle change to earn less money. One commentator, Juliet Schor, termed these people "downshifters," characterizing them as exhausted by work and desiring more time at home. A segment of that group, termed "simple-livers," found consumption beyond a certain level to be undesirable, and consciously limited what they bought along with what they earned (Schor 1998, 113–15, 136–39).

Other movements focus on responsible consumption as a way to limit what they see as the negative aspects of consumerism. The slow food movement is typical of this. Arguing that current food creation systems, like fast food chains that commodify food, are environmentally wasteful, inefficient, and the cause of obesity, proponents of slow food advocate that Americans buy locally and cook their foods rather than buy premade food. In consuming food responsibly, smart consumers can reduce waste and create environmentally sustainable consumption patterns that better benefit the world. Like the slow food movement, many modern consumer movements do not challenge consumerism directly, but instead argue for judicious consumption, that is, for people to learn about where they buy from and what they are buying (Bittman 2013).

Likewise, American intellectuals have long been critical of the effects of consumerism on American life. Famously, at the turn of the century Thorstein Veblen attacked the practice of "conspicuous consumption," in which Americans around him were showing their wealth through buying luxury items. But the changes brought about after World War II spurred the most sustained debate about the merits of consumerism (Blaszczyk 2009, 3–4).

Initially, many American intellectuals were deeply critical of the effects of affluence. In the 1950s, intellectuals like Harold Rosenberg, along with prominent thinkers in the Frankfurt School such as Theodor Adorno, argued that the "mass culture" of postwar society cultivated a passive, alienated, conformist public that mindlessly consumed products. In one of the best-known critiques, Dwight MacDonald argued that the proliferation of mass culture threatened the existence of art by replacing thought-provoking materials with mindless entertainment (Horowitz 2012, 19–33).

Most of these criticisms stressed the passive nature of the consumer, arguing that consumption threatens or replaces individual agency. But by the 1960s and 1970s, intellectuals gradually came to see the ways in which people could use consumer goods in active ways. Tom Wolfe's *The Kandy Kolored Tangerine-Flake Streamline Baby* (1963), for example, was an examination into working-class teenagers in

Los Angeles who customized hot rods. Wolfe found in this subculture and emerging artistic form, one that showed how consumer products could be used to generate creativity and art. On the other end of the class spectrum, pop artists in the 1960s created works of art that appropriated and satirized images from mass culture, both demonstrating the creative potentials of consumer items and also blurring the lines between high art and popular culture by exploring the symbolic values inherent in consumer images. Movements like these stressed the positive potentials of consumer culture as a system for exploring creativity and identity (Horowitz 2012, 219–34, 280–84).

More recently, criticisms have been leveled against consumerism not for its deleterious effects on American culture, but for more practical reasons. Critiques in the 1970s often focused on the ways in which consumerism and the waste it produced were toxic to the environment. In the mid-1990s, however, Juliet Schor offered a critique based around American work habits. Schor believed that the proliferation of media representations of Americans has led to an American obsession with "keeping up with the Joneses." By working alongside people who make more money, or by watching television and seeing affluent characters, the modern American feels compelled to "keep up" with everyone else, forcing many Americans to work more than it is necessary, leading to an everlasting cycle of working to afford commodities that one can never enjoy because they are always working (Schor 1998, 4–34). Schor's solution is to opt out of this consumer lifestyle by intentionally working less and buying less, in effect challenging the assumption that Americans should always collect more goods to achieve happiness (Schor 1998, 145–167).

James Livingston, a professor of history at Rutgers, has more recently written a defense of consumerism. Livingston argues that our resistance to consumer society stems from outdated ideas about the necessity of work and the benefits of frugality. In an age of abundance like postwar America, consumer goods allow us to experience gratification, teach us generosity, and allow us to fashion identities. Advertising might stimulate desires for consumer goods, as Schor argues, but Livingston questions why this is in fact bad. Instead, he stresses how advertising offers us utopic visions of life beyond the workplace. More importantly, consumer goods and advertising allow people to fashion identities outside of work and carve out a sphere of their lives in which they have freedom to fulfill their dreams. Ambivalence over buying and spending, Livingston contends, is a relic of a morality based on the Protestant work ethic, but now that we live in an era of affluence, we should learn to enjoy the treasures that consumption offers us (Livingston 2011, 128–34, 151–61, 172–79).

Schor and Livingston present two arguments that are emblematic of the current debate over the good of consumer culture to American lives. This debate, however, is not settled, and just as some Americans continue to argue the tenets of Occupy Wall Street to those who will listen, others buy Chick-fil-A sandwiches in support of a business that espouses the Christian values they find important. Whatever Americans feel about the effects of consumerism, few alternatives to consumerism present themselves as viable options for reform. Instead, consumerism is indelibly a part of American politics and has played a major role in how Americans interact with each other and the society as a whole.

See also Advertising, Political; American Dream; Class and Politics; Individualism; Popular Culture and Politics; Youth and Politics.

Aaron George

Bibliography

Belasco, Warren James. 2006. *Appetite for Change: How the Counterculture Took On the Food Industry*. Ithaca, NY: Cornell University Press.

Bittman, Mark. 2013. "Slow Food Quickens the Pace." *New York Times* (March 26). http://opinionator.blogs.nytimes.com/2013/03/26/slow-food-quickens-the-pace/?ref=markbittman&_r=1. Accessed May 22, 2014.

Blaszczyk, Regina Lee. 2009. *American Consumer Society, 1865–2005*. Wheeling, IL: Harlan Davison Inc.

Breen, T.H. 2004. *The Marketplace of Revolution: How Consumer Politics Shaped American Independence*. New York: Oxford University Press.

Bush, George W. 2003. "Remarks to Airline Employees in Chicago Illinois." September 27, 2001. *Public Papers of the Presidents: George W. Bush, 2001, Vol. II*. Washington, DC: United States Government Printing Office.

Cohen, Lisabeth. 2003. *A Consumers' Republic*. New York: Vintage Books.

Cross, Gary. 2000. *An All Consuming Century*. New York: Columbia University Press.

Gitlin, Todd. 2012. *Occupy Nation*. New York: Itbooks.

Glickman, Lawrence. 1997. *A Living Wage: American Workers and the Making of Consumer Society*. Ithaca, NY: Cornell University Press.

Glickman, Lawrence. 2009. *Buying Power: A History of Consumer Activism in America*. Chicago: University of Chicago Press.

Horowitz, Daniel. 2012. *Consuming Pleasures*. Philadelphia: University of Pennsylvania Press.

Hsu, Tiffany, Laura Hautala, and William D'Urso. 2012. "Chick-fil-A Fans and Critics Take to the Streets." *Los Angeles Times* (August 1). http://articles.latimes.com/2012/aug/01/business/la-fi-chick-fil-a-day-20120802. Accessed May 22, 2014.

Leach, William. 1993. *Land of Desire*. New York: Pantheon Books.

Lears, Jackson. 1994. *Fables of Abundance*. New York: Basic Books.

Livingston, James. 2011. *Against Thrift: Why Consumer Culture Is Good for the Economy, the Environment, and Your Soul*. New York: Basic Books.

Moreton, Bethany. 2009. *To Serve God and Walmart: The Making of Christian Free Enterprise*. Cambridge, MA: Harvard University Press.

Noble, Barbara Presley. 1992. "Gay Group Asks Accord in Job Dispute." *New York Times* (November 25). http://www.nytimes.com/1992/11/22/business/at-work-and-now-the-sticky-floor.html. Accessed May 22, 2014.

Schor, Juliet B. 1998. *The Overspent American*. New York: Harper Perennial.

Sommer, Jeff. 2012. "The War against Too Much of Everything," *New York Times* (December 22). http://www.nytimes.com/2012/12/23/business/adbusters-war-against-too-much-of-everything

.html?pagewanted=all&_r=0. Accessed October 31, 2014.

Turner, Fred. 2006. *From Counterculture to Cyberculture*. Chicago, IL: University of Chicago Press.

Wyatt, Edward, and Ben Protess. 2011. "Foes Revise Plan to Curb New Agency." *New York Times* (May 5). http://www.nytimes.com/2011/05/06 /business/06consumer.html. Accessed May 22, 2014.

Young, Kyla M. 2013. "Out at the Barrel: The Search for Citizenship at Cracker Barrel Old Country Store." Electronic Thesis, Ohio State University. https://etd.ohiolink.edu/. Accessed May 22, 2014.

Conventions. *See* Nominating Conventions

CORPORATE BEHAVIOR AND POLITICS

In the beginning—that is, in the days of the nation's founders—corporations could not make any political or charitable contributions or spend money to influence legislation. Corporate charters (licenses to exist) were granted for a limited time and could readily be revoked for violating laws. Corporations, which included towns, churches, associations, and universities, could engage only in activities necessary to fulfill their chartered purpose. They could not own stock in other corporations or own any property that was not essential to fulfilling their chartered purpose. Corporations were often terminated if they exceeded their authority or caused public harm. Owners and managers were responsible for criminal acts committed on the job (Reclaim Democracy 2004).

This relatively tame version of the corporation began to change during the Industrial Revolution. In the mid-19th century, a landmark U.S. Supreme Court decision, *Santa Clara County v. Southern Pacific R.R. Co.* (1866), granted corporations "personhood," meaning that they could enjoy many of the rights and responsibilities of individuals. Those rights included ownership of property, the signing of binding contracts, and payment of taxes. As the Court affirmed in a separate case two years later, "corporations are merely associations of individuals united for a special purpose and permitted to do business under a particular name" (*Pembina Mining Co. v. Pennsylvania*, 1888). Thus did corporations achieve a break from their colonial past along with a greater degree of control over their business activities—not to mention increased influence over politicians and the courts (Brown 2003).

Nearly 150 years after the *Pembina* ruling, Republican presidential candidate Mitt Romney uttered the now famous line "corporations are people, my friend." Romney was seeking to quell calls for raising taxes on corporations and using the revenue to provide greater assistance to people. Unlike his critics in the audience, Romney did not see—or did not publicly acknowledge—the difference between people and corporations. Each, he insisted, would be harmed by increased taxes, and each deserved an equal measure of respect and fairness in the way they were treated.

Romney's perspective, and his boldness, might have been helped by a Supreme Court ruling, *Citizens United* (2010), that came out the year before his talk. In this landmark case the Court, in a 5–4 decision, stated that not only are corporations legal persons whose rights may not be infringed, but they are entities that are entitled to unlimited spending in the political arena, primarily in the form of advertising. These political ads, the Court cautioned, must concern ideas or causes ("social welfare"), not calls to vote for particular candidates or to join particular parties. The ruling formally endorsed the creation of so-called super-PACS, political action committees (corporations) focused on the collection of money to advance the messages *behind* the candidates but not, strictly speaking, the candidates themselves or their political parties. But as most anyone who has ever seen or heard such ads knows, these PAC-sponsored advertisements typically make it imminently clear which candidate stands for the idea or goal being promoted and which one stands against to it. *Citizens United* essentially gave corporations a dominant voice, if not *the* dominant voice, in American politics (although, to be sure, the ruling also treats labor unions and other associations as on par with corporations).

Beyond PACs: Corporate Behavior in America

PACs are corporate entities designed specifically to influence the outcome of elections and the makeup of legislative agendas. They aim to persuade—and to please, by means of the partisan images and messages they employ in their public announcements. The story of PACs is largely the story of campaign finance and the regulation of elections. That subject is treated separately in the present encyclopedia under the heading "Campaign Finance." But there is another story concerning corporations in the United States that has to do with business corporations in the traditional sense and their place in the American political economy. That is the main subject of the present entry.

It is widely recognized that the 1950s and 1960s were good times for the American economy and the American way of life. Workers could look forward to good pay and strong benefits (health care, pensions), and businesses thrived by entering into long-term commitments with their employees, their customers, their suppliers, and their shareholders. Profits and investors' interests were key components of the picture, but they were by no means the only components. If a business wanted to grow, it had to invest in the community as much as it did in the corporate balance sheet. States and localities in which businesses operated received their fair share in the form of regular corporate taxes. It was a system that seemed to work well for everyone and that few questioned or criticized. The U.S. economy became the envy of the world (not for the first time, nor for the last).

This state of affairs began to erode in the 1970s, however, brought on in part by an economic downturn. It was aided in its decline by a new brand of economic thinking, at the center of which stood Milton Friedman and others at the University of Chicago, and by a group of conservative critics that included William F. Buckley Jr. and Irving Kristol. These thinkers and commentators argued for a rebellion, of sorts, that gave precedence to the workings of the free market and the interests of business leaders. As a result, corporations began to set up lobbying organizations in Washington and to join new, conservative associations such as the Business Roundtable and the National Federation of Independent Business. Political and economic think tanks such as the Cato Institute and the Heritage Foundation promoted an antilabor, pro-business policy agenda. The order of the day among corporate elites became the preference of business over government, of commerce over consumers, of employers over employees, of stockholders over the local citizenry (Smith 2012).

With the election of Ronald Reagan in 1980 and the opening of the "Reagan Revolution," this new business vision took center stage. There was a strong emphasis on the lowering of tax rates and the elimination of many taxes; on the weakening of union organizing principles and the expansion of nonunion businesses; on the reduction or elimination of the minimum wage; on changing over from traditional pensions to new 401(k) plans, which shifted financial risks from employers to employees; on business cost-cutting measures aimed, in part, at local suppliers, who were often replaced by overseas firms; and on the need to pay top executives great sums as reward for increased profits and satisfied shareholders, even as other measures of company health might suffer. During the 1980s and into the 1990s, businesses and their supporters in government played a key role in shifting the societal paradigm toward acceptance of deregulation of industry, privatization of government functions, the offshoring of production facilities, and the phenomenon known as globalization, or the flow of capital, goods, and labor across borders. The purpose of government, it was argued, was to "get out of the way" so that businesses could thrive.

One area that grew during this period was the hostile takeover. Private equity firms specialized in identifying companies that were deemed to be underperforming on the basis of their stock prices and other factors. An equity firm would acquire such a company, take it into bankruptcy, write off its debts (shedding many or most of its divisions and its employees), and then resell it as a smaller, leaner, potentially profit-making enterprise. The biggest losers were often employees and retirees, because bankruptcy allows a corporation to break labor contracts and reduce pension debt. Shareholders often lost as well, because a hostile takeover is, by design, driven by external interests. The ones who profited most were the equity firms themselves.

Whether such "turnarounds" of companies produced lasting positive or negative effects from an economic standpoint remains a hotly debated subject today (Fisman 2012; Weissmann 2012).

In any case, by the start of the 21st century the corporation that had once held sway across the nation was hardly visible anymore, replaced by a global entity that pitted states and cities against one other as they bid on how far they would go to drop tax requirements in exchange for employment opportunities. In one case, for example, General Motors (GM) was offered free buildings, worker training programs, tax breaks, and even cash rewards if the company retained a plant in a Michigan community (Ypsilanti). A total of $200 million in incentives was provided, with company officials lauding this "win/win situation" and promising a bright future. Within only a couple of years, however, the firm had decided to pull out and was seeking to liquidate its assets. That the economic crisis of 2008–2009 hit GM and this community hard is well known and perhaps a mitigating factor. But that GM and other companies like it may continue to cost state and local governments up to $80 billion a year in unrealized returns, under favorable tax conditions, is less widely known (Story 2012).

Corporate Organization and Involvement in Politics

The corporation is managed, administered, and controlled by various stakeholders. The stakeholders such as the shareholders (owners of stock), boards of directors, and managers run the corporation and shape and execute the strategies and day-to-day operations. The other stakeholders such as employees, customers, suppliers, regulators, and society at large are also interested in proper management of the corporation. The objectives of sound corporate governance include economic efficiency and maximization of shareholder value and may include other goals as assigned by the regulators and the society. To achieve such objectives, the shareholders, boards of directors, and managers need to be honest, trustworthy, and respectful of the letter and spirit of the law. Sometimes, however, demands of the various stakeholders can conflict, giving rise to complex moral and ethical dilemmas.

For many managers, the ideal form of business regulation is the absence of any regulation. They believe that as soon as the government gets involved in private markets, it hinders the otherwise free flow of commerce. This is especially true in the United States, where business hostility to regulation is generally stronger than in Europe and elsewhere (see Prasad 2013). But this hostility is misplaced. Although certainly there are outmoded and counterproductive regulations, there also are policies and systems in place that support private markets. Markets do not exist in and of themselves; rather, they are human creations that rely on underlying rules and enforcement mechanisms to help level the playing field, spell out expectations, address business failures, and protect citizens from unscrupulous actors.

For many government officials, and for most members of the public, corporations are the organizations that provide jobs, grow the economy, and provide the nation and its citizens with the financial means to achieve progress and attain the American dream. They also are organizations that have a strong hand in shaping public policy. When most people think of corporate involvement in politics, they think of direct lobbying. It is true that many large companies spend tens of millions of dollars a year on efforts to influence state and federal legislation. Some of them maintain well-funded Washington offices as well as an array of state government relations specialists spread throughout the country. But lobbying is only one way in which corporations manage their public policy environment. A 2011–2012 study by the Foundation for Public Affairs examined all of the ways in which companies participate in politics. The four most common strategies were making federal Political Action Committee (PAC) contributions, hosting visits by public officials or candidates at company locations, participating in coalitions, and lobbying and "relationship-building" by senior executives. Other popular strategies included attending candidate fund-raisers, engaging in grassroots activism (such as facilitating town hall meetings), making state PAC contributions, and relationship-building by non–public affairs employees.

Yet these are not the only options available to businesses. More than half of the companies surveyed noted that they hosted get-out-the-vote drives during election years, and some firms published political newsletters, trained employees on political involvement, hosted candidate debates, or supported issue-oriented advertising. Many companies get involved in politics indirectly through their regional and national trade association memberships (Foundation for Public Affairs 2013).

In their political activities, as in their business activities, most companies seek to stay within the letter of the law, even while they may push the limits of business ethics and social acceptability. They may, for example, help write, through top-level lobbying organizations, the very laws that are intended to protect citizens from corporate misbehavior (Ferguson 2012). Or they may merely exploit existing legal loopholes or use less than perfect transparency in describing their operations. Such secretive, self-serving behavior is, some have argued, endemic to the corporate form (Bakan 2004).

At the same time, there are pressures at work in society that help to hold businesses accountable and keep them honest. Besides regulatory bodies such as the Securities and Exchange Commission, the Environmental Protection Agency, and similar government agencies, there are many professional watchdog groups such as Consumers Union, the Better Business Bureau, and the Center for Responsive Politics. The field of journalism has long served as an independent watchdog of business and politics, and with the Internet and social media at its disposal, it continues to do so with more vigor than ever. The laws in the United States that deal with business are many and varied, and they include recently reinforced protections for corporate whistleblowers—that is, individuals who identify illegal practices taking place within a corporation. The group WikiLeaks, known for its release of classified government documents, also has released material on businesses. One final potentially corrective force is a recent trend toward "corporate social responsibility," where companies seek to behave as good citizens in all respects—commercially, environmentally, and socially. When corporations begin to see that it is in their own best interest to act admirably in society, then all of their stakeholders—not just stock owners and executives—stand to benefit.

Varieties of Corporate Misconduct

Corporate misconduct and crime can produce economic and social harms as well as environmental damage and physical injury or death to individuals. There are several ways to categorize the various types of corporate crime, but almost any categorization would include monopolistic practices (antitrust violations), fraud, tax evasion, economic exploitation, price fixing, price gouging, false advertising, unfair labor practices, unsafe working conditions, unsafe environmental practices, and unsafe consumer products. These are examined here.

Antitrust Violations

When firms collude on prices, product features, or market territory, the central economic assumption that buyers and sellers hold regarding the benefits of market competition is violated. These firms are acting in concert with one another rather than in competition. The consequences of collusion first became visible in the United States at the end of the 19th century, when the so-called robber barons in industries such as oil, steel, and railroads created industrial giants that held disproportionate power in the marketplace. Lawmakers responded to the growing popular political pressure at that time by enacting the foundational U.S. antitrust legislation, the 1890 Sherman and the 1914 Clayton Acts, and by establishing the Interstate Commerce and the Federal Trade Commissions in 1887 and 1914, respectively. Antitrust regulations and the agencies charged with enforcing them have been regularly altered through legislation and case law since then. While the definitions of anticompetitive behavior and the technical means for measuring and preventing such behavior have changed over the past century, the basic, underlying aim has not: U.S. antitrust regulations promote competition and discourage monopolization. They seek, in short, to enhance market competition.

Recent antitrust cases often have involved large high-tech companies. In 2000, for example, Microsoft was found by a federal judge to hold a monopoly in the market for personal computer operating systems, in part because the company had integrated its Internet Explorer web browser into its Windows operating system in such a way as to limit access to competing browsers. Initially, the judge in the case called for Microsoft to be broken up into smaller corporate entities, but as the legal process advanced, a less drastic penalty was agreed to (*U.S. v. Microsoft Corp.*, 2001). More recently, one of Microsoft's chief rivals, Apple, and several publishers were found guilty of engaging in anticompetitive behavior in the e-book market. The charges concerned the way this group conspired to undersell Amazon.com, with its Kindle reader, by offering less expensive e-books designed for Apple's iPad (Van Voris 2012). Another major tech firm, Google, on the other hand, was recently cleared in an antitrust investigation looking at how that company arranges its search results—purportedly in such a way as to favor its own products and services (Alden 2013).

Fraud, Tax Evasion, and Economic Exploitation

Fraud, tax evasion, and economic exploitation have serious consequences for both society and individuals because they allow companies to unfairly increase their profits, lessen their tax burdens, and undercompensate their staffs and other stakeholders. Fraud covers violations of the Internal Revenue Code, primarily, and involves corporations deceiving the government, private investors, or other parties.

To take a recent example, Congress and the Securities and Exchange Commission (SEC) have investigated the actions of the Wall Street investment firm Goldman Sachs, among others, in the lead-up to the 2008–2009 financial crises. Goldman was alleged to have sold high-risk, shaky investment products (namely, mortgage-backed securities based on subprime loans) while at the same time hedging its bets that these products would fail in the market, thus allowing the firm to profit at investors' expense. Company officials were on record as calling these investments "crap" (or worse), and yet they promoted them to outside investors as legitimate opportunities. There were also allegations that Goldman (and others) deceived the rating agencies that assist consumers in evaluating financial products. By July 2010, Goldman had decided to settle the case with the SEC—for the sum of $550 million (a relatively small amount for such a

firm). One week later, Congress passed, and President Barack Obama signed, the Dodd-Frank Wall Street Reform and Consumer Protection Act, a law aimed at restricting the very kinds of practices that caused Goldman and the others to be investigated.

For decades, tax reduction strategies have been used by corporations to help them lower their tax burdens. The use and abuse of tax shelters, or financial mechanisms designed for the sole purpose of creating losses to deduct for tax purposes, took off in the 1990s, as accounting and law firms created and promoted tax shelter plans for individuals and corporations with high taxable incomes. Such tax shelters create large tax write-offs and, consequently, bring in substantial fees to the consulting firms that market and help implement them. It may cost a tidy sum to purchase the services required to set up and execute these schemes, but if they save a company $2 million in taxes, it is deemed worth the expense.

When corporations engage in illegitimate tax shelter schemes, they are, in essence, stealing from the U.S. Treasury. Over the years, tens if not hundreds of billions of tax dollars have been lost. Recently, the IRS and Congress have taken a firm position with legislation to impede tax shelters. They have, for example, mandated that Swiss banks no longer conceal the names of their U.S. depositors, and they have investigated technology companies, such as Apple, for allocating revenue and intellectual property offshore to avoid domestic taxes (Duhigg and Kocieniewski 2012; Lattman 2012). There are numerous other examples of tax evasion as corporations continue to exploit loopholes in the tax code.

As for economic exploitation, one can do no better than to look (again) at the rise of subprime mortgages. Under these home loans, borrowers who could not qualify for traditional government-insured loans were able to obtain mortgages. In marketing the American dream, real estate agents and brokers stood to make bigger commissions by selling larger loans. All that was needed was a way to qualify consumers for the mortgages, which in the case of the subprime market often included an inflated property appraisal. A wide range of comparatively risky loans were created and approved by bank regulators, even though the loans were impossible for millions of Americans to afford.

These included adjustable-rate mortgages (which start at a very low interest rate and jump to up to 10 times the rate after a short introductory period), "no doc" or unverified financial information loans, and other complex and risky options. Nor was the inability to provide a down payment a problem, because the loan closing costs and additional fees could all be added to the mortgage. Thus did low-income and largely urban minorities become the first casualties of the ensuing economic crash of 2008–2009.

Meanwhile, Wall Street investment firms were buying, packaging, and reselling these subprime mortgages to institutional investors (banks, insurance companies, mutual funds). Major rating agencies such as Moody's and Fitch were seduced by the lucrative business and seemingly rubber-stamped their approval.

Eventually, however, the housing bubble burst and the riskiest mortgage-backed securities became worthless. Investors wanted to reduce their losses, prompting banks and mortgage companies to initiate foreclosure proceedings. This created a domino effect whereby home sale prices fell further and increased investors' losses. In an attempt to stabilize the housing market, the U.S. Congress provided over $200 billion to the home mortgage finance giants Fannie Mae and Freddie Mac, which purchased delinquent mortgages. But the subprime mortgage catastrophe continued to unfold, its cost eventually exceeding $1 trillion.

Price Fixing, Price Gouging, and False Advertising

In price fixing, companies that are supposed to be competitors collude to manipulate the cost of products or services, keeping them artificially high and thereby maximizing profits. Archer Daniels Midland, for example, was convicted in the 1990s of price fixing commodities used in common processed foods. The company paid a $100-million antitrust fine (and became the subject of a major motion picture, *The Informant!*, starring Matt Damon). Similarly, Hoffman-La Roche, a drug manufacturer, was fined $500 million for attempting to fix the price of some vitamins worldwide. More recently, Barclays Bank and UBS paid fines in excess of $350 million and $1.2 billion, respectively, for their roles in a rate-rigging scandal

involving the Libor (London Interbank Offered Rate), an interest rate standard used by banks and other financial institutions.

Price gouging involves taking advantage of consumers during times of scarcity of products (as in an emergency), or charging excessively high prices on the basis of owning monopolies or otherwise manipulating the market. American corporations have long been accused of taking advantage of the poor, for example. "Many food chains find that it costs 2 or 3 percent more to operate in poor neighborhoods, yet low-income consumers pay between 5 and 10 percent more for their groceries than those living in middle-income areas" (Simon 2007, 12). During times of scarcity of products, price gouging is frequent. In 2004, the southeastern coast of the United States was hit by a number of hurricanes. In the aftermath of the storms, the Florida Department of Agriculture and Consumer Services received more than 3,000 complaints of price gouging by hotels, gas stations, and other retail service providers.

False advertising is nothing new, either. Consumers in the United States have been deceived into purchasing billions of dollars of products or services that never lived up to their claims. Food products giving false nutritional values and products claiming certain utility through false demonstrations are examples of false or deceptive advertising. Before reforms were enacted in 2009, credit card companies routinely promoted cards with no fees in bold print yet hid, in small type, additional charges and important information such as high interest rates on new purchases.

Unfair Labor Practices and Unsafe Working Conditions

Not allowing labor to unionize, strike, or collectively bargain are three examples of unfair labor practices. The result, arguably, is the loss of millions of dollars by employees who cannot negotiate or who are passed over for promotion on the basis of race, ethnicity, gender, or age. One of the largest alleged exploiters of labor in the United States is Walmart; the allegations of wrongdoing against the retailer are many and varied (Lichtenstein 2006). Charges of unfair labor practices make up most of the charges filed against the company, although there have also been reports of violations of health coverage among Walmart employees. Walmart has taken notice and made some changes.

In 2011, the Bureau of Labor Statistics, a division of the U.S. Department of Labor, reported 3 million work-related illnesses and injuries nationwide and another 4,700 workplace fatalities. It has been argued that such numbers are the consequence of businesses refusing to pay for proper safety measures and of federal and state governments failing to enforce safety regimens (Reiman 2007). Although the numbers have been on a downward trend in recent years, undoubtedly there is still room for improvement.

Unsafe Environmental Practices

The most prevalent form of corporate crime may be pollution. Corporations account for a large share of environmental violations. Today, they manufacture more toxic waste than ever, nearly a ton per person annually, and improper disposal of this deadly waste occurs in perhaps 90 percent of cases (Friedrichs 2009). The detrimental consequences of this are obvious: about 25 percent of U.S. residents will get cancer in their lifetimes, and a study by Cornell University finds that roughly 40 percent of deaths worldwide can be attributed to environmental pollutants (Segelken 1998). Pollution has also been linked to health problems other than cancer—problems like birth defects, heart and lung disease, and sterility. The Exxon Valdez oil spill in 1989 and the BP–Deepwater Horizon spill in 2010 are two of the worst cases of environmental pollution in world history. In 1991, Exxon pleaded guilty to criminal charges and paid a $100 million fine, followed three years later by payment of $5 billion in punitive damages. In the case of BP–Deepwater Horizon, investigations were ongoing as of mid-2013; but even in the early stages questions were raised about the readiness and safety status of key pieces of equipment used by the company in extracting oil from the Gulf of Mexico. Both criminal cases and civil suits ensued.

Unsafe Consumer Products

Although corporations may not intend to harm consumers, their desire to maximize profits often leads them to cut corners when it comes to product safety. Everything from the food we eat, to the medicines we take, to the vehicles we drive, to any of the products we use on a daily basis can be dangerous to our health and well-being. According to the Consumer Product Safety Commission (2003), whose charge it is to protect the public from risks posed by hazardous products, injuries, deaths, and property damage from consumer product incidents cost us more than $70 billion annually. Deaths occurring from unsafe products or product-related accidents are estimated to number 70,000 annually (Consumer Product Safety Commission 2003).

The Consumer Product Safety Commission oversees 15,000 different products to protect the public from harm. More than 800 persons die annually from materials that are not guarded against flammability, and another 800 perish and 18,000 are injured from unsafe equipment (Consumer Product Safety Commission 2003). Tougher laws, increased prosecution, heftier fines, and negative publicity help to alleviate the problem over time, but incidents continue to occur.

Consumer products imported into the United States from foreign companies have fueled a number of recent safety warnings. According to Schmidt (2007), roughly 25,000 shipments of food arrive in the United States each day from over 100 countries; the FDA inspects about 1 percent of these imported foods, down from 8 percent in 1992. The U.S. Department of Agriculture, on the other hand, inspects about 16 percent of imported meats and poultry, but about 80 percent of the U.S. food supply is the responsibility of the FDA (Schmidt 2007). The Centers for Disease Control and Prevention estimates that there are 5,000 deaths and 76 million illnesses caused by unsafe food in the United States annually (Schmidt 2007).

Conclusion

The business corporation has been a subject of controversy and public scrutiny ever since its development. It cannot be considered simply as a passive albeit necessary component of the free-market economy. Rather, it is an institution that, however much it may have been shaped by economic history, is also an instrument of economic and social power. A few corporations have developed a social perspective that goes beyond the usual objective of immediate profit making and is aimed instead at contributing to the well-being of society, but such a perspective is fairly rare. It is true, too, that many, perhaps even most, corporations practice philanthropy in one form or another, but oftentimes such measures are modest compared to the total revenues controlled by these corporations. These and other complex issues will continue to be examined in the future by social scientists seeking to understand the scope and nature of the modern corporation.

See also Banking Policy and Politics; Campaign Finance; Globalization; Interest Groups and Lobbying; Privatization and Deregulation; Public–Private Partnerships; Tax Policy and Politics; Trade Policy and Politics.

Michael Shally-Jensen

Bibliography

Alden, William. 2013. "Google's Antitrust Victory." *Dealbook* (January 4). http://dealbook.nytimes.com/2013/01/04/googles-antitrust-victory/. Accessed May 22, 2014.

Bakan, Joel. 2004. *The Corporation: The Pathological Pursuit of Profit and Power*. New York: Free Press.

Brown, Bruce. 2003. *The History of the Corporation*. Sumas, WA: BF Communications.

Carroll, Archie B., et al. 2012. *Corporate Responsibility: The American Experience*. New York: Cambridge University Press.

Consumer Product Safety Commission. 2003. *2003 Annual Report*. http://www.cpsc.gov//PageFiles/122069/2003rpt.pdf. Accessed October 31, 2014.

Duhigg, Charles, and David Kocieniewski. 2012. "Inquiry into Tech Giants' Tax Strategies Nears End." *New York Times* (January 4), B1, B4.

Ferguson, Charles H. 2012. *Predator Nation: Corporate Criminals, Political Corruption, and the Hijacking of America*. New York: Crown Business.

Fisman, Ray. 2012. "Private Equity vs. Private Jets." *Slate* (May 14). http://www.slate.com/articles/business/the_dismal_science/2012/05/private_equity_are_firms_like_bain_capital_good_or_bad_for_jobs_and_the_economy_.html. Accessed May 22, 2014.

Foundation for Public Affairs. 2013. *The State of Corporate Public Affairs 2011–2012*. Washington, DC: Foundation for Public Affairs.

Friedrichs, David O. 2009. *Trusted Criminals: White Collar Crime in Contemporary Society*. 4th ed. Belmont, CA: Wadsworth.

Geis, Gilbert. 2011. *White-Collar and Corporate Crime: A Documentary and Reference Guide*. Santa Barbara, CA: Greenwood Press.

Heal, G.M. 2008. *When Principles Pay: Corporate Social Responsibility and the Bottom Line*. New York: Columbia University Press.

Lattman, Peter. 2012. "Swiss Bank Pleads Guilty to Helping American Tax Dodgers." *New York Times* (January 4), B5.

Lichtenstein, Nelson. 2006. *Wal-Mart: The Face of Twenty-First Century Capitalism*. New York: New Press.

Prasad, Monica. 2013. "Land of Plenty (of Government)." *New York Times* (March 2). http://opinionator.blogs.nytimes.com/2013/03/02/land-of-plenty-of-government/?_r=0. Accessed May 22, 2014.

Reclaim Democracy! 2004 *Our Hidden History of Corporations in the United States*. http://reclaimdemocracy.org/corporate-accountability-history-corporations-us/. Accessed May 22, 2014.

Reiman, Jeffrey. 2007. *The Rich Get Richer and the Poor Get Prison: Ideology, Class, and Criminal Justice*. 8th ed. Boston: Allyn & Bacon.

Rosoff, Stephen, Henry N. Pontell, and Robert Tillman. 2009. *Profit without Honor: White Collar Crime and the Looting of America*. 5th ed. Upper Saddle River, NJ: Prentice Hall.

Schmidt, Julie. 2007. "US Food Imports Outrun FDA Resources." *USA Today* (March 8).

Segelken, Roger. 1998. "Environmental Pollution and Degradation Causes 40 Percent of Deaths Worldwide." *Cornell News* (September 30).

Simon, David R. 2007. *Elite Deviance*. 9th ed. Boston: Pearson/Allyn & Bacon.

Smith, Hedrick. 2004. *Tax Me If You Can*. Documentary. Boston: PBS (a Frontline coproduction with Hendrick Smith Productions).

Smith, Hedrick. 2012. *Who Stole the American Dream?* New York: Random House.

Story, Louise. 2012. "The Empty Promise of Tax Incentives." *New York Times* (December 2), A1, A30–A31.

U.S. v. Microsoft Corp., 253 F.3d 34 (D.C. Cir. 2001).

Van Voris, Bob. 2012. "U.S. Files Antitrust Lawsuit against Apple, Hachette." Bloomberg.com (April 11). http://www.bloomberg.com/news/2012-04-11/u-s-files-antitrust-lawsuit-against-apple-hachette.html. Accessed May 22, 2014.

Weissmann, Jordon. 2012. "Is Private Equity Bad for the Economy?" *The Atlantic* (January 11). http://www.theatlantic.com/business/archive/2012/01/is-private-equity-bad-for-the-economy/251245/. Accessed May 22, 2014.

Will, Susan, Stephen Handelman, and David C. Brotherton, eds. *How They Got Away with It: White Collar Criminals and the Financial Meltdown*. New York: Columbia University Press.

CORRUPTION IN POLITICS

The United States is no stranger to corruption. In the 1840s when the American party system was in its formative years, "the material advantages of party victory (in patronage) . . . were . . . immense" (Josephson 1938, 72). Two decades later things had gotten worse: "In response to the grosser tactics of bribery which showed themselves during the 1860s, the impulse of the professional politicians was to give regard to their own vested interests and allow the competing groups to *bid against* each other for their charters [i.e., government contracts and licenses]" (Josephson 1938, 102).

At the end of the 19th century, the leader of the Tammany Hall political machine in New York City, George Washington Plunkitt, even distinguished between "honest" and "dishonest" graft. The former included patronage jobs and inside information on business so that followers and the boss himself could benefit from political office. "I seen my opportunity and I took it," Plunkitt argued (Riordan 1948, 5). "Dishonest graft"—"blackmailin' gamblers, saloon-keepers, disorderly people," selling nominations for public office to the highest bidder, eating the "poison" of violating "the Penal Code Tree"–was evil (Riordan 1948, 3–4, 41, 98–99). But it was rampant in most American big cities, according to Lincoln Steffens, a journalist

who was one of a small band of "muckrakers" who uncovered misdeeds in political life in the early 19th century. In Minneapolis, a state that is now one of the least corrupt, " police graft was . . . a deliberate, detailed management of the police force, not to prevent, detect, or arrest crime, but to protect, share with, and direct the criminals" (Steffens 1931, 376).

By 2013 the United States was rated as one of the more honest countries in the world by Transparency International, a research organization that presents annual ratings of the relative corruption of countries. The American score was 73, with Somalia (8) being the most corrupt country and Denmark (91) the most honest. The United States ranked 19th out of 183 countries. Many European countries rank ahead of the United States, but most other nations have more perceived corruption.

The United States is now relatively uncorrupt. In Uslaner (2008) I argue that corruption is part of an "inequality trap." This "trap" is based upon these reinforcing linkages (see also You 2005):

inequality → low trust → corruption → more
inequality

The poor become trapped as clients to their patrons in corrupt societies. The well off "redistribute" society's resources to themselves and entrench themselves in power by controlling all of society's institutions (Glaeser, Scheinkman, and Shleifer 2003, 200–201). The poor who depend upon powerful leaders for their livelihood—and for justice—have almost no opportunity to challenge the balance of power (Scott 1972, 149). Corruption stems from inequality and reinforces it.

Glaeser, Scheinkman, and Shleifer (2003, 200; see also You 2005, 45–46) argue that

inequality is detrimental to the security of property rights, and therefore to growth, because it enables the rich to subvert the political, regulatory, and legal institutions of society for their own benefit. If one person is sufficiently richer than another, and courts are corruptible, then the legal system will favor the rich, not the just. Likewise, if political and regulatory institutions can be moved by wealth or influence, they will favor the established, not the efficient. This in turn leads the initially well situated to pursue socially harmful acts, recognizing that the legal, political, and regulatory systems will not hold them accountable.

Similarly, You and Kaghram (2005, 138) argue: "The rich, as interest groups, firms, or individuals may use bribery or connections to influence law-implementing processes (*bureaucratic corruption*) and to buy favorable interpretations of the law (*judicial corruption*)."

Inequality breeds corruption by (1) leading ordinary citizens to see the system as stacked against them; (2) creating a sense of dependency of ordinary citizens and a sense of pessimism for the future, which in turn undermines the moral dictates of treating your neighbors honestly; and (3) distorting the key institutions of fairness in society, the courts, which ordinary citizens see as their protectors against evil-doers, especially those with more influence than they have (Uslaner 2002, 181–83, 2008, 42–43, 49; see also Glaeser, Scheinkman, and Schleifer 2003 and You and Khagram 2005).

Generalized trust is the belief that "most people can be trusted" as opposed to "you can't be too careful in dealing with people." Generalized trusters have faith not only in people they know but also in strangers, who may be different from themselves. Such trust stems from optimism and a sense of control: the world is a good place, it is going to get better, and you can make it better. When people trust others who are different from themselves, they are more likely to do good deeds (charitable contributions and volunteering time) and to look on minorities and immigrants—people different from the majority population—favorably. They see others as part of their "moral community" and thus believe that they should treat them fairly, although trust is *not* the same thing as honesty. Trust and inequality are strongly linked: the strongest determinant of generalized trust over time in the United States, across American states, and cross-nationally is the level of economic inequality.

When inequality is high, people will restrict their trust to in-groups (particularized trust). Particularized trusters strongly distrust outsiders. They fear that people of different backgrounds will exploit them—and

in a dog-eat-dog world, you have little choice to strike first before someone exploits you. Gambetta (1993) argues that the Mafia took root in southern Italy because there were strong in-group ties and weak generalized trust there. Varese (2001, 2) makes much the same argument about the Russian Mafia: "If trust is scarce, and the state is not able or willing to protect property rights, it is sensible to expect a high demand for non-state, private protection. The existence of a demand for protection does not, however, necessarily imply that a supply of protectors will emerge."

Low levels of generalized trust should lead to greater corruption. When people don't trust people who are different from themselves—and reserve their trust for their own kind (particularized trust)—they will feel less guilty about acting dishonestly to people who are not part of their moral community. Where inequality is high, people do not see a common fate with members of out-groups, whether they define these groups in economic or ethnic or racial terms. If you and I do not share interests or a fate in common, my acting dishonestly toward you will not trouble me as much as my behaving badly toward those whose destiny I share will.

I shall summarize the evidence on the inequality trap, both cross-nationally and in the United States, especially across the American states. I show that trust and inequality are strongly related to corruption and that lower levels of inequality in the United States over time have led to a reduction in corruption from 1916 to 1974. Inequality has increased significantly since then (Uslaner 2012). I also argue that the main policy alternative that would reduce inequality, promote trust, and limit corruption is universal public education (Rothstein and Uslaner 2005; Uslaner 2008, Chapter 9). And I show that as education became more widespread in the United States, inequality fell and so did corruption.

The Inequality Trap in the United States

The United States was a highly unequal society in the early 20th century. In 1916 the top 0.1 percent earned 10 percent of the nation's income, and the top 1 percent had 19 percent of the income (Piketty and Saez 2003, Table A1 and Figure 4). And corruption was widely considered rampant. Aside from the "muck-raking" journalism of Steffens and a handful of others, Glaeser and Goldin (2006) compiled data on mentions of fraud in *The New York Times*. The number of mentions in the early 19th century (on a three-year moving average) was approximately 0.18, down substantially from almost twice that amount at the turn of the century, but still twice as high as the late 1960s (the series ends in 1974). As I shall show, corruption and inequality are strongly related. As America became more equal, it became less corrupt.

What is striking about this result is the decline in corruption. It is not easy to conquer dishonesty in government or in the broader society. The argument underlying the inequality trap is precisely that it is a trap. For most countries, high inequality, low trust, and high levels of corruption persist over time (Uslaner 2008, 26–27). Corruption is difficult to conquer because both inequality and trust levels persist over time. The United States may be an exception to this fate—either because it was able to reduce inequality (though not permanently). Or it may not be so exceptional—we may just have better data over time to trace this linkage.

Whatever the story is, people see corruption as linked to both trust and inequality. And Americans are not quite so willing to admit that corruption has been sharply reduced. In the 2004 American National Election Study, only 8 percent of respondents said that hardly any political leaders are corrupt (Uslaner 2008, 222). This finding is not atypical: in a 2012 survey by the Pew Research Center for the People and the Press, it was found that 54 percent of respondents believed that most officials in the United States are corrupt compared to just 31 percent who said that they were honest (Pew Research 2012). Ordinary Americans see far more corruption than do elites, as reported in Transparency International's Corruption Index. While elite respondents rank the United States 24th out of 183 countries, the American public sees a bit more corruption. In the 2013 Global Corruption Barometer—a survey of people in 107 countries—the United States ranked 31st, with a mean score of 3.97 on a five-point scale (Transparency International 2013).

I analyzed responses to the 2004 ANES survey in Uslaner (2008, 222–24). Both generalized trust and perceptions of increasing inequality are strongly linked to the belief that most people in government are crooked. Trust and the belief that there is a large change in the income gap between the rich and the poor are two of the strongest predictors of how many officials are crooked (after confidence in business and whether elections make politicians pay attention to what ordinary people think). Even though the United States does not have high levels of corruption by international standards, people do link trust and inequality to malfeasance in government—perhaps because they are not quite as sanguine about honesty in government as those who prepare the Transparency International rankings.

Measuring Trust and the Link to the Past

Public opinion surveys give us an idea of how people think about corruption. But can we measure malfeasance directly? The problem with attempting to measure corruption is that if it is done at all well, it is not observable. There are many critiques of elite perceptions as measures of corruption (summarized in Uslaner 2008, 12–15). However, there are few alternatives in most cases. In the United States, however, there *is* an objective measure of corruption—the indictment and conviction rates of public officials (Meier and Holbrook 1992). In 1997, according to this measure, the most corrupt states were Georgia (with 441 convictions) and New York (102 convictions), the least corrupt (no convictions) being Delaware, Kansas, Nevada, Rhode Island, and Vermont. In 1983 New York had the most convictions (681) followed by Tennessee (102), with no convictions in Indiana and Vermont.

The story of the inequality trap is "stickyness" in corruption as well as inequality and trust. But there is considerable variation over time in conviction rates. The rate in 1983 is almost perfectly correlated with the 1989 figures, but only modestly with the 1990 numbers and barely at all with the 1994 rates.

An alternative method of measuring corruption is newspaper reporters' subjective estimates of corruption (Boylan and Long 2001), which is closest to international estimates of corruption by Transparency International. The Boylan-Long measures for 47 states in 1999 have Rhode Island and Louisiana as the most corrupt. The Dakotas and Colorado rank as the most honest, with Minnesota 7th and Wisconsin 12th.

Rhode Island has a traditional patronage-oriented Democratic machine that is dominant in state politics. Charges of corruption are common. Former Providence mayor Buddy Cianci has served jail sentences for both assault (he was charged with attacking his wife's alleged lover with a lit cigarette, an ashtray, and a fireplace log) and racketeering, extortion, conspiracy, and witness tampering. He resigned following his first conviction but won reelection anyway.

Data on perceptions by reporters are subject to the same criticisms as those from elites in cross-national research. However, both have the same strength: the rankings make sense. Rhode Island and Louisiana are widely considered to be among the most corrupt states, as reporters tell us. But the conviction rates for Rhode Island are uniformly low. In 1992 there were just five convictions in Louisiana. While the reporters' rankings exist only for one year, there is little evidence of consistency over time for conviction rates. Prosecution indicators may reflect the personal priorities of prosecutors (Boylan and Long 2001, 3–4), and it may simply be more difficult to gain an indictment and conviction in a heavily corrupt state. The correlations between these measures are not strong. The reporters, on the other hand, seem to have gotten it right.

In the Louisiana of Huey Long and his brother Earl, everything was for sale—especially political influence. Earl believed that this was a formula for winning the hearts and minds of voters. "Someday Louisiana is going to get 'good government.' And when they do, they ain't going to like it," he once said (quoted in Kolbert 2006).

Former Louisiana governor Edwin Edwards, convicted of 17 counts related to political corruption, speaks to the media outside the federal courthouse in Baton Rouge, January 8, 2001. (AP Photo/Bill Haber)

Louisiana's corrupt government did not end with the end of the Long dynasty (in the 1950s for the state house, in the 1970s in the Congress). A recent four-term governor, Edwin Edwards, was sentenced to 10 years in prison in 2001 for racketeering. But before he was convicted, he was tried multiple times for a variety of different crimes and won reelection nevertheless. The capital city, New Orleans, is widely considered to be one of the most corrupt in the nation. Former senator John Breaux, while a member of the House, was once asked if his vote could be bought. He replied, "No, but it can be rented" (Edsall 1983). Former representative Billy Tauzin said (referring to the devastation of Hurricane Katrina), "Half of Louisiana is under water and the other half is under indictment" (*New York Daily News* 2005).

Louisiana has one of the highest levels of inequality of any state. It ranks last on the Census Bureau household Gini index for 1989 (the Gini index is a measure of income distribution); and in Langer's (1999) review of Gini indices in the states from 1976 to 1995, Louisiana ranked last in the 50 states 11 times, 49th 5 times, 48th 3 times, and 47th once. Louisiana's school system has the fewest number of computers per student in the country and the second highest share of adults who did not finish high school; it is also the only state not to pay for the defense of indigent people charged with crimes, leading to stays in jail of up to nine months before trial (*New York Daily News* 2005). Louisiana ranked 35th out of 40 states on trust in the 1980s, and 34th out of 44 in 1990.

Rhode Island doesn't fit the pattern quite as well. It ranked 30th of 44 states on trust in 1990. But its level of inequality is not so high: it ranked 19th in the 1989 household Gini and in the state-level Gini for 1990. However, it was relatively equal in 1969 (ranking 11th) but less so in 2004 and 2009 (ranking 30th and 31st).

The least corrupt states have the most trusting populations. In 1990 the least corrupt sate, South Dakota, ranked sixth on trust, while the third and fourth least corrupt states, North Dakota and Minnesota, ranked second and seventh on trust. In the 1989 household Ginis, South Dakota ranked third and North Dakota ninth. Over time, there is less consistency in these Gini indices across the least corrupt states.

Overall, I find considerable support for linkages among trust, inequality, and perceived corruption (Uslaner 2008, 226–27). Another indicator of inequality, the ratio of blacks living in poverty compared to poor whites (from Hero 2007), is an even stronger predictor of corruption in the American states. The most powerful determinant of corruption is the structure of the party system: parties that focus more on patronage than on developing policy—the "traditional party organization" variable in Mayhew (1986)—are far more likely to be found in the most corrupt states.

These are all contemporaneous determinants of corruption. My "inequality trap" argument is based upon the idea that corruption persists over long periods of time so that causes can be traced back in time. This view fits in well with Steffens's (1931, 407) argument that "the graft and corruption of politics . . . must be not an accidental consequence of the wickedness of bad men, but the impersonal effect of natural causes."

We can trace contemporary levels of corruption to larger cultural and economic forces in American history. These factors include the following:

- Historical support for clean government, as reflected in the statewide percentage of the 1924 presidential vote for Progressive candidate Robert LaFollette. LaFollette and the Progressives strongly focused on clean government and institutional reform. Steffens (1931, 462, 463) wrote that he "did all that he did for his public purposes" and that his "career . . . is the story of the heroism it takes to fight in America for American ideals."

- The share of the LaFollette vote in a state is a "noisy" indicator of support for political reform since people may support candidates for a variety of reasons unrelated to political reform, including the party's ideology. It is the best measure there is and works well—and are also surrogate measures for trust.

- The share of a state's population in 1880 whose parents were born in Scandinavia. The Nordic countries are the most trusting, the most equal, and the least corrupt (Uslaner 2008, 214–17). And the American states that with the largest populations of Nordics are also the most equal, have the highest levels of trust, and the least corrupt. They were also the most likely to have given LaFollette larger vote shares in 1924. Steffens (1931, 462) wrote that "Scandinavians, Germans, old Americans . . . were . . . honest men who, like the big, bad crooks in the cities, meant well and they had ideals."

- The "big bad crooks" in the cities were the sources of corruption. States with large cities will be more corrupt—so I include a measure of population density in the 1920s.

- A more educated population will be more trusting (Uslaner 2002, Chapter 4). Education is the social policy most likely to lead to greater equality (Rothstein and Uslaner 2005, 47, 51, 63). And greater access to education—over time and contemporaneously—leads to far less corruption (Uslaner and Rothstein 2013). The corrupt political machine in at least one big city—New

York—came to an end in the 1950s and early 1960s. Immigrants had been highly dependent upon local political leaders, but their children received free university education—and then formed the Reform movement that ousted corrupt leaders (Uslaner 2008, 236–41). My historical measure of education is the percentage of the workforce that holds professional jobs in 1920—since higher-status occupations largely depend upon more education.

The measures I use (as well as the years selected) come from Glaeser and Goldin (2006). And these historical measures predict contemporary (1999) corruption and the LaFollette vote well.

Even as the relationship is not overwhelming, there is a clear linkage between reporters' corruption perceptions in 1999 and the LaFollette vote in 1924

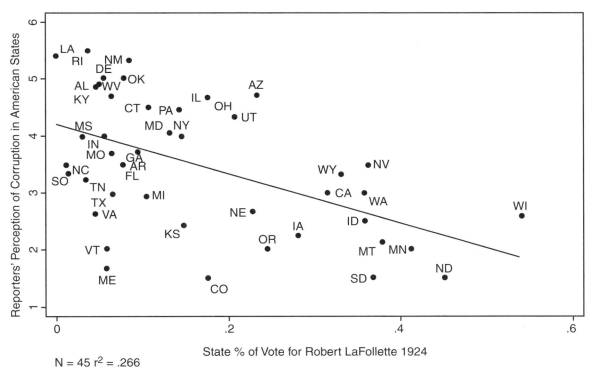

N = 45 r² = .266

Reporters perception of corruption in American states by 1924 LaFollette vote in the American states. States perceived to be high in corruption (and which are low in their LaFollette vote) fall into the upper left quadrant, while states perceived to be low in corruption (and high in their LaFollette vote) fall into the lower right quadrant.
Source: Uslaner (2008, 229)

(see Figure 3). In the Midwest, where support for re-form movements was strongest, the relationship seems especially powerful.

The professionalization of workers in 1920 significantly predicts lower corruption almost 80 years later, as does (even more strongly) the population density in the same year. The share of parents born in Scandinavia in 1880 is a significant predictor of corruption perceptions more than a century later, so that the state with the greatest Scandinavian heritage (South Dakota) would be predicted to have a score 1.18 less on the reporters' corruption scale (ranging from 1.5 to 5.5) than the state with the lowest share of Nordics in 1880 (North Carolina). This amounts to "making" Louisiana into Utah or Maryland—a substantial effect, especially given such a long time frame.

There is substantial evidence that the legacy of the past shapes corruption in the present across the American states. States with the strongest support for reform and with the most professionalized workforce in the 1920s had the most honest government eight decades later. Population density in 1920 continued to exert a powerful influence on corruption.

Curbing Corruption: The Policy Response

How do we reduce corruption? We take action to reduce inequality and the best way of doing this is through universal free education. Outside the United States, Hong Kong, Singapore, Taiwan, and Botswana all reduced corruption through a stronger rule of law,

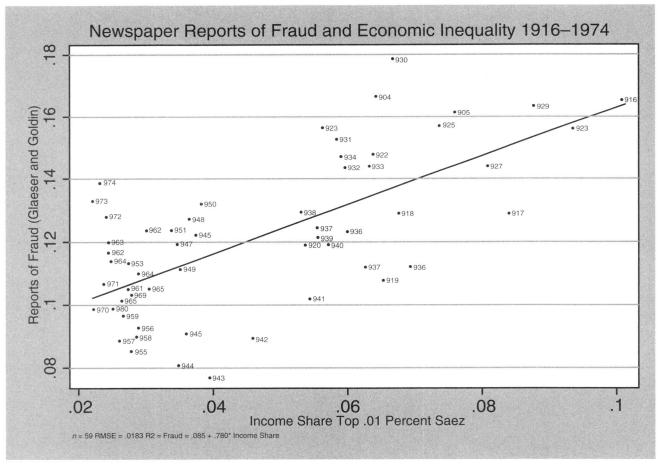

Newspaper reports of fraud and economic equality 1916–1974. As the top .01 percent's share of national income increases, so too do accounts of corruption.

to be sure, but more critically through investment in programs designed to reduce inequality and provide more social services (Uslaner 2008, 242–43). Education builds trust, but more critically it frees people from reliance on corrupt leaders for their sustenance.

The access of the children of immigrants to a free education at the City University of New York in the mid-20th century was essential in the toppling of the corrupt Tammany Hall machine in Manhattan. Rothstein (2007) argues that the adoption of universal education in the mid-19th century led to the long-term fall in corruption.

When inequality is high, so is corruption. In Figure 4, I plot the Glaeser and Goldin (2006) measure of corruption (fraud mentions in *The New York Times*) against the income share of the top. 01 percent of the population from Saez (with the first digit of the year deleted to improve readability). The years included are 1916–1974. The Glaeser and Goldin data cover the years 1816–1974; the Saez measure is from 1916 to 2010. So the overlapping years are from 1916 to 1974. The relationship between the two measures is strong: when the top. 01 percent received more than 10 percent of national income. As its share fell to just under 3 percent of national income by the 1950s through the early 1970s, corruption stories fell by half.

Education is the great equalizer. In Figure 5, I plot the school enrollment rates in the United States and corruption citations from 1816 to 1974. This is a longer time series—but we see a similar picture to inequality and corruption. When education levels were lower—at the beginning of the time series—corruption reports

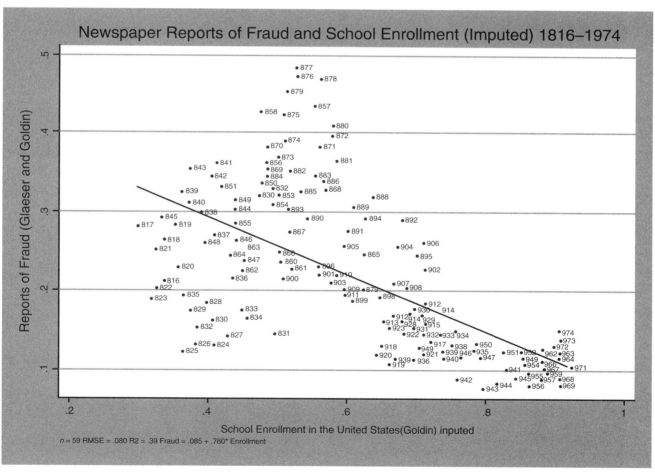

Newspapers reports of fraud and school enrollment (imputed) 1816–1974. As school enrollment increases, accounts of corruption decrease.

were more frequent. As the United States moved toward virtually universal education, reports of corruption fell dramatically—by a factor of almost four.

I used a cutoff of 1974 because there was almost no movement in the share of children enrolled in elementary schools (at 90 percent or more). It is difficult to establish a causal order between educational enrollment and inequality. When school enrollment is at 90 percent or less, education and inequality are almost perfectly correlated.

Thus, if we want to curb corruption, the means to do so are (1) increase educational enrollment and (2) reduce inequality.

See also Bureaucracy and American Political Culture; Ethics in Government; Inequality and Politics; Interest Groups and Lobbying; Scandals in Politics; Term Limits.

Eric M. Uslaner

Bibliography

Boylan, Richard T., and Cheryl X. Long. 2001. "A Survey of State House Reporters' Perception of Public Corruption." Unpublished manuscript, Department of Economics, Washington University, St. Louis.

Edsall, Thomas B. 1983. "Democrats' Lesson: To the Loyal Belong the Spoils." *Washington Post* (January 14), A7.

Gambetta, Diego 1993. *The Sicilian Mafia: The Business of Private Protection*. Cambridge, MA: Harvard University Press.

Glaeser, Edward L., and Claudia Goldin. 2006. "Corruption and Reform: Introduction." In Edward L. Glaeser and Claudia Goldin, eds. *Corruption and Reform: Lessons from America's Economic History*. Chicago: University of Chicago Press.

Glaeser, Edward L., Jose Scheinkman, and Andrei Shleifer. 2003. "The Injustice of Inequality." *Journal of Monetary Economics* 50: 199–222.

Glaeser, Edward L., and Bruce A. Ward. 2006. "Myths and Realities of American Political Geography." Discussion paper 2100, Harvard Institute of Economic Research. http://scholar.harvard.edu/files/glaeser/files/hier2100.pdf. Accessed May 19, 2014.

Goldin, Claudia. 2006. "School Enrollment Rates, by Sex and Race: 1850–1994." Table Bc 438–446. In Susan B. Carter, Scott Sigmund Gartner, Michael R. Haines, Alan L. Olmstead, Richard Sutch, and Gavin Wright, eds. *Historical Statistics of the United States, Earliest Times to the Present: Millennial Edition*. New York: Cambridge University Press. http://dx.doi.org.proxy-um.researchport.umd.edu/10.1017/ISBN-9780511132971.Bc1-509. Accessed May 19, 2014.

Hero, Rodney. 2007. *Racial Diversity and Social Capital*. New York: Cambridge University Press.

Josephson, Matthew. 1938. *The Politicos*. New York: Harcourt, Brace, and World.

Kolbert, Elizabeth. 2006. "The Big Sleazy: How Huey Long Took Louisiana." *The New Yorker* (June 12). http://www.newyorker.com/printables/critics/060612crbo_books. Accessed May 19, 2014.

Langer, Laura. 1999. "Measuring Income Distribution across Space and Time in the American States." *Social Science Quarterly* 80, no. 1: 55–67.

Mayhew, David R. 1986. *Placing Parties in American Politics*. Princeton, NJ: Princeton University Press.

Meier, Kenneth J., and Thomas M. Holbrook. 1992. "'I Seen My Opportunities and I Took 'Em:' Political Corruption in the United States." *Journal of Politics* 54 (February): 135–55.

Pew Research. 2012. "Growing Gap in Favorable Views of Federal, State Governments." April 26. http://www.people-press.org/2012/04/26/growing-gap-in-favorable-views-of-federal-state-governments/. Accessed December 20, 2013.

Piketty, Thomas, and Emmanuel Saez. 2003. "Income Inequality in the United States, 1913–1998." *Quarterly Journal of Economics* 118: 1–39.

Riordan, William L. 1948. *Plunkitt of Tammany Hall*. New York: Knopf.

Rothstein, Bo. 2007. "Anti-Corruption: A 'Big-Bang' Theory." Working Paper no. 3. Gothenburg: University of Gothenburg.

Rothstein, Bo, and Eric M. Uslaner. 2005. "All for All: Equality, Corruption, and Social Trust." *World Politics* 58: 41–72.

Scott, James C. 1972. *Comparative Political Corruption*. Englewood Cliffs, NJ: Prentice-Hall.

Steffens, Lincoln. 1931. *The Autobiography of Lincoln Steffens*. New York: Literary Guild.

Teachout, Zephyr. 2014. *Corruption in America: From Benjamin Franklin's Snuff Box to Citizens United*. Cambridge, MA: Harvard University Press.

Transparency International. 2013. "Corruption Perception Index." http://cpi.transparency.org/cpi2013/results/. Accessed December 20, 2013.

"The Ugly Truth: Why We Couldn't Save the People of New Orleans." 2005. *New York Daily News* (September 5). http://www.nydailynews.com/front/story/343324p-292991c.html. Accessed May 19, 2014.

Uslaner, Eric M. 2002. *The Moral Foundations of Trust*. New York: Cambridge University Press.

Uslaner, Eric M. 2008. *Corruption, Inequality, and the Rule of Law*. New York: Cambridge University Press.

Uslaner, Eric M. 2012. "Income Inequality in the United States Fuels Pessimism and Threatens Social Cohesion." Working Paper Center for American Progress, Washington, DC. http://www.americanprogress.org/wp-content/uploads/2012/12/Uslaner.pdf. Accessed May 19, 2014.

Uslaner, Eric M., and Mitchell Brown. 2005. "Inequality, Trust, and Civic Engagement." *American Politics Research* 31: 868–94.

Uslaner, Eric M., and Bo Rothstein. 2013. "The Historical Roots of Corruption." www.gvpt.umd.edu/uslaner/historicalrootscorruptionoctober2012.doc. Accessed May 19, 2014.

Varese, Frederico. 2001. *The Russian Mafia: Private Protection in a New Market Economy*. Oxford: Oxford University Press.

You, Jong-Sung. 2005. "A Comparative Study of Income Inequality, Corruption, and Social Trust: How Inequality and Corruption Reinforce Each Other and Erode Social Trust." Unpublished Draft of PhD Dissertation, John F. Kennedy School of Government, Harvard University. http://ksghome.harvard.edu/~youjong/dissertation%20contents.htm. Accessed May 19, 2014.

You, Jong-Sung, and Sanjeev Khagram. 2005. "A Comparative Study of Inequality and Corruption." *American Sociological Review* 70 (February): 136–57.

COURTS AND COURT POLITICS

In the United States, the judicial branch makes binding policy through the legal decisions it produces. The process by which the courts make these legal decisions has been the subject of a great deal of study and controversy. Law is a critical component of any society, and American society is no exception. The law structures the interactions among all members of society, as well as the institutions and groups that form within society. These rules provide predictability in our world, as we know what consequences to expect in a number of different situations.

Law is one of the most recognizable outputs of the American political process, by which society decides "who gets what, when, and how" (Lasswell 1958). All of the engines of government are involved in this process to one degree or another, either through passing statutes, writing administrative rules, or developing policies for the execution of the laws. But when there is some disagreement about how the law ought to be construed or applied, it is the judicial branch that we look to for answers.

Courts adjudicate disputes involving local ordinances, laws of Congress, actions of state bureaucracies, and constitutional questions. The courts have very little space for autonomous law-making. However, through the decisions they make, courts make important contributions to our understanding of laws at all levels of the legal hierarchy.

The Judiciary and Political Development

The Constitution created only one federal court: the Supreme Court of the United States. Article III of the Constitution is quite short, and it provides very little foreshadowing of what the federal judiciary would ultimately become. The Constitution prescribes the selection of federal judges and the Court's federal jurisdiction, but it leaves the rest up to Congress. This situation may have been due to the fact that delegates to the Constitutional Convention were not in agreement as to how the judiciary should be organized. Some delegates preferred a single federal court, while others anticipated the need to develop a fully formed federal judiciary to run parallel to the state systems.

One of the first bills passed by the new Congress was the Judiciary Act of 1789. It is here that we see the structure of the federal court system take shape. The

Judiciary Act created 13 federal district courts, which served as the trial courts in the federal system. These courts had a single judge each. The act also created three circuit courts, and these courts had no judges. Instead, judges would be borrowed from the Supreme Court and the district courts. This meant that the Supreme Court justices had to travel around the country to perform their duties. Travel was much less luxurious than it can be nowadays, and this made the job of Supreme Court justices quite a bit less desirable. Today's federal court system maintains this structure, although circuit riding was abolished in 1891. There are now many more federal courts, and each court is staffed with a team of federal judges.

The original Supreme Court had just three justices, but this number grew over the years. According to the Constitution, Congress has the authority to expand or contract the size of the Supreme Court bench; it has declined to do so since 1869. Franklin Delano Roosevelt attempted to convince Congress to expand the bench substantially in the face of Supreme Court resistance to his New Deal Policies, but even the FDR-friendly Congress was unwilling to go along with the plan. The Courts of Appeals have retained their monikers as "circuit courts," even though circuit riding has long since been abandoned. There are currently 12 circuits. Eleven of these encompass a number of states, and the 12th has geographic jurisdiction over the District of Columbia (the D.C. Circuit). There is a 13th Court of Appeals called the Federal Circuit. It is also located in the District of Columbia but, unlike the rest of the Courts of Appeals, it does not have geographic jurisdiction. Instead, it has subject matter jurisdiction over a number of issues of federal law.

The aforementioned courts are all appellate courts, which consider questions of law. The federal judiciary also has 94 federal judicial district courts, which conduct trials and decide matters of fact. These courts are the general jurisdiction trial courts of the system. Their jurisdiction is mandatory, which means that they must deal on the merits with each case that comes to them. In addition to these general jurisdiction district courts, there is also a system of federal bankruptcy courts as well as a Court of Federal Claims and a Court of International Trade.

Law and Judicial Philosophy

The ability of the Supreme Court to set binding precedent in its interpretation of the Constitution is the source of its law-making power. But Americans tend to disagree about whether, how, and how much the Court should use its interpretive powers to adjust the meaning of the Constitution to fit today's world. Our Constitution is quite brief, and in many of its prescriptions it is very vague. In modern times, most people accept that interpreting the Constitution's provisions is a necessity of the Court's job. But if we concede that the justices have to engage in this kind of interpretation, how should they do it? If the Constitution is unclear on something, how should the justices go about filling in the blanks? Many argue that the judges should use something called "originalism." The overarching strategy in originalism is to limit the amount of discretion that judges have in deciding what the big concepts of constitutional law require in our modern-day life.

Most originalists today use the strategy of original meaning. Here, the judge asks what a reasonable person at the time had understood these words to mean. This means that today's judges don't have to try to "get into the heads of" and "divine the intentions of" people who have been dead for centuries. Instead, they can look to the common language of the time. This is also not without difficulty, of course. We do not even have a dictionary of American English until the 1820s, which is about 40 years after the Constitution was ratified. But the argument is that this strategy, while imperfect, allows us to anchor the meaning of the Constitution's provisions. The originalist argument is generally popular among Americans, particularly those with conservative or libertarian ideological leanings (Greene, Persily, and Ansolabehere 2009).

Critics of originalism, on the other hand, find the appeal to historical standards to be quite troubling. As societal standards change, we begin to feel uncomfortable with the idea that the Constitution might allow things that we now find unacceptable. For example, when the Constitution was written, slavery was a fact of life, accepted or at least tolerated by the Constitution's authors. The "living constitutionalism" philosophy argues that each generation needs to interpret the words of the Constitution in terms of its meaning and intent *today*, not at the time of the provision's ratification. This approach alleviates the problem of having a Constitution that otherwise holds the government responsible by outdated standards.

But this is not without its problems, either. Originalism is an attempt to tie our understanding of the Constitution to a mostly immovable anchor. But, in living constitutionalism's attempt to unhook today's Constitution from these outdated moorings, it has a hard time finding an alternative anchor point. The Constitution is the supreme law of the land mostly because it is very difficult to change. The provisions of the Constitution cannot be changed by Congress or the president; instead, we must use the onerous amendment process. This is how we are able to maintain the continuity of the law.

Living constitutionalism allows judges to use contemporary societal standards as it interprets the meaning of constitutional provisions. Sometimes, this leads to results that probably aren't in keeping with what the framers of the provisions would have anticipated. For example, the Court in *Roe v. Wade* (1971) essentially "found" a right to reproductive privacy in the various different provisions of the Constitution dealing with protection against unreasonable searches, First Amendment protections of speech and conscience, and more. Justice Blackmun's majority opinion concedes that "the Constitution does not explicitly mention any right of privacy." Indeed, either of the originalist approaches would fail to find such a protection in the provisions where the majority finds this right.

The originalist complaint about this process has a lot to do with the process of "finding" these more modern interpretations for the Constitution's provisions. Instead of the interpretation being tied to the document itself, judges in the living constitution tradition must find some other mechanism for interpreting the Constitution. How do they do this? It doesn't make much sense to rely solely on some concept like "contemporary community standards" or something like that, because the judge has little claim to being an expert on this. Indeed, the Congress, the president, state legislators, and governors seem in a much better position to represent the will of the people.

Models of Legal Decision Making

Complementing these normative questions about how judges ought to approach the decision-making process, there is a large body of work dedicated to empirical investigation of the way judges actually perform their jobs. Indeed, researchers have been trying to develop a complete theory of judicial decision making, which has been going on for quite some time. In many respects, it has been successful. The major contributors have been proponents of the traditional legal model, the personal attribute model, the attitudinal approach, and various rational actor models. Together, these have yielded an enormous list of factors that have been hypothesized to contribute to the understanding of judicial behavior, with various degrees of empirical support.

The legal model of Supreme Court decision making is traditionally associated with the legal positivist tradition, emphasizing the mechanical role of the judge in the application of the law. More recently, judicial behavior scholars have developed a more sophisticated contemporary version of this tradition, most often referred to as post-positive legalism. This perspective shares one thing in common with its more deterministic predecessor—namely, the assertion that decisions of the justices should be understood largely in terms of the dictates of the laws that speak to the dispute in question. All told, the legal model argues that the decisions judges make are made mostly on the basis of the judges' knowledge of the relevant laws (in the legal positivist tradition) or, alternatively, from knowledge of the judges' understanding of the relevant laws (in the post-positivist tradition). In short, this model of judicial decision making argues that judges are constrained by the law. The decisions the judges make, then, are largely a result of what the law says.

The traditional legal model, holding that case facts and precedent serve as the sole determinants of the outcome of litigation, was called to task by Pritchett's *The Roosevelt Court* (1948). Pritchett identified policy preference as an important explanatory variable, along with some of the traditional legal factors involved in understanding judicial outcomes. In other words, he argued that Supreme Court justices make decisions at least in part according to the view about what the nation's policy ought to be. He stopped short of an empirical test of such factors, but other researchers quickly stepped in to conduct statistical analyses (Baum 2003).

The attitudinal model represents a significant break from the legalist traditions. Developed in response to the American legal realist movement, the attitudinal model is the culmination of a large and varied behavioralist tradition. Political scientists, intrigued by Pritchett's introduction of legal realist theory to the discipline, sought to find ways to empirically validate or invalidate this politicizing revelation about the judiciary.

The earliest attempts to scientifically analyze judicial behavior led researchers to probe such explanatory variables as social background characteristics (Schmidhauser 1962), policy-oriented attitudes and values (e.g., Schubert 1965), conception of the judicial role (e.g., Grossman 1968), and the dynamics of small-group membership (e.g., Snyder 1958). Each of these approaches arose out of the search for satisfactory statistical evidence to predict the votes of judges. Small-group dynamics research is arguably closer to the rational choice tradition than the others are, while the role orientation approach is closer to the legalist tradition. In terms of Supreme Court research, the attitudinal model has survived the others, largely because of its impressive ability to explain behavior. The attitudinal model derives its leverage by concentrating on individuals—specifically on the *differences* between individuals in terms of policy orientations.

The rational choice tradition, like the attitudinal tradition before it, grew largely out of theoretical advances in other fields of research. Rational choice theorists, most notably William Riker (1962), were beginning to develop a positive political theory, applying the assumptions of rational choice to political behavior and phenomena. These assumptions, although stated differently by different researchers, largely center on (1) the ability of actors to rank alternatives in terms of their goal preferences and (2) the ability of actors to select from available alternatives to maximize the attainment of these goals (see Epstein and Knight 2000). The focus of the theory is on the individual, but the theory emphasizes the similarities between individuals instead of their differences. In the

context of judicial decision making, this difference is usually manifested in the concentration on strategy as shaped by institutions. Although this is different from the attitudinal model, most incarnations of judicial strategy include explicit provisions for individual attitudes and goals.

While the attitudinal model asserts that Supreme Court justices are able to pursue their policy preferences unconstrained, rational choice theorists respond that this is too simplistic. Instead, the justices are constrained by institutional features of the court itself, as well as by the court's place in the system of government more generally. While the seeds of rational choice can be found in the early work of Schubert (1965) and Pritchett (1961), the first explicit application of rational choice theory to judicial decision making is found in Murphy's *Elements of Judicial Strategy* (1964). Although the trend toward rational choice theory in the other American political science subdisciplines grew at a fever pitch, judicial scholars largely abandoned the approach. The empirical rewards of the more behavioral strategies were more immediately apparent. It was not until the work of economist Brian Marks (1989) that rational choice once again grabbed the attention of the judicial subfield.

Marks, followed by reputable political scientists from various subdisciplines, reintroduced rational choice theory to the judicial subfield (Ferejohn and Shipan 1990; Ferejohn and Weingast 1992). Some argue that there is now a distinct trend toward rational choice theory in the study of Supreme Court decision making (Epstein and Knight 2000). Certainly, with a number of significant strategy-based models of decision making emerging in the past decade, the approach occupies an important space in the contemporary literature.

The result is a renewed debate about the appropriate paradigm for understanding judicial decision making on the Supreme Court. Traditional proponents of the attitudinal model have been reinvigorated, responding to the challenge of the rational choice theorists (i.e., Segal and Spaeth 2002). While compelling reasons for employing a rational choice approach in lower court studies are well understood, the case for abandoning the attitudinal model at the Supreme Court level is not nearly as clear-cut.

But while the attitudinal model tells us how Supreme Court justices are expected to vote on the merits, it has a harder time helping us understand processes that happen before, during, and after the merits stage. Proponents of the rational choice approach to studying judicial politics have developed many theories about the constraints on U.S. Supreme Court justices. Constraints are imposed either by external actors limiting the expression of judicial preferences (Epstein and Knight 2000) or by the judges upon themselves and each other (Maltzman, Spriggs, and Wahlbeck 2000).

Proponents of applying strategic, rational choice-based theories to the Supreme Court largely argue that such an application affords researchers the ability to describe more than simply the votes on the merits (Epstein and Knight 2000). For example, the decision of a litigant to pursue a remedy through the filing of a petition for a *writ of certiorari* is an external constraint on the judges that is not explicitly addressed by the attitudinal model (McGuire, Smith, and Caldeira 1999). Other such external constraints include the effects of public opinion, congressional policy positions, and more. In addition to this, there are internal constraints on the justices such as collegiality, equity, efficiency, and strategic considerations of the positions of others. The adoption of the rational choice approach allows for an understanding of judicial constraints, while not abandoning the idea that judges have (and use) policy preferences to make decisions (Shapiro 1995).

Proponents of the attitudinal model do not concede much to this argument. Segal and Spaeth (2002) take up the cause against using rational choice models of Supreme Court behavior. First among their criticisms of this approach is the stringency of the assumptions that are inherent in rational choice models. This is a familiar argument from critics of rational choice theory as applied to political behavior generally (Green and Shapiro 1994). Perhaps more damning, however, is their contention that the empirical evidence simply fails to bear out the hypotheses derived from these strategic theories (Segal and Spaeth 2002).

The research has begun to come full circle. Several scholars have started to take a fresh look at the traditional legal model variables, integrating them with the lessons learned from other empirical work. Segal (1984) has examined Supreme Court search and seizure cases from the perspective of the legal model. In this research, he uses a multivariate model in an attempt to bring order to the seemingly chaotic realm of Fourth Amendment litigation. His findings suggest that traditional legal characteristics do matter in these particular cases. Aliotta (1988) applies a similar approach to equal protection cases. Although her legal variables do not correspond in any meaningful sense with those used by Segal (1984), she does find that they add explanatory power to the attitudinal variables. George and Epstein (1992) also find evidence to support the inclusion of traditional legal variables in models of capital punishment cases.

The lesson here, of course, is that competing models of judicial decision making are only "competing" to the extent that they are incompatible in their approach to a particular task. A reliance on attitudes is important in most functioning strategic models, and this pairing can be extremely helpful in understanding decision-making behavior in courts other than the U.S. Supreme Court. If nothing else, it reminds us that judicial decision making involves a complex mixture of legal reasoning, policy goals, and institutional constraints.

See also Constitution and Constitutionalism; Crime, Punishment, and Politics; Supreme Court, United States.

Rebecca Gill

Bibliography

Aliotta, Jilda M. 1988. "Combining Judges' Attributes and Case Characteristics: An Alternative Approach to Explaining Supreme Court Decision-Making." *Judicature* 71: 277–81.

Baum, Lawrence. 2003. "C. Herman Pritchett: Innovator with an Ambiguous Legacy." In N. Maveety, ed. *The Pioneers of Judicial Behavior*. Ann Arbor: University of Michigan.

Epstein, Lee, and Jack Knight. 2000. "Toward a Strategic Revolution in Judicial Politics: A Look Back, A Look Ahead." *Political Research Quarterly* 53, no. 3: 625–61.

Ferejohn, John, and Charles Shipan. 1990. "Congressional Influence on Bureaucracy." *Journal of Law, Economics and Organization* 6: 1.

Ferejohn, John, and Barry Weingast. 1992. "A Positive Theory of Statutory Interpretation." *International Review of Law and Economics* 12: 263–79.

George, Tracey, and Lee Epstein. 1992. "On the Nature of Supreme Court Decision Making." *American Political Science Review* 86: 323–37.

Green, Donald P., and Ian Shapiro. 1994. *Pathologies of Rational Choice Theory: A Critique of Applications in Political Science.* New Haven, CT: Yale University Press.

Greene, Jamal, Nathaniel Persily, and Stephen Ansolabehere. 2009. "Profiling Originalism." *Columbia Law Review* 111: 356–418.

Grossman, Joel B. 1968. "Dissenting Blocs on the Warren Court: A Study in Judicial Role Behavior." *Journal of Politics* 30, no. 4: 1068–90.

Lasswell, Harold D. 1958. *Politics: Who Gets What, When and How.* New York: Meridian Press.

Maltzman, Forrest, James F. Spriggs II, and Paul J. Wahlbeck. 2000. *Crafting Law on the Supreme Court: The Collegial Game.* Cambridge: Cambridge University Press.

Marks, Brian. 1989. "A Model of Judicial Influence on Congressional Policymaking: Grove City College v. Bell." PhD Dissertation, Washington University.

McGuire, Kevin T., Charles E. Smith Jr., and Gregory A. Caldeira. 1999. Ambiguities in Measuring and Modeling the U.S. Supreme Court. Paper read at American Political Science Association, Atlanta, Georgia.

Murphy, Walter F. 1964. *Elements of Judicial Strategy.* Chicago: University of Chicago Press.

Pritchett, C. Herman. 1948. *The Roosevelt Court: A Study in Judicial Politics and Values, 1937–1947.* New York: Macmillian.

Pritchett, C. Herman. 1961. *Congress versus the Supreme Court.* Minneapolis: University of Minnesota Press.

Riker, William H. 1962. *The Theory of Political Coalitions.* New Haven, CT: Yale University Press.

Schmidhauser, John R. 1962. "*Stare Decisis*, Dissent, and the Background of the Justices of the Supreme Court of the United States." *University of Toronto Law Journal* 14: 194.

Schubert, Glendon A. 1965. *The Judicial Mind: The Attitudes and Ideologies of Supreme Court Justices, 1946–1963.* Evanston, IL: Northwestern University Press.

Segal, Jeffrey A. 1984. "Predicting Supreme Court Cases Probabilistically: The Search and Seizure Cases, 1962–1981." *American Political Science Review* 78: 891–900.

Segal, Jeffrey Allan, and Harold J. Spaeth. 2002. *The Supreme Court and the Attitudinal Model Revisited.* Cambridge: Cambridge University Press.

Shapiro, Martin M. 1995. "From the Section Chair." *Law and Courts* 5: 1.

Snyder, Eloise. 1958. "The Supreme Court as a Small Group." *Social Forces* 36, no. 3: 232–38.

CRIME, PUNISHMENT, AND POLITICS

The United States currently ranks as the most punitive nation in the world, prompting questions about the political, social, and cultural environment that led to such high incarceration rates. It has now been well documented that the U.S. increase in punitiveness was not a direct result of rises in crime. Instead, it reflects laws and policies that increased both the scope of those involved in the criminal justice system and the severity of punishment they received. Hence, punishment and politics in the United States are inherently intertwined with one another. Apart from the direct impact of politics on punishment (and the collateral consequences that follow), punishment also influences politics through policy feedback effects. These include both direct mechanisms, such as state laws that prevent felons from running for office, serving on juries, and voting, and indirect mechanisms, such as the general decline in civic engagement that follows contact with the criminal justice system. In short, politics and punishment are mutually reinforcing.

The Big Rise in American Punishment

Incarceration

From the mid-1970s until 2009, the U.S. prison population grew at rates unprecedented in history. Since 2009 the rate of incarceration has slowly begun to decline, but the United States remains the world's leader in incarceration. Apart from its size, two other striking features of the U.S. prison population are its demographic makeup and its recent disconnection from rates of crime. Figure 6 shows the rate of violent crime and rate of incarceration in the United States. As this figure illustrates, the violent crime rate peaked in the 1990s, yet incarceration continued growing despite almost two decades of declining crime rates (Shannon and Uggen 2014). Moreover, the incarceration rate is similarly unrelated to other types of crime such as property crime. Changes in sentencing, rather than crime, have been responsible for rising incarceration rates.

The demographic composition of the prison population is also noteworthy. Although only about 13 percent of the U.S. population is African American and about 17 percent is Hispanic (U.S. Census 2012), a full 38 percent of those incarcerated in state and federal prisons are African American and 21 percent are Hispanic (Mauer 2014). Further, although slightly over half of the U.S. population is female, women make up only 7 percent of the prison population (though their rates of incarceration have been growing at rates faster than men's). Put another way, white males have a 6 percent lifetime chance of serving time in prison, Hispanic males have a 17 percent chance, and black males have a 32 percent chance (Mauer 2014).

Beyond Incarceration

Nevertheless, the correctional population is made up of far more people than just those incarcerated in prisons. In fact, two thirds of Americans under correctional supervision are monitored in the community while on probation and parole. In 2009 one in every 32 adults was under some form of correctional supervision (Pew

U.S. Incarceration & Violent Crime Rates

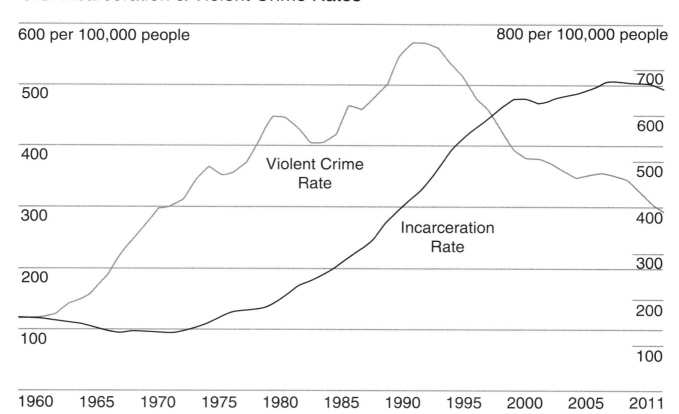

Incarceration and crime (Shannon and Uggen 2014). The incarceration rate continues to climb despite a drop in crime rates.

Sources: BJS, State and Federal Prisoners, 1925–1985; BJS trends since 1980 (http://bjs.ojp.usdoj.gov/content/glance/tables/incrttab.cfm); Uniform Crime Rates (http://www.ucrdatatool.gov/).

U.S. Incarceration Populations

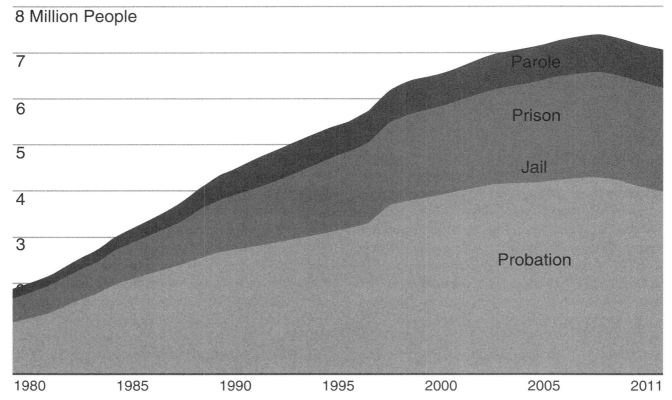

U.S. correctional populations (Shannon and Uggen 2014). Parolees make up the bulk of those under supervision, followed by those in prisons, jails, and on probation.

Sources: Bureau of Justice Statistics, Annual Probation Survey, Annual Parole Survey, Annual Survey of Jails, Census of jail Inmates, and National Prisoner Statistics Program, 2000–2011.

Center on the States 2009). Figure 7 breaks down the U.S. correctional population by type of supervision. As this figure illustrates, the majority of those supervised are on probation, followed by prison, jail, and parole.

Although it is easy to think of all of these forms of punishment as related and growing simultaneously, some important distinctions should be noted. First, although rates of incarceration and probation have grown over the same time period, these populations have not grown at the same pace. Moreover, there is much state-level variation; some states with high rates of incarceration have low rates of probation and vice versa (Phelps 2013). Also, 16 states and the federal system eliminated discretionary parole (Bureau of Justice Statistics 2014), and during this same period, there

has been a general decline in the granting of executive clemency by presidents and governors (Gill 2010).

Consequences for Individuals

Arrests, Fines, and Fees

Aside from the obvious loss of liberty that the criminal justice system imposes on individuals, myriad other less obvious consequences also ensue. For instance, as Harris, Evans, and Beckett (2010) point out, the United States has become more punitive not just in terms of the number under correctional supervision, but also in terms of the other punishments individuals receive. From 1991 to 2004 there was a dramatic increase (25 percent) in the number of prisoners facing court-imposed monetary sanctions (e.g., fines, fees, and restitution). These monetary sanctions further disadvantage people with criminal records, leading to poor credit ratings, new warrants, re-incarceration, and exacerbated racial inequality. Furthermore, one does not need to be convicted to be negatively impacted by involvement with the criminal justice system. Lageson and colleagues (2014) find that even a minor arrest with no conviction results in a 4 percentage point drop in the rate of "callbacks" from employers. This is especially pertinent, as a recent study by Brame et al. (2012) found that by age 18 between 15.9 percent and 26.8 percent of youth had been arrested or taken into custody, and by age 23, these percentages had increased to between 25.3 percent and 41.4 percent.

Collateral Sanctions

On top of the formal punishments such as fines and imprisonment, many more "invisible sanctions" follow from arrest and conviction. People can lose access to public housing, custody of their children, and public assistance, while nonresidents can even be deported (Ewald and Uggen 2012). With regard to deportation, the Supreme Court has begun to blur the longstanding distinction between direct and collateral consequences. In *Padilla v. Kentucky* (2009), defense counsel had assured the defendant, Mr. Padilla, that he would not be deported were he to plead guilty to a drug distribution charge in Kentucky. After pleading guilty, Padilla learned that he did indeed face automatic deportation. He filed for post-conviction relief, claiming that he would have gone to trial had he received accurate information from his attorney. On appeal, the Supreme Court ruled in favor of Padilla. The Court recognized deportation as a serious penalty, albeit a "civil" rather than a "criminal" consequence. Justice Stevens, who wrote the majority opinion, nevertheless attempted to circumscribe the ruling: "This decision will not open the floodgates to challenges of convictions obtained through plea bargains" (p. 3). The extent to which this decision will affect other collateral consequences remains to be seen.

Other collateral sanctions that individuals face include banishment, whereby individuals convicted of minor offenses are banned from public spaces (Beckett

and Herbert 2010), and either automatic or discretionary restrictions on occupational licensing, federal benefits, federal student loans, educational tax credits, occupational restrictions, housing restrictions and eviction, to name a few (Ewald and Uggen 2012). Even when an individual is not explicitly banned from an occupation via licensing or legal restrictions, those with a criminal record face discrimination finding work—a disadvantage that is magnified for minority men, especially African Americans (Pager 2003). People convicted of crimes also face serious political collateral consequences, typically forfeiting their right to vote, serve on juries, run for public office, possess firearms, and serve in the military (Ewald and Uggen 2012).

Explaining Mass Incarceration

Scholars have attempted to explain punishment in many ways. In 1939, decades before the era of American mass imprisonment, Rusche and Kirchheimer crafted a theory of punishment based on economic and labor market conditions. More recently, King, Massoglia, and Uggen (2012) applied this theory to criminal deportations in America, finding that prior to the era of mass incarceration there was a lengthy period (1941–1986) in which the rate of unemployment and the rate of deportation were very closely correlated. This supports the premise that deportations had been used to help control the labor market. In more recent years, however, factors such as incarceration rates have been more closely associated with criminal deportations.

David Garland (1990) was among the first and most influential scholars to address the juggernaut of mass incarceration. Drawing on the work of other prominent social theorists, Garland identified how institutions of punishment reflected cultural meanings and social relations. By 2001, well into the punishment boom, Garland had crafted a nuanced explanation of mass incarceration in the United States and England, pointing to the social conditions of late modernity, the decline of penal-welfarism, the corresponding increase of neoliberal politics, and other large-scale "indices of change" that increased penal control. Scholars have also tried to understand U.S. punishment at a lower level, focusing on state-level penal variation. For example, Greenberg and West (2001) focused on the relationship between poverty policies, religious composition, and political beliefs on state rates of incarceration—illustrating, for instance, that penal conservatism leads to growth in imprisonment. Jacobs and Helms (1996) similarly demonstrated that Republican political leadership and election-year politics helped to explain increases in imprisonment rates.

A contrasting understanding of punishment was articulated by Feeley and Simon in 1992. Feeley and Simon explained American punishment as a "new penology" that focused more on managing the risks of dangerous populations and administrative control than on punishing individual offenders. Later, Simon (2007) extended this analysis to explain how politicians became dependent on law-and-order politics and rhetoric for success. As Simon (2007) explains, political success was contingent on forceful anticrime rhetoric; law and order politics had changed from *an* issue to *the* issue. A more critical neo-Marxian explanation has been articulated by Beckett and Sasson (2004), who draw on Gramsci's concept of hegemony to explain the role of media and discourse in the war on drugs and ensuing high rates of punishment. They describe the shift from the welfare state to the "security state" as a hegemonic project of the ruling class, in which representatives of the capitalist class seek popular consent through cultural and ideological mechanisms rather than coercion, shaping public opinion via education and mass media.

Other scholars focus more squarely on race in understanding U.S. punitiveness. Loic Wacquant (2000) identifies mass incarceration as the fourth "peculiar institution" designed to control African Americans in the United States. Following slavery, Jim Crow laws, and urban ghettos, mass incarceration can be viewed as the latest system of racial control to emerge in America. Similarly, Michelle Alexander (2012) has famously called punishment "The New Jim Crow," highlighting the centrality of race in criminal justice and showing how the collateral consequences faced by former prisoners are comparable to the legal barriers faced by African Americans in the Jim Crow era. Relatedly, Michael Tonry (2011) explains racialized punishment in the United States as stemming from the Southern Strategy of politicians invoking law-and-order rhetoric to gain support from white voters and crime policies that disproportionately impact minorities—as opposed to racial differences in drug use or criminal behavior.

Finally, scholars have examined U.S. punishment using a comparative lens in cross-national work. Sutton (2004) compared 15 affluent capitalist democracies and found that politics and labor market structure, though not labor market supply, engendered higher imprisonment rates. Tonry (1999), on the other hand, argues that U.S. rates of imprisonment are so high because of American moralism and the structural characteristics of U.S. government that make punishment policies highly susceptible to moral panics. In a comparison between the United States and Germany, Savelsberg (1994) explained macro-level political and legal decision making as resulting from both the production of public, political, and academic knowledge and micro-level political and legal decisions. Finally, Farrington, Langan, and Tonry (2004) conducted a cross-national study compiling information on crime rates and convictions for six crime categories in eight Western industrialized countries, allowing for comprehensive international comparisons.

State-Level Differences

While the United States leads the world in incarceration, the nation's high overall punishment rate obscures great differences across the states. Punishment in America is both racial and spatial, with states in the Northeast and to some extent the Midwest maintaining relatively low rates of punishment, while Southern states have consistently higher rates. On the other hand, states in the north central region tend to have relatively low incarceration rates but very high rates of racial disproportionality. In addition to the quantitative research summarized in the preceding section, scholars have also conducted case studies on individual states to understand how punishment processes operate at a more micro-level. Goodman, Page, and Phelps (2014), for instance, focus on the interaction between state and national politics and actors in explaining California trends. Joshua Page (2011) similarly demonstrates how a powerful alliance between victim rights groups and the California Correctional and Peace Officers Association led to both the adoption of punitive policies and resistance to changing these policies. In Texas, Campbell (2011) points to the role of prosecutor groups and political actors (especially the governor). In Arizona, Mona Lynch (2009) shows how prison condition litigation and state politics shaped punishment in the American Sunbelt. Vanessa Barker (2006) compares California, Washington, and New York, examining how democratic processes and organization led to great variation in imprisonment. Despite these state and regional differences, however, there are similarities as well. Campbell and Schoenfield (2013) used comparative historical methods to formulate a political explanation of punishment, which included information from both state-level case studies and national studies in tandem. This research found three historical developments that fueled mass incarceration: national political competition, federal crime control policy, and federal court decisions.

How Punishment Deepens Inequality

As referenced earlier, the consequences of punishment are not equally dispersed throughout the U.S. population. Some groups, especially young African American men, bear the brunt of U.S. crime policies. Since this segment of the population is already disadvantaged relative to other groups, punishment tends to exacerbate social inequalities. As Pettit (2012) and Pettit and Western (2004) illustrate, statistics on the improving economic conditions of African American men have been misleading since incarcerated populations are not counted. This coincides with Alexander's (2012) claim that mass imprisonment disproportionately impacts communities of color, leading to the sort of large-scale group disadvantages that existed during the Jim Crow era (such as lack of political power, employment, and education). Supporting this argument, Pettit and Western demonstrate that incarceration has exacerbated the black–white wage gap by up to 58 percent.

With regard to health, Schnittker and John (2007) find that post-release incarceration has a negative impact on many health limitations, explaining racial health outcomes to a small extent, while explaining overall health disparities more broadly. Moreover, the consequences of imprisonment are not limited to those who are personally incarcerated. Clear (2007) shows how entire communities are weakened when a large share of the residents are imprisoned, while Wakefield and Wildeman (2014) identify a great range of detrimental consequences for the children of incarcerated parents. At the same time, the welfare system and the criminal justice system have become more deeply intertwined, exacerbating the disadvantages faced by the poor (Gustafson 2009; Schram et al. 2009).

Political Consequences

As we have demonstrated, politics affects punishment both directly and indirectly. Less explored, however, is the reverse—how punishment, in turn, affects politics. Uggen and Manza (2002) point to felon disenfranchisement laws as one direct example of how punishment systematically affects political outcomes. Uggen and Manza find evidence that these laws have benefitted Republicans, in part due to the racial disproportionality in disenfranchisement and race differences in partisan preference. They estimate that disenfranchisement may have affected the outcomes of seven U.S. Senate elections and one presidential election, namely the narrow victory of George Bush over Al Gore in 2000. Just as imprisonment rates and racialized punishment vary by state, so does felon disenfranchisement. Figure 8 shows a cartogram from Uggen, Shannon, and Manza (2012), which distorts area boundaries for the percentage of the voting age population that is disenfranchised in 2010. As the figure shows, states in the South (such as Florida) disenfranchise far greater portions of their populations than do states in the Midwest and Northeast.

A similar line of research explores the relationship between punishment and other forms of political and social participation. Weaver and Lerman (2010) examine how criminal justice interactions ranging from being questioned by police to serving time in prison have affected civic engagement outcomes such as registration, voting, and other political and civic participation. Overall, the more severe the interaction with the criminal justice system, the less likely they were to engage civically. Sarah Brayne (2014) extends this line of research to show how criminal justice contact also reduces interactions with banks, hospitals, and other social institutions. These studies support the idea that not only does punishment prohibit individuals from participating politically, but it also discourages them from wanting to engage. More generally, these findings align with work by Mettler and Soss (2004), who make a broader argument about the relationship between policies and politics.

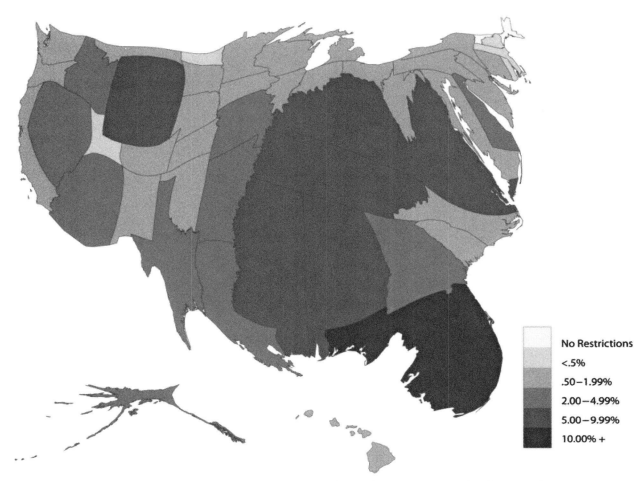

No Restrictions
<.5%
.50–1.99%
2.00–4.99%
5.00–9.99%
10.00% +

Felon disenfranchisement as percentage of voting age population by state, 2010. The diagram shows disproportionate disenfranchisement of felons in southern states.

Conclusion

Punishment in the United States has changed dramatically in recent decades. The consequences of this change have been profound for both individuals and entire segments of the population, exacerbating existing inequalities. Scholars have attempted to explain the rise in American punitiveness in many ways, all of which acknowledge a central role for politics in creating and sustaining this phenomenon. While punishment is a product of politics, however, it also affects political outcomes. These reciprocal feedback effects have made for a close connection between politics and punishment—both in explaining the rise of mass incarceration and in projecting its far-flung effects.

See also Corporate Behavior and Politics; Drug Policy and Politics; Guns and Politics; Inequality and Politics; Poverty and Politics; Race, Ethnicity, and Politics; Violence and Politics.

Veronica L. Horowitz and Christopher Uggen

Bibliography

Alexander, Michelle. 2012. *The New Jim Crow: Mass Incarceration in the Age of Colorblindness*. New York: The New Press.

Barker, Vanessa. 2006. "The Politics of Punishing Building a State Governance Theory of American Imprisonment Variation." *Punishment & Society* 8, no. 1: 5–32.

Beckett, Katherine, and Theodore Sasson. 2004. *The Politics of Injustice: Crime and Punishment in America*. Thousand Oaks, CA: Sage Publications.

Beckett, Katherine, and Steve Herbert. 2010. *Banished: The New Social Control in Urban America*. New York: Oxford University Press.

Brame, Robert, et al. 2012. "Cumulative Prevalence of Arrest from Ages 8 to 23 in a National Sample." *Pediatrics* 129, no. 1: 21–27.

Brayne, Sarah. 2014. "Surveillance and System Avoidance: Criminal Justice Contact and Institutional Attachment." *American Sociological Review* (April 4). Doi: 10.1177/0003122414530398.

Bureau of Justice Statistics. 2014. "Reentry Trends in the U.S.: Releases from State Prison." http://www.bjs.gov/content/reentry/releases.cfm. Accessed April 20, 2014.

Campbell, Michael C. 2011. "Politics, Prisons, and Law Enforcement: An Examination of the Emergence of 'Law and Order' Politics in Texas." *Law & Society Review* 45, no. 3: 631–65.

Campbell, Michael C., and Heather Schoenfeld. 2013. "The Transformation of America's Penal Order: A Historicized Political Sociology of Punishment." *American Journal of Sociology* 118, no. 5: 1375–423.

Clear, Todd R. 2007. *Imprisoning Communities: How Mass Incarceration Makes Disadvantaged Neighborhoods Worse*. New York: Oxford University Press.

Ewald, Alec, and Christopher Uggen. 2012. "The Collateral Effects of Imprisonment." In Joan Petersilia and Kevin Reitz, eds. *The Oxford Handbook on Sentencing and Corrections*. 83–103. New York: Oxford University Press.

Farrington, David P., Patrick A. Langan, and Michael H. Tonry. 2004. "Cross-National Studies in Crime and Justice." U.S. Department of Justice, Office of Justice Programs, Bureau of Justice Statistics.

Feeley, Malcolm M., and Jonathan Simon. 1992. "The New Penology: Notes on the Emerging Strategy of Corrections and Its Implications." *Criminology* 30, no. 4: 449–74.

Garland, David. 1990. *Punishment and Modern Society: A Study in Social Theory*. Chicago: University of Chicago Press.

Garland, David. 2001. *The Culture of Control: Crime and Social Order in Contemporary Society*. Chicago: Oxford University Press.

Gill, Molly M. 2010. "Clemency for Lifers: The Only Road Out Is the Road Not Taken." *Federal Sentencing Reporter* 23, no. 1: 21–26.

Goodman, Philip, Joshua Page, and Michelle Phelps. 2014. "The Long Struggle: An Agonistic Perspective on Penal Development." *Theoretical Criminology*, forthcoming.

Greenberg, David F., and Valerie West. 2001. "State Prison Populations and Their Growth, 1971–1991." *Criminology* 39, no. 3: 615–54.

Gustafson, Kaaryn. 2009. "The Criminalization of Poverty." *The Journal of Criminal Law and Criminology* 99, no. 3: 643–716.

Harris, Alexes, Heather Evans, and Katherine Beckett. 2010. "Drawing Blood from Stones: Legal Debt and Social Inequality in the Contemporary United States." *American Journal of Sociology* 115, no. 6: 1753–99.

Jacobs, David, and Ronald E. Helms. 1996. "Toward a Political Model of Incarceration: A Time-Series Examination of Multiple Explanations for Prison Admission Rates." *American Journal of Sociology* 102, no. 2: 323–57.

King, Ryan D., Michael Massoglia, and Christopher Uggen. 2012. "Employment and Exile: U.S. Criminal Deportations, 1908–2005." *American Journal of Sociology* 117, no. 6: 1786–825.

Lageson, Sarah Esther, Mike Vuolo, and Christopher Uggen. 2014. "Legal Ambiguity in Managerial Assessment of Criminal Records." *Law and Social Inquiry*, forthcoming.

Lynch, Mona. 2009. *Sunbelt Justice: Arizona and the Transformation of American Punishment*. Stanford, CA: Stanford University Press.

Mauer, Mark. 2014. "Facts about Prisons and People in Prisons." http://sentencingproject.org/doc/publications/inc_Facts%20About%20Prisons.pdf. Accessed April 14, 2014.

Mettler, Suzanne, and Joe Soss. 2004. "The Consequences of Public Policy for Democratic Citizenship: Bridging Policy Studies and Mass Politics." *Perspectives on Politics* 2, no. 1: 55–73.

Padilla v. Kentucky, 559 U.S. (2009).

Page, Joshua. 2011. *The Toughest Beat: Politics, Punishment, and the Prison Officers Union in California*. New York: Oxford University Press.

Pager, Devah. 2003. "The Mark of a Criminal Record." *American Journal of Sociology* 108, no. 5: 937–75.

Pettit, Becky. 2012. *Invisible Men: Mass Incarceration and the Myth of Black Progress*. New York: Russell Sage.

Pettit, Becky, and Bruce Western. 2004. "Mass Imprisonment and the Life Course: Race and Class Inequality in U.S. Incarceration." *American Sociological Review* 69, no. 2: 151–69.

Pew Center on the States. 2009. "One in 31: The Long Reach of American Corrections." Washington, DC: The Pew Charitable Trusts.

Phelps, Michelle. 2013. "The Paradox of Probation: Understanding the Expansion of an 'Alternative' to Incarceration during the Prison Boom." PhD Dissertation, Princeton University, Princeton, NJ.

Savelsberg, Joachim J. 1994. "Knowledge, Domination, and Criminal Punishment." *American Journal of Sociology* 99, no. 4: 911–43.

Schnittker, Jason, and Andrea John. 2007. "Enduring Stigma: The Long-Term Effects of Incarceration on Health." *Journal of Health and Social Behavior* 48, no. 2: 115–30.

Schram, Sanford F., et al. 2009. "Deciding to Discipline: Race, Choice, and Punishment at the Frontlines of Welfare Reform." *American Sociological Review* 74, no. 3: 398–422.

Shannon, Sarah S., and Christopher Uggen. 2014. "Visualizing Punishment." In Douglas Hartmann and Christopher Uggen, eds. *Crime and the Punished*. New York: W.W. Norton, pp. 42–62

Simon, Jonathan. 2007. *Governing through Crime: How the War on Crime Transformed American Democracy and Created a Culture of Fear*. New York: Oxford University Press.

Sutton, John R. 2004. "The Political Economy of Imprisonment in Affluent Western Democracies, 1960–1990." *American Sociological Review* 69, no. 2: 170–89.

Tonry, Michael. 1999. "Why Are U.S. Incarceration Rates So High?" *Crime & Delinquency* 45, no. 4: 419–37.

Tonry, Michael. 2011. *Punishing Race: A Continuing American Dilemma*. New York: Oxford University Press.

Uggen, Christopher, and Jeff Manza. 2002. "Democratic Contraction? Political Consequences of Felon Disenfranchisement in the United States." *American Sociological Review* 67, no. 6: 777–803.

Uggen, Christopher, Sarah Shannon, and Jeff Manza. 2012. "State-level Estimates of Felon Disenfranchisement in the United States, 2010." Washington, DC: Sentencing Project.

U.S. Census Bureau. 2012. "State and County Quickfacts: USA." http://quickfacts.census.gov/qfd/states/00000.html. Accessed April 15, 2014.

Wacquant, Loic. 2000. "The New 'Peculiar Institution': On the Prison as Surrogate Ghetto." *Theoretical Criminology* 4, no. 3: 377–89.

Wakefield, Sara, and Christopher James Wildeman. 2014. *Children of the Prison Boom: Mass Incarceration and the Future of American Inequality*. Oxford: Oxford University Press.

Weaver, Vesla M., and Amy E. Lerman. 2010. "Political Consequences of the Carceral State." *American Political Science Review* 104, no. 4: 817–33.

CRISES, EMERGENCIES, AND POLITICS

A crisis is something that most people and organizations try to avoid. In general, a crisis is some type of breakdown in a system that creates stress (Perry 2007). People tend to associate crises with negative factors. For instance, corporations frequently experience financial loss and reputational damage from crises such as industrial accidents and product recalls (Coombs 2012). Crises are related to emergencies. An emergency is a situation that demands immediate action because there is a threat to health, life, property, and/or the environment. Emergencies usually are sudden and create an urgent need for relief or assistance. Castles (2010) refers to emergencies as "black swans" because they are statistical outliers—unusual events. Examples of emergencies could include a tornado wreaking devastation on a town, terrorist attacks, armed conflicts, or an economic depression. An emergency might evolve into a crisis, and some crises have an emergency component. For example, a tornado could become a crisis if it damages the ability of private and public organizations to deliver goods and services. An industrial accident could be an emergency if it threatens the health and safety of employees and community members living near the facility.

While distinct on some levels, crisis and emergencies belong to the same general class of external shocks that create periods of disorder (Nohrstedt and Weible 2010). Though there are distinctions, researchers commonly use the terms "crisis" and "emergency" interchangeably (Boin and 't Hart 2010), especially in the political context. People and organizations typically seek to avoid such external shocks. In politics, however, crises often are cultivated and emergencies are often exploited to build support for a policy or a candidate. A crisis or an emergency can, in that sense, be a political resource. The present entry follows the lead of Boin and 't Hart (2010) by treating crises and emergencies as similar concepts.

Threatening situations can be used to pursue a political objective. Some have argued that crises serve a key role in creating major policy changes: they expose problems and create the need for change (e.g., Birkland 1997). However, research has shown mixed results for crises as events that actually drive policy changes (Nohrstedt and Weible 2010). The creation of significant policy change is more often a function of a politician's skill at exploiting a crisis than it is the mere existence of a crisis. A crisis is a necessary but not a sufficient condition to generate significant policy change. Exploiting a crisis is a function of communication. The skill in how politicians communicate about a crisis often determines the success or failure of that crisis as a stimulus for significant policy change. But politics is also competitive—meaning that other politicians will challenge any efforts to exploit a crisis and seek to defend the status quo. The result can be a more skilled opponent blocking efforts to create change by means of a crisis.

Crises as a Political Resource in Policy Making

Political researchers have demonstrated a keen interest in exploring how crises actually influence policy

making. More precisely, researchers have studied the factors that determine whether a crisis comes to be translated into significant, as opposed to incremental, policy change. Significant policy change is a critical topic because it is, of course, difficult to accomplish (Castles 2010). Much early research in this area concerned presidential rhetoric, because of its importance with respect to policy and policy change. Later research shifted to framing—that is, arranging or adjusting a message to serve a purpose—and the inclusion of other political actors besides presidents.

Presidential rhetoric was the first research area to be examined in terms of the way crises can be leveraged to create policy change. The power of presidents lies in their ability to persuade others to follow or support their preferred courses of action. Presidents find crises can be useful political tools that help to create a "persuasive advantage" (Bostdorff 1994, 5). Consider the example of a president seeking to pursue a particular course of action but being unsure whether he or she can generate the necessary support for that action. A crisis is then discovered that threatens the country in some respect. In due course, the president's desired course of action is presented as the perfect response to that crisis. Thus is a crisis used to craft the rationale for a president's policy. Presidents have used crises in this way to justify their actions, particularly the need for military intervention (Bostdorff 1994).

The concept of the "focusing event" is often used in this context. A focusing event is "an event that is sudden, relatively rare, can be reasonably defined as harmful or revealing the possibility of potentially greater future harms, inflicts harms or suggests potential harms that are or could be concentrated on a definable geographical area or community of interest, and that is known to policy makers and the public virtually simultaneously" (Birkland 1997, 22). Not all crises qualify as focusing events. For instance, there are thousands of tornadoes each year in the United States. A typical tornado is not a focusing event because it is relatively common. However, a massive tornado that destroys an entire town is a comparatively rare phenomena and can be considered a focusing event. Politicians, likewise, need to articulate why "their" crisis is a focusing event if they hope to tap into public sentiment and exploit the potential of that crisis for steering policy or changing policy directions.

There are four advantages to be gained from a crisis serving as a focusing event: (1) having the attention of the public (or various publics); (2) generating a sense of urgency; (3) uniting people behind a common cause or purpose; and (4) emphasizing the need for short-term actions. By means of its attention-getting and urgency-creation functions, a crisis serves to provide a rationale for immediate action. Such action can include policy changes. The focusing event also helps to generate support for the policy change. People are led to conclude that they should rally around the action (policy change) even if it requires short-term sacrifice. Crises have served as common rationales for a variety of policy changes and administrative actions such as budget expenditures or the reorganization of governmental agencies. Consider how the Patriot Act altered

policies following the terrorist attacks of 9/11. International issues are commonly used when presidents seek to promote a crisis. International issues, even today, are remote and people rely on the expertise of the government to interpret those issues.

Crises also can be used by Presidents to distract people from problems. If a particular political problem seems to be hurting a president, the appearance of a crisis creates a distraction in the sense that it demands everyone's attention. In most instances, international problems have been used to distract people from domestic problems. When the news media follow such crises, people tend to lose interest in the troublesome domestic issue and attend instead to the new international crisis. People forget about the local problem in favor of the larger concern. By managing crises effectively, presidents and other political actors can rebuild political support (Bostdorff 1994). Distraction through

President George W. Bush meets with his national security advisers in the White House situation room on September 20, 2001. (AP Photo/White House, Eric Draper)

use of crisis works because both the news media and the populace have a limited attention span and tend to concentrate on the latest and greatest issue.

Kuypers (1997) articulated the view of crises as a means for presidents to *frame* issues. In general, a frame tells people how to interpret an event by emphasizing certain aspects of the event and ignoring or downplaying other aspects. A frame is valuable in politics because defining the problem also helps to define the solution. A crisis establishes a frame according to which action, not debate, is required. Presidents can advance policies by framing situations *as* crisis and taking immediate action in the desired direction. Presidents simply need to promote the right crisis to justify the actions they wish to take or the policy they want to implement. Framing works best when a crisis is slow and ambiguous. A slow crisis gives the president's team time to craft the right crisis frame while the ambiguity of the crisis allows for latitude in how the frame is ultimately crafted. In contrast, event-based crises and emergencies, such as natural disasters, are more resistant to framing because of the obvious need for action (Kuypers 1997).

Boin, 't Hart, and McConnell (2009) extended framing to other politicians besides presidents with their "crisis exploitation theory." This theory builds from the idea of agenda setting (i.e., identifying and building support for particular issues) and sees political framing as a contest, of sorts. Crises are a means of placing a policy change on the agenda by drawing attention to the need for that change. Politicians attempt to utilize crisis rhetoric to generate political support to create an actual policy change. However, multiple political actors compete to establish the frame for understanding the crisis. Three types of frames have been among the most widely discussed: (1) denial, (2) threat, and (3) opportunity. A "denial" frame is one that suggests that there is no crisis; denial seeks to prevent others from using a crisis to stimulate change. A "threat" frame acknowledges that a crisis exists and even allows that the crisis may form a threat, but it does not see the need for instituting change. Finally, an "opportunity" frame recognizes that a threat exists and welcomes the need for change to address the problems raised by the crisis.

There are also the matters of significance and causality to consider. Significance has to do with whether a crisis is regarded as something worth attending to or is regarded, rather, as something that can easily be dismissed. (A denial frame seeks to minimize crisis significance; a threat frame recognizes the significance of a crisis; an opportunity frame tries to maximize significance to encourage change.) Causality, in turn, concerns that which precipitated the crisis. Endogenous (or endogenic) crises are those that result from existing policies or what politicians—the status quo—did or did not do. An economic downturn not directly related to international markets would be an endogenous crisis. Exogenous (or exogenic) crises, on the other hand, are those that result from external factors and would include natural disasters and terror attacks. (An opportunity frame would emphasize exogenous causality, while a threat frame favors endogenous causality.)

Crises, then, can have applications for policy making. Crisis exploitation theory views crisis frames as competition between those seeking to create policy change and those trying to prevent policy change. Crisis rhetoric can be used to incite people to change or to calm people into quiescence. Politicians of the status quo try to resist efforts by those seeking change or try to minimize such efforts through advancing incremental change. A crisis that is minor and exogenous does not require action; the status quo argues for keeping the current system in place. A crisis, however, that is framed as significant and endogenous indicates the need to change the status quo; such crises suggest that the status quo has failed. Significant exogenous crises can be used to argue for change, as well. Though the cause may be external, measures might be implemented that can reduce the likelihood of a crisis repeating itself. Significant crises are forms of focusing events. When properly exploited, a focusing event can result in significant policy changes. However, the mere occurrence of a focusing event does not guarantee that there will be any form of change, significant or incremental. Rather, politicians must effectively exploit the crisis to stimulate political change. Moreover, competing crisis frames emerge naturally owing to the conflict inherent in politics (Boin, 't Hart, and McConnell 2009).

The tradition news media are participants in the framing contest. The news media constitute a resource that politicians can utilize in efforts to frame a crisis.

Essentially, politicians seek to influence news media coverage so that that coverage supports their preferred crisis frame. This is part of the "skillful exploitation" of crises by politicians (Nohrstedt and Weible 2010). The winner is determined by which frame garners the strongest support from the public (or publics).

The contest between opposing factions can extend beyond the framing of the crisis. If a crisis creates a frame that demands action, politicians can use symbolic action to create quiescence. This symbolic reassurance calms agitated publics while not creating any substantive changes (Edelman 1985). Symbolic action creates the illusion of change and can create the same quiescence effect as a material change. Policies are created, typically incremental change, but new policies do not materially alter the current situation. However, people see a new policy—the symbolic action—has been implemented and return to a quiescent state. They are reassured that action has been taken to address the crisis and move on to other concerns (Coombs and Holladay 2011). In the framing competition, symbolic reassurance is a vital resource for those political actors seeking to prevent change. When opponents have created an active call for change because of a crisis, symbolic reassurance addresses that call without significant change, thereby protecting the status quo. Politicians might lose the battle to frame the crisis but can still succeed in framing the means to address the problems presented by the crisis.

Crises and Performance

Event-based (exogenous) crises, typically emergencies, sometimes demand that substantive action be taken by politicians. When thousands of people are left homeless after a natural disaster, politicians cannot "frame away" the need for action. As noted, such crises are difficult to frame because their frames arise naturally and dominate media coverage of the emergency.

Such event-based crises, then, add a performance dimension to a situation. The crisis becomes an emergency demanding attention—some action must be taken. A common example is the need to provide relief and aid to people impacted by natural disasters. Common actions after an emergency include evacuating people, providing temporary shelter, providing food and water, and repairing the infrastructure damage created by the emergency.

However, performance also precedes the emergency. Part of crisis/emergency management is preparation and mitigation. Preparation is designed to have people ready to react when an emergency occurs. First responders and potential victims should be prepared. First responders must have the training and resources to be prepared. Potential victims should have plans in place and know in advance their responsibilities during an emergency. Mitigation involves efforts to reduce the damage from an emergency or the likelihood of its occurrence. Politicians can create policies and allocate resources to aid mitigation. Policy examples include strengthening building codes in areas subject to hurricanes and having zoning regulations that prevent construction in flood zones. Allocation of resources includes projects to prevent flooding and purchasing equipment for first responders. After an emergency, the news media help to reveal whether politicians have acted to help or to hinder preparation and mitigation. Problems involving decades of political neglect in the area of prevention and mitigation only intensified the damage caused by Hurricane Katrina in 2005.

Politicians are judged on their performance in an emergency. The initial evaluation will be on the response to an emergency. For instance, the Bush administration was severely criticized for its ineffective response during hurricane Katrina. The evaluation of the crisis performance adds to the framing process. An effective crisis performance bolsters the status quo because the political actors are viewed as having met the challenge and fighting off the crisis successfully. Subsequently, any efforts toward prevention and mitigation are examined to determine whether politicians have taken the necessary steps. Some responsibility for an emergency will fall to a politician who cannot successfully place blame on external events. Effective crisis performance tends to promote quiescence or at least limit any change to incremental change. An ineffective crisis performance reinforces the position of change advocates regarding the flawed nature of the status quo and arguments for altering it. That is, ineffective crisis performance reinforces the view that significant change is needed.

Crisis and the Effects on Political Careers

As with policy change, crises can also have an effect on political careers, including the outcome of elections (Boin, 't Hart, and McConnell 2009). The effects of crises on political careers include (1) damage, (2) reinvigoration, and (3) escape. "Damage" means that a crisis has resulted in the decline of a politician's reputation or career. "Reinvigoration" occurs when a politician benefits from the crisis. "Escape" is when a politician avoids blame for a crisis or can diffuse the blame across a large number of political actors (Boin, 't Hart, and McConnell 2009).

Timing and commissions influence the effect of crises on political careers. A crisis can be more damaging to a political career the closer it occurs to an election, hence the importance of timing. Commissions, in turn, are used to investigate major crises. A commission investigation can be led by politicians or by experts. Incumbent politicians fare better with expert-led commissions, while opponents benefit more from politician-led commissions. A crisis is more likely to favor an incumbent when the politician has a reserve of pre-crisis political capital, has effectively communicated his or her frames, and has been in office a short time. A crisis favors an opponent when there is an endogenous cause for the crisis, when incumbents have been in office a long time, and when incumbents have had recent bad press (Boin, 't Hart, and McConnell 2009).

Conclusion

Politics has an interesting relationship with crises and emergencies. On the one hand, politicians sometimes want to avoid or distance themselves from crises, much like their counterparts in the corporate world. On the other hand, politicians frequently seek crises because of their value as a political resource. It is rather unique to politics that researchers have identified efforts to create crises and to exploit crises. Crises can be used to advance one's own policy agenda or career or to damage an opponent's policy agendas or career.

As a political resource, crises have three clear functions: (1) agitation, (2) symbolic reassurance, and (3) distraction. Agitation flows from a crisis being a focusing event. Politicians use a crisis to agitate their publics and create a demand for policy change. The crisis is framed as significant and a result of the actions or inactions of current officials. The crisis is exploited as a way to force action on policy changes. Symbolic reassurance is the counter to agitation. Symbolic reassurance tries to frame the crisis as minor and a result of uncontrollable external factors. If action is needed, symbolic actions (incremental change) are offered as an effective solution to the demands generated by the crisis. Distraction occurs when a crisis is identified to switch attention away from a current problem that is harm to certain politicians. The utilization of crises as a political resource has implications for policy change. Effective crisis exploitation can result in significant policy changes or actions that prevent such changes.

Certain types of crises (emergencies) will demand substantive action. Substantive action adds a performance component to crises. Politicians who excel at performance enhance their reputations and careers while those that fail experience a decline in both. Crises in politics are a complex phenomenon whose effect depends on competing efforts to frame the crisis and perform effectively when called upon to act. Crises do not stand alone but are a function of how they are interpreted. Interpretations of crises can have significant effects on policy decisions and political careers.

See also Disasters and Politics; Disinformation, Deception, and Politics; Fear Tactics in Politics; Leaders and Leadership; Political Communications; Scandals in Politics; Surveillance, Society, and Politics; Terrorism, Torture, and Politics; Theater and Ritual in American Politics.

W. Timothy Coombs

Bibliography

Birkland, Thomas A. 1997. *After Disaster: Agenda Setting, Public Policy, and Focusing Events.* Washington, DC: Georgetown University Press.

Boin, Arjen, and Paul 't Hart. 2010. "Organising for Effective Emergency Management: Lessons from Research." *Australian Journal of Public Administration* 69, no. 4: 357–71.

Boin, Arjen, Paul 't Hart, and Allan McConnell. 2009. "Crisis Exploitation: Political and Policy Impacts of Framing Contests." *Journal of European Public Policy* 16, no. 1: 81–106.

Bostdorff, Denise M. 1994. *The Presidency and the Rhetoric of Foreign Crisis*. Columbia: University of South Carolina Press.

Castles, Francis G. 2010. "Black Swans and Elephants on the Move: The Impact of Emergencies on the Welfare State." *Journal of European Social Policy* 20, no. 2: 91–101.

Coombs, William T. 2012. *Ongoing Crisis Communication: Planning, Managing, and Responding*. 3rd ed. Thousand Oaks, CA: Sage.

Coombs, William T., and Sherry J. Holladay. 2011. "Self-Regulatory Discourse: Corrective or Quiescent? *Management Communication Quarterly*" 25, no. 3: 494–510.

Downs, Anthony 1972. "Up and Down with Ecology: The 'Issue-Attention Cycle.'" *The Public Interest* 29: 39–50.

Edelman, Murray J. 1985. *The Symbolic Uses of Politics*. Urbana-Champaign: University of Illinois Press.

Kuypers, Jim A. 1997. *Presidential Crisis Rhetoric and the Press in the Post-Cold War World*. Westport, CT: Praeger.

Nohrstedt, Daniel, and Christopher M. Weible. 2010. "The Logic of Policy Change after Crisis: Proximity and Subsystem Interaction." *Risk, Hazards & Crisis in Public Policy* 1, no. 2: 1–32.

Perry, Ronald W. 2007. "What Is Disaster?" In Havidan Rodriguez, Enrico L. Quarantelli, and Russell R. Dynes, eds. *Handbook of Disaster Research*. New York: Springer, pp. 1–15.

Strömbäck, Jesper, and Lars W. Nord. 2006. "Mismanagement, Mistrust and Missed Opportunities: A Study of the 2004 Tsunami and Swedish Political Communication." *Media Culture and Society* 28, no. 5: 789–800.

Taleb, Nassim N. 2010. *The Black Swan: The Impact of the Highly Improbable*. 2nd ed. New York: Random House.

CULTURAL PLURALISM

While cultural pluralism has always been present in the United States, the concept of "cultural pluralism" first entered the lexicon of American political culture in the early 20th century. In general, cultural pluralism refers to the coexistence of multiple ethnic groups within one country that maintain different customs, identities, religious beliefs, and/or languages. Cultural pluralism is a two-sided concept. On the one side, it focuses on the degree to which immigrants and other subcultures retain their unique identities, beliefs, and practices, blend and mix their cultural practices with mainstream American cultural values, or shed their unique identities, beliefs, and practices as they assimilate into mainstream American culture. And on the other side, it focuses on whether American mainstream culture can and should accommodate and recognize the diversity it contains or whether diversity should be suppressed and minimized by promoting a shared public culture that emphasizes a singular set of shared values, a common language and history, and a unifying American identity.

Cultural pluralism is a socio-demographic fact in the United States, especially as the country becomes more diverse along ethnic, racial, and religious lines in the 21st century (Bowler and Segura 2012). But how Americans *react* to this fact reveals a deep and ongoing conflict in American political culture: opponents view it as a disintegrating and divisive force that undermines a shared and unifying American political culture by emphasizing differences rather than similarities (Huntington 2004; Schlesinger 1992); and proponents see it as a way to recognize and embrace the diversity that adds richness to American cultural life while guarding against excessive homogenization and conformity that overlooks the unique cultural contributions of various ethnocultural groups (Walzer 1990).

In recent years, the term "multiculturalism" has been used in much the same way that "cultural pluralism" was and is used; they are basically synonyms. Whether it is called cultural pluralism or multiculturalism, disputes about the proper relationship between cultural diversity and social unity are a permanent fixture of American political culture (Merelman, Streich, and Martin 1998).

The Historical Roots of Cultural Pluralism

Cultural pluralism has always been a feature of American political culture. Colonial America was characterized by a religious pluralism that sparked debates between those who preferred to establish an official religion as part of a dominant political culture in each colony (and later, each state) and those who promoted disestablishment as a way to ensure religious pluralism, toleration, and the separation of church and state. In addition, colonial America witnessed vigorous debates about whether American culture was forged by an English cultural mold or whether it was an entirely new and unique culture that could accommodate various ethnic and national groups.

These ethnic and religious components of cultural pluralism were both evident in arguments about whether various European immigrants coming to colonial America could be absorbed and assimilated. During this period two competing motifs emerged. The first motif is restrictive and looked upon certain ethnic or national groups (then called "races") as a cultural threat to a dominant political culture. For example, in 1751 Benjamin Franklin expressed this motif when he argued that German immigrants threatened to overwhelm a Pennsylvanian culture based on Anglo norms, customs, and the English language:

> [W]hy should the Palatine Boors be suffered to swarm into our Settlements, and by herding together establish their Language and Manners to the Exclusion of ours? Why should Pennsylvania, founded by the English, become a colony of *Aliens*, who will shortly be so numerous as to Germanize us instead of our Anglifying them, and will never adopt our Language or Customs, any more than they can acquire our Complexion. (Quoted in Bowler and Segura 2012, 235)

In contrast, there was a second, more expansive, motif that argued that all European immigrants could be successfully assimilated into a new American culture. For example, in his 1782 essay "What is an American?" J. Hector St. John de Crèvecoeur argued that American culture was not simply a modified English culture but instead totally unique in its ability to melt various European immigrants into a new "race" of people who shared a brand new American culture and identity:

> [W]hence came all these people? They are a mixture of English, Scotch, Irish, French, Dutch, Germans, and Swedes. From this promiscuous breed, that race now called American have arisen. . . . What, then, is the American, this new man? He is either an European, or the descendant of an European; hence that strange mixture of blood, which you will find in no other country. I could point out to you a family whose grandfather was an Englishman, whose wife was Dutch, whose son married a French woman, and whose present four sons have four wives of different nations. *He* is an American, who, leaving behind him all his ancient prejudices and manners, receives new ones from the new mode of life he has embraced, the new government he obeys, and the new rank he holds. Here individuals of all nations are melted into a new race of men. (Quoted in King 2000, 15)

Unlike Franklin, Crèvecoeur argued that American culture is a brand new byproduct of the merging and fusing of plural immigrant groups, including the Germans that Franklin dreaded. Indeed, he introduced the theme what would eventually become the "melting pot" metaphor that describes how immigrants shed their old customs and identities as they adopt their new American identity, ideals, and customs.

These motifs have remained permanent themes in American political culture. Those who invoke the restrictive motif typically argue that the proper response to the cultural threat posed by undesired immigrants is to ban or limit their immigration on the assumption that they are inherently different and inferior, unable and/or unwilling to assimilate into American political culture, and threaten to undermine mainstream American political culture based on Anglo-Saxon heritage, the English language, and Protestant religious values (Huntington 2004). Over time, this motif has been invoked by those who sought to ban or strictly limit the immigration of groups such as the Irish in the 1850s, the Chinese (and then other Asians) from 1882 through the 1950s, Southern and Eastern Europeans from the 1920s to the 1960s, and Mexicans and Central Americans from the 1980s to the present.

And while the original version of the expansive motif focused exclusively on assimilating European immigrants into a new American culture, by the mid-1800s this motif was modified to include all people, not just those of European descent. For example, Ralph Waldo Emerson hailed the United States as the "asylum of all nations" that drew strength from "the energy of the Irish, Germans, Swedes, Poles, and Cossacks, and all the European tribes—of the Africans, and the Polynesians" (quoted in Hollinger 1995, 87). By broadening Crèvecoeur's expansive motif to include non-Europeans, Emerson helped establish the idea that American political culture is based on values, principles, and ideals that are not exclusively European but open to and adoptable by all who come to America regardless of their nationality, religion, ethnicity, or race.

Cultural Pluralism versus Assimilation in the Early 20th Century

The restrictive and expansive motifs remained prominent in the early 20th century as new immigrants came to America from Southern and Eastern Europe. The restrictive motif was invoked by political leaders who viewed these new immigrants as inferior, prone to criminality, and therefore a threat to the dominant Anglo-Saxon culture that should be kept out of the United States (King 2000, 50–81). And the expansive motif was reiterated in Israel Zangwill's metaphor of the melting pot to emphasize the assimilating, integrating power of American political culture. Like Emerson, Zangwill includes non-Europeans to the list of people eligible for melting into American culture:

> [T]here she lives, the great Melting Pot. . . . Ah, what a stirring and a seething! Celt and Latin, Slav and Teuton, Greek and Syrian— black and yellow. Yes, East and West, and North and South,—how the great Alchemist melts and fuses them with his purging flame! Here shall they all unite to build the Republic of Man and the kingdom of God. Ah, what is the glory of Rome and Jerusalem where all nations and races come to worship and look back, compared with the glory of America, where all races come to labor and look forward. (Quoted in King 2000, 15–16)

The melting pot helps fuse and forge a new American political culture that is forward looking and able to absorb culturally diverse immigrants, assimilate them, and make them "Americans." Old customs, traditions, and identities are erased and new ones take their place.

Despite Zangwill's praise of its alchemic power, political leaders in the early 20th century invoked the melting pot solely as a way to assimilate various European immigrants into American culture while simultaneously banning immigration from Asia, restricting immigration from Eastern and Southern Europe, and relegating African Americans to second-class citizenship under the legally sanctioned racial segregation of the Jim Crow era (King 2000). Moreover, in the 1910s the federal government, educational institutions, civic groups, and major industries adopted a range of "Americanization" policies designed to encourage European immigrants to shed their old customs, languages, and national loyalties and adopt new customs, the English language, and patriotic attachment to the United States. These efforts were motivated by the idea that unassimilated immigrants represented a threat to American culture and stability. During World War I these Americanization programs were intensified due to the fear that immigrants remained loyal to their old countries. For President Woodrow Wilson, "Any man who carries a hyphen about him carries a dagger that he is ready to plunge into the vitals of this Republic" (Kennedy 1980, 87). In other words, Italian Americans, German Americans, and so on, must assimilate and become loyal Americans.

Cultural pluralism emerged as a reaction against these Americanization policies that pressured immigrants to shed their old customs, religions, and languages and become Americans. As such, cultural pluralism as a sociological and normative framework represents a distinct third motif because it not only defended immigration but argued that immigrants should be allowed to retain their unique cultural attributes as they establish roots in the United States.

Sociologist Horace Kallen first defined cultural pluralism in a 1915 essay, "Democracy *versus* the Melting Pot." For Kallen, the enforced assimilation of Americanization policies was unnecessary and counterproductive. It denied the United States a source of diversity in the name of assimilating immigrants into a homogeneous identity that reflected the cultural norms of Anglo-Protestant elites. For Kallen, the question was: "What do Americans will to make of the

United States—a unison, singing the old British theme 'America', the America of the New England School? or a harmony, in which that theme shall be dominant, perhaps, among others, but one among many, not the only one?" ([1915] 1924, 188). In contrast to Americanization programs that emphasized a unison that suppressed ethnic differences, Kallen defended the ethnic harmony and diversity of cultural pluralism. Indeed, this pluralist harmony allowed Jews, Poles, and Italians to become Jewish Americans, Polish Americans, and Italian Americans. In contrast to President Wilson, Kallen argued that the hyphen united rather than divided by creating a "democracy of nationalities" and a "multiplicity in a unity" ([1915] 1924, 124). Kallen argued that cultural pluralism is beneficial for immigrants who were able to sustain their cultural practices as well as be perfectly compatible with an American culture based on a shared commitment to democratic principles and institutions. He concluded that social tension was not inherently due to the ethnic diversity of cultural pluralism but a byproduct of denying certain ethnic groups equal economic and political opportunities (Kallen [1915] 1924, 120–24).

Another advocate of cultural pluralism was Randolph Bourne. In his 1916 essay "Trans-national America," Bourne observed that "foreign cultures have not been melted down or run together, made into some homogeneous Americanism, but have remained distinct but coöperating to the greater glory and benefit, not only of themselves but of all the native 'Americanism' around them" ([1916] 1999, 113). For Bourne, Americanization policies promoted assimilation into a bland, homogenizing, mass consumer culture of cheap entertainment, leading him to conclude that "[w]e have needed the new peoples . . . to save us from our own stagnation" ([1916] 1999, 109). Moreover, he worried that heavy-handed efforts to promote assimilation would backfire, leading immigrants to assert their ethnic identity in "strident and unwholesome ways" ([1916] 1999, 122). Echoing Kallen, Bourne argued that effective integration occurs not when assimilation and homogenization are enforced, but when all groups are granted equal respect, rights, and opportunities. This can be achieved when "no national colony within our America feels that it is being discriminated against or that its cultural case is being prejudged. This strength of cooperation, this feeling that all who

are here may have a hand in the destiny of America, will make for a finer spirit of integration than any narrow 'Americanism' or forced chauvinism" ([1916] 1999, 119). Echoing Kallen, Bourne argued that the United States is a "world-federation in miniature" that contains "the most heterogeneous peoples under the sun" ([1916] 1999, 117). And instead of basing national unity on cultural uniformity, Bourne argued that America is a culturally diverse nation held together by shared political ideals, goals, and an intellectual sympathy that "will unite not divide" ([1916] 1999, 119).

In sum, cultural pluralists were critical of Americanization programs that pressured immigrants to shed their old cultures, assimilate, and become "Americans." Instead, cultural pluralists argued that shared political, social, and economic ideals and goals were sufficient to hold a culturally diverse nation together. In addition, cultural pluralists highlight how balancing diversity and unity is a two-way process: immigrants eventually integrate, learn English, and adopt elements of mainstream American culture (even if they retain their unique cultural traditions and languages) but mainstream American culture revitalizes and renews itself by adopting and absorbing elements of various ethnic subcultures.

From Cultural Pluralism to Multiculturalism

The contrast between assimilation/Americanization and cultural pluralism in the 1910s focused exclusively on European immigrants, failing to address the unequal status of African Americans, Asian Americans, Native Americans, and Latinos (Glazer in Melzer, Weinberger, and Zinman 1998, 18–22). This began to change in the 1960s–1970s as these groups pushed for equal rights, social recognition of their unique cultural identities, and inclusion in educational curricula. In 1972 Congress authorized the ethnic heritage studies program, influenced by testimony from academics that argued that the Anglo-Saxon emphasis of elementary and secondary education ignored other groups and understated the pluralistic nature of American society (King 2000, 266–67).

By the 1980s multiculturalism emerged as a new and improved form of cultural pluralism. Multiculturalism is similar to the cultural pluralism of the 1910s.

Both resist the homogenizing emphasis of the melting pot metaphor, defend the benefits of cultural diversity, and criticize the social exclusion of groups deemed unassimilable. However, multiculturalism raises new issues that traditional cultural pluralism ignored, namely, multiculturalism moves beyond cultural pluralism's emphasis on European immigrants by highlighting the benefits of acknowledging, including, and respecting the various literary, social, cultural, and political contributions of women and people of color in the United States. Despite the self-image of the United States as an "immigrant nation," not all Americans are descended from Europeans who voluntarily came to America. Instead, many Americans are descended from people who were forcibly brought to the United States as slaves, forcibly removed from their land as a result of Manifest Destiny, and many others who faced legalized discrimination and political exclusion if their ancestors did not come from Europe. To move beyond the framework of European immigrants and their descendants as the norm to which others must conform, advocates of multiculturalism have sought to replace the assimilationist melting pot with new metaphors such as mosaic, kaleidoscope, stir-fry, or salad bowl to better symbolize how diversity and unity coexist. In short, by the 1980s the European ethnic diversity of cultural pluralism gave way to a much wider range of racial, cultural, and ethnic diversity of multiculturalism (Hollinger 1995).

As an educational reform movement, multiculturalism seeks to "celebrate diversity" by including previously excluded groups in the curriculum. Reformers sought to expand the literary canon beyond Milton and Shakespeare to include the works of African American writers such as Toni Morrison and James Baldwin. Courses in U.S. history and social studies were reoriented away from a "Eurocentric" emphasis on the history of European American men toward a multicultural approach that emphasized the contributions of women and people of color. Many American universities established departments and programs in Chicano Studies, Women's Studies, Afro-American Studies, and so on, and required students to take at least one course in non-European history. Such reforms not only diversify the curriculum, but they also expand students' understanding of and respect for the various groups that contributed to American culture and history, generate a sense of inclusion and pride among students who learn

Varieties of Multiculturalism

Like all concepts, multiculturalism is highly contested and defined in multiple ways by critics and supporters alike. The various definitions of multiculturalism can be placed on a spectrum, with mild versions on one end and strong versions on the other. The most mild and noncontroversial form of multiculturalism is the fact that as the U.S. becomes more diverse, so too has its cuisine and music. Americans of all backgrounds enjoy the foods, spices, dances, and music that are brought to the United States by diverse immigrants. Indeed, salsa outsells ketchup as the most popular condiment. Moderate forms of multiculturalism argue that ethnic and cultural groups can and should keep their cultural traditions alive, even while adapting to mainstream American culture. This approach also emphasizes how different cultures blend, mix, borrow, overlap, and create hybrid cultural forms such as "Tex-Mex" and "Spanglish." The strongest, and most controversial, form of multiculturalism assumes that each cultural group should be kept distinct and separate, otherwise dominant group values will extinguish the values of marginalized subcultures. For example, in the 1980s "Afrocentrism" was introduced as a way to reject external, "Eurocentric" values and norms while defending unique African values and norms. For critics, this reestablished the discredited idea of "separate but equal" as well as denied the many ways in which American and African American culture and history are intertwined. As the United States becomes more diverse, there will be ongoing debates about how to ensure that diversity is represented in educational curricula, popular culture, and legislative bodies.

about the diverse people who contributed to American society, and promote "cross-cultural literacy" that enables students to interact with people from diverse cultural backgrounds.

While there are many opponents of multiculturalism, Arthur Schlesinger Jr. highlights many of their concerns in his book *The Disuniting of America* (1992). For Schlesinger, multiculturalism is a "gesture of protest against the Anglocentric culture" that "threatens to become a counter-revolution against the original theory of America as 'one people,' a common culture, a single nation" (1992, 43). Renewing the goal of assimilating immigrants into the melting pot, Schlesinger argues that the genius of the United States was in creating a "brand-new national identity, carried forward by individuals who, in forsaking old loyalties and joining to make new lives, melted away ethnic differences" (1992, 13). Moreover, it is an "unassailable fact" that "for better or worse, American history has been shaped more than anything else by British tradition and culture" (1992, 53). Indeed, Schlesinger fears that by attempting to instill pride in African American history, multiculturalism undermines a shared American history and generates a cultural separatism that "crystallizes racial differences and magnifies racial tension" (1992, 53). Critical of the multicultural defense of hyphenated identities that allow cultural diversity and political unity to coexist (Walzer 1990), Schlesinger argues that educational institutions should emphasize a shared culture, history, and a unifying "American" identity.

For advocates of multiculturalism, Schlesinger and other critics exaggerate the degree to which diversity ignores shared values and history. Instead, multiculturalists argue that diversity is not inherently a threat to social cohesion. Rather, the real threat to social cohesion is the assimilationist framework that demands conformity to a white Anglo-Saxon norm, ignores the many contributions of women and people of color, and overlooks how cultural diversity can flourish within a unifying political framework.

Ongoing Controversies

Cultural pluralism and multiculturalism are entwined with several academic and political debates. First, immigration has revived the debate about restriction, assimilation, and cultural pluralism/multiculturalism. Some worry that immigration from Central America and Asia will undermine a shared political culture based on the English language, unifying American identity, and Anglo-Saxon, Protestant, and individualist norms (Huntington 2004). Others argue that these new immigrants, like the European immigrants of earlier eras, will spur economic creativity and revitalize an American political culture based on shared ideals and principles (King 2000).

Second, multiculturalism in public education remains controversial. For example, in 2010 Arizona banned ethnic studies courses in public high schools. The law specifically bans classes that "are designed primarily for pupils of a particular ethnic group" or "promote resentment against a race or class of people" (PBS 2013). Lawmakers argued that a popular Mexican American studies program in Tucson undermined a shared American history and identity, exacerbated racial conflict, generated mistrust, and resulted in separatism. Defenders of such programs argued that they improve retention and graduation rates, are open to all students, highlight a more complex understanding American history and society, and instill pride in students who see people from their ethnic or racial group as major contributors to American society (PBS 2013).

And third, there are debates about accommodating cultural pluralism in the realms of commercial and public life. Businesses know the United States is increasingly diverse and have started advertising to ethnic markets by using different cultural imagery and languages. And in public life, there is an increasing awareness that various national and religious holidays must be recognized. So, Cinco de Mayo is celebrated along with St. Patrick's Day. And Muslim holy days such as Eid al-Fitr, the Hindu festival of Diwali, and Jewish holy days such as Yom Kippur can be celebrated alongside various Christian holidays. Critics of multiculturalism argue that such practices undermine the importance of the English language and Christianity as core elements of American political culture.

Conclusion

American political culture contains a deeply rooted, ongoing debate about how to reconcile and balance various forms of ethnic, religious, and cultural pluralism on the one hand with unifying values, ideals, and principles on the other. Contrary to arguments that ethnic and racial groups must assimilate into a mainstream that is based on a narrow Anglo-Saxon norm, cultural pluralism and multiculturalism are conceptual lenses that seek to defend the coexistence of ethnic subcultures and racial groups within an overarching framework of economic opportunity, social inclusion, and equal rights. But how these subcultures maintain themselves over time, whether they coexist, overlap, or conflict with each other, and whether they are eventually assimilated into mainstream American culture will remain important issues. As the United States becomes more diverse, it must find new ways to balance diversity and unity. After all, the national motto "*E Pluribus Unum*" ("out of many, one") reminds us that the United States has always struggled to forge a unified nation out of its diverse people.

See also Affirmative Action; American Dream; Civil Rights; Culture Wars; Desegregation and Politics; Immigration and Politics; National Identity; Nationalism.

Gregory W. Streich

Bibliography

Bourne, Randolph. 1999. "Trans-national America." In C. Resek, ed. *War and the Intellectuals: Collected Essays, 1915–1919*. Indianapolis: Hacken, pp. 107–23.

Bowler, Shaun, and Gary Segura. 2012. *The Future Is Ours: Minority Politics, Political Behavior, and the Multiracial Era of American Politics*. Thousand Oaks, CA: CQ Press.

Glazer, Nathan. 1997. *We Are All Multiculturalists Now*. Cambridge, MA: Harvard University Press.

Hollinger, David. 1995. *Postethnic America: Beyond Multiculturalism*. New York: Basic Books.

Huntington, Samuel. 2004. *Who Are We? The Challenges to America's National Identity*. New York: Simon and Schuster.

Kallen, Horace. 1924. *Culture and Democracy in the United States*. New York: Boni and Liveright.

Kennedy, David, 1980. *Over Here: The First World War and American Society*. New York: Oxford University Press.

King, Desmond. 2000. *Making Americans: Immigration, Race, and the Origins of the Diverse Democracy*. Cambridge, MA: Harvard University Press.

Melzer, Arthur, Jerry Weinberger, and M. Richard Zinman, eds. 1998. *Multiculturalism and American Democracy*. Lawrence: University Press of Kansas.

Merelman, Richard, Greg Streich, and Paul Martin. 1998. "Unity and Diversity in American Political Culture: An Exploratory Study of the National Conversation on American Pluralism and Identity." *Political Psychology* 19: 781–807.

PBS. 2013. "Need to Know: Banned in Arizona." http://www.pbs.org/wnet/need-to-know/video /need-to-know-february-15-2013/16294/. Accessed: July 19, 2013.

Schlesinger, Arthur. 1992. *The Disuniting of America: Reflections on a Multicultural Society*. New York: W.W. Norton.

Walzer, Michael. 1990. "What Does It Mean to Be an American?" *Social Research* 57: 591–614.

CULTURE WARS

The "culture wars" are a major source of conflict in contemporary American political culture. In general, the term "culture wars" describes a political environment that is polarized along religious and cultural fault lines, and these divisions are visible in conflicts surrounding issues such as abortion, prayer in public schools, how science and history are taught in public high schools, gun control, and same-sex marriage. This wide range of issues is often filtered through the lens of political partisanship that pits Democratic and liberal "blue" states against Republican and conservative "red" states. While the culture wars do indeed divide Americans along ideological and partisan lines, they cannot be reduced to simple partisan conflict. Rather, scholars have argued that the culture wars actually reflect deeper cultural tensions in American political culture. However, despite the conventional wisdom that the United States is increasingly paralyzed by the culture wars, there is some evidence that the continual reference to the culture wars by political elites and media pundits actually exaggerates the degree to which average Americans are divided and distracts Americans from recognizing that on many issues there is actually a stable consensus. In short, the culture wars are real, but they are fought among a small segment of the overall American public.

Origins of the Culture Wars

One early salvo in the culture wars was the 1925 Scopes Trial, formally known as *The State of Tennessee v. John Thomas Scopes*. At issue was whether Mr. Scopes violated the state of Tennessee's "Butler Act" which banned the teaching of Charles Darwin's theory of evolution in schools that received state funding. Instead, Tennessee public schools taught that the origin of humans and animal species should be explained on the basis of "creationism," drawn from the book of Genesis in which God created the earth and all its creatures in seven days. And while Tennessee continued to ban the teaching of evolution, this case revealed an underlying conflict in American political culture between modernists who see science and evolution as compatible with religious faith and fundamentalists who take the Bible as the revealed and unerring word of God that takes priority over human knowledge. The conflict between evolution and creationism reemerged in *Epperson v. Arkansas* (1968), a case in which the U.S. Supreme Court struck down an Arkansas state law prohibiting the teaching of evolution. The Court ruled that Arkansas' ban on evolution in favor of creationism amounted to a state endorsement of a particular religious viewpoint and therefore violated the Establishment Clause in the First Amendment of the U.S. Constitution. The conflict over science and faith in science curricula remains a central fault line in the culture wars.

While particular battles in the culture wars have deep historical roots, most scholars agree that the culture wars began in the 1960s, a decade that revealed multiple conflicts and schisms in American social and political life. The civil rights movement pitted advocates of racial equality and integration against defenders of racial inequality and segregation. The Women's Liberation Movement brought to the surface a conflict between advocates of gender equality and equal opportunity for women and those who defended traditional

gender roles and patriarchy. And the embrace of "sex, drugs, and rock and roll," most noticeably visible in the emergence of "hippies" and the counterculture, was seen by middle America as an attack on the social and moral fabric of the country. In all these cases, conflicts were evident between those who advocated change, progress, equality, greater individual freedom, and a more expansive and inclusive society against those who resisted change and defended the status quo, traditions, and existing social hierarchies.

The U.S. Supreme Court issued other important decisions in the 1960s that would spur the formation of the modern conservative movement. In *Engel v. Vitale* (1962) the Court ruled that nondenominational prayer in public schools was a violation of the Establishment Clause in the First Amendment. In *Engel*, the Court affirmed the doctrine of the separation of church and state and stated that even religiously neutral prayer risked putting "indirect coercive pressure upon religious minorities." Critics of this decision included religious leaders and social conservatives who continue to advocate for prayer in public schools. From their perspective, the *Engel* decision took God out of public schools, which they see as a major factor in the decline of traditional morality. And in *Griswold v. CT* (1965), the Supreme Court ruled that a Connecticut couple had a right to "marital privacy" and struck down a Connecticut law banning the use of "any drug, medicinal article or instrument for the purpose of preventing conception." The *Griswold* case remains important and controversial because the Court concluded there is an individual right to privacy that emanates from the U.S. Constitution. A few years later in *Roe v. Wade* (1973) the Court ruled that the right to privacy protects a woman's right to an abortion in the first trimester of a pregnancy without state interference. Ever since *Roe v. Wade*, social and religious conservatives in the "pro-life" movement have dedicated themselves to overturning the decision while the "pro-choice" movement has sought to defend it and keep abortion safe and legal.

The remainder of the 1970s saw the emergence of conservative organizations such as the Moral Majority that opposed abortion, opposed the Equal Rights Amendment, and supported returning prayer to public schools. Ronald Reagan's 1980 presidential campaign mobilized many of these religious and social conservatives, bringing them into an emerging Republican coalition in which they continue to play an important role. The 1970s also saw organizations such as People for the American Way mobilize social liberals and progressives to counteract the conservative movement and protect the right to privacy, equal rights for women, and the separation of church and state.

Recent Fault Lines in the Culture Wars

While the culture wars started in the 1960s and early 1970s, they have escalated and expanded into new territory ever since.

First, ever since *Roe v. Wade* (1973) the battle over reproductive rights and abortion has been a central battle in the culture wars. Beginning in the 1980s, social and religious conservatives have not been successful in overturning *Roe v. Wade* but they have succeeded in passing additional regulations that limit access to abortions at the state level (e.g., no public funding of abortions, waiting periods, parental consent for minors). In addition, abortion became an important part of the nomination process to the federal judiciary. In 1987 the U.S. Senate rejected President Reagan's nominee to the Supreme Court, Robert Bork, on grounds that his views were too conservative and outside the mainstream. While Bork was a highly regarded legal scholar, he was unabashedly conservative in his interpretation of the Constitution (e.g., he concluded that there was no constitutional right to privacy and that many laws banning discrimination against women and racial minorities had little constitutional basis). Conservative organizations such as the Moral Majority lobbied strongly for Bork in their attempt to steer the Supreme Court in a more conservative direction, while liberal groups such as the People for the American Way mobilized opposition to Bork. Ever since the Bork nomination, Supreme Court nominations have been entangled with the question of whether a nominee would uphold or overturn *Roe v. Wade*. And in the election of 2012, debates surrounding access to abortion, public funding of Planned Parenthood, and access to contraception once again revealed a major fault line in the culture wars, with social conservatives taking strong stands against these issues.

Second, debates surrounding "family values" have also been a major battle in the culture wars. Indeed, 1992 was a pivotal year for the family values debate. One reason is the political reaction to the Los Angeles Riots that occurred after the acquittal of the Los Angeles police officers who were video-taped beating and kicking an unarmed African American man named Rodney King. Vice President Dan Quayle stated that one cause of the riots was that too many children were being raised by single mothers rather than in traditional families with father figures. Quayle singled out the sitcom *Murphy Brown* for featuring a story line in which the lead character chose to have a baby as a single mother. Quayle criticized the show for glamorizing single mothers as a "lifestyle choice," thus mocking traditional family values. While Quayle's conservative supporters agreed that the decay of family values helped explain the Los Angeles Riots, his critics argued that the real causes of the riots were broader social problems such as police brutality, poverty, and failing public schools. This debate is embedded in an ongoing culture war battle in which social conservatives argue that divorce rates, single parents, and the demise of traditional family values are the main source of social decay, and in response liberals and progressives argue that stagnant wages, chronic unemployment, and underfunded public schools are to blame.

The year 1992 was also important because of Patrick Buchanan's speech at the Republican National Convention in Houston, Texas. While President George H.W. Bush was running for reelection on a message of ushering in a kinder, gentler nation, Buchanan rallied conservatives to defend traditional morality against what he saw as the permissive liberalism of Bill and Hillary Clinton:

> The agenda that [Bill] Clinton & [Hillary] Clinton would impose on America: abortion on demand, a litmus test for the Supreme Court, homosexual rights, discrimination against religious schools, women in combat units. That's change, all right. But that's not the kind of change America needs. It's not the kind of change America wants. And it's not the kind of change we can abide in a nation we still call "God's country" . . . Friends, this

election is about more than who gets what. It is about who we are. It is about what we believe and what we stand for as Americans. There is a religious war going on in this country. It is a cultural war, as critical to the kind of nation we shall be as the Cold War itself. For this war is for the soul of America. And in that struggle for the soul of America, Clinton & Clinton are on the other side, and George Bush is on our side. (Buchanan 1992)

In classic "us versus them" style, Buchanan artfully portrayed Republicans as defenders of traditional morality against the Democrats as opponents of family values. While Buchanan rallied social conservatives in the Republican Party, it is equally likely that his strident rhetoric pushed social moderates away from the Republicans, ironically allowing Democratic president Bill Clinton to get reelected in 1996. While Buchanan failed in his 1992 and 1996 quests for the presidency, he remains an important conservative culture warrior.

Most recently, this "family values" debate has revolved around the question of same-sex marriage. Social and religious conservatives defend what they see as a traditional definition of marriage as one man and one woman, and oppose same-sex marriage as an affront to biblical morality. Indeed, many states have passed laws and constitutional amendments banning same-sex marriage. On the other hand, progressives, liberals, and even a few small-government conservatives have started to build stronger public support for same-sex marriage both as a matter of equal rights and a recognition that this will help strengthen the "family values" of love and commitment. Indeed, support for same-sex marriage has risen from 35 percent in 2001 to 49 percent in 2012, while opposition has fallen from 57 percent in 2001 to 40 percent in 2012 (Pew Forum 2012). Support has been driven by younger Americans who are twice as likely as older Americans to support same-sex marriage. Underneath, however, the religious cleavages of the culture war are still evident. By 2012 only 19 percent of white evangelical Christians supported same-sex marriage, but 52 percent of Catholics, 54 percent of white Mainline Protestants, and 73 percent of religiously unaffiliated Americans

support same-sex marriage (Pew Forum 2012). While overall public support is shifting on this issue, there remains strong opposition from religious and social conservatives as well as organizations such as the Family Research Council.

A third front in the culture wars includes ongoing debates surrounding science standards in public high schools. When states establish science standards for their public high schools, the battle lines of the culture wars are evident. On the one hand, scientists and educators (with support from groups such as the National Center for Science Education [NCSE]) argue that students should be taught the scientific consensus surrounding the theory of evolution and that creationism and intelligent design are nonscientific religious interpretations of the origin of human beings. And on the other hand, social and religious conservatives (with support from groups such as the Discovery Institute) argue that students should be taught the limits of Darwin's theory and exposed to alternative theories such as creationism and intelligent design. The Discovery Institute has argued that science textbooks should "teach the controversy" between intelligent design and evolution, but the NCSE responds by saying that there is no controversy to be taught because there is a solid scientific consensus behind evolution. In addition, conservative legislators have introduced legislation requiring that high school science classes include materials casting doubt on global warming. And groups such as the NCSE respond by highlighting the scientific consensus that global warming is real and that human activity is a contributing factor.

And a fourth flashpoint in the culture wars is the annual debate surrounding holiday greetings: "Merry Christmas" versus "Happy Holidays." This debate reflects an ongoing argument whether the United States is a "Christian nation" or a religiously plural nation. Social and religious conservatives argue that "Happy Holidays" takes Christianity out of the Holy Season, since Jesus is the "Reason for the Season." Indeed, pundits like Bill O'Reilly suggest that "Happy Holidays" amounts to a "war" on Christmas and is an indication that Christians are besieged in an increasingly secular society (O'Reilly 2007). On the other hand, for some American "Happy Holidays" is a greeting that covers both Christmas and New Year's greetings. However, "Happy Holidays" has also become the greeting of choice for people, public entities, and corporations that want to recognize the increasing religious pluralism of the United States since Christmas, Kwanzaa, and Hanukkah occur during the same period of the calendar year.

The Underlying Causes of the Culture Wars

It is clear that the culture wars are fought on a variety of hot-button social and cultural issues. But the culture wars are a symptom of deeper conflicts in American political culture. Explanations of these deeper sources of conflict are often expressed in dichotomies: fundamentalists versus secularists; traditionalists versus progressives; conservatives versus liberals; the Coasts versus the Heartland; elites versus middle Americans; and of course, Red versus Blue.

One of the deeper causes of the culture wars was identified by James Davison Hunter in his book *Culture Wars: The Struggle to Define America* (1991). For Hunter, underneath the culture wars is a debate about the "matter of moral authority" and the "basis by which people determine whether something is good or bad, right or wrong, acceptable or unacceptable, and so on" (Hunter 1991, 42). Ultimately, this deeper conflict revolves around two competing impulses, each with its own worldview. On the one hand there is the impulse of "orthodoxy," which is "the commitment on the part of adherents to an external, definable, and transcendent authority. Such objective and transcendent authority defines, at least in the abstract, a consistent, unchangeable measure of value, purpose, goodness, and identity, both personal and collective" (Hunter 1991, 44). And on the other hand, there is the impulse toward "cultural progressivism" in which "moral authority tends to be defined by the spirit of the modern age . . . [f]rom this standpoint, truth tends to be viewed as a process, as a reality that is ever unfolding" (Hunter 1991, 44). Hunter then adds:

> It nearly goes without saying that those who embrace the orthodox impulse are almost always cultural conservatives, while those who

embrace progressivist moral assumptions tend toward a liberal or libertarian social agenda. . . . For the practical purposes of naming the antagonists in the culture wars, then, we can label those on one side cultural conservatives or moral traditionalists, and those on the other side liberals or cultural progressives. (Hunter 1991, 46)

Another insight from Hunter is that the culture wars are not just an interfaith battle but rather an intra-faith battle between the orthodox and progressive impulses within each of the major American religious traditions. As a result, for example, evangelicals join with conservative Catholics in their shared opposition to abortion and same-sex marriage, while many mainstream Protestants and liberal Catholics support abortion rights and same-sex marriage.

These interreligious and intra-religious dynamics are increasingly evident in voter preferences. Beginning in 2000 it has become increasingly clear that religious conservatives have become central players in the Republican coalition while religious moderates and religiously unaffiliated voters have shifted into the Democratic coalition (White 2003). Indeed, how frequent a person attends religious services has become a relatively accurate predictor of their presidential vote. Exit polls from the 2012 election show that among those who attend religious services "weekly" 39 percent voted for Barack Obama and 59 percent voted for Mitt Romney, among those who attend services "occasionally" 55 percent voted for Obama and 43 percent voted for Romney, and among those who "never" attend religious services 62 percent voted for Obama and 34 percent voted for Romney. And among born-again Christians, only 21 percent voted for Obama but 78 percent voted for Romney (CNN 2012). Numbers such as these illustrate how the underlying religious dynamics of the culture wars have reshaped the electoral coalitions of the two major parties in the United States

A second deeper cause of the culture wars has recently been examined by E.J. Dionne in his book *Our Divided Political Heart: The Battle for the American Idea in an Age of Discontent* (2013). Dionne notes that American political culture rests on two tenets that coexist but are often at odds: individualism and community. On the one hand, Americans love individual liberty and freedom. After all, the iconic image of the "rugged individual" is central to American political culture. But on the other hand, Americans recognize the need for community and the responsibilities it entails. Likewise, the New England town hall meeting filled with civic-minded citizens is also an iconic image in American political culture. And while excessive individualism undermines the bonds of community, the bonds of community often constrain and squelch individualism and individual freedom. Nevertheless, Dionne argues that Americans must find a way to balance individual freedom and the bonds of community. If not, contemporary American politics will continue to be poisoned by hyper-individualism that embraces liberty but rejects the responsibilities that citizens have toward each other as members of the American polity.

Are the Culture Wars Real or Overhyped?

Cable television news and talk radio stations are filled with arguments about the culture wars. But the pundits and hosts on those channels and stations are not just reporting and analyzing the culture wars, they are very often "culture warriors" themselves. For instance, FOX News pundit Bill O'Reilly regularly defends conservatives and "traditionalists" from "secular-progressives" (O'Reilly 2007). While the audiences of these channels and stations may get whipped up and motivated to join the culture wars, they may not represent "middle America." Indeed, even while describing the competing impulses of orthodoxy and progressivism that animate the culture wars, James Davison Hunter admits that "most Americans occupy a vast middle ground between the polarizing impulses of American culture" (Hunter 1991, 43). It is these moderate Americans in the middle that often rebuke culture warriors when they take positions that are too extreme.

Scholars such as Morris Fiorina and Alan Wolfe argue that the culture wars pit political elites against each other while the vast majority of Americans remain moderate, centrist, pragmatic, and unpersuaded by culture war rhetoric (Fiorina 2010; Wolfe 1998).

To be sure, politicians and pundits often fan the culture wars to get votes or to increase their audience share and sell books. But Fiorina finds that political elites and their rhetoric are often more divided than the general American public. For instance, contrary to the culture wars that rage around the issue of same-sex marriage, there is an emerging consensus that it should be legalized. Similarly, on the question of abortion, Gallup surveys illustrate that over the last two decades there has remained a slim but consistent majority (currently standing at 53 percent) of Americans who believe that *Roe v. Wade* should *not* be overturned and a consistent minority (currently 29 percent) who believe it *should* be overturned (Saad 2012). In short, among average Americans there is a modest or growing consensus on issues such as abortion and same-sex marriage, but the rhetoric of political activists, elites, and media pundits gives the impression that the entire nation is engulfed in the culture wars (Fiorina 2010; Hunter and Wolf 2006).

Conclusion

Politics is a contest between those who promote social change and those who defend the status quo. So it is with the culture wars. What makes the culture wars unique is that the political debate revolves around a range of hot-button issues that are seen through cultural and religious frameworks. This leads progressives and liberals to embrace social change while conservatives and traditionalists oppose it. What progressives and liberals see as building a more inclusive, tolerant, and pluralistic society in which all people have equal treatment and respect under the law, social and religious conservatives see as an attack on institutions, traditions, customs, and Judeo-Christian morality that holds American society together. While some Americans join with political elites and media pundits to fight various battles of the culture wars, this should not overshadow the fact that there is a moderate, stable, and practical streak in American political life that continues to hold the United States together despite the dire predictions of the culture warriors.

See also Abortion and Politics; Church–State Relations; Evolution, Creationism, and Politics; Family,

State, and Politics; Gay and Lesbian Culture and Politics; Guns and Politics; Partisanship and Polarization; Prayer and Religious Symbols in Public Places

Gregory W. Streich

Bibliography

Buchanan, P. 1992. "Address to the Republican Convention." http://www.americanrhetoric.com/speeches/patrickbuchanan1992rnc.htm. Accessed May 24, 2014.

CNN, 2012. "President: Full Results." http://www.cnn.com/election/2012/results/race/president. Accessed May 24, 2014.

Dionne, E. J. 2013. *Our Divided Political Heart: The Battle for the American Idea in an Age of Discontent*. New York: Bloomsburg.

Fiorina, M. 2010. *Culture War? The Myth of a Polarized America*. 3rd ed. New York: Pearson, Longman.

Hunter, J. D. 1991. *Culture Wars: The Struggle to Define America*. New York: Basic Books.

Hunter, J. D. 1995. *Before the Shooting Begins: Searching for Democracy in America's Culture War*. New York: The Free Press.

Hunter, J. D., and A. Wolfe. 2006. *Is there a Culture War? A Dialogue on Values and American Public Life*. Washington, DC: Brookings Institution Press.

O'Reilly, B. 2007. *Culture Warrior*. New York: Broadway Books.

Pew Forum. 2012. "Changing Attitudes on Gay Marriage." http://features.pewforum.org/same-sex-marriage-attitudes/slide3.php. Accessed May 24, 2014.

Pew Research. 2012. "Behind Gay Marriage Momentum, Regional Gaps Persist." http://www.people-press.org/2012/11/09/behind-gay-marriage-momentum-regional-gaps-persist/. Accessed May 24, 2014.

Saad, L. 2012. "Majority of Americans Still Support Roe v. Wade Decision." http://www.gallup.com/poll/160058/majority-americans-support-roe-wade-decision.aspx. Accessed May 24, 2014.

White, J. K. 2003. *The Values Divide: American Politics and Culture in Transition*. Washington, DC: CQ Press.

Wolfe, A. 1998. *One Nation, After All*. New York: Viking.

CYBERSECURITY AND POLITICS

President Barack Obama has described cyber threats as one of the most serious economic and national security challenges that we face as a nation, and has called for greater efforts at cybersecurity. Cybersecurity can be described as measures taken to protect a computer or computer system against unauthorized access or attack. Oftentimes, this unauthorized access or attack can take the form of viruses, worms, hacking, spyware, and malware. While its definition may seem simple, its scope is enormous. Americans rely on a digital infrastructure of computer networks, grids, wireless and satellite signals, and broadband network to pay bills, shop, make bank transactions, pay taxes, and power enormous telecommunication networks and power grids. It is a great irony that, as Obama pointed out, the technologies that empower Americans to create and build also empower others to disrupt and destroy.

The ability of individuals, companies, and countries to secure their systems from cyber-attack presents challenges not only to security experts but also to everyday Americans as they struggle to understand how measures aimed at increasing cybersecurity affect their fundamental civil liberties, such as personal privacy and freedom of speech. While many Americans may feel that their online transactions are secure and private, massive data breaches by computer hackers into personal and credit card information for millions of customers at major retailers have cast doubt on the security of computer networks. A recent study by computer technology company Hewlett-Packard reported that, of the 180 mobile applications it examined for both iOS software and Android operating systems, close to half of the applications either failed to use encryption or used it incorrectly, thereby potentially exposing sensitive data.

Data security has become what one Forbes analyst called the "arms race" between attackers and businesses, each trying to change its tactics and approaches with technological advancements. Although most policy analysts and scholars argue that cyber-attacks are a serious issue, many disagree on how widespread the attacks are, who is behind them, and their impact on financial, military, and governmental spheres of business.

Post 9/11 Cyber Fears

While analysts and policy makers recognized the threat of cybercrime and cyber-attacks during the onset of widespread Internet use in the 1990s, public discourse about the severity of cyber threats, or fears of cyberterrorism, sharply increased after the terrorist attacks of 9/11. Many Americans wondered that if computer hackers could penetrate computer systems, couldn't terrorists do the same? Thus, the idea of cyberterrorism, or the use of computer network tools to damage or shut down critical national infrastructures such as energy and transportation grids and government operations, quickly became a subject of national attention. Since critical infrastructure in the United States is networked through computers, the potential threat from cyberterrorism was considered by some to be very alarming, in both academic circles and pop culture. The threat of a massive cyber-attack on major infrastructure, for example, was depicted in popular American films like "Live Free or Die Hard"; in it, actor Bruce Willis's character joins forces with a young hacker to bring down a cyber-terrorist bent on taking control of U.S. transportation, power, and natural gas distribution grids.

Further attention was brought to the possibility of cyberterrorism when in 2002, Al Qaeda documents recovered by U.S. troops suggested cyber-attacks on various targets, including the electrical grid. Recovered laptops by U.S. troops also indicated that Al Qaeda members spent time on websites offering programming instructions for digital switches that run a number of grids, including ones for power, water, and communications. One computer seized at an Al Qaeda office contained models of a dam, made with structural architecture and engineering software that enabled the planners to simulate its catastrophic failure. Although the information did not show that Al Qaeda was planning a cyber-attack, it did show that information on the programming of critical infrastructure was being accessed online.

While there is no universal definition for cyberterrorism, the FBI has defined it as premeditated, politically motivated attack against information, computer systems, computer programs, and data, which results in violence against noncombatant targets; a cyber-terrorist attack is designed to cause physical violence or extreme financial harm.

It is important to differentiate among cyber-terrorist attack, hacking, and "hacktivism." Hacking is conducted online to manipulate or exploit vulnerabilities in computer operating systems and other software. Hackers tend *not* to have political agendas and typically use tactics such as e-mail attacks, computer break-ins, and computer viruses and worms. Viruses can have global impact. The "I Love You" virus that originated in the Philippines in the spring of 2000 spread worldwide in one day, infecting 10 percent of all computers connected to the Internet and causing billions of dollars in damage. The virus spread quickly among users of Microsoft Outlook and corporate networks that use the Microsoft Exchange e-mail server because it sent a copy of itself to every e-mail address in a recipient's Outlook address book.

Other cyber assault techniques include the use of "spyware," which records keystrokes and collects information, such as passwords, without user knowledge. Spyware software goes undetected, collecting various types of personal information and Internet habits. Malicious codes disrupt normal computer functions and can open a backdoor for a remote attacker to take control of the computer without the owner knowing that his or her computer has been compromised. There is some fear that individual hackers may sell their computer skills to countries and terrorist groups, regardless of the political interests involved, thereby allowing them to rent high-tech computer skills, such as "botmasters" for large amounts of money. "Hacktivist," on the other hand, break into or "hack" computer systems for a politically or socially motivated purpose. Their goal is to support a political agenda, and their activity often includes defacing websites or stealing and leaking classified government information. Hactivists may use the same tools and techniques as hackers, but their goals are often to overload e-mail servers and hack into websites to send a political message.

As concern over terrorist attacks has declined, fears about American vulnerability to cyber-attacks have grown. Renewed attention to cybersecurity and cyber threats appeared when, in October 2012, Defense Secretary Leon Panetta stated that the United States was facing the possibility of a "cyber Pearl

Harbor." According to Panetta, "an aggressor nation or extremist group could use these kinds of cyber tools to gain control of critical switches. . . . They could derail passenger trains, or even more dangerous, derail passenger trains loaded with lethal chemicals. They could contaminate the water supply in major cities, or shut down the power grid across large parts of the country" (Panetta 2012).

While many experts point to physical destruction that could be brought on by a cyber-attack, others warn that the attacks are more likely through stealing data that can undermine confidence in U.S. banking or communications systems.

Data Theft

In December 2013, the nation's third-largest retailer, Target Corporation, announced that during the year's busy holiday retail period, personal information of over 110 million people was stolen. The data theft included payment card information for 40 million customers and personal data such as names, e-mail and residential addresses of 70 million others. As expected, the stolen Target customer information quickly reached the black market in the form of fraudulent credit cards available for purchase. By mid-December, shortly after hackers first breached Target, fraud experts tracked a significant increase in the number of stolen card numbers on black market websites. Shortly after the Target data breach was announced, luxury retailer Neiman Marcus announced that hackers had invaded its systems over a period of several months in a breach that involved 1.1 million credit and debit cards. Furthermore, the malware (software designed to damage or disable computers) installed on terminals in Neiman Marcus stores appeared to be the same malware that infiltrated Target's systems.

The Target and Neiman Marcus retail data breach was not the first of its kind. T.J. Maxx and Marshall's retail companies experienced similar data breaches over an 18-month period from 2005 to 2007, when 45.6 million credit and debit card numbers were stolen by cyber intrusions. The consequences of the Target data breach may continue for years. According to security experts, one potential threat is that hackers could piece together customers' stolen information for identity theft or for use in a spear phishing attack. The latter occurs when hackers send customized e-mails to victims asking them to click on a link or download an attachment that, when opened, gives hackers access to their computers.

Reports of cyber incidents continue to rise yearly. The Federal Bureau of Investigation reported that in 2013 it uncovered around 20 cases of cyber-attacks against retailers. The FBI warns that the worst is yet to come. It recently warned retailers about the possible spread of malicious malware that can penetrate credit-card swiping machines in retail stores. Credit-card swiping machines connect to a company's computer network typically through the Internet. The malware software scans memory in search of track data from payment cards that may be unencrypted. The continuing threat of major data breaches has led to political debate in both the business community and Capitol Hill regarding whether to adopt a "smart card" or "chip-and-pin" system in the United States to replace magnetic strips on credit cards. Widely used in Europe, chip-and-pin credit cards and debit cards are embedded with a microchip on which the card information is stored. Instead of swiping and signing a credit card to make payments, retail machines read the chips and cardholders enter PIN codes to verify their identities. The benefit of the chip-and-pin system is the difficulty in making counterfeit cards.

One of the many challenges posed by cybercrime is its difficulty to trace the attacks. Often it takes months to pinpoint the origin of attacks since they are generally routed through computer servers all over the world. Security experts can often track where communications come from, and sometimes even a user's Internet address, but hackers often use many computers and push their efforts through multiple countries. In the Target investigation, initial reports indicated that stolen card data was offloaded via FTP communications to a location in Russia and several "drop" locations, the drop locations being compromised computers in the United States and worldwide used to house the stolen data until accessed by the perpetrators.

In addition to personal data theft, the loss of intellectual property is a significant issue facing companies and universities who spend billions of dollars in research and development (R&D). Some universities claim that there are millions of hacking attempts per week, with upward to 100,000 attempts made per day by foreign countries, especially by China. Universities and their professors are awarded thousands of patents in areas such as medicine and medical devices, computer and environmental technology, agriculture, and aviation. By stealing data, countries like China save billions of dollars and years of expensive R&D. The problem of data theft is so serious that some universities no longer allow professors to take laptops abroad. Many companies and universities suggest that employees take loaner devices like laptops to China and Russia, not to enable Bluetooth, and to remove their battery from cell phone while in meetings, operating under the assumption that the electronics will be compromised. Some recent estimates indicate that more than 90 percent of cyber espionage in the United States originates in China.

In 2013, *The Washington Post* leaked a classified report that hackers accessed designs for more than two dozen major U.S. weapons systems. A report released by Mandiant, a Virginia-based IT security company, in early 2013, identified the People's Liberation Army, a secret Chinese military unit, as the most likely group behind the hacking of computer networks for many U.S. industries. While the Chinese Defense Ministry has denied the accusations, the frequency of Chinese cyber-attacks on U.S. computer networks has only increased the intensity of the strained diplomatic relationship between the United States and China.

Cyber Warfare

As electronic technology has advanced, so has the ability to conduct cyber warfare as an alternative or complement to conventional warfare. Cyber warfare is a type of politically motivated, information warfare, which involves hacking to conduct espionage or to sabotage systems. Cyber warfare expert Richard A. Clarke defined cyber warfare in his 2010 book as "actions by a nation-state to penetrate another nation's computers or networks for the purposes of causing damage or disruption." Threats of cyber warfare can range from the spread of propaganda and website defacement to espionage and infrastructure disruption. Among the array of cyber threats seen today, only

government-sponsored programs are developing capabilities with the future prospect of causing widespread, long-duration damage to critical infrastructures.

One type of cyber warfare is the use of Distributed Denial-Of-Service (DDOS) attacks, which happen when multiple computer systems overload a website with so many incoming messages that it shuts down, denying service to users. In April 2007, computer systems in Estonia began to experience DDOS attacks on its electronic infrastructure. For over a month, these attacks penetrated Estonian websites, including government ministries, banks, telecommunications companies, and Internet service providers. In one of the attacks, a flood of bogus messages shutdown the e-mail server of the Parliament. In Estonia, the attacks were magnified by the infiltration of computers around the world with software known as "bots," which were banded together in networks (or "botnets") to perform the attacks. Botnets are computers infected with malicious code that can be controlled from remote locations from the Internet. Technology analysts believe that up to 1 million computers may have been involved in the botnet used to bring down Estonian websites. Two years later, in the summer of 2009, three waves of DDOS attacks were targeted at U.S. and South Korean governmental and media websites, including the Pentagon and White House. While these incidents did not result in data theft, they caused disruption that prevented people from carrying out transactions, purchasing items, or conducting business. To many Americans, the cyber-attacks in Estonia and the United States illustrate the vulnerability of a country's dependence on information technology.

Cyber threats can also come from national governments. Iran has long alleged that the United States and Israel are orchestrating a secret cyber war of sabotage against its nuclear program. The *Stuxnet* virus, discovered in 2010, was a sophisticated computer worm designed to search for controllers that regulate the machinery in factories and power plants. The worm targeted Microsoft Windows machines and networks by compromising the programmable logic controllers, allowing the worm's creators to spy on the industrial systems and causing gas centrifuges used for enriching uranium to spin out of control and self-destruct. While *Stuxnet* affected several countries like India,

Indonesia, and Azerbaijan, its greatest impact was in Iran. Although the authors of *Stuxnet* have never been officially identified, it is widely believed to have been created by the United States and Israel. In 2012, *The New York Times* reported that *Stuxnet* was part of operation *Olympic Games*, a covert and still unacknowledged campaign of sabotage by means of cyber disruption, directed at Iranian nuclear facilities. The *Stuxnet* virus was first time the United States used cyber weapons to disable infrastructure in another country. It was done without a bombing campaign, only with computer code.

Stuxnet was followed by the malware infection, *Flame*, which was discovered by cybersecurity experts in 2012. Designed for cyber espionage rather than industrial sabotage, *Flame* could gather data files, change computer settings, turn on computer microphones to record conversations overs Skype, take screen shots and copy instant messaging and keyboard strokes. Its ability to avoid detection led to it being undiscovered for five years. Its primary targets were the computers of high-ranking officials in Iran and other parts of the Middle East. *Flame*, like *Stuxnet*, is also believed to be created by the United States and Israel.

Conclusion

In February 2013, President Obama signed an executive order promoting the sharing of information about cyber threats between the government and private companies that oversee critical infrastructure such as dams, chemical plants, and electrical grids. While the order promotes information sharing, it does not set minimum requirements for the protection of crucial infrastructure networks since that would require congressional approval. Legislation to set up minimum requirements was defeated the previous year when the Cybersecurity Act of 2012 failed to overcome a Republican-led filibuster in the U.S. Senate. The bill would have allowed the Department of Homeland Security to enforce minimum protection standards. Opposition to the bill was led by the U.S. Chamber of Commerce, one of the largest lobbying groups in the United States, and other business groups that argued that the passage of the bill would add excessive government interference and regulation to the operations of privately held companies. In addition, there was concern that companies would give too much customer information to the government. Again, the bill revealed the uneasy balance between the need for security and maintenance of personal privacy. After former National Security Agency (NSA) contractor Edward Snowden revealed that major telecommunications and technology companies were transferring data on Americans to the NSA, the bill was shelved. Ironically, Snowden extracted classified government information from an NSA facility unequipped with up-to-date software, exposing how insecure top secret government computer networks are, while revealing the workings of U.S. surveillance programs.

While many security experts believe that the probability of a well-coordinated, serious cyber terror attack in the near future is low, most agree that it could bring a devastating blow to the U.S. economy. Despite all the fear of the damage of a cyber-attack, scholars point to the fact there has been no recorded instance of a terrorist cyber-attack on U.S. public facilities, transportation systems, nuclear power plants, power grids, or other key components of the national infrastructure. Cyber-attacks are common, but they have not been conducted by terrorists and they have not sought to inflict the kind of damage that would qualify them as cyberterrorism. For the most part, cyber-attacks take the form of criminal theft rather than destruction. Experts in both government and private sectors, however, continue to realize the need to address vulnerabilities in the electronic infrastructure of the United States.

See also Infrastructure and Politics; Intelligence Community and Politics; Internet, Society, and Politics; National Security Policy and Politics; Privatization and Deregulation; Surveillance, Society, and Politics.

Sara Hower

Bibliography
Blum, Justin Blum. 2005. "Hackers Target US Power Grid." *Washington Post* (March 11), E01.
Brenner, Joel. 2011. *America the Vulnerable: Inside the New Threat Matrix of Digital Espionage, Crime, and Warfare.* New York: Penguin Press.

Bumiller, Elisabeth. 2013. "Pentagon Expanding Cybersecurity Force to Protect Networks Against Attacks." *New York Times* (January 28), A7.

Clarke, Richard A., and Robert K. Knake. 2012. *Cyber War: The Next Threat to National Security and What to Do about It.* New York: HarperCollins.

Finn, Peter. 2007. "Cyber Assaults on Estonia Typify a New Battle Attack." *Washington Post* (May 19), A01.

Gross, Michael Joseph. 2013. "A Declaration of Cyber-War," *Vanity Fair* (April). www.vanityfair.com/culture/features/2011/04/stuxnet-201104. Accessed December 5, 2013.

Hower, Sara B. 2011. "Cyberterrorism." In Lori Johnson, Kathleen Uradnik, and Sara B. Hower, eds. *Battleground: Government and Politics.* Santa Barbara, CA: ABC-CLIO.

Landler, Mark, and John Markhoff. 2007. "Digital Fears Emerge after Data Siege in Estonia." *New York Times* (May 29). www.nytimes.com/2007/05/29/technology/29estonia.html. Accessed October 10, 2013.

Lewis, James A., J.D. McCreary, and Maren Leed. 2013. "Offensive Cyber Capabilities at the Operational Level: The Way Ahead." Washington, DC: Center for Strategic and International Studies.

Love, Richard A. 2007. "The Cyberthreat Continuum." In Maryann Cusimano Love, ed. *Beyond Sovereignty: Issues for a Global Agenda.* 3rd ed. Belmont, CA: Thompson Wadsworth.

McElroy, Damien, and Christopher Williams. 2012. "Flame: World's Most Complex Computer Virus Exposed." *The Telegraph* (May 28). www.telegraph.co.uk/news/worldnews/middleeast/iran/9295938/Flame-worlds-most-complex-computer-virus-exposed.html. Accessed February 26, 2014.

Panetta, Leon. 2012. Remarks by Secretary Panetta on Cybersecurity to the Business Executives for National Security, New York City, October 11. www.defense.gov/transcripts/transcript.aspx?transcriptid=5136. Accessed February 17, 2014.

Perez-Pena, Richard. 2013. "Universities Face a Rising Barrage of Cyberattacks." *New York Times* (July 17), A1.

Rotberg, Robert I. 2003. *When States Fail: Causes and Consequences.* Princeton, NJ: Princeton University Press.

Sanger, David E. 2012. "Obama Order Sped Up Wave of Cyberattacks against Iran." *New York Times* (June 1), A01.

Sanger, David E. 2013. "In Cyberspace, New Cold War." *New York Times* (February 25), A1.

Schmidt, Michael S., and Nicole Perlroth. 2013. "Obama Order Gives Firms Cyberthreat Information." *New York Times* (February 13), A16.

Schwartz, John. 2001. "A Nation Challenged: The Computer Networks; Cyberspace Seen as Potential Battleground." *New York Times* (November 23). www.nytimes.com/2001/11/23/business/nation-challenged-computer-networks-cyberspace-seen-potential-battleground.html?pagewanted=2. Accessed February 28, 2014.

Verton, Dan. 2003. Black Ice: The Invisible Threat of Cyber-terrorism. New York: Osborne/McGraw-Hill.

Weimann, Gabriel. 2006. *Terror on the Internet: The New Arena, the New Challenges.* Washington, DC: USIP Press.

Wilson, Clay. 2008. "Botnets, Cybercrime, and Cyberterrorism: Vulnerabilities and Policy Issues for Congress." *CRS Report for Congress.* www.fas.org/sgp/crs/terror/RL32114.pdf. Accessed February 27, 2014.

D

DEATH PENALTY AND POLITICS

One of the most controversial issues in criminal justice, and in American society at large, is the death penalty. For most people who support the death penalty, the execution of killers (and people who commit other horrible acts) makes sense. Death penalty supporters frequently state that executions do prevent those executed from committing heinous crimes again and that the example of executions probably prevents most people who might contemplate committing appalling crimes from doing so. In addition, many death penalty supporters simply believe that people who commit such crimes deserve to die—that they have earned their ignominious fate.

For opponents, the death penalty issue is about something else entirely. For many opponents, the level of death penalty support in the United States is a rough estimate of the level of maturity of the American people. The not-so-subtle implication is that a mature, civilized society would not employ the death penalty. Opponents maintain that perpetrators of horrible crimes can be dealt with effectively by other means and that it makes little sense to kill some people, however blameworthy they may be, to teach other people not to kill. These opponents argue that although the perpetrators of terrible crimes may deserve severe punishment, that punishment need not be execution. They also fear that, given the hundreds of cases of wrongfully convicted people that organizations like the Innocence Project have brought to light—including 18 individuals on death row—it is possible that innocent persons could be executed.

Background

The first person executed in what is now the United States was Capt. George Kendall, a councillor for the Virginia colony. He was executed in 1608 for being a spy for Spain. The fact that he was executed was not particularly unusual, because the death penalty was just another one of the punishments brought to the New World by the early European settlers.

Since Kendall's execution in 1608, more than 19,000 executions have been performed in what is now the United States under civil (as opposed to military) authority. This estimate does not include the approximately 10,000 people lynched in the 19th century. Nearly all of the people executed during the past four centuries in what is now the United States have been adult men; only about 3 percent have been women. Ninety percent of the women were executed under local as opposed to state authority, and the majority (87 percent) were executed prior to 1866. About 2 percent of the people executed have been juveniles—that is, individuals who committed their capital crimes prior to their 18th birthdays. Most of them (69 percent) were black and nearly 90 percent of their victims were white (Bohm 2011).

It is important to understand that all of the significant changes in the practice of capital punishment in the United States—culminating in its complete abolition in some jurisdictions—are the result of abolitionist efforts. Pressure from abolitionists caused Pennsylvania in 1794 to repeal the death penalty for all crimes except first-degree murder. Between 1794 and 1798, Virginia and Kentucky joined Pennsylvania in abolishing the death penalty for all crimes except first-degree murder; New York and New Jersey abolished the penalty for all crimes except murder and treason. Virginia and Kentucky, both slave states, confined the reforms to free people; slaves in those states were still subject to a long list of capital crimes. When New Jersey, Virginia, and Kentucky severely restricted the scope of capital punishment, they also appropriated funds for the construction of their first prisons; Pennsylvania and New York had established prisons earlier. Still, a half-century would pass before the first state abandoned capital punishment entirely.

Between 1800 and 1850, U.S. death penalty abolitionists also helped change public sentiment about public executions, especially among many northern social elites. In 1800, public hangings were mostly solemn events regularly attended by members of all social classes and touted as having important educational value. But by midcentury, members of the upper classes were staying away from them because in their minds they had become tasteless, shocking, rowdy, sometimes dangerous, carnival-like spectacles.

Another problem with public hangings during this period was that attendees were increasingly sympathizing with the condemned prisoners, weakening the position of the state. Indeed, some of those who met their fate on the gallows became folk heroes. Increasing acceptance of the belief that public executions were counterproductive because of the violence they caused was yet another change. Stories were circulated about the violent crimes being committed just before or after a pubic hanging by attendees of the event.

For these reasons, Connecticut, in 1830, became the first state to ban public executions. Pennsylvania became the second state to do so in 1834. In both states, only a few authorized officials and the relatives of the condemned were allowed to attend. By 1836, New York, New Jersey, Massachusetts, Rhode Island, and New Hampshire had enacted similar policies. By 1860, all northern states and Delaware and Georgia in the South had shifted the site of executions from the public square to an enclosed jail yard controlled by the sheriff and deputies. By 1890, some states had moved executions to inside the jail or a prison building. The last public execution was held in Galena, Missouri, in 1937.

A major change took place in the legal jurisdiction of executions during the time of the Civil War. Before the war, all executions were conducted locally—generally in the jurisdiction in which the crime was committed. But on January 20, 1864, Sandy Kavanagh was executed at the Vermont State Prison. He was the first person executed under state as opposed to local authority. This shift in jurisdiction was not immediately adopted by other states. After Kavanagh, there were only about two state- or federally authorized executions per year well into the 1890s; the rest were locally authorized. That pattern would shift dramatically during the next 30 years. In the 1890s, about 90 percent of executions were imposed under local authority, but by the 1920s, about 90 percent were imposed under state authority. Today, all executions except those conducted in Delaware and Montana and by the federal government and the military are imposed under state authority. Texas has carried out the most executions of any state, although Oklahoma, Florida, Ohio, and Arizona also regularly execute persons convicted of murder (Table 1).

States with No Death Penalty (and Year Abolished)

Alaska (1957)
Connecticut (2012)
Hawaii (1957)
Illinois (2011)
Iowa (1965)
Maine (1887)
Maryland (2013)
Massachusetts (1984)
Michigan (1846)
Minnesota (1911)
New Jersey (2007)
New Mexico (2009)
New York (2007)
North Dakota (1973)
Rhode Island (1984)
Vermont (1964)
West Virginia (1965)
Wisconsin (1853)

Legal Decisions by the U.S. Supreme Court

Furman v. Georgia

On January 17, 1972, Furman's lawyers argued to the Supreme Court that unfettered jury discretion in imposing death for murder resulted in arbitrary or capricious sentencing in violation of their client's Fourteenth Amendment right to due process and his Eighth Amendment right not to be subjected to cruel and unusual punishment. Furman's challenge proved successful, and on June 29, 1972, the U.S. Supreme Court set aside death sentences for the first time in its history. In its decision in *Furman v. Georgia, Jackson v. Georgia*, and *Branch v. Texas* (all three cases were consolidated and are referred to here as the *Furman* decision), the Court held that the capital punishment statutes in the three cases were unconstitutional because they gave the jury complete discretion to decide whether to impose the death penalty or a lesser punishment in capital cases. The majority of five justices pointed out that the death penalty had been imposed arbitrarily, infrequently, and often selectively against minorities. A practical effect of *Furman* was the Supreme Court's voiding of 40 death penalty statutes and the sentences of more than 600 death row inmates in 32 states. Depending on the state, the death row inmates received new sentences of life imprisonment, a term of years, or, in a few cases, new trials.

It is important to note that the Court did not declare the death penalty itself unconstitutional. It held as unconstitutional only the statutes under which the death penalty was then being administered. The Court implied that if the process of applying the death penalty could be changed to eliminate the problems cited in *Furman*, then it would pass constitutional muster.

The backlash against *Furman* was immediate and widespread. Many people, including those who had never given the death penalty issue much thought, were incensed at what they perceived as the Supreme Court's arrogance in ignoring the will of the majority and its elected representatives. They clamored to have the penalty restored. Obliging their constituents, the elected representatives of 36 states proceeded to adopt new death penalty statutes designed to meet the Court's objections. The new death penalty laws took two forms. Twenty-two states removed all discretion from the process by mandating capital punishment upon conviction for certain crimes (mandatory death penalty statutes). Other states provided specific guidelines that judges and juries were to use in deciding if death were the appropriate sentence in a particular case (guided discretion death penalty statutes).

Woodson v. North Carolina *and* Gregg v. Georgia

The constitutionality of the new death penalty statutes was quickly challenged, and on July 2, 1976, the Supreme Court announced its rulings in five test cases. In *Woodson v. North Carolina* and *Roberts v. Louisiana*, the Court voted 4–5 to reject mandatory statutes that automatically imposed death sentences for defined capital crimes. Justice Potter Stewart provided the Court's rationale. First, Stewart admitted that "it is capricious to treat similar things differently" and that mandatory death penalty statutes eliminated that problem. He added, however, that it also "is capricious to treat two different things the same way." Therefore, to impose the same penalty on all convicted murderers, even though all defendants are different, is just as capricious as imposing a penalty randomly. To alleviate the problem, then, some sentencing guidelines were necessary. Thus, in *Gregg v. Georgia, Jurek v. Texas*, and *Proffitt v. Florida* (hereafter referred to as the *Gregg* decision), the Court voted 7–2 to approve guided discretion statutes that set standards for juries and judges to use in deciding whether to impose the death penalty. The Court's majority concluded that the guided discretion statutes struck a reasonable balance between giving the jury some direction and allowing it to consider the defendant's background and character and the circumstances of the crime.

It is noteworthy that the Court approved the guided discretion statutes on faith, assuming that the new statutes and their procedural reforms would rid the death penalty's administration of the problems cited in *Furman*. Because guided discretion statutes, automatic appellate review, and proportionality review had never been required or employed before in death penalty cases, the Court could not have known whether they would make a difference. Now, more than 30 years later, it is possible to evaluate the results. A large body of evidence indicates that the reforms have had negligible effects.

Coker v. Georgia *and* Eberheart v. Georgia

The Supreme Court has repeatedly emphasized that the death penalty should be reserved for the most heinous crimes. In two cases decided in 1977, the Court, for all intents and purposes, limited the death penalty to aggravated or capital murders only. Aggravated or capital murders are murders committed with an aggravating circumstance or circumstances. Aggravating circumstances (or factors) or special circumstances, as they are called in some jurisdictions, refer "to the particularly serious features of a case, for example, evidence of extensive premeditation and planning by the defendant, or torture of the victim by the defendant." At least one aggravating circumstance must be proven beyond a reasonable doubt before a death sentence can be imposed. (To date, all post-*Furman* executions have been for aggravated murder.) The Court ruled in *Coker v. Georgia* that the death penalty is not warranted for the crime of rape of an adult woman in cases in which the victim is not killed. Likewise, in *Eberheart v. Georgia*, the Court held that the death penalty is not warranted for the crime of kidnapping in cases in which the victim is not killed. Traditionally, both rape and kidnapping have been capital crimes regardless of whether the victim died.

Lockett v. Ohio *and* Bell v. Ohio

One of the changes to death penalty statutes approved by the Court in *Gregg* was the requirement that sentencing authorities (either juries or judges) consider mitigating circumstances before determining the sentence. Mitigating circumstances (or factors), or extenuating circumstances, refer "to features of a case that explain or particularly justify the defendant's behavior, even though they do not provide a defense to the crime of murder" (e.g., youth, immaturity, or being under the influence of another person). The requirement that mitigating circumstances must be considered has been the subject of several challenges. The first test was in 1978 in the cases of *Lockett v. Ohio* and *Bell v. Ohio*. In those cases, one of the issues was whether defense attorneys could present only mitigating circumstances that were listed in the death penalty statute. The Court held that trial courts must consider any mitigating circumstances that a defense attorney presents, not just those listed in the statute. The only qualification to this requirement is that the mitigating circumstance must be supported by evidence.

Pulley v. Harris

In *Pulley v. Harris* (1984), the Court decided that there was no constitutional obligation for state appellate courts to provide, upon request, proportionality review of death sentences. Since *Pulley*, many states have eliminated the proportionality review requirement from their statutes, whereas other states simply no longer conduct the reviews.

Lockhart v. McCree

In *Lockhart v. McCree* (1986), the Court ruled that prospective jurors whose opposition to the death penalty is so strong that it would prevent or substantially impair the performance of their duties as jurors at the sentencing phase of the trial may be removed for cause. Stated differently, as long as jurors can perform their duties as required by law, they may not be removed for cause because they are generally opposed to the death penalty. To date, *Lockhart v. McCree* is the latest modification to the Court's earlier *Witherspoon* decision. In *Witherspoon v. Illinois* (1968), the Court rejected the common practice of excusing prospective jurors simply because they were opposed to capital punishment. The Court held that prospective jurors could be excused only for cause. That is, jurors could be excused only if they would automatically vote against imposition of the death penalty, regardless of the evidence presented at trial, or if their attitudes toward capital punishment prevented them from making an impartial decision on the defendant's guilt.

McCleskey v. Kemp

The most sweeping challenge to the constitutionality of the new death penalty statutes was *McCleskey v. Kemp* (1987), wherein the Court considered evidence of racial discrimination in the application of Georgia's death penalty statute. Recall that in the *Furman* decision, racial discrimination was cited as one of the problems with the pre-*Furman* statutes. The most compelling evidence was the results of an elaborate statistical analysis of post-*Furman* death penalty cases in Georgia. That analysis showed that Georgia's new statute produced a pattern of racial discrimination based on both the race of the offender and the race of the victim. In *McCleskey*, the Court opined that evidence such as the statistical analysis—which showed a pattern of racial discrimination—is not enough to render the death penalty unconstitutional. By a vote of 5 to 4, it held that state death penalty statutes are constitutional even when statistics indicate they have been applied in racially biased ways. The Court ruled that racial discrimination must be shown in individual cases—something McCleskey did not show in his case. For death penalty opponents, the *McCleskey* case represented the best, and perhaps last, chance of having the Supreme Court again declare the death penalty unconstitutional.

Atkins v. Virginia

In *Atkins v. Virginia* (2002), the Court ruled that it is cruel and unusual punishment to execute the mentally retarded. A problem with the *Atkins* decision is that the Court did not set a standard for what constitutes mental retardation. That issue was left to the states to decide. Texas became the first to test the law when it pursued, successfully, the execution (in 2009) of Bobby Wayne Woods, a convicted murderer, who had an IQ of between 68 and 86.

Roper v. Simmons

In *Roper v. Simmons* (2005), the Court held that the Eighth and Fourteenth Amendments forbid the imposition of the death penalty on offenders who were under the age of 18 at the time their crimes were committed.

Baze v. Rees

In this case (2008) the Court ruled that execution by lethal injection did not constitute "cruel and unusual punishment" and therefore was acceptable under the U.S. Constitution. (Some states, however, have begun to question the chemical "cocktail" used in lethal injection after a few instances of slowed and/or seemingly painful death.)

The Situation Today

Globally, the death penalty is trending toward abolition. As of this writing, more than half of the countries in the world—100 of them—have abolished the death penalty in law or practice. Another 48 have effectively abandoned it in practice (or at least have not applied it in 10 years or more). All of the major U.S. allies except Japan have abolished the death penalty. On the other hand, only 40 countries and territories have retained the death penalty and continue to apply it; seven countries allow it (on paper), but only in extraordinary circumstances (such as war).

In the United States, 19 jurisdictions (including the District of Columbia) do not have a death penalty, and among the 31 jurisdictions that do have one, only a handful use it more than occasionally and almost all of them are located geographically in the South. More than 70 percent of all post-*Furman* executions have occurred in the South. Still, executions are more concentrated than the 70 percent figure suggests. Five states—Texas, Virginia, Oklahoma, Missouri, and Florida—account for 65 percent of all post-*Furman* executions; three states—Texas, Virginia, and Oklahoma—account for 53 percent of them; Texas and Virginia account for 45 percent of them; and Texas alone accounts for 36 percent of them. Thus, the death penalty today is a criminal sanction that is used more than occasionally in only a few nonwestern countries, a few states in the U.S. South, and two U.S. border states. This is an important point because it raises the question of why those death penalty—or more precisely, executing—jurisdictions in the world need the death penalty, whereas all other jurisdictions in the world—the vast majority—do not.

In the states noted previously, the death penalty has proved stubbornly resilient and will probably remain a legal sanction for the foreseeable future. One reason is that death penalty support among the U.S. public, at least according to the major opinion polls, remains relatively strong. According to a recent Gallup poll, for example, 60 percent of adult Americans favored the death penalty for persons convicted of murder, 35 percent opposed it, and 5 percent did not know or refused to respond (Gallup 2013). But the trend is toward declining support for it; Gallup notes that the figures mentioned are the lowest they have been in 40 years. Support for the death penalty among Republicans stands at 80 percent, among Independents at 60 percent, and among Democrats at 47 percent.

The abiding faith of death penalty proponents in the ability of legislatures and courts to fix any problems with the administration of capital punishment is one reason for its continued use in some places. However, the three-decade record of fine-tuning the death penalty process remains ongoing. Legislatures and courts are having a difficult time "getting it right," despite spending inordinate amounts of their resources trying.

Many people support capital punishment even though they are ignorant of the subject. It is assumed by abolitionists that if people were educated about capital punishment, most would oppose it. Unfortunately, research suggests that educating the public about the death penalty may not have the effect the abolitionists desire. Although information about the death penalty can reduce support for the sanction—sometimes significantly—rarely is the support reduced to less than a majority, and the reduction in support may be only temporary.

Two major factors seem to sustain death penalty support in the United States: (1) the desire for vindictive revenge and (2) the symbolic value it has for politicians and law enforcement officials. According to a 2010 Gallup poll, 50 percent of all respondents who favored the death penalty provided retributive reasons for their support: 37 percent replied "An eye for an eye/They took a life/Fits the crime," and another 13 percent volunteered "They deserve it." The reasons offered by the next largest group of death penalty proponents (by only 11 percent each) were "Save

taxpayers money/Cost associated with prison" and "Deterrent for potential crimes/Set an example." No other reasons were given by more than 10 percent of the death penalty proponents (Gallup 2010).

Conclusion

The choice of "An eye for an eye" has been called *vindictive revenge* because of its strong emotional component. Research shows that the public supports the death penalty primarily for vindictive revenge. Those who responded "An eye for any eye" want to repay the offender in kind for what he or she has done. Research also shows that people who support the death penalty for vindictive revenge are generally resistant to reasoned persuasion. That is, they are less likely to change their position on the death penalty when confronted with compelling evidence that contradicts their beliefs.

Politicians continue to use support for the death penalty as a symbol of their toughness on crime. Politicians who oppose capital punishment are invariably considered soft on crime. Criminal justice officials and much of the public often equate support for capital punishment with support for law enforcement in general. It is ironic that although capital punishment has virtually no effect on crime, the death penalty continues to be a favored political silver bullet—a simplistic solution to the crime problem used by aspiring politicians and law enforcement officials. In sum, although the global trend is toward abolishing the death penalty, pockets of resistance in the United States remain and will be difficult to change.

See also Crime, Punishment, and Politics; Drug Policy and Politics; Public Opinion; Terrorism, Torture, and Politics.

Robert M. Bohm

Bibliography
Acker, James R., Robert M. Bohm, and Charles S. Lanier, eds. 2003. *America's Experiment with Capital Punishment: Reflections on the Past, Present and Future of the Ultimate Penal Sanction.* 2nd ed. Durham, NC: Carolina Academic Press.
Bakken, Gordon Morris. 2010. *Invitation to an Execution: A History of the Death Penalty in the United*

States. Albuquerque: University of New Mexico Press.

Banner, Stuart. 2002. *The Death Penalty: An American History*. Cambridge, MA: Harvard University Press, 2002.

Bedau, Hugo, and Paul Cassell, eds. 2004. *Debating the Death Penalty: Should America Have Capital Punishment?* New York: Oxford University Press.

Bohm, Robert M. 2011. *Deathquest: An Introduction to the Theory and Practice of Capital Punishment in the United States*. 4th ed. Cincinnati, OH: Anderson, 2011.

Gallup. 2010. "Death Penalty." www.gallup.com /poll/1606/death-penalty.aspx. Accessed March 4, 2014.

Gallup. 2013. "U.S. Death Penalty Support Lowest in More Than 40 Years." www.gallup.com/poll /165626/death-penalty-support-lowest-years.aspx. Accessed March 4, 2014.

Haney, Craig. 2005. *Death by Design: Capital Punishment as a Social Psychological System*. New York: Oxford University Press.

Sundby, Scott E. 2007. *A Life and Death Decision: A Jury Weighs the Death Penalty*. New York: Palgrave Macmillan.

DEBATES, PRESIDENTIAL

While Americans often associate political debates with the advent of television, what may be the most infamous of all debates occurred long before this era. During the 1858 Senate race in Illinois, Republican Senate nominee Abraham Lincoln engaged in a series of seven debates against Democratic incumbent Sen. Stephen Douglas. These debates took place in congressional districts around the state, and the candidates debated such wide-ranging topics as the abolition of slavery and the Mexican–American War. The format was unusual, with each candidate posing several questions to the other. While Lincoln lost his race for the Senate, the popularity he gained throughout the North during these debates set the stage for his successful run for the presidency two years later.

In the modern era, the first nationally televised presidential debate was held during the campaign of 1960, which pitted Massachusetts senator John F. Kennedy against Vice President Richard Nixon. On September 26, 1960, Nixon and Kennedy faced each other in the studios of station WBBM in Chicago, Illinois. CBS News reporter Howard K. Smith moderated the debate. Sixty-six million viewers tuned in to watch the candidates speak. Democratic nominee Kennedy appeared youthful and healthy and had a relaxed demeanor in front of the camera. His manner was confident and knowledgeable, and his personal charm was evident to those who viewed the event on their television screens. Most importantly, Kennedy seemed at ease answering difficult questions regarding foreign and domestic policies. Prior to the debate, political observers had wondered whether the young senator's political inexperience might prove a liability. Equally important, Kennedy used the forum as a means to allay concerns that as a Roman Catholic, he would be obligated to follow the decrees of the pope, effectively giving the Vatican control of the White House.

Exhausted by a long campaign tour and recovering from a recent illness, Nixon looked tired, drawn, and pale in comparison to Kennedy, with sweat clearly visible on his forehead at times. This had the unwanted effect of making Nixon appear nervous and even dishonest, in response to some questions. In the end, Kennedy prevailed in the minds of the majority of those who watched the first debate on television, while those who listened to the debate on the radio perceived Nixon to be the victor. Even though three more debates between Kennedy and Nixon followed, the first debate proved crucial in persuading swing voters to take a chance on the untested Kennedy. Kennedy went on to narrowly defeat Nixon in both the popular and Electoral College vote in what remains the closest election in recent history.

Debate Emerges—In Fits and Starts

Sixteen years would pass before the next presidential candidate debate. President Lyndon Johnson refused to give Republican nominee Barry Goldwater a platform for his ideas during the campaign of 1964. Burned by the 1960 debates, Republican nominee and frontrunner Richard Nixon refused to debate Democratic nominee Hubert Humphrey or American Independent

Party candidate George Wallace during the campaign of 1968. Far ahead in the polls, President Richard Nixon saw no advantage in debating Democratic nominee George McGovern during the campaign of 1972.

Nixon's resignation in 1974 as a result of the Watergate scandal (and the resignation of his initial running mate, Spiro Agnew, after he was indicted on tax charges) catapulted Michigan representative Gerald Ford into the presidency. Two years later, Ford was running for a full term, and he agreed to participate in a series of debates against Democratic nominee Jimmy Carter. These debates were sponsored by the nonpartisan League of Women Voters. Both candidates were heavily dependent on public funding for their election bids and thus were eager for whatever free media coverage was available. The most memorable moment in the Ford-Carter debates occurred during the second debate on foreign-policy issues. *New York Times* reporter Max Frankel asked Ford a question about the Soviet Union's domination of Eastern Europe. To the surprise of everyone watching (including Carter), Ford responded, "There is no Soviet domination of Eastern Europe." Ford was given an opportunity to clarify his remarks, yet he still insisted that the Soviet Union did not dominate Poland, Romania, and Yugoslavia. It took more than a week for the Ford campaign to clarify Ford's comments. Ford's gaffe taught future presidential candidates an important lesson. Candidates needed to prepare for almost every question and stick carefully to a script when answering debate questions. Similar to 1960, the 1976 debates helped Carter overcome public doubts over his ability to deal with complex foreign-policy and domestic issues. Equally important, Carter was able to convince voters that he looked presidential. Carter went on to narrowly defeat Ford on Election Day.

Debates in the 1980s

During the campaign of 1980, President Jimmy Carter initially refused to debate former actor and Republican nominee Ronald Reagan, much as President Johnson had refused to debate Barry Goldwater in 1964. The Carter campaign defended its decision by arguing that President Carter needed to remain in the White House to deal with pressing international and domestic problems, including the ongoing Iran hostage crisis. Carter's strategy backfired; the public came to perceive Carter as a hostage in the White House. As the polls tightened between Carter and Reagan, the Carter camp decided that Carter had no choice but to debate Reagan. Reagan had already debated independent candidate John Anderson (a moderate Republican who had lost his party's nomination to Reagan). Presidential historians credit Reagan's performance in the October 28 debate as crucial to his landslide victory over Carter. Reagan delivered a number of carefully rehearsed sound bites to remind voters of the nation's severe economic problems and the declining standard of living for millions of Americans. Particularly noteworthy was the question Reagan posed to his viewing audience: "Are you better off than you were four years ago?"

Riding high in the polls and having attained a reputation as the Great Communicator, Reagan did not shy away from debating Democratic nominee Walter Mondale in the campaign of 1984. To the surprise of many observers, Reagan fared rather poorly in the first debate. Speculation swirled over whether Reagan's age might be slowing him down. Yet, in the October 21 debate, Reagan returned to form, dispelling any doubts that he had lost his touch with the American people. Reagan would go on to defeat Mondale in a landslide.

During the campaign of 1988, Republican nominee George H. W. Bush was initially reluctant to debate Democratic nominee Michael Dukakis. By the first debate on September 25, Bush had come back from a double-digit deficit in the polls to hold a small lead over his opponent. Neither Bush nor Dukakis committed any major gaffes during the first debate. By the second debate on October 13, Dukakis found himself trailing in the polls by a significant margin. The Bush campaign had successfully defined Dukakis as yet another Northeast liberal who was soft on crime. In one of the most controversial questions in presidential debate history, the moderator of the debate, Bernard Shaw of the CNN, asked Dukakis whether he would still oppose the death penalty if his wife "were raped and murdered," an oblique reference to the Bush campaign's Willie Horton ad (which described how the convicted felon Horton had been released on weekend furlough in Governor Dukakis's home state of Massachusetts, only to commit further violent crimes). Dukakis responded with an emotionless and scripted answer that reflected his long opposition to the death penalty: "No, I don't, Bernard. And I think you know that I've opposed the death penalty during all of my life. I don't see any evidence that it's a deterrent, and I think there are better and more effective ways to deal with violent crime. We've done so in my own state. And it's one of the reasons why we have had the biggest drop in crime of any industrial state in America; why we have the lowest murder rate of any industrial state in America." Dukakis's lack of emotion when asked to contemplate the death of his wife was not well received by political commentators or the public at large. Bush went on to soundly defeat Dukakis.

The League of Women Voters withdrew its sponsorship of the final debate of the 1988 campaign, declaring that "the demands of the two campaigns would perpetrate a fraud on the American voter." League president Nancy Neuman noted: "it has become clear to us that the candidates' organizations aim to add debates to their list of campaign-trail charades, devoid of substance, spontaneity, and honest answers to tough questions." In particular, the league objected to the 16-page negotiated agreement between the candidates demanding control over questioners, the composition of members of the audience, and access for the press, among other things. The candidates refused to debate under any other conditions, and the League backed out of the debate.

Debates in the 1990s

In the aftermath of the league's decision, the major political parties established the nonprofit Commission on Presidential Debates (CPD). Because the major parties control the composition of the CPD, it is not a

Presidential candidates Bill Clinton (standing, left), George H.W. Bush (seated, center), and Ross Perot (seated, right) present their arguments to a studio audience during a debate, October 16, 1992. (AP Photo/Stephan Savoia)

nonpartisan group. The presence of independent candidate Ross Perot in 1992 created problems for the commission. While they would have liked to exclude Perot, he had strong support in public opinion polls and therefore could not reasonably be excluded. The CPD also made a major change in the format of the debates by permitting citizens in the audience to directly ask the candidates questions in a format known as the town-hall meeting.

The first debate using the town-hall meeting format took place on October 15, 1992, at the University of Richmond in Virginia. President George H.W. Bush received considerable criticism for looking at his watch several times during the debate, giving the appearance that he was bored and not interested in the questions being posed by the audience. In sharp contrast, Bill Clinton welcomed the opportunity to directly interact with members of the audience and demonstrated an ability to identify with their concerns. Perot also made a strong impression in the debate, showing a mastery of information about the budget deficit that helped to increase his standing in the polls. Perot's running mate, Admiral James Stockdale, did not fare as well in the vice presidential debate, apparently falling asleep at one point. Stockdale is, however, remembered for asking the rhetorical question, "Who am I? Why am I here?"

During the campaign of 1996, Democratic incumbent Bill Clinton debated Republican nominee Bob Dole on two occasions, once with a single moderator and once when citizens directly asked questions of the candidates. Perot, running as a candidate for the newly created Reform Party, was excluded from the debates and unsuccessfully sued to have the CPD eliminated on the grounds that as the sole vehicle for the debates, it was inherently biased against third parties. Both Clinton and Dole were experienced and well informed; as a consequence, the debates had little effect on the polls.

Debates in the 2000s and 2010s

During the campaign of 2000, once again, a popular third-party candidate (Green Party nominee Ralph Nader) was excluded from the debates. The CPD had formulated specific criteria to limit third-party participation, including requiring that candidates have a reasonable chance at earning the 270 electoral votes needed to win the presidency and demonstrate (through at least five independent national opinion polls) public support of at least 15 percent of the electorate. Democratic nominee Al Gore faced Republican nominee George W. Bush in three separate debates. Prior to the October 3 debate, Gore held an eight-point lead in the polls. However, Gore sighed audibly at several points during the debate, also rolling his eyes (which he later claimed was due to an asthma attack) and thus creating the impression that he was bored. This helped Bush, who was able to convince voters that he was engaged and enthusiastic about the office of the presidency. Postdebate polls showed the gap between Gore and Bush narrowing. Viewership for the final two debates dropped sharply, suggesting that voters did not feel that additional useful information would be gleaned from the later debates. The vice presidential debate between Democrat Joe Lieberman and Republican Dick Cheney focused on foreign policy, an area of strength for both candidates, and the collegial atmosphere created by the candidates and their knowledgeable responses were an asset for both of their running mates, who were generally perceived to be less experienced in this area. The 2000 election ended with Al Gore winning the popular vote and narrowly losing the Electoral College after the Supreme Court effectively awarded Florida's disputed electoral votes to George W. Bush.

During the campaign of 2004, very little of note occurred during the debates of Republican incumbent George W. Bush and Democratic nominee John Kerry. Both candidates were careful not to stray from well-crafted responses, and broke little new ground. Once again, Nader was excluded from participating in the debates and was even arrested and removed from the audience, despite possessing a ticket to attend (for which he later sued).

In the campaign of 2008, the presidential debates between Democratic nominee Barack Obama and Republican nominee John McCain probably benefitted Obama far more than his opponent, in that they provided Obama with an opportunity to demonstrate his intellect and his presidential demeanor to the general public. McCain made no substantive gaffes; rather, he simply stood to benefit less, as voters were already familiar with his background from his long time in the

Senate and his earlier run for the presidency in 2000. McCain was already a known (and well-respected) quantity. However, at one point McCain inexplicably wandered around the stage, a lapse in form that was noticed.

The most eventful debate of the campaign of 2008, and also the most viewed, involved the vice presidential candidates Joe Biden and Sarah Palin. Palin's political experience prior to the debate consisted of her two years as Alaska governor and her previous time spent as mayor of the tiny Alaska town of Wasilla. She was a complete political unknown. Biden, on the other hand, had a long career in the Senate and had run in the primaries against Obama and Clinton, so, like McCain, he was a known quantity. Biden was placed in a difficult position—should he respond to the barrage of attacks delivered by Palin, or would it look more dignified to ignore them? Palin tended to avoid the questions asked by the moderator, instead giving folksy, canned replies on themes that she wanted to emphasize. At one point, Palin used a thinly veiled reference to Ronald Reagan when she responded to a comment by Biden by saying, "there you go again, Joe." On several occasions, Palin winked at the camera.

Palin explained her role in the campaign in a pitch to middle America: "One thing that Americans do at this time, also, though, is let's commit ourselves just every day American people, Joe Six Pack, hockey moms across the nation, I think we need to band together and say never again. Never will we be exploited and taken advantage of again by those who are managing our money and loaning us these dollars." The debate appeared to be a draw; pundits were wondering if Palin would commit a major mistake, and she did not, largely because she relied on rehearsed answers to questions that were not necessarily asked of her. Obama went on to easily defeat McCain, in a large part because voters blamed the Republicans for the poor state of the economy. Palin's role is more controversial. Some analysts argue that she was critical in mobilizing the evangelical Christian base of the party, who tended to be lukewarm about McCain. Others note that Republican voter turnout overall was down in 2008, potentially because some Republicans found McCain's choice of a running mate too unattractive. Several notable conservatives, including Christopher Buckley, Andrew Sullivan, John Dean, and Colin Powell, expressed support for Obama in 2008, and many of these individuals were critical of the selection of Palin.

During the campaign of 2012, Obama debated Republican nominee Mitt Romney in a series of three debates, while Biden debated Republican vice presidential nominee Paul Ryan. In the first Obama-Romney debate, Obama surprised viewers by not appearing fully engaged, a departure from his usual practice. As a result, the Obama campaign watched a solid lead in the polls before the debate drop considerably after the debate. In the second, town-hall-style debate, both candidates performed reasonably well, but Romney ended up being criticized for mishandling a question about the September 2012 attack on the U.S. diplomatic mission in Benghazi, Libya. Romney insisted that Obama had been late in identifying the attack as a terrorist attack, whereas the debate's own moderator, CNN's Candy Crowley, confirmed that, indeed, the president had characterized the attack as a terrorist one. In the third and final debate, Romney was thought by some viewers to be stumbling over his lines more than usual and was caught perspiring on camera, reminding some of Richard Nixon in the famed 1960 debate.

Conclusion

The concerns of the League of Women Voters have been borne out by the character of modern debates. Eager to avoid damaging gaffes, presidential and vice presidential debates have become heavily scripted events, with candidates rarely straying from talking points, even if those talking points are not responsive to the questions they are being asked. While debates remain a ritual for all presidential and vice presidential candidates, whether they contribute much useful information to voters is questionable. Polls tend to show that voters feel that their own party's candidate had the strongest performance, regardless of the actual content of the debate.

See also Campaigns and Campaigning; Nominating Conventions; Presidency and Presidential Politics; Television News, Opinion, and Politics; Vice Presidency.

Robert North Roberts, Scott John Hammond, and Valerie A. Sulfaro

Bibliography

Commission on Presidential Debates. 2012. "Debate History." www.debates.org/index.php?page=debate-history. Accessed May 5, 2014.

Jamieson, Kathleen Hall, and David S. Birdsell. 1990. *Presidential Debates: The Challenge of Creating an Informed Electorate*. New York: Oxford University Press.

Lincoln-Douglas Debates. 2002. University of Nebraska–Lincoln. lincoln.lib.niu.edu/lincolndouglas/index.html. Accessed May 5, 2014.

Marietta, Morgan. 2009. "The Absolutist Advantage: Sacred Rhetoric in Contemporary Presidential Debate." *Political Communication* 26, no. 4: 388–411.

Minow, Newton N., and Craig L. LaMay. 2008. *Inside the Presidential Debates: Their Improbable Past and Promising Future*. Chicago: University of Chicago Press.

Schroder, Alan. 2008. *Presidential Debates: Fifty Years of High-Risk TV*. New York: Columbia University Press.

DEBT, DEFICIT, AND POLITICS

The words "debt" and "deficit" have been hot topics in American politics for a long time, but much confusion surrounds both terms. Try talking to people about the "government debt." Numbers scare most people, especially big numbers such as those found in the U.S. budget and those that mark our national debt. Though vitally important in any discussion of government (or one's own finances), these topics are not fully explained and are often avoided by media sources. When one understands their meaning and how they are used in government, one gains a greater understanding of the nature of our political system and how American society has changed over the past 30 to 40 years.

> **"Deficit"**—The yearly amount the United States (or an individual) overspends in one year.
>
> **"Debt"**—The total of all accumulated yearly deficits.

Starting with a commonsense definition, "deficit" is the amount one spends in excess of one's income. It is no different for government. When expenditures exceed income from taxes, fees, and all sources, including borrowed funds, there is a deficit. The government normally passes a yearly budget displaying an estimate that shows how short of funds it will run and how much it will have to borrow. Over the past 40 years the United States has spent more than it takes in nearly every year, and those yearly deficits add up. These accumulated deficits become "debt." Most individuals have some debt through a home mortgage or a car loan. When individuals borrow money, a clear plan is usually established to pay the lender back. The United States continually borrows money from many sources and adopts a staggered repayment schedule depending on the type of debt it has borrowed and from whom it has borrowed.

When it comes to debt and deficits, the U.S. budget, the deficit, and the debt have become political theater for both parties in Congress, whose leaders squabble over who is the biggest saver, the more efficient spender, or the best monitor of the public trust. The budget and the size of the deficit are always controversial political topics at the forefront of nearly every discussion about government. Politicians on the inside see the machinations of how debt and deficits work in the U.S. budget, but the public is not privy to these discussions and is left to seek understanding of these concepts through media reports that are usually simple, basic, and incomplete. An attempt at clarifying the issues involved in our debt and deficits is made in the present entry.

History and Demographics

The United States of America has had some degree of national debt since the days of the Revolutionary War, when the country borrowed money from France, Holland, and Spain to fight the British (United States Bureau of the Public Debt 2012). Since then, the debt has grown, contracted, and grown again. During the 1920s the United States ran a small surplus, and did so again in 1947–1948, 1956–1957, and 1999–2000 (Budget of the United States 2012a). Table 2 shows how our debt has grown at crucial periods in our history.

> Debt is a common feature of our American culture. In the late 1990s and after 2000, most Americans freely used credit cards for anything and everything. Credit card spending

Table 2 U.S. Debt and Percentage of Gross Domestic Product

Period	Total Debt	Percentage of Gross Domestic Product
1790	75 million	35.0
1835	0.0	0
1865	2.7 billion	35.0
1920	22.0 billion	36.0
1945	260.0 billion	90.0
1980	1.0 trillion	37.0
2012	16.3 trillion	105.0

Source: U.S. Office of Management and Budget.

rose from $1.2 trillion in 2000 to $2.4 trillion (projected) in 2012, and the total card debt outstanding is $870 billion (projected) (United States Census Bureau 2012).

There are multiple reasons for our deficit and debt. Our demographics have changed. In 1970, 203 million people lived in the United States but in 2012, 330 million called the United States their home (Statistical Abstract of the United States 2012). Our public is aging; by 2030, 70 million people will be over 65, creating a challenging environment for two of our costliest programs: Social Security and Medicare (Budget of the United States 2012a). Downturns in the economy create newly unemployed and increase the demand for social services at the state and federal levels. New services and programs have been added, agencies have grown and expanded their jurisdiction, and more sub-offices have been created. Since 1977, four new cabinet departments, those of Energy (1977), Education (1980), Veterans Affairs (1989), and Homeland Security (2002) have been created. In addition, the Bush administration signed a new and costly Medicare drug benefit program into law in 2003. More programs and offices equals more spending.

Keynesianism

When a government spends more for programs and services, more money is injected into the economy. When the government goes into a deficit to increase this spending, it is called "Keynesianism" after British economist John Maynard Keynes. Keynes's theory proposes that when the government is a more active player in purchasing goods and services, money flows into the economy and produces growth. The resultant economic growth produces jobs which produces employed individuals who pay income taxes and buy more goods and services. Keynes thought that the overall benefit would be positive even when governments engaged in deficit spending. In fact, Keynes thought governments should deficit-spend. Most governments today are engaged in deficit spending through a relationship with their central banks, a topic that will be explored later.

Keynes (1883–1946) advocated for governments to deficit-spend in order to put money into the sagging economy but was not concerned about the resulting deficit or debt. Keynes believed that when the economy grew, tax revenues would offset the deficits and debt (BiographyOnline.com 2012).

Today

Deficit spending, through Keynesian policies, is a part of every budget cycle and almost a "given" in American politics. In 2010, the Obama administration passed the *Patient Protection and Affordable Care Act*, a large program to provide government-subsidized health insurance and an expansion of Medicaid to those individuals who have no health insurance. Also, since 1991, America has conducted three expensive wars whose cost is approximately $3 trillion: the 1991 Gulf War, the Iraq war, and the invasion of Afghanistan (Budget of the United States 2012a). In addition, technology has come to the U.S. government which has undergone a revolution in how the offices do their work. Government agencies have reorganized themselves and their records electronically and established an Internet presence. These changes have consumed trillions in expenditures.

Complicating Factors

Other factors make the debt and deficit issue more confusing than it needs to be. One such factor is that the U.S. government makes its own rules on how much it overspends in any given year, how much it borrows, how much interest it pays, and when loans will be paid back. The amount the government overspends, or the deficit target, is usually determined by the interplay between the president and the Congress, by congressional politics, and by the possibility of borrowing from external sources. Over the years it has become the norm to spend more than the country takes in as revenue. Yearly deficits have become politically acceptable. Most of the media reports regarding the yearly deficit relay one of at least four different types of deficits, namely, the off-budget deficit. In the off-budget deficit, certain programs, in this case Social Security and Medicare, are left out of the budget figures. The reported off-budget deficit has been about $1 trillion each year from 2008 to 2013. If we put those programs back into the budget, the picture looks far worse with a yearly deficit in the multitrillions.

> The U.S. government records different types of budget deficits depending on their purpose at the time. They are the On-Budget Deficit, the Off-Budget Deficit, the Federal Funds Deficit, and the Consolidated Deficit. Each has its own purpose beyond the scope of this article (Collender 1991).
>
> The Generally Accepted Accounting Principles (GAAP), if used in the U.S. budget, would require the government to fully show what is owed to the Social Security and Medicare trust funds. Under GAAP rules our national debt would come closer to $100 trillion, and not the $16.3 trillion that the off-budget figures show (Cauchon 2006).

However, government reports the deficit according to its own rules and not the accounting rules that private businesses must use, and this is a crucial difference. Businesses account for all of their revenue and debts and include those that will come due at some point in the future according to the Generally Accepted Accounting Principles (GAAP). If the U.S. government used the GAAP rules, the deficit each year would run closer to $4 trillion $5 trillion. In addition, if we considered what is owed to those funds (Social Security and Medicare), our total debt would be far more

than the reported $16 trillion in late 2012. In the past, the U.S. government tapped federal civil service workers' pensions to offset a temporary shortfall when time was of the essence (Barr 2006; Goldfarb 2011). The government replaced its employees' pension funds with more "IOUs."

> **"Entitlement"** programs—Technically, an entitlement program is one in which all persons who may or may not have contributed to the program may receive benefits from it. Social Security was created in 1935 and in the years immediately thereafter there were about four workers for every beneficiary. In 2012, there were about two and one half workers for every beneficiary, and no money remained in the trust fund because Congress had spent it, replacing the money with "IOUs." Social Security is not, technically, an entitlement program because all workers pay into its trust fund (Budget of the United States 2012a).

The reason that Social Security trust funds are taken out of the budget should be obvious—there is no money in the trust fund, just government-backed "IOUs." Since the Social Security program was created in 1935, more money has flowed into the Social Security Trust fund than was needed to pay then current beneficiaries, and the excess was simply too big a temptation for Congress. In the ensuing years, Congress spent all of the excess revenue, leaving the Social Security Trust fund with a large future liability that will come due when those working now (and contributing to the Trust fund) will retire. The GAAP rules say that the United States must account for the value of that long-term liability, but the responsible U.S. officials say that it does not. The government has countered this concern by noting that it could "always cancel" the Social Security and Medicare programs (Cauchon 2006). Acceptance of the deficit-spending norm means that governments, regardless of their party, can promise more goods and services to their constituents, even though the money will have to be borrowed or created. When all expenditures are considered, neither political party, when it has had control of both houses of Congress over the past 30 years, has produced a balanced budget (Budget of the United States 2012b).

Another issue that produces misunderstandings about debt and deficits is that there are two categories of spending in the U.S. budget: "mandatory" and "discretionary" (Budget of the United States 2012c). Mandatory spending includes all entitlement programs (Social Security, Medicare, Medicaid, Food Stamps, etc.), interest on the debt, and a few other programs. This portion of the budget ranges from 62 percent to 67 percent and is on autopilot, meaning that, as long as individuals meet the eligibility criteria, the spending for these benefits goes forth regardless of how much or how little money is available in the Treasury or allotted to the program in the budget. When there are more claims than there are funds, deficit spending occurs. Generally, these programs are automatic because Congress does not reauthorize or sometimes even consider them during budget negotiations (Wildavsky and Caiden 2001). If claims for benefits exceed available funds by, for example, $200 billion, then the government and its creditors must make an agreement on how to fund the benefits. Mandatory program spending, though essential for many people to live, is highly contributory to the national deficit and debt.

> "Mandatory" spending is program spending for which Congress has created eligibility criteria and for which money leaves the Treasury in payments to individuals and businesses. Most Americans feel these social programs are essential and deserved and proposals to reduce benefits are met with disdain (Cauchon 2006).

However, if those few programs are mandatory and account for about two-thirds of the budget, then everything else the government does falls in the "discretionary" category. That is exactly the case. Administration of the cabinet departments, all of the independent agencies such as NASA and the Environmental Protection Agency, must be paid for from discretionary funds left in the budget. National defense of the country is discretionary, federal education programs are discretionary, Homeland Security is discretionary, Interior, Transportation, and Commerce department spending, and so on are all discretionary. These agencies do not run entitlement programs. Congress debates *around* these topics when engaged in budget talks, and true debates about program substance are infrequent. Unfortunately, too, the mandatory portion of the budget is growing faster than current revenues can sustain.

Easy Money

To enable the creation of sufficient money to operate when revenues are inadequate, the U.S. government goes to the Federal Reserve banking system. The "Fed" as it is often called is a private cartel of banks that have agreed to manage the finances of the United States. The Federal Reserve System was formed in 1913 with the passage of the Federal Reserve Act and is not part of the U.S. government (Federal Reserve System of the United States 2003; Griffin 2002). The Federal Reserve works with Congress and the Treasury department to produce "money." When the president or Congress wants or needs to spend more money than is available, the Fed authorizes the Treasury to print a Treasury bond or bill for a certain amount of money, say $100 billion. The Fed then takes those bonds and tries to sell as many of them as it can to willing buyers in the open market. Many of the buyers of U.S. Treasury securities are foreign countries such as China. If the Fed cannot sell them all, it "buys" the remainder and adds the amount of the unsold bonds to its balance sheet. With the new money created from the issuance of debt, the Congress and the president can continue to spend. The Fed thus creates money out of U.S. debt (Griffin 2002). U.S. pension funds are one of the largest holders of this type of debt.

> Contrary to public opinion, the Federal Reserve System is not an agency of the U.S. government. A group of wealthy industrialists and U.S. senators took a train to Jekyll Island, Georgia, in 1913 and hatched out a complicated plan whereby private banks would authorize the printing of currency, a.k.a. "Federal Reserve Notes." The group felt that the new system would prevent currency shortages at banks around the country and therefore financial panics would be eliminated (Griffin 2002).

"Black ops" programs are popularized as the stuff of secret agents and, indeed, that is sometimes the case. An example of a once-"black" program now in common use is the "L-Rad" Acoustic Wave Generator now in use by police and military units. The device, a large disc mounted on the rear of a heavy jeep or personnel carrier, emits a low-frequency sound wave into a group of people and makes them feel queasy or nauseous. They disperse quickly (mindjustice.org)

In addition, one part of the budget is so highly classified that only a few individuals know exactly what line items it includes. That part of the budget is devoted to covert, or "black" operations—"black ops." The items in this part of the budget are secret and never reported to the media on the premise that disclosure would jeopardize national security. Almost all of these items are for the Defense Department or the Department of Homeland Security and its suboffices, such as the National Security Agency or the Defense Advanced Research Projects Agency. When these budget items are made public, they are usually heavily redacted so that it is impossible to tell what they are. Estimates of expenditures range from $50 billion to over $1 trillion (Shachtman 2010). Covert programs are unlikely to show up as their true purpose and may be listed in the budget as something else.

Another factor that complicates the debt and deficit topic is that the congressional and presidential timetable for producing the budget is almost two years long, includes many stakeholders, and is fraught with burdensome reporting and complex requirements (Keith 1996). In 1921 Congress passed the *Budget and Accounting Act* that gave power to the president to begin the budget process every year. Formerly Congress held this power. Over one year in advance, the Office of Management and Budget (OMB) sends budget instructions to the federal cabinet departments and agencies (United States Office of Management and Budget 2012). Each agency builds its budget request based on what the department secretary or agency head believes is needed, what programs it is responsible for, and how the president directs it. (The agencies and departments are part of the executive branch.) Millions

of pages of forms must be completed by the agencies as they submit their budget requests to OMB. OMB then presents those requests in one package to the president, who then adjusts them as he sees fit. At this point the budget requests may be vague and general or very specific. When the president concludes his review and makes his adjustments, he presents his budget request to Congress.

"Compromise" between the parties in congress and between the branches of government, was, until about 1990, taken for granted. The party leaders, the rank and file congressmen and women, and the president expected that compromise would be reached and the wheels of government would move forward. Somewhere in the 1990s the atmosphere changed and partisan bickering and intransigence increased. Compromise is now lost somewhere in the trash-talking in the media and government output has slowed (Wildavsky and Caiden 2001).

Congress then begins work on its own version of the budget, and the members belonging to the president's party usually seek to move the items on his agenda forward. In both houses of Congress, the party with the most members, the majority party, also controls all committees, and Congress does most of its works in committees. If the president's party is not in control of either the House or the Senate, then the president's budget package moves forward slowly, if at all. If Congress is controlled by the president's party, his agenda moves forward more rapidly. When both the executive and legislative branches are controlled by the same party, more budgets are completed on time and there is less friction. It is unclear whether, over time, same-party budgets are larger or smaller than budgets produced by executive and legislative branches of different parties, a status known as "divided government." In times of divided government, both parties "dig in" and hold fast to their positions, generally refusing to compromise. While our government is in such a state, no budgets are produced or passed and the U.S. government runs on a series of "continuing resolutions." A continuing resolution simply allows expenditures for all budget items to go forward at the rate at which they stood the last time a budget was passed. Therefore, when the parties in control of the White House and the Congress are different, spending is likely to remain on autopilot to keep the government running and the benefits and services flowing while the two parties argue over what the country should do. Without the continuing resolution procedure, the U.S. government would be forced to shut down as it did briefly in 1995 and 1996, sending millions of workers home and delaying billions in benefits. However, when running on a continuing resolution, the Treasury must find the money to continue to spend on previously legislated programs even if that means borrowing from all available sources. Therefore, partisan intransigence promotes overspending and poor accountability on the debt and deficit issues.

Three other factors that help us understand our debt and deficits are those of (1) annularity, (2) balance, and (3) comprehensiveness—the so-called abc's of budgeting (Wildavsky and Caiden 2001). After World War II and until the 1980s, Congress considered the entire budget every year. Committee and floor debates brought discipline and accountability to the process. Budgetary balance was a factor that meant a lot more to elected officials than it does today. In fairness, it must be remembered that our economy was booming and tax revenues flowed freely into the Treasury. After the dot-com bust of 2000 and the financial crisis of 2008, tax revenues dropped sharply as businesses failed and millions lost their jobs, their homes, and their future financial security. Retail sales declined and the tax revenues with them. In recent decades, both presidents Bush and Obama have resorted to Keynesian spending to boost economic activity, each with minor success. Keynesian spending, while perhaps a boost to a sagging economy, increases deficits and, therefore, debt.

> The "fiscal cliff" was the term used to denote the precise moment at which the U.S. government would run out of money to operate because the country had reached the debt ceiling, or the statutorily imposed limit on borrowing, and could not legally borrow more.

> The "sequester" is a government measure to make small cuts in certain predetermined programs. When congress and President Obama failed to reached a budget agreement, the sequester automatically kicked in, lowering the expenditures by a small amount (The White House 2013).

Finally, until 2013, the U.S. government had a self-imposed limit on how much it could borrow. This limit was called the "debt ceiling." In late 2012, most controversy surrounded the lifting of this ceiling to allow the government to borrow in excess of the ceiling and thus continue spending through continuing resolutions. The condition of reaching the debt ceiling and running out of money to operate was called the "fiscal cliff." Many a talking head weighed in on the consequences of the United States "going over the fiscal cliff." Dire predictions abounded of service shutdowns, benefit interruptions, and even deaths of those who could not obtain needed public health care. In early 2013 President Obama, the Republican-controlled House of Representatives, and the Democratically controlled Senate abolished the debt ceiling such that now Congress is not required to pass a law that expressly raises the debt ceiling and the government can borrow as much as the market is willing to lend, continue to spend freely, and increase our national debt (Borrowing Limit Raised Officially 2013).

See also Banking Policy and Politics; Budget Politics; Recession and Politics; Social Security and Politics; Tax Policy and Politics.

Barbara L. Neuby

Bibliography

Bankrate.com. 2013. "Financial Security Index Survey." February 25. http://www.bankrate.com/finance/consumer-index/financial-security-charts-0213.aspx. Accessed May 24, 2014.

Barr, Stephen. 2006. "Retirement Fund Tapped to Avoid National Debt Limit." *Washington Post* (March 8), D4.

BiographyOnline.com. 2012. Keynes, John Maynard. http://www.biographyonline.net/writers/keynes.html. Accessed May 24, 2014.

"Borrowing Limit Raised Officially." 2013. *New York Times* (February 5), A14.

Budget of the United States. 2012a. Table 3.1 "Outlays by Super-function and Function." U.S. Office of Management and Budget, Washington, DC.

Budget of the United States. 2012b. "Historical Perspective." U.S. Office of Management and Budget, Washington, DC.

Budget of the United States. 2012c. Table 1.1 "Summary of Receipts, Outlays, Surpluses or Deficits 1798–2017." U.S. Office of Management and Budget. Washington DC.

Cauchon, Dennis. A. 2006. "What's the Real Federal Deficit?" *USA Today* (August 3), 1.

Collender, Stanley. E. 1991. *The Guide to the Federal Budget*. Washington DC: The Urban Institute Press.

Federal Reserve System of the United States. 2003. "The Structure of the Federal Reserve System." Last Modified July 8. http://www.federalreserve .gov/pubs/frseries/frseri.htm. Accessed May 24, 2014.

Goldfarb, Zachary. 2011. "Treasury to Tap Pensions to Help Fund Government." *Washington Post* (15 May). http://www.washingtonpost.com/busi ness/economy/treasury-to-tap-pensions-to-help-fund-government/2011/05/15/AF2fqK4G_story .html. Accessed May 24, 2014.

Griffin, G. Edward. 2002. *The Creature from Jekyll Island*. Westlake Village, CA: American Media.

Keith, Robert. 1996. "A Brief Introduction to the Federal Budget Process." Congressional Research Service. http://www.4uth.gov.ua/usa/english/laws/leg proc/96-912.htm. Accessed May 24, 2014.

LRAD Corporation. 2013. "LRAD 100X." http:// www.lradx.com/site/content/view/207/110. Accessed May 24, 2014.

Shachtman, Noah. 2010. "Pentagon's Black Budget Tops $56 Billion." February 1. http://www.wired .com/dangerroom/2010/02/pentagons-black-budget-tops-56-billion/. Accessed May 24, 2014.

Statistical Abstract of the United States. 2012. "Table 1. Population and Area: 1790–2010." 8.

The White House. 2013. "What You Need to Know about the Sequester." http://www.whitehouse.gov /issues/sequester. Accessed May 24, 2014.

United States Bureau of the Public Debt. 2011. "Our History." Last Modified December 22. http:// www.publicdebt.treas.gov/history/history.htm. Accessed May 24, 2014.

United States Census Bureau. 2012. "Table 1188 Credit Cards-Holders, Number, Spending, and Debt, 2000–2009 and Projected for 2012." http://www.census.gov/compendia/statab/2012 /tables/12s1188.pdf. Accessed May 24, 2014.

United States Office of Management and Budget. 2012. "Budget Concepts and Process." http:// www.whitehouse.gov/sites/default/files/omb/bud get/fy2012/assets/concepts.pdf. Accessed May 24, 2014.

Wildavsky, Aaron, and Naomi Caiden. 2001. *The New Politics of the Budgetary Process*. New York: Addison Wesley.

Williams, W. John. 2010. "Financial Statements of the US Government." ShadowStats.com. http://www .shadowstats.com/article/no-340-2010-financial-statements-of-the-us-government. Accessed May 24, 2014.

DEMOCRACY

The word "democracy" literally means rule by the people (*demos-archy*). Its origins lie in the city states of ancient Greece. Though not usually associated with democracy, the city of Sparta adopted a popular assembly system of government around 600 BC (Hornblower 1992, 1). It was in the city of Athens, however, where democracy first flourished. The great architects of Athenian democracy, Solon and Kleisthenes, produced political reforms that led eventually to the establishment of regular assembly meetings around 508 BC.

Democratic government has historically been enmeshed in controversy. If democracy involves rule by the people, just who are the people who enjoy this right to rule? The Greek word "demos" (people) contains an apparent ambiguity. It can refer either to the citizenry or to the many poor (the masses) (Farrar 1992, 17). The Greek philosopher Aristotle understood democracy in this latter sense and distinguished it from aristocracy and oligarchy (rule by wealthy elites), and monarchy (rule by a single leader). Today, however, democracy is generally understood to involve citizen participation in the political process, and the conditions of citizenship in most contemporary democracies are generously understood to include native-born individuals as well as those individuals who have completed an established naturalization process.

But controversy remains; for even if it is possible to be clear on who qualifies as a citizen, there is still reason to ask why citizens are qualified to have a voice in political decision making. The standard alternative to democracy is meritocracy, or rule by elites best qualified to make key political decisions. The first and perhaps foremost defender of meritocracy was the Greek philosopher Plato, who likened political rule to sailing a ship. Sailing a ship, Plato argued, requires a division of labor in which the most able sailors (typically the ship's captain) make key decisions and the less able sailors carry them out. Making key decisions about how best to sail a ship is not something that should be left to a vote of the crew because the crew will likely lack the knowledge and expertise required to make wise decisions. The same can be said, Plato argued in his famous dialogue, *The Republic*, for the ship of state.

The right to rule, Plato concluded, should be put in the hands of those most able to rule. Because the people lack the wisdom to rule effectively and justly, Plato concluded that democracy was an undesirable form of government. This cynicism toward democracy as a viable form of government dominated Western political thought until a new spirit of democracy emerged during the French Revolution of 1789. This new spirit, and the concurrent revitalization of democratic government, now dominates the political landscape of the West and beyond. Democratic government is now commonly regarded as an integral aspect of the legitimacy of modern states, and even states that allow little or no citizen involvement in the political process attempt to avail themselves of this sense of legitimacy by appropriating the label of democratic government.

Why Democracy?

But is the popularity that democracy now enjoys really deserved? To pose this question is to ask why anyone should think it proper to prefer democracy to meritocracy. There are several reasons advanced in support of this preference. First, democracy seems like the most reasonable political strategy for checking possible abuses of political power when this power is lodged exclusively in the hands of minorities. Meritocracy is desirable only if elites rule wisely and unselfishly, but it degenerates into a form of tyranny if elites rule in a manner that champions their own interests at the expense of the remainder of the population. Democracy is an attractive form of government because it permits a population to guard against the tyranny of minorities and elites.

But if democracy equates to rule by the will of the majority, a new form of tyranny is on the horizon—tyranny of the majority. The threat of majority tyranny can be abated somewhat, however, if the population of a state is large. The larger the population, the more diverse it is likely to be, and the more diverse a population, the less likely that a majority will emerge that is in agreement on all, or even a great many, policy issues (Hamilton. Madison, and Jay 1961, 77–84). A second and more structural way to guard against majority tyranny is to adopt principled limitations on the power of government by means of a strategy of constitutionalism and/or adherence to a system of civil liberties. This strategy, popular in the United States, is rather undemocratic, however, for principled limitations upon the power of government in a democracy may actually prohibit political decisions favored by a majority of the citizenry, thus frustrating the will of the majority.

A second argument for preferring democracy to meritocracy makes appeal to the view that persons are their own best authority on what is good for them. This view holds that persons know their own best interests better than anyone else, and therefore, they should have input into any and all decisions that affect them (Dahl 1989, 100). Because political decisions invariably affect all citizens, it follows that citizens should have input into all political decisions. Democracy is that form of government that allows such citizen input. Therefore, democracy is to be preferred over meritocracy.

This seems like a good argument, but one might question whether persons really are their own unquestioned authorities on their best interests. Modern societies rely upon a division of labor, and people often need to seek the advice of others to determine what is best for them. Professionals like doctors and lawyers, for example, have an expertise that most people need at least some of the time to determine their best interests. But doctors and lawyers do not make decisions for people; they provide advice. People must then decide if they will follow this advice. Democratic politics ideally functions similarly. People with the expertise required to assess the costs and benefits of political decisions may, and perhaps should, offer their advice to the citizenry, and the citizenry must then decide what political decisions should be made. But there remains the problem of determining how citizens can reasonably assess the advice of political experts. Moreover, if people simply follow the advice of experts, they are no longer clearly the sole authorities of what is good for them, and this justification for democracy collapses.

Forms of Democracy

If democracy involves citizen participation in political decision making, it becomes important to consider how much, and what kind of, participation is required of the citizenry. In general, the greater the citizen involvement in political decision making, the more democratic a state will be. A state in which all political decisions are made collectively by the citizenry is more democratic than a state in which the citizens are only nominally or indirectly involved in decision making.

Consider first the type of involvement citizens might have. For full citizen participation in government, three conditions must be satisfied. First, all citizens must have access to the agenda setting process—this is the *agenda setting* condition. Agenda setting involves the introduction of those issues that the citizenry must decide upon. Political participation is diminished if a minority of individuals are able to determine what issues will be put forward for acceptance or rejection by the general citizenry when it is decision-making time. So, the more open the access to the agenda, the more democratic the state will be. Ideally, all citizens should be allowed to introduce issues on the agenda for consideration.

Second, all citizens should be permitted to express themselves with regard to the desirability or undesirability of all issues placed on the agenda—this is the *discussion and deliberation* condition. Discussion and debate should be expanded as much as possible under democratic government. The interests and concerns of all citizens should be heard, discussed, and considered. This assures that the interests and thoughts of all citizens receive a public hearing. Discussion and deliberation also provide an important educational function for democratic decision making. Through the process of debate and discussion, the costs and benefits policy proposals will have for the state are sharpened, refined, and better understood. Expanding debate and discussion also minimizes the influence of entrenched political interests and thus allows for the greater possibility of the formation of a public interest that ranges beyond the private interests of the parties most immediately concerned, positively or negatively, with policy proposals.

Third, all citizens should be permitted a voice in the decision-making process—this is the *decision-making* condition. Discussion and deliberation must end sometime, and when it does, it is time to vote. Voting determines whether a policy proposal placed on the political agenda will be accepted or rejected. But the voting process produces some important questions. While all citizens should be permitted to vote, one might still ask if all citizen votes should be weighted equally—a "one person, one vote" condition. One might also ask about the size of the vote required to accept or reject a particular policy proposal. If a simple majority is required, then a policy proposal would pass if 50 percent of the voting population plus one voted in favor of it. If a super-majority is required, then greater voter support for a policy proposal becomes necessary. For example, a super-majority might require two-thirds of the voting population's support to pass some proposal.

Weighted voting will make sense if it is believed that the decision-making input of experts, or better-informed individuals, should be accorded greater weight in the decision process than the weight to be accorded to nonexperts or to individuals with less interest in or concern for decision outcomes. If it is believed, however, that the interests and concern of all citizens should stand equal in the decision-making process, then votes should be weighted equally. This is the dominant sentiment in most contemporary democratic states, including the United States.

Reliance upon super-majorities will make sense if it is believed that the status quo should be preserved unless there is a strong public sentiment in favor of change of some sort. Super-majorities protect against the winds of change driven by transient majorities and introduce a more conservative element into the decision-making process. The more dramatic the outcome of some policy proposal at issue, the more sense it makes to rely upon a super-majority to affect change. In the United States, for example, a super-majority is required to amend the Constitution, though in less significant policy questions a simple majority will ordinarily suffice.

A democratic process in which all three conditions of democracy are maximally satisfied is called a *direct democracy*. In a direct democracy, the citizenry is completely self-governing. The political agenda is open to everyone. Discussion and deliberation is open to everyone and is taken seriously. And decisions are made according to the principle of majority rule. If the point of democratic government is to enable citizen self-government, then direct democracy is the most ideal form of democracy. If, however, it is infeasible or undesirable to have recourse to direct democracy, then it might be preferable to employ systems of *indirect democracy* where citizen involvement in the democratic process is lessened or diminished. The most common form of indirect democracy is *representative democracy*.

In representative democracy citizens do not engage directly in political decision making; instead they select, usually by means of an election, representatives to do this work for them. This means that representative democracy requires the formation of political institutions (legislatures) where the representatives of the citizenry can meet to do the job of governing. Representative democracy has the virtue of making the policy formation process more efficient and timely. It also takes a substantial amount of the burden of government off the backs of the citizenry, thus freeing up time for other pursuits. But recourse to representative democracy also raises challenging questions about how the representative process should work. The following are among the most challenging of these questions:

Who should be represented? How should representatives be chosen or selected? And, finally, what does the job of representation involve?

1. *Who should be represented?* The obvious answer to this question is that the citizens should be represented, and representatives are ideally supposed to function as proxies for the interests of the citizens they represent. It is hardly possible, however, for one person to represent all the differing interests that might happen to be present in the citizenry as a whole, and consequently, the job of representation must be apportioned in some way by breaking up the general citizenry into distinct constituencies. This apportionment might be done in a variety of ways. Representation might be based upon geographical districting, as it typically is in the United States, or it might be based upon the electoral support political parties receive at election time. These two strategies may also be blended to allow party support to determine representation in specified districts.

Suppose for the moment representatives are chosen by election. Elections are necessary only if there is competition for the job of representative within a specific constituency. Competition of this sort might be open and unstructured, or it might be organized along party lines. Parties tend to form because citizens with similar or overlapping interests have reason to pool their votes to have the greatest chance of winning competitive elections. If representatives are chosen from geographical districts, it could be decided that the winner will be that individual who receives the largest number of votes cast. This can be called the "winner take all" (or "first past the post") electoral system and is typical of the electoral process in the United States.

But representatives might also be chosen according to the proportion of votes a given party's candidate receives in an election. If, for example, five parties run candidates for five elective offices and each party receives 20 percent of the overall votes cast, each party would be entitled to one seat. This type of electoral process is typically called a system of proportional representation (Weale 2007, 130). Proportional representation increases the representation of minority parties and interests, while a winner take all system expands the representation of the more dominant parties and interests within the electoral constituency.

2. *How should representatives be chosen or selected?* In American politics, elections are the standard method for the selection of representatives. But representatives may also be chosen by lot or by some alternative random strategy. If representatives are randomly selected from the general body of citizens, anyone may be called into government service, and the general concerns of the population would then be well represented. If representatives are chosen by means of an electoral process, the selection process becomes competitive, and the campaign process will help educate the general citizenry on issues and provide voters with the opportunity to choose candidates who will most effectively represent their interests. Competitive elections make the political process adversarial and encourage party formation.

3. *What does the job of representation involve?* Representatives may elect to perform the duties of their office in two possible ways. First, they may suppose representation involves faithfully following and implementing the policy wishes and concerns of their electoral constituency. Second, they may follow their own conscience and help shape policy they believe necessary and appropriate. If competitive elections are used to select representative, the electorate should have a reasonable sense of the political views of the winner, and the winner should have some sense of the political wishes and concerns of the electorate. This information facilitates the process of representation and may encourage representatives to blend the two strategies of representation into a distinctive style of representation.

Challenges to Democracy

Democracy has three great enemies: size, time, and expertise. Direct democracy demands much of the citizenry. Citizens must put in the time required to inform themselves on policy proposals, listen to the concerns and interests of their fellows, and engage in the deliberative process. It follows that direct democracy seems best suited to small political units. As the size of the citizenry increases, logistical problems become more daunting. Ideally, direct democracy requires the opportunity for all citizens to assemble and hear one another out, but this opportunity is lost when the citizenry becomes so big that general assembly is no longer possible or feasible. Similarly, time constraints also become problematic as the citizenry grows in size. Discussion and deliberation is unworkable if everyone in a large state is allowed to discourse even for a short time on policy proposals because of the amount of time this would take.

Perhaps in an age where technological developments have expanded greatly the ability to communicate with others, some of these logistical difficulties may be overcome or at least moderated (Barber 1984, 273–78). But the problem of expertise would still remain. Modern societies are mutual support systems. Because people cannot do everything for themselves, they depend upon the contributions of others while developing their own talents and abilities to make their own contributions to others. Mechanics are necessary to fix cars. Lawyers are required to help make contracts. Doctors meet a population's medical needs; plumbers keep the drains going, and so forth. Politics also depends upon expertise. Modern states face economic problems, energy problems, international relations challenges, environmental issues, and so forth. The challenges of policy formation in these and many other areas of concern are daunting and demanding. Expertise is required if these challenges are to be met. If policy makers are not to be at the mercy of the experts in these various fields, they must develop an element of expertise of their own. But it is hardly possible for the general citizenry to become experts in each of the various policy fields that political decision making must cover. Thus, the need for expertise also diminishes the feasibility of direct democracy.

As noted earlier, the standard complaint against democracy is that the general citizenry is likely to act unwisely, capriciously, or intolerantly. The meritarian objection to democracy is that the general citizenry lacks the knowledge and sophistication to govern wisely and therefore political power should be handed over to appropriate elites. But contemporary challenges to democracy do not echo these meritarian concerns; instead, they introduce practical problems that require compromises to the ideal of democracy to sustain some degree of political participation by the general citizenry. Because direct democracy seems hardly feasible in large modern states, it is necessary to make do with indirect democracy.

Representative democracy overcomes the challenges of time and size by limiting the number of participants in legislative assemblies and thus enabling them to function in a workable fashion. But the problem of expertise remains. To meet this problem, either trained experts must be encouraged to enter the electoral process and run for office, or those individuals who do become representatives of the citizenry must be accorded the training that allows them to become expert in at least some of the key policy areas requiring political attention. In places like the United States today, the meritarian threat to democratic politics comes in the form of an entrenched bureaucratic system that controls most (if not all) of the knowledge and information required for effective decision making. To meet this threat, democratic assemblies in the United States must depend upon representatives who have the opportunity to develop an element of expertise on their own and the inclination to insert the concerns of the general citizenry into the policy formation process.

Democracy in the United States

The first democratic experiment in what is now the United States arguably appeared in the colony of Rhode Island in the middle part of the 17th century. This was, however, a radical departure from standard political practice in colonial America. The notion of democracy retained its historic negative connotation, even in America, through the period of the formation of the U.S. Constitution. The democratic spirit in America began to grow only with western migration. The ready availability of land in the west, the inevitable self-sufficiency of western settlements, and the emergence of distinctive regional interests all facilitated the emergence of the democratic spirit in America.

The architects of the U.S. Constitution remained suspicious of democracy, which they understood largely in terms of direct democracy. James Madison, for example, insisted that the federal union of states should be viewed as a republic and not as a democracy. Democracy, in Madison's judgment, was ill-suited to the fledgling United States because the size of the union made it unworkable (Hamilton, Madison, and Jay 1961, 81–84). Consequently, the Constitution, as drafted and ratified, blended elements of elite control with principles of representative government. Citizen participation in the political process in the early days of the union was restricted to the election of members of the House of Representatives. In addition, citizen eligibility for democratic participation was limited to white, male, property owners over the age of 21.

As the spirit of democracy grew throughout the land, changes were introduced to permit increased citizen selection of political leaders and to expand the suffrage by removing the freeholder requirement and including women, minorities, and those 18 years of age and older in the ranks of eligible voters. Americans still do not govern themselves, but they do select the people who do govern them by means of a system of representation. American democracy does not demand excessive political participation from the citizenry, and citizens are left free to determine their own degree of political involvement. But it does demand that the right of participation be extended to all those who qualify as citizens regardless of race, religion, ethnicity, gender, sexual preference, or political point of view. The ideal of equality drives the spirit of democracy in America.

See also Citizenship and Politics; Constitution and Constitutionalism; Electoral College; Political Parties; Redistricting; Voting and Politics.

Craig L. Carr

Bibliography

Barber, Benjamin. 1984. *Strong Democracy*. Berkeley: University of California Press.

Birch, Anthony H. 1993. *The Concepts and Theories of Modern Democracy*. London: Routledge.

Carr, Craig L. 2007. *Polity: Political Culture and the Nature of Politics*. Lanham, MD: Rowman & Littlefield.

Dahl, Robert. 1989. *Democracy and Its Critics*. New Haven, CT: Yale University Press.

Dahl, Robert. 1998. *On Democracy*. New Haven, CT: Yale University Press.

Dunn, John. 2005. *Democracy: A History*. New York: Atlantic Monthly Press.

Farrar, Cynthia. 1992. "Ancient Greek Political Theory as a Response to Democracy." In John Dunn, ed.

Democracy: The Unfinished Journey. Oxford: Oxford University Press, pp. 17–40.

Hamilton, A., J. Madison, and J. Jay. 1961. *The Federalist Papers.* New York: Mentor Books.

Hornblower, Simon. 1992. "Creation and Development of Democratic Institutions in Ancient Greece." In John Dunn, ed. *Democracy: The Unfinished Journey.* Oxford: Oxford University Press, pp. 1–16.

Saward, Michael. 1998. *The Terms of Democracy.* Cambridge: Polity Press.

Tilly, Charles. 2007. *Democracy.* Cambridge: Cambridge University Press.

Weale, Albert. 2007. *Democracy.* Houndmills, UK: Palgrave Macmillan.

DEMOCRATIC PARTY

The Founding Fathers knew they wanted a republican form of government that would secure the blessings of liberty for themselves and their posterity. But in the beginning, political parties were not on their horizon. In *Federalist Paper* #10, James Madison condemns the evils of political faction but recognizes their inevitability: "Liberty is to faction what air is to fire."

So it was impossible to eliminate faction without destroying liberty. Both were part of the political process. Later, during Washington's second administration, Madison helped Jefferson found the Republican Party, which historians commonly call the Democratic-Republican Party because of its historical ties to the modern Democratic Party.

To understand why political parties are vital to the democratic process, it is necessary to understand the organizational basis of political power and what functions political parties play in organizing government. According to Wilfred Binkley (1962), political parties are organizations that nominate candidates and contest elections in hopes of selecting governmental personnel and influencing public policies.

This is perhaps why it is extremely difficult for governments to operate without them, at least in a democracy. The crucial role they play may also help explain a famous dictum by E.E. Schattschneider (1942, 1): "Political parties created democracy and modern democracy is unthinkable save in terms of the parties."

The Democratic Party is the oldest party in the world and has been the dominant party in American politics with the exception of the third and fourth party systems (1860–1932). In this essay, we discuss how the Democratic Party has evolved over the course of American history, the political constituencies that have waved its banner, where the party stands on different policy issues today, its political contributions to American government and politics, and the challenges it faces.

History of the Democratic Party

Given the association of the modern Democratic Party with strong activist government, it is ironic that it began as an opposition party to the federalist policies of George Washington and Alexander Hamilton. But this was in keeping with its early republican philosophy of limited and constitutional government.

Under the leadership of Madison and Jefferson, it united an unlikely coalition of farmers, yeoman workers, and plantation owners under the banner of states' rights and slavery. Adding to its early difficulties, Federalists saddled it with the epithet of the Democratic-Republican Party because they associated democracy with mob rule. It was only later that the word "Democratic" came to be a badge of honor.

But what really established the dominance of the Democratic-Republican Party was the ability of its leaders to establish an organizational base. This included setting up the first political machines and recruiting new immigrants like Swiss expatriate Albert Gallatin, Jefferson's secretary of the Treasury. What also helped was the failure of the Federalist Party to recruit many new followers.

Under the leadership of Andrew Jackson, the Democratic-Republican Party expanded its electoral base to include the Border people. According to the historian David Hackett Fischer (1989), the name "Border" derives from the fourth and by far the largest wave (c. 290,000) of British settlers who migrated to America from northern England, Scotland, and Northern Ireland between 1718 and 1775. They settled largely in the Appalachian backcountry and the southern and western territories that eventually became known as the Border states.

Fischer calls Andrew Jackson the first Border chieftain who became president. His victory over the British in the Battle of New Orleans was one of the few bright spots in the needless and highly unpopular War of 1812, which culminated in the sacking and burning of Washington, DC, by angry British troops from Canada.

Jackson was known for introducing the spoils system in American politics. Critical historians tend to associate it with two tenets: (1) "To the victor go the spoils." (2) "There is not a job that cannot be performed by a party hack."

The former members of the Democratic-Republican Party who opposed "King" Jackson's patronage politics and his populist domestic and foreign policies became known as Whigs. The supporters of his and his successor's policies became known as Jacksonian Democrats. In 1844 they formally renamed the party as "The Democratic Party," the name that has stuck to this day.

Faced with growing sectional and regional differences over slavery and economic policy, the Democratic Party splintered into a northern and southern wing in the elections of 1860. Lincoln may have saved the Union, but his victory with only 39 percent of the popular vote was largely responsible for the secession of southern states that quickly followed. During the Civil War (a.k.a. "The War Between the States"), Confederate leaders did everything they could to avoid factional and partisan disputes.

But after the end of Reconstruction in 1877, white supremacists took control of the southern wing and imposed Jim Crow laws that made conservative one-party rule possible (Burnham 1970). The "solid" Democratic South also made the Democratic Party competitive in the House and the Senate. The more liberal northern wing used machine politics to recruit new immigrant groups and take control of large central cities like New York, which went bankrupt under the corrupt Tammany Hall machine in 1871.

Only two Democratic candidates were elected president between 1860 and 1932. Grover Cleveland alternated in and out of the White House for two split terms. Woodrow Wilson served two consecutive terms because of a split in Republican ranks between liberal Republicans, who backed Teddy Roosevelt, and conservatives, who backed the incumbent and former vice president under Roosevelt, William Howard Taft.

In the elections of 1932 the Democratic Party re-established its dominance in American politics by cobbling together a New Deal Coalition of economic have-nots: white southerners, white ethnics, labor, liberals, and racial minorities. It was an ultimate rainbow coalition that united whites, blacks, Protestants, Catholics, and Jews as well as northerners and southerners.

In 1929, per capita income in the South was only half of the national average. White ethnics were struggling to rise up the immigrant ladder. Labor leaders could recruit workers into their unions. But without laws to protect their collective bargaining rights and a glut of immigrant workers who could be hired to break strikes, there was little they could do to raise worker wages and improve working conditions. Without a strong and active national government, liberals could not compete with conservative business interests. At this time blacks and other racial minorities were largely at the social margins of American society.

This coalition was largely dominant in national politics from 1932 to 1994 with two minor exceptions. Republicans controlled both houses of Congress for two years following the 1946 midterm elections and then again in 1952 under the former Supreme Allied Commander and war hero Dwight David Eisenhower, who ran as an "omnibus" candidate.

In 1964, Lyndon Johnson reached out to African American voters and promised to establish a "Great Society" but alienated many white southern and white ethnic voters in the process. This election has been characterized by Walter Dean Burnham (1970) as a "converting" election, one where the majority party remains in power but the political coalitions of the two parties change.

By 1994 white southerners were ensconced in the Republican Party and white ethnics were half-way there. As a result, the New Deal Coalition was reduced to what was left of organized labor, white liberals, and a growing constituency of racial and ethnic minorities, primarily African Americans.

Nonetheless, the Democrats were able to win the White House in 1976, 1992, and 1996 by nominating two southern-favorite-son candidates, Jimmy Carter and Bill Clinton. They were also inadvertently helped by Gerald Ford's controversial pardon of Richard Nixon and Ross Perot's Reform candidacy that split off Republican voters in the 1992 and 1996 elections.

What few commentators noted at the time was the electorate's changing racial and social makeup. Expansionist immigration policies and differential fertility rates were slowly but inexorably reducing white electoral dominance. What has also helped the Democrats in recent elections is their ability to carry the electoral votes of 18 "safe" states and the District of Columbia, which comprise 247 of the 270 that are needed to win the presidency.

These demographic and electoral trends finally came together for the Democrats in 2008 with the nomination of an African American candidate for president and a perfect Democratic storm: two unpopular wars, a financial panic, a tepid economy, and rising unemployment and underemployment. Under the slogan of "Change You Can Believe In," Barack Obama forged a new majority–minority coalition of African American, young, liberal, single-female, Latino, and immigrant voters. In the 2008 and 2012 elections, African Americans and young people under 30 were two key swing groups that were able to provide the margin by victory by themselves. If Obama had run in 1992, he would have been defeated by a far different electorate.

Though few saw it at the time, the groundwork for the Obama coalition was laid years before by the 1965 Immigration Amendments and the representational reforms introduced by the 1968 McGovern-Fraser Commission. The immigration amendments replaced a national quota system that restricted both the numbers and diversity of immigrants with one that freely admitted immigrants from around the world based on existing international pressures to immigrate and the goal of family reunification. South Dakota senator George McGovern and Minnesota Congressman Donald Fraser were liberal Democratic reformers who chaired a commission that was created in the wake of the tumultuous 1968 Democratic Convention in Chicago. Both wanted the party to reach out to young people, women, and racial minorities.

McGovern rejuvenated his state's Democratic Party organization and used it to win election to the U.S. Senate. The son of a Methodist minister and a history professor at South Dakota's Wesleyan College,

he opposed the Vietnam War on moral grounds and gained the Democratic nomination for president in 1972 largely on the basis of representational reforms he helped champion. In his acceptance speech, he declared that America might have to lose the Vietnam War to save its own soul. He was crushed in the general election by Richard Nixon, who won 61 percent of the popular vote to McGovern's 39 percent. McGovern could not even carry his home state, winning only the electoral votes of Massachusetts.

Under the sway of party liberals like McGovern and Fraser, the Democratic Party has pursued a representational strategy, as opposed to a service strategy that was followed by the Republican Party under the Republican national chairman Ray Bliss, who picked up what was left of the party's electoral base after the Goldwater debacle of 1964.

This representational strategy has been further extended by party liberals like President Obama, Senate majority leader Harry Reid, House minority leader Nancy Pelosci, and New York senator Charles Schumer, all of whom favor amnesty and a path to citizenship as a way of reaching out to Latinos and new immigrant voters.

The Changing Democratic Coalition

Since its inception, the political constituencies of the Democratic Party have evolved over time. Initially, it was the party of indolent white slave owners and rural-small-town residents, who were largely self-sufficient and dependent on their own hard labor. Now it is primarily the party of racially and ethnically diverse urban residents, organized labor, and professional groups, who have become increasingly dependent on government regulation, jobs, and welfare benefits.

This transformation in the political constituencies of the Democratic Party has forced historians and political scientists to distinguish between the party's root and instrumental goals. Historically, the Democratic Party has stood for the interests and well-being of the so-called common man.

From the beginnings of the Republic until 1880, these interests were perhaps best served by a Jeffersonian philosophy of limited and constitutional government, legislative dominance, and states' rights. With the onset of the industrial revolution and growing urbanization, these interests were better served by a Hamiltonian philosophy of strong government, executive dominance, and national supremacy. So while the instrumental goals of the Democratic (and Republican) Party have changed over time, it can be argued that the root goals have remained essentially the same.

In his analysis of post–World War II elections, Burnham (1970) argues that in many states, the Democratic Party has largely become a top-bottom coalition. This is because many white ethnic groups that have traditionally voted Democratic—for example, Jews, Greeks, and Italians—live in large metropolitan areas where there are more opportunities for higher education and good-paying jobs (Greeley 1976). They are joined by white mainline liberals, many of whom have postgraduate degrees and professional jobs that depend on government funding, such as education and social welfare. Those that are at the bottom are largely racial and ethnic minorities, such as African Americans, Latino Americans, and now increasingly new immigrant groups from third-world countries.

And just as the Republican Party has been largely reduced to the party of "white Europeans," the Democratic Party is coming to look more and more like the party of the "nonwhite rest-of-the-world" (Connelly and Kennedy 1994). A breakdown of the Democratic coalition by ethnicity is instructive. Since 1972 the University of Michigan Survey Research Center has collected National Election Study data on ethnicity. By classifying respondents into different ethnic groups, it is possible to see which are trending Republican and which are going Democratic.

Since whites split their votes between the two major parties, there is no racial or ethnic group whose members give the Republican Party majority support. So-called mainline groups, who trace their ancestries to the British Isles or northern Europe, provide the Republican Party a bare plurality of support. About 47 percent identify with the Republican Party. But 42 percent identify themselves as Democrats.

By contrast there are four major racial-ethnic groups where majorities identify themselves as Democrats: African Americans (84 percent), Latin Americans (59 percent), Greater Middle East (57 percent), and white ethnic (53 percent). Those who do not identify with another ethnic group besides "American" give plurality support to the Democratic Party (47 percent to 36 percent), while Asian Americans give only a slight plurality of support to the Democrats (43 percent to 42 percent). This breakdown suggests that under current immigration policies, the Democratic Party's political dominance will only continue to grow (Lieske, Hasecke, and Fisher 2013).

Democratic Policy Preferences

Democrats generally prefer more government intervention on social welfare, foreign policy, and civil rights issues but less on social-cultural issues. As Thomas and Mary Edsall (1991) argue in *Chain Reaction*, where voters' stand on most issues depends on where they sit. Because Democratic voters generally have lower levels of education and income, they tend to be more dependent on government-supported jobs and welfare benefits. Conversely, better-educated and more affluent Republican voters are less likely to need them.

For all practical purposes, the Democratic Party has become the liberal party in American politics, while the Republican Party has become the conservative party. Both trends have been driven by political polarization and partisan sorting (Abramowitz 2013). But these in turn appear to be driven by three primary forces.

Perhaps the most important is that Democratic primaries and caucuses are decided for the most part by very liberal and partisan voters. On average less than 20 percent of the eligible electorate vote in direct primaries. In the Democratic Party, the overwhelming majority are liberal ideologues. A second cause seems to be the joint effects of the country's growing levels of racial-ethnic diversity and income inequality, both of which are strongly correlated with political polarization and partisan sorting themselves. A third possible factor is the growing importance of social identities in American electoral politics, which seem to be largely driven by ethnic nepotism and competition (Lieske, Hasecke, and Fisher 2013).

Candidates for the Democratic Party's nomination on stage prior to the first presidential primary debate in Orangeburg, South Carolina, April 2007. From left: former senator Mike Gravel (D-Ala.), Sen. Barack Obama (D-Ill.), Sen. Christopher Dodd (D-Ct.), former senator John Edwards (D-S.C.), Rep. Dennis Kucinich (D-Ohio), Sen. Joe Biden (D-Del.), Governor Bill Richardson (D-N. Mex.), and Sen. Hillary Rodham Clinton (D-N.Y). (AP Photo/J. Scott Applewhite)

Liberal dominance in Democratic primaries also means that Democratic presidential aspirants must take liberal positions on three key litmus tests: (1) affirmative action, (2) abortion, and (3) gay rights. The first is of fundamental importance to African American voters. The second is very important to single women and young people. Finally, the third is important to a mobilizing gay community and liberals. In the 2008 Democratic primaries, all 10 candidates for the Democratic nomination, including General Wesley Clark, were pro-affirmative action, proabortion, and pro-gay rights.

Political Contributions of the Democratic Party

Among other accomplishments, the Democratic Party deserves credit for helping lay the foundations for a two-party system and legitimating the long-standing British tradition of a loyal opposition. On the negative side, it is the party that has been most closely associated with political machines, machine politics, and the patronage system. But with the exception of the post-reconstruction era in the South, it is also a party that for the most part has championed the well-being and interests of the common person.

Today, most Democrats believe that government is the solution to the social and economic ills that beset Americans, as opposed to the belief by many Republicans that government itself is the problem. So it is a party that likes to see itself as improving the lot of economic have-nots by policies of government intervention on social welfare, foreign policy, and civil rights issues.

However, its internationalist policies have gotten the country bogged down in two very costly and unpopular civil wars, Korea and Vietnam. They have also forced national leaders to do away with the draft and defend the country and police the world with arguably a more compliant and obedient professional military that does not question orders made by their commander in chief.

Despite Jefferson's professed love of limited government and states' rights, his support of the Louisiana Purchase did more to expand the territory of the United States than any other president. The Democratic Party also deserves credit for championing the principle of the social safety net and finally establishing the social welfare state in America during the 1930s, nearly 50 years after it was implemented in Bismarck's Prussia.

Democrats can also take credit for passing long-needed civil rights legislation like the 1965 Voting Rights Act and the 1968 Fair Housing Act. However, because of strong opposition from southern conservatives, the 1964 Civil Rights Act would not have been passed without the support of northern Republican moderates.

During the Johnson years, the Democrats expanded the welfare state into education, health care for the poor and elderly, income maintenance programs for the poor and unemployed, and urban renewal. In 2009, under unified control of the Congress and the White House, they were finally able to implement their dream of universal health care by passing the Affordable Health Care Act. However, they were unable to get even one Republican in either chamber to support the measure.

For now the jury is still out on the meaning and implications of the party's expansionist immigration policies. These include passage of the 1965 Immigration Amendments, the 1980 Refugee Act, and the 1990 Immigration Act. Not only have these legislative acts radically altered the racial and ethnic distribution of the United States. They have also greatly added to the costs of federal, state, and local governments.

Challenges

One major challenge the party will continue to face in the short run is rising Republican opposition to the growing costs of the welfare state. It will also become more difficult for the Democrats to portray themselves as the "party of the common man" when they pursue immigration policies that increase unemployment and underemployment. The huge and growing national debt they will leave at the end of the second Obama administration—more than doubling it to an estimated $20 trillion—will also make it difficult for them to deflect Republican charges that they are the "tax and spend" party.

A second challenge is satisfying all the constituent groups in their diverse coalition. Latinos mostly compete with blacks, and Asians mostly compete with whites for a dwindling number of good-paying jobs. Catholics favor national policies that promote Christian morality, while Jews want policies that establish a secular state. In Israel where Jews are a majority, they prefer a Jewish state. Finally, more and more young Americans are finding themselves competing with new immigrants and their children for jobs that require a college education or postgraduate degree.

A third challenge is how to reconcile a growing number of contradictions in its public policies that are not lost on conservative critics. The costs of policing the world impose limits on further expansions of the welfare state. Adding millions of new immigrant workers to the labor force will only make it more difficult to reduce unemployment and welfare rolls. A rapidly growing population, largely fueled by immigration, will further despoil the environment. American companies will continue to outsource jobs as long as Democrats go along with policies of free trade and economic globalism.

Perhaps a final challenge is how to rein in the excesses of liberal ideologues who define the party and what it stands for. In the long run, it cannot continue to expand the welfare state and increase the number of recipients who do not pay their way by constantly growing the national debt.

See also Factions and Intraparty Conflict; Liberals and Liberalism; Political Parties; Progressives, Progressivism, and President Barack Obama; Republican Party; Third Parties

Joel Lieske and Melanie Furey

Bibliography

Abramowitz, Alan. 2013. *The Polarized Public?* Upper Saddle River, NJ: Pearson.

Binkley, Wilfred E. 1962. *American Political Parties: Their Natural History.* New York: Knopf.

Burnham, Walter Dean 1970. *Critical Elections and the Mainsprings of American Democracy.* New York: Norton.

Connelly, Matthew, and Paul Kennedy. 1994. "Must It Be the Rest Against the West?" *Atlantic Monthly* 274 (December): 61–84.

Edsall, Thomas, and Mary Edsall. 1991. *Chain Reaction.* New York: W.W. Norton.

Fischer, David Hackett. 1989. *Albion's Seed.* New York: Oxford University Press.

Greeley, Andrew. 1976. "The Ethnic Miracle." *Public Interest* 45: 20–36.

Lieske, Joel, Edward Hasecke, and Kasey Fisher. 2013. "The Changing American Voter and Party System." Paper delivered at the 2013 State of the Parties Conference.

Schattschneider, Elmer Eric. 1942. *Party Government.* New York: Rinehart.

Deregulation. *See Privatization and Deregulation*

DESEGREGATION AND POLITICS

Prior to the 1954 *Brown v. Board of Education* Supreme Court decision, 17 states had laws requiring the segregation of black and white students in schools. The pursuit of school desegregation—first to remedy existing segregation and later to address a variety of related public and private actions—has been shaped by both legal decisions and politics at the federal, state, and local levels. This has led to uneven implementation and, in recent decades, to growing resegregation of schools (Orfield, Kucsera, and Siegel-Hawley 2012). School desegregation has, over time, been affected by changing jurisprudence, which mandates or constrains local political efforts. In addition, federal and state policies have largely furthered desegregation efforts in recent years, although these have become limited in scope.

The Development of the Law

In *Brown v. Board of Education*, the Supreme Court combined legal challenges to legally mandated school segregation from four districts. The segregation practiced in each case had been upheld—sometimes reluctantly—by lower courts due to the precedent of *Plessy v. Ferguson*, an 1896 case involving the segregation of passengers in railroad cars. The cases were first argued in 1952, but the justices were undecided and held them over to be reargued in 1953. In the interim, the chief justice died and was replaced by Earl Warren, previously governor of California. As portrayed in Richard Kluger's detailed analysis of the decision, there was intense behind-the-scenes work done by Warren, who had assigned the decision to be written by himself and believed it was important to render a unanimous decision so as to not give southern states any support for resisting the Court's decision. As a result, the final decision was eloquent in declaring that separate was "inherently" unequal, but put off any discussion about how such constitutional violations would be remedied. Nevertheless, a triumphant Thurgood Marshall, who had led the challenge to segregation, declared that schools would be desegregated within five years (Patterson 2001).

A year later, in a decision commonly known as *Brown II*, the Supreme Court directed that the best way to oversee compliance with *Brown* was to remand desegregation cases back to local district courts so that judges who understood the local context could devise desegregation remedies. They also infamously wrote that the decision should be complied with "with all deliberate speed," which was a marked change from the typical assumption that constitutional violations would be remedied immediately. It also meant that desegregation would have to proceed district by district, which often presented tremendous expense and difficulty for black plaintiffs who wished to challenge existing school segregation. Because of this, along with state responses such as "pupil placement laws" that made it virtually impossible in practice for black students to attend schools with whites, a decade after the *Brown* decision, only 0.2 percent of black students in the South attended majority white schools (Frankenberg, Lee, and Orfield 2003). In fact, in some states, it took until 1963 before any schools in the state were integrated.

In the late 1960s, the Supreme Court began to finally define what desegregation required of districts, indicating irritation with districts that had resisted desegregation for more than a decade. In *Green v. County School Board of New Kent County*, the Supreme Court declared that the time of token desegregation had to end, and dual school districts (e.g., black and white systems of schools within a district) needed to be eliminated "root and branch." The Court specified six factors that districts needed to address in terms of equity to be fully desegregated: students, staff, faculty, transportation, facilities, and extracurricular activities. Several years later, in the 1971

Swann v. Charlotte-Mecklenburg decision, the Supreme Court went further, declaring that in addition to the freedom-of-choice plans that *Green* had identified as subterfuge to avoid widespread desegregation, neighborhood school plans that resulted in segregated schools owing to segregated neighborhoods also did not meet the constitutional requirement of *Brown*. Instead, the Court ordered the use of cross-town busing of students, using noncontiguous zones where needed to fully integrate large districts. Finally, in 1973, the Court in *Keyes v. Denver, Colorado*, found that districts were still responsible for segregation that existed even if there were no laws mandating segregation as was the case in southern states. *Keyes* also first extended desegregation rights to Latino students. Thus, in a short time span, the Court had become a champion of school desegregation, increasingly prescribing wide-ranging strategies and judging compliance by outcomes.

This progress was quickly halted in 1974, in a split decision, and has been marching steadily backward ever since. The 1974 *Milliken v. Bradley* decision overturned lower court rulings that had required a metropolitan desegregation remedy for the segregation in the Detroit public schools. The Supreme Court held that since suburban districts had not been found liable for the segregation existing within Detroit, they did not bear responsibility for helping to remedy the segregation. In dissent, now-justice Thurgood Marshall predicted that exempting the suburbs from desegregation responsibility would lead to separate black and white schools—a prediction that accurately foreshadowed the demographics of schools decades later. Even with the subsequent *Milliken II* (1977) decision that devoted more resources to Detroit as a partial remedy to the harms of segregation, the district today has few white students while nearby suburban districts remain overwhelmingly white (see, e.g., Freund 2007).

In the 1990s, the Supreme Court issued three decisions that have resulted in the ending of scores of desegregation cases (Orfield and Eaton 1996). These cases lessened the standards that districts had to meet to be judged "unitary" or to have eradicated the dual system of segregated schools. The cases held that districts should be judged on whether they had made "good faith" efforts to desegregate, that they were not responsible for changing demographics in the district, and that court oversight could end even when it was likely that districts would resegregate. It is unclear exactly how many districts have since been declared unitary or how many remain under order (Le 2010), but these decisions have contributed to reductions in school integration in the South where most desegregation cases were in place (Reardon et al. 2012).

Finally, in an ironic twist on its recent jurisprudence in which the Court had emphasized the importance of ending federal court oversight in favor of returning local control to school districts, the Supreme Court prohibited districts from *voluntarily* implementing certain types of school integration policies (which had been adopted because districts wanted to maintain diverse schools). In a fractured, lengthy decision, the Court held that while the goals of voluntary integration policies were permissible, the means the districts were using harmed students because they used the student's racial status as part of the decision about school assignment. Essentially, the Court held that the use of a student's race/ethnicity to integrate schools was just as harmful as using race to assign students to segregated schools as was done prior to *Brown*. This decision, along with other decisions by the federal courts, has led many to be extremely hesitant about any use of race-conscious policies in K-12 student assignment.

Federal Politics

While the *Brown* decision was the impetus for school desegregation, the judicial branch was not solely responsible for the transformation of southern schools by the early 1970s. As mentioned, a decade after *Brown*, there was only token desegregation that had occurred in the South. Yet, the next several years brought key legislative policies that, when coupled with executive enforcement of desegregation, caused widespread desegregation compliance: the South, by 1970, had a higher percentage of black students attending majority white schools than was the case in any other region.

The 1964 Civil Rights Act was the first piece of legislation pertaining to school desegregation compliance. Title VI of the Civil Rights Act permitted the federal government to withhold federal funds that were to go to school districts that were not complying with desegregation remedies. The following year, as part of President Lyndon Johnson's War on Poverty, the Elementary and Secondary Education Act (ESEA) was passed. While not directly addressing school segregation, ESEA dramatically increased the federal money going toward education.

In addition to legislation, the executive branch enforcement of desegregation during the Johnson administration was another reason compliance with desegregation orders became more comprehensive. The Office of Civil Rights (OCR) within the Department of Health, Education and Welfare (HEW) was tasked with implementing the provisions of the Civil Rights Act and began to focus increasingly on the results of school policies in terms of racially balancing schools to receive federal funds. OCR and HEW officials, drawing on desegregation compliance requirements spelled out in lower court decisions, helped to increase the share of black students in formerly all-white schools by 1968. The U.S. Civil Rights Commission was another important federal actor at this time that issued reports on the status of desegregation.

During the Nixon administration, the Emergency School Aid Act (ESAA) was passed with bipartisan support from a Democratic Congress and the Nixon White House. The ESAA expressly forbid funding for busing students to schools to comply with desegregation orders, but instead directed money toward interventions that would improve the educational experiences of students in newly diverse schools. Hundreds of millions of dollars supported a wide array of programs and supports to make desegregation more successful: teacher training, curriculum development, and research on how to improve race relations. One part of the ESAA, for example, was the Magnet School Assistance Program (MSAP) that began in the mid-1970s and is still in existence. MSAP is a competitive grant program that supports the development or restructuring of magnet schools that are designed to reduce or eliminate racial isolation. The program was extremely popular, and districts often went beyond what was required in terms of desegregating students and teachers to gain the funding. ESAA ended in 1981, but MSAP was restored in the 1980s.

The political tide at the federal level turned against desegregation slightly before the courts' support of more extensive desegregation efforts began receding. Although there were a few desegregation measures during the Nixon administration, this administration is generally regarded as beginning the retreat from desegregation enforcement efforts though appointment of federal judges who were hostile to desegregation efforts, weakening the enforcement of desegregation remedies, and running on a "southern strategy" that demonized "forced busing." This trend continued under President Ronald Reagan who ended ESAA, which provided desegregation funding. The shift from desegregation and equity was further cemented by the release of *A Nation at Risk* in 1983, a report focusing on educational excellence not equity.

The last sustained, progressive attention by a federal administration was that of President Johnson's, despite the fact that students of color are a large and growing percentage of the public school enrollment—and the many changes in the educational landscape since that time. The hope among civil rights advocates of major changes by the Obama administration has not yet been borne out, though there are several policies to note. Most pertinent to desegregation is the guidance the Departments of Education and Justice released in December 2011 about the use of race-conscious policies in K-12 education. This guidance replaced a letter issued by the Bush administration's OCR that restrictively interpreted a 2007 case, *Parents Involved v. Seattle* (which knocked down race-conscious assignment). The Obama administration guidance highlighted what was legally permissible in terms of policies to create diverse schools and reduce racial isolation, but significantly also described the importance of pursuing such goals and described effective strategies based on districts' experiences and research findings. In addition, Secretary of Education Arne Duncan has spoken of the importance of school diversity, and the Education Department allows competitive grant programs to include as a competitive funding priority an incentive for schools or districts that are pursuing diversity. Yet, many programs do not yet include such incentives, and some existing programs may inadvertently incentivize segregation.

State Politics

Initially after *Brown*, the role played by states was to resist compliance with desegregation as much as possible. This occurred in a variety of ways. States implemented policies that were seemingly race-neutral but had the effect of maintaining rigid segregation in schools, such as freedom-of-choice or pupil placement laws that required students who wished to transfer to other-race schools to satisfy a dozen or more requirements. In some places, governors tried to prevent desegregation from happening—most famously in Little Rock, Arkansas, in 1957—and the federal government became involved to ensure that court orders to desegregate were followed. Finally, there was also state support in several southern states for private academies that enrolled white students who wished to avoid public schools subject to even token desegregation, including in parts of Virginia where the public schools closed rather than have any racial mixing.

In a more promising role, a handful of states have adopted policies to proactively support racial desegregation. Racial imbalance laws are in place in a few states, with the first being adopted in Massachusetts in 1965. There is not much evidence that such laws are currently being enforced, and there is also debate about whether such laws are still needed. Minnesota is a unique example in that it has a state desegregation rule that has, for example, led school districts to collaboratively form interdistrict desegregation partnerships. The state has also historically provided integration funding to support local desegregation initiatives. However, the integration funding is currently in jeopardy. There are also six to eight existing interdistrict transfer programs, some of which exist with state financial support and are instrumental in creating diverse schooling experiences for urban students of color who transfer to largely white suburban districts.

As is the case at the federal level, such pro-diversity policies are relatively small in scale in comparison to

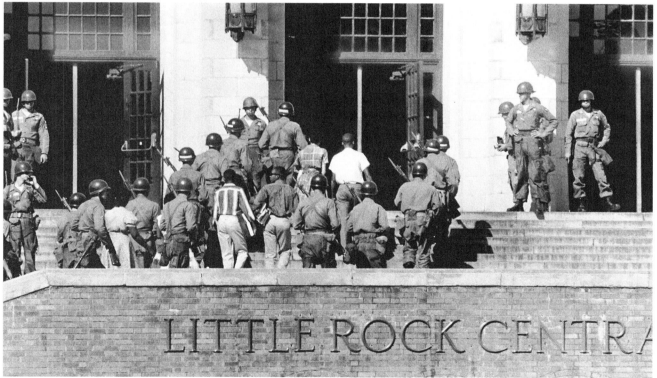

African American students walk up the steps to Central High School in Little Rock, Arkansas, September 25, 1957. They are flanked by U.S. Army soldiers carrying out President Dwight D. Eisenhower's order to enforce a federal court ruling integrating the school. The school district's lawsuit, *Cooper v. Aaron* (1958), was an additional unsuccessful attempt to delay the process of desegregating Arkansas schools. (Bettmann/Corbis)

other state education initiatives, and there are many other policies that may exacerbate racial isolation. For example, in Wisconsin, the Chapter 220 program is an integration-focused interdistrict transfer plan that sent students of color from Milwaukee to largely white participating suburban districts. More recently, Wisconsin has implemented an interdistrict choice plan that is more popular due to more funding that goes along with the program, but it does not have any desegregation guidelines and may exacerbate an already segregated metropolitan area.

Thus, while there has been relatively little attention paid to the role of states as it pertains to desegregation, over the last six decades there have been ways in which states have both furthered and impeded desegregation.

Local Politics

The differences in local politics differ widely across jurisdictions, depending on many factors such as legal history, type of jurisdiction (e.g., countywide vs. municipal district), demographics, and other characteristics. It is impossible to fully describe all such responses, so I briefly focus here on local politics during two distinct eras of desegregation: court-ordered desegregation and voluntary integration.

During the era of court-ordered desegregation, many school districts initially resisted compliance with *Brown* and subsequent court decisions as long as possible, or proposed remedies that would create the most upheaval in an effort to show that desegregation would not work. As experience with desegregation grew, and there were not constant reassignments to comply with court orders, in many districts, some of the elements of desegregation plans, such as magnet schools, were actually quite popular. Some districts, like Charlotte, North Carolina, which had fought vehemently against widespread desegregation (e.g., *Swann* case), turned desegregation into part of their identity as a district and fought efforts to be declared unitary.

As many districts once under court order have been declared unitary, the vast majority of new desegregation policies going forward will be those voluntarily implemented. While some districts like Wake County, North Carolina, have had voluntary desegregation policies in places for decades, many are more recently adopted. However, these policies are under increased scrutiny after *Parents Involved* struck down two such policies that used race-conscious controlled choice to assign students to schools. One of the districts, Jefferson County Public Schools (JCPS) in Louisville, Kentucky, had first adopted voluntary integration policies after it was declared unitary in 2000 because it valued the educational and social benefits of the desegregation plan it once fought to avoid implementing. JCPS has subsequently adopted a new voluntary integration policy that complies with current jurisprudence. Illustrating the diverse experiences of localities, the other district whose policy was struck down in *Parents Involved*, Seattle Public Schools, abandoned efforts to voluntarily desegregate and instead adopted a neighborhood schools policy. Thus, while there are important legal guidelines affecting local policies, the politics of the districts as it pertains to diversity vary substantially in terms of the district's desire to pursue policies in an arena that is seen as somewhat risky.

Other Policies

Finally, although not focused on here, it is important to note that school desegregation has been and still is affected by social policies beyond those of education. In particular, because of the local control of education, schools are strongly linked to geographic residence. Thus, housing policies have a substantial impact on school composition. There have been some limited efforts to design housing and education desegregation policies in coordination, and some scholars suggest that efforts to desegregate schools must also include neighborhood desegregation efforts to be sustainable. However, there has been minimal enforcement of the Fair Housing Act, despite its requirement that communities take affirmative action to further integration. Given growing restrictions on what policies school districts can implement, focusing on housing integration efforts is an important policy option for desegregation advocates.

Conclusion

The last six decades of desegregation illustrate the complexity of using the courts to accomplish social reform. *Brown* dramatically reshaped public education and, by extension, many aspects of the public sphere. These 60 years, however, have witnessed uneven progress and the challenges of pursuing such comprehensive change with a variety of political actors involved and whose interests toward desegregation have shifted over time. Today, desegregation varies widely, reflecting the vast differences in the local districts in which desegregation occurs. Yet, there is much left to be done to fulfill the promise of *Brown* and to realize the benefits for students and society of providing integrated education for all students.

See also Affirmative Action; Civil Rights; Cultural Pluralism; Education Policy and Politics.

Erica Frankenberg

Bibliography

Frankenberg, E., C. Lee, and G. Orfield. 2003. *A Multiracial Society with Segregated Schools: Are We Losing the Dream?* Cambridge, MA: The Civil Rights Project at Harvard University.

Freund, D. 2007. *Colored Property: State Policy and White Racial Politics in Suburban America.* Chicago: University of Chicago Press.

Lamb, C. M. 2005. *Housing Segregation in Suburban America since 1960: Presidential and Judicial Politics.* New York: Cambridge University Press.

Le, C. Q. 2010. "Racially Integrated Education and the Role of the Federal Government." *North Carolina Law Review* 88: 725–86.

Orfield, G., and S. Eaton. 1996. *Dismantling Desegregation: The Quiet Reversal of* Brown v. Board of Education. New York: The New Press.

Orfield, G., J. Kucsera, and G. Siegel-Hawley. 2012. *E Pluribus Separated: A Diverse Society with Segregated Schools.* Los Angeles: UCLA Civil Rights Project/Proyecto Derechos Civiles.

Patterson, J. T. 2001. *Brown v. Board of Education: A Civil Rights Milestone and Its Troubled Legacy.* New York: Oxford University Press.

Reardon, S., et al. 2012. "*Brown* Fades: The End of Court-Ordered Desegregation and the Resegregation of American Schools." *Journal of Policy Analysis and Management* 31, no. 4: 876–904.

DISABILITY AND POLITICS

Most texts and encyclopedias on politics ignore disability. Not long ago, most texts and encyclopedias omitted mention of sexual minorities. Some omitted mention of race, gender, and class. (And where differences were mentioned, the reference was often brief and superficial). With changing definitions and approaches came change in whether much of America was included in "politics," but also in how it was included. This entry summarizes the disability community's increasingly active participation in American politics.

Definitions and Approaches

Most discussions of disability and politics begin by discussing definitions and approaches. This entry is not an exception. "Disability" can be a label assigned to a disfavored group or to pioneers in human enhancement. In current American law and policy, though, "disability" usually means limitation in ability to perform functional tasks (e.g., walking).

Disability politics reflects dozens if not thousands of overlapping approaches, lenses, frames, or models. We group them into four categories. The approaches frequently coexist and overlap. Coalitions may embrace seemingly contradictory principles, but share common concerns (e.g., access to employment, health care, education, and housing).

Shifts in vocabulary accompany evolving definitions and approaches. "Handicapped," "challenged," "infirm," "patient," "client," or "invalid" are still used to describe disabled people, but less frequently. The "person-first" trend (e.g., "person labeled as having a psychiatric disability"; "Americans with Disabilities Act") partly grew from recognition that "disability" may mean that individuals are ignored. A later sentiment is that the person-first vocabulary is condescending. (Members of no other group are "people" before their characteristics. Analysts do not refer to "a person labeled as female, Irish, or heterosexual.") We sometimes use the person-first acronym for people with disabilities (PWDs) but we will often put disability first ("disabled people").

Contexts and Influences on U.S. Disability and Politics

Contexts and influences on U.S. disability and politics can be compared to categories used by British artist/activist Ju Gosling. What we group as separate "rights" approaches are part of Gosling's "social model." Gosling has an "administrative model" that we group with "medical approaches." Since "disability" includes every religion, level of education, age, ethnicity, region, class, gender, sexuality, etc., these factors are relevant to public policy.

Charity   "I organise social events for non-disabled people. This raises money to create jobs for non-disabled people. Then we provide the disabled people whom we think are deserving with the things that we think they need."

Medical   "I invent and administer tests to classify disabled people according to what I think are their impairments. Then I carry out experiments to try to make them more like me. If I fail, I try to identify and kill them before they are born."

Social   "I fight against prejudice, discrimination and disabling environments. I fight for equal rights legislation and better health and social care provision. I also fight to eliminate the poverty, abuse, violence and war that cause the majority of impairments."

Source: Gosling, Ju. 2003. "Helping the Handicapped." http://sinnlos.st/help/index.html.

Moral Approaches

The moral obligation of nondisabled people is a common American political theme. The theme of disability as a punishment is less frequent, although not uncommon. Thus, disability may be a source of obligation for non-disabled people to "help" or a just punishment. Media stereotypes may reinforce ideas of disabled characters being sinister and prone to criminality, on the one hand, or as needy and pitiful on the other.

Religions and charities sometimes link disability to their appeals to serve the needy. Many of the factors historically associated with someone being needy such as poverty, inferior education, and "unsightly" appearance were particularly characteristic of the disabled population.

Medical and Vocational Approaches

A second set of approaches suggest that the disabled population can be made "better" by medical care. With better scientific knowledge, medical care will improve, and therefore disabled people's lives will benefit. That care can be used either to remedy the person's disability or to change the person so that the person can engage in productive labor.

These approaches have been influential in the 20th and 21st centuries with a network of departments of vocational rehabilitation, and federal programs devoted to rehabilitation. Attitudes toward returning veterans' reintegration have often been significant in policy changes. Increasingly in the United States, veterans with disabilities will enter the civilian workforce, although support services are uneven.

Rights-Based Approaches

Especially after World War II, activists, scholars, and policy makers suggested that disabled people were individuals or a class entitled to rights. Laws sometimes followed, with rights language used in many, for example, the 1990 Americans with Disabilities Act (ADA). Rights language is also used by women, racial, ethnic, sexual minorities, and other groups to question education, institutionalization, and welfare policies.

Civil rights rhetoric is powerful in the United States, and disability rights are often cast as civil rights. Rights to health care, housing, education, employment, and many others raise broader "human rights" concerns. The United Nations Convention on the Rights of Persons with Disabilities (CRPD) lists rights for which disability advocates in the United States have long advocated.

Social-Cultural Approaches

Some approaches challenge the sufficiency of rights language. They posit emergence of a disability culture with values to which nondisabled Americans should subscribe. In addition to (or rather than) rights or opportunities, these approaches emphasize social change. Whereas rights language focuses on courts and government, a disability community may prosper independent of government institutions.

For instance, American historian Paul Longmore and psychologist Carol Gill wrote on "disability culture." Many people in major metropolitan areas, especially recently, identify with disability culture, overlapping with their claiming of rights. Some aspects of globalization and austerity measures threaten the survival of a "disability community." But other aspects of globalization, including improved information and communication technologies, contribute to the growth of an international disability culture.

Disability is no longer seen exclusively from a "deficit" approach and is a sign of resistance against a society (and politics) that disables people. Rather than impediments to the future, disabled people are the pioneers of new developments in education, prosthetics, architecture, and other fields.

Recent Disability Policy

Our previous section on rights approaches discussed the influence of returning veterans and the civil rights movement. Many cases and laws were a response to these influences.

Most of the first legislative changes obligated government, but only in some respects, and not restaurants, shopping malls, or sports arenas. The 1968 Architectural Barriers Act and 1973 Rehabilitation Act reflect the limits to legislative changes. While these acts affect government, particularly federally funded buildings and programs, a widespread pattern of private discrimination persisted.

The Rehabilitation Act was hampered by problems of implementation. Although its Section 504 prohibited discrimination on the basis of "handicap," implementing regulations were not issued until later. Four years after the law's adoption, the implementing regulations were finally issued after occupation of federal buildings in San Francisco, Washington, DC, and elsewhere.

Today as amended, the Rehabilitation Act provides standards and funding for Centers for Independent Living (CILs). CILs provide "essential ('core') services" of information and referral (e.g., for employment), independent living skills training (e.g., food preparation), peer counseling, and advocacy (for individual consumers and for "systems change"). Some CILs (though not others) also provide home modification information, equipment repair, recreational programs, and personal assistance services.

The 1975 Education of All Handicapped Children Act was subsequently amended and is today known as the Individuals with Disabilities Education Act (IDEA). IDEA includes great aspirations such as "zero reject," and "least restrictive environment." The aspirations are hampered by inadequate funding and uneven commitment from local educational authorities.

Although some Court decisions aided the disability civil rights movement, this was not always the case. In 1982 The Supreme Court heard *Board of Education of Hendrick Hudson Central School District v. Rowley*. Three years later, the Court heard *City of Cleburne v. Cleburne Living Center, Inc.* In both cases, the Supreme Court decisions limited the future application of disability rights.

The disability rights movement more often achieves change through disability protests and the legislative process than through the courts. ADAPT (originally American Disabled for Accessible Public Transit, then American Disabled for Attendant Programs Today, concerned with all disability rights issues) was founded in 1983. Disability activism is typically decentralized, so spontaneous protests emerged in major cities. Sometimes, but not always, local CILs or ADAPT chapters play significant roles.

A growing disability rights lobby included groups founded in the 1960s and 1970s, such as the Disability Rights Education and Defense Fund (DREDF, founded 1979), organizations founded later, such as the American Association of People with Disabilities (founded 1995), and older organizations whose activism increased with time, such as the American Foundation for the Blind (founded 1921).

In 1990, the ADA was enacted. Early drafts were written in the National Council on the Handicapped, today the National Council on Disability (NCD), then led by Justin Dart. Support for the ADA came from several members of Congress, among them the ADA's chief sponsor, Iowa senator Tom Harkin. A new legion of disability activists encouraged Bob Dole, Tony Coelho, Steny Hoyer, Major Owens, and Steve Bartlett to support Dart and Harkin.

Disfavor of actions "for" but not "by" disabled people is reflected in an emerging disability media. The "Disability Rag and ReSource," later the "Ragged Edge" and "Electric Edge" e-zine, "Mainstream," and "Mouth" gave voice to writers with disabilities. "New Mobility," the most commercially successful disability periodical, continues to shape and be shaped by American political culture. Broadcast media also reflect the disability rights movement's emergence. Pacifica stations and syndicated shows such as "On a Roll" and "Disability Matters" carried messages from an increasingly active disability community. Simultaneously, the major media slowly made small changes and concessions.

The disability press and lobby confronted what has been described as a "pendulum" or "backlash" from courts and policy makers. Many older statutes were updated, with new sections added to the Rehabilitation Act (e.g., Section 508 promoting web access in 1998), and the Americans with Disabilities Act Amendments Act (2008). With the political struggles came slowly increasing recognition that disability issues are not exclusively matters for medicine and social work. Physicians and social workers operate within a social and political context. Developments in the laboratory or academy can empower or marginalize the disability community.

Policy Dilemmas

Disability-related political issues such as immigration, employment, education, transportation, and assisted

---

Some Flashpoints

Candidates and issues reflect disability politics. Some candidates are open, sometimes affirming about their disabilities (e.g., Tammy Duckworth and James Langevin) or family members' disabilities (e.g., Cathy McMorris Rodgers and Sarah Palin's children with Down syndrome). The Obama administration touts its appointment of PWDs and explicitly included disability issues in its 2012 campaign. Social Security, stem cell research, the Affordable Care Act, funding for inclusive education, personal assistance, and assisted suicide are flashpoints.

Education Funding	Aspirations outpace achievement when it comes to education. Although IDEA was based on a 40% federal–60% state formula for financing, the federal portion was always below 20%. In examining "special education law" Ruth Colker and others suggest that it works much better for those who need it less, while services are less often available to poor students and their families.
Personal Assistance	In 1999, the Supreme Court held in *Olmstead v. LC* that Lucille Curtis and Elaine Wilson were illegally discriminated against since they wished to live independently rather than in the Georgia State Hospital. States devise plans to implement *Olmstead*, but the NCIL, the National Disability Rights Network, and other organizations point to serious weaknesses.
Assisted Suicide	Many disability rights groups, for example, Not Dead Yet and DREDF, contend that assisted suicide policies discriminate against PWDs. Seemingly neutral doctors undervalue life with a disability, authorizing assisted suicides of "terminal" people. Oregon was the first state to permit assisted suicide (1994). Washington followed through referendum (2009). The practice received judicial support in Montana (2009) and New Mexico (2014). Vermont's legislature approved of assisted suicide (2013). Several other states defeated similar proposals.

suicide may seem new. However, most issues accounting for the current salience of disability politics are rooted in earlier eras.

Disability is a fundamental part of the American and global experiences. Upon close examination, most aspects of the American experience have international causes or consequences. The topic of disability and politics can be appreciated through examination of U.S. foreign policy and war, development, and the building of international law.

War and peace have major consequences for disability and politics. What in earlier wars was inadequately described as "shell-shock" (some individuals diagnosed had not been near "shells") is now subsumed under post-traumatic stress disorder, a disabling condition. Traumatic brain injury has been described as a "signature injury" of the wars in Afghanistan and Iraq. Tinnitus is a medical term for hearing injuries that are now especially common. A large population now expects employment, recreation, and full social participation.

The United States vacillates between enthusiasm and hostility to United Nations activities promoting group rights of women, ethnic minorities, children, and persons with disabilities. The United Nations CRPD was drafted in New York and signed by U.S. president Obama. The Senate, however, refuses to approve the treaty by a constitutionally required two-thirds vote. U.S. participation in the convention system is now a priority for many nongovernmental groups such as the DREDF,

the National Council on Independent Living (NCIL), and the U.S. International Council on Disabilities.

"Independent living," "self-advocacy," and "de-institutionalization" are three prevalent ideas in disability politics. Sen. Robert Kennedy's description of the Willowbrook State School as a "snake pit" in 1965 was followed by a move away from large institutions, but barriers to independent living remain.

American politics confronts issues of life with a disability in many ways. Ongoing debates concern the use of capital punishment and assisted suicide. Prominent disability rights advocates including the Bazelon Center for Mental Health Law in Washington, DC, successfully argued that use of capital punishment against people with intellectual disabilities was unconstitutional. Their successful argument was that intent to commit capital offenses was unclear at best. The Supreme Court agreed in *Atkins v. Virginia* (2002).

A key concept in the ADA is nondiscrimination, either by governments (including government supported schools) or by "public accommodations" such as shopping malls, sports stadiums, and restaurants. The general rules, however, are unevenly implemented as noted by the courts, legislatures, and the media.

For instance, in a 2001 Supreme Court case, *Alabama v. Garrett*, a five-judge majority held that the ADA's employment provisions could not be used by plaintiffs (a nurse and a security guard) who had been state employees. The NCD, the major media, and other

Differing Views on Accomplishments to Date

"I am grateful for the Americans with Disabilities Act, which has heralded a new era of civil rights in this country. I think the Americans with Disabilities Act is the most useless, empty, unenforceable law of the last quarter-century. It ranks up there as one of the most pansy-assed excuses for a White House news conference in U.S. history."

—John Hockenberry

"[The Convention on the Rights of Persons with Disabilities] will provide the leverage, the hook, that we need in order to push other countries to pass laws or improve their laws or raise their standards for the protection of people with disabilities up to the standard that we have already adopted in the United States of America."

—Secretary of State, John Kerry

Hockenberry, John. *Moving Violations: War Zones, Wheelchairs, and Declarations of Independence*. Page 88. Kerry, John. Testimony to Senate Foreign Relations Committee, November 21, 2013 http://www.state.gov/secretary/remarks/2013/11/217894.htm.

Some Key Laws

Year	Law	Description
1973	Rehabilitation Act	Expands vocational rehabilitation services for and mandates federal responsibilities to PWDs.
1975	Individuals with Disabilities in Education Act (IDEA)—originally Education of all Handicapped Children Act	Guarantees a "free appropriate public education" (FAPE), regardless of disability, in the least restrictive environment. Seeks to prepare students with disabilities for employment and independent living.
1977	Implementing Regulations for Rehabilitation Act, §504	Prohibits discrimination on the basis of disability in federally funded programs or employment.
1990	Americans with Disabilities Act (ADA)	The legislative culmination of the disability rights movement. It provides remedies for abuses of PWDs' civil rights. The act's five titles cover employment (Title I), public entities/transportation (Title II), public accommodations (Title III), telecommunications (Title IV), and miscellaneous provisions (Title V).
2002	Help America Vote Act	Created in response to the 2000 presidential elections. Provides for access to polling locations and the voting machine/software for PWDs.
2008	Americans with Disabilities Act Amendments Act (ADAAA)	Passed by Congress in response to judicial decisions interpreting the ADA, which Congress felt severely limited the rights of PWDs. Broadens the definition of disability and requires courts interpreting the ADA to focus on whether there was discrimination rather than whether the individual is disabled.

Some Key Supreme Court Cases

Year	Case	Description
1982	. . . Hendrick Hudson Central School District v. Rowley, 458 U.S. 176	Concerned provision of a sign language interpreter for a deaf student. The Court held that a state satisfies its duty of FAPE by providing sufficient support services for children with disabilities to progress rather than to maximize potential.
1985	City of Cleburne v. Cleburne Living Center, Inc., 473 U.S. 432	Invalidated a Cleburne, Texas, zoning ordinance used to deny a construction permit for a group home for adults with mental disabilities. The Court held that the law violated the Fourteenth Amendment's equal protection clause. It rejected the contention that people with mental disabilities are a quasi-suspect class, as they are a "large and diversified group." In his separate opinion, Justice Marshall disagreed, arguing that there should be higher scrutiny in examining laws concerning people with mental disabilities.
1999	Olmstead v. L.C., 527 U.S. 581	Individuals with disabilities have the right to live in the community rather than in institutions. Interpreting the ADA's Title II, the Court found that institutionalization lowers PWDs' quality of life. Deinstitutionalization is a "reasonable accommodation" under the ADA.
2001	Board of Trustees of the University of Alabama v. Garrett, 531 U.S. 356	The Court found Congress had not overcome states' Eleventh Amendment immunity when enacting the ADA; therefore, Patricia Garrett and Milton Ash were unable to bring ADA employment discrimination claims against Alabama.
2002	Atkins v. Virginia, 536 U.S. 304	The Eighth Amendment's prohibition of cruel and unusual punishment includes execution of persons labeled "mentally retarded."
2004	Tennessee v. Lane, 541 U.S. 509	Access to the courts is a fundamentally protected right of people with disabilities under Title II of the ADA.

sources consistently indicate that barriers to equal access are still widespread.

Full and direct participation means more people speaking for themselves who were formerly excluded. It means removing barriers to participation. In 2002 the Help America Vote Act called for an end to "separate but equal" voting, with disabled people guaranteed access to the polls. A 2004 court decision, *Tennessee v. Lane*, acknowledged disabled people's fundamental rights to access courtrooms, specifically where trials were held on second floors of buildings without an elevator.

The minimal changes following adoption of non-discrimination legislation lead many disability rights advocates to suggest that more government action is necessary. They call for renewed attention to old guarantees, extension of some current ones, and addition of new reforms.

One subject of prominent current concern, the Social Security Act, was adopted in 1935, later amended to include Social Security Disability Insurance (SSDI). (SSDI is financed from deductions from wages and is greater than Supplemental Security Income). The adoption and evolution of both programs reflect the connection of disability and politics and conflicting perceptions of "rights."

Minimum wage legislation contains an exception for "sheltered workshops," allegedly because a subminimum wage enables transition into the workforce. Some organizations like the Salvation Army and Goodwill employ workers at subminimum wages, with criticism by the National Federation of the Blind, the NCIL, and other groups.

The linkage between economic rights and civil rights is apparent in debates over the Affordable Care Act (ACA). In 2010 Congress adopted the ACA (popularly known as "Obamacare"). The ACA includes a mandate that no one can be denied health insurance because of a preexisting condition.

Future Directions and Conclusion

This final section is speculative. Familiarity with disability's past and present in American political culture provides a basis for reasoned speculation. Does "disability" have a future in American politics? Some advocates of a "medical approach" envision a world of cure and prevention (perhaps aided by sterilization or assisted suicide policies). Utopia or dystopia, the techno-medical future is not going to happen. Some advocates of vocational and rights approaches envision a world in which disability no longer determines opportunities. Such a world is also unlikely.

What kind of future? There are many plausible alternatives. Although it seems trite to say "the future depends on us," it does. One very likely, but not inevitable scenario was summarized in Blaser's 1996 *Futurist* article, "A Brilliant Future with Disabilities." We have been very successful at keeping people alive with disabilities. When people live longer, they will acquire more disabilities. A task of public policy is to capitalize on these developments.

We know that especially with regard to disability, the world and the United States are, and will continue to be, more "lumpy" than "flat." New media, speech-related technology, prosthetics, advancements in medical care, recreation, and mobility all reflect the tension between potential, physical access, and actual usage. Social, economic, and cultural disparities hamper implementation.

Many disability advocates embrace concepts of "crip politics" and "universal design." Other advocates embrace one term but not the other, while others are leery of both terms. Some advocates for those with learning disabilities, AIDS, and the deaf community are skeptical of disability efforts, while other advocates suggest that such efforts will grow and become universal. Disability and politics is important now and will become even more so.

See also Cultural Pluralism; Grassroots Activism; Protest Movements; Veterans and Politics.

Arthur Blaser and Samuel Schleier

Bibliography

Bagenstos, Samuel. 2009. *Law and the Contradictions of the Disability Rights Movement*. New Haven, CT: Yale University Press.

Barnartt, Sharon, and Richard Scotch. 2001. *Disability Protests: Contentious Politics, 1970–1999*. Washington, DC: Gallaudet University Press.

Black, Edwin. 2003. *War against the Weak: Eugenics and America's Campaign to Create a Master Race*. New York: Four Walls Eight Windows.

Blanck, Peter, et al. 2005. *Disability Civil Rights Law and Policy*. St. Paul, MN: Thomson/West.

Blaser, Arthur. 1996. "A Brilliant Future with Disabilities." *The Futurist* 30, no. 5 (September/October).

Colker, Ruth. 2013. *Disabled Education: A Critical Analysis of the Individuals with Disabilities Education Act*. New York: New York University Press.

Fleischer, Doris Zames, and Frieda Zames. 2011. *The Disability Rights Movement: From Charity to Confrontation—Updated Edition*. Philadelphia: Temple University Press.

Haller, Beth. 2010. *Representing Disability in an Ableist World: Essays on Mass Media*. Louisville, KY: The Advocado Press.

Hockenberry, John. 1995. *Moving Violations: War Zones, Wheelchairs, and Declarations of Independence*. New York: Hyperion.

Hofstadter, Richard. 1959. *Social Darwinism in American Thought*. New York: George Braziller, Inc.

Johnson, Mary, and Barrett Shaw, eds. 2001. *To Ride the Public's Buses: The Fight That Built a Movement (Disability Rag Reader)*. Louisville, KY: The Advocado Press.

Krieger, Linda Hamilton. 2006. *Backlash against the ADA: Reinterpreting Disability Rights*. Ann Arbor: University of Michigan.

Longmore, Paul. 2003. *Why I Burned My Book and Other Essays on Disability*. Philadelphia: Temple University Press.

Neudel, Eric, director. 2011. *Lives Worth Living: The Great Fight for Disability Rights*. Natick, MA: Storyline Motion Pictures.

Nielson, Kim. 2013. *Disability History of the United States*. Boston: Beacon Press.

Russell, Marta. 1998. *Beyond Ramps: Disability at the End of the Social Contract*. Monroe, ME: Common Courage Press.

Scotch, Richard. 2001. *From Good Will to Civil Rights: Transforming Federal Disability Policy*. 2nd ed. Philadelphia: Temple University Press.

Shapiro, Joseph. 1994. *No Pity: People with Disabilities Forging a New Civil Rights Movement*. New York: Random House, Inc.

Shaw, Barrett, ed. 1994. *The Ragged Edge: The Disability Experience from the Pages of the First 15 Years of The Disability Rag*. Louisville, KY: The Advocado Press.

Switzer, Jacqueline Vaughn. 2003. *Disabled Rights: American Disability Policy and the Fight for Equality*. Washington, DC: Georgetown University Press.

DISASTERS AND POLITICS

Disasters, by definition, are disruptive events. They alter our everyday activities and normal interactions with others. Disasters are caused by many different types of circumstances and situations. Some disasters—such as tornadoes, floods, hurricanes, and earthquakes—occur because of fluctuations in weather patterns or layers in the earth's surface. These events are referred to as natural disasters because they are not directly produced by human activities or behaviors. Natural disasters represent both the most common and the most disruptive types of disasters. Some natural disasters have limited, concentrated impacts on small numbers of people, while others inflict far-reaching damages on extensive populations across massive geographic areas and national boundaries. It can be extremely difficult to predict exactly when and where natural disasters will occur, as well as how extensive their impact might be.

Other disasters are the product of our own actions and behaviors. They can be the consequence of societal advances and developments, or they can result from more idiosyncratic activities. Such disasters include travel-related mishaps, infrastructure failures, technological breakdowns, and hazardous material accidents. They also include disasters that happen because of individual or collective acts of violence and terrorism. Like natural occurrences, human-created disasters occur very frequently, and they can have extremely severe impacts on affected populations. Similar to natural disasters, it is often difficult for us to prepare for and respond to these types of disasters in an effective manner.

Regardless of what causes them, disasters are often highly visible events that attract immediate media coverage and public attention. They can generate conditions that are difficult, and often impossible, for citizens to ignore. When a snow storm knocks out the electricity in a neighborhood, the residents living in the affected area are definitely aware of the situation. When a bridge collapses, commuters and local businesses are clearly affected by the problem and have to adjust their normal transportation routes accordingly. Furthermore, information about these kinds of situations is easily and readily transmitted by the news media. Disasters are exactly the type of events that the media spotlight. They are unusual, different, spectacular, and at times even horrific. They also provide compelling visual images for mass circulation. So, the problem is visible not only to those who are immediately affected by the situation but to the vast majority of the American population as well.

When an occurrence is identified as a "disaster," the term itself immediately signals that something terrible and calamitous has occurred. The urgency and severity of the situation is automatically understood. In addition, the term "disaster" implies an unusual, extraordinary event that private individuals may not be able to handle on their own. In addition, disasters can occur without warning. They can strike at virtually any time (i.e., in any season, any month, or any time of day) and they can erupt in a variety of different forms (e.g., as the consequence of too little rain—droughts—or too much rain—floods). The unpredictable and highly variable nature of such events contributes further to their symbolic appeal. More specifically, it provides additional justification for broader, collective intervention. Individuals simply may not know how to handle such unusual, extraordinary circumstances because they have never experienced them before.

Disasters possess all of the elements that readily propel them onto the political agenda for collective action. Disasters are, by definition, unsettling, problematic situations; they are often almost impossible to predict with any accuracy (such as the timing of an earthquake, the explosion in a chemical plant, the exact path of a hurricane, a bridge failure, or an act of terrorism); they can affect innocent, blameless citizens; and they are often extremely difficult to manage. Finally, many disasters create problems that can only realistically be addressed and managed by government. When a severe thunderstorm causes massive damage in an area, private utility companies can repair broken electrical lines and (eventually) restore power. But they cannot deal with contaminated water

supplies, broken telephone lines, or disrupted sewer services. Similarly, when a fire in a local business destroys the surrounding homes and property, private volunteer groups can effectively distribute clothing and food to fire victims. But they do not have the authority to tell local citizens to evacuate before the fire spreads, the capability to help residents relocate during the incident, or the resources to help people rebuild after the disaster occurs). Often times, it is the government that has the technical capability, the appropriate resources, and the authority to coordinate a range of disaster-related responses. Thus, many disaster situations tend to be viewed as governmental responsibilities because there are no other viable alternatives to handle them in the private sector.

Thus, there are important reasons why government gets involved in disaster situations. First, disasters can cause extraordinarily severe and patently obvious societal problems. The economic, physical, and emotional costs of these events can reach such high levels that they cannot be ignored or overlooked. Second, disaster situations can become highly politicized issues: they reveal the extent to which public figures are willing and able to respond to citizens' needs. Disasters also contain extremely important symbolic elements: individual people tend to view these events as cataclysmic, life-threatening, and beyond their own control. Finally, many disasters, particularly the larger, cataclysmic events, generate problems that the private sector simply cannot handle.

How the Government Responds to Disasters

Every year hundreds of disasters occur in the United States. Although some of these situations are handled by individual citizens, private businesses, or nonprofit organizations, governments play a prominent role in helping people deal with these events. To prepare for and respond to any type of disaster situation in an effective manner, the United States has developed a fairly complex emergency response process. This system has evolved over the years as the scope and severity of emergencies have increased. Yet, the basic framework has remained fairly stable. The system involves local, state, and national governments;

it incorporates a mix of public, private, and nonprofit agencies; and it rests upon a set of policies and procedures designed to guide activity during any type of disaster situation.

Basically, the U.S. governmental disaster relief process is designed to work from the "bottom up." It begins at the local level and follows a series of pre-specified steps up through the state and ultimately the national government. Municipal and county governments are the first link in the chain. Their job is to deal with emergencies that occur within their jurisdictions. The basic assumption is that disaster response will be handled primarily by local emergency management agencies, and related organizations, such as law enforcement units, fire departments, ambulance services, and civil defense coordinators. But there is also a recognition that disasters place exceptionally large burdens on local communities' officials. Therefore, they may be forced to look elsewhere for guidance and assistance with their response procedures.

If the capabilities of one community are overwhelmed, local officials can seek help from other neighboring jurisdictions. Over the last decade, a number of city and county governments have developed regional compacts and cooperative agreements to facilitate the flow of aid from one community to another. These regional compacts can play an extremely important role in helping to mobilize and coordinate response efforts both within and across local jurisdictions. Hence, they have become an important component of the intergovernmental response process.

Local governments can also turn to higher governmental levels if their resources are totally exhausted. Specifically, they can ask state officials and state organizations for additional guidance and assistance. For their part, state governments have the ability to mobilize extra assets and larger-scale organizations to deal with situations that local officials cannot handle. The responsibilities and obligations of each state government are set forth in that state's emergency preparedness/response plan. These plans contain a number of common elements: they specify the processes that will be used to guide the deployment of statewide resources; they delineate the types of support available for local disaster relief operations; and they describe the roles and responsibilities of various state officials

(i.e., the governor, emergency preparedness personnel, and law enforcement officials) during a disaster situation.

To provide a degree of uniformity across the nation, the federal government imposes some conditions on all state systems. These federal requirements are designed to ensure that the same basic features exist in states across the nation. For example, a single state agency must be placed in charge of emergency preparedness, homeland security, and disaster relief to provide one specific point of contact for emergency operations within every state. These state organizations play a critical role in the intergovernmental response process. They are responsible for coordinating all state-level activities and ensuring that the state maintains a coherent and effective system for dealing with disasters. Moreover, one of their most important functions is to serve as the main liaison between local jurisdictions and the federal government.

In addition to the state emergency management/homeland security agency, the governor plays a key role in disaster preparedness and response at the state level. There is some variation from state to state in this respect, but most state governors have fairly expansive powers during disaster situations: they can declare a "state of emergency"; they can order evacuations of residents; they specify the conditions under which the state's National Guard can be mobilized; and they determine how essential resources will be reallocated across the state to disaster-stricken areas. Governors can also request assistance from other states either through informal arrangements or more formally established interstate mutual aid assistance compacts.

The last step in the intergovernmental response process is the direct involvement of the national government. The conditions under which the federal government can intervene are specified in legislative statutes and executive orders. These policies indicate when and how the national government can become involved in a disaster situation. For the vast majority of situations, the federal government becomes directly and actively engaged when a state or territorial governor makes a formal request for assistance. A governor's request for federal assistance is first reviewed and evaluated by the Federal Emergency Management

President Barack Obama (second from left), FEMA administrator Craig Fugate (left), and Mayor Glenn Lewis (center) and Governor Mary Fallin (right) along with other state officials visit a neighborhood in Moore, Oklahoma, impacted by a tornado in 2013. (Jocelyn Augustino/FEMA)

Agency (FEMA). Based upon their reading of the situation, FEMA officials prepare a recommendation for the president. Then, it is up to the president of the United States to officially decide whether the magnitude of a crisis really is beyond the capacity of state and local governments to warrant federal involvement. If so, he issues a formal declaration that a "major disaster" has occurred.

A "major disaster" declaration by the president has far-reaching, significant consequences. It indicates that a severe event exceeding the capabilities of state and local governments has occurred. Moreover, it suggests that the disaster warrants the involvement of the federal government. A presidential declaration is vitally important to the residents, businesses, and communities directly affected by a disaster: it is a necessary first step for their obtaining federal aid. To the general American public, that is, those who are not directly affected by the disaster, a presidential declaration of a major disaster situation is also significant. It indicates that a major event has occurred, requiring the involvement of the federal government.

A presidential disaster declaration also has a profound impact on the nature of subsequent relief efforts. The declaration of a "major disaster" paves the way to an array of federal assistance and the possible infusion of federal funds. However, not all forms of federal assistance will be forthcoming, even if a "major disaster" is declared. Instead, an assessment is made during each particular situation to determine what type of support is warranted (i.e., temporary shelter, emergency medical care, direct cash grants, debris removal, housing supplements) and who will receive it (e.g., will aid go to individual citizens, private businesses, and/or public facilities).

Once a "major disaster" has been declared, the president appoints a Federal Coordinating Officer (FCO) to serve as the federal government's representative to the stricken area. In general, the FCO is responsible for coordinating all subsequent response/recovery efforts.

The FCO has a great deal of discretion over the nature and scope of governmental actions in a particular disaster situation. Of course, the FCO does not act alone in organizing, directing, and implementing relief activities. Instead, he or she provides overall direction to the activities of emergency management officials at the federal, state, and local levels. To start the process, the federal government signs an agreement with the governor of the affected state. This agreement includes a plan that outlines federal, state, and local responsibilities in the recovery effort; identifies the exact nature of federal assistance that will be provided; and specifies how federal resources can be employed.

At this stage of the process, FEMA begins to work directly with state (and local) officials involved in the disaster. Since 2005, the primary mechanism for ensuring intergovernmental cooperation has been the National Incident Management System (NIMS). NIMS is a comprehensive framework for emergency management that is designed to apply across all jurisdictional levels and all types of disasters. It establishes a unified command system at the onset of a crisis situation so that the actions of all public and private agencies are coordinated and focused on achieving the same basic objectives.

In addition to coordinating efforts across governmental levels, FEMA serves as a clearinghouse for mobilizing the actions of other federal assistance programs. FEMA also administers several programs on its own. For example, the agency can make temporary housing available, or provide tents and mobile homes, and rent money to people whose homes have been damaged or destroyed. It can also distribute cash grants to individuals and families who are in need but ineligible for other types of aid. And it can make funds available to government agencies and private companies to restore or replace their disaster-stricken facilities and property.

It is important to point out that the federal government is not supposed to step in and take charge during most major disaster situations. Instead, it should stay in the background, providing general guidance, financial support, and technical assistance to lower governmental units. This bottom-up process—starting at the local level, moving up through the states, and ultimately to the national government if necessary—is believed to work best for the vast majority of disasters.

However, the federal government does have the ability to assume a more proactive role during natural disasters. The September 11, 2001, terrorist attacks made it clear that some events (i.e., major catastrophic situations) can immediately overwhelm the capabilities of state and local governments. During such situations, it would be difficult, even impossible, for the traditional "bottom-up" framework to work effectively. Therefore, federal officials cannot wait for a response to work its way up through the intergovernmental framework. Instead, the national government should become involved at an earlier stage so that critical resources can flow more quickly and easily into the stricken area. For this type of situation, this means that the federal government deploys personnel, resources, and equipment proactively as a disaster is developing to help state and local and jump-start the process.

Regardless of how the response unfolds, federal officials are still supposed to work directly with state, and local, officials to assess the severity of the situation, to determine the type of assistance needed, and to facilitate the distribution of aid to affected populations and areas. Local, state, and national governments are supposed to share emergency management responsibilities and work together to implement disaster relief policies. Private and nonprofit organizations are also very involved in the nation's emergency management system. But the foundation for the system is based on the multilayered structure of American government.

The previously described system depicts how the governmental response is *supposed* to work. Ideally, there exists a well-coordinated, integrated management system that will automatically handle each and every emergency, no matter when or where it occurs. In reality, however, the process operates quite differently during each disaster situation.

First, different perspectives often develop across different governmental levels which affect the way the governmental response process works. On the one hand, local and state officials feel that their responsibilities have ended once they pass the response up to the federal government. On the other hand, federal officials view the system as a team effort where the three units of government have separate, but clearly interdependent and continuous, obligations. Second, emergency management officials are often unable to coordinate the actions of other participants in the process. There are simply too many agencies and officials involved in disaster relief operations. Each has its own set of rules, regulations, and policies, with different leadership, personnel, and organizational structures. Third, disaster relief operations are severely underfunded throughout the entire intergovernmental system. At the local and state levels, many emergency management agencies operate on limited budgets, with small staffs or part-time personnel. Similarly, FEMA—the lead federal agency in most major disasters—has a staff of only several thousand trained reservists who can be deployed to any given disaster situation and a tiny operating budget (especially compared to other federal agencies) to cover all of its day-to-day, disaster-related activities. Moreover, the funds available to FEMA for major emergencies—contained in the Disaster Relief Fund—are kept so low that Congress must appropriate additional, supplemental money before the federal government can mobilize or sustain an adequate response. And, in recent years, Congress has been reluctant to increase federal funding for disaster assistance as the number of federally declared major disasters has grown, raising concerns about the growing role of the federal government in such circumstances.

Disaster Politics, Political Leadership, and the Impact on Governmental Performance

Disasters are political events with major consequences for public officials and governmental systems. When a disaster occurs, the public's attention is riveted on that event. This situation, in turn, provides a window of opportunity for governmental activity. Public officials can use a disaster situation to demonstrate their willingness to tackle tough, difficult problems. Their actions will almost always receive instant public attention and media coverage. Moreover, it is virtually impossible to oppose or criticize an official who steps in and takes charge of a disaster situation to help stricken citizens and communities.

Political leadership is particularly important for understanding governmental actions during disasters and overall performance of the disaster response process. Political leaders are often involved in determining whether a situation qualifies as a disaster. Through their words and actions, a given situation is identified and defined as a disaster. This may be based on objective factors (i.e., the scope or severity of the event), or it can be a reflection of more subjective considerations (e.g., pressures to take charge or to claim ownership or an issue). Regardless of the motivations behind it, political leadership is extremely important for drawing attention to a particular disaster, getting the situation on the policy agenda, and setting the stage for subsequent actions to address it. Without the "push" from political leaders, it is unlikely that some disasters will be acknowledged or that any follow-up actions will be taken.

Disasters also produce conditions that allow political leaders to show their concern for the needs and demands of the citizens they serve. Disaster victims may encounter problems that they have never before experienced. In addition, individual citizens are often unprepared or unequipped to handle these difficulties on their own. Public officials are simply in a much better position to channel necessary resources to help those in need. Political leaders who successfully address disaster-related problems are rewarded. They can dispense particularized benefits to constituents and use these as a resource to facilitate their reelection efforts or to advance their political careers. In contrast, public officials who are unwilling or unable to act during a disaster situation can get blamed for the way they handled the situation. If they hesitate or delay to act when an emergency erupts, they may be depicted as being unresponsive to the needs of their constituents. If they are bewildered or confused by the situation that develops, they may appear to be unprepared and out of touch, or even incompetent and uncaring. These negative images of political leadership—actually, the lack of political leadership—are extremely difficult to change and overcome. They can have serious negative political repercussions for public officials.

Political leadership can also have broader consequences. When political leaders and public officials demonstrate strong and effective leadership during a major crisis, this presents a positive picture of government's overall capabilities. Unfortunately, when the reverse scenario occurs (i.e., political leaders appear to be indifferent or unwilling to assist), this projects a negative impression of governmental incompetence and unresponsiveness. Such actions (or inactions) in a disaster situation can have profound and lasting impacts on a political system. They can affect more general public impressions of governmental performance, influencing citizens' confidence in government's ability to address pressing policy issues.

See also Cities and Politics; Coastal Zones, Economics, and Politics; Governors and Gubernatorial Politics; Infrastructure and Politics; State and Local Politics.

Saundra K. Schneider

Bibliography
Rubin, Claire, B., ed. 2012. *Emergency Management: The American Experience 1900–2010.* 2nd ed. Boca Raton, FL: CRC Press.

Schneider, Saundra K. 2011. *Dealing with Disaster: Public Management in Crisis Situations.* New York: M.E. Sharpe, Inc.

Sylves, Richard T. 2008. *Disaster Policy and Politics: Emergency Management and Homeland Security.* Washington, DC: CQ Press.

Waugh, William L., Jr., and Kathleen J. Tierney, eds. 2007. *Emergency Management: Principles and Practices for Local Government.* Washington, DC: ICMA Press.

DISINFORMATION, DECEPTION, AND POLITICS

Disinformation is the preferred form of deception in American politics. As the comedian George Carlin quipped, "the government doesn't lie, it engages in disinformation." According to the *American Heritage Dictionary of the English Language, disinformation* is "deliberately misleading information announced publicly or leaked by a government or especially by an intelligence agency to influence public opinion or the government in another nation."

Disinformation in American politics is nothing new. *The Onion* probably had it right when it reported that "Presidents Washington through Bush may have lied about key matters." Even "Honest Abe" was not above using disinformation to achieve his political ends. In early 1865, several members of Congress wanted to postpone voting on the abolition of slavery if the Confederacy was ready to negotiate an end to the American Civil War. But Lincoln was able to get the Thirteenth Amendment passed by telling Congress, "So far as I know, there are no [Confederate] peace Commissioners in the City, or likely to be in it," when, in fact, he knew that three peace commissioners actually were on their way to Fort Monroe, Virginia (see Goodwin 2005, 688).

Beginning with World War II, however, the use of disinformation became standard practice in American politics. Presidents Roosevelt, Johnson, and George W. Bush each deceived the American people to gain support for entering and/or escalating foreign wars. Presidents Nixon and Clinton each famously attempted to cover up scandals by lying. In

President George W. Bush addresses the nation aboard the aircraft carrier USS *Abraham Lincoln*, May 1, 2003. Beneath a sign proclaiming "Mission Accomplished," Bush declared major fighting over in Iraq following the fall of Baghdad. (AP Photo/J. Scott Applewhite)

fact, political deception has become so prevalent in the last few years that we no longer expect to hear the truth from politicians. The standard joke is, "How can you tell if a politician is lying? . . . His or her lips are moving."

This entry will look at why politicians deceive, how they deceive, whether they are ever justified in deceiving, and whether it is even still possible to deceive the highly skeptical American electorate.

Why Do Politicians Deceive?

Politicians often try to deceive the public to garner support for policies that are unpopular, but that they deem to be necessary for the good of the nation. For instance, to escalate the Vietnam War, President Johnson lied about there having been an unprovoked attack by the North Vietnamese on the USS *Maddox* in the Gulf of Tonkin (see Mearsheimer 2011, 47–49). When the policy in question is military action, politicians may engage in *fearmongering* (see Mearsheimer 2011, 45–62). That is, they may inflate the danger of some external threat. For instance, prior to the second Iraq War, the second Bush administration famously deceived the American public about there being weapons of mass destruction (WMDs) in Iraq (see Carson 2010, 212–23; Mearsheimer 2011, 49–55). Vice President Dick Cheney claimed that "there is irrefutable evidence that [Saddam] has once again set up and reconstituted his program to take uranium . . . so that it will function as the base material as a nuclear weapon." A few months later, Secretary of State Colin Powell told the UN that "there can be no doubt that Saddam Hussein has biological weapons and the capability to produce more, many more."

It must be noted that the Bush administration may not have *intended to deceive* the American public about there being WMDs in Iraq. They may very well have believed that Saddam Hussein had such weapons. But it is now clear that the evidence for there being WMDs in Iraq was less than conclusive. Thus, it is clear that the Bush administration did intend to deceive the American public about *how much evidence* they had for there being WMDs in Iraq (see Carson 2010, 217).

Politicians also engage in deception to keep the existence of unpopular policies secret (see Mearsheimer 2011, 66). For instance, because he recognized the

serious threat that Adolf Hitler posed, Franklin D. Roosevelt was doing everything he could in 1941 to provoke the German military into firing on American ships so that he would have an excuse to declare war. But public opinion in the United States was strongly opposed to entering the war. So, in one of his fireside chats, FDR told the American people, "we have sought no shooting war with Hitler. We do not seek it now" (see Carson 2010, 210–11). Also, to end the Cuban Missile Crisis, "Kennedy agreed to the Soviet demand that the United States pull its nuclear-armed Jupiter missiles out of Turkey" (Mearsheimer 2011, 66). But he then publicly denied that there had been such an agreement. Most recently, in a Senate hearing, Director of National Intelligence, James Clapper, lied about the extent to which the communications of American citizens are under government surveillance (see Bamford 2013).

Politicians also engage in deception to cover up embarrassing facts that might harm their careers. For instance, when the journalist Jim Lehrer asked President Clinton about his (now well-documented) relationship with a White House intern, Clinton replied, "There is not a sexual relationship" (see Saul 2012, vii). He later went on television and told the American public, "I did not have sexual relations with that woman, Miss Lewinsky." Similarly, while running for president in 2008, John Edwards lied about not having an extramarital affair and an illegitimate child. Also, during his presidential campaign, "JFK purposely denied the variety of physical troubles that had hospitalized him nine times in the late 1950s" (Dallek 2010, 12).

Edwards's lies about his sex life and Kennedy's lies about his health exemplify yet another category of political deception. Candidates for public office often lie to get elected. The 2012 presidential campaign was rife with such lies. As the journalist Charles Blow (2012) points out, "this election may go down in history as the moment when truth and lies lost their honor and stigma, respectively." In addition to trying to cover up their own scandals, candidates often engage in fearmongering about their opponent. For instance, the Romney-Ryan campaign tried to convince the electorate that President Obama planned to gut the popular Medicare entitlement program (see Stanley 2012). Also, in the last days of the campaign, Romney ran an ad claiming that Chrysler was moving Jeep production to China (thereby suggesting that his opponent was causing American jobs to be sent overseas) even though it was easy to verify that this claim was false (see Blow 2012).

Finally, politicians sometimes attempt to deceive the American public simply because that is the only way to effectively deceive others. For instance, the Eisenhower administration lied about the mission of its U-2 spy planes because it did not want to reveal to the international community that the United States was violating Soviet airspace (see Mearsheimer 2011, 88–89). Also, Clapper may only have lied to Congress about government surveillance to hide from our enemies how we look for terrorists.

How Do Politicians Deceive?

The main form of political disinformation is the *lie*. You lie when you say something that you believe to be false with the intent to deceive your audience (see Mearsheimer 2011, 16). For instance, FDR was lying when he said, "we have sought no shooting war with Hitler." Members of the Bush administration lied about how much evidence they had for there being WMDs in Iraq. Also, Clapper lied to Congress despite his subsequent claim that he had just chosen to respond in the "least untruthful manner."

But there are many other forms of political disinformation. Most notably, it is possible to deceive people by saying something *true* as well as by saying something false (see Saul 2012). For instance, Lincoln's statement about the peace commissioners was literally true. Confederate peace commissioners were not in Washington, DC, or on their way to Washington, DC. But his statement led the members of Congress to mistakenly conclude that the Confederacy was not yet ready to end the war.

When a politician sticks to the truth, but cloaks it in misleading language and/or selectively emphasizes only certain facts, it is known as *spin* (see Carson 2010, 57–58). For instance, it was true that Obama's budget decreased funding for Medicare by $716 billion. However, Paul Ryan chose to describe this as "funneling money out" of the program rather than as "reducing expected future increases in payment to private insurance companies." Also, he neglected to mention that his own budget plan included similar anticipated savings from Medicare.

In most cases, the deceptive politician wants his audience to understand what he says and then to draw a false conclusion. But sometimes, he intends to be *misunderstood*. For instance, when Clinton said, "There *is* not a sexual relationship" (emphasis added), he meant that there was *currently* no such relationship (which was true), but he wanted people to conclude that there never had been such a relationship.

In his bestseller *On Bullshit*, the philosopher Harry Frankfurt (2005) discusses yet another form of disinformation that is "short of lying." According to Frankfurt (2005, 33–34), it is a "lack of connection to a concern with truth—this indifference to how things really are—that I regard as the essence of bullshit." One of Frankfurt's (2005, 16–18) main examples is a bullshitting politician:

Consider a Fourth of July orator, who goes on bombastically about "our great and blessed country, whose Founding Fathers under divine guidance created a new beginning for mankind." He would be lying only if it were his intention to bring about in his audience beliefs that he himself regards as false, concerning such matters as whether our country is great, whether it is blessed, whether the founders had divine guidance, and whether what they did was in fact to create a new beginning for mankind. But the orator does not really care what the audience thinks about the Founding Fathers, or about the role of the deity in our country's history, or the like. The orator intends his statements to convey a certain impression of himself. He wants them to think of him as a patriot, as someone who has deep thoughts and feelings about the origins and the mission of our country, who appreciates the importance of religion, who is sensitive to the greatness of our history, whose pride in that history is combined with humility before God, and so on.

Much of the disinformation spread during the 2012 presidential campaign arguably falls into this category. For instance, Mitt Romney certainly did not appear to be concerned with whether or not the claims made in his political ads were true. As was quickly pointed out by several sources, and as Romney himself either knew or could easily have discovered, Chrysler was actually adding jobs in the United States. Much like Frankfurt's Fourth of July orator, it appears that Romney just wanted to convey to certain segments of the electorate that he shared their values and concerns (see Stanley 2012).

Although Frankfurt contrasts bullshitting with lying, it must be noted that these two categories do overlap. For instance, if the orator made a claim that he *knew* to be false (such as that Washington chopped down a cherry tree or that Chrysler was sending American jobs overseas), it would be a lie. But it would also be bullshit because he still would not care whether or not what he said was true. In addition, while bullshitters typically misrepresent their "own thoughts, feelings, or attitudes," this is not always the case. For instance, the orator may very well believe that he is a patriot, and he may even be a patriot. But even so, the speech is still bullshit because the orator does not care whether or not what he literally says is true, or whether or not people believe it. Also, it still counts as disinformation. As Frankfurt (2005, 54) explains, what the bullshitter "does necessarily attempt to deceive us about is his enterprise. His only indispensably distinctive characteristic is that in a certain way he misrepresents what he is up to."

While we often focus on the deceptive things that politicians *say*, disinformation is often *visual*. In fact, misleading images and doctored photographs are frequently used in American politics. For instance, a photograph published during the 2004 presidential campaign appeared to show John Kerry and Jane Fonda sharing the stage at an anti-Vietnam war rally. But it was really a composite of two separate photographs taken at two separate events (see Farid 2009, 98).

It is also important to note that deceptive politicians do always not personally deliver their own disinformation. They frequently get someone else to do it for them. This is often an individual or an organization that knowingly and willingly conspires with the politician. But politicians sometimes trick someone into innocently passing along the disinformation. For instance, former White House press secretary Scott McClellan claims that certain members of the Bush administration intentionally gave him false information to relay to the press corps (see Shear 2008). Indeed, the government may actually be able to legally compel citizens to spread disinformation against their will. For instance, the Patriot Act allows the FBI to send "National Security Letters" which require recipients to deny that they have received such a letter (see Doctorow 2013).

As in the cases discussed so far, the goal of disseminating political disinformation is usually to mislead people into believing the content of the information (and/or something that can be inferred from that content). But sometimes, the goal is simply to mislead people in to believing that *other people believe* the content. For instance, as the philosopher Peter Ludlow (2013) points out, private intelligence agencies have developed systems for the government "that allowed one user to control multiple online identities ('sock puppets') for commenting in social media spaces, thus giving the appearance of grass roots support." In some cases, it is even part of the plan to reveal that the information is false. For instance, a private intelligence firm developed a proposal for the Chamber of Commerce to undermine the credibility of one of its critics, a group called Chamber Watch. The proposal called for first creating a "false document, perhaps highlighting periodical financial information," giving it to a progressive group opposing the Chamber, and then subsequently exposing the document as a fake to "prove that U.S. Chamber Watch cannot be trusted with information and/or tell the truth."

Is Deception in Politics Ever Justified?

Most people think that lying and deceiving are usually bad things to do. The main reason is that deception often causes (unjustified) harm to the people who are deceived. For instance, deceptive advertising can lead consumers to waste money on products that are ineffective or possibly even unsafe (see Carson 2010, 182–90). But deception does not always have such bad consequences. Elected leaders often have the ability to do great good by engaging in a bit of deceit. For instance, the world might still be under the yoke of Nazi tyranny if FDR had not used some trickery to get the United States into World War II (see Carson 2010, 228).

The idea that political deception might be morally permissible if it is done for the greater good goes back to Plato's (2004, 100) idea of the "noble lie." In Book 3 of the *Republic*, Socrates suggests that the rulers of a city tell the people that the gods have placed a certain sort of metal (gold, silver, or iron) in each person's soul. This metal determines the person's station in life (rulers, those who help the rulers, farmers, and other craftsmen, respectively). According to Socrates, telling this false story to the people is justified because it "would have a good effect, by making them care more for the city and for each other."

By contrast, the lies told by political candidates for public office might simply appear to be self-serving acts of manipulation that are no more justified than any other type of deceptive advertising. But such lies can also potentially be defended as "noble lies." After all, a candidate cannot serve the public good in the way that FDR did unless he or she first gets elected. As the philosopher Michael Walzer (1973, 164) puts it, "they can do no good themselves unless they win the struggle, which they are unlikely to do unless they are willing and able to use the necessary means."

In addition, some forms of political disinformation can potentially be defended on other grounds. As the philosopher Anita Allen (1999, 162) points out, there is a "widespread moral belief and religious doctrine that lying sometimes is a morally justifiable response to others seeking information to which they have no right." Thus, Clinton might have been justified in using deception to protect his own privacy.

However, there are several reasons to think that, much like lying and deception in general, political deception is usually unjustified. Even if it is done for the public good, political deception can be especially problematic in a democratic nation such as the United States. For a democracy to function properly, citizens need access to accurate and comprehensive information about the public sphere and the workings of government (see Mearsheimer 2011, 84). Otherwise, they will be unable to make informed choices about which candidates to vote for and about which policies to support. Moreover, as Allen (1999, 163) notes, "one of the most compelling arguments against lying by government officials is that dishonesty by those in public life potentially undermines trust in government." Such loss of trust can potentially undermine a democracy (see Mearsheimer 2011, 85–86).

Political deception can also lead the deceptive politicians themselves to make decisions that have bad consequences. Decision making is typically enhanced by having full information and being exposed to diverse viewpoints. Think of Lincoln's "team of rivals" (see Goodwin 2005). By contrast, when policies are kept secret and are not openly discussed, leaders may not learn why certain policies are unlikely to be a good idea. Bad polices can easily result if leaders are isolated in a "White House bubble." Moreover, even if a particular case of political deception has the good *immediate* consequences that are intended, it can set a bad precedent for the future. For instance, FDR's use of deception no doubt made it easier for Johnson and Bush to use deception to get the United States into foreign wars that were much less justified and much less successful (see Carson 2010, 229).

Furthermore, even if most people can justify the use of deceit to keep private matters confidential, it is not clear that politicians can. For instance, if a president (or a candidate for president) suffers from health issues that might easily incapacitate him or her while in office, the American public has a legitimate right to know (see Dallek 2010, 11–14). In fact, it might even be suggested that the electorate ought to be privy to many other details of a politician's personal life. Such details are potentially relevant when voters are evaluating the wisdom and intelligence of candidates for public office. For instance, if a politician makes decisions in his or her personal life that exhibit a lack of good judgment (such as having illicit sexual relationships), it might suggest a lack of good judgment more generally.

Finally, since bullshit is now so prevalent in American political discourse, it is worth noting that Frankfurt (2005, 60–61) claims that there is an important sense in which bullshit can actually be worse than other forms of disinformation. Since the liar aims to mislead people whereas the bullshitter just does not care whether people are misled, lies might seem to be more dangerous at first glance. However, by indulging in bullshit ourselves and tolerating it from our politicians, our "normal habit of attending to the ways things are may become attenuated or lost." Thus, Frankfurt concludes that "bullshit is a greater enemy of the truth than lies are."

Is Deception in Politics Effective Anymore?

Although politicians often have some motivation to deceive (e.g., to get public support for their policies and to get elected in the first place), they have to weigh these potential benefits against the potential costs to their reputations if their deceit is discovered (see Tullock 1967, 133–43). However, as the philosopher Jason Stanley (2012) notes, Americans "no longer expect consistency and honesty from politicians, and the savvy political campaigner recognizes that there is no cost to making statements that contradict even their most well-known beliefs." We are arguably living now in what the historian Eric Alterman (2004, 305) calls a "post-truth political environment." Indeed, distrust in American political discourse has reached the level where a member of Congress actually shouted out "You lie!" at the president while he was addressing a joint session of Congress (see Sullivan 2009).

In this sort of environment, politicians do not have to pay a significant cost for engaging in deception. But since politicians also cannot expect the American public to simply believe what they say, it is not immediately clear why they should bother disseminating disinformation. Nevertheless, even though their statements are unlikely to be believed outright, politicians often have good reason to tell lies.

First, despite the general distrust of politicians, politicians can often get at least some people to believe what they say. Politicians typically address very big audiences (see Tullock 1967, 137). It is not going to be surprising if a few of these people are quite credulous. Thus, even if a politician says something that is extremely implausible or that can easily be shown to be false, some people may be convinced, and they may be the swing voters who turn an election.

Second, even in contexts where people are not inclined to believe what is said, it is still possible to influence their beliefs and their behavior with deceptive statements. For instance, if I am playing poker in Vegas, I am not just going to believe my opponent when he or she claims to have a really strong hand. Even so, he or she is not necessarily wasting his or her breath. His or her comment might increase my uncertainty just enough to cause me to fold. Similarly, even

though there is a lot of distrust of politicians in America, they can still influence people with their lies. For instance, even if a political ad does not convince me that a particular candidate would dismantle Medicare or Social Security, I might still not vote for him or her just because I am now uncertain about what he or she would do if elected.

Finally, even if the politician cannot get anyone to actually believe what he or she says, there can still be an important point to a politician making false statements. As noted earlier in the discussion of bullshit, saying certain things can be a very good way to convey information about who you are and about what your values are. So, even though political disinformation may not be quite as effective at deceiving us as it was when FDR duped the American people in 1941, it is probably here to stay.

See also Advertising, Political; Debates, Presidential; Ethics in Government; Fear Tactics in Politics; Information Leaks and Politics; Political Communications; Scandals in Politics; Television News, Opinion, and Politics.

Don Fallis

Bibliography

Allen, Anita L. 1999. "Lying to Protect Privacy." *Villanova Law Review* 44: 161–87.

Alterman, Eric. 2004. *When Presidents Lie*. New York: Viking.

Bamford, James. 2013. "They Know Much More Than You Think." *New York Review of Books*. http://www.nybooks.com/articles/archives/2013/aug/15/nsa-they-know-much-more-you-think/. Accessed May 22, 2014.

Blow, Charles M. 2012. "Liberty to Lie." *New York Times*. http://campaignstops.blogs.nytimes.com/2012/11/01/liberty-to-lie/. Accessed May 22, 2014.

Carson, Thomas L. 2010. *Lying and Deception*. New York: Oxford University Press.

Dallek, Robert. 2010. "Presidential Fitness and Presidential Lies: The Historical Record and a Proposal for Reform." *Presidential Studies Quarterly* 40: 9–22.

Doctorow, Cory. 2013. "How to Foil NSA Sabotage: Use a Dead Man's Switch." *Guardian*. http://www

.theguardian.com/technology/2013/sep/09/nsa-sabotage-dead-mans-switch. Accessed May 22, 2014.

Farid, Hany. 2009. "Digital Doctoring: Can We Trust Photographs?" In Barbara Harrington, ed. *Deception*. Stanford, CA: Stanford University Press, pp. 95–108.

Frankfurt, Harry G. 2005. *On Bullshit*. Princeton, NJ: Princeton University Press.

Goodwin, Doris K. 2005. *Team of Rivals*. New York: Simon & Schuster.

Ludlow, Peter. 2013. "The Real War on Reality." *New York Times*. http://opinionator.blogs.nytimes.com/2013/06/14/the-real-war-on-reality/. Accessed May 22, 2014.

Mearsheimer, John J. 2011. *Why Leaders Lie*. New York: Oxford University Press.

Plato. 2004. *Republic*. Translated by C. D. C. Reeve. Indianapolis: Hackett.

Saul, Jennifer M. 2012. *Lying, Misleading, and What Is Said*. Oxford: Oxford University Press.

Shear, Michael D. 2008. "Ex-Press Aide Writes That Bush Misled U.S. on Iraq." *Washington Post*. http://articles.washingtonpost.com/2008-05-28/politics/36783592_1_press-secretary-bush-white-house-president-bush. Accessed May 22, 2014.

Stanley, Jason. 2012. "Speech, Lies, and Apathy." *New York Times*. http://opinionator.blogs.nytimes.com/2012/08/30/speech-lies-and-apathy/. Accessed May 22, 2014.

Sullivan, Andrew. 2009. "The British Counter-Example." *The Atlantic*. http://andrewsullivan.theatlantic.com/the_daily_dish/2009/09/the-british-counterexample.html. Accessed May 22, 2014.

Tullock, Gordon. 1967. *Toward a Mathematics of Politics*. Ann Arbor: University of Michigan Press.

Walzer, Michael. 1973. "Political Action: The Problem of Dirty Hands." *Philosophy & Public Affairs* 2: 160–80.

DRUG POLICY AND POLITICS

On July 17, 1971, President Richard Nixon delivered a special message to the United States Congress. The abuse of illegal drugs, Nixon declared, constituted America's "public enemy number one," and he announced the beginning of a war against illegal drug use. Nixon's declaration of a war on drugs, an aggressive metaphor that has endured, came at a time when drug use in the United States had grown rapidly within a short period. The counterculture of the 1960s had embraced marijuana, and to a lesser extent LSD, and growing numbers of young Americans were experimenting with amphetamines and heroin. As the war in Vietnam intensified in the late 1960s, an increasing number of veterans returned to the United States with experiences of heroin use in Southeast Asia. Soldiers' drug use in Vietnam prompted fears that military personnel would continue to use drugs once they returned home. Yet, while Nixon's declaration of a war on drugs was a result of the tumultuous early 1970s, the federal government had been actively trying to control psychoactive drug use in the United States for over half a century before 1971.

The Harrison Act

During the 19th century, no federal laws regulated the use of psychoactive drugs in the United States. Opium-based medicines were widely available and their use was common among many segments of the population—not least among middle-class white women, many of whom used morphine to dull pain and allay anxieties. The late 19th century witnessed the rise of the first laws targeting drug users in the United States. These laws were passed not by the federal government but by states and municipalities across the country. One of the earliest American drug laws was passed in California in the 1870s in response to Chinese immigrants' smoking of opium. As Chinatowns grew in several American cities, laws prohibiting opium smoking spread, often wrapped in racist anti-Chinese rhetoric. Both cocaine and opiates were widely available in the late 19th and early 20th centuries; despite many states' attempts to regulate the use of these drugs, addiction rates were remarkably high compared to early 21st-century patterns.

The unregulated sale of opiates and cocaine would come to a close in the early 20th century, however, as a wide range of reform interests came together in what has become known as the Progressive Movement. One of the movement's major legislative achievements, The Pure Food and Drug Act of 1906, required medicine manufacturers to disclose whether their products contained drugs such as morphine or cocaine. The 1906 law did not, however, restrict the public's access to these drugs—that occurred eight years later. In 1914, the U.S. Congress passed the country's first national drug law. The Harrison Narcotics Tax Act, signed into law by President Woodrow Wilson, came into force in March 1915 and created the first federal framework of drug control in the United States. The Harrison Act required physicians, druggists, and manufacturers of drugs to register and document the sale of a range of psychoactive drugs, including heroin, morphine, and cocaine.

Originally, the Harrison Act simply stated that physicians had to register their transactions, and many continued to prescribe opiates to their addicted patients. The Supreme Court, however, through three related decisions, greatly narrowed physicians' discretion to dispense drugs. These three cases, *U.S. v. Jin Fuey Moy* (1916), *U.S. v. Doremus* (1919), and *U.S. v. Webb* (1919), largely ended physicians' rights to prescribe drugs to their addicted patients. Many cities and states, concerned about addicts suddenly cut off from supplies of opiates they were addicted to, established municipal clinics, beginning in 1915, where drugs could be dispensed legally to addicts. These were places where addicts were allowed to buy opiates (usually morphine) at a low cost without fear of being arrested. The federal government came to oppose the clinic system, however, and by 1923 federal agents had shut down the last remaining clinic. As licit supplies decreased, an illicit market grew.

The Classic Era of Narcotic Control

Historian David Courtwright has called the period from 1923 to 1965 the Classic Era of Narcotic Control, characterizing it as a period of "simple, consistent, and

rigid" drug laws. This period marked the end of Progressive Era reforms. Ironically, rates of drug use had already declined significantly from their peak by the 1910s, as many drug users scaled back their use in response to undesirable effects they experienced or witnessed in others. Despite the decreased levels of drug use, the image of the drug user remained a cause of concern for policy makers. The junkie, presented in the media as a heroin-addicted young urban male from a working-class background with a propensity for violence and crime, became an American stereotype during the Progressive Era. This popular image could be invoked by politicians and policy makers to bolster support for their policies, and one of the architects of the public's perception of drugs and of drug users was Harry J. Anslinger.

In 1930, the drug enforcement arm of the federal government was reorganized, and the Federal Bureau of Narcotics was created, with Commissioner Harry J. Anslinger at its helm. Anslinger is mainly remembered for his efforts to ban the use of marijuana, a drug whose availability in the United States rose in the 1920s and 1930s after spreading across the border from Mexico through the American Southwest and into the urban centers of the North. In the mid-1930s the American media presented sensational stories about the dangers of marijuana; in response, Congress passed the Marijuana Tax Act of 1937, adding marijuana to the list of drugs banned by the federal government.

While World War II disrupted the global supply of illegal drugs, smuggling routes were quickly reestablished after the war, and the late 1940s and early 1950s witnessed the rise of the Cold War and an accompanying fear of subversive activities in the United States. In response to increased heroin use in these years, Congress passed two pieces of drug legislation in the early postwar years: the Boggs Act of 1951 and the Narcotics Control Act of 1956. Both acts established harsh mandatory minimum sentences for anyone convicted in federal courts of violating the Harrison Act. The Narcotics Control Act of 1956 included a provision enabling juries to impose the death penalty in cases where adult defendants were charged with selling heroin to minors.

Methadone

Originally developed by German scientists in the late 1930s, methadone is a synthetic alternative to morphine, heroin, and some other drugs derived from opium; therefore, it is useful as an analgesic, or pain reliever. Used by the German army during World War II, methadone was introduced to the United States in 1947 and was marketed as an analgesic. In the early 1960s, two researchers at Roosevelt University in New York, Marie Nyswander and Vincent Dole, began trials using methadone as a way to treat heroin addiction. Because methadone acts on the same receptors in the brain as opiates available on the street, the drug can be used as an alternative to heroin. One of the benefits of methadone is the fact that because it is longer-acting than heroin, it can be administered less frequently (once a day vs. two to three times a day), and it relieves the addict from the need for heroin. Known as Substitution Treatment or Methadone Maintenance Therapy, methadone programs help create structure and stability in the lives of addicts. This treatment method has become an important tool in the treatment of opiate addiction. President Nixon saw methadone maintenance as an inexpensive form of treatment that promised to reduce street crime by getting heroin addicts into treatment. His office created the National Institute on Drug Abuse, which funded the establishment of methadone clinics in many American cities. Methadone maintenance has remained a useful tool in the treatment of opiate addiction ever since.

Drug Use and the 1960s Counterculture

The early 1960s marked a distinct shift in federal thinking about drug policy. During the 1950s a small cadre of liberal critics, mainly within academic circles, began questioning the increasingly punitive aspects of American drug laws. In 1962, President John F. Kennedy announced a White House Conference on Narcotics and Drug Abuse. The conference's final report heralded a shift to less punitive policy toward addiction with more room for rehabilitation. Another break with the past occurred in August 1962, when Harry J. Anslinger retired. Meanwhile, two physicians in New York City, Vincent Dole and Marie Nyswander, were experimenting with methadone, a synthetic opiate, which they found to be useful for the treatment of heroin addiction. In 1966 Congress passed the Narcotics Addict Rehabilitation Act, opening the possibility for addicts to undergo treatment instead of serving time in prison.

But drug use continued to expand into the late 1960s. This trend coincided with rising levels of crime, as well as African American uprisings in a number of American cities, especially following the assassination of Dr. Martin Luther King Jr. This unrest and political turmoil all seemed to come together at the Democratic Nati-onal Convention in 1968, where riot police fought demonstrators in the streets of Chicago. As the Republican candidate for president that year, Richard Nixon sensed the appeal of a law and order campaign to the electorate.

The 1970s and the War on Drugs

Nixon was a shrewd politician: the war on drugs was not simply a response to rising levels of drug use, but a calculated political effort to bolster the newly elected president's support among his political base. More than anything else, Nixon was worried about reducing crime and disorder, which he tied to drug use, urban riots, opposition to the Vietnam War, and the "hippie" movement. These elements all seemed to threaten conventional morality, and, combined with the specter of addicted Vietnam veterans, Nixon's appeal to law and order drew support from the "silent majority," who he believed felt threatened in the same way. While Nixon is credited with starting the war on drugs, his actual policy solutions were surprisingly moderate, as he funneled significant amounts of money into drug treatment programs in addition to domestic and international police efforts. Nixon signed into law the Comprehensive Drug Abuse Prevention and Control Act of 1970, a complete revamping of the nation's drug laws. Three years later, in 1973, the Drug Enforcement Administration (DEA) was created, replacing the previous agencies responsible for enforcing federal drug laws.

Not until the 1970s did popular opposition to the punitive approach to drug policy begin to be voiced. From a small number of academics in the 1950s and 1960s, a swelling mass of individuals and groups came out in support of drug law reform in the 1970s. In 1970, the National Organization for the Reform of Marijuana Laws (NORML), one of the first organizations to challenge American drug policies, was founded. It saw a range of early successes, as states as diverse as Alaska, Mississippi, and Oregon decriminalized the use and possession of marijuana in the late 1970s. Marijuana enjoyed widespread popularity throughout the decade.

This tolerant attitude reached its peak during the administration of Democratic president Jimmy Carter. Carter's drug policy advisor, Peter Bourne, a British-born physician, favored legalizing marijuana use and it was widely believed that the question was *when* it would happen, not *if*. However, because of the growing consumption of drugs in the United States and the concomitant rise of drug smuggling from outside the United States, American foreign policy was increasingly influenced by the war on drugs. For example, the Carter administration supported a government program in which marijuana plantations in Mexico were sprayed from the air with the herbicide Paraquat. Much of this marijuana was destined for the American markets and fears arose that smoking marijuana with Paraquat residue would cause harmful effects. This alarm created tensions between the administration and drug-reform-minded Americans, NORML in particular. The tension came to a head in 1978, when Peter Bourne was publicly accused of having used cocaine at a party held by NORML, and the accusations—which seem to have been accurate—proved too controversial for a man in Bourne's political position. After Bourne was forced to leave the administration, the Carter

White House lost most of its political capital to enact drug reform. This event symbolically ended the relative liberalism toward drugs in the 1970s.

Ronald Reagan: "Just Say No"

A new force was on the rise within the nation's conversation about drugs. As some parents discovered their teenage children were using marijuana, they mobilized other parents; this effort grew into the Parent Movement. With other groups such as Mothers Against Drunk Driving, the Parent Movement fought for more stringent drug laws and a move away from legal tolerance and social acceptance of drug use. As Carter's drug reform ideas were laid to rest after the 1978 controversy, a new conservative star from California was on the ascent. Ronald Reagan, former actor turned politician, had a history of fighting the counterculture from when he was governor of California. He, like President Nixon, understood the power of drugs as a political issue.

Elected president in 1980, Reagan quickly established his conservative bona fides by declaring that drugs were a threat to national security and he promised to scale up the war on drugs. Influenced by the Parent Movement, Reagan dismissed any attempts to decriminalize marijuana. First Lady Nancy Reagan adopted drug abuse as her signature issue, popularizing the slogan "Just Say No" to schoolchildren all across America. She supported the drug education program called Drug Abuse Resistance Education, which brought police officers into schools across the United States to advocate drug abstinence. While Ronald Reagan's early war on drugs had focused mostly on marijuana and teenage drug use, the popular use of cocaine had risen since the early 1970, peaking in about 1980.

Cocaine had largely been absent from the American drug scene after its heyday around the turn of the 20th century. In the early 1970s, however, cocaine found a new niche in the American drug marketplace. It was generally viewed as a problem-free drug used mainly by upwardly mobile white professionals. But by the early 1980s cocaine's addictive properties began to be recognized as problematic patterns of use became apparent. The popularity of cocaine in the United States also helped fuel organized crime in

Nancy and Ronald Reagan at their California ranch, "Rancho del Rio." The First Lady brandishes a sign on which is written the antidrug campaign slogan "Just Say No." (Pete Souza/White House/Sygma/Corbis)

the Latin American countries where the illegal production took place. The immense profits gained by those controlling the illegal trade spurred the creation of ruthless criminal enterprises like the Cali and Medellin cartels in Colombia. Smuggled through Central America and the Caribbean, cocaine reached America's southern border, which increasingly became the site of drug-related violence.

Just as cocaine use seemed to be waning, a new form of the drug appeared that would spread its use even further. Crack cocaine, which resulted from a simple mix of cocaine and baking soda, was sold in small rocks for as little as $10 a piece. When smoked, crack cocaine produced a cheap and intense, yet short-lasting, high. Crack found its market largely in poor neighborhoods of color in large cities, areas that had been devastated by deindustrialization and by

economic hardships often made worse by the cutting of social service budgets. While most of the cocaine profits were made by kingpins beyond the reach of American law enforcement, the money generated by crack cocaine sales in poor communities created ample opportunities for young men to make a living—a living that involved violence and turf wars, and, for many, a violent death.

A widely publicized event further fueled the antidrug hysteria of the decade. Len Bias, a basketball player at the University of Maryland, was drafted by the Boston Celtics during his senior year. A promising young star, Len Bias had captivated sports fans across the United States. In 1986, the nation was shocked to learn that he had died of an apparent cocaine overdose in his dorm room. Although Bias had used powder cocaine, not crack, the incident nevertheless prompted a wave of anticrack hysteria in Congress. Politicians from across the political spectrum seized the opportunity to be seen as tough on drugs and deliberations began in Congress to pass a tough new drug bill. In the fall of 1986, congressional hearings provided politicians the opportunity to show they were tough on drugs, and in the end, the Anti-Drug Abuse Act of 1986 was signed into law by President Reagan. This law included a range of mandatory minimum sentences and the notorious crack/powder cocaine sentencing disparity: individuals arrested for possession of crack cocaine would be sentenced much more harshly than those arrested for possessing an identical weight of powder cocaine.

The American level of incarceration had begun to climb in the early 1980s. The Anti-Drug Abuse Act of 1986 would send increasing numbers of nonviolent drug offenders to prison. While rates of drug use are similar among white and black Americans, the fact that crack cocaine was largely sold in poor communities of color led to an increasing rate of African Americans being incarcerated.

In 1988, in the midst of what came to be referred to as the crack epidemic, Congress passed yet another drug bill, The Anti-Drug Abuse Act of 1988, which further penalized drug users and created the Office of National Drug Control Policy (ONDCP). The director of ONDCP is a cabinet-level post; the head of the office is colloquially known as the Drug Czar.

A Growing Reform Movement

While the drug laws of the 1980s were passed with overwhelming bipartisan support, critics increasingly began to voice their opposition to what came to be seen as draconian and sometimes counterproductive penalties. Kurt Schmoke, a Democrat elected mayor of Baltimore, Maryland, in 1987—a city with a long history of problems related to drug use and illegal drug markets—voiced his opposition to the war on drugs and began advocating drug decriminalization as a way to deal with his city's problems. While the counterculture's political home was on the Left, and voices questioning the war on drugs are more commonly found in the Democratic Party, some notable conservatives and Republicans also opposed drug laws, though on libertarian grounds. William F. Buckley, founder of the conservative weekly *The National Review*, published an editorial in which he declared the "war on drugs" lost. Some other conservatives, such as the Nobel-prize-winning economist Milton Friedman and the psychiatrist Thomas Szasz, also embraced drug legalization.

Harm Reduction

"Harm Reduction" refers to a set of policies that aim to reduce the physical and social harms associated with the use of psychoactive drugs. Supporters of Harm Reduction view addiction as a matter of public health, not criminal justice. Needle exchange programs have become a centerpiece of a Harm Reduction policy toward drug users. Clean needles help curb the spread of HIV/AIDS, and needle exchange programs strive to be nonjudgmental and safe environments for active drug users, a demographic group with various needs and problems. Needle exchanges also often refer drug users to drug treatment programs, such as Methadone Maintenance Therapy. Federal funding for needle exchange has always been politically controversial. In 1988, Congress passed a law forbidding the federal government to fund needle exchange, despite mounting evidence of its effectiveness. In 2009, President Obama signed into law a bill lifting the ban on federal funding of needle exchange. But the ban again became federal law when it was included as a minor piece of the 2012 budget bill, which Obama signed to end a fractious debate on the federal budget. Thus, drug reform remains politically controversial in the United States.

The 1980s brought another dimension to the American drug policy discussion. In 1981 the first cases of AIDS were discovered in Los Angeles, California, and it was quickly understood that the disease was transmitted not only through unprotected sex but also through the sharing of hypodermic syringes, a common practice among injection drug users. As a response, in some cities activists began distributing clean needles and other injection equipment in an effort to slow the spread of HIV, the virus that causes AIDS, in drug-using populations. Needle exchange was controversial since it appeared to condone drug use, and though these efforts were denied federal funding, activists continued their work. Needle exchange would become a centerpiece of a public health–centered policy toward drug use, often referred to as Harm Reduction.

Despite dissenting voices on both the Left and the Right, however, the war on drugs continued to be waged in the 1990s, with few politicians willing to embrace a change in direction. An important change occurred in 1996, when the voters of California, through a referendum, legalized the use of marijuana for medicinal purposes. While virtually every politician in the state of California, as well as national politicians, opposed this effort, the voters supported the idea, and as a result marijuana dispensaries selling marijuana began opening across the state. As California took the lead, many states followed suit, and by 2013 some 18 states and Washington, DC, had legalized medicinal use of marijuana. The federal government, however, still did not recognize the legality of medical marijuana and, through the DEA, continued to raid venues where marijuana was sold in California. As increasing numbers of states legalized medical marijuana, however, their governors and their representatives in Congress began questioning the meddling in their state's affairs by the federal government.

Conclusion

During the 2012 election, three states offered their voters the opportunity to legalize marijuana for recreational use: Colorado, Oregon, and Washington. In two of them, Colorado and Washington, a majority of the voters decided to make marijuana use legal, thus breaking with the history of drug policy in the United States. The legalization of marijuana proved to have strong support among the American electorate, and polls taken in 2012 suggested that an outright majority of Americans supported the legalization of marijuana use.

Nevertheless, drug policy remains a complicated and controversial subject, as several recent episodes have shown. In the mid- to late 2000s, a new stimulant popularly called Bath Salts appeared in the United States, producing a national panic and a rush to ban the substance. While marijuana use seemed poised to become legal in several states, other substances such as Bath Salts, heroin, and amphetamines will likely remain illegal and subject to political controversy.

See also Biotechnology and Politics; Popular Culture and Politics; Public Health and Politics.

Amund Tallaksen and Caroline Jean Acker

Bibliography

Acker, Caroline Jean. 2000. *Creating the American Junkie: Addiction Research in the Classic Era of Narcotic Control*. Baltimore: The Johns Hopkins University Press.

Alexander, Michelle. 2012. *The New Jim Crow: Mass Incarceration in the Age of Colorblindness*. New York: The New Press.

Campbell, Nancy D. 2007. *Discovering Addiction: The Science and Politics of Substance Abuse Research*. Ann Arbor: The University of Michigan Press.

Courtwright, David T. 2001. *Dark Paradise: A History of Opiate Addiction in America*. Cambridge, MA: Harvard University Press.

Courtwright, David T., Herman Joseph, and Don Des Jarlais, 2012. *Addicts Who Survived: An Oral History of Narcotic Use in America before 1965*. Knoxville: The University of Tennessee Press.

Frydl, Kathleen J. 2013. *The Drug Wars in America, 1940–1973*. New York: Cambridge University Press.

Hentoff, Nat. 1968. *A Doctor among the Addicts*. New York: Rand McNally.

Herzberg, David. 2010. *Happy Pills in America: From Milltown to Prozac*. Baltimore: The Johns Hopkins University Press.

Kuzmarov, Jeremy. 2009. *The Myth of the Addicted Army: Vietnam and the Modern War on Drugs.* Amherst: The University of Massachusetts Press.

MacCoun, Robert J., and Peter Reuter. 2001. *Drug War Heresies: Learning from Other Vices, Times, and Places.* New York: Cambridge University Press.

Musto, David F. 1999. *The American Disease: Origins of Narcotic Control.* New York: Oxford University Press.

Nelkin, Dorothy. 1973. *Methadone Maintenance: A Technological Fix.* New York: George Braziller.

Provine, Doris Marie. 2007. *Unequal under Law: Race in the War on Drugs.* Chicago: The University of Chicago Press.

Rasmussen, Nicolas. 2009. *On Speed: The Many Lives of Amphetamine.* New York: The New York University Press.

Reinarman, Craig, and Harry G. Levine. 1997. "Real Opposition, Real Alternatives: Reducing the Harms of Drug Use and Drug Policy." In Craig Reinarman and Harry G. Levine, eds. *Crack in American: Demon Drugs and Social Justice.* Berkeley: University of California Press, pp. 435–66.

Reuter, Peter, and Jonathon Caulkins. 1995. "Redefining the Goals of National Drug Policy: Recommendations from a Working Group." *American Journal of Public Health* 85, Part I: 1059–63.

Schneider, Eric. 2008. *Smack: Heroin and the American City.* Philadelphia: The University of Pennsylvania Press.

Simon, Jonathan. 2009. *Governing through Crime: How the War on Crime Transformed American Democracy and Created a Culture of Fear.* New York: Oxford University Press.

Spillane, Joseph F. 2000. *Cocaine: From Medical Marvel to Modern Menace in the United States, 1884–1920.* Baltimore: The Johns Hopkins University Press.

Weimer, Daniel. 2011. *Seeing Drugs: Modernization, Counterinsurgency, and U.S. Narcotics Control in the Third World, 1969–1976.* Kent, OH: Kent State University Press.

Western, Bruce. 2007. *Punishment and Inequality in America.* New York: Russell Sage Foundation Publications.

E

ECONOMIC POLICY AND POLITICS

Both politically and substantively, economic matters have become central elements of American politics. Since at least the 1930s, presidents have come to be seen by the public as the "managers of prosperity" (Dolan, Frendreis, and Tatalovich 2008, 2–3), and presidents, and those who wish to become president, spend a great amount of effort discussing and working on economic matters. Since modern polling began in the 1930s, economic matters rank at or near the top of Americans' concerns in public opinion polls, displaced from the top position only by national security concerns during wars or episodes of high international tension.

The present entry discusses economic politics and policy in six parts. First, the goals of economic policy are discussed, economic concerns are grounded in American political culture, and the significant economic theories that structure economic policies are presented. Next, the key actors in economic policy making are identified, and the tools of economic policy making are described. Finally, the entry concludes by examining economic politics and policy as it relates to the Great Recession of 2007–2009, the most significant economic challenge faced by the United States since the Great Depression of the 1930s.

The Goals of Economic Policy

There is a broad consensus within American political culture in support of core elements of the American economy such as private property, the efficacy of markets, and the superiority of capitalism as an economic organizing principle. Beyond this, American political leaders promote policies designed to pursue a variety of economic goals. Many of these goals are broadly embraced, even where the proposed means to the desired ends differ. Other goals are themselves sources of political controversy.

Four goals are broadly accepted across the political spectrum and have been sometimes described as the "Golden Quadrangle" (Peters 1986, 157). These are economic growth, full employment, stable prices, and a positive balance of international trade. Economic growth generally refers to growth in the gross domestic product (GDP), which is the sum of all goods and services produced within the country. When GDP grows at a rate faster than the rate of population growth, the larger GDP means that some or many members of society may be better off, without these gains coming from other people's losses. Using the familiar metaphor of a pie, the pie gets larger, allowing all pieces of the pie to either stay the same or get larger. The second goal, full employment, means that all people seeking work can be employed. Interestingly, because of things like geographic mobility and temporary gaps in employment when switching jobs, the full employment level is not the same as a zero level of unemployment. Rather, in recent decades economists have generally regarded an unemployment level of about 4 percent as representing the full employment level. The third element of the Golden Quadrangle, stable prices, means that aggregate price increases are modest, averaging less than 2 percent per year. Americans are most familiar with the problem of inflation, when price increases are much higher than this, but the reverse—generally falling prices, or deflation—also creates problems for the economy. Finally, the fourth broadly embraced goal, a positive balance of international trade, means that the dollar values of goods and services exported (produced in the United States and purchased by those outside the United States) are greater than the dollar value of imports (foreign-produced goods and services purchased by entities in the United States). While for much of the 20th century the United States experienced trade surpluses (exports greater than imports), trade deficits have been the norm for the last 20 years.

Political leaders sometimes pursue other economic goals that are more controversial. One such goal is promoting structural change to the economy, for example, using government investments to create a "green" economy or develop key industries like electronics or machine tools. When this takes on a comprehensive character, this type of policy is sometimes referred to as a national industrial policy. While such policies, which imply close cooperation between industry and government (including both investment and the management of competition), have been utilized effectively in many developed or emerging economies in East Asia, these efforts are often opposed within U.S. politics on the grounds that they interfere with the operations of the market. This opposition springs from the great faith placed in market mechanisms, coupled with a belief that government intervention is usually ineffective or counterproductive. In practical political terms, Republicans are more likely to oppose such policies, while Democrats are more likely to favor them. The roots of these partisan differences will be discussed in the next section.

An economic issue that has received increasing attention during the last two decades is the unequal distribution of income and wealth in the United States. Statistics indicate that inequalities of income (yearly earnings) and wealth (accumulated assets) have been increasing in the United States since about 1980, reversing a trend toward greater equality that was seen for about five decades from the early 1930s until the late 1970s. Although this has led many to argue for a goal of reducing income and wealth inequalities in the United States, this has proven to be an even more controversial policy than a national industrial policy.

Economic Issues and American Political Culture

While there is broad support for private property, market-based economies, and free enterprise, Americans display a range of attitudes relating to the need for and purposes of government intervention in the economy. These divisions can be usefully described in terms of liberal and conservative beliefs, and the core of these differences centers around the extent to which people believe that private actors operating in a market economy produce the best possible outcomes for American society. Liberals are more likely to believe that market outcomes can lead to outcomes that are generally preferable, though flawed, and they believe that government action is required to address these market imperfections. Conservatives are skeptical about the benefits of government efforts to influence markets, and they tend to regard such interventions as running counter to core American beliefs about individual freedom and the superiority of free markets to central planning or control of the economy.

The differences in liberal and conservative beliefs also align with contemporary political party differences, with Democrats being more likely to favor government intervention in the economy, to promote both economic and noneconomic goals, and Republicans opposing this intervention on the grounds that it is unnecessary, ineffective, or harmful to economic goals like job creation. These partisan differences have been apparent in recent debates over the 2009 economic stimulus package, raising the minimum wage, and efforts to reduce income inequality.

Economic Theories Underlying Economic Policy in the United States

Historically, four different economic theories have influenced economic policy, although none has ever been used exclusively to guide public policy, and today elements of all four can be seen in policy discussions and actions. The four economic theories are laissez-faire economics, Keynesian economics, monetarism, and supply-side economics.

Laissez-Faire Economics

The oldest of the four is laissez-faire economics, which is also referred to as classical economics (or neoclassical economics, in a more recent variant). This can be traced back to Adam Smith, a Scottish economist who first advanced these ideas in his book *The Wealth of Nations*, published in 1776 (Smith 1999). Reacting to an earlier set of ideas called mercantilism, Smith argued for limited government interference in an economy organized around free markets, which he suggested would yield more goods produced at lower prices and increase the well-being of a nation. While the United States never completely adopted the idea of very limited government activity, particularly in regard to the development of a national infrastructure and new industries, for much of U.S. history the application of laissez-faire (French for "leave it alone") principles promoted policies of limited government intervention in the market economy.

Keynesian Economics

A significant problem for the laissez-faire approach is that the performance of the U.S. economy fluctuated on a regular basis between periods of economic expansion and economic contraction, a phenomenon known as the business cycle. Economists have traced these fluctuations and have identified 32 cycles of these fluctuations between 1854 and the present (National Bureau of Economic Research 2014). Laissez-faire economics argues that private markets should stabilize at an equilibrium point that maximizes economic output, so these fluctuations—particularly the deep contractions known as "panics" or "depressions"—pointed to flaws in the laissez-faire model. In the midst of the Great Depression (1929–1940 in the United States), a new set of ideas, Keynesian economics, began to gain currency. As developed by a British economist, John Maynard Keynes, this theory explained these macroeconomic fluctuations as emanating from too little or too much aggregate demand for goods and services within a national economy (Keynes 1936). Keynes argued that economic activity (represented as the aggregate supply of good and services) rises and falls to meet demand, so the remedy for these economic fluctuations

is to manipulate the aggregate demand, a task Keynes felt could be undertaken only by the government. The mechanism for this government manipulation of demand was government fiscal policy (spending and taxing decisions), and Keynes laid out scenarios whereby governments should run overall deficits during downturns and surpluses during expansions. More significantly, Keynesian economics established a positive, interventionist role for government, in contrast to the mainly passive role in the laissez-faire model. Between the passage of the Employment Act of 1946 and the early 1970s, Keynesian economics came to dominate the thinking of policy makers of both parties in the United States and many other Western nations.

Monetarism

Just as Keynesian economics was being broadly embraced, it was challenged both by a seemingly insoluble economic problem and by an alternative theory of economic policy making. The economic problem was the simultaneous appearance of recession (economic contraction) and price inflation, a phenomenon termed stagflation, which could be neither explained by nor solved effectively by Keynesian ideas. The alternative theory, monetarism, was advanced most effectively by American economist Milton Friedman (Friedman and Schwartz 1963). Monetarism held that fluctuations in the supply of money translated into fluctuations both in overall economic activity and in prices, and thus, the regulation of the economy should rest primarily on regulation of the money supply rather than on manipulation of aggregate demand. The chief policy prescription flowing from this theory is that the government should take actions that yield a steady growth of the money supply within a narrow percentage range, essentially equal to the long-term growth rate sought for the economy.

Supply-Side Economics

Since the 1980s, a fourth significant economic theory has become part of economic policy discussions. Supply-side economics focuses on incentives to those who produce goods and services ("suppliers") and argues that incentives and disincentives to suppliers affect investment and employment decisions. In contrast to the demand-side argument of Keynesian economics, supply-side economics sees these incentives as the key to influencing the level of economic activity. Political rhetoric based on these ideas argues for reductions in marginal tax rates and in regulations as the means to stimulate the economy, and this viewpoint has been very influential among Republicans, especially during the presidencies of Ronald Reagan, George W. Bush, and Barack Obama (in the latter case, in opposition to the president).

Economic Theory and Practice

As a practical matter, economic theory always represents a mixture of approaches. Over time, the main lines of thought underlying policy are something of an overlay of all of the theories described earlier. In the past 30 years, Keynesian economics has been the dominant approach to addressing economic contractions, especially among Democrats, while monetarism has been embraced broadly in terms of controlling inflation. Supply-side ideas have formed the underpinning of Republican opposition to raising taxes and support for cutting marginal tax rates. Even so, laissez-faire ideas, which match up well with core American cultural ideas in support of limited government, continue to promote skepticism of the benefits of government intervention in the economy. As the final section of this entry details, all of these ideas can be seen in the debates and policy actions in response to the major economic downturn in 2008 that has come to be called the Great Recession.

Key Actors in Economic Politics and Policy

Although many institutions play a role in the development and implementation of economic policy, four key executive branch institutions are especially significant: the president, the Executive Office of the President (EOP), the Treasury Department, and the Federal Reserve System.

The President

The most important of these is the president, to whom the American public looks to secure prosperity and toward whom the public expresses disappointment when this fails to materialize. Economic policy proposals represent an important part of each president's domestic policy agenda, and the American public places great emphasis on economic matters when evaluating candidates during presidential elections. The successful 1992 presidential campaign of Bill Clinton famously featured a sign with three phrases in the national campaign headquarters, of which the second phrase, "The economy, stupid," was designed to remind members of the campaign team to focus on this issue in their campaign messaging.

Executive Office of the President

The president's ability to devise and executive economic policy is significantly enhanced by units within the EOP, especially the Council of Economic Advisors and the Office of Management and Budget. The first of these units consists of a council composed of three economists, supported by a staff of economists and other professionals. The council plays a critical role in forecasting future economic conditions and providing advice to the president on how to address potential economic challenges. The Office of Management and Budget provides expert advice on budgetary matters and oversees the preparation and execution of the annual federal budget on behalf of the president, a critical element in fiscal policy.

Treasury Department

Established in 1789, the Treasury is one of the oldest cabinet departments in the federal government. The secretary of the Treasury serves as one of the president's chief advisors on economic matters, while the department he or she oversees implements key aspects of economic policy, such as managing the national debt, collecting tax revenues, and paying the government's bills.

Federal Reserve System

The Federal Reserve System, created in 1913, performs the functions of a central bank for the United States. Organized into 12 regional banks and overseen by a Board of Governors appointed to long and staggered terms, the Federal Reserve System, or Fed, is a key part of the nation's banking system. The Fed has significant regulatory powers with respect to the banking system and has direct control over policies related to money supply. With influence over interest rates and the availability of credit, the Fed has played a key role in developing and implementing policies to combat the economic problems associated with the Great Recession and its aftermath.

Other Actors

Other actors, both inside and outside of the government, play important roles in developing or implementing economic policy. Working with the president, Congress establishes tax laws, national debt limits, annual spending, and economic regulations through the legislative process. The Departments of Labor and Commerce have responsibility for implementing policies designed to provide training to workers and promote business opportunities. Interest groups and think tanks outside of the government provide commentary and critiques of economic issues and policies, and many new ideas are first proposed by these nongovernmental actors.

Tools of Economic Policy

There are three principal policy tools that the government utilizes to pursue the goals of economic policy identified earlier. These tools are fiscal policy, monetary policy, and regulatory policy.

Fiscal Policy

Fiscal policy is composed of the taxing and spending decisions made by the federal government. The U.S. government operates with an annual budget, so each year Congress must pass, and the president must sign, laws establishing spending for the following year. Major changes to the tax code are made less frequently. Fiscal policy can be used in a variety of ways to influence the economy. Taken as a whole, the total level of spending and taxation is the instrument for altering aggregate demand, the key intervention dictated by Keynesian economics. In addition, the specific features of the tax code—who pays what under various circumstances—can be used to influence income and wealth inequality and to promote or discourage certain kinds of private actions. The levels of taxation on various income levels, known as the marginal tax rates, are one of the chief objects of supply-side economics. Finally, the specific things the government chooses to address with spending programs—infrastructure, military spending, education, social safety net programs—can directly influence matters like poverty, social mobility, and future economic activity enabled by current investments.

Monetary Policy

Monetary policy is composed of policy actions designed to increase or decrease the supply of money within the U.S. economy, something that has come to be seen as a powerful influence on inflation, interest rates, and the ability of the economy to grow or contract. Development and implementation of monetary policy is the responsibility of the Federal Reserve System, especially its central coordinating unit, the Board of Governors. Monetary policy decisions by the Fed in the early 1980s are credited with curing the high levels of inflation that ravaged the U.S. economy during the 1970s. During the Great Recession and its aftermath, the Fed's monetary and credit policies have been the most important tools employed to stimulate the economy and have made the Fed chairman, Ben Bernanke, a highly visible and significant figure in U.S. politics.

Regulatory Policy

Regulatory policy is composed of rules established by the government to alter the behavior of individuals and corporations in ways that produce outcomes viewed as more socially desirable. Many of the regulations affecting the economy are designed to have a specific economic impact, such as rules designed to promote competition, while others have an impact on the economy, even though the primary intent of the regulation is noneconomic, such as reducing pollution. Many types of economic regulations are administered by boards or commissions that operate relatively independently of Congress and the president, although the underlying laws are, of course, passed by Congress and signed by the president. Examples include the Security and Exchange Commission, which regulates the securities market, the National Labor Relations Board, which oversees regulations related to collective bargaining by unions, and the Federal Reserve System. Other regulations are administered by executive branch agencies reporting to the president, and, since the presidency of Ronald Reagan, presidents of both parties have maintained greater control on the regulations established by these executive departments and agencies. In fact, the review of these potential regulations and the president's power to appoint heads of regulatory agencies are important methods by which the president can influence policy even when a hostile Congress does not wish to pass new legislation.

Economic Policy and the Great Recession

In December 2007, the economy reached a turning point and began a period of economic contraction that lasted until June 2009. Although the GDP began to expand again at that point, the pace of economic expansion was slow, and the unemployment rate did not peak at 10 percent until four months later, remaining relatively high for several years more, and not dropping below 7 percent until December 2013. The duration, extent of contraction, and slow pace of recovery made this economic downturn the worst contraction (also known as a recession) since the Great Depression of 1929–1940. As a result, this economic contraction has come to be known as the Great Recession, and the reaction of the public and policy makers to this economic challenge illustrates much of what has been discussed earlier.

In political terms, much of the public's anger at the deteriorating economy and rising unemployment was directed originally at President George W. Bush and his Republican Party. The president's public approval ratings slumped, and the subsequent presidential election victory of Democrat Barack Obama over Republican John McCain can be partially attributed to the public's dissatisfaction. In turn, the persistence of high levels of unemployment throughout 2009 and 2010 weakened President Obama's public standing and

contributed to the Republican's regaining of control of the House of Representatives in the 2010 midterm election. These relationships between the economy, the public's attitudes, and election results are often observed (see Tufte 1978), although the severity of the downturn magnified these political effects.

The roles of different actors and the policy responses crafted can be understood in terms of the underlying theories and policy tools described earlier. In 2008, Congress and President Bush engineered a one-time $150 billion tax rebate program, in line with Keynesian prescriptions to stimulate demand. This was followed with a much more massive Keynesian-based $700-billion fiscal stimulus package, proposed by President Obama and enacted by a Democratic Congress in the spring of 2009. While a source of much political debate, this package is generally regarded as reducing the peak level unemployment rate by around 1 percentage point. Throughout this time period, the Fed played a prominent role, first in engineering changes to the banking system designed to prevent massive bank failures and later in reducing interest rates to near zero in hopes of stimulating economic activity. The onset and severity of the Great Recession is thought by many to be the result of failures in economic regulatory policy in the securities, banking, and housing areas (see McLean and Nocera 2010), and a final response of Congress and the president was to pass a law dictating major changes to the regulatory framework overseeing financial matters.

See also Budget Politics; Debt, Deficit, and Politics; Inequality and Politics; Privatization and Deregulation; Tax Policy and Politics.

John P. Frendreis

Bibliography

Dolan, Chris J., John Frendreis, and Raymond Tatalovich. 2008. *The Presidency and Economic Policy*. Lanham, MD: Rowman and Littlefield.

Friedman, Milton, and Ann Jacobson Schwartz. 1963. *A Monetary History of the United States, 1867–1960*. Princeton, NJ: Princeton University Press.

Keynes, John Maynard. 1936. *The General Theory of Employment, Interest, and Money*. New York: Harcourt, Brace.

McLean, Bethany, and Joe Nocera. 2010. *All the Devils Are Here: The Hidden History of the Financial Crisis*. New York: Portfolio/Penguin.

National Bureau of Economic Research. 2014. "US Business Cycle Expansions and Contractions." http://www.nber.org/cycles/cyclesmain.html. Accessed May 19, 2014.

Peters, B. Guy. 1986. *American Public Policy: Promise and Performance*. 2nd ed. Chatham, NJ: Chatham House.

Smith, Adam. 1999. *The Wealth of Nations*. New York: Penguin.

Tufte, Edward R. 1978. *Political Control of the Economy*. Princeton, NJ: Princeton University Press.

EDUCATION POLICY AND POLITICS

At the beginning of the 20th century, the role of government in schooling was to provide free public schools for children. So it was at the fin de siècle. What, then, changed? In 1900, schools were almost entirely the creatures of local governments. States played little role in their financing and operations, and the federal government was wholly absent. Come 2000, the role of local governments in schooling had ebbed, while the role of state governments and the federal government had grown. Expressed as dollars, in 1900, local governments provided more than 80 percent of school funds; state governments contributed the rest. The federal government contributed none. By 2000, localities provided 43 percent of school funds, states 48 percent, and the federal government 9 percent.

These funding figures exhibit the growth of state influence over the schools. To cite just a few examples, state governments set high school graduation requirements, operate student learning testing and assessment programs, and dictate the certification requirements for teachers.

However, these numbers obscure arguably the most profound transformation in education policy and the government's role with respect to schooling, which is the dramatic rise in the power of the federal government to influence school operations. During the 20th century, the federal government went from having no role whatsoever to playing some part in virtually every aspect of schooling. Policies and actions of the federal government have affected schools' curricula and school policies toward minority (racial, language) and handicapped children, provided school lunches, funded cultural and arts programs and drug and alcohol abuse deterrence programs, and more. Furthermore, the growth of state education agencies and their development into highly professionalized entities was spurred, largely, by the federal government. Increasingly, the roles of state and local governments have been sculpted by actions of the federal government. As will be seen, the growth of the federal government's role in schooling has come through two means: federal court decisions and federal grants-in-aid policies.

The Colonial Era and After

Government's role as the provider of free education developed in fits and starts since the earliest settlement of North America. Though many children were educated by their parents or in private academies, some early localities and colonies did provide schools. In 1642, the Massachusetts Colonial Court decreed that, owing to the "great neglect of many parents and masters, in training up their children in learning and labor, and other employments, which may be profitable to the commonwealth," we the court "do hereby order and decree, that in every town, the chosen men appointed to manage the prudential affairs . . . shall henceforth stand charged with the redress of this evil." The leaders of the towns could be fined and punished if they failed to remedy illiteracy among children, who were thought ignorant of "the principles of religion and the capital laws of this country."

The establishment of public schools was encouraged by the land management policies of the earliest federal governments of America. For example, the Northwest Ordinance of 1785 provided for the sale of western lands by the federal government. As a condition of sale, it required that "there shall be reserved [a lot in] every township, for the maintenance of public schools within the said township." During the 19th century, the growth of government-sponsored schools accelerated. Many local governments, often nudged by states and zealous educators, established simple schools that would provide rudimentary educational skills training, such as reading and writing. Progress, though, was uneven, particularly in rural and low-income communities, where limited tax bases and the agrarian way of life inhibited the development of modern schools.

Government Provision but Not Compulsion

Private schools have existed since European settlers arrived in North America. While all levels of government have recognized a community interest in the education of children, this has not meant that government has an absolute power to compel student attendance to government-funded or "public" schools. This limited power was stated forcefully by the Supreme Court in *Pierce v. Society of Sisters* (268 U.S. 510 [1925]), when it struck down an Oregon law that required parents to send their children to a public school. The Court declared:

> We think it entirely plain that the Act of 1922 unreasonably interferes with the liberty of parents and guardians to direct the upbringing and education of children . . . under their control. As often heretofore pointed out, rights guaranteed by the Constitution may not be abridged by legislation which has no reasonable relation to some purpose within the competency of the state. The fundamental theory of liberty upon which all governments in this Union repose excludes any general power of the state to standardize its children by forcing them to accept instruction from public teachers only. The child is not the mere creature of the state; those who nurture him and direct his destiny have the right, coupled with the high duty, to recognize and prepare him for additional obligations.

Throughout the 20th century, this antagonism between the professed interests of communities in schooling children and the rights of parents over their children has recurred. Frequently, these disputes have been litigated and judges have had to rule on nettlesome issues, such as the right of parents to homeschool their children.

Development of Federal Involvement in Schooling

In its enumeration of the powers of the federal government, the U.S. Constitution makes no mention of schooling or education. Moreover, the Tenth Amendment of the Constitution declares: "The powers not delegated to the United States [government] by the Constitution, nor prohibited by it to the states, are reserved to the states respectively, or to the people." How, then, was the federal government able to assume a role in schooling? In great part, the vehicle has been grants-in-aid. Put succinctly, a grant-in-aid is an offer of funding by the federal government to states or localities. In exchange for the funds, the recipient of the grant must expend it on the purposes stipulated by the grant and obey the grant's mandates (i.e., "conditions of aid"). Thus, grants-in-aid have provided the primary means through which the federal government has leapt over the federalism divide, which purported to separate governing responsibilities between the federal and state governments, and assumed a role in schooling.

Growth of the Federal Role in Schooling, 1917–1958

In a pattern that was to be repeated during the 20th century, the establishment of the first major federal education policy was spurred by a crisis. As the federal government began to draft men to fight in World War I, it found that 25 percent of them were illiterate. President Woodrow Wilson, a PhD and former university president, found this troubling and favored education legislation to remedy this problem. He believed that the modern industrial economy and military needed workers and soldiers who were literate and skilled in industrial trades. Thus, one month before the United States formally entered World War I, President Wilson signed the Smith-Hughes Vocational Act on February 23, 1917.

The Smith-Hughes Act appropriated money "to be paid to the respective states for the purpose of co-operating with the states in paying the salaries of teachers, supervisors, and directors of agricultural subjects, and teachers of trade, home economics, and industrial subjects, and in the preparation of teachers of agricultural, trade, industrial, and home economics subjects." The act established the surprisingly powerful Federal Board for Vocational Education, which was empowered to set the requisite qualifications for an individual to be hired as a vocational education teacher. The board also could withhold federal funds from schools that violated federal education standards of what constituted appropriate agricultural, home economic, vocational, and industrial educational curricula. The statute mandated that states set up state vocational education boards that would work with the federal board.

Despite this breakthrough, however, the federal government's role changed little over the next three decades. During the Great Depression, agencies such as the Public Works Administration (PWA), the Civilian Conservation Corps, and the National Youth Administration provided emergency funding to cash-strapped schools. In 1934, emergency aid reached approximately $2 million to $3 million per month. By 1940, PWA had helped local and state authorities build 12,704 schools with 59,615 classrooms. This brief expansion of the federal role in schooling, though, contracted once the Great Depression passed.

Between 1946 and 1958, the scope of federal involvement expanded. On June 4, 1946, the School Lunch Act was signed into law by President Harry S. Truman. The law declared it "to be the policy of Congress . . . to safeguard the health and well-being of the Nation's children and to encourage the consumption of nutritious agricultural commodities and other foods, through grants-in-aid." The school lunch program required schools to provide low-cost or free lunches to children; in exchange, schools receive cash subsidies and food from the Department of Agriculture.

Impact Aid was enacted into law four years later (1950). This policy grew out of a 1940 program to fund infrastructure projects (sewers, recreational facilities, etc.) in areas where the federal government had a large presence (e.g., military installations, federal agencies). Mobilization for World War II created a huge growth in the size of the federal workforce. Military facilities occupied large swaths of land, which removed them from state and local tax rolls. (States and localities may not tax the federal government.) In time, the presence of these facilities and workers brought forth children who needed schooling. Impact Aid was devised to reimburse these federally affected areas. Each year, today, communities provide the federal government with data on costs (e.g., educational costs) and receive reimbursement based upon a formula.

The launch of the *Sputnik* satellite by the Soviet Union on October 4, 1957, set off a media and political firestorm in the United States. While President Eisenhower downplayed the significance of the event, many inside and outside of Congress whipped up a frenzy. Sen. Lyndon B. Johnson made especially worrisome claims. Control of space, he told the press, would make for control of the world, as the Soviets would have the power to control the weather and raise and lower the levels of the oceans. (Such ideas were not so far-fetched at the time.) The schools were blamed for this situation. Prominent persons, such as former president Herbert Hoover and Sen. Henry Jackson, claimed that Soviet schools were producing far more brainpower than U.S. schools. In the name of national defense, many said, more federal education aid was needed. Less than a year later, the National Defense Education Act (NDEA) became law on September 2, 1958. Much of the NDEA benefited colleges, showering them with funds for research grants for technical training and advanced studies. Public high schools also benefited. Secondary schools were given funds to identify able students who should be encouraged to apply for federal scholarships for collegiate study in foreign languages, mathematics, and science.

Despite this growth in the federal role, many attempts to expand it further failed. Between 1935 and 1950, dozens of bills were introduced into Congress to provide general aid to public schools. Some of the bills would have raised teachers' salaries; others would have provided grants and low-interest loans to districts that needed to build bigger and more modern schools. In a hint of things to come, a number of bills were introduced that would have provided federal monies to create a floor in per-pupil spending. This latter proposal would have helped poor school districts, where property values were low, leaving schools grossly underfunded. All of the proposals to increase and equalize school funding stalled in Congress, blocked by members who saw little sense of propriety in an expansion of the federal role in schooling.

The Promotion of Equity in Schooling, 1954–1975

For much of its existence, the federal government did little to expand access to schooling for special needs and nonwhite children. On occasion, the U.S. Congress provided aid. For example, in 1864, the federal government helped found the Columbian Institution for the Deaf, Dumb, and Blind, which later became Gallaudet University. The federal government also aided in the development of schools for nonwhites. Subsequent to treaties signed with Native American tribes, the federal government funded and operated schools on Indian reservations. The federal government aided blacks by chartering Howard University in 1867. At the close of the Civil War, the federal government also forced confederate states to rewrite their constitutions to include provisions to require states to provide schooling for all children. (Previously, many black children and those in isolated rural areas lacked access to schooling.) Between 1954 and 1975, however, the federal government moved to the fore in expanding access to schooling.

The federal government's first major effort at ensuring equity in education came in the form of a Supreme Court decision. The case, *Oliver Brown et al. v. Board of Education of Topeka et al.*, popularly known as *Brown v. Board of Education*, came on May 17, 1954. The Court noted that education was "perhaps the most important function of state and local governments." That said, it denied that states and localities could require children to attend racially segregated schools. Separate schooling was "inherently unequal," said the Court, and violated the Fourteenth Amendment's due process clause. States must, the Court declared, make schooling "available to all on equal terms." The upshot of the *Brown* case was the gradual demolition of states' racially segregated schooling. The *Brown* decision and those federal court decisions that followed it led to the federal policy of busing children to achieve racial desegregation. This policy was largely abandoned after 1980.

In the wake of America's "discovery of poverty" and rising violence in urban areas, the federal government greatly expanded its role in schooling and its funding of schooling through the enactment of the Elementary and Secondary Education Act (ESEA) of 1965. The act lifted the federal contribution to school funding to over 8 percent of total school funding. The ESEA provided funds for a number of school programs, the largest of which was Title I (also known as Chapter I). This program provided funds for schools to expend on compensatory education programs for nonwhite and poor children. The ESEA also provided funds to help state education agencies professionalize their operations. Over time, ESEA funds and mandates helped build state agencies into formidable educational administration agencies.

The federal government further expanded its role as promoter of equity in schooling with the enactment of the Bilingual Education Act of 1968 and the Education for All Handicapped Children Act of 1975. Both of these acts established programs to help public schools to better teach underserved children. The former act provided funds for instruction in English and foreign languages. The latter act forbade school systems from excluding children with mental or physical handicaps from schools and provided funds for programs to help school these children.

Finally, the federal government expanded its role further when it forbade states from denying schooling to the children of illegal immigrants. When the state of Texas enacted a statute to deny children of illegal immigrants the right to attend school, the Supreme Court struck it down. In *Plyler v. Doe* (1982), the Court stated that, although these children did not have a fundamental right to schooling, the law did deny the children the equal protection under the law guaranteed by the Fourteenth Amendment to the Constitution because it erected "unreasonable obstacles to advancement on the basis of individual merit."

The Proliferation and Diversification of Federal Involvement, 1976–2010

Over the next quarter of a century, the federal role in schooling became more diversified. The Office of Education was replaced by the Department of Education in 1979. This upgrading of federal administration solidified the federal government's role in a number of areas, including compensatory education, bilingual education, vocational education, and educational research. New grants-in-aid programs proliferated; by the end of the century, the federal government funded school programs in arts education, physical fitness, school technology, antidrug and alcohol-dependency classes, character education courses, and more.

During this period, criticism arose over the efficacy of federal programs, such as Title I of the ESEA. In response, the federal government began creating policies to increase student learning as measured by tests. Congress enacted Goals 2000 in 1994 and amended the ESEA's Title I grants-in-aid program via both the Improving America's Schools Act of 1994 and the No Child Left Behind (NCLB) Act of 2002. Under the new Title I of NCLB, the conditions of aid required states and localities to experiment with school choice or voucher programs. That is, funds were provided for the development of privately operated but open-to-all charter schools. The new Title I also required local school districts to permit students attending underperforming schools to choose the public school they attended. As a further condition of aid, these policies required states to develop accountability

President Bush signs the No Child Left Behind education reform act into law on January 8, 2002. In attendance are (left to right) Representative George Miller (D-Calif.), Senator Edward M. Kennedy (D-Mass.), Secretary of Education Rod Paige, Senator Judd Gregg (R-N.H.), and Representative John Boehner (R-Ohio). (AP Photo/Ron Edmonds)

systems consisting of academic standards and tests that would be used to hold schools accountable for student learning. By 2009, however, school districts and government officials were faced with a flood of "failing schools" under NCLB guidelines, and policy makers worked to adjust the accountability strictures and to move ahead with an allied program, Race to the Top, aimed at rewarding schools for demonstrating efforts to improve.

Ongoing Debates, 2010–Present

The school-reform movement, of which NCLB is a part, includes not only an emphasis on private charter schools and school choice but also efforts to challenge teachers and teachers' unions to embrace change (de-unionization), national standards, and market-based solutions (privatization). In the wake of NCLB and the reform movement, the field of education was quickly pervaded by teacher assessment tools and concepts from business administration, including cost–benefit analyses of failing schools and school programs.

The only problem is that such measures had never been tried before, at least not on a national scale. Moreover, over the last decade there has emerged a body of evidence suggesting that these reforms may have problems of their own. Although some charter schools continue to excel, as a group they do not outperform traditional public schools. Meanwhile, teachers and their unions have a strong presence in many high-performing public schools, even as many union-free charter schools based on business principles perform poorly or have failed entirely. In addition, as school districts continue to stress rote preparation ("teaching to the test") in anticipation of standardized testing and school evaluation, they continue to push, at the same time, for revising the national benchmarks downward. Several scandals have broken in recent years involving school principals or district superintendents accused of altering test results to achieve higher ratings for their schools. Finally, student achievement has not risen significantly over the past 12 or 13 years under NCLB and related reforms.

As things stand at present, lawmakers in Washington, DC, seem unable to agree on where to turn next. NCLB was to have been reauthorized—or replaced—in 2007, but because there is no consensus regarding it or its potential replacement, the law remains in a state of limbo. It continues to be operational even while it is thought to be unachievable at best and misdirected at worst. By 2012, up to 32 states had been granted waivers by the federal government in exchange for promises to continue working toward achieving reforms.

Conclusion

States and localities provide the vast majority of funds for public schools. It is these two levels of government that have the greatest power to prescribe schools' curricula, set the compensation and standards for the licensure of teachers and administrators, and oversee day-to-day school operations. Nevertheless, as the federal government has assumed a larger and larger role, more and more of what states do occurs within a context set by the federal government. Through court decisions and grants-in-aid programs, the federal government, despite its modest contribution to school funding, has taken a broad and significant role in the public schools.

Over the past few years another test-based initiative called the Common Core has arisen. Sponsored by the National Governors Association and the Council of Chief State School Officers, the Common Core program promotes statewide educational standards in language arts and mathematics in line with similar efforts toward achieving consistent learning standards and school and teacher accountability. Some 44 states have adopted the Common Core since 2009, when the initiative first got off the ground. At the same time, by 2014 there was already serious pushback on the part of parents, students, and teachers who claimed that yet another version of "teaching to the test" was unwelcome and in fact detrimental to the goal of educating young people. A number of states ended up repealing or rolling back testing requirements based on complaints from constituents and meager results in terms of test score improvements. Even U.S. education secretary Arne Duncan allowed that "testing issues today are sucking the oxygen out of the room in a lot of schools" (Alvarez 2014). Others called for a shift from a culture of testing to a culture of learning. As a result, education policy today is in flux and is likely to remain so in the near future as parents, educators, and policymakers wrestle with these issues.

See also Youth and Politics.

Kevin R. Kosar and Michael Shally-Jensen

Bibliography

Alvarez, Lizette. 2014. "States Listen as Parents Give Rampant Testing an F." *New York Times* (November 30): A1, A16.

Angus, David L., and Jeffrey E. Mirel. 1999. *The Failed Promise of the American High School, 1895–1995*. New York: Teachers College Press.

Fusarelli, Bonnie C., and Bruce S. Cooper. 2009. *The Rising State: How State Power Is Transforming Our Nation's Schools*. Albany: State University of New York Press.

Howell, William G., ed. 2005. *Besieged: School Boards and the Future of Education Politics*. Washington, DC: Brookings Institution Press.

Kosar, Kevin R. 2005 *Failing Grades: The Federal Politics of Education Standards*. Boulder, CO: Lynne Rienner.

Manna, Paul. 2010. *Collision Course: Federal Education Policy Meets State and Local Realities*. Washington, DC: CQ Press.

McCluskey, Neal P. 2007. *Feds in the Classroom: How Big Government Corrupts, Cripples, and Compromises American Education*. Lanham, MD: Rowman & Littlefield.

Ravitch, Diane. 2011. *The Death and Life of the Great American School System: How Testing and Choice are Undermining Education*. New York: Basic Books.

Rhodes, Jesse H. 2012. *An Education in Politics: The Origin and Evolution of No Child Left Behind*. Ithaca, NY: Cornell University Press.

Vinovskis, Maris A. 2009. *From a Nation at Risk to No Child Left Behind: National Education Goals and the Creation of Federal Education Policy*. New York: Teachers College Press.

Elections. *See* Campaign Finance; Campaigns and Campaigning; Debates, Presidential; Electoral College; Initiatives and Referendums; Midterm Elections; Nominating Conventions; Primaries and Caucuses; Recall Elections; Voter Turnout; Voting and Politics

ELECTORAL COLLEGE

The "Electoral College"—the name which custom has given to the constitutional system for electing the U.S. president—is among the least understood of the nation's political institutions. Much of its mystery owes to the uniquely specialized role assigned to it by the Constitution. Every four years it is summoned into being for the brief and sole task of establishing who the next president will be. Upon completion of that task the body is extinguished, until the next presidential election calls it forth once again.

Adding to the confusion is that the Electoral College is not in fact one body but 51 separate bodies meeting simultaneously in the several state capitols and in Washington, DC. The earliest uses of the term confirm the system's plural nature, referring to it as so many "different Electoral Colleges" (Farrand 1966, vol. 3, 383).

There is, moreover, reason to doubt the propriety of using the word "college," which suggests deliberation, independent judgment, and choice in its work. A good deal of time has passed since the Electoral College system behaved in that manner, if indeed it ever did. The electors who chose George Washington did not need to deliberate or even to choose. That the great general would be the first president was a foreordained conclusion, and no one stood against him. The men whose votes made John Adams the second president, in the nation's first true presidential contest, were largely known to be committed to him *prior* to being chosen as electors. And as early as the election of 1800, voices were heard insisting that presidential electors were supposed "to *act*, not to think" (Gregg 2008, 30). Thus, the notion of an "independent elector" has been mainly mythical, while the phenomenon of the pledged elector has been around almost from the beginning.

How the Electoral College Works

The notion of electors as mere delegates is assumed in the operation of the Electoral College as it functions today and has functioned in every state at least since the Civil War. When citizens enter the voting booth to choose between the presidential candidates, they are in fact choosing a slate of electors pledged to vote for that candidate. For all intents and purposes these electors serve as a mechanism that turns the votes of the most citizens in the most states into a constitutionally established choice for the next president.

While these elections take place on a state-by-state basis, each state has a different number of electors. The number of state electors exactly reflects the total number of the state's representation in Congress. As every state has two senators and at least one member in the House of Representatives, likewise every state is guaranteed at least three presidential electors. And as states with larger populations have many more members in the House, so they will end up with many more electors. (California, for instance, has 55, 17 more than Texas, the next largest state in the Union.)

This arrangement gives populous states the most influence in electing the president, but it also gives smaller states more influence than they would have had if the allocation were based on population alone. Because the Constitution leaves it up to states to decide how their electoral votes were to be chosen, states quickly learned that the best way to maximize their influence was to give all their electors to a single statewide favorite. Only the states of Maine and Nebraska have chosen not to adopt this "winner-take-all" method—choosing instead to divide their electors, one for each congressional district and two for the statewide winner.

After the addition of the District of Columbia's three electors, granted to it by the Twenty-Third Amendment, the total number of presidential electors became 538. The Constitution requires that a winning candidate must receive a majority of these electors. If no candidate receives the required majority (that is, at least 270 electoral votes), a contingency plan exists that allows the president to be chosen by the House of Representatives and the vice president to be chosen by the Senate. Instead of individual congressmen and senators each receiving a vote, however, a single vote is awarded to each state delegation and must be cast as a unit.

How the Electoral College Came to Be

It is common for political scientists to observe that the Electoral College never worked exactly as the Constitution's framers had intended. Less well known is just how it was intended to work and how this unusual electoral procedure came to be. The delegates to the Constitutional Convention were determined to construct a vigorous national government with both the authority to make national policy and the ability to enforce it. It was the lack of such ability—due to a lack of any true executive power in the government—which mainly caused these leading Americans to consider the Articles of Confederation to be an irredeemable failure.

The construction of an adequate executive arm of the government was therefore one of the top priorities of the framers, but it was by no means obvious how they could accomplish it without giving up altogether on republican (i.e., non-monarchical) government. History had provided no example of executive power that was effective, safe, *and* republican. The example of safe and effective executive power most readily at their disposal was the hereditary British monarchy. The republican examples from the ancient world proved far from safe. And the majority of the American state governors—the only republican examples available to them from the modern world—were often ineffective due to a high degree of dependence on the state legislatures. There was also, moreover, the desire that only fit (or "virtuous") characters would be able to attain this critically important office.

The construction of the presidency would be guided, then, by the attempt to strike a proper balance between these three basic goals—"republicanism, independence, and virtue" (Gregg 2008, 3). In effect, however, the framers were searching for a way to recreate the safety and effectiveness of the British king within a wholly republican constitution.

The common republican practice of letting the legislature select the executive was generally understood to be problematic for independence, but the convention had a difficult time settling on another option. Direct national popular election was proposed early on by James Wilson but was rejected as "impracticable" (Farrand 1966, vol. 1, 69). If it could be made to work, this mode would seem to meet all three of the framers' goals (especially that of independence). Wilson's proposal the next day to use "electors" instead was clearly intended to retain the benefits of popular election while overcoming the objections regarding its feasibility.

The inability to make legislative selection compatible with executive independence eventually brought the convention around to support the modified form of Wilson's proposal for electors that we now know as the Electoral College. In fashioning this institution, however, the framers not only believed that they had discovered a method of securing executive independence that also possessed the same republican legitimacy as direct election. They also thought they had found a way to make that selection more deliberate and less vulnerable to demagoguery than it would be in a direct popular election—the same "deliberate sense of the community" bestowed upon the legislative process by having a bicameral Congress—thereby increasing the likelihood that the best individuals would be chosen for the nation's highest office. And because the electors would cast their votes in their home states instead of all meeting in the national capitol, it was thought to protect against the dangers of "corruption and cabal."

How the Electoral College Has Changed

Over the more than 200 years since its construction, the constitutional *form* of the Electoral College has changed very little, but its *operation* did adapt with the development of American democracy in two very significant ways. Because the Constitution left the manner of choosing presidential electors to the state legislatures, most of these began by making the choice themselves. This arrangement soon proved out of step with the democratic ethos, and the states all eventually switched to popular selection of electors. As the states began to adopt this change, they saw that they could maximize their voting power by also adopting the winner-take-all system.

Thus, as elections expert Andrew Busch has noticed, these two changes went hand in hand and had their greatest surges in the democratic "party-building eras of Jefferson and Jackson" (Busch 2008, 32). By 1828 only South Carolina continued to choose its electors through its state legislature, and by 1836 it was also the only state that did not use the winner-take-all method. In large part, these two early developments established the modern Electoral College and gave American presidential elections their plebiscitary character.

The Election of 1800

Thomas Jefferson and his running mate, Aaron Burr, both received the same amount of electoral votes when they ran together in 1800. Instead of conceding to Jefferson, the ambitious Burr insisted that the nation might have wanted him to be president. Since it fell to the House of Representatives to choose between them, many of the outgoing Federalists voted for Burr instead of Jefferson, resulting in another virtual tie. In the end, Alexander Hamilton intervened on behalf of Jefferson, despite the fact that Jefferson was his political archenemy and despite the fact that up to that time he had always had good relations with Burr, his fellow New Yorker. Hamilton insisted that political principle must come before personal feelings. When Hamilton again intervened against Burr in a later election, it led to the famous duel that ended his life.

The earliest reform to the institution, however, was to the constitutional form itself. The Twelfth Amendment was instituted to patch a flaw in the Electoral College that nearly caused a constitutional crisis of having no legitimate presidential winner. This flaw resulted from the mistaken assumption that presidential elections would be nonpartisan affairs. As such, none of the framers foresaw that presidential and vice-presidential candidates would run together on a "party ticket." Under the original constitutional procedure, the electors were to cast two ballots for the president, representing, so to speak, their first and second choices for the office. (The second ballot had to be a different name than the first ballot, and one of the two had to be from a different state than the elector.) The candidate winning a majority of electors and the most ballots became president, and the runner-up became vice president.

In the 1800 election this system caused a tie between the two candidates from the Democratic-Republican Party. This meant that there was no constitutionally decisive winner, despite the fact that the party ticket presented Thomas Jefferson for president and Aaron Burr for vice president. The contingency election in the House of Representatives likewise failed to establish a winner in 35 successive ballots, until Jefferson (with some critical and unexpected help from Alexander Hamilton) was finally able to get the necessary majority.

As astute students of English history, the founding generation would have known that few things were more dangerous to the civil peace than an interregnum. The Twelfth Amendment was instituted to prevent such a crisis, and according to its constitutional alterations every election since has required the electors to cast "distinct ballots" for president and vice president.

In an important sense, the 1800 election and its troubles were also part of the democratization that was dramatically shaping American politics. Modern political parties were not anticipated because there was not yet at the framing any example of how a modern democratic polity would operate. America was the first one. To later observers, parties seem the necessary and inevitable outgrowth of democratic politics. Thus, the Twelfth Amendment did not seek to alter the Electoral College so much as to adjust it to the reality of democratic party politics.

Controversial Elections and Calls for Reform

Controversial elections have often served as a spur to electoral reform and have sometimes led people to question the Electoral College's legitimacy as a constitutional or democratic institution. In 1824 Andrew Jackson and his supporters thought he had been wrongly deprived of a presidential victory when a four-way race prevented an Electoral College majority from forming and the contingent election in the House of Representatives gave the presidency to John Quincy Adams. A furious Jackson questioned the legitimacy of the entire process, calling for the abolition of the Electoral College among other things.

While Jackson may have been the first to voice doubt about the institution's democratic legitimacy, his anger was primarily directed at the party caucus nominating process, which failed to produce a clean two-way race, and the backroom deals he thought responsible for Adams's victory in the House. While reforms to the party system and to the nominating process ensued—replacing "King Caucus" with the national party convention—criticism of the Electoral College was soon forgotten.

On the eve of the Civil War, in the aftermath of another presidential election, South Carolina's official "Declaration" of the causes for secession suggested that Abraham Lincoln's victory was the result of Electoral College manipulation. The Republican Party, it argued, found within the Constitution's form of electing the president a means by which to undermine "the Constitution itself." Though taking the posture of a defense of the *spirit* of the Constitution and, by implication, of the *intention* of the Electoral College, this Declaration points to a severe operational defect, so severe that fixing it was not even suggested as an option.

The election of 1860 had also been a four-way race. But unlike 1824, this was primarily the result of a sectional split in the Democratic Party, which so weakened it outside the southern states that Lincoln won most of the other states, giving him a majority in the Electoral College. Though he also received more popular votes than any other candidate, they amounted to less than 40 percent of nation's total, and he had not even appeared on the ballot in some of the southern states. Thus, in the words of this "Declaration," a "sectional party" was able to capture the presidency, which was to its thinking ipso facto illegitimate.

Widespread voter fraud, party dysfunction, and sectional distrust left over from the Civil War nearly turned the election of 1876 into a bloody constitutional crisis. A very close election, President Grant had to send troops to keep the peace in the states undergoing their final vote tabulations, as each side attempted to bribe, forge, and stuff the ballot box to ensure victory. When three southern states sent multiple and conflicting returns, leaving the election inconclusive, an ad hoc bipartisan commission was convened to sort it out. When it narrowly held for Republican Hayes over Democratic Tilden, voting along partisan lines, Democrats refused to accept the decision. The crisis was averted only when Southern Democrats agreed to support Hayes in return for a promise to end Reconstruction. To prevent something like this from happening again, Congress passed the Electoral Count Act of 1887, which established many of the rules by which the electoral count is now certified.

Since then there have been controversial elections but none that threatened to break the dam of legal and constitutional procedure and endanger the civil peace. When charges of voter fraud and other irregularities surfaced in the 1960 election, the issue was dropped once the lawyers concluded that nothing could be proved in time for the December 12 deadline for certification of electors required by the Electoral Count Act of 1887.

There have been two elections (for which there are reliable numbers) in which the Electoral College winner received fewer nationwide popular votes than his opponent. In 1888, when Grover Cleveland lost in this fashion to Benjamin Harrison, the people hardly seemed to notice. Cleveland himself when asked to what he attributed his loss said: "It was mainly because the other party got more votes," meaning, of course, more votes in the Electoral College (Gregg 2008, 118). In the absence of 1824's moribund nomination process and suspicions of corrupt bargaining, 1860's deep sectional resentment and distrust, or 1876's widespread fraud, the people seemed fully willing to accept the legitimacy of the Electoral College even when it produced a president who did not receive a national electoral plurality.

Things were somewhat different 112 years later when the 2000 election made George W. Bush the nation's second nonplurality-winning president. But while Al Gore was not so gracious as Cleveland, and many of his supporters claimed that Bush "stole the election," the brunt of their attack was directed not at the Electoral College itself but at the state of Florida, the U.S. Supreme Court, and the Republican Party. The Electoral College, however, did not escape unscathed, and voices were heard calling for its abolition and replacement by some other form of direct, national plebiscite. People now seemed more likely to doubt the institution's legitimacy and to view it as outdated and undemocratic.

The Election of 2000

In the run-up to the 2000 election, many political prognosticators thought that it was so close that Gore might win the Electoral College but lose the national popular vote. The Gore camp began assembling arguments defending the legitimacy of this unusual scenario, but the end result turned out to be the exact *opposite of what was predicted. The election was closest* in the state of Florida whose 25 electoral votes would decide who would be president. After weeks of postelection litigation and partial recounts, the Supreme Court halted the counting, citing the impossibility of completing a consistent and fair recount in time for the December 12 deadline for certifying electors. When Florida halted the counting Bush led Gore by a mere 537 votes, 0.0009 percent of the votes cast in the state. The final tally in the Electoral College was 271 for Bush and 266 for Gore.

The Debate over Whether to Abolish the Electoral College

The greater tendency at the turn of the millennium to suspect the democratic bona fides of the Electoral College follows upon a century of periodic attempts (some academic, some political) to discredit and abolish it. The basic premise of Electoral College opponents is a simple one. Only the purest reflections of the popular will merit the name "democracy," and that which is democratic is always good. Because the Electoral College does not and was not intended to reflect the raw, unfiltered will of a national majority, it is therefore illegitimate and must be eliminated. Thus, it is sufficiently determinative for the opponent of the Electoral College to say that it "violates the principle of equality, one of the most fundamental tenets of democracy" (Edwards 2005, xvi).

The Electoral College is thought to violate this principle of equality and stands condemned as undemocratic because of the following characteristics: It gives individual votes in smaller states greater proportional weight than those in larger states. By counting states as units, due to the winner-take-all system, it lumps the votes of state minorities in with that of the majority and effectively "disenfranchises" them. It causes the candidates to pay more attention to key "battleground" states and discourages voter turnout in safely "red" or "blue" states. And it allows for the possibility of a winner who has not received the greatest number of the nation's votes.

Skeptics of Electoral College reform tend to doubt that a purist approach to democracy is ever a good thing, much less that it should be taken as the default position. Such thinking misunderstands not only the Constitution's provision for electing the president, they argue. It misunderstands the entire presidential office and most of the rest of the Constitution. Indeed, it is contrary to the very idea of representative and constitutional government. If the Electoral College must be changed on this basis, it is hard to see why the following constitutional arrangements would not also need to be scrapped: the difficult amendment process, equal state representation in the Senate regardless of population, the guarantee of at least one member in the House no matter how small the state, the federal judiciary's virtual life appointments and almost complete insulation from the popular will, and the lengthy terms of senators and presidents.

According to defenders, these complicated constitutional arrangements—of which the Electoral College is only one—are what allow democratic government to rule in a moderate, effective, stable, and just manner over such a large territory with so many diverse interests, ideas, and habits. The role of the Electoral College in this process, they believe, is the combined product of purposeful design and incremental adaptations to the changing political environment. At the high tide of the movement to abolish the Electoral College in the mid-1950s, then senator John F. Kennedy warned that such a move could upset "the whole solar system of power. If it is proposed to change one of the elements of the system, it is necessary to consider the others" (Gregg 2008, 59).

Unconvinced by these objections, critics continue to oppose the Electoral College, arguing that the benefits in legitimacy will outweigh any costs incurred to the structural balance of constitutional power. They point to opinion polls that suggest a consistent majority of the American people agree with them. The general lack of understanding about what the Electoral College is and what it does, however, makes these poll results of questionable significance. Absent some more urgent sense of the institution's failings, it seems unlikely that the high hurdles necessary for a constitutional amendment can be overcome.

For the foreseeable future then, the American people will continue to choose its presidents through the Electoral College system, just as it has done for the past two and a quarter centuries. Foreign observers will continue to be intrigued by this unique institution, and many American citizens as well will continue to be puzzled by its operation. But every four years much of the planet will continue to watch and wait to see how it will channel the will of the American people, as it chooses the next president of the United States.

See also Constitution and Constitutionalism; Democracy; Federalism.

Anthony D. Bartl

Bibliography

Busch, Andrew E. 2008. "The Development and Democratization of the Electoral College." In Gary L. Gregg II, ed. *Securing Democracy: Why We Have and Electoral College.* Wilmington, DE: ISI Books.

Edwards, George C. 2005. *Why the Electoral College Is Bad for America.* New Haven, CT: Yale University Press.

Farrand, Max. ed. 1966. *The Records of the Federal Convention.* 4 vols. New Haven, CT: Yale University Press.

Gregg, Gary L., II, ed. 2008. *Securing Democracy: Why We Have an Electoral College.* Wilmington, DE: ISI Books.

Emergencies. *See Crises, Emergencies, and Politics; Disasters and Politics*

ENDANGERED SPECIES ACT, HABITAT LOSS, AND POLITICS

Passed by the 93rd Congress with strong bipartisan support and signed into law by President Nixon, the Endangered Species Act (ESA) of 1973 protects species at risk for extinction and their habitats. The ESA established a process by which species are listed as "threatened" or "endangered" based on the best available scientific evidence and are protected against threats to their existence. The law defines endangered as "in danger of extinction throughout all or a significant portion of its range." A species is designated as threatened if it is "likely to become an endangered species within the foreseeable future throughout all or a significant portion of its range."

Conflicting values and political fights over the utilization of land, water, old growth forests, and other natural resources have characterized ESA history. As the National Research Council (1995, 17) concluded in its report to Congress, "Many of the conflicts and disagreements about the ESA do not appear to be based on scientific issues. Instead, they appear to result because the act—in the committee's opinion designed as a safety net of last resort—is called into play when other policies and management strategies or their failures, or human activities, in general, have led to the endangerment of species and populations."

At the heart of the conflict are competing valuations of wildlife and the natural environment. Environmentalists see ESA as a critical tool for restoration of ecosystems and preservation of biodiversity. The ESA "gave nature, in all its forms, a right to exist" (Roman 2011, 62); the act conferred on endangered species a claim to habitat and to protection from harm. Opponents, including agribusiness, oil and gas, development and hunting interests, and the wise use and property rights movements, view the law as an affront to economic growth, property rights, and individual liberty. The fight over the ESA also has become a proxy war over government regulation, federalism, and climate change.

History of the ESA

The United States was the first country to enact a national law to protect endangered species with the 1966 Endangered Species Preservation Act, which preceded the ESA. The 1966 endangered species law allowed the use of conservation funds to purchase land to protect endangered species. The new law required the listing of some species, but did not protect these species beyond the boundaries of federal wildlife refuges. The 1969 Endangered Species Conservation Act extended the scope of protections by regulating interstate and foreign commerce in endangered species and instructed the Department of the Interior and the State Department to convene an international conference to address these issues, which resulted in a multilateral treaty, Convention on International Trade in Endangered Species of Wild Fauna and Flora (CITES).

The ESA of 1973 implements the CITES. While CITES lists species solely on the basis of the risks caused by commercial trade, the ESA addresses a broader range of threats to species survival. These threats include destruction and modification of habitat; overharvesting; disease or predation, including invasive species; inadequacy of existing regulatory mechanisms; and other natural and man-made factors. The designation of critical habitat and development of recovery plans are required for listed species. Recovery plans include population goals, timetables, and estimated costs.

The United States Fish and Wildlife Services (FWS), which is located in the Department of the Interior, is responsible for ESA administration primarily for land and freshwater species. The National Marine Fisheries Service (NMFS), which is housed in the Department of Commerce, administers the law for most marine, estuarine, and diadromous species. Currently, 1,524 U.S. species are listed, including 650 animal species and 874 plant species (U.S. Fish and Wildlife Services 2014). Of these species, 77 percent are covered by active recovery plans.

The ESA requires federal agencies consult with the FWS and NMFS to "insure that actions authorized, funded or carried out by such agency is not likely to jeopardize the continued existence" of protected species. The act prohibits the "taking" of these species on federal and nonfederal lands and forbids engaging in commerce in endangered species. Taking is defined as "to harass, harm, pursue, hunt, shoot, wound, kill, trap, capture or collect, or attempt to engage in any such conduct." Courts have interpreted the prohibitions on taking or harming protected species to encompass significant habitat modification, which has expanded the scope of ESA protections. Criminal and civil penalties enforce these prohibitions.

The ESA empowered nongovernmental organizations (NGOs) with provisions requiring public availability of information and allowing citizen petitions and lawsuits. Consideration of species for listing or delisting may be initiated by FWS, NMFS, or citizen petition. Citizen lawsuits also can be used to enforce agency implementation of the act. Both environmental NGOs and NGOs representing economic interests have used these provisions to their advantage.

The ESA takes a precautionary approach. Listings are made on the basis of the best scientific data available, not scientific certainty. In addition, the delisting of a species is subject to judicial review.

Causes of Extinction

Overharvesting was the primary factor in extinctions and species depletions in the 1800s. Increases in population, consumption, and economic growth presented new threats to species in the 1900s, which continue today. Habitat loss, degradation, and fragmentation, which have been driven by development, ranching, agriculture, pollution, and extraction of natural resources, are the primary causes of species extinction and vulnerability. See Table 5. Habitat destruction is responsible for threats to the survival of as many as 85 percent of imperiled species (Wilcove et al. 1998).

Invasive species also are a leading cause of species extinction. An estimated 45 percent of imperiled species are threatened by competition with or predation from the introduction of invasive species (Wilcove et al. 1998). Invasive species also pose a disease threat.

Table 5   Causes of Species Endangerment and Extinction

Habitat loss, fragmentation, and degradation
   Development
   Ranching and livestock overgrazing
   Agriculture
   Mineral, gas, and oil extraction
   Logging
   Pollution
   Disruption of fire ecology
   Roads and infrastructure
   Water development, including reservoirs, dams, aquaculture, and navigational access
   Aquifer and wetlands depletion
Invasive species
Climate change
Disease
Overexploitation, including harvest
Outdoor recreation and tour development, including off-road vehicles
Military activities
Vandalism

Sources: Czech and Krausman (2001) and Wilcove et al. (1998).

Climate change is another major threat to species survival. By some estimates, 15 percent to 37 percent species would be "committed to extinction" by 2050 as a result of climate change (Thomas 2004). While the Intergovernmental Panel on Climate Change (IPCC) declined to project the percentage of species that may face extinction, a recent IPCC report stated, "A large fraction of both terrestrial and freshwater species faces increased extinction risk under projected climate change during and beyond the 21st century, especially as climate change interacts with other stressors, such as habitat modification, over-exploitation, pollution, and invasive species" (Intergovernmental Panel on Climate Change 2014, 15).

Preservation of Species

The ESA employs a species approach to biodiversity. Some scientists have criticized the limits of species-based conservation for preservation of biodiversity and advocated for landscape, community management, or ecosystem approaches as alternatives. The capacity of the ESA to respond to indirect causes of species extinction such as invasive species and climate change also has been questioned. Others maintain that species are the appropriate focus since species regulate the environment, and the loss of diversity negatively affects ecosystem functioning. Despite this disagreement, most concur that the ESA's species prioritization and management approach has been successful.

The ESA has been credited with preventing the extinction of at least 227 species (Scott et al. 2006, 31). Of all ESA-listed species, 98 percent still survive (U.S. Fish and Wildlife Service 2013). Thirty species or distinct population segments of species have been delisted as a result of recovery, including the bald eagle, peregrine falcon, and American alligator (U.S. Fish and Wildlife Services 2014). Dozens of additional species have been reclassified from endangered to threatened. Only 10 species have become extinct after ESA listing.

ESA opponents claim that the low level of species recovery points to the ineffectiveness of the law. However, according to Suckling, Greenwald, and Curry (2013), 90 percent of species in their analysis are recovering at the rate set out in recovery plans.

The ESA embeds values about which species are most deserving of protection. Through much of ESA history vertebrates have enjoyed greater protections. As Roman (2011, 63) describes, the FWS was "slow to stray beyond the big and the beautiful." The 1966 law protected only vertebrate species. In 1969, protections were extended to invertebrates and in 1973 to plants. In the past decade, invertebrates and plants have exceeded vertebrates in listings, although they remain underrepresented relative to the risks they face. The designation of distinct population segments for protection remains available only for vertebrates. Plants on private lands are exempted from take prohibitions. The advantaged status of birds, mammals, and fish derives from more positive social constructions and greater representation by interest groups; in turn, allocation of recovery efforts reflects these values and political power (Czech and Krausman 2001).

ESA listings have not been able to keep pace with threats to species. Ten times more known U.S. species are threatened with extinction than are protected under the ESA (Wilcove and Master 2005). The average length of time to list a species is 11 years (Greenwald, Suckling, and Taylor 2006, 62). At least 42 species have become extinct as they waited for listing determinations. As Scott et al. (2006, 22) observe, "we are not getting ahead of the extinction curve."

Political Evolution of the ESA

As originally enacted, the ESA is prohibitive (Yaffee 1982). It bans federal and private actions that threaten the destruction of species and their habitats. As Chief Justice Burger wrote in the Supreme Court's opinion in *TVA v. Hill* (1973), which granted an injunction against the Telleco Dam because of the threat that the dam posed to the snail darter fish, the "plain intent of Congress in enacting this statute was to halt and reverse the trend toward species extinction, whatever the cost."

Following passage of the ESA and other environmental laws, industry-led opposition emerged. This opposition has particularly manifested in the wise use and property rights movements. Motivated by anti-regulation and anti-federal government views and economic interests, these forces have attempted to shift the debate from species preservation to job loss, individual liberty, and economic costs. They have pursued legal challenges, claiming that ESA violates the takings clause of the Fifth Amendment by not providing compensation for loss of land uses. Although these legal claims largely have been unsuccessful, the framing of ESA as an economic issue has been pervasive.

Over the past 40 years, the battle between environmental and economic interests over ESA has been joined in legislative, administrative, and judicial venues. As a result, a series of legislative and administrative changes have "transform[ed] the prohibitive statute into a more flexible permitting system" (Goble 2006, 23). Congressional amendments in 1978 placed new requirements on listing procedures, including expanded notice and hearings, withdrawal of listings upon which there had been no action after two years, and designation of critical habitat concurrent with listings. Upon taking office, President Reagan suspended issuance of all rules, including ESA listings. By executive order, the Reagan administration in 1981 conditioned listings and other agency rules on economic impact analysis.

In a victory for environmentalists, Congress in 1982 amended the ESA to make scientific evidence the sole basis for listing decisions. While listing determinations are made solely on the basis of biological and ecological criteria, economic impacts are considered in the designation of critical habitat. The 1982 amendments further increased the power of NGOs by setting a deadline by which the FWS and NMFS have to respond to citizen petitions.

At the same time, the 1982 amendments weakened ESA take provisions, permitting increased incidental take of members of protected species and habitat degradation in exchange for habitat conservation plans to protect land elsewhere for species. Additional reforms under Department of the Interior secretary Bruce Babbitt in the Clinton administration allowed the agency to negotiate agreements and issue more incidental take permits to facilitate development on nonfederal land. Some attribute the durability of the ESA to the increased flexibility and incentive-based approach of these reforms. Others maintain that these modifications are counter to the intent of the act.

Congress remains a battleground for ESA. After multiple extensions, the authorization for ESA expired in 1992. Continued legislative efforts to circumscribe ESA authority have prevented consideration of a full reauthorization of the law. ESA requirements remain in force with funds requested and appropriated each year. However, agency requests often fall short of the resources necessary to address the listing backlog and species recovery needs. Moreover, following the election of Republican majorities in the House and Senate in 1994, Congress enacted a moratorium on listings between 1995 and 1996 through the appropriations process.

Since the 1990s, dozens of bills have been introduced to require cost–benefit analysis; eliminate fines and imprisonment for habitat destruction; remove protections, prevent listings, and terminate recovery efforts for certain species; reduce litigation; enact compliance exemptions; and devolve enforcement to states. Removal of federal protection for gray wolves in Idaho and Montana by Congress in 2011 as a result of pressure from livestock and hunting interests marked the first congressionally mandated delisting. Although other measures to weaken the ESA have failed to win congressional approval, the formation of an Endangered Species Act Congressional Working Group (2013), led by ESA opponents, signals an intensified effort for legislative modification.

The Science and Politics of Implementation

Although Congress has set deadlines and specifications for listings, the law leaves ample room for administrative discretion in implementation. Spending priorities, listing delays, classification of species as threatened rather than endangered, delays in critical habitat designation, incidental take permits, and the boundaries of habitat designation are some of the staff-level decisions that shape ESA implementation (Yaffee 1982).

Additional sources of discretion are found in the evaluative criteria used to designate species for protection and evaluate their recovery. Vucetich, Nelson, and Phillips (2006) identify "endangered," "threatened," "recovery," "distinct population segment," "in danger of," "foreseeable future," and "significant proportion of range" as vulnerable to normative judgments.

The placement of ESA opponents in key administrative positions has further limited ESA implementation. During the administration of President George W. Bush, a FWS official was forced to resign in a scandal in which investigators found that she tampered with scientific evidence, improperly removed endangered species and habitats from protections, overrode the recommendations of the agency's biologists, and gave internal agency documents to industry lobbyists.

Reflecting these politics, the listing rates under presidential administrations vary substantially. They range from a high of 65 listings per year under President Clinton to a low of 8 per year under President George W. Bush (U.S. Fish and Wildlife Services 2014).

In the face of agency resistance and resource constraints, environmental NGOs have played an increasingly important role in ESA implementation. Citizen action has been responsible for a significant portion of the species listings, particularly in the past two decades. Of all species listed between 1974 and 2003, 54 percent were listed as a result of citizen petitions and an additional 17 percent after lawsuits (Greenwald, Suckling, and Taylor 2006, 55). Although administrative regulations under the Clinton administration limited the use of citizen petitions, the activities of environmental organizations continue to spur listing consideration and decisions.

In response to citizen petitions, the FWS in 2007 proposed to list the polar bear as threatened because of the risk posed to polar bear habitat by global warming. Only after two lawsuits did the FWS take final action on the petition, listing polar bear as threatened in 2008. The terms under which polar bear was listed highlight ESA challenges in the face of climate change and industry opposition. The polar bear listing rule exempts greenhouse gas emissions from regulation under the

A biologist in Canada prepares a gray wolf for transport to the United States as part of a 1996 initiative to reintroduce gray wolves to Yellowstone National Park. (U.S. Fish & Wildlife Service/Luray Parker)

ESA. The rule also prevents lawsuits claiming incidental take of polar bears as a result of power plants outside of Alaska. Legislation has been introduced to delist the polar bear and to prohibit further consideration of greenhouse gasses in ESA implementation.

In 2011, a federal district court judge approved a historic settlement of 13 consolidated cases requiring the FWS to make decisions on hundreds of species by 2018. In exchange, the Center for Biological Diversity and WildEarth Guardians agreed to not pursue further legal action on behalf of these species. To reduce the influence of NGOs, ESA opponents in Congress have fought unsuccessfully to eliminate administrative and judicial appeal provisions.

Delisting proposals also are a focal point of political fights. Once recovery goals for a species are met, an assessment is conducted to determine if there is present or threatened destruction or curtailment of species habitat or range, if the species is subject to overutilization, if disease or predation poses a risk, if existing regulatory mechanisms outside of ESA provide adequate protection, and if other natural or man-made factors affect continued existence. A species can be delisted if these risks are not present.

NGOs such as the Pacific Legal Foundation and the Mountain States Legal Foundation, which are aligned with the wise use movement, have filed petitions and lawsuits to delist numerous plant and animal species, including the gray wolf, Pacific Northwest orca, and Inyo California Townhee. These legal foundations have represented farm bureaus, cattleman's associations, and hunters among others in these actions.

The definition of recovery on a "significant portion of range" has been at the center of key delisting controversies. Although gray wolves occupy less than 15 percent of their historic range, the FWS in 2013 proposed the delisting of remaining protected gray wolf populations, declaring that recovery had been achieved in the wolves' "current range." Critics assert that recovery should be tied to the restoration of the species in its historic range rather than the range in which it currently exists and that threats to the existence of gray wolves continue. Bruskotter et al. (2014, 2) argue, "The ESA is intended to mitigate reductions

in range, not merely describe them." Bald eagles, for example, were not delisted until they were restored to their historic range pre-colonization.

The Future of ESA

Despite the mobilization of a variety of economic interests that have challenged the law and legislative and administrative changes that have modified its implementation, the ESA remains largely intact and has strong public support. According to recent polls, two-thirds of Americans want to see the ESA strengthened or unaltered (Center for Biological Diversity 2014). Supporters have recommended improvements to reduce administrative discretion and enhance species protections. Environmental advocates and scientists have called for greater designation and protection of critical habitat in recovery plans; clearer standards for the listing, delisting, down-listing, and recovery of species; formal tracking systems to monitor conservation plans and agreements; and removal of economic criteria from consideration in critical habitat designations. The prioritization of funding among recovery plans, improved risk assessment, consideration of ecosystem services in listing decisions, and en mass species listings are additional recommendations. The future of ESA as well as the survival of many at-risk species may depend more on politics than ecological or biological considerations.

See also Climate Change and Politics; Environmental Policy and Politics; Green Movement and Politics; Mining and Politics; National Parks, Wilderness Areas, and Politics; Water Policy and Politics.

Jennifer L. Jackman

Bibliography

Bruskotter, Jeremy, et al. 2013. "Removing Protection for Wolves and the Future of the U.S. Endangered Species Act (1973)." *Conservation Letters* (December 26).

Center for Biological Diversity. 2014. "A Wild Success." February. http://www.biologicaldiversity .org/campaigns/esa_wild_success/pdfs/A_Wild_ Success.pdf. Accessed May 19, 2014.

Czech, Brian, and Paul R. Krausman. 2001. *The Endangered Species Act: History, Conservation Biology, and Public Policy*. Baltimore: Johns Hopkins University Press.

Endangered Species Act Congressional Working Group. 2014. Report, Findings and Recommendations. February 4. http://esaworkinggroup.hastings.house.gov/uploadedfiles/finalreportandrecommendations-113.pdf. Accessed May 19, 2014.

Goble, Dale D. 2006. "Evolution of At-Risk Species Protection." In J. Michael Scott, Dale D. Goble, and Frank W. Davis, eds. *The Endangered Species Act at Thirty: Conserving Biodiversity in Human-Dominated Landscapes, Volume 2*. Washington, DC: Island Press.

Greenwald, D. Noah, Kieran F. Suckling, and Martin Taylor. 2006. "The Listing Record." In Dale D. Goble, J. Michael Scott, and Frank W. Davis, eds. *The Endangered Species Act at Thirty: Renewing the Conservation Promise, Volume 1*. Washington, DC: Island Press.

Intergovernmental Panel on Climate Change Working Group II. 2014. "Climate Change 2014: Impacts, Adaptation, and Vulnerability, Summary for Policy Makers." March 31. http://ipcc-wg2.gov/AR5/. Accessed May 19, 2014.

National Research Council. 1995. *Science and the Endangered Species Act*. Washington, DC: National Academy Press.

Roman, Joe. 2011. *Listed: Dispatches from America's Endangered Species Act*. Cambridge, MA: Harvard University Press.

Scott, J. Michael, et al. 2006. "By the Numbers." In Dale D. Goble, J. Michael Scott, and Frank W. Davis, eds. *The Endangered Species Act at Thirty: Renewing the Conservation Promise, Volume 1*. Washington, DC: Island Press.

Suckling, Kieran, Noah Greenwald, and Tierra Curry. 2013. *On Time, On Target: How the Endangered Species Act Is Saving America's Wildlife*. Washington, DC: Center for Biological Diversity.

Thomas, Chris D., et al. 2004 "Extinction Risk from Climate Change." *Nature* 427: 145–48.

U.S. Fish and Wildlife Services. 2013. Defining Success under the Endangered Species Act. July 12. http://www.fws.gov/endangered/news/episodes/bu-04-2013/coverstory/index.html. Accessed May 19, 2014.

U.S. Fish and Wildlife Services. 2014. "Species Reports." http://ecos.fws.gov/tess_public/. Accessed April 13, 2014.

Vucetich, John A., Michael P. Nelson, and Michael K. Phillips. 2006. "The Normative Dimension and Legal Meaning of Endangered and Recovery in the U.S. Endangered Species Act." *Conservation Biology* 20, no. 5: 1383–90.

Wilcove, David S., et al. 1998. "Quantifying Threats to Imperiled Species in the United States." *BioScience* 48, no. 8: 607–15.

Wilcove, David S., and Lawrence L. Master. 2005. "How Many Endangered Species Are There in the United States?" *Frontiers in Ecology and the Environment* 3, no. 8: 414–20.

Yaffee, Steven Lewis. 1982. *Prohibitive Policy: Implementing the Federal Endangered Species Act*. Cambridge, MA: MIT Press.

ENERGY POLICY AND POLITICS

Abundant and reasonably priced energy is essential to the American and world economies. Yet conflicts over rising energy prices and the environmental impacts of energy use, such as urban air pollution, oil spills, and climate change, have sparked a new interest in energy policy at both the federal and state levels. Whether the issue is dependence on other nations for the oil that we use, how best to encourage production and use of different energy resources in the country (e.g., through use of government regulation, subsidies to particular energy resources, tax credits to consumers, or reliance on the free market), or what to do about climate change, government policy makers increasingly face critical decisions about a subject they rarely confronted previously.

The purpose of this article is to review efforts over the past four decades to develop national energy policies that address such concerns, to explain the rise and fall of energy issues on the national political agenda, and to highlight the continuing need to design and approve a long-term and broadly supported national energy strategy for the nation.

The Energy Crisis of the 1970s and Its Effects

The United States has long struggled with energy resource challenges, particularly how best to meet a growing need for energy to power the economy. Yet for most of the decades prior to the 1970s, concern over energy use and public policy was confined largely to energy producers and agencies of government. The primary concerns during this period focused on prices and competition within each energy sector, particularly coal, oil, and natural gas. This approach served the interests of energy producers by stabilizing markets and ensuring profits while also providing reliable energy supplies at an affordable cost to the American public (Davis 1993; Goodwin 1981; Kraft 2011).

Nuclear power was something of an exception to this pattern because of its connection to national security. Federal policies such as the Atomic Energy Acts of 1946 and 1954 shielded the technology from the marketplace and to some extent from public scrutiny to help ensure rapid growth of its use. The Atomic Energy Commission and its successor agencies, the Nuclear Regulatory Commission and the Department of Energy (DOE), vigorously promoted nuclear power as an important component of the nation's energy mix (Duffy 1997).

These policy-making arrangements began to change after 1973 as the public and a wider range of interests became involved in energy decisions. In October 1973, members of the Organization of Petroleum Exporting Countries (OPEC) initiated an oil embargo in retaliation for the U.S. decision to assist Israel by supplying it with weapons and other war material during the Yom Kippur war. That embargo lasted until March 1974, and it disrupted oil supplies in the United States and substantially raised the price of oil.

The longer-term impact of the 1973 embargo was the political leverage that OPEC acquired by its capacity to set a world price for oil through its members' agreement on production levels. Industrialized nations relied heavily on OPEC for their oil, and oil price increases were a significant factor in high levels of inflation in the 1970s and the economic recession related to it. It would not be too much of an exaggeration to say that inflation and the recession were instrumental in President Jimmy Carter's loss to Ronald Reagan in the 1980 election.

As a consequence of these developments, energy issues rose quickly on the political agenda. Policy makers also began to think about the advantages of an overall national policy on energy use, especially the need to reduce dependency on other nations for U.S. energy resources. Presidents Richard Nixon, Gerald Ford, and Jimmy Carter all called for achieving American energy independence, both for national security and for economic reasons. In 1975, Congress approved the Energy Policy and Conservation Act that created new fuel efficiency requirements, the Corporate Average Fuel Economy (CAFE) standards, for motor vehicles, and also authorized the Strategic Petroleum Reserve to stockpile oil for future emergencies as one way to limit oil price shocks to the American economy.

Carter went further than his predecessors in proposing a National Energy Plan in 1977, and calling upon Congress to enact it as a comprehensive national energy policy that emphasized a strong governmental role rather than continuing a pattern of relying on the private sector. His plan also looked more to energy conservation than to the traditional options of increasing domestic supplies of energy. However, the complex plan, with 113 separate provisions on energy taxes, efficiency standards, utility rate reforms, and spending priorities, drew little support in Congress (especially in the Senate) as energy producers, industry, utilities, consumer groups, labor, and environmentalist all found something in the plan to dislike. Despite his appeals to the American public, where he referred to the plan as the "moral equivalent of war," Carter got only part of what he asked for. Congress approved these policies as the National Energy Act of 1978 (Kash and Rycroft 1984; Kraft 1981). The president was successful in increasing government funding for renewable energy resources, conservation, and efficiency initiatives, and he also established the DOE, which consolidated previously independent agencies into the new cabinet department.

The limited policy actions of the 1970s set the stage for repeated efforts in subsequent decades to formulate

President Jimmy Carter speaks about his energy policy against a backdrop of solar panels at the White House, June 1979. (AP Photo/Harvey Georges)

and approve a diverse array of national energy and climate change policies. Most of these proposals were as controversial as the parallel efforts in the 1970s, and they often bitterly divided the two major parties and the nation itself over the necessity of governmental action and the preferred direction for energy policy. Because they deal with fundamental questions related to economic growth, environmental protection, the role of government, and American lifestyles, these debates are very likely to continue for some time.

In addition to specific energy policies, the nation's use of energy was affected by the environmental protection policies adopted during the 1970s. Energy extraction, transportation, refinement, and use invariably affect environmental quality and public health. For example, coal mining can ravage the land and poison the waters around mines, and burning it to produce electricity is a leading cause of air pollution, water pollution, and climate change. Even cleaner sources

of energy, such as nuclear power, can affect the environment. Nuclear reactors produce highly radioactive waste that must be isolated from the biosphere for thousands of years. As Congress and the states adopted a new generation of environmental policies to deal with these risks, they also constrained the production of energy and raised its costs.

As a result of these new concerns and economic forces, energy issues have risen and fallen on the political agenda since the 1970s, depending on their immediate effects and how much they stir public concern. For example, despite President Carter's innovative actions in the 1970s, President Ronald Reagan and Congress eliminated most of the new funding for renewable energy sources and conservation initiatives while increasing government subsidies for nuclear power. Reagan even removed the solar panels that Carter had installed on the White House to symbolize his administration priorities. Reagan and his

Energy, Values, and Politics

U.S. responses to the energy challenges since the 1970s illustrate that governments may choose *not* to adopt formal policies and thus leave decisions about energy production and use to individuals, corporations, and the marketplace. Such choices allow traditional American values of individual liberty, states' rights, and maintenance of a free market to dominate. In this sense, energy policy is about which set of values wins out.

There are echoes of such value conflict in many presidential election campaigns, including the most recent one, the 2012 contest between President Barack Obama and Governor Mitt Romney, the Republican Party nominee. Romney campaigned against Obama's efforts to invest in renewable energy resources, to impose higher automobile fuel efficiency standards, to hold off on the Keystone XL pipeline for transporting Canadian tar sands oil to the Gulf of Mexico pending further environmental review, and to impose modest restraints on domestic energy production both off-shore and on federal lands.

Decisions *not* to adopt or expand energy policies also are made because policymakers are unconvinced that government involvement is needed or legitimate, the level of controversy over proposals makes agreement impossible, or there is insufficient public demand to take action. Under these conditions, government officials find it easier to do little or nothing rather than face a public and energy industry concerned chiefly with short-term costs. This kind of complacency has been a major feature of U.S. energy policy over the past four decades.

conservative advisors sought instead to limit government involvement in energy issues and to rely instead on the free market. The administration also tried to dismantle the DOE. One journalist described the Reagan policy strategy as "duck, defer, and deliberate" (Hogan 1984). However, declining energy prices at the time provided little incentive for policy makers to take any further action in the 1980s, and once again the public and its leaders lost interest in the subject (Kraft 2011).

Energy Policy for the 20th Century

Despite what many would call the backward steps of the Reagan administration, most presidents and other policy makers have sought to respond to public concern over the rising cost of energy, and especially the price of gasoline, and to some of the more visible environmental impacts of energy use. Their efforts can be seen in reactions to events such as the *Exxon Valdez* tanker accident and oil spill in Alaska in 1989, which led to adoption of the Oil Pollution Act, with new regulations on tanker safety, and the Deep Water

Horizon/BP oil spill in the Gulf of Mexico in 2010. The BP accident led to major changes by President Barack Obama's administration in regulation of off-shore oil drilling and to realignment of what had been a fairly weak regulatory office in the Department of the Interior.

Presidents George H.W. Bush, Bill Clinton, George W. Bush and Obama all addressed energy issues in these ways, but without fundamental changing U.S. energy policy or energy use. Some 85 percent of U.S. energy consumption continues to come from fossil fuels. Until recently, U.S. dependence on imported oil continued to stand above 60 percent, far above the levels that provoked great concern during the 1970s. Dependence on oil imports declined significantly during President Obama's administration to nearly 40 percent by 2012 as U.S. oil production rose dramatically in the wake of higher oil prices that stimulated increased exploration of new oil fields, the economic slowdown of 2008 to 2012 that reduced energy demand, and a new generation of fuel-efficient vehicles reached the market.

The common factor across all of these presidencies in limiting action on a national energy policy has been the persistent low saliency of energy-related issues, including climate change, and often intense opposition by the fossil fuel industry to additional regulation that might increase the costs of energy (Guber and Bosso 2013; Kraft 2011). When prices are low, or least are seen as reasonable, and no immediate crises present themselves, Americans tend to lose interest in the subject, as do policy makers (Feldman 1996). As a result, there has been a lack of political will to approve comprehensive and long-term national energy policies or policies to address climate change. The reluctance continued even as overwhelming scientific consensus emerged on climate change and the serious risks it poses to the environment, public health, and the economy (Selin and VanDeveer 2013). To the extent that the United States responded strongly to energy problems and climate change, it was at the state level, where states such as California took energy conservation and efficiency and climate change far more seriously than did the federal government (Rabe 2010).

A brief recounting of energy policy efforts and achievements since the 1980s underscores these arguments. George H.W. Bush's administration pushed for a National Energy Strategy in 1989, seeking a balance of conservation and production, but including drilling for oil in the Arctic National Wildlife Refuge (ANWR), a nonstarter for environmentalists. After highly contentious debate and lobbying by energy interests and automobile companies (which opposed high fuel efficiency standards), Congress approved the Energy Policy Act of 1992. It was a massive bill that called for greater energy conservation and efficiency in electric appliances, building, lighting, plumbing, industrial motors, and heating and cooling systems, among other measures, in addition to spurring energy production.

The Clinton administration sought to advance energy policy to compensate for deficiencies in the 1992 law. Through executive orders it imposed new energy efficiency and greenhouse gas emissions limitations on federal agencies. The president also proposed increasing energy taxes over a five-year period based on heat output or British thermal units (BTU) to discourage use. The so-called BTU tax was an instant political failure as it was greeted by a tidal wave of opposition on Capitol Hill by industry groups, farmers, energy-producing states, and consumers. In the end, Congress would agree only to a 4.3 cent a gallon increase in the federal gasoline tax, despite the lowest market price for gasoline in a generation and far higher gasoline taxes in most other developed nations.

When Republicans gained control of Congress after the 1994 elections, they went further by blocking the Department of Transportation from reviewing or changing federal fuel economy standards, largely to prevent President Clinton from raising mileage requirements. The administration did initiate a clean car program called the Partnership for a New Generation of Vehicles that established a joint government–automobile industry program to coordinate research on development of a "supercar" that could get 80 miles per gallon with low-pollutant emissions. That effort helped to spur development of hybrid vehicles, the first of which reached the U.S. market in 2000. In 2002, however, the George W. Bush administration ended the program in favor of hydrogen-based or fuel cell-power vehicles that never caught on.

The Bush administration, as widely expected, developed its own national energy plan under the direction of Vice President Dick Cheney. It called for significant increases in use of fossil fuels and nuclear power, easing of environmental regulations that could inhibit energy production, and, once again, drilling for oil in ANWR. After a long and bitter battle in Congress, with Democrats strongly opposed to the Bush plan, Congress approved much of it in 2005 as gasoline and other fuel prices began to climb again. However, the bill included no new fuel efficiency standards for vehicles, nor any efforts to reduce greenhouse gas emissions, nor did it impose any requirements on electric utilities to push them toward use of renewable energy sources, as the states had begun doing. The ANWR provision was deleted as well.

The Energy Policy Act of 2005 provided billions of dollars in federal tax credits and other subsidies to energy producers as an incentive to generate more energy, a provision that one journalist dubbed "spectacular giveaways" to the energy industry (Kraft 2011). It also provided some new, although short-term, tax deductions or credits for consumers who purchased new renewable power systems for their homes, improved home energy efficiency, or bought hybrid vehicles. There were more generous provisions of this kind for commercial buildings, as well as research and development funds intended to increase energy efficiency, diversify energy supplies, and reduce environmental impacts of energy use.

Just a year later, however, President Bush declared in his State of the Union message that the United States remained "addicted to oil, which is often imported from unstable parts of the world." He announced several new energy initiatives, but continued to oppose higher fuel efficiency requirements. Late in 2007 Congress agreed on a modest energy package in the Energy Independence and Security Act of 2007. It set new fuel economy standards of 35 miles per gallon by 2020, the first significant change in the CAFE standards since 1975; this would be replaced within two years by a more ambitious effort in the Obama administration. Congress also sought to increase the supply of alternative fuels by setting a renewable fuel standard requiring production of at least 36 billion gallons of biofuels by 2022. In retrospect, this action is widely view as a flawed decision that converted much of the nation's corn crop to ethanol without any real gains in energy efficiency or reduction in greenhouse gas emissions.

Finally, the Obama administration could claim several significant advances in national energy policy even if it failed to secure congressional approval of a climate change policy in 2010. The House passed a comprehensive climate and energy bill in 2009, but the Senate never took up the measure. Obama's signature achievement was closely tied to the February 2009 economic stimulus measure, the American Recovery and Reinvestment Act. Included in it was a massive and historic energy package of more than $80 billion in spending initiatives, tax incentives, and loan guarantees to promote energy efficiency, renewable energy sources, fuel-efficient vehicles, mass transit, and clean coal. Just as important, the administration brokered an unprecedented agreement with an ailing auto industry to substantially increase fuel efficiency standards, bringing the goals of the 2007 energy legislation to

new vehicles on an accelerated schedule. Following a second round of negotiations, by 2012, the administration finalized new standards that will bring a fleet average of 54.5 miles per gallon for cars and light-duty trucks by 2025. It remains to be seen whether a Republican majority, claiming both houses of Congress beginning January 2015, will go along with these policies or attempt to reverse them.

Conclusions

Despite the lack of sustained concern and political interest in the subject, many energy experts believe that it is imperative for the United States and other nations to develop such energy policies for economic, national security, and environmental reasons. Energy resources are central to economic development and also vital to U.S. security interests, as repeated U.S. intervention in Middle Eastern conflicts suggests. Indeed, in recent years, the Department of Defense, the Central Intelligence Agency, and other intelligence agencies have warned repeatedly that global energy and climate change issues may pose serious national security threats to the nation (Matthew 2013). As the evidence of climate change and other environmental effects of energy use mounts, it is becoming clearer that the United States and the world will need to reduce excessive reliance on fossil fuels.

It is for these reasons that debates over energy policy in recent years have turned on the responsibility of government to expand efforts in energy conservation and efficiency in transportation, building construction, lighting, and urban design; to further develop traditional energy sources (both fossil fuels and nuclear power) to meet the short-term goals of energy independence and low costs; to spur technological innovations that can reduce the environmental impacts of energy use; and to initiate a long-term transition to sustainable energy resources, including wind, solar, geothermal, and biofuels.

See also Air Quality and Politics; Climate Change and Politics; Environmental Policy and Politics; Green Movement and Politics; Nuclear Power and Politics; Oil, Natural Gas, and Politics.

Michael E. Kraft

Bibliography

Davis, David Howard. 1993. *Energy Politics.* 4th ed. New York: St. Martin's Press.

Duffy, Robert J. 1997. *Nuclear Politics in America: A History and Theory of Government Regulation.* Lawrence: University Press of Kansas.

Feldman, David Lewis, ed. 1996. *The Energy Crisis: Unresolved Issues and Enduring Legacies.* Baltimore: Johns Hopkins University Press.

Goodwin, Craufurd D., ed. 1981. *Energy Policy in Perspective: Today's Problems, Yesterday's Solutions.* Washington, DC: Bookings Institution.

Guber, Deborah Lynn, and Christopher J. Bosso. 2013. "'High Hopes and Bitter Disappointment': Public Discourse and the Limits of the Environmental Movement in Climate Change Politics." In Norman J. Vig and Michael E. Kraft, eds. *Environmental Policy.* 8th ed. Washington, DC: CQ Press.

Hogan, William H. 1984. "Energy Policy." In Paul R. Portney, ed. *Natural Resources and the Environment.* Washington, DC: Resources for the Future.

Kash, Don E., and Robert W. Rycroft, eds. 1984. *U.S. Energy Policy: Crisis and Complacency.* Norman: University of Oklahoma Press.

Kraft, Michael E. 1981. "Congress and National Energy Policy: Assessing the Policy Process." In Regina S. Axelrod, ed. *Environment, Energy, Public Policy: Toward a Rational Future.* Lexington, MA: Lexington Books.

Kraft, Michael E. 2011. "Energy and Natural Resource Policies." In Michael E. Kraft, ed. *Environmental Policy and Politics.* 5th ed. New York: Pearson Longman. Chapter 6.

Matthew, Richard A. 2013. "Environmental Security." In Norman J. Vig and Michael E. Kraft, eds. *Environmental Policy.* 8th ed. Washington, DC: CQ Press.

Rabe, Barry G., ed. 2010. *Greenhouse Governance: Addressing Climate Change in America.* Washington, DC: Brookings Institution Press.

Selin, Henrik, and Stacy D. VanDeveer. 2013. "Global Climate Change: Beyond Kyoto." In Norman J. Vig and Michael E. Kraft, eds. *Environmental Policy.* 8th ed. Washington, DC: CQ Press.

U.S. Department of Energy. n.d. www.energy.gov. Accessed May 24, 2014.

ENVIRONMENTAL POLICY AND POLITICS

American environmental policy and politics emerged as a subject of interest largely in the late 1960s and 1970s as the nation began developing the foundation for governmental action on an increasingly important array of emerging environmental and natural resource problems. From air and water pollution to the health risks of toxic chemicals, a remarkable set of public policies was adopted in an uncharacteristically short period of time.

The reasons for these actions can be traced to rising public concern in a society of increasing affluence and education, increased media coverage of the problems, improvements in scientific understanding, and the rise of a broadly supported environmental movement. The last was evident in sharply rising membership in groups such as the Sierra Club, National Audubon Society, the Wilderness Society, and the Natural Resources Defense Council. Taken together, these forces helped to define the problems, set the political agenda, and mobilize the public, thus paving the way for policy makers at both the national and state levels to set in place a new generation of policies. Most of the key policies were approved between 1969 and 1976, an unexpected political and public policy development in light of the normal incremental policy-making process found in the United States (Andrews 2006; Kraft 2011; Vig and Kraft 2013).

The purpose of the present entry is to describe and explain these public policy and political developments and the effects they have had over the past four decades; to identify the concerns that have arisen over the policies, particularly by the business community and political conservatives; and to highlight the remaining challenges in what many experts call the third era of environmental policy, centering on the pursuit of sustainable development both in the United States and globally (Eisner 2007; Fiorino 2006; Mazmanian and Kraft 2009).

Both the economic impacts of the legacy policies of the 1970s and the character of this new generation of environmental problems have prompted an ongoing search for new policy approaches that offer an alternative to the conventional command-and-control or regulatory approach that has dominated environmental protection policy over the last 40 years. These policy ideas, such as greater use of market-based approaches, flexible regulation, information disclosure in environmental health policies (Bennear and Coglianese 2013; Kraft, Stephan, and Abel 2011; Olmstead 2013), and reliance on collaborative decision making in natural resource management (Gerlak, Heikkila, and Lubell 2013), merit serious consideration for their potential, but also careful assessment to determine how effective they have been or are likely to be in the future.

Background

Environmental policy encompasses a wide range of governmental actions that deal with environmental quality or the use of natural resources. It includes the traditional focus on the conservation or efficient use of natural resources such as public lands and waters, wilderness, and wildlife. Federal policies dealing with these issues date back to the 19th century and were further developed and refined in the 20th century. These actions resulted in adoption of the Wilderness Act of 1964, the National Environmental Policy Act of 1969, the Endangered Species Act of 1973, and two central federal lands policies in 1976: the Federal Land Policy and Management Act and the National Forest Management Act (Andrews 2006; Kraft 2011; Vig and Kraft 2013).

Since the 1960s, both in the United States and other developed nations, environmental policy has also been understood to include the environmental protection efforts of government, such as air and water pollution control to protect public health. Key federal policies in this category include the Clean Air Act Amendments of the 1970s, the Clean Water Act of 1972, the Safe Drinking Water Act of 1974, the Resource Conservation and Recovery Act of 1976 (the nation's chief policy on hazardous waste), the Toxics Substances Control Act of 1976, and the Comprehensive Environmental Response, Compensation, and Liability Act of 1980, commonly referred to as the Superfund (which was to facilitate the cleanup of abandoned chemical waste sites).

All of these acts are designed to set and enforce national environmental quality standards that are to protect the public from unreasonable risk from pollution and toxic and hazardous chemicals. Other acts of the same kind deal with controls on the use of pesticides and herbicides, the level of agricultural chemicals allowed in food (the Food Quality Protection Act of 1996), provisions for siting and building national repositories for nuclear waste from commercial nuclear power plants (the Nuclear Waste Policy Act of 1982 and its amendment in 1987), and disclosure to the public of information regarding industrial release of toxic chemicals (the Superfund Amendments and Reauthorization Act of 1986).

As this brief listing of key laws suggests, U.S. environmental policy is not found in any single decision or statute. Rather it is the aggregate of laws, plus the regulations, and court precedents related to them, and it also includes the attitudes and behavior of public officials charged with making, implementing, and enforcing them. A range of political and economic forces have shaped the decisions to adopt and carry out these policies over time, and as a result, the United States now has a disparate and uncoordinated collection of environment-related policies adopted at different times and for different purposes. That is, there is no single environmental policy, but rather a complex array of environmental policies that often conflict with one another, and are not necessarily coordinated with other actions that can affect environmental quality and public health. The way these policies are carried out also varies from one state to another as public values and the political culture of each state affect what policy makers are willing or able to do at any given time (Rabe 2013).

Defined more broadly, environmental policy may include much more than statutes on clean air and water and on toxic chemicals. For example, it might encompass government action at any level, from local to international, that affects energy use, transportation, agriculture and the food supply, the design of cities, human population growth, and the protection of earth's ecological, chemical, and geophysical systems.

The reasons for this policy breadth are easy to understand. The energy sources on which we rely (primarily fossil fuels such as coal, oil, and natural gas) can have significant environmental consequences, including air pollution and climate change. The transportation systems we use, such relying primarily on private vehicles, can have major effects on land use and air pollution as well as on energy consumption. Cities can be designed in a way that encourages efficient use of energy, public transportation, provision of abundant green spaces, and adoption of sustainability goals and plans, or they can be built in a way that leads to the kind of haphazard development and sprawl that one finds in nearly every major city in the nation. The rising human population has major effects on nearly every environmental concern because people require energy, housing, clothing, food, clean water, and many other resources to meet their needs. The point is that, viewed in a comprehensive way, as the concept of sustainability or sustainable development implies, environmental policy encompasses all of these concerns and more (Mazmanian and Kraft 2009; Vig and Kraft 2013).

Whether we choose to define environmental policy narrowly or broadly, these various kinds of government policy actions represent society's collective decision to pursue certain environmental goals or objectives and to use particular tools (e.g., regulation, financial incentives, or information disclosure) to achieve them. As is the case with other public policies, from education to health care, these policy choices inevitably reflect the prevailing public values or political culture, such as the extent to which the public favors governmental intervention in the economy through a regulatory process or how the public and policy makers view the relative importance of environmental protection and economic growth at any given time (Kraft and Furlong 2012).

Public opinion on environmental policy today reflects this competition among values, often yielding a mixed verdict on how much regulation the public desires, particularly during a time of economic hardship, such as the period from 2008 to 2012. Much depends, of course, on how the issues are framed at any given time, that is, on how they are presented to the public and the nature of political debate over the subject (Guber and Bosso 2013). Because of fundamental conflicts over core values, the two major political parties today have strongly divergent views about

Costs and Benefits of Environmental Regulation

One of the more surprising developments over the past four decades is the increasingly partisan nature of environmental policy. Where once the two parties were not that far apart on the issues, today they often disagree strongly on both the goals of public policy and the means to be used. These conflicts reflect the different values held by key constituencies within each of the two parties, and a decided move to the right by the Republican Party, which is evident on a wide range of issues in recent years (Below 2013; Guber and Bosso 2013).

Disagreements over the extent of regulation or the power of the U.S. Environmental Protection Agency (EPA) to act are at the center of these conflicts, for example, over whether and to what extent the agency should regulate mercury and greenhouse gas emissions from coal-fired power plants. Democrats and environmentalists tend to favor strong regulations and defend them as essential to protect public health. They also argue that the health and environmental benefits of regulation greatly exceed the costs that will be imposed on the power plants. In contrast, Republicans and business leaders, particularly executives in the coal industry, tend to criticize such regulations as an unwarranted and costly intrusion into the energy marketplace. These kinds of disputes can be followed in publications such as *The New York Times* and *The Wall Street Journal* or in professional newsweeklies such as *CQ Weekly* or the *National Journal*. The EPA itself (www.epa.gov) is a good source for background information, and the agency reports frequently on economic analyses of the costs and benefits of all of its major regulatory initiatives.

environmental protection policies (Below 2013). In contrast, during the 1970s, the two parties were much closer together on the issues, and the American public strongly supported environmental protection efforts (Daniels et al. 2013).

Moreover, increasingly, environmental policy extends beyond national policies and includes the establishment of major international accords that seek to protect the Earth's ozone layer, limit transboundary movement of toxic chemicals and hazardous wastes, conserve biological diversity, and reduce the risks of global climate change, among other goals (Chasek, Downie, and Brown 2010; O'Neil 2009). Regional environmental accords also are increasingly common, most notably and successfully in the European Union, which generally has adopted tougher requirements than that found in the United States.

Sometimes governments also choose *not* to adopt formal policies and thus implicitly leave many or most decisions about certain environmental and resource problems (e.g., the level of energy use or action on climate change) to individuals, corporations, and the operations of the free market. Such decisions may be made because policy makers are not convinced that government involvement is needed or legitimate, or because the level of controversy over proposals makes agreement impossible. Hence governments find it easier to do nothing in the short term, an outcome that is common in the international arena when nations cannot come to an agreement on what to do in light of their often divergent national interests (Kraft 2011).

The Evolution of Environmental Policy and Politics

As noted at the beginning of this article, the problems that environmental policies are intended to address have changed substantially over time, as have the set of policy approaches and tools that governments have relied upon and the political and institutional context in which policy making and implementation take place. Many students of environmental policy recognize at least three different generations of public policies, and some see this evolution as a fundamental shift from one policy era or epoch to another.

During the 1970s, for example, the problems were defined largely as air and water pollution, and later toxic chemicals and hazardous wastes. The preferred solution in the United States was federally driven regulation of industry through what became known as "command-and-control" policies, in which the federal government and the states set environmental quality standards and enforce them as provided in the laws (Rabe 2013). These kinds of policies, such as the Clean Air Act and Clean Water Act, achieved many of their objectives over time as measured by substantial improvements in air and water quality that have been reported in analyses by the U.S. EPA, other government agencies, and private organizations. For example, urban air quality has improved dramatically from the 1970s to the 2010s, and we continue to see major gains in air quality as vehicle fuel efficiency improves and cities rely more on mass transit.

At the same time, these bedrock policies could not fully deal with existing problems. Costs often were high and noncompliance by industry with policy mandates has not been unusual, leaving the states and the federal government struggling to figure out how to improve compliance without imposing too great a burden on the affected industries and the workers and communities dependent on them. This has been particularly so as the budgets of environmental agencies have remained insufficient to fully implement the range of policies given to them (Vig and Kraft 2013). The prospects of increasing funding for environmental programs seem poor in light of continuing federal and state budgetary constraints and a general public preference for reducing government expenditures to help deal with continuing federal deficits and the national debt.

Moreover, the policies as designed could not handle newer problems such as nonpoint sources of pollution (e.g., runoff from agricultural land and urban surfaces) where regulation was impractical. Indeed, the EPA has reported in recent years that most of the remaining problems of surface water quality in the nation stem from nonpoint sources, not directly from industry as was the case in the 1970s. Thus, many analysts have concluded that the bedrock policies of the 1970s have important weaknesses that must be addressed to deal with contemporary environmental problems (Kraft 2011; Mazmanian and Kraft 2009; Vig and Kraft 2013).

Throughout the 1980s and 1990s, policy scholars and policy makers defined the problems somewhat differently than they had been understood in the 1970s, and they offered a range of ideas for reform both in pollution control and in natural resources policies. They emphasized the promotion of efficiency and effectiveness through regulatory flexibility, greater cooperation between government and industry, and the use of new policy approaches such as market incentives and information disclosure. Especially in the United States, they also tended to favor devolution of policy responsibilities from the federal government to the states and greater collaboration among stakeholders.

Controversy has swirled around many of these proposals from the second generation of environmental policy, in part because environmentalists often saw them as a rolling back of environmental policy goals while representatives from business and some state and local governments argued they did not go far enough to grant them the flexibility they sought to improve environmental performance. Reform of the major statutes from the 1970s also proved difficult because of deep partisan divisions over the issues and a resulting policy gridlock (Eisner 2007; Klyza and Sousa 2008; Vig and Kraft 2013).

By the late 1980s and into the 1990s, a third generation or era in environmental policy began, with strong roots in the concept of sustainability. It didn't replace the first two eras so much as it built upon the foundations that they laid and incorporated new ways of thinking about environmental problems, policy goals, and the best means for achieving them. For example, from this perspective much value is placed on comprehensive and integrated analysis of the way in which human activities affect natural systems and, in turn, how society depends on the healthy functioning of such systems, such as purification of air and water or the stabilization of climate. It is in this period that scholars and policy makers began to see that environmental problems had to be considered in relation to population growth, energy use, land use, transportation patterns, the design of cities, agriculture and water use, and many other practices (Mazmanian and Kraft 2009).

In addition, a global rather than merely local, regional, or national perspective emerged as a key element in this view of environmental policy. Global problems such as loss of biodiversity, population growth, climate change, and growing water scarcity emerged at international meetings from the 1970s to the 2000s and helped to build a new policy agenda for the 21st century. The most visible signpost of the new outlook was the United Nations Conference on Environment and Development, the Earth Summit, held in Rio de Janeiro in 1992, and its legacy is apparent in the approved plan of action, *Agenda 21*. This broad commitment to sustainable development continued at several follow-up meetings, including the World Summit

Secretary of State Colin Powell speaks at the World Summit on Sustainable Development in Johannesburg, South Africa, September 2002. (AP Photo/Pedro Ugarte)

on Sustainable Development, held in Johannesburg, South Africa, in 2002 and the Rio-Plus 20 meeting in Rio de Janeiro in 2012. These meetings drew new attention to the need to improve social and economic conditions in the world's poorest countries while also fostering economic growth and environmental protection, as reflected in the UN Millennium Development Goals. The Kyoto Protocol on climate change, adopted in 1997, and to be replaced by a newly negotiated treaty, is a leading example of these trends in global environmental policy (Brown 2010; O'Neill 2009; Vig and Kraft 2013).

New Directions in Environmental Policy

The implications of this shift to sustainability or sustainable development, and also of international action on global environmental problems, are profound. They range from the redesign of industrial processes to the promotion of sustainable use of natural resources, such as energy. Successful policies are likely to require new kinds of knowledge and new methods of analysis as well as an unprecedented level of cooperation among nations. For the student of environmental policy and politics, there will be much to follow in the coming years.

These developments are a reminder that the study of environmental policy involves more than understanding politics, the processes of policy making, or the institutions of government. It requires knowledge of economics, ethics, environmental science, sociology and American cultural values, public administration, and law, among other fields. The more environmental policy is seen in the larger context of sustainability, the more we need to recognize the importance interdisciplinary analysis of environmental problems and the range of variables that can affect environmental policy adoption, implementation, and impact at all levels of government.

See also Air Quality and Politics; Biotechnology and Politics; Climate Change and Politics; Energy Policy and Politics; Farming, Food, and Politics; Green Movement and Politics; Mining and Politics; Nuclear Power and Politics; Oil, Natural Gas, and Politics.

Michael E. Kraft

Bibliography

Andrews, Richard N. L. 2006. *Managing the Environment, Managing Ourselves: A History of American Environmental Policy*. 2nd ed. New Haven, CT: Yale University Press.

Below, Amy. 2013. "Parties, Campaigns, and Elections." In Sheldon Kamieniecki and Michael E. Kraft, eds. *The Oxford Handbook of U.S. Environmental Policy*. New York: Oxford University Press.

Bennear, Lori S., and Cary Coglianese. 2013. "Flexible Approaches to Environmental Regulation." In Sheldon Kamieniecki and Michael E. Kraft, eds. *The Oxford Handbook of U.S. Environmental Policy*. New York: Oxford University Press.

Brown, Lester R. 2010. *Plan B 4.0: Mobilizing to Save Civilization*. New York: W.W. Norton.

Chasek, Pamela S., David L. Downie, and Janet Welsh Brown. 2010. *Global Environmental Politics*. 5th ed. Boulder, CO: Westview Press.

Daniels, David P., et al. 2013. "Public Opinion on Environmental Policy in the United States." In Sheldon Kamieniecki and Michael E. Kraft, eds. *The Oxford Handbook of U.S. Environmental Policy*. New York: Oxford University Press.

Eisner, Marc Alan. 2007. *Governing the Environment: The Transformation of Environmental Regulation*. Boulder, CO: Lynne Rienner.

Fiorino, Daniel J. 2006. *The New Environmental Regulation*. Cambridge, MA: MIT Press.

Gerlak, Andrea K., Tanya Heikkila, and Mark Lubell. 2013. "The Promise and Performance of Collaborative Governance." In Sheldon Kamieniecki and Michael E. Kraft, eds. *The Oxford Handbook of U.S. Environmental Policy*. New York: Oxford University Press.

Guber, Deborah Lynn, and Christopher J. Bosso. 2013. "Issue Framing, Agenda Setting, and Environmental Discourse." In Sheldon Kamieniecki and Michael E. Kraft, eds. *The Oxford Handbook of U.S. Environmental Policy*. New York: Oxford University Press.

Kamieniecki, Sheldon, and Michael E. Kraft, eds. 2013. *The Oxford Handbook of U.S. Environmental Policy*. New York: Oxford University Press.

Klyza, Christopher McGrory, and David Sousa. 2008. *American Environmental Policy, 1990–2006: Beyond Gridlock*. Cambridge, MA: MIT Press.

Kraft, Michael E. 2011. *Environmental Policy and Politics*. 5th ed. New York: Pearson Longman.

Kraft, Michael E., and Scott R. Furlong. 2012. *Public Policy: Politics, Analysis, and Alternatives*. 4th ed. Washington, DC: CQ Press.

Kraft, Michael E., Mark Stephan, and Troy D. Abel. 2011. *Coming Clean: Information Disclosure and Environmental Performance*. Cambridge, MA: MIT Press.

Layzer, Judith A. 2011. *The Environmental Case: Translating Values into Policy*. 3rd ed. Washington, DC: CQ Press.

Mazmanian, Daniel A., and Michael E. Kraft, eds. 2009. *Toward Sustainable Communities: Transition and Transformations in Environmental Policy*. 2nd ed. Cambridge, MA: MIT Press.

Olmstead, Sheila M. 2013. "Applying Market Principles to *Environmental Policy*." In Norman J. Vig and Michael E. Kraft, eds. *Environmental Policy*. 8th ed. Washington, DC: CQ Press.

O'Neill, Kate. 2009. *The Environment and International Relations*. New York: Cambridge University Press.

Rabe, Barry G. 2013. "Racing to the Top, the Bottom, or the Middle of the Pack?" In Norman J. Vig and Michael E. Kraft, eds. *Environmental Policy*. 8th ed. Washington, DC: CQ Press.

Rosenbaum, Walter A. 2011. *Environmental Politics and Policy*. 8th ed. Washington, DC: CQ Press.

U.S. Department of Energy. n.d. www.energy.gov. Accessed May 24, 2014.

U.S. Environmental Policy Administration. n.d. www.epa.gov. Accessed May 24, 2014.

Vig, Norman J., and Michael E. Kraft, eds. 2013. *Environmental Policy: New Directions for the Twenty-First Century*. 8th ed. Washington, DC: CQ Press.

ETHICS IN GOVERNMENT

On August 9, 1974, President Richard M. Nixon, "marred by dust, and sweat, and blood," became the first president of the United States of America to resign from office. Flashing that infamous double peace sign, Nixon loaded onto Army One, taking with him what remained of American trust in the integrity of government (Nixon 1974). Our obsession with public ethics and corruption was born in the moment the 37th president was forced to walk away in the midst of an ethical and legal scandal. Or so the story goes; the truth is markedly more complex. American perceptions of what constitutes ethical behavior in the public sector and how firmly public integrity ought to be safeguarded have changed dramatically over time. To understand the contemporary American approach to public ethics, it is critical to understand our country's roots.

Ethics in the Design

The contemporary American preoccupation with enforcement of public ethics would seem peculiar to the early Americans. In both colonial America and the early Republic, controls against corruption were seen as fundamentally built into government. Ethics was considered fundamental to government in Colonial America and often enforced by means of a religious test. Public confessions of faith were treated as prerequisites to the voting franchise within the church and the colony (Locke 1995, 15–16). The underlying assumption was that good standing within the faith ensured moral character. It was commonly held that ethical behavior among public officials could not be enforced from without, but must come from within. As William Penn, founder of Pennsylvania, put it, "Governments, like clocks, go from the motion men give them, and as governments are made and moved by men, so by them they are ruined too. Wherefore governments rather depend upon men than men upon governments" (Penn 2006, 257).

While much of their approach to political life was drawn from the contemporary thought of the Enlightenment, early Americans also drew heavily from classical political thought. The central pursuit of life for the great minds of the ancient world was *arete*. Arete captures notions of both excellence and virtue, and the realization of individual potential (Sandoz 2001, 99).

A fine example of *arete* in action comes from Plato's *Crito*. In this powerful dialogue, Socrates has been sentenced to death for the crimes of corrupting the minds of the youth of Athens and preaching false doctrines about the Gods. Socrates at age 70 is awaiting his execution in an Athenian jail. His friend Crito comes to him and tells him he can bribe the right individuals and help Socrates escape to safety. Both know of Socrates's innocence, yet Socrates insists he has a moral duty to the City State of Athens to remain in jail and accept his conviction and sentence. He is willing to sacrifice his life to uphold his duty to obey the laws of Athens (Plato 1937, 434–35).

Here we see the duty, obligation, and the pursuit of one's potential bound up with the state. Drawing on both classical thought and exemplars, and their own protestant ethic, early Americans viewed the greatest check against corruption to be the selection of men who, like Socrates, embodied deep virtue (Locke 1995, 16).

With the First Amendment to the Constitution, the use of religious tests for public office was officially banned, though the other ingredients to the righteousness recipe remained intact. This young country needed a stronger focus on the rights of speech including the right to vote. One noted dissenter on the limited voting franchise was James Sullivan. A Massachusetts jurist and politician, Sullivan argued forcefully that all those who were governed ought to have some mechanism by which to consent to the laws by which they were governed.

In 1776, John Adams responded to Sullivan's assertions by pointing out that not all voices may be represented at once, that the majority of necessity must be allowed to speak for the whole even if the minority disagrees on a public matter. Adams (who became the second president of the United States in 1797) argued in favor of excluding other voices. Excluding women, for example, he justified on the basis that their, "Delicacy renders them unfit for . . . the hardy Enterprizes of War, as well as the arduous cares of State." Likewise, he argued, those men who are "wholly destitute of Property, are also too little acquainted with public Affairs to form a Right Judgment, and too dependent upon other Men to have a Will of their own" (Adams 1996, 82).

Adams's argument highlights a central concern of the Founding Fathers—the notion of dependency. Dependency, too, is drawn from classical political thought, in which liberty is defined as absence of dependence upon the will of another. Dependence on another was anathema to the political ideals of the early Republic. Moreover, creating the conditions that promote dependence (e.g., extending the vote to landless men), would make "a fine encouraging Provision for Corruption" (Adams 1996).

Racing to Stay Behind

During the first two decades of its history, the nation followed the blueprint set forth by its founders. It was a nation led by landed gentry, a natural aristocracy. These leaders freely engaged in a variety of activities, the ethics of which were little questioned.

Alexander Hamilton, for example, not only enabled the nascent country to refinance its debts through the creation of a national bank but also used his positional authority to help business associates persuade private banks to finance trade associations and generally engaged in a highly convoluted dance that recognized few barriers between the public and private sectors (Roberts and Doss 1997, 6). While some contemporaries (e.g., Thomas Jefferson) questioned the virtue of Hamilton's approach, they were few in number.

By the 1820s, however, Americans were beginning their first redefinition of public ethics. In the aftermath of the Napoleonic Wars, America experienced a serious economic crash which produced an enduring depression, and widespread foreclosures, bankruptcies, and unemployment throughout the 1820s. Much of the blame for the events was placed squarely on the banks and banking industry and all things associated therewith—especially the ruling political aristocracy (Locke 1995, 19–20).

By the 1820s, most states had broadened the franchise, extending the right to vote to those without property or financial means. The combination was a perfect storm that swept Andrew Jackson into the presidency in 1828. Jackson effectively turned public sector ethics on its head, not by defining what was ethical but by defining what was corrupt. In words that seem clearly aimed at the founding aristocracy, Jackson argued:

It is to be regretted that the rich and powerful too often bend the acts of government to their selfish purposes. "Distinctions in society will always exist under every just government . . . but when the laws undertake to add to these natural and just advantages artificial distinctions, to grant titles, gratuities, and exclusive privileges, to make the rich richer and the potent more powerful, the humble members of society—the farmers, mechanics, and laborers—who have neither the time nor the means of securing like favors to themselves, have a right to complain of the injustice of their Government" (Jackson 1909, 590).

This may be the beginnings of the modern American definition of political corruption. Jackson's words are a direct assault on the Hamiltonian view that commerce, and the sustaining thereof by government, is inherently virtuous (Chan 2006, 215–16).

Corruption, according to Jackson, is the abusive use of the public infrastructure of the state to enlarge the prosperity of the already prosperous. What is most striking, however, is Jackson's solution. Jackson did not, as a modern reader might expect, require public officials to disclose conflicts of interest. Instead, Jackson argued forcefully in his First Annual Message in 1829 for the regular rotation of public officials to ensure that an entrenched class did not develop. In remarks that seem to serve as a direct counterpoint to John Adams, Jackson wrote:

> There are, perhaps, few men who can for any great length of time enjoy office and power without being more or less under the influence of feelings unfavorable to the faithful discharge of their public duties. Their integrity may be proof against improper considerations immediately addressed to themselves, but they are apt to acquire a habit of looking with indifference upon the public interests and of tolerating conduct from which an unpracticed man would revolt. (Jackson 1909, 448)

Jackson challenged the ethics of virtue as a protection against corruption, at least over time. It may be said that the system created by Jackson had its roots in classical thought as well. *Victori Spolia*, "to the victor go the spoils," was a notion as inherent to classical Rome as anything Cato offered. Jackson did not invent the spoils system (which awards political supporters with government jobs and appointments upon

the election of their candidate to office), but he did enshrine it as a key feature of 19th-century American politics (Roberts and Doss 1997, 10). Today, the spoils system is held up as the essence of government corruption, and in 1832, it was viewed as desperately needing reform.

The Spoils and the Spoiled

An overlooked outcome of the Civil War was the relative expansion of the power of the national government. As President Lincoln reached for new power and authority, and uncoupled old limitations to meet the challenge of preserving the Union during the course of the Civil War, he also created opportunities for fraud. Immediately after the Civil War, there is significant evidence to validate this ancient maxim. The maxim warns that the larger the state, and the more its powers and statutes, the greater the potential for graft, and thus the more likely openings for opportunistic individuals seeking personal benefits from the public coffers. Likewise, when grafters hold the keys of government, they are likely to find new and exciting ways to drag money from the public (Goel and Nelson 1998, 117).

It is estimated that of the approximately $50,000,000 worth of government contracts executed during the Civil War, some $17,000,000 were lost to fraud and graft. The urgencies of war made rampant fraud possible, but that does not mean that all public contractors were complicit in the fraud (Franklin 2013, 8). Indeed, it coincides with ancient Roman senator Tacitus's views that the greater the quantity of fraud and corruption, the greater the preponderance of laws designed to address fraud and corruption (Hunter 1980, 47).

In 1863, Congress passed the False Claims Act (FCA), which imposed harsh fines on anyone found guilty of intentionally defrauding the military. Moreover, the law, created in a time before the creation of the Department of Justice, offered citizen-whistleblowers a bounty equal to half the amount recovered from the fraudulent contractor. While the approach of the FCA has deep historical roots that predate the Civil War by centuries, this particular legislation carried greater heft and urgency than any previous enforcement mechanism of its kind. In many respects, the FCA marks the beginning of modern American public ethics regulation. In fact, the FCA remains in effect and has become a powerful mechanism for deterring defense contract fraud (Meador and Warren 1998, 462).

Despite reforms such as FCA, the postwar period was marked by rampant profiteering and corruption. Over the next several decades, demand for reform intensified as the spoils system became an ever more glaring example of the excesses and corruption of the Gilded Age. As is often the case, no traction was made until tragedy struck. On July 2, 1881, President James Garfield was shot by Charles J. Guiteau, a disgruntled office seeker who felt he was owed a position for his support of the Garfield campaign (Thierault 2003, 60).

With the public and lawmakers now able to make a direct tie between the spoils system and the death of a president, calls for reform reached critical mass. In 1883, Congress passed the Pendleton Act, which served as the first major civil service reform. The Pendleton Act shifted acquisition of government jobs away from the spoils or patronage system and toward merit-based appointment (Thierault 2003, 50–68). Similar reforms were adopted by the states, though reforms were slow to come to major cities where political "bosses" still controlled public offices and government jobs (Menes 1996, 64–66).

Progressive Reform and the Modern Era

From 1881 on, demands for public sector reform only intensified. Among the hard-won victories of the Progressive Era (approximately 1890–1820) were the following:

- *The Seventeenth Amendment.* Prior to 1913 U.S. senators were elected by members of their respective state legislatures. Many substantiated cases of U.S. senators acquiring votes in exchange for money or favors led to the Seventeenth Amendment, which provides for the direct election of U.S. senators.
- *Municipal Civil Service Reform.* In 1914, the International City Managers Association was formed to serve as a credentialing body for professional city managers. City managers were seen as a solution to the problem of corruption at the local government level.
- *Campaign Finance Reform.* One of the unintended consequences of the Pendleton Act was that candidates and political parties had to turn increasingly to businesses, trade associations, and labor unions for campaign donations to replace the financial support previously received from aspiring government appointees. The Tillman Act of 1907 and the Federal Corrupt Practices Act of 1925 laid the groundwork for limiting direct campaign contributions from private companies, and other interests.

These and many other reforms changed the tenor and definition of public ethics. Ethics were increasingly enforced through law and policy, punishments, and fines. However, many holes were left, and many laws poorly enforced. It would take slow progress, followed by a serious scandal decades later, for teeth to be added to these regulations.

Watergate

On its surface, the Committee for the Re-election of the President (CRP) was little more than a fundraising and support organization to President Nixon's 1972 reelection campaign. In reality, it was a fully operational political skunkworks, designed to win the election at any cost. The committee's activities were wide ranging, but included money laundering, wiretapping, sabotage, forgery, leaking false information, theft, and burglary (Bernstein and Woodward 1972, 1). It was the last of these activities that eventually exposed the inner workings of the committee and launched the greatest political scandal in American history. In breaking into headquarters of the Democratic National Committee located at the Watergate Hotel on June 17, 1972, the CRP made the fatal mistake of getting caught. Over the next two years, the sordid details of their activities slowly came to light.

The consequences of the Watergate scandal, including the attempts of the White House to cover up the president's involvement therein, cannot be overstated. In May 1972, in response to the Gallup Poll question, "Let me ask you how much trust and confidence you have at this time in the executive branch headed by the president," 73 percent of respondents replied a "Great Deal" or "Fair Amount" (Gallup 2013). By April 1974 that figure had dropped to 40 percent. In fact, the most enduring combined legacy of Watergate and the Vietnam War may be the deep, corrosive distrust of government those events bred in the American consciousness.

This persistent distrust has been the primary shaping factor in public ethics reform since Watergate. In 1971, Congress passed the Federal Election Campaign Act (FECA), which set more stringent disclosure requirements for federal campaign contributions. However, it did not create a dedicated enforcement body to ensure compliance. The fact that the Watergate break-in was financed by illegal campaign contributions made vivid the need for an enforcement entity (Wertheimer 1986, 87–88).

In the wake of the Watergate scandal, Congress amended FECA in 1974, creating the Federal Elections Commission to regulate campaign finance and election laws. It also set limits on campaign contributions, limits on candidate spending, and strengthened provisions that allowed for public financing of presidential election campaigns. This last provision was seen as a way of leveling the playing field and of granting presidential candidate a measure of independence from donors (Wertheimer 1986, 87–88).

In 1976, under *Buckley v. Valeo*, the Supreme Court struck down FECA's provisions limiting candidate spending, stating that spending was a form of political free speech, and therefore protected by the First Amendment. However, the Court also upheld large portions of the legislation, arguing that Congress had legitimate authority to regulate contributions, and require disclosure of donations to prevent corruption or even the appearance of corruption (*Buckley v. Valeo*, 1976).

Valeo is perhaps most notable for this admission, that even the appearance of corruption can erode public trust and undermine the legitimacy of representative government. This same concern has shaped much of public ethics regulation since Watergate, but it is also an extension of the definition of ethics and corruption that materialized during the Progressive Era.

It is only in recent years that this view has come to be challenged.

Corruption Control versus Effectiveness

Another legacy of Watergate was the enactment of the Ethics in Government Act of 1978, which eventually centered on a new entity, the Office of Government Ethics. From the cascading influence of this act, it appears to focus on the mechanics of ethics in our governmental processes. Some of the ethical mechanics began in 1993 when the Clinton-Gore administration formed the National Performance Review (NPR) to streamline the federal government, making it more efficient, nimble, and responsive to the public. The NPR, which was led by Vice President Gore, identified numerous inefficiencies, many of which could only be described as absurd. One such example highlighted by Gore was the General Services Administration's nine-page specification on the requirements for a government ashtray, which among many other stipulations stated, "It must be square or round and made of clear glass. If square, it must have a minimum of four cigarette rests, spaced equidistant around the periphery and aimed at the center of the ash receiver, molded into the top" (Stone 2003, 82).

The effort to reinvent government ethics under Clinton-Gore was not without controversy. Critics viewed their efforts as the hollowing out of government. After all, rules such as the detailed specifications for ashtrays were a product of the public demand to eliminate fraud and profiteering (Watkins and Arrington 2007, 42). The NPR report illuminates one of the fundamental paradoxes of American political culture.

Basically, the broad mission of the U.S. Office of Government Ethics (OGE) is to foster high ethical standards for executive branch employees and strengthen the public's confidence that the government's business with taxpayer dollars is conducted with impartiality and integrity. The OGE is designed to prevent and resolve conflicts of interest and to promote high ethical standards for executive branch employees. Specifically, the office is responsible for over 4 million civilian employees and uniformed service members in over 130 executive branch agencies. The office is also over a financial disclosure and compliance system. Education and training of more than 5,700 ethics officials and other executive branch employees is also a duty of the office. Specifically, there are approximately 5,700 ethics officials working across 133 agencies. The OGE does not establish the ethics program for each of the 133 agencies. Rather, the head of each governmental agency has responsibility for that agency's ethics program. In addition to a new employment sector in ethics, the act created mandatory, public disclosure of financial and employment history of public officials and their immediate family. It mandated restrictions on lobbying efforts by public officials for a set period after leaving public office. It also requires that an Ethics Pledge be signed by every government appointee (United States Office of Government Ethics 2014). The Office of Government Ethics has no oversight or role in the legislative or judicial branches of the federal government. It also has no role in state or local government ethics programs. Legislative and judicial ethics are enforced on both a national and state basis through a variety of programs (National Conference of State Legislatures 2014).

The third branch of government, the judiciary, has looked to ethics commissions and state codes for many years. The American Judicature Society was founded in 1913 to protect the ethics and integrity of the American justice system. The primary work of the society focuses on judicial ethics. Most states have a volunteer board known as the Judicial Conduct Commission. Members of this commission are responsible for reviewing complaints of unethical behavior by judges and recommending sanctions or even disbarment if the complaints are proven. Members of these commissions are generally selected by all three branches of government: the governor, the legislature—both the house and the Senate, and the judiciary (American Judicature Society 2013).

Both Hamilton and Jackson

Over time, we have become both Hamilton and Jackson, both robber baron and progressive reformer. Americans demand that government operate like, and support the expansion of, business. At the same time

Americans demand that graft and corruption be rooted out at all costs. As many scholars have pointed out, these two goals are often diametrically opposed.

In seeking to assure that not a single dime or dollar of taxpayer money is misused, we build regulatory structures, paperwork, red tape, enforcement agencies, policies, and procedures that make government inefficient. Likewise, when we seek to make government more nimble and innovative, we open greater opportunities for fraud and theft (Anechiarico and Jacobs 1996, 193–94).

In 2010, the Supreme Court in *Citizens United v. FEC* rolled campaign finance reform back nearly a century, by permitting corporations to directly spend money for purposes of political advocacy (though it did not allow for corporate donations directly to campaigns). In a short decision, the Court stated, "We now conclude that independent expenditures, including those made by corporations, do not give rise to corruption or the appearance of corruption" (*Citizens United v. Federal Election Commission*, 2010).

Citizens United and the more recent *McCutcheon v. FEC* have cleared the way for a more Hamiltonian view of public ethics to achieve dominance. This leaves us with the question, what approach to public ethics should we embrace?

Tensions will always exist among public values. Efficiency and integrity are no exception. In the past century, and particularly in the past 40 years, America has turned increasingly toward compliance-based programs backed by fines and penalties. Americans may now be entering a period where, to realize all our public aspirations, we must reinvent public ethics once again (Graaf and van der Wal 2010, 625).

Integrity-based ethics systems used by some countries and organizations "focus on what is achieved, rather than policing and punishing errors or bad behavior" (Graaf and van der Wal 2010, 625). Incentive programs like the whistleblower bounty provided under the FCA can empower citizens to enforce compliance, rather than enforce compliance through heavy-handed regulations and red tape. Alternatively, we may look to other models, such as the governance model of long-lived Benedictine monasteries, which focus on the inward, intrinsic motivations of monks to assure performance while upholding ethical behavior (Inauen 2010, 641).

As this entry has shown, Americans are amazingly adept at reinvention. America has changed its definition and its approach to ensuring public integrity numerous times, and many tools lay open either underutilized or yet unused.

See also Bureaucracy and American Political Culture; Campaign Finance; Corporate Behavior and Politics; Corruption in Politics; Public Opinion; Scandals in Politics.

Elaine E. Englehardt and Luke Peterson

Bibliography

Adams, J. 1996 (1776). "Letter to James Sullivan." In John J. Patrick, ed. *Founding the Republic: A Documentary History*. Westport, CT: Greenwood.

American Judicature Society. 2013. Center for Judicial Ethics. www.ajs.org/judicial-ethics/. Accessed April 30, 2014.

Anechiarico, F., and J. B. Jacobs. 1996. *The Pursuit of Absolute Integrity: How Corruption Control Makes Government Ineffective*. Chicago: University of Chicago Press.

Bernstein, C., and B. Woodward. 1972. "FBI Finds Nixon Aides Sabotaged Democrats." *Washington Post* (October 10).

Buckley v. Valeo, 424 U.S. 1 (1976).

Chan, M. D. 2006. *Aristotle and Hamilton: On Commerce and Statesmanship*. Columbia: University of Missouri.

Citizens United v. Federal Election Commission, 558 U.S. (2010).

Franklin, John Hope. 2013. *Reconstruction after the Civil War*. 3rd ed. Chicago: University of Chicago Press.

Gallup. 2013. "Trust in Government." www.gallup.com/poll/5392/trust-government.aspx. Accessed April 29, 2014.

Goel, R. J., and M. A. Nelson. 1998. "Corruption and Government Size: A Disaggregated Analysis." *Public Choice* 97, nos. 1–2 (October).

Graaf, G. de, and Z. van der Wal. 2010. "Managing Conflicting Public Values: Governing with Integrity and Effectiveness." *The American Review of Public Administration* 40, no. 6 (August).

Hunter, W. B. 1980. *A Milton Encyclopedia*. Vol. 8. Lewisberg, PA: Bucknell University Press.

Inauen, E., et al. 2010. "Monastic Governance: Forgotten Prospects for Public Institutions." *The American Review of Public Administration* 40, no. 6 (May).

Jackson, A. 1909 (1832). "Veto Message." In J. D. Richardson, ed. *A Compilation of the Messages and Papers of the Presidents, 1789–1908: 1841–1849*. Vol. 2. Washington, DC: Bureau of National Literature and Art.

Locke, H. G. 1995. "Ethics in American Government: A Look Backward." *The ANNALS of the American Academy of Political and Social Science*.

Meador, P., and E. Warren. 1998. "The False Claims Act: A Civil War Relic Evolves into a Modern Weapon." *Tennessee Law Review* 65, no. 2 (Winter).

Menes, R. 1996. "Limiting the Reach of the Grabbing Hand. Graft and Growth in American Cities, 1880 to 1930." In E. L. Glaeser and C. Goldin. *Corruption and Reform: Lessons from America's Economic History*. Chicago: University of Chicago Press.

National Conference of State Legislatures. 2014. Separation of Powers—Legislative Oversight. www.ncsl.org/research/about-state-legislatures/separation-of-powers-legislative-oversight.aspx. Accessed April 30, 2014.

Nixon, R. 1974. "Address to the Nation Announcing Decision to Resign the Office of President of the United States." August 8, 1974. http://www.pbs.org/newshour/spc/character/links/nixon_speech.html. Accessed April 30, 2014.

Penn, W. 2006 (1682). "Frame of Government with Laws Agreed Upon in England." In Jon L. Wakelyn, ed. *America's Founding Charters: Primary Documents of Colonial and Revolutionary Era Governance*. Westport, CT: Greenwood Press.

Plato. 1937. "Crito." In *The Dialogues of Plato*. Vol. 1. Translated by B. Jowett, B. New York: Random House.

Roberts, R. N., and M. T. Doss. 1997. *From Watergate to Whitewater: The Public Integrity War*. Westport, CT: Praeger.

Sandoz, Ellis. 2001. *A Government of Laws: Political Theory, Religion, and the American Founding.* Columbia: University of Missouri Press.

Stone, B. 2003. *Confessions of a Civil Servant.* Oxford: Rowman & Littlefield.

Thierault, S. M. 2003. "Patronage, the Pendleton Act, and the Power of the People." *Journal of Politics* 65, no. 1 (February).

United States Office of Government Ethics. www.oge.gov. Accessed April 30, 2014.

Watkins, A. L., and C. E. Arrington. 2007. "Accounting, New Public Management and American Politics: Theoretical Insights into the National Performance Review." *Critical Perspectives on Accounting* 18, no. 1 (January): 33–58.

Wertheimer, F. 1986. "Campaign Finance Reform: The Unfinished Agenda." *Annals of the American Academy of Political and Social Science* 486 (July).

Ethnicity. *See Race, Ethnicity, and Politics*

Evangelicals. *See Protestants, Evangelicals, and Politics*

EVOLUTION, CREATIONISM, AND POLITICS

Creation stories explain not only the origin of the world but also how people ought to live and worship. One creation story, common in various ways to the Jewish, Christian, and Islamic traditions, is of a divinity with absolute transcendence on whom humans and the world are wholly dependent. Thus, when science, within the ambit of the Christian tradition, became committed to a theory of the world's formation by means of evolutionary change, there arose a major confrontation between science and religion, particularly in the United States, that has yet to be fully resolved. Attempts at resolution have taken at least three forms: fundamentalist affirmation of creationism, a religion-rejecting affirmation of evolution, and efforts to adjudicate some intermediate position.

Roots of the Debate

"How did the world come to be?" is a very old question. Aristotle (384–322 BCE) thought of everything in the world as having an end goal or purpose—for example, trees grow leaves to capture sunlight, sharks have fins to swim, and so on—and that there must be some first cause that produces this effect. For Aristotle this cause or "unmoved mover" was conceived as part of the cosmos. By contrast, the Judeo-Christian-Islamic creation story tells of a wholly transcendent God who gave intelligence to the world but is beyond complete human comprehension. The medieval Christian theologian Thomas Aquinas (1224–1274), for instance, used Aristotelian-like arguments to demonstrate the existence of a first mover God who functions throughout time to make the world as it is, but he did not think reason alone could prove God created the world at some point in the past. Divine revelation, as found in the Bible, was the basis for such a belief. At the same time, following a tradition of interpretation that goes back to the use of metaphors in the Bible, especially as developed by biblical commentators such as Philo Judaeus of Alexandria (20 BCE–50 CE) and Augustine of Hippo (354–430), Aquinas adopted a nonliteral interpretation of the creation story. Six days need not have been six 24-hour periods, nor need there have been two individuals named Adam (which in Hebrew simply means "man") and Eve.

In the wake of the work of natural philosophers such as Nicolaus Copernicus (1473–1543) and Isaac Newton (1642–1727), new theories about the cosmos began to explain physical phenomena in ways that did not require a Prime Mover, divine or otherwise. Although some later interpreters of the punishment by the Roman Catholic Church of Galileo Galilei (1564–1642) made it into a conflict between religion and science (and there is evidence to the contrary), over the next 200 years God was out of favor in European intellectual circles as an explanation for terrestrial events. As part of the Enlightenment promotion of science, philosophers defended the possibility of explaining *all phenomena* in natural scientific terms. Theorists such as Pierre Laplace (1749–1827) sought to understand the world through physical causes alone. When Napoleon asked about his work, noting how he never once mentioned God, Laplace reportedly replied that he had "no need of that hypothesis." This approach became known as naturalism. Half a century later, Charles Darwin (1809–1882) and the theory of evolution extended naturalistic explanation from the physical to the biological realm.

It was Darwinian evolution, much more than Galilean astronomy or Laplacian physics, that some 19th- and early 20th-century American thinkers felt presented a deep challenge to Christian beliefs. If human beings are at most indirect creations of a God who sets in motion evolutionary processes, it becomes increasingly difficult to give much meaning to the idea of humans as created "in the image" of God (Genesis 1:27), and God himself becomes an increasingly remote or abstract reality.

Darwin's theory, which proposes that humans as well as all other species evolved over millions of years from simpler life forms, created a challenge for some Christians, who were already heatedly engaged in debates over the literal interpretations of the Bible and the separation of church and state. In 1860, after publication of Darwin's *Origin*, a famous debate on evolution took place in London between Bishop Samuel Wilberforce (opposing) and Thomas H. Huxley (supporting). The effect was to draw a line between Christian belief and scientific theory. In England and Europe this opposition became less and less severe as liberal Christian theologians worked to reconcile the two views, often simply by saying that God could use evolution or any way he chose as a means of creation. In the United States, however, political differences compounded arguments over the separation of church and state and the literal interpretation of the Bible and led to a much more heated and extended debate, with "creation" and "evolution" represented as the key protagonists.

Emerging Social and Political Realities

These North American difficulties can be traced back to what is called the fundamentalist movement to reaffirm the literal truth of the Bible. This movement, with which 45 percent of North Americans identified in 1991 (and more than one-third continue to do today), has given rise to three major creationist oppositions

to biological evolution: Scopes trial–era creationism, creation science, and intelligent design (ID). The emergence of this movement and its different viewpoints provide the basic framework within which the creationism versus evolution debate has developed.

Within a few decades after publication of *On the Origin of Species* (1859), Darwin's ideas were becoming widely accepted in both the scientific and the public arenas. Among the greatest official opposition to evolution was the fundamentalist movement in early 20th-century America. This movement was in part a reaction to the German theological movement toward a cultural, historical, and literary interpretation of the Bible, using creation as a test case. The rise of science and technology for these first fundamentalists seemed to bring with it a deterioration of traditional human values.

Christian fundamentalists wished to preserve the "fundamentals" of Christianity as defined by widely distributed booklets called *The Fundamentals*, published between 1910 and 1915. Not all of the booklets were antievolutionary; some maintained that a divine creator and evolution could coexist. Yet it was the fundamentalist movement that broke open the evolution and creationism debate and caused it to spill into the realms of politics, law, and education.

A challenge to some recently passed Tennessee legislation against the teaching of evolution, the 1925 Scopes trial was the first clash of creationism and evolution in the courtroom. William Jennings Bryan, a former presidential candidate and liberal politician known for supporting workers' rights, prosecuted a high school biology teacher, John T. Scopes, for teaching evolution. Bryan, a Christian fundamentalist and creationist, won the case and effectively inhibited the teaching of evolution in U.S. high schools; by 1930 evolution was not taught in 70 percent of American classrooms. Yet the newspaper reporting of events during the Scopes trial left a very different impression on the American public. The evolutionists were set against the fundamentalists, who were portrayed as foolish religious zealots. Decades later, the popular play *Inherit the Wind* (1955) satirically presented the ruling of the trial as being in violation of free speech and freedom of conscience. Despite the negative image of the fundamentalists, evolution was infrequently taught in high school classrooms.

American lawyer and politician William Jennings Bryan argues for the prosecution during the "Scopes Monkey Trial" in Dayton, Tennessee, 1925. (Hulton Archive/Getty Images)

School Board Controversies

Ground Zero in the evolution versus creationism debate is state school boards throughout the nation, particularly in states that have elected highly conservative legislatures. Many of these state efforts take the form of "academic freedom" bills, which encourage the use of creationist material in the science curriculum.

Often students are protected in such bills for subscribing to a particular view. They are also encouraged to develop "critical thinking skills" on controversial issues and thus invited to discuss the strengths and weaknesses of "existing scientific theories" (i.e., evolution). In many cases, not only evolution but also global warming, human cloning, and stem cell research are named as theories to be questioned. Between 2004 and 2011, about 40 such bills were filed in 13 states.

In Louisiana, for example, following a U.S. Supreme Court ruling, *Edwards v. Aguillard* (1987), that ruled the state's "balanced treatment" law unconstitutional (because it favored a particular religion, Christianity), there have been repeated efforts to reintroduce a pro-creationist curriculum—though opposition continues. In Kansas, in 2005, the state board of education approved new standards mandating a balanced treatment, but two years later a new school board membership rejected the revised standards and returned to a view geared toward "natural explanations" of observed phenomena. In Texas, the state school board has been at the center of controversy as debate rages over placing creationist views in textbooks along with views that question climate change and other scientific findings.

The launch of Sputnik in 1957—the world's first satellite—by the Soviet Union stimulated a desire to intensify science education in the United States. In the years leading up to Sputnik, more and more evidence had been gathered by scientists around the world to support evolutionary theory, and James Watson and Francis Crick had identified and explained the existence of DNA. Consequently, the teaching of evolution was determined by the National Science Foundation (NSF) to be integral to the best science education. School boards across the country were pressured by their communities to choose new, up-to-date textbooks with the NSF stamp of approval. Evolution once again became a prominent theme in biology textbooks for political reasons.

It was during this time that a second major form of the creationism versus evolution debate arose. In the decade before American scientific education was refocused by the space race, Henry M. Morris, a trained engineer, began defending creationism with science. His most famous work, *The Genesis Flood* (1961), cemented the modern creation-science movement. In 1970 Morris established the Institute for Creation Research, which continues to be active today. The institute "equips believers with evidences of the Bible's accuracy and authority through scientific research." The most decisive blow to creation science being taught in the science classroom, however, came in 1981 when a law that required it to be taught in Arkansas public schools alongside evolution was struck down as a violation of the separation of church and state. The trial, *McLean v. Arkansas Board of Education*, was dubbed "Scopes II."

Recent Developments

Since the 1980s the creationism versus evolution debate has taken on a number of new dimensions. Of particular importance are theories of ID, which claims to be based on science, and a religion-rejecting affirmation of evolution that is also understood by its defenders to be based on science.

A central concept for ID is the *inference to design*. ID is different from creation science in that proponents of ID do not claim outright that the designer is the God of Genesis. They do claim that the religious belief that gives impetus to their work is justified because it is equivalent to the evolutionists' belief in naturalism. For ID proponents, searching for origins by way of purely physical causes (naturalism) is no more objective than doing so by way of a combination of physical causes and probabilities.

Given the current scientific evidence, ID proponents argue, to infer that a species must have been designed is more reasonable than to say it evolved. University of California at Berkeley law professor Phillip E. Johnson attempts to shoot holes in evolutionary theory in *Darwin on Trial* (2010). Supporting Johnson's work, biologist Michael Behe in *Darwin's Black Box* (2006) explains in detail his notion of the "irreducible complexity" of particular physical bodies from which we can infer a designer. Guillermo Gonzales and Jay Richards alert us to the finely tuned conditions necessary for life in *The Privileged Planet: How Our Place in the Cosmos Is Designed for Discovery* (2004). The coordinating and funding agency for research in ID is the Discovery Institute.

On the other side of the debate are evolutionists who believe evolutionary theory proves the nonexistence of God. Perhaps the most famous current religion-rejecting evolutionists are Richard Dawkins, author of the best-selling *The God Delusion* (2008), and Daniel C. Dennett, author of the best seller *Breaking the Spell: Religion as a Natural Phenomenon* (2007). They argue that the theory of evolution is strong enough to explain how species and complex bodies evolved. Given a world that can be explained using naturalist processes, they see a conflict between religion and science that is insurmountable. How can these creation stories be true, when we know how the world creates itself? Sam Harris, in *The End of Faith* (2005), highlights the divide between religious fundamentalism and rational thought or human reason.

Although there is no certainty as to the origin of species, mainstream scientists are convinced that evolutionary theory is the key to understanding such origins. If evolutionary theory is correct, and scientists are someday able to explain the origins of life using it, does this rule out God? There are possible syntheses between the two positions, as religious thinkers and scientists outside North America have more readily explored, because one does not necessarily rule out the other. Considering the evidence for both theories unfortunately seems far less popular in some circles than the desire to generate heat (rather than light) on the subject, and so the debate continues.

See also Biotechnology and Politics; Church–State Relations; Culture Wars; Prayer and Religious Symbols in Public Places; Protestants, Evangelicals, and Politics; Religion and Politics.

Michael J. Bendewald

Bibliography

Barbour, Ian G. 2000. *When Science Meets Religion.* San Francisco: Harper Collins.

Behe, Michael J. 2006. *Darwin's Black Box: The Biochemical Challenge to Evolution.* 2nd ed. New York: Free Press.

Dawkins, Richard. 2008. *The God Delusion.* Reprint ed. New York: Mariner Books.

Dennett, Daniel C. 2007. *Breaking the Spell: Religion as a Natural Phenomenon.* New York: Penguin.

Discovery Institute. www.discovery.org. Accessed May 19, 2014.

Gonzales, Guillermo, and Jay Richards. 2004. *The Privileged Planet: How Our Place in the Cosmos Is Designed for Discovery.* Washington, DC: Regnery.

Harris, Sam. 2005. *The End of Faith: Religion, Terror, and the Future of Reason.* Reprint ed. New York: Norton.

Institute for Creation Research. www.icr.org. Accessed May 19, 2014.

Johnson, Phillip E. 2010. *Darwin on Trial.* Rev. ed. Downers Grove, IL: IVP Books.

National Center for Science Education. nsce.com. Accessed May 19, 2014.

Pennock, Robert T., ed. 2001. *Intelligent Design Creationism and Its Critics: Philosophical, Theological, and Scientific Perspectives.* Cambridge, MA: MIT Press.

Scott, Eugenie C. 2009. *Evolution vs. Creationism: An Introduction.* 2nd ed. Berkeley: University of California Press.

Woodward, Thomas. 2006. *Darwin Strikes Back: Defending the Science of Intelligent Design.* Grand Rapids, MI: Baker Books.

EXECUTIVE PRIVILEGE

Although the term "executive privilege" was not used in the debates over the U.S. Constitution, it was understood early in the administration of George Washington that there might be suitable occasions where the president could deny Congress executive documents. Whether the president prevails depends on many factors, particularly the determination of Congress and its committees to press for information. Significant tools are available to the legislative branch when it asks for documents: committee hearings, committee subpoenas, holding executive officials in contempt (with potential fines and jail sentences), and when public opinion turns against the president. Frequently the courts become involved in deciding the reach of executive privilege, but most document disputes are settled politically between the elected branches. There are many examples, to be discussed, where a potential "victory" for the executive branch carries so many downsides that it decides to capitulate and release requested documents.

Allocation of Powers

The U.S. Constitution established a general structure for government. It did not attempt to settle every type of imaginable dispute that might develop nor did it try to identify all the powers of the three branches. It provided for certain express powers, such as the power of Congress to appropriate funds and the president's power to nominate federal officers. But it also contemplated that all three branches would have additional *implied* powers. For example, the president has the express duty to see that the laws are faithfully executed. If the head of an executive department is unable or unwilling to carry out a statute, the president has the implied power to remove that individual. Congress has the express power to legislate. To do that in an effective and informed manner, it has the implied power to investigate. The constitutional system is protected because implied powers must be drawn reasonably from express powers. Nevertheless, there are plenty of opportunities for express and implied powers to produce conflicts among the branches.

The Supreme Court has recognized the constitutional authority of Congress to investigate (*McGrain v. Daugherty* in 1927) and the president's authority to withhold information (*United States v. Nixon* in 1974). Those powers would exist with or without court rulings. Both of the elected branches from the start concluded that certain powers are necessarily implied for the effective functioning of government. The difficult and unpredictable issue is what happens when two implied powers collide (Rozell 2010). A lengthy study by Herman Wolkinson in 1949, expressing the executive branch position, asserted that federal courts "have uniformly held the President and the heads of departments have an uncontrolled discretion to withhold the information and papers in the public interest, and they will not interfere with the exercise of that discretion" (Wolkinson 1949, 103).

That statement, incorrect when written, is even less true today as a result of litigation and political precedents established over the past six decades. Similarly inaccurate is Wolkinson's claim that "in every instance where a President has backed the refusal of a head of a department to divulge confidential information to either of the Houses of Congress, or their committees, the papers and the information requested were not furnished" (Wolkinson 1949, 104). Committee may go into executive session to receive confidential information. Wolkinson further asserted that Congress could not, "under the Constitution, compel heads of departments by law to give up papers and information, regardless of the public interest involved; and the President is the judge of that interest" (Wolkinson 1949, 107). Congress has coercive powers that can override executive determinations, including those of the president.

Neither Congress nor the president has incontestable authority to withhold information or force its disgorgement. Both branches have figured out how to reach accommodations that satisfy their mutual interests. In 1982, President Ronald Reagan issued general guidelines when responding to congressional requests for information: "Historically, good faith negotiations between Congress and the Executive Branch have minimized the need for invoking executive privilege, and this tradition of accommodation should continue as the primary means of resolving conflicts between the Branches" (Reagan 1982, paragraph 1).

Political confrontations between Congress and the executive branch attract the media, which loves a good fight. Knockdown battles dominate the press and remain within our collective memory, but less attention is devoted to the quiet cooperative efforts that characterize much of executive–legislative relations. Government cannot function in a constant state of strife, agitation, and enmity. Lawmakers and agency officials search for methods to break deadlocks and move public policy forward (Stathis 1986).

Precedents during the Washington Administration

In 1790, during the First Congress, lawmakers debated a request from Robert Morris to investigate his conduct as Superintendent of Finance during the Continental Congress. The House created a five-man committee to pursue the inquiry. Some senators objected that the matter should be left to the president who had already appointed three commissioners to investigate. Rep. James Madison disagreed, insisting that the House "should possess itself of the fullest information in order to doing [*sic*] justice to the country and to public officers" (Fisher 2004, 7). The House committee conducted an inquiry and issued a report on February 16, 1791 (*Annals of Congress* 2: 2017).

Another political collision over documents occurred in 1790 when Treasury secretary Alexander Hamilton asked Congress to compensate Baron von Steuben for his services during the Revolutionary War. Hamilton sought a lump sum of $7,394.74, an annuity for life, and "a moderate grant of land" (Fisher 2004, 8). A Senate committee, created to investigate the matter, discovered that the Continental Congress had already given Steuben $7,000. When Hamilton proved uncooperative in allowing access to public documents, the Senate had all the leverage. It could simply refuse to pass the bill for Steuben. Offended by Hamilton's conduct, the Senate deleted the lump sum of $7,000, reduced the annuity to $1,000, and eliminated any notion of a grant of land. In 1790, Congress settled on a bill that granted Steuben an annuity of $2,500 for life.

A major issue during the Washington administration concerned a decision by the House on March 27, 1792, to appoint a committee to inquire into the heavy military losses suffered by troops of Maj. Gen. Arthur St. Clair fighting with Indian tribes. Out of 1,400

U.S. troops, 657 were killed and another 271 wounded (Chalou 1975, 1: 3–101). The House empowered the committee to call for such persons, papers, and records as may be necessary to assist the inquiry. Some members of the House thought the investigation should be conducted by President Washington, but a motion to that effect was rejected. According to the account of Secretary of State Thomas Jefferson, President Washington convened his cabinet to consider the House request.

The cabinet agreed, first, that the House was an inquest, and therefore might institute inquiries; second, that it might call for papers generally; third, that the executive ought to communicate such papers as the public good would permit, and ought to refuse those the disclosure of which would injure the public; and, fourth, that neither the committee nor the House had a right to call on the head of a department, whose person and papers were under the president alone, but that the committee should instruct its chairman to move that the House address the president (Fisher 2004, 10).

The president's cabinet also concluded in this particular case there was no document that should *not* be properly produced to the House. President Washington instructed Secretary of War Henry Knox to provide all the documents to the House it requested. He also thought it appropriate for St. Clair to make himself available to the House. St. Clair prepared a written statement and submitted it to the House. The general principle of executive privilege had been established, but Washington was advised that he could refuse papers "the disclosure of which would injure the public." The injury had to be to the public, however, not to the president or his associates. The St. Clair precedent did not mean that presidents could withhold information from Congress simply because it might embarrass the administration or reveal improper and illegal activities.

The St. Clair investigation is well known. So is the decision of President Washington in 1795 to withhold from the House documents related to the Jay Treaty, arguing that it is excluded by the Constitution from the treaty process. What is less known is that several years earlier, Washington treated the House on equal grounds, constitutionally, on the matter of a treaty with Algiers to pay ransom for allowing U.S. ships to move safety in the Mediterranean. He considered borrowing money to pay the ransom, but Secretary of State Jefferson advised against it. Washington would later have to go to Congress to seek an appropriation to pay for the loan and Congress might decline. Moreover, Jefferson reasoned that just as senators expect to be consulted before a treaty, the House had the same interest, particularly if they had to pass legislation to authorize and fund the treaty.

Following Jefferson's advice, Washington forwarded to both the Senate and the House confidential letters that he asked lawmakers to keep secret. Whatever information he sent to the Senate he sent to the House, which went into secret session to consider the treaty. For several days the House debated the confidential documents. With close cooperation between the two branches, Congress authorized and funded the treaty with Algiers. The treaty included an annual amount to be paid to the Dey of Algiers (Fisher 2004, 32–33).

This experience demonstrates the lack of honesty of President Washington in 1796 when he refused to give the House documents on the Jay Treaty. He advised that the Senate had the exclusive role to participate as a member of the legislative branch in treaty matters. He reasoned that the only ground on which the House might request documents regarding treaty instructions and negotiations would be impeachment, "which the [House] resolution has not addressed" (Fisher 2004, 35). Three points. First, his decision to withhold documents from the House was not an exercise of executive privilege. He had already transmitted the treaty documents to the Senate. Second, he had treated the House equally with the Senate on the Algerine treaty. Third, the House was not requesting documents as part of the treaty process. It was deciding whether to pass legislation to authorize and fund the treaty. The House had a right to whatever papers it needed to make an informed judgment.

Shortly after Washington's message to the House denying access to the papers, Rep. Thomas Blount introduced two resolutions (both adopted 57 to 35), stating that although the House had no role in making treaties, whenever a treaty depends on laws passed by Congress (as with the Jay Treaty), "it is the Constitutional right and duty of the House of Representatives, in all such cases, to deliberate on the expediency or inexpediency of carrying such Treaty into effect, and to determine and act thereon, as, in their judgment, may be most conducive to the public good" (Fisher 2004, 37). In other words, if the president refuses to release documents that the House has requested about the treaty, the House may block implementation of the treaty. Over the years, many presidents have invited members of the House and the Senate to participate in treaty negotiation to ensure legislative support.

Congressional Leverage

In *McGrain v. Daugherty* (1927), the Supreme Court described the congressional power of inquiry as "an essential and appropriate auxiliary to the legislative function." Often committees can obtain the information they need from the executive branch without using a subpoena to force testimony or the release of agency documents. Yet the issuance of a subpoena may be indispensable for an authorized investigation. Federal courts give great deference to congressional subpoenas. If the inquiry falls within the legitimate legislative sphere, such investigative activities are immune from judicial interference.

A committee subpoena may require the production of agency documents and the attendance of an executive official at a hearing. Committee subpoenas have the same force as if they were issued by the House or the Senate. If a witness refuses to testify or produce papers in response to a subpoena, the committee may vote to report a resolution of contempt to the floor, where the full House or Senate can pass a contempt citation. The power to hold someone in contempt is an implied power of Congress. In *Anderson v. Dunn* (1821), the Supreme Court ruled that without this power the legislative branch would be "exposed to every indignity and interruption that rudeness, caprice, or even conspiracy, may mediate against it." If either house votes for a contempt citation, the president of the Senate or the Speaker of the House shall certify the facts to the appropriate U.S. attorney, "whose duty it shall be to bring the matter before the grand jury for its action" (2 U.S.C. § 194). Individuals who are convicted of contempt are subject to fines up to $100,000 and one year in prison.

It is rare for an executive official to wholly sidestep a committee subpoena. The official might appear if only to invoke the Fifth Amendment right not to incriminate himself or herself. If a witness invokes that constitutional right, Congress can force testimony by granting the witness either partial or full immunity. During the Iran-Contra investigation in 1987, Congress offered partial immunity to several witnesses. The record is strong that committee subpoenas, if lawmakers are persistent, are effective in gaining access to agency testimony and documents (Fisher 2004, 95–109).

Similarly, issuance of a contempt citation by the House or the Senate is usually sufficient to force cooperation by the executive branch. Even with a contempt citation looming, the pressure is likely to lead to a compromise settlement that gives Congress access to documents (Fisher 2004, 112–26). However, on three occasions from 1982 to the present time, the executive branch refused to give Congress documents even in the face of a contempt action. Furthermore, after the House passed a contempt citation, the Justice Department refused to go to a grand jury, as provided by statute. Instead, it argued that once the president invokes executive privilege, his decision prohibits prosecution. The first two examples involved investigation into the Superfund scandal in 1982 (involving the misuse of federal toxic site cleanup funds) and the firings of U.S. attorneys (allegedly on political grounds) in the George W. Bush administration (Rozell 2010, 101–3, 169–81).

The third example resulted from a House investigation of the "Fast and Furious" gunrunning program during the Obama administration. Under this program, the Alcohol, Tobacco, and Firearms agency allowed close to 2,000 assault weapons to leave U.S. gun shops and enter into Mexico to trace them. The congressional effort to obtain documents from the executive branch led the House to hold U.S. attorney general Eric Holder in contempt, at which point President Obama invoked executive privilege and the Justice Department announced there would be no effort to bring Holder before a grand jury (Fisher 2013).

When the Justice Department refuses to prosecute someone held in contempt by the House or Senate, Congress can authorize a civil suit to force compliance with the contempt statute. In the case of Superfund, the House gained access to the agency documents it needed. With regard to the dispute over U.S. attorneys, the House won an important victory in federal district court but the appellate court placed a stay on the case to permit negotiations with the next administration under Barack Obama (Rozell 2010, 177–79). The House Judiciary Committee obtained additional information from the executive branch on the issue of U.S. attorneys. As for Fast and Furious, the House has filed a civil action and it will be some time before the case is resolved in court.

One other point about congressional leverage. In 1986, President Reagan refused to give the Senate Judiciary Committee certain internal memos that his nominee for chief justice, William Rehnquist, had written while serving in the Justice Department as head of the Office of Legal Counsel (OLC) from 1969 to 1971. The reason for invoking executive privilege is to protect the confidentiality and candor of legal advice submitted to presidents and their assistants (Kamen and Marcus 1986, A1). Rehnquist agreed to the release of the memos, but the White House did not, preferring to bolster presidential authority under executive privilege. The administration's constitutional theory ran against a hard fact. Democrats on Senate Judiciary gained the support of several Republican members to subpoena the OLC documents. Not only was Rehnquist's confirmation at stake, but the Senate had planned to vote on both Rehnquist and Antonin Scalia as associate justice on August 14.

An op-ed by Sen. Ted Kennedy put the matter succinctly: "Rehnquist: No Documents, No Senate Confirmation" (Kennedy 1986, Part II, 5). Sen. Paul Laxalt, Republican of Nevada, negotiated with the administration to see if a compromise could be reached (Kurtz and Marcus 1986, A1). In an effort to move the Rehnquist and Scalia nominations forward, President Reagan agreed to allow committee access to some of Rehnquist's OLC memos. Under the agreement, six senators and six staff members were allowed to read the memos (Kurtz and Kamen 1986, A1, A14). Later the committee requested and received additional documents prepared by Rehnquist when he worked in the Justice Department (Fisher 2004, 76–77). The Senate confirmed Rehnquist and Scalia on September 17, 1986.

Supreme Court Involvement

As already noted, the Supreme Court has provided helpful guidance in defining the powers of Congress over subpoenas and contempt citations. An especially high-profile ruling was issued by the Court during the Watergate burglary scandal. During his impeachment proceedings, President Richard Nixon insisted on the right to withhold information from a congressional inquiry if he determined that the release of such documents would violate the constitutional doctrine of executive privilege. Faced with subpoenas from the House Judiciary Committee, he argued that release of presidential conversations to Congress would undermine the independence of the executive branch and jeopardize operations in the White House. A line had to be drawn somewhere, he said, and he would be the one to do it. The committee could receive some documents, but not all, and Nixon would decide whether the documents needed to be edited before release (Lavovitz 1978, 201–6).

One of Nixon's first actions was to object to the appearance of White House counsel John Dean at congressional hearings. Nixon said that "no President could ever agree to allow the Counsel to the President to go down and testify before a committee" (Nixon 1973, 160). Within a short time, however, he allowed not only Dean to testify but 21 other White House officials (Fisher 2004, 59–60, 199–200). These hearings enabled Congress to learn about listening and recording devices installed in the White House. Nixon fought against release of the tapes, invoking executive privilege. In *United States v. Nixon* (1974), the Supreme Court held that in a criminal case, where defendants need information to protect their rights in court, the president's general authority over agency information could not override the specific need that defendants have for evidence.

Some of the Watergate tapes ended up in the hands of District Judge John Sirica, who presided over the trial of the Watergate burglars. He wondered why the Justice Department was content to prosecute only those arrested in the burglary. Who else was involved? Who had planned and financed the burglary? In listening to the tapes, Sirica heard unmistakable evidence of obstruction of justice at high levels. At a March 22, 1973,

The Senate Committee on Presidential Campaign Activities convenes in May 1973 to hear testimony related to the break-in at the Watergate complex. President Nixon sought to protect taped White House conversations under the principle of executive privilege—to no avail. (Library of Congress)

meeting with other White House officials, Nixon said: "And, uh, for that reason, I am perfectly willing to—I don't give a shit what happens. I want you to stonewall it, let them plead the Fifth Amendment, cover-up or anything else, if it'll save the plan" (Sirica 1979, 162). The "plan" was to save the Nixon presidency. With release of the tapes, Nixon recognized that a House vote on impeachment was inevitable and saw no grounds for support in a Senate trial. He announced his resignation on August 8, 1974, effective the next day.

Ongoing Document Battles

Whether lawmakers actually receive agency documents depends on their willingness, skills, and perseverance. Agencies have plenty of ways and incentives to delay access, hoping lawmakers and committees will turn to other things. Congressional success is greatly improved when committees act in bipartisan

manner to get the documents they need. Faced with an unwanted investigation, presidents and agencies will typically promise to "cooperate fully" while at the same time perfecting efforts "to blunt, to parry, and to outlast accusations against them" (Tiefer 1998, 146). Agencies are adept at flooding committees with thousands of documents that are of marginal or extraneous interest, or some so heavily redacted that they are useless to the committee.

Congress has the theoretical edge because of the abundant tools at its disposal. To convert theory to success requires from lawmakers and their staff an intense focus and staying power to cope with a long and frustrating battle for documents. What is needed from committees is an abiding commitment to honor their constitutional purpose. Antonin Scalia, while serving as the head of the OLC, put the matter well during Senate hearings in 1975. When congressional and presidential interests collide on the search for documents, the answer is likely to lie in "the hurly-burly, the give-and-take of the political process between the legislative and the executive. . . . [W]hen it comes to an impasse the Congress has means at its disposal to have its will prevail" (Scalia 1975, 87).

See also Constitution and Constitutionalism; Presidency and Presidential Politics; Separation of Powers; State Secrets and Politics.

Louis Fisher

Bibliography

Annals of Congress. This series covers congressional debates from 1789 to 1824.

Chalou, George C. 1975. "St. Clair's Defeat, 1792." In Arthur M. Schlesinger Jr. and Roger Bruns, eds. *Congress Investigates, 1792–1974.* 5 vols. New York: Chelsea House.

Fisher, Louis. 2004. *The Politics of Executive Privilege.* Durham, NC: Carolina Academic Press.

Fisher, Louis. 2013. "Obama's Executive Privilege and Holder's Contempt: 'Operation Fast and Furious.'" *Presidential Studies Quarterly* 43: 167–85.

Kamen, Al, and Ruth Marcus. 1986. "Reagan Uses Executive Privilege to Keep Rehnquist Memos Secret." *Washington Post* (August 1).

Kennedy, Edward M. 1986. "Rehnquist: No Documents, No Senate Confirmation." *Los Angeles Times* (August 5).

Kurtz, Howard, and Al Kamen. 1986. "Rehnquist Not in Danger over Papers." *Washington Post* (August 6).

Kurtz, Howard, and Ruth Marcus. 1986. "Democrats Seek to Subpoena Papers." *Washington Post* (August 2).

Lavovitz, John R. 1978. *Presidential Impeachment.* New Haven, CT: Yale University Press.

Nixon, Richard M. 1973. *Public Papers of the Presidents, 1973.* Washington, DC: Government Printing Office.

Reagan, Ronald. 1982. Memorandum to the Heads of the Executive Departments and Agencies. "Procedures Governing Responses to Congressional Requests for Information." November 4.

Rozell, Mark J. 2010. *Executive Privilege: Presidential Power, Secrecy, and Accountability.* 3rd ed. Lawrence: University Press of Kansas.

Scalia, Antonin. 1975. "Executive Privilege—Secrecy in Government." Hearings before the Subcommittee on Intergovernmental Relations of the Senate Committee on Government Operations, 94th Cong., 1st Sess.

Sirica, John J. 1979. *To Set the Record Straight.* New York: Norton.

Stathis, Stephen W. 1986. "Executive Cooperation: Presidential Recognition of the Investigative Authority of Congress and the Courts." *Journal of Law and Politics* 3: 183–294.

Tiefer, Charles. 1998. "The Specially Investigated President." *University of Chicago Law School Roundtable* 5: 143–204.

Wolkinson, Herman. 1949. "Demands of Congressional Committees for Executive Papers." Part 1. *Federal Bar Journal* 10: 103–50.